Selected Writings of Lord Acton

VOLUME II

ESSAYS IN THE STUDY AND WRITING OF HISTORY

Lord Acton

Selected Writings of Lord Acton

VOLUME II

ESSAYS IN THE STUDY AND WRITING OF HISTORY

by
John Emerich Edward Dalberg-Acton
First Baron Acton

edited by J. Rufus Fears

LibertyClassics

Indianapolis

Liberty*Classics* is a publishing imprint of Liberty Fund, Inc., a foundation established to encourage study of the ideal of a society of free and responsible individuals.

The cuneiform inscription that serves as the design motif for our end-papers is the earliest-known written appearance of the word "freedom" (*ama-gi*), or "liberty." It is taken from a clay document written about 2300 B.C. in the Sumerian city-state of Lagash.

Frontispiece photograph from The Bettmann Archive Inc., New York, New York.

Cover art is the frontispiece from *Lord Acton and His Circle* published in 1906 by Longmans, Green & Co., New York, New York.

Library of Congress Cataloging in Publication Data

Acton, John Emerich Edward Dalberg-Acton, Baron,
1834–1902.
Selected writings of Lord Acton

Includes bibliographical references and index.
Contents: v. 1. Essays in the history of liberty.
1. Liberty—Addresses, essays, lectures. 2. History—
Study and teaching—Addresses, essays, lectures.
3. Historiography—Addresses, essays, lectures.
4. Aphorisms and apothegms—Addresses, essays, lectures.
5. Liberalism—History—19th century—Addresses, essays,
lectures. I. Fears, J. Rufus. II. Title.
D15.A25A25   1985   907.2   85-4522

ISBN 0-86597-048-3

ISBN 0-86597-049-1 (pbk.)

10 9 8 7 6 5 4 3 2 1

Contents

Biographical Note

LORD ACTON (1834–1902). Historian and political thinker, John Emerich Edward Dalberg-Acton was one of the most significant figures in the intellectual and political life of Victorian England. A Roman Catholic, he was educated in Munich under the Catholic church historian Ignaz von Döllinger. From 1858 until 1871, through his personality, editorial activities, articles, and reviews, he assumed a major role in the Liberal Catholic movement. Although he was briefly a member of Parliament, his main political influence was exercised as an admirer, friend, and confidant of the Liberal Prime Minister William Gladstone. As Regius Professor of Modern History at Cambridge from 1895 to 1902, Acton was instrumental in transforming the writing of history in England from a form of belles lettres into a rigorously scientific discipline based on the model of German scholarship.

While emphasizing complete objectivity in the pursuit of historical truth, Acton was deeply concerned with the need for moral judgment in history and with the meaning of history. This meaning he found in the concept of human freedom. For Acton, "the idea of liberty is the unity, the only unity of the history of the world, and the one principle of a philosophy of history." Although his planned *History of Liberty* never came to fruition, the lectures, essays, and reviews that he did write are more than sufficient to establish him as a thinker of supreme importance in the intellectual heritage of classical Liberalism. It is an importance of more than historical interest. His powerfully original analysis of the nature of individual and political freedom and of the forces that foster and threaten that freedom speak to the most profound concerns of the late twentieth century.

The Essays in This Volume

For Lord Acton, the idea of liberty was the key to history.[1] Acton's concept of liberty was the unifying theme of the essays collected in the first volume of this edition. His idea of history is the leitmotiv of the lectures, articles, and reviews brought together in this second volume. In every sense, the two volumes are complementary. Acton's understanding of liberty was the product of his historical studies and thought, while almost everything he wrote and said about history related in some way to the course and meaning of human freedom.

Acton devoted a lifetime to the study of history. Acton's studies in Munich, under Ignaz von Döllinger from 1850 until 1857, coincided with the period in which German scholarship transformed history from a form of belles lettres into a scientific discipline.[2] This transformation rested upon three discoveries, truths that remain the basis of sound historical methodology: critical evaluation of the sources, the preference of primary to secondary sources, and impartiality.[3] For Acton, Leopold von Ranke (1795–1886) was the representative of the age that instituted the modern study of history.[4] "For his most eminent predecessors, history was applied politics, fluid law, religion exemplified, or the school of patriotism. Ranke was the first German to pursue it for no purpose but its own."[5]

For Ranke, history had no purpose other than the pursuit of truth; the only goal of the historian was to discover what had actually happened in the past. To achieve this goal, Ranke taught history "to be critical, to be colourless, and to be new."[6] Historians such as Livy

---

[1] Acton, *Selected Writings of Lord Acton: Volume II: Essays in the Study and Writing of History*, Fears, ed., p. 524.

[2] Acton, *Correspondence*, p. 24.

[3] Acton, *Selected Writings*, II, pp. 527–531.

[4] Acton, *Selected Writings*, II, p. 533.

[5] Acton, *Selected Writings*, II, p. 331.

[6] Acton, *Selected Writings*, II, p. 533.

in his *History of Rome* or Machiavelli in his *History of Florence* are not primary sources. They are, to use Acton's analogy, hearsay evidence. Before the modern historian can admit their testimony, before he can believe what they say about events in Rome or in Florence, he must subject them to the most searching cross-examination. Only after such a critical analysis can the historian decide where he may safely follow a secondhand account, where he must reject it.

Ranke taught that history should be new as well as critical. He taught historians to get out of the library and the study and to work in archives. "All the printed books in the world . . . still leave the student upon the threshold of general History."[7] Critical dissection of secondhand accounts will take the historian only so far. He must himself roll up his sleeves and cull his facts from primary sources, from the unpublished and even secret records and documents of the actual events.[8]

Ranke also taught historians to be impartial. The true historian does not read his opinions, beliefs, and prejudices into the sources. He draws his opinions and beliefs from the facts and he writes "with so much scruple, and simplicity, and insight, as to carry along with [him] every man of good will and . . . compel his assent." Hero-worship was one casualty of such impartiality; admiration of "great men" was to be avoided "as the last ditch of prehistoric prejudice." Nor is there room for national feeling or religious dogma in scientific history; the account of the Battle of Waterloo, in a true historian, will be one that "satisfies French and English, Germans and Dutch alike,"[9]

It was Ranke who dominated Acton's thoughts in "The Study of History," delivered as his Inaugural Lecture as Regius Professor at Cambridge, in 1895. But Acton was well aware that he owed far more to Döllinger.[10] It was Döllinger who taught him the art of historical thinking. It was Döllinger who led him to understand that the study of history "fulfils its purpose even if it only makes us wiser, without producing books, and gives us the gift of historical thinking, which is better than historical learning. It is a most powerful ingredient in the

---

[7] McElrath, p. 128.

[8] Acton, *Selected Writings*, II, pp. 334–335.

[9] Acton, *Selected Writings*, II, p. 530. The quotation on the Battle of Waterloo is taken from Acton's letter to contributors to the *Cambridge Modern History*. Published in part in Acton, *Lectures on Modern History*, pp. 315–318.

[10] Döllinger, III, p. 179.

ormation of character and the training of talent, and our historical judgements have as much to do with hopes of heaven as public or private conduct."[11]

In becoming politically impartial, the study of history did not cease to be useful in politics. Indeed, in Acton's view, the most intimate relationship existed between the sciences of politics and history. "The science of politics is the one science that is deposited by the stream of history, like grains of gold in the sand of a river; and the knowledge of the past, the record of truths revealed by experience, is eminently practical, as an instrument of action and a power that goes to the making of the future."[12] As a student in Munich, Acton had viewed his historical studies as being supremely utilitarian.[13] He believed that his knowledge of history and of German historical science would enable him to be of the greatest service to his country and to his church. With this end in view, he returned to England in 1857 and began his involvement in the journalism of Liberal Catholicism. The great majority of his contributions to the *Rambler*, the *Home and Foreign Review*, and later to the *Chronicle* and the *North British Review* are historical in character. Even when he wrote on current events, it was from the vantage point of a historian and with the conviction that to report on the present would lead him to understand better the past.[14]

The first half of this volume brings together a wide range of Acton's work from this first period of his life as a historian, from 1858 to 1871. It was a period marked on the one side by the beginning of Acton's association with the *Rambler* in 1858, and on the other by the Vatican Council of 1870 and its aftermath, including the demise of the last of the organs of Liberal Catholicism, the *North British Review*.[15] The first four pieces have not been reprinted since their original publication; in fact, they are not even listed in previous bibliographies of Acton's writings.[16] Included are two long essays and two shorter book reviews.

---

[11] Acton, *Selected Writings*, II, pp. 513–514.

[12] Acton, *Selected Writings*, II, pp. 504–505.

[13] Acton, *Correspondence*, p. 27.

[14] Acton-Simpson, II, p. 9.

[15] Acton's association with the *Rambler* and other liberal Catholic journals is briefly discussed in Acton, *Selected Writings of Lord Acton, Volume I: Essays in the History of Liberty*, Fears, ed., pp. xxii–xxiv.

[16] Acton's contributions to these journals were unsigned. The difficulties that this creates for bibliographers and the resulting shortcomings of published Acton bibliographies are discussed in Acton, *Selected Writings*, I, pp. xxiv–xxvii.

The first of the long essays appeared in the *Dublin Review* in 1858 when Acton was twenty-four. It used a discussion of M. A. Poirson's *Histoire du Règne de Henri IV* (Paris, 1856) as the springboard for an analysis of aspects of the policies of Henry IV, that king of France who "launched his country in a course in which principle was subordinate to expediency but which was eminently congenial to the national character and conducive to the national greatness."[17] The second of these longer essays was published in the *Rambler* in 1861: "Expectation of the French Revolution" explored the implications of Acton's belief that "there is a prophetic office in history, and our notions of the future are shaped according to our experience of the past. . . . The past acts upon our conduct chiefly by the views of the future which it suggests, and the expectations it creates."[18]

Equally provocative were Acton's comments in two short book reviews published in the *Rambler* for July and August 1858. A review of R. K. Philp's *History of Progress in Great Britain* gave Acton the occasion to evaluate a form of history much in vogue today: "The demand that the historian should inform us as to the condition of the people has become a commonplace of newspaper criticism. . . . It is a tendency which can hardly produce any durable effect on historical writing, because it is opposed, not to the dignity, but to the unity of history. . . . Great political and intellectual revolutions have occurred without really affecting the social existence of the people, which remains unchanged often for centuries. The real substance of history, which is going altogether out of fashion, the great march of public events, is yet very far from being so thoroughly understood . . . that the historian need seek elsewhere materials for interesting his readers."[19]

Acton's review of P. A. Chéruel's *Marie Stuart et Catherine de Médicis* provided the opportunity to deal with another school of historical thought which he found equally misguided: the "great man" approach to history. Acton returned to this theme in reviews of Carlyle's *History of Friedrich II of Prussia* and of S. R. Gardiner's *History of England, 1603–1616*, both reprinted here for the first time.[20] But Ranke, not Carlyle, was Acton's model: in an article entitled simply "Ranke," written for the *Chronicle* for July 20, 1867, and republished here for the first time,

---

[17] Acton, *Selected Writings*, II, pp. 6, 3–30.
[18] Acton, *Selected Writings*, II, pp. 39, 38–62.
[19] Acton, *Selected Writings*, II, pp. 31–32, 31–33.
[20] Acton, *Selected Writings*, II, pp. 34–37, 63–66, 163–164.

Acton evaluated the contribution of Ranke within the context of a review of his *Englische Geschichte vornehmlich im sechszehnten und siebzehnten Jahrhundert.*[21]

Along with this new material are collected several of Acton's other historical contributions to the *Bridgenorth Journal,* the *Rambler,* the *Home and Foreign Review,* and the *North British Review,* articles that have long been counted among the most important that Acton ever wrote. Acton's Narration of "The Rise and Fall of the Mexican Empire" was counted to be the finest public lecture which he ever delivered.[22] "The Protestant Theory of Persecution,"[23] "Mr. Goldwin Smith's *Irish History,*" and "Secret History of Charles II"[24] discussed the history of freedom of conscience and religious tolerance. His essay "The Massacre of St. Bartholomew," published in 1869, dealt equally with an event fundamental in the history of religious intolerance. It also developed another theme of major significance to Acton's perception of the function of history: the idea of moral judgment in history.[25]

The last of Acton's historical contributions to the *North British Review* was his essay "The Borgias and Their Latest Historian," a discussion of the seventh volume of Ferdinand Gregorovius's *History of Mediaeval Rome,* written after the Vatican Council and the promulgation of the dogma of papal infallibility. Here, Acton discussed the pontificate of Alexander VI, a pope who "declared that his authority was unlimited, that it extended over all man and all things." Sinful he may have been, but the Borgia Pope filled "a great space in history, . . . [and] the system which Luther assailed was the system which Alexander VI had completed and bequeathed to his successors."[26]

As was true of almost all of Acton's historical contributions in this first period, "The Borgias and Their Latest Historian" was inspired by contemporary concerns. The pontificate of Alexander VI was a signal phase in the history of the Papacy as a secular power. It thus spoke directly to Acton's intense concern in this period of his life with the temporal power of the church. As a truly free church was essential to a free state, so temporal power—the possession of an actual physical

---

[21] Acton, *Selected Writings,* II, pp. 165–172.
[22] Acton, *Selected Writings,* II, pp. 173–197.
[23] Acton, *Selected Writings,* II, pp. 98–131.
[24] Acton, *Selected Writings,* II, pp. 67–97, 132–162.
[25] Acton, *Selected Writings,* II, pp. 198–240.
[26] Acton, *Selected Writings,* II, pp. 250, 242, 241–258.

territory ruled by the Pope as sovereign—Acton believed, was essential
to the liberty of the church.[27] His view was opposed to the realities of
politics in nineteenth-century Europe. In 1860 the larger part of the
Papal States was annexed to the newly unified kingdom of Italy. After
occupation by Italian troops and a plebiscite in 1870, Rome became
the capital of the kingdom of Italy, and the Papal States disappeared
from the political map of Europe.

Equally opposed to the dominant currents of the time was Acton's
mission to make Catholics understand that science and Liberalism,
that the pursuit of truth and liberty, served the true ends of the
church.[28] This sense of calling, the wellspring of Acton's literary
productivity in the period from 1858 to 1870, was a source that abruptly
ran dry with the Vatican Council of 1870 and the promulgation of
papal infallibility. The next years were the most trying of Acton's life.
He was pressured by the Catholic hierarchy to submit to a decree
which he regarded as "the common refuge of those who shunned . . .
the liberal influence in Catholicism."[29] If he did not submit, he believed
himself certain to be excommunicated. In fact, he avoided both
submission and excommunication; but he was convinced that all his
work of the last decade had been without consequence. Such circumstances and feelings were not inducements to scholarly productivity,
and for almost fifteen years Acton wrote little for publication. It was
in this period that he acquired the reputation of being "the most
learned Englishman alive" and of never writing anything.[30]

However, his research continued, and the second half of this volume
brings together those essays and studies that gained Acton a reputation
as one of the foremost historians of his time. In 1877, he not only
delivered his lectures on the history of freedom but also published a
detailed study of the divorce of Henry VIII from Catherine of Aragon.
In theme, this article is not unrelated to Acton's earlier work, for it
dealt with a critical episode in the relationship of Church and State.
An exercise in the new science of history, it showed how much new
light the use of archival material could cast upon a story as frequently
told as that of Wolsey and the divorce of Henry VIII. Both the essay
on Wolsey and two brief reviews from this period (*Geschichte des Concils*

[27] Acton, *Church and State*, p. 86; Acton, *The History of Freedom*, p. 373.
[28] Acton-Simpson, II, p. 195.
[29] Acton, *Freedom and Power*, p. 302.
[30] Louise Creighton, *Life and Letters of Mandell Creighton*, (London, 1913), I, p. 275.

von Trent and "Review of the Spanish Calendar") which appeared in *The Academy* in 1876 reflected Acton's own mastery of a wide range of archival material and his insistence that historical certainty depends on the substitution of documents for historians.[31]

After this article on Henry VIII, nine years passed before another substantial historical article appeared in print. Significantly, it did not appear in the kind of literary journal that had served as the vehicle for Acton's earlier historical essays. Acton now chose instead to write for the *English Historical Review*, which he had helped to found in 1886. A journal for scholars, its goal was to elevate the level of historical research in England. It intended to make history a professional discipline in England, and it fulfilled this goal even if it failed in its other aim of interesting the general public in serious historical writing.[32] The first issue of the *English Historical Review* carried a thirty-five-page article by Acton, "German Schools of History." Commenting on it, Mandell Creighton, the editor of the journal, said, "Acton has written a survey of German historians which will at once command attention all over the continent and will, I think, secure our reputation abroad as first rate. . . . [Acton's article is] the sort of thing that takes your breath away, a philosophical criticism of all German historians of this century, most brilliant."[33]

The writing of history was equally at the center of the second major article that Acton contributed to the *English Historical Review*. His 1890 essay, "Döllinger's Historical Work," as erudite as his "German Schools of History," was all that Acton ever published of an intended biography of his teacher.[34] In this period Acton also contributed a series of lengthy review articles to the *English Historical Review* and to the *Nineteenth Century*. Each provided Acton the opportunity to bring the fruits of years of research and reading to bear upon a question of enduring interest to him. Thus a review of Henry Charles Lea's *History of the Inquisition of the Middle Ages* permitted Acton to deal at length with a central issue in the history of freedom of thought and religious intolerance.[35] The history of the Inquisition was a consuming interest

[31] Acton, *Selected Writings*, II, pp. 259–311, 312–319, 320–324. Acton described his archival researches in the period 1864–1868 in a Cambridge lecture published in McElrath, pp. 127–140.

[32] Creighton, *Life and Letters of Mandell Creighton*, I, pp. 333–344.

[33] Creighton, *Life and Letters of Mandell Creighton*, I, p. 339.

[34] Acton, *Correspondence*, p. 72; *Selected Writings*, II, pp. 412–461.

[35] Acton, *Selected Writings*, II, pp. 392–411.

for Acton, and it formed an intellectual link between Acton's two great historical passions, the history of freedom and the history of the Papacy.[36] In 1887, one year before his review of Lea, Acton had written a lengthy review of Mandell Creighton's *History of the Papacy during the Period of the Reformation,* volumes III and IV. In an earlier, brief review Acton had spoken favorably of the first two volumes of the work, and as editor of the *English Historical Review* Creighton asked Acton to review the later volumes.[37] The resulting unfavorable review took Creighton aback. Creighton was prepared to publish the review as it stood, but after correspondence, Acton undertook to soften and to clarify his expression of opinion. Both the review and the correspondence between Acton and Creighton about the review deserve study; both are published here. It was in this correspondence that Acton penned his most famous aphorism: "Power tends to corrupt, and absolute power corrupts absolutely."[38]

The great point at issue between Acton and Creighton was the role of moral judgment in history. "It is the office of historical science to maintain morality as the sole impartial criterion of men and things, and the only one on which honest minds can be made to agree." "Great men," in Acton's view, "are almost always bad men."[39] Nothing so debased the moral currency as did the tendency of historians to excuse the immoral acts of great men on the grounds of expediency, success, statesmanship, and patriotism. Acton returned to this point in his review of Talleyrand's *Memoirs*[40] and in his introduction to L. A. Burd's edition of Machiavelli's *The Prince,*[41] both published in 1891, where he attacked Talleyrand, the great practitioner of expediency, and Machiavelli, the great theoretician of expediency. For Acton, thoughts on morality and conscience were never far from the history of liberty, and in his 1895 review of Robert Flint's *Historical Philosophy in France and French Belgium and Switzerland,* Acton left no doubt that he regarded the development of liberty as "the soul of history."[42]

[36] John Loose, *A Guide to the Acton Papers in the Cambridge University Library,* (Ms. Cambridge, 1971) p. 29.

[37] The review of Volumes I and II of Creighton's *History of the Papacy* was published in *The Academy* 22 (1882), pp. 407–409.

[38] Acton, *Selected Writings,* II, pp. 365–391, 383.

[39] Acton, *Selected Writings,* II, p. 374, 383.

[40] Acton, *Selected Writings,* II, pp. 462–478.

[41] Acton, *Selected Writings,* II, pp. 479–495.

[42] Acton, *Selected Writings,* II, pp. 496–503.

In 1895, Acton assumed the Regius Professorship of Modern History at Cambridge, one of the most prestigious chairs of history in the scholarly world and his first real academic position. He was without earned academic degrees. In 1872, the University of Munich had awarded him an honorary doctorate; and he also held honorary doctorates from Cambridge and Oxford, awarded respectively in 1888 and 1889. In 1890 he had been elected as an Honorary Fellow of All Souls College, Oxford. The appointment as Regius Professor was a tribute to his enormous and deserved reputation for learning. He turned out to have been a splendid choice. The *Times* obituary echoed the general sentiment in writing: "During the time he filled [the Regius] chair he did work that cannot fail to have considerable influence on the future of historical science in England, and makes us regret that some similar post had not been given him earlier in life."[43] Doubts about his ability to communicate his vast learning vanished. His lectures were thronged, and with the instincts of a born teacher Acton learned the joy of enthralling an audience with the romance and the science of history.[44] His students found "inspiration as well as knowledge" in his lectures; "no professor was ever more accessible. He was willing to give advice to anyone, and nobody who consulted him went away empty."[45]

Apart from his Inaugural Lecture on the study of history, Acton published nothing during his years at Cambridge. Much of his time was consumed by his duties as planner and first editor of the *Cambridge Modern History,* which Acton undertook as the nineteenth-century historian's bequest to the twentieth century.[46] Its title referred to more than the time span covered in the volumes. The work itself was to be a monument to the new science of history. This great collaborative history marked the onset of the twentieth century and its cult of experts. Each chapter, to be written by the best man in the field, was to be totally impartial and totally up-to-date.[47] It was a grand vision

[43] London *Times* (June 20, 1902) p. 12. John Figgis and Reginald Laurence prefaced their edition to Acton's *Lectures on Modern History* with an appreciation of "Lord Acton as a Professor" (ix–xix). See also Alan Bell, "Lord Acton Gets His Chair," *Times Literary Supplement* (February 8, 1974) p. 137; and Robert Schuettinger, *Lord Acton: Historian of Liberty* (LaSalle, Illinois, 1976) pp. 153–178.

[44] Acton's letter of February 8, 1895, to his daughter Annie; Add. Mss. 8121, Box 20.

[45] Figgis and Laurence, preface to Acton's *Lectures on Modern History,* pp. ix, xiii,

[46] Add. Mss. 5699; cited in Gertrude Himmelfarb, *Lord Acton: A Study in Conscience and Politics* (Chicago, 1952) p. 223.

[47] G. N. Clark discusses "Origin of the *Cambridge Modern History,*" *Cambridge Historical Journal* 8 (1945) pp. 57–64.

but one that Acton did not live to see realized. When he became ill in April 1901, the first volume had still not issued from the press, and Acton's own contributions were still unwritten. More personal monuments to his years at Cambridge were his *Lectures on the French Revolution* and his *Lectures on Modern History,* published after his death but originally delivered in the ordinary course of his duties as Regius Professor.

The first volume of the present collection of Acton's writings reprints substantial selections from his *Lectures on Modern History* and one of his lectures on the French Revolution. This second volume of the collection concludes with the last of Acton's essays to be published in his lifetime, his Inaugural Lecture, "The Study of History." As Acton's lectures on the history of freedom provide an ideal introduction to his concept of liberty, so his "The Study of History" is the supreme summary of a lifetime devoted to historical thought.[48]

A gulf of thirty-seven years separated the man addressing his first Cambridge professorial lecture from the fervent young Catholic scholar who believed he could do good by writing books.[49] It was a gulf of more than time. The years had brought the most tragic disappointments, estrangement from his church and from his teacher, Döllinger. His pessimism over the defeat of federalism and the course of democracy in America equalled his dismay over the failure of Liberalism and the triumph of absolutism in the church. He felt completely alone in his intellectual and ethical stance. He had learned to be surprised at praise, for he knew how unsympathetic his teaching must be to "the philistine, the sordid, the technical, the faddist, the coward, the man of prejudice and passion, and the zealot."[50] But despite time, disappointment, and isolation, a profound continuity of thought existed between the ideas of the young Acton who wrote for the *Dublin Review* and the *Rambler* and those expressed by the sixty-one-year-old Regius Professor.

From Acton's earliest essays and reviews to his Inaugural Lecture, certain basic ideas appear as central themes in his historical thought. To begin with, there was his belief in the unity of history. In his Inaugural Lecture, he told his audience that he found "wisdom and depth in the philosophy which always considers . . . history as one consistent epic." For Acton, the unity of history was not to be found in anonymous social and economic forces and certainly not in the

---

[48] Acton, *Selected Writings,* II, pp. 504–552.

[49] Döllinger, I, pp. 339, 346.

[50] Acton's letter of October 30, 1895, to his daughter Annie; Add. Mss. 8121, Box 20.

deeds of great men; the key to the unity of history lay in ideas. Ideas, not personalities and not force, are "the spiritual property that gives dignity and grace and intellectual value to history."[51] And of those ideas that give history its power to act positively on "the ascending life of man," liberty is the greatest. Liberty, to Acton, was "the palm, and the prize, and the crown" of history. "Liberty is the one ethical result that rests on the converging and combined conditions of advancing civilization."[52] In the gradual increase of freedom, Acton saw the real meaning of progress. And in the progress of liberty, Acton saw the working out of God's plan for mankind and the surest proof of the proposition that history is the true demonstration of religion.[53] In liberty Acton found more than the key to the unity of history. He found the key to the unity of his life as a Catholic, as a Liberal, and as a historian. He defined Liberty as the reign of conscience, and he believed that Liberalism was ultimately founded on the idea of conscience, upon the idea that man must live by the light within, must prefer the voice of God to the voice of public opinion. From his commitment to the necessity of moral judgment in history arose his impatience with the "great man" school. His earliest essays and reviews dealt severely with the tendency among historians, statesmen, and men of religion to substitute expediency for principle and to take success rather than morality as the measure of men and causes. In the intimate historical connection between the ideas of liberty, conscience, and morality, Acton found the justification for a final aspect of his historical thought: his belief in progress and his conviction that the history of these ideas would reveal a constant progress and justify the ways of God to man.

Acton closed his inaugural address at Cambridge with the lesson of a lifetime of historical thought: "Whatever a man's notions [of modern history] are, such, in the main, the man himself will be. Under the name of History, they cover the articles of his philosophic, his religious, and his political creed. They give his measure; they denote his character. . . . [I]f we lower our standard in History, we cannot uphold it in Church or State."[54]

It is Acton's monument that he never lowered that standard.

J. Rufus Fears

[51] Acton, *Selected Writings*, II, p. 506.
[52] Acton, *Selected Writings*, II, pp. 523, 521.
[53] Acton, *Selected Writings*, II, pp. 521–523.
[54] Acton, *Selected Writings*, II, p. 552.

Editor's Note

This three-volume edition of Lord Acton's *Selected Writings* presents a full compendium of what is most important and most enduring in his thought. Each of these volumes is self-contained, with its own front matter and index. Volume I collects Acton's published writings on the history of liberty. Volume II brings together published lectures, articles, and reviews relating to the study and writing of history. Volume III presents a wide range of material to illustrate Acton's views on historical and contemporary issues in religion, politics, and morality. Volume I also contains a special foreword to the entire edition.

The bibliographical footnotes that accompany each essay are identical in character with those in Volume I. They are intended to indicate the title, place of original publication, and subsequent reprints of each essay included in this volume. In the case of unsigned articles, I have also indicated my authority for ascribing the piece in question to Acton. The problems facing the bibliographer of Acton's work are outlined in Volume I, pp. xxiv–xxvii. A list of abbreviations may be found on pp. xxiv–xxv of this volume. The decision of the publisher was to reprint Acton's previously published writings with only minor typographical corrections. Accordingly, apart from an introductory footnote giving the provenance of each essay, there are no editorial comments in the text, and the editor has not provided translations of Acton's numerous quotations in foreign languages.

My interest in Acton began during my tenure as a Guggenheim Fellow and has grown naturally out of my scholarly research on the history of liberty in the ancient world and the interpretation of classical freedom in nineteenth-century historiography. The preparation of this edition was made possible by an extended period of research with the Acton papers in the Cambridge University Library. I wish to thank the Syndics of Cambridge University Library and to express my deep appreciation to the staff of the Library for their remarkable efficiency

and unfailing courtesy. I owe an equal debt of gratitude to the Master
and Fellows of Christ's College for the warm hospitality extended me
during my stay in Cambridge.

J. Rufus Fears
Bloomington, Indiana

J. Rufus Fears is Professor of History at Indiana University.

List of Abbreviations

Acton, *Church and State*   Acton, John Emerich Edward Dalberg, First Baron. *Essays on Church and State*. Edited by Douglas Woodruff. London, 1952.

Acton, *Correspondence*   ———. *Selections from the Correspondence of the First Lord Acton*. Edited by John Figgis and Reginald Laurence. London, 1917.

Acton, *Freedom and Power*   ———. *Essays on Freedom and Power*. Edited by Gertrude Himmelfarb. Boston and Glencoe, Illinois, 1948.

Acton, *Historical Essays*   ———. *Historical Essays and Other Studies*. Edited by John Figgis and Reginald Laurence. London, 1908.

Acton, *History of Freedom*   ———. *The History of Freedom and Other Essays*. Edited by John Figgis and Reginald Laurence. London, 1907.

Acton, *Lectures on French Revolution*   ———. *Lectures on the French Revolution*. Edited by John Figgis and Reginald Laurence. London, 1910.

Acton, *Lectures on Modern History*   ———. *Lectures on Modern History*. Edited by John Figgis and Reginald Laurence. London, 1906.

Acton, *Liberal Interpretation of History*   ———. *Essays in the Liberal Interpretation of History*. Edited by William McNeill. Chicago, 1967.

Acton-Simpson   Altholz, Josef, Damian McElrath, and James Holland, eds. *The Correspondence of Lord Acton and Richard Simpson*. Cambridge, 1971–1975.

Add. Mss.   Acton Papers. Cambridge University Library.

Döllinger   Döllinger, Johann Ignaz von. *Briefwechsel*. Edited by Victor Conzemius. vols. I–III. Munich, 1963–1971.

McElrath   McElrath, Damian. *Lord Acton: The Decisive Decade 1864–1874: Essays and Documents*. Louvain, 1970.

xxiv

Paul   Paul, Herbert, ed. *Letters of Lord Acton to Mary Gladstone.* New York and London, 1904.

Ryan   Ryan, Guy. *The Acton Circle, 1864–1871: The 'Chronicle' and the 'North British Review.'* Diss. University of Notre Dame, 1969.

Shaw   Shaw, W. A. *A Bibliography of the Historical Works of Dr. Creighton, late Bishop of London, Dr. Stubbs, late Bishop of Oxford, Dr. S. R. Gardiner, and the late Lord Acton.* London, 1903.

Wellesley   *The Wellesley Index to Victorian Periodicals, 1824–1900.* Edited by Walter Houghton. Toronto and London, 1966–1979.

Selected Writings of Lord Acton

VOLUME II

ESSAYS IN
THE STUDY AND
WRITING OF HISTORY

[1]
Review of Poirson's *Histoire du Règne de Henri IV*

Of this work we shall have very little to say excepting that it is by far the most elaborate existing account of an important period, and throws considerable light upon the measures by which Henry IV and his ministers restored the French monarchy after the convulsions of the religious wars. The author is more at home in details than in matters of greater moment; and the tendency both of his studies and of his opinions is such as enables him to represent his hero in the most favourable manner and to ignore or palliate his greatest faults. He professes himself a Gallican of the school of Bossuet; but his Gallicanism in reality more nearly resembles that of the school of Richer or Dupin, and is marked by a contemptuous dislike of the authority of the Holy See. No principles could be more convenient to a writer who is determined, according to the traditional practice of biographers, to be the panegyrist of Henry, and none more utterly preclude a just appreciation of some of the principal features of his reign and character. Another serious deficiency is the little use M. Poirson has made of any but exclusively French sources of information. He has therefore, with all his industry, done little to explain the position of France towards other powers, and the part which Henry took in the great questions which agitated Europe in his time. We propose to examine one or two questions in which he has failed to connect the general policy of Henry with his attitude towards the religious movement.

The policy which was introduced by Henry IV and which so materially contributed to the greatness of his house, was a natural consequence of the circumstances under which he obtained his crown.

Auguste Poirson, *Histoire du Règne de Henri IV*, 3 vols. (Paris: Louis Colas, 1856). This review was published in the *Dublin Review* 44 (March 1858): 1–31. *Wellesley* II: 61; Döllinger I: 140.

He owed it neither to the arms of the Huguenots nor to the consent of the Catholics, but to the influence of a third party which represented, more accurately than either, the national temper and the future policy of France. The Catholic League, led by the princes of the house of Guise, refused to acknowledge a protestant king, and succeeded in excluding him until he undertook to be instructed in the Catholic doctrines. Yet the Leaguers were but a part, and latterly a small part of the Catholics of France. The mediaeval theory of public law which they revived and so resolutely maintained, had been everywhere conspicuously defeated during the preceding age. It was opposed to the tendency of the times and was particularly distasteful to a nation whose brilliant fortunes have seldom been purchased by preferring duty to interest, or right to expediency. At the same time the aid which the league received from Spain alarmed the patriotism of many Catholics, whilst the revolutionary fanaticism of some of its leaders excited the legitimate disgust of many more. From about the time of the death of Henry III a third party stands forth, as distinct from the League in its politics, as from the Huguenots in religion, which, deriving its strength from the increasing exhaustion of the country, and from the declining ardour of the contest, gradually prevailed over the enemies of Henry. These were the *Politiques* who did so much to introduce into political affairs that disregard for religious considerations with which all Europe became afterwards familiar. Various shades of opinion and various motives of interest combined to form this party, but they were united in the common tendency to strengthen to the utmost the royal authority and to support the claim of the king of Navarre. It included the greater portion of the magistracy, bred in the spirit of the Roman law, and generally hostile to all the remnants of feudal independence. It was still more efficiently supported by the clergy. A majority of the bishops had never joined the League. The spirit of Gallicanism was roused by the reaction against it to seek its natural protector in an absolute sovereign, and the alliance inauspiciously commenced between the house of Bourbon and the church of France, which so greatly promoted the transitory splendour and the ruin of both. Finally the party of the Politiques was embraced by all who were devoid of the enthusiasm of the conflict, and who desired, at all hazards, to bring it to an end. This party were naturally driven to join the Huguenots, until their common object was attained by the victory of Henry. After his death, considerations of political interest similar to those which had led to their separation from the League, led to a still more determined hostility against their Protestant allies.

Had Henry become a Catholic earlier than he did he would have lost all the political advantages of the step. His conversion took place at a time when it had become obvious that he could not otherwise be king of France, but when his enemies had sufficiently experienced the difficulty of opposing him. He knew the danger of doing it prematurely, though he knew that it could not ultimately be avoided. "No cannon," he said with his usual levity, "would make a breach in the walls of Paris but the canon of the Mass." If he had joined the Catholics before he had made himself formidable to them, he would have gained nothing. He would have become completely dependent on them; he would have irrecoverably forfeited his credit with the Protestants, and the civil war would have continued as before. As it was, he was able to preserve to the end the fidelity, if not the confidence, of both parties, and to prevent their antagonism from injuring the state. He did not owe so much to either as to be dependent on one alone; but he made the power and the interests both of Catholics and Protestants subservient to his own, and succeeded so well in conciliating both that his enemies could enlist no religious sympathies on either side against him. He was indeed singularly qualified, both by his virtues and his defects, to maintain the equivocal and difficult position from which he derived his extraordinary influence. He recovered in great measure the ground that he had lost with the Protestants by his conversion. They soon perceived that the change of his religion was but a superficial change, and that he had not given up his early attachments. After the Edict of Nantes had been granted they began anew to entertain hopes which Henry did not live to dissipate, and which occupy a place so prominent in the history of his latter years. Nor did the same observation which reconciled the Protestants produce a corresponding alienation of the Catholics. The levity of the king in all religious matters, his scandalous life, and the notorious temporal advantages which accompanied his conversion, seem to have excited no permanent mistrust. The ablest of the Leaguers sat with Sully at his council board. The Pope accepted his mediation in the dispute with Venice. The greatest divine and the greatest saint of the age recommended him, by the influence of their example, to the confidence of the Catholic world. Cardinal Duperron was his intimate adviser, and his most efficient advocate with the court of Rome; while St. Francis of Sales, whom

Henry knew and revered, repeatedly expressed the warmest admiration for him, and bitterly lamented his death.[1]

Time has torn down the veil which, in his own day, concealed the real character of this famous prince. We who are able to judge how completely both Catholics and Protestants were deceived in him, can appreciate the marvellous skill with which he blinded all his contemporaries; and our notion of his ability rises as the idea of his virtues fades away. But for his sudden death it is probable that his next proceedings would have disclosed more of the truth to the world.

The recognition of Henry as king of France, immediately followed by his conversion, could be claimed as a victory neither by the Protestants nor the Catholics, and the interests of neither religion exclusively determined the policy of the new reign. The great controversy of the sixteenth century raised those states which were the most decided and vigorous partizans of the contending principles to an unexampled height of power. The same dispute which ruined Germany by dividing it, made Spain and England, the champions of the old and of the new religion, the foremost powers in Europe. What Spain and England gained by adopting religion as a motive of policy, was obtained by France by the exclusion of religion from politics. Whilst others were making sacrifices for a spiritual cause, Henry gained great political advantages by neglecting spiritual for temporal objects, and thus anticipating the other powers in a policy which was afterwards pursued by all. As king of a Catholic country, he could not contest the championship of the Reformation with Elizabeth; and by adopting as his own the cause of the Church, he would have placed himself under the undisputed hegemony of Spain. In seeking his own advantage, regardless of the consequences to the interests of the Church, Henry sought and enjoyed the friendship of Catholic as well as Protestant states. He launched his country in a course in which principle was subordinate to expediency, but which was eminently congenial to the national character and conducive to the national greatness. So well did it suit the interests of France that it continued to be even more energetically pursued when bishops and cardinals were at the head of the affairs, and when the Church of France, by the piety and learning of her clergy, was the first in the world. But from that day forward

---

[1] (Hamon) Vie de St. François de Sales. 1854. i. p. 636. Nothing in this interesting book is more interesting than the account of the saint's visit to Paris in 1602, and of his intercourse with the king and his court, Livre 3. chap. 4.

France has been an uncertain friend and a frequent enemy of the Church, and has borne by courtesy only the name of a Catholic power.

There is one point in particular where the consequences of this system are still felt by the whole of Christendom.

The Turks had made good their footing in Europe in consequence of the schism between the Greek and Latin churches; and it was manifest that the security of their conquests, and the chance of extending them depended on the continuance of similar differences among the Christian states. The Reformation provided this permanent source of division, and the revolt of so many countries from the Pope put an end to the terror with which the Turks had been accustomed to regard him as the great author of all the alliances against them. They came therefore to consider the Protestants as their best friends, and the eagerness with which the Protestants sought their friendship amply justified the opinion. At the time when the fall of Rhodes seemed to deprive Christendom of its last bulwark, when the imminence of the danger inspired even the monks with warlike ardour, when the Franciscans offered to raise an army by sending a soldier from each of the forty thousand monasteries of their order, the Protestant clergy were denouncing the iniquity of the Turkish war. Luther had declared that to fight with the Turks was to fight against God, and his saying was frequently used on the Turkish frontier, to the great detriment of the christian cause. He found it necessary to justify himself, and wrote a book in which, with characteristic audacity, he attributed the reverses of the Christian arms to the part which the clergy had taken in the war. "So long," he said, "as a cross or a crucifix should appear on the Christian standard, it was no more to be followed than the devil."[2] At a time when the Church was the only promoter of a war, which most of the states looked upon with dread, the practical effect of such doctrines could not be doubtful. The French Protestants appear to have regarded the Turks with equal favour. Brantome[3] relates that during the civil wars Coligny sent several gentlemen of his party to Constantinople, "pour faire quelque haute entreprise" with Soliman, but the death of the Sultan crossed their plans. Similar opinions prevailed in England, for we find Sir Henry Wotton preferring the Turks to the Catholics: "But to return to the Spanish league with the peers of France, I think no good christian can think better of them

[2] Vom Krieg wider den Türken, p. 21.
[3] Mémoires, IX, p. 218.

than of a Turk; and I am of opinion that the league and amity of Turkish Infidels is more to be esteemed than the friendship of these Leaguers."[4]

In consequence of this good understanding Protestants were received with favour in Turkey. It was usual to ask the prisoners taken on the Danube and the Drave whether they were Lutherans or Papists, and their treatment differed according to the answer they gave. Nor did this preference arise from political causes alone. Paleologus relates an interview with the Cadi of Chios who asked him if he was not a Lutheran, because "Nos Lutheranos defendere solemus, quoniam melius de Deo sentire videntur et (nobiscum) parum dissentiunt; multum autem dissentiunt Papistae."[5] In Hungary Protestantism kept pace with the progress of the Turkish arms, and flourished under their protection. The Protestant preachers declared publicly that the victories of the Turks were permitted in order to assist the growth of the Gospel. Turkish officers sometimes attended at their sermons, and always decided in their favour when disputations with the Catholics were held before them.[6]

France was, of all the great powers, the least dangerous to the Turks and the least exposed to their hostility. It was natural, therefore, for Francis I to unite with Soliman in his war against their common enemy Charles V. The progress of Protestantism in France strengthened these friendly dispositions. Selim congratulated Charles IX on the marriage of his sister with the king of Navarre, "as he was a Huguenot and a great enemy of the Pope and of the king of Spain." He was greatly disconcerted at the news of the massacre of St. Bartholomew, in which his best allies seemed to have been exterminated. But when there was a prospect that a Calvinist might become king of France, the Turks began to expect great things from his friendship, and in 1577 Sultan Murad offered to send 200 galleys to his aid. When Henry ascended the throne of France he resolved to turn this friendship to account. His own maritime weakness rendered the alliance of a great naval power highly desirable. "I will not," he wrote to his ambassador, "be reproached and envied for this alliance as my predecessors were, without deriving any advantage from it."[7] He was as willing as the

---

[4] The State of Christendom, 1657, p. 140.
[5] Reussner Epist. Turc. III, p. 143.
[6] Fessler Geschichte der Ungarn VII. p. 517. Fessler was an apostate Capuchin.
[7] Lettres missives de Henri IV. iv. p. 497.

Protestants had been to invoke Turkish help against the Christian powers, and it is as much to the absence of religious sentiments from his policy as to the Reformation itself that the Turks owe their permanent establishment in Europe. This contempt of the principles which all Christian nations obeyed prevailed in France long before the visible decline of the Ottoman Empire under Murad III and Mahomet III had dissipated the universal terror which it had so long inspired; and it was still displayed in the ignominious conduct of Lewis XIV when the old alarm was revived by the last aggressive effort of the Turks, and even Protestant princes followed Sobieski to the relief of Vienna. It was never more strikingly displayed than by Henry IV. In 1593 he wrote as follows to his ambassador at Constantinople:

"A esté bien à propos que vous ayés cogneu ses intentions, (he is speaking of the English envoy,) affin de vous tenir doresnavant plus serré avec luy, en ce que vous aurès à traicter, sans luy dire chose qu'il puisse interpreter ny divulguer à mon desadvantage, pour faire tomber le blasme sur moy, du mal que la chrestienté peut recevoir par les armées et forces du dict Grand Seigneur . . . et aux offices que vous ferez envers eulx, qui doibvent principalement tendre à faire tourner ses forces contre celuy qui me travaille injustement, comportez-vous aussi de fasçon et avec une telle discretion qu'il ne paroisse rien à la veue et aux yeux des autres princes chrestiens, qui leur puisse donner occasion de m'estimer instigateur ny cause de faire entrer en la chrestienté un si grand orage, mesme au dommage de ceux desquels j'en ai reçeu aulcuns offices."[8]

This referred to his endeavours to obtain the assistance of a Turkish fleet against Spain. His ambassador was told to remind the Sultan that if the Spaniards succeeded in depriving him of the crown of France there would be nothing to prevent them from turning their arms against Turkey. France, he says truly enough, was ever the chief obstacle to the designs of Spain against the Turkish empire.[9] He perceived nothing in this admission to be ashamed of; but he got little from the Turks except their good opinion. He and the Great Mogul were the only princes whom the Sultan honoured with the imperial title of Padishah. The feebleness and inaction of Sultan Mahomet caused him great concern. He urges his Ambassador to make every effort "affin de l'eschauffer et persuader de mettre la main à la

[8] Ibid. p. 34–35.
[9] Ibid. p. 89.

besogne."[10] The result of these efforts was the victorious campaign of Mahomet in Hungary in 1596, when in the great battle before the walls of Erlau fifty thousand Christians fell. Henry rejoiced at his success and was inconsolable at his reverses. In order to understand the moral worth of these sentiments of the most Christian king, we must remember the barbarity with which the war on the Danube was carried on, that capitulations were not observed, that large garrisons were massacred, that the Hungarian women filled the harems of Turkey, and that the nobles carried poison about them to escape the mutilation and the hopeless slavery which were the lot of the Christian captive.[11]

When at length all hope of effectual assistance from the Turks was dispelled by the decline of their power; and the odium of their alliance was no longer outweighed by the profits derived from it, Henry's friendship was converted into enmity, and he conceived the design, which he did not live to attempt, of their expulsion from Europe. He himself had made it impossible by making Turkey through his alliance a necessary member in the European system, and by diminishing the authority of religion over the policy of public men.

This indifference to religion as a determining cause of political conduct had indeed been already shown by the predecessors of Henry. The advantages which the division of Europe by the Reformation offered to a state, which, taking part against neither side should use each in turn against the other, were soon understood and accepted in France. It was a line of conduct which the circumstances of the time suggested, but it found a peculiarly fit and competent instrument in the person of the king. He was made to be the organ of a system in which religion had no place rather than to be a leader in a religious war. The great passions of the time did not touch him. He had none of the uncompromising, devoted zeal of the Guises and the Chatillons. He was a man of few prejudices and of fewer principles, and his passions were subject to his interests. But as the line of policy which he followed was made possible and attractive to him by that position of affairs which Protestantism had produced, Protestantism had some influence at first in directing it. The Protestant cause coincided for a time with the interests of France. Henry had little capacity for religion.

---

[10] Ibid. p. 452.

[11] This is the origin of the little flask suspended at the shoulder which is still a part of the costume of the Hungarian nobility.

Though not a sceptic, and in his own opinion, at least during the last ten years of his life,[12] a Catholic, his superficial and epicurean nature had none of the cravings which religion alone can satisfy. He had no sympathy for the enthusiasm of the times, and as he did not share it he was able to employ it for his own advantage. It is impossible to prove, what many have tried to prove, that he was really a Catholic or really a Protestant, for it is impossible to prove that he was really susceptible of religious conviction. His real sentiments were of a kind that might be interpreted either way. So far as he was open to religious belief he was a Catholic, but where he was actuated in his public conduct by notions derived from religion, he was a Calvinist. It was productive of serious consequences that his early impressions had been received under the influence of Calvinism, and that most of his private friends were Calvinists. It made it natural that he should depend chiefly on Protestant states for support, which opened in some degree the way for their influence, and it enabled the Protestants to turn his religious indifference against the Church by concealing their own plans under the disguise of solicitude for his interests.

The passions of nations and the interest of princes had caused the triumph of the Reformation throughout the North of Europe. It had prevailed in Sweden over the resistance of the people, and in Scotland over the power of the throne. In England its success was bound up with the rights of an able and popular Sovereign, in Denmark with the influence of a powerful aristocracy, in Holland with the cause of Independence. Nearly all the states of Germany had adopted it at the price even of personal liberty. It confined the power and menaced the existence of the few Catholic princes that remained. It was rapidly gaining ground in the hereditary dominions of the house of Austria, it had penetrated the Slavonic states to the frontiers of Muscovy, and seemed about to prevail in Poland. It had been adopted by all who sought an instrument for the subversion either of liberty or authority, and its adherents were still increasing in numbers, and were seldom deficient in zeal.

---

[12] Richelieu says in his Mémoires I, p. 10 ed. Michaud: "Il confessa à la Reine qu'au commencement qu'il fit profession d'être catholique, il n'embrassa qu'en apparence la vérité de la religion pour s'assurer en effet sa couronne; mais que, depuis la conférence qu'eut à Fontainebleau le cardinal Duperron avec Duplessis-Mornay, il détestoit autant par raison de conscience la créance des Huguenots, comme leur parti par raison d'état." The conference in question was held in 1600.

Catholicism, on the other hand was upheld by no great power excepting Spain, and Spain was fast sinking in the unequal contest with hostile nations and revolted provinces, with the innumerable enemies that for temporal or religious causes were united against her. The leaders of the great Catholic Reformation, Paul IV and Pius V, St. Ignatius and St. Charles, were dead. Their efforts and their example joined to the renewed activity of the religious orders could scarcely protect Italy from the new doctrines. There was not a single country beyond the Alps, even among those which had not renounced their allegiance, where Protestantism was not making progress. And this was the time when the Turkish frontier was in sight of Vienna, and when Turkish fleets ravaged the coasts of Italy. The Church and the whole civilisation of the world had not seen such peril when Attila was in Lombardy, or Abderrahman on the Loire.

All felt the importance of the contest which raged in France. It seemed that the victory of the Protestants there must be followed by their victory in all those states where they had gained a footing; whilst, if the Catholics prevailed they would be able to prolong the great struggle on more equal terms. Even the fierce strife in the Low Countries stood still for a time while Philip withdrew his armies to a more decisive battle field. Even the parsimonious Elizabeth lavished treasure in order that a Huguenot might be her Brother of France. Adventurers thronged from Germany, from Switzerland, and the Netherlands, some for pay and some for conscience-sake, to lend their swords to the princes who were contending for the splendid prize.

It appears to us that the great change which just then followed in the fortunes of Protestantism cannot be attributed entirely to the vigour of the Catholic reaction. The Protestants lost the day but the Catholics did not in reality win it. Their weakness was but a secondary cause of the success of the Reformation, and their strength was not the chief cause of its defeat. The secret of its rapid growth and of its sudden check lies in the principles themselves. It is to be sought even more in the nature of the doctrines, than in the circumstances of the time.

Every great heresy has power to attract men for a time, and the attraction of Protestantism was more intense and more general than any other because its chief doctrine seemed practically to permit the gratification of the passions. But, like every heresy, the sources from which it drew its vitality acted but for a time, and its attractiveness declined when its benefits had been once enjoyed, and when its consequences were fully understood. The principle of separation and insubordination from which it started became a principle of dissolution and anarchy. Some of its promises were found to be delusive, others could produce no permanent effect and could be fulfilled but once for all. Those causes precisely by which the extreme rapidity of its early progress can be explained could excite no lasting enthusiasm, and attracted only by their novelty. The errors of the Protestant doctrines began soon to develop their consequences. Calvinism not only robbed Lutheranism of all its conquests excepting Germany and Scandinavia, but stopped its progress in Germany itself, and penetrated into its stronghold, the court of Saxony. The dissensions among the Lutherans themselves, which had begun before the death of Luther, afterwards greatly increased. They were pacified at length by the adoption of the Formula Concordiae, a confession so carefully drawn up that all could subscribe it who professed to be followers of Luther. But this artificial concord, whilst it put an end to the scandal of dissension, arrested at the same time completely both the development and propagation of the doctrines. Calvinism everywhere engaged in conflict with the Catholics, and possessing in its synods some kind of organized authority, remained longer in a united and rampant state. But soon after the period of which we speak occurred the great Arminian separation, in consequence of which Calvinism divided against itself, and checked in its growth as it had checked the growth of Lutheranism, ceased to be an aggressive power. From that time the swords of the Protestants were turned against each other. The war of Religion had become a war of sects. The executions of Crell, of Barneveld, of Laud, were a pledge that the fierceness of the great revolution had subsided, and that the spirit of division was beginning to produce its natural fruit. Where the Reformation had been a popular movement, it was rendered impotent by internal differences. Where it was the work of the princes, it had, sooner or later, the people against it. Men began to waver in their attachment to a system which introduced a tyranny far more oppressive than the discipline which had been cast off with the authority of the Church. The dissolution began at the heart. Where Lutheranism had taken its rise it began first to decline. There is no doubt that at a very early period a great part of the German Lutherans longed to return to the old religion.

Amongst the causes which made the end of the sixteenth century the turning-point in the history of Protantism we must reckon the circumstance that it was only then that the doctrinal controversy was virtually decided. The new doctrines required time to display their real character and consequences. It was not until they had been fully developed by controversy that they could be completely understood and successfully refuted by the Catholic divines. During the first period of the Reformation no great dogmatical works appeared. Luther himself put forth no regular system, and he greatly modified his teaching, for the purpose of reconciling, not the Catholics but the Zwinglians. Most of his doctrines were subordinate to the great central dogma of Justification. He carried on the movement chiefly by means of tracts, pamphlets, and commentaries. His followers readily shifted their ground, their works were rather aggressive than constructive, and they confined themselves generally to the discussion of a few distinct points. Their adversaries were obliged to follow their example in order to combat them on their own ground. It was long after the death of the founders of Protestantism, when the doctrines of the Church had been defined by the Council of Trent, that the great Catholic writers, Bellarmin, Stapleton, Duperron, produced those great theological works by which the intellectual discomfiture of Protestantism was accomplished, and its decline greatly accelerated.

All these circumstances are anterior to the great Catholic revival, and opened the way for its action. Certain it is that the marvellous attraction which the Protestant doctrines of Justification and Predestination had exercised during a great part of the sixteenth century suddenly ceased. Whilst it lasted Protestantism conquered the greatest obstacles. Neither defeat nor persecution could arrest its victorious career. Henceforth no victory could help it on. The vigour of the movement was exhausted, and neither great promises and great hopes, nor the severity of a vindictive persecution, have ever brought about a considerable apostasy, or prevented the gradual recovery by the Church, of much that she had lost.

When the Protestants seemed on the point of becoming supreme in France, the spell by which their success had been obtained was already broken. But their hopes were too sanguine and too much justified by the external aspect of things, to be at once abandoned upon the abjuration of their chief. That event however, joined to the evident decrease in the vitality of the movement and the diminished ardour of its converts, naturally led to a larger introduction of political elements in order to assist and to disguise their designs. When wholesale secessions to the Reformed Faith by force from above or by tumult from below were no longer heard of, it was natural to seek other means of extending it. Political combinations made up for the declining efficacy of religious zeal in carrying on the work. The pulpit had done its part, and the turn of the sword had come; the statesman had taken the place of the preacher. This was the general character of the period from 1598 to 1648, from the peace of Vervins and the edict of Nantes to the peace of Westphalia. The contest which was waged during the greater part of those fifty years for the political predominance of Protestantism in Europe, was not less fierce than that by which its doctrines had established themselves in particular countries. The temporal interests which were mingled more largely with the zeal for the dogma did not damp the ardour of their defenders, but the period had gone by when Protestantism throve in spite of oppression, and its victories in the field were compensated by losses of another description.

The leaders of the Protestant movement during this period were the Calvinists. The followers of Luther never succeeded in forming a fixed and definite dogmatic system of their own. They were scarcely reconciled to the idea of a complete and final separation from the Church. They clung to the hope that the Catholics would accept the Confession of Augsburg, and in that hope Melanchthon, the author of the Confession, advised his mother not to change her religion. For a long time attempts to accommodate the Protestant to the Catholic system form the only intellectual activity in the stagnant existence of German Lutheranism. Calvinism on the other hand, from the comparative completeness and consistency of the system, and from the circumstances under which it forced its way in France where the Church was already so completely under the control of the state as to be no object of envy or cupidity, consciously aimed at the destruction of Catholicism. It connected itself with the memory of the mediaeval heresies and was assisted in its course by the remains of their revolutionary enmity to Church and state. It flourished chiefly in those parts where the execution of the Albigenses was not yet forgotten. From its first appearance in France it stood in a menacing and hostile attitude to the government; for the French kings were already absolute, and the authority which they possessed over the Church in their dominions removed one great temptation which led princes to join the new faith. This was the cause of the singular sincerity and fierceness of the French Calvinists, who had more martyrs and more assassins amongst them than any other denomination of Protestants. In France, in England, and in the Netherlands, where the Reformation had been first preached by Lutherans, the Calvinists prevailed over them. Lutheranism came to be looked upon as the national Teutonic form of Protestantism. In Hungary, the Germans were Lutherans, and the Magyars Calvinists. But even in Germany Lutheranism could not hold its ground. Melanchthon, with the whole body of the Humanists, seceded to the Swiss Reformation. In Saxony itself the growth of Calvinism was only stopped by the execution of the Calvinistic chancellor. Anhalt, Hesse, Brandenburg, exchanged the system of Luther for the system of Calvin. The Palatinate, after having changed its religion four times with the accession of each new Elector, remained Calvinist at last. The Lutherans, furious at the losses inflicted on them by their Protestant brethren, turned from the Catholic controversy to an enemy nearer home, and extended to the Calvinists all their hatred of the Church. There was a lull in the conflict between Catholics and Lutherans which made the counter Reformation possible in Germany. But the Calvinists were foremost wherever the contest with Catholic Europe was carried on. The greatest works which have been written against the Church were produced by them. Many of their greatest warriors wielded with equal energy the pen and the sword.

The most conspicuous of these at the time of Henry IV was Duplessis-Mornay, who was called not unjustly the Pope of the Huguenots. He possessed in an equal degree the confidence of the Protestants and of the king. He had served under Henry during the war, and he continued to serve him still more effectually by his influence after the peace. He was the champion of Calvinism against Duperron in the famous conference of Fontainebleau. In his polemical writings, the most celebrated of which is the *Mysterium Iniquitatis,* his hatred of the Church makes up for the deficiency of his learning. He was the chief of those who perseveringly endeavoured to carry the religious quarrel on to another ground. A statesman as well as a soldier and controversialist, he perceived before any of his party the advantage which they would derive from the position and character of Henry. With this view he was the principal author of the tranquillity of the Huguenots during his reign. At the same time he spared no pains to dispose the king in favour of the policy which would suit their ends. For many years he devoted himself to the organization of a great final effort of the Protestants against the Church. To that end he developed an activity and vigilance which nothing could surpass. He corresponded not only with the leaders of his party in France, but also with the king and his ministers, with the chief men among the Protestants in every country in Europe, with the ministers of foreign princes, and with several of the foreign princes themselves. Besides his correspondents he had agents and emissaries wherever he judged that anything of importance was to be done. He was consulted by many of the German princes and by the leaders of both parties in the Netherlands. The Protestant diplomatists in the service of Henry received his instructions and reported to him as regularly as to the Government. His plans were pursued with an energy as comprehensive and as intense as those of the king. Their ends agreed, for each needed the support of the other against the great Catholic power. This knowledge gave him confidence. No occasion, he thought, could ever be more favourable to strike a great blow. The downfall of the Church seemed to him inevitable. "Our forces," he writes, "will be sufficient to seek the pope in Rome."[13] On another occasion he says: "You know the work at which I am labouring according to my poor ability. I have reports every day from its chief directors who are pushing it on, prudently and powerfully, according to the measure of their gifts. . . . I am making the same efforts in the Low Countries and everywhere else."[14] "I omit nothing in Germany, in England, in the Low Countries, through letters, through friends, *opportune, importune,* to the right and to the left. In divers places I am led to hope that God will co-operate, if He pleases."[15] He repeatedly declares that the king might be depended upon for active assistance when the time came. His great hopes were founded upon the projects which he knew that his friends were recommending to the king, and it is in this vast conspiracy, organised by the Huguenot leader, that the designs which Henry was preparing to execute at the close of his reign find their explanation.

Henry began to entertain these designs as soon as peace was restored to France, and he never lost sight of them. The humiliation of Spain was their chief aim, for he was surrounded on all sides by the Spanish dominions and opposed by Spanish influence. He could form no plan for the aggrandisement of France of which Spain was not the object. The inference to which these circumstances inevitably led was confirmed

[13] Mémoires de Duplessis-Mornay, 1824. x. p. 321.
[14] Ibid. p. 342.
[15] Ibid. p. 352.

by his resentment against the Power which had nearly deprived him of his throne, and by the natural antipathy of the founder of the new system of European politics against the representative of the old.

The peace of Vervins was concluded by Philip II from exhaustion. His sincerity was secured by the absolute necessity of the measure. Under Philip III everything was done to conciliate France. Alliances were proposed against the Protestants, and against the Mahometans. A marriage was proposed between Henry's daughter and an Infant of Spain, and they were to receive the crown of the Netherlands, provided Henry would aid in reducing them. But he had more to expect from the help of the Protestants against the Spaniards than from that of the Spaniards against the Protestants, and he remembered that he had derived assistance from the Low Countries when Spain was exerting herself to keep him from the throne. The embassy which proceeded to Paris for the purpose of negotiating the match was fruitless. But it appears from the memoirs of the time, that the dignity and the skill of the Spanish envoy made a great impression. Henry became irritated at last and swore that when once in the saddle he would breakfast at Milan, hear Mass in Rome, and dine at Naples. "At that rate," answered the Spaniard, "your Majesty might arrive for Vespers in Sicily."

In spite of all these pacific efforts of the Spaniards Henry pursued his plan of uniting in a great league all those powers whom religious, political, or commercial interests rendered jealous of either branch of the House of Habsburg. The proposal of this plan had been favourably received by Elizabeth and James, and it had been accepted by all the Protestant powers, by Sweden, Denmark, and the Netherlands. But the most important and active members of the confederacy were the German Calvinists. Their connection with Henry began at the time of the religious wars, and arose from the military dependence of France upon the German soldiers during the period which beheld the passage from the feudal to the modern system of warfare.

From a very early period, when Germany ceased to exert over her neighbours the authority which the populousness and the valour of the nation would have justified, the German soldiers who could find no employment at home flocked to the service of richer and less warlike states. During the latter period of the middle ages there was scarcely a war in Europe where the German mercenaries were not conspicuous. They fought at Poitiers for the king of France, and at Stoke for the house of York. Their reputation did not decline with this decline of the Empire. When the Emperors no longer led their armies into Italy, the German warriors continued to seek employment in the petty wars of the Italian Republics. Werner of Urslingen, Captain of the Great Company, who bore on his breastplate the honest and significant device, "*Nemico di Dio, di pietà e di misericordia,*" was the first of a long line of German condottieri famous for their barbarity, but known, as Boccaccio[16] admits them to have been, for their fidelity to their engagements. The revolution in the art of war, which was marked by the introduction of artillery and of infantry, was first carried into effect in Germany, and the Germans were thenceforward considered the most formidable enemies and the most valuable allies. At Pavia their pikemen destroyed for ever the reputation of the Swiss. A necessary change soon followed in the cavalry. Light horsemen, armed with heavy pistols first appear in the wars of the Reformation in Germany. They were mostly Protestants from Pomerania and Franconia, and the simplicity of their equipment enabled great numbers to join them who were too poor to purchase defensive armour. These were the Reistres who played so great a part in the wars of Religion in France.

The French nobility were longer in adapting themselves to a mode of warfare which supplanted that by which they had maintained their power and their renown. Their old supremacy was lost in the encounter with the English bowmen at Créci, and with the Flemish clubmen at Courtrai.[17] It was long before a national infantry arose in France. An attempt of Charles VII in 1448, and another of Francis I in 1534 to raise regular foot soldiers in the country, signally failed. The pikemen of Picardy and Gascony were alone found to be available. Francis acknowledged in 1536, that either by design or neglect his predecessors

[16] Decamerone Giornata viii. Novella 1.

[17] The battle of Créci was won by the English foot. There were no horse on the English side. Froissart (part i. cap. 130) says it was the first battle of the kind. The English were victorious so long as their tactics had the advantage of novelty. From the want of cavalry all their battles at that time are defensive. Villani (Cronica 1845 ii. p. 68) says of the battle of Courtrai (1302); "Di questa sconfitta abbassò molto l'onore, e lo stato, e fama dell' antica nobiltà e prodezza de' Franceschi, essendo il fiore della cavalleria del mondo isconfitta e abbassata da' loro fedeli, e dalla più vile gente che fosse al mondo, tesserandi, e felloni, ed altre vili arti e mestieri, e non mai usi di guerra, che per dispetto e loro viltade, da tutte le nazioni del mondo i Fiamminghi erano chiamati conigli pieni di burro; e per queste vittorie salirono in tanta fama e ardire, che uno Fiammingo a piè con uno godendac in mano, avrebbe atteso due cavalieri franceschi."

had allowed the military spirit of the nation to degenerate to such a degree, that he was unable to carry on war without the aid of foreign troops. "We are strong," he says, "in cavalry, but not in infantry; for it has been considered wiser to leave the people to the pursuit of agriculture and the arts of peace."[18] His general Tavannes,[19] declares that the French kings thought it dangerous to put weapons in the hands of the people, and preferred to give money to foreigners than arms to their subjects. In the same age, another French general, Montluc,[20] stimulated the courage of his soldiers before a battle by reminding them that if they won the day they would be the first Frenchmen who had ever fought with the Germans and were not defeated. The kings of France, in their progress towards absolute power, encountered the greatest obstacle in the feudal nobility. This obstacle could not be vanquished by a feudal army, and they were therefore driven to raise troops in the neighbouring states, where a great force of infantry already subsisted. The importance of these mercenaries was so great that Francis was accustomed to relax his severity towards the disciples of the Reformation whenever a new war obliged him to have recourse to his Protestant allies. It was in this manner that Henry IV had become connected with the princes of Anhalt and of the Palatinate, who encouraged him in his plans against Spain and invoked his aid in an enterprise against the Empire. The common pretext of these designs was still the exorbitant power of the House of Austria, which, it was pretended, menaced the independence of Europe. It was generally supposed that the union in the same family of the Spanish and Imperial crowns rendered it formidable to the other states. But in reality the Emperor was the most feeble sovereign in Europe, and a great source of weakness to his Spanish relative. Whilst in France and Spain and England absolute monarchy was rising on the ruins of feudalism, in Germany the contrary process took place, and the supreme authority gradually declined. In the contest between the emperors and the popes the cause of the church had been upheld in Germany by the great feudal aristocracy. When the papacy prevailed over the House of Hohenstaufen the nobles shared the victory. For several years they remained without an Emperor, and the power which

---

[18] Barthold, Deutschland und die Hugenotten i. p. 18. Carew Relation of the state of France, in Birch, Negotiations p. 427.

[19] Mémoires de Tavannes ed. Michaud. p. 64, 83.

[20] Commentaires de Montluc ed. Michaud. p. 67.

they at last committed to Rudolph of Habsburgh was but the shadow of what had been. Maximilian I was so poor that the administration of justice was suspended for want of funds, and on one occasion certain state papers could not be removed because there was not money enough in the imperial treasury to hire a cart. He described in a pointed saying the character of the four great monarchs: "The king of France is a king of asses, for they bear whatever he imposes on them; the king of Spain is a king of men, for they obey him only in what is just; the king of England is a king of angels, for he governs justly and they obey willingly; but we are a king of kings for they obey us only when they please." He said before his accession that he would not be a king of money but a king of the people, but in the peculiar constitution of the empire he was left sometimes without money and sometimes without troops. Charles V derived all his power from his Spanish crown. In Germany he was once without an army, and narrowly escaped being captured by the rebellious Protestants. During his lifetime the Reformation reduced his power in Germany to such a degree that only the name remained. At the end of the sixteenth century the imperial authority was confined to the hereditary states. Even there the power of the emperor was less than that of other sovereigns, and even of his own vassals, over their subjects. It had never fallen so low as when the Protestant princes made its oppressiveness the pretext of their league with France. Rudolph II who then occupied the throne, was the most feeble and incapable of his race. He had lost Hungary and Transylvania. Austria, Styria and Tyrol had become independent territories under the archdukes Mathias, Ferdinand and Maximilian. Bohemia, where the emperor resided, was distracted by religious factions, and he was forced to make concessions to the Protestants, by which, without satisfying their pretensions, he exhibited and confirmed his own weakness. A few years later, he was forced to resign even the Bohemian crown, and yet was emperor, though without a court, an army, or a home. A number of petty princes differing in religion and in their interests, agreeing only in their contempt for the imperial authority and in the resolution of governing their dominions with absolute sway, appeared in the place of the empire which had been for five hundred years the foremost power in Christendom. Such was Germany at a time when her neighbours, France, and Sweden, and Turkey, were at the height of their power and their ambition. Henry and his allies were incited by the weakness, not by the strength of the empire, to attempt its destruction. He professed that he was obliged to provide for the safety of his descendants, and therefore, by way of securing peace to Europe, at a time when perfect tranquillity prevailed, he prepared a mighty war. The object of the war is described in the memoirs of Sully, and is known in history as the "Grand Dessein." Of this design the memoirs give several draughts. It was substantially as follows:

Europe was to be divided into fifteen states; six hereditary monarchies, six elective monarchies, and three republics. The hereditary monarchies were France, Spain, England, Sweden, Denmark, and Lombardy, which was to be formed by giving the duchy of Milan to the House of Savoy. The elective monarchies were the Empire, the Papal States with the addition of Naples, Venice, sometimes reckoned as a fourth republic, which was to obtain Sicily, Poland, Hungary, and Bohemia, which included Silesia and Moravia. The Helvetic confederation was to obtain Tyrol, Alsace, and Upper Burgundy; the Belgic confederation was to embrace the whole of the Netherlands; and the Italic confederation was to be formed out of the smaller states and cities of central Italy.

These states were to constitute the Christian republic. Their affairs were to be conducted by several assemblies, and by a great Federal council of 64 members, to which the greater states were to send four deputies apiece, and each of the lesser states, including even the several petty states of the Italic confederation, two. The office of this Assembly was to preserve peace among the members of the European republic, by watching and advising the government in all of them, and to secure equal toleration for Catholics, Lutherans, and Calvinists. The forces of this formidable confederacy were to be directed towards the expulsion of the Turks and of the schismatics from Europe.

Many historians have denied that this extraordinary project was ever seriously entertained. Siri calls it an absurd project injurious to the memory of a great king. Hénault says: "cela a bien l'air d'une chimère." Flassan calls it "une fantaisie." The Jesuit D'Avrigny endeavours to shew its improbability. Michelet thinks it a ridiculous plan drawn up by the secretaries of Sully. Ranke considers it a vague scheme, by a very incompetent person for the expulsion of the Turks. It rests, however, by no means on the questionable authority of Sully's memoirs alone. Amongst others Wolf, in his Life of Maximilian of Bavaria (ii. p. 534) gives a version of it from several manuscripts. It may however be shown that there is nothing improbable or inexplicable about the plan, which should lead us to doubt that it was ever intended to be carried into execution. We propose to show that its chief provisions coincide with the known intentions of Henry, whilst they were partly justified by the course which affairs subsequently took, and that they were exceedingly well adapted for the accomplishment of hopes of which we have already mentioned the existence.

At the time of his death Henry was on the point of starting on an expedition which was to end in the humiliation of both branches of the house of Habsburg. For more than twelve years he had laboured to form a league for this purpose among the German Protestants; but although the Calvinists eagerly seconded him, it was with great difficulty that the Lutherans could be induced to join them. They had a stronger aversion for the Calvinists than for the Catholics, and they felt that there was more reason to fear a powerful ally like the king of France than an enemy so feeble as the emperor. At length Henry succeeded in forming the Protestant Union, which was afterwards so active in provoking the thirty years' war. He immediately seized the occasion of the disputed succession of Juliers and Cleves to set on foot an army sufficient for the conquest of the empire. Indeed it was very generally believed that his real object was the imperial crown. It is mentioned as a report by Cardinal Bentivoglio[21] and by the Polish historian Piasecius,[22] and it was suspected by Henry's great ally, Maurice of Orange.[23] The Austrians had long been aware of the existence of such a design. It is spoken of so early as 1599 in a letter from the archduke Maximilian to the archduke Mathias. In 1608 the Lutheran Elector of Saxony, knowing that it was a favourite plan of the Calvinists, again put the Emperor on his guard. Warnings and rumours came from several quarters. So lately as 1851 a contemporary document was discovered and published which discloses all the details of the scheme.[24] In order to remove the opposition of the Catholic duke of Bavaria, and to enlist him on the side of the enemies of Austria, he received an offer of the imperial dignity for himself.[25] The chief support that Henry relied on in carrying out his designs was that of the German Calvinists

[21] Relationi 1646, p. 462.
[22] Chronica Gestorum 1645. p. 268.
[23] Winwood's Memorials, iii. p. 157.
[24] Historisch politische Blätter xxvii. p. 77.
[25] Mémoires de Sully ed. Michaud ii. p. 337.

who offered to make him Emperor.[26] He looked forward also to an insurrection of the Protestants in the Austrian dominions, whom he promised to aid and to protect. This is the reason why the policy of Henry seems so greatly to have favoured the Protestants. They were his principal auxiliaries in his ambitious designs upon Germany, and he favoured their cause for the same reason that he had favoured the Turks against the emperor. This very project of destroying the Austrian power by their help is the substance of the Great Design, according to which the house of Austria was to be deprived of the empire, of Sicily, Naples, Milan, Franche-Comté, Belgium, Tyrol, Bohemia, Moravia, Silesia, Carinthia and Styria. The assistance which was expected from a revolt of the Protestants in Austria would be rewarded by that article of the scheme which secured to them perfect toleration. Again, we know from the memoirs of the Duke de Nevers (ii. p. 840) that the Spanish possessions in the north of Italy were destined, as the plan declares, for the duke of Savoy.

The great object of the European republic was to be, according to the design, the war against the Turks. This also exactly agrees with what we know to have been the intention of Henry. We have seen that he threw over the Turks as soon as they ceased to be useful allies. Zinkeisen, in his excellent history of the Ottoman empire (iii. p. 862) has published a very remarkable paper presented by a Greek to Henry in 1609, in which, on condition of receiving certain definite assistance from France, he pledges himself that the Greeks shall rise to the number of sixty thousand men, and shows how the Turks might be driven out of Europe, and the crown of Byzantium placed on the head of the king of France. It is certain that this document was seen by Henry, and the author of it says, that he was induced to present it because he knew that the king was desirous of undertaking such an expedition in the East.[27] Turkey was already the sick man of the European family. "Keep me well informed," writes Henry to his envoy at Constantinople, "of all that takes place, and I will hold myself in readiness to take advantage of the changes that may occur."[28] "These injuries and offences, constantly repeated, instead of infinite proofs of good will which they have received from me, are insupportable, and

---

[26] Aretin Bayern's Auswärtige Verhältnisse i. p. 88.

[27] "Che la Majestà Christianissima ha animo di impiegarsi alle imprese di detto Levante, et è desiderosissimo per tal imprese."

[28] Lettres Missives de Henri IV. vi. p. 3.

oblige me to take revenge, as you will tell them that I am resolved to do. . . . I shall alter my counsels and my conduct, and am resolved to do worse in joining those who have sworn the ruin of his empire."[29]

The high position and the increase of territory which the Design assigns to the pope, are inconsistent with its general tendency, yet they confirm its authenticity, for it is certain that such concessions were actually intended both by Henry IV and by the great Dutch statesmen Barneveld and Grotius. It was of great importance to Henry to remove all causes of jealousy of his power by enlisting on his side all the sympathies and interests that were in any way opposed to the house of Habsburg. He contrived to combine the political aspirations of the Catholic states with the religious ambition of the Protestants, and his peculiar position and singular skill enabled him to reconcile the two. In order to make sure of the Catholics it was indispensable to have the pope on his side. For this purpose he represented to him that none but a Catholic prince should be eligible to the imperial throne, that the existing rights and privileges of the Catholic clergy should be everywhere secured, and that the Protestants should not be permitted to spread in the countries where they had not yet penetrated. At a time when the Church was surrounded by so many perils, and when her existence in so many countries was threatened, it appeared a considerable relief that so much should be secured by the guarantee of the French king. Under these conditions Paul V promised his co-operation.[30]

We have seen that the design tended ever to promote the known policy of Henry. The practicability of some of its dispositions, which may at the time have appeared extravagant and incredible, has been proved by later events. They were partly such as had become inevitable since the moderating influence of the Holy See over the conduct of princes had passed away, and they would have become still more necessary after the great changes which were proposed in the distribution of states. The theory of the balance of power, the parity of the three confessions, the territorial independence of the princes of the empire, and the idea of the great central council, were anticipations of what was afterwards realized in the peace of Westphalia and in the frequent congresses of the Holy Alliance.

But although the execution of this design would have satisfied the

[29] Ibid. pp. 287–288.
[30] Schmidt. Geschichte der Deutschen viii. p. 294.

utmost ambition of Henry, its real significance lies not in the fact that it would have raised France to the first place among the nations, but in this, that it was to bring about the certain triumph of the Protestant religion in the form of Calvinism. Sully, next to Mornay the most eminent Huguenot in France, was the king's confidential adviser in all important matters, and especially in his foreign policy. His whole financial administration aimed at the collection of a sufficient amount of treasure for the war which he expected as eagerly as the king. We learn from his memoirs that his zeal so far surpassed the expectations of Henry that the latter was taken by surprise when he was informed of the sums which had been accumulated, and when he learned how completely all things were prepared for the opening of the campaign. The whole plan was indeed his work. Henry gave him the leading ideas in order that he might work them out and prepare the means of executing them. They were developed and matured in his mind in the course of many years, and were reproduced in the shape of what was called the Great Design. This combination of Sully's ideas with those of the king explains much that seems obscure. We see how Sully took advantage of the ambition of his master and of his need of Protestant support to prepare in appearance indeed the supremacy of France, but in reality the predominance of Protestantism in Europe. By his influence the schemes which Duplessis-Mornay had so busily promoted were made a part of the state policy of France. Each portion of the Design was intended either to promote or to disguise the triumph of the Swiss Reformation. The destruction of the Austrian and the reduction of the Spanish power would have removed the chief obstacle that set bounds to its progress. The new kings of Bohemia and Hungary would be Protestants. The Catholic provinces of Tyrol and Franche-Comté were to fall under the power of Switzerland, the stronghold of Calvinism. The Catholic Netherlands were to become subject to the United Provinces. The toleration of Protestantism would have led to its victory in the Austrian dominions. The principle of toleration would have told virtually only in favour of the Protestants. It would be enforced only in those countries where they were still struggling for equal rights. The Catholics would have gained nothing by it. In England such a law would at that time have been powerless against the terror of Elizabeth and the prejudices of James, and it would have been profoundly incompatible with the intolerant spirit of the Anglo-Saxon race. In other countries it would have been useless for the protection of Catholics where there were none to protect. But whilst the law of toleration protected the Protestants against the Catholics, by confining it to the Lutherans and Calvinists, the further increase of those sects would have been prevented which had already so much injured the Protestant cause. It appears therefore that the plan was remarkably well fitted for the attainment of the real ends which its projectors had in view. It would have increased prodigiously the power of the Protestants by the arms of the king of France. Had they ever acquired the position which this arrangement would have given them, they might have used it, and there is no doubt that they would have used it for the utter destruction of the Catholic Faith. It would have been in their power to realize the doctrine of Calvin that the dominion of the earth belonged to the Elect. The equality which the Protestants demanded would no sooner have been obtained, than it would have been developed into a decided supremacy in Europe. When they had prevailed abroad they would necessarily have become supreme at home; for France was to be the chief author of their triumph, and in France it was they who originated and directed the movement. Sully, his son Rosny, Lesdiguières, Rohan, La Force, who were all Huguenots, were to have the chief commands. Lesdiguières, who was to invade the Milanese in conjunction with the Duke of Savoy, received orders, to prevent suspicion, to appoint as many Catholic officers as possible.[31] The precaution was not unreasonable, considering that all the Protestant powers were on Henry's side, and that all his enemies were Catholics.

It is surprising that none of the historians who have written on these times should have understood that the real drift of the scheme was such as we have described it. Under the circumstances it was neither extravagant nor unnatural. There is an inconsistency between those parts of it which it was really intended to carry out and those which were introduced for the purpose of recommending it to such as were not in the secret, which gives it an unreal and contradictory appearance. It is obvious that in many of the details the author has accommodated his own design to the ideas of the king, or has modified it according to the caution which it was necessary to observe. Such artifices to render the scheme acceptable at first were, for instance, the dignity which was given to the pope, the absence of any claim to territorial

---

[31] Mémoires de Nevers, ii. p. 868.

increase on the part of France, and the plan of a crusade against the Turks. It was not entirely sincere, and it was not meant to be final, or to be the limit of ambition of its authors, but its leading ideas were seriously entertained, and with good reason, as the means of obtaining further advantages. We do not therefore doubt that it really proceeded from the great statesman of the Calvinists. A remodelling of Europe and of European policy had become necessary by the decline of the institutions and habits of the middle ages. Schemes not less bold and extensive than that of the Huguenot leader were projected in the succeeding age by Gustavus Adolphus for the supremacy of Lutheranism, and by Wallenstein for that of the Catholic Empire.

Independently of the advantages which it promised to France and to the Protestant religion, the design clearly betrays the influence of those revolutionary ideas which the Reformation, and especially the progress of Calvinism, had produced. Democracy had had a great part in the religious revolution of the Dutch, whilst in France the Calvinists put forth a theory of government derived partly from the writings and partly from the principles of the Reformers, which anticipated by two hundred years the doctrines of Rousseau and the practise of Robespierre. Those principles of public law which were represented in France by Languet and Duplessis-Mornay, in Scotland by Knox and Buchanan, in Austria by Tschernembl, were carried into action on a wider field by the instigators of a design which aimed at the overthrow of established rights and existing institutions all over Europe. The revolutionary energy which inspired it may be understood from the conduct of the remnant of the League of Henry IV in the thirty years' war. When that great rebellion broke out, the vast extent of these schemes became manifest, and it appeared what prodigious consequences followed the crime of Ravaillac. It was one of the most portentous moments in the history of the world. There is something awful in the details which innumerable authorities have preserved of the death of the king. Five days later he was to have departed on an expedition for which 300,000 men were under arms, and which must have changed the face of the world and altered the course of history. It was when a passion more ignoble than ambition arose to hasten the execution of his sanguinary enterprise that retribution overtook him. On the day of his death he felt much uneasiness, and was troubled like Caesar with forebodings and warnings. La Force, who was with him all the day and who remained alone with the body after his death, says in his memoirs

(i. p. 221.); "comme s'il eût pressenti son malheur, il dit, se portant la main sur le front: *Mon Dieu! j'ai quelque chose là-dedans qui me trouble fort. Il revint dans la chambre de la Reine, et lui dit: Je ne sais ce que j'ai, mais je ne puis sortir d'ici.* La Reine fit tout ce qu'elle put pour le retenir, mais il ne voulut pas rester." Before stepping into his carriage he dismissed his guards, who, as a matter of course, were preparing to accompany him. Then as he drove towards the arsenal, a narrow street through which he must pass was blocked up by some carts. Most of the servants went forward to clear the way; some had already gone on to meet the carriage by a shorter road. One remained, but as Ravaillac approached the carriage wheel he had turned aside to fasten his garter. Seven persons were in the coach with Henry, yet no one saw the assassin strike the blow! No wonder that a deed so incredible in its actual details, and in its consequences so weighty, should have been attributed to the instigation of many persons who seemed to be benefitted by it. Suspicion fell indiscriminately on all who were thought to have anything to gain by Henry's death, on the Jesuits, of course, on the Spaniards, hardly less inevitably, on Epernon, on the pope, on the queen herself. It was a great opportunity to test the efficacy of torture. For thirteen days the murderer suffered every torment which was known to the executioners of that day. He constantly denied that he had any accomplice, and when at last, after having been burnt with hot irons, and with molten lead poured into his wounds, he was about to be torn in pieces by wild horses, he begged for absolution only under the condition that he had spoken the truth. Few facts in history are established by more certain evidence than that the murder of Henry IV was the act of a single man.

We have entered upon only a few of the questions which Mr. Poirson appears to us to have imperfectly understood. We will notice but one thing more. Like all the admirers of Henry he constantly praises him for his tolerant principles. Yet, as we have indicated already, there is no doubt that he would not long have tolerated the Protestants in France. The Revocation of the Edict of Nantes was foreseen by him who gave it. The certainty of this has caused recent Protestant writers in France to judge his character with great severity.[32] Richelieu has recorded the advice which Henry gave the queen when he was about to leave her Regent on starting for the wars. Therein occurs the

[32] Haag: La France Protestante V. art. Henry IV and Read, Henri IV et Daniel Chamier, 1854 passim.

following passage:[33] "Sooner or later she would be obliged to come to blows with the Huguenots, but she was not to give them light causes of discontent, for fear they might begin the war before she was prepared to finish it. For his own part, he had had much to endure from them because they had been of some slight service to him, but his son would one day chastise their insolence."

[33] Mémoires de Richelieu ed. Michaud i. p. 14.

[2]
Review of Philp's *History of Progress in Great Britain*

Mr. Philp is a writer who, at least, is not ashamed of his opinions. People may be taken in as to the value of his book, but nobody can be deceived as to his intentions. It were well if he knew his subject as well as he knows his own mind about it. "No one," he says, "has yet ventured to assert, and laboured sufficiently to prove, that history is a stern record of struggles between the contracted policy of kings and priests, and the nobler aims of mind and labour, and that to the victories of the latter the British nation owes the greatness which commands for her the admiration of the world." But Mr. Philp has luckily been moved to compassion by this grievous deficiency in our literature; and it is a comfort to think that his book "will be a real history of the British people, with special regard to their struggles against oppression, bigotry, intolerance, and ignorance"—such a book, in short, as we have long felt the want of. "It will be shown that the steps of progress have been sternly opposed by the pulpit, the sword, and even by popular clamour; it will also be shown that none of the countless predictions of revolution, ruin, infidelity, and national decline have been fulfilled." In all this rigmarole there is one point which deserves to be noted. The demand that the historian should inform us as to the condition of the people has become a commonplace of newspaper criticism. Many attempts have been recently made to satisfy it. Chambers's work on Scottish history, which we noticed last month, is a book of this kind. It is a tendency which can hardly produce any durable effect on historical writing, because it is opposed, not to the dignity, but to the unity of history. Only those facts and elements in

Robert Kemp Philp, *The History of Progress in Great Britain, Part I* (London: Houlston and Wright, 1858). This review was published in the *Rambler* 10 (July 1858): 63–65. *Wellesley* II: 775.

the people's life which bear on the actual progress of events can be admitted into an historical work. The whole mass of details is without limit and without connection, and would serve only to illustrate illustrations. These studies have formed themselves very properly into a distinct antiquarian pursuit. They are of service to the historian, who can use what he wants, without incorporating the whole into his works. They are the background of history, not a part of history itself. The stream of events scarcely touches them. Great political and intellectual revolutions have occurred without really affecting the social existence of the people, which remains unchanged often for centuries. The real substance of history, which is going altogether out of fashion, the great march of public events, is yet very far from being so thoroughly understood and sucked dry that the historian need seek elsewhere materials for interesting his readers. But inasmuch as it requires a very much greater mental exertion, both in the writer and the reader, than the collection of details, it is naturally less popular.

It is in reality the notion of perpetual progress which lies at the bottom of this style of historical writing. It comes from admiration of the present, not of the past. The writer who brought it into vogue was Lord Macaulay. Whilst his imaginative faculty placed him at the head of the picturesque historians, his political sentiments made him the partisan of the theory of progress. "Those who compare the age on which their lot has fallen with a golden age which exists only in their imagination, may talk of degeneracy and decay; but no man who is correctly informed as to the past, will be disposed to take a morose or desponding view of the present" (*History of England,* vol. i. p. 3). "No ordinary misfortune, no ordinary misgovernment, will do so much to make a nation wretched, as the constant progress of physical knowledge, and the constant effort of every man to better himself, will do to make a nation prosperous" (p. 290). This is precisely the same principle which Mr. Philp and others have carried to an extreme. This indulgence in self-gratulation and admiration of the present time bodes no good for the future. The partisans of the theory of indefinite progress forfeit all the advantage which is to be got from the contemplation of those points on which former ages were superior to our own. A certain manly discontent and regret can alone produce vigorous efforts for real improvement. Men of this school are never put to shame by the greatness of old. They generally hold it cheap. Moral greatness, judged by their standard, is of very little real use. It does not promote what in their eyes is the first consideration—material well-being. Hence the worship of intellect rather than virtue, and especially of that kind of intellect which manifests itself in tangible results—the genius of Newton, Watt, or Arkwright. Each event and period of history must be viewed in its own native light. It is the business of historians every where to furnish us with this light, without which each object is distorted and discoloured. We must distrust our knowledge of every period which appears to us barbarous. It appears so as long as we have not found the key to its real character. For the same reason that other nations were barbarians in the eyes of the Greeks, other ages seem barbarous to us. We are unable, and care not, to understand and sympathise with them. The true view of history is the reverse of this narrowness. Its chief purpose is to break down the idolatry of a particular age and stage of development, and to awaken a generous catholic appreciation of mankind in every period and phase of its existence. All the books that are written to celebrate our age at the expense of those which have preceded it, will in a few years become obsolete and ridiculous. Future generations will have a keen eye for our failings when they have corrected them, and will not be dazzled by our discoveries when they have been surpassed. To these writers the peculiarities of the past are interesting only in so far as they have been superseded, and the comparison with our own time is drawn only when it is to the advantage of the present. This tendency is equally perverse in history and in politics. It seeks in the past only opportunities of despising it, and overlooks in the present what most needs improvement. These men see in history only the reflection of themselves. They endeavour to illustrate, not an age, but an opinion—to establish the truth, not of facts, but of an idea. But no science can flourish that is not cultivated for its own merits, and no work can live that is not written for the sake of its professed subject.

[3]

Review of Chéruel's *Marie Stuart et Catherine de Médicis*

A book containing some new facts and many old falsehoods. The author had the good luck to discover, in a country-house in Normandy, a number of letters of French ambassadors at the court of Elizabeth, of the years 1575 to 1586. The majority are from Castelnau (Mauvissière), of whose correspondence during his first embassy we gave a specimen in our last Number. They are interesting chiefly for the light they throw on the policy of France in the drama which terminated in the death of Queen Mary. M. Chéruel, however, who shows no particular vocation or competency for the task of judging her conduct, has appended so much of his own matter as was wanted to make up a goodly volume. As the letters he has published are really valuable, we can only regret that he should have thought fit to add any thing of his own. In order to show what his opinions are worth, we need only say that he calls Mignet "the most conscientious" of Mary's biographers (p. 49), "whose learning and impartiality it is impossible to question" (p. 46).

It was the fate of Mary Stuart to be the victim of a party who have always been the foulest calumniators that ever agreed in a lie. The writers by whom their accusations have been repelled, extended to her character the interest which her fate excites. But the day is past when a writer who accepted the judgment of her enemies, or the enthusiasm of some of her admirers, could lay claim to the title of an historian. In the middle ages historians, as well as naturalists, kept their eye upon the action of God in the world, and discerned in all things the

Pierre Adolphe Chéruel, *Marie Stuart et Catherine de Médicis* (Paris: Hachette, 1858). This review was published in the *Rambler* 10 (August 1858): 134–136. *Wellesley* II: 775.

manifestation of His power. Their attention was not distracted by the multitude of details. Then came the time of minute research, in which the study of details concealed the unity of idea, and the action of Providence was lost sight of. This was a subordinate view both of nature and history: in the one it led to materialism; in the other to the disappearance of the design and action of God behind the conflict of human will. It gave a prominence to individuals, by which the unity of the subject was destroyed. The explanation of human intentions and character became the key to all history, all disputes turned upon the merits of individuals, and there was an endless field for the exercise of partisan ingenuity. But now men have learnt that there is a greater drama enacting than that which is presented by the fate of the individual actors. In a play, or a novel, the general public are content with details: they tremble with Partridge at the ghost, and remember of Falstaff only his paunch and his jokes; few are able to distinguish the idea which it is the design of the author to bring out in his whole work. So in history it is characteristic of a popular and superficial view to discuss the lives and fortunes of particular persons, and to overlook the great stream of universal history. There are so many trees, says a German proverb, that one cannot see the wood. Partiality in judging great historical characters, and anxiety to identify principles and persons, implies a very imperfect idea of history, and, among Catholics, a very imperfect trust in religion: it shows that they cannot distinguish that which is essential from that which is accidental—the greatness of God from the weakness of man. It can rarely happen that a principle must stand or fall with the reputation of an individual; and, in the case of Catholics, the cause is always immeasurably above the champion—we judge men by their fidelity to the cause, not the cause by the virtues of its defenders. No Catholic is as good as his religion. It is the only case in which there is not the slightest inducement to represent friends and enemies otherwise than as they are. Hence perfect impartiality is possible only among Catholics; but among Catholics it is also imperative. Because St. Thomas died a martyr, we are not tempted to deny that he wavered at Clarendon; nor because St. Augustine was the greatest doctor of the West, need we conceal the fact that he was also the father of Jansenism.

So it is with Queen Mary. Almost every action of her reign proved her unworthiness to be the protector of the great cause with which her fate was identified. She owed that position to her birth only; not to her fitness for it. Her whole character betrayed the influence of that state of European society which was the chief secondary cause of the progress of the Reformation. For nearly half a century before that event the condition of religion, even in Italy, was deplorable. Men like St. Francis of Paul and Savonarola shone like meteors in the midst of an all but universal depravity. The Catholic reformation began at the head before it reached the members. Most providentially Luther, and not Calvin, was the leader of the Protestant movement when Leo X presided over the church. The Lutheran Reformation was followed by a visible deterioration of morals; when, a generation later, Calvin appeared at the head of a reformed party, conspicuous for sternness, consistency, and moral power, he encountered at the head of the Church a spirit very different from that of Leo, and there was never even an apparent moral superiority on the part of the reformers over the rulers of the Church. In France the temper of the Medicean age survived by fifty years its disappearance from the court of Rome. When Mary lived and reigned in Paris, the Council of Trent, the Jesuits, and the religious wars, had not yet infused the spirit of the Catholic revival into the court and nation. It was the character of the place where she had been educated—not, indeed, in its worst form, but with all its levity, thoughtlessness, and sensuality—that she carried with her to Scotland, to encounter the most powerful, devoted, and consistent fanatic that Calvinism ever inspired. In the fatal conflict that ensued between Protestantism, in its most formidable champion, and the feeblest defender of the Church, we cannot always bestow our respect and sympathy on the side which has our wishes. It is only the expiation of her last years, her captivity and death, that invest Mary Stuart with the interest which attaches to her name. We may apply to her an admirable saying of Burke, when reproached by a cynical friend with his eulogy on Marie Antoinette (Works, vol. i. p. 573, ed. 1852): "I really am perfectly astonished how you could dream, with my paper in your hand, that I found no other cause than the beauty of the Queen of France (now, I suppose, pretty much faded) for disapproving the conduct which has been held towards her, and for expressing my own particular feelings. I am not to order the natural sympathies of my own heart, and of every honest breast, to wait until all the jokes of all the anecdotes of the coffee-houses of Paris, and of the dissenting meeting-houses of London, are scoured of all the slander of those who calumniate persons, that afterwards they may murder them with impunity. . . . Am I obliged to prove judicially the virtues of all those I shall see suffering every kind of wrong and contumely and risk of life, before I endeavour to interest others in their sufferings; and before I endeavour to excite horror against midnight assassins at back-stairs, and their more wicked abettors in pulpits?"

[4]
Expectation of the
French Revolution

There is nothing which so favourably distinguishes modern from ancient historians as the importance which they allow to the immaterial metaphysical agents in human affairs, and their attempts to trace the progress of ideas, as well as the succession of events, and the reaction of one upon the other. Among those ideas which are at once causes and effects, which influence one series of events by reflecting another, the most important, but the most difficult to estimate, are the ideas which a nation entertains of its history. In its interpretation of its own experience it forms and expresses its notion of its own character and destiny, of its appointed part in the world and in the designs of God, and the lessons, the warnings, and the tendencies, by which it consents to be guided. These notions become a part as well as a result of its nature and of its history, and irresistibly direct its conduct. It is not, therefore, without reason that a living historian has reproduced in its legendary and poetic garb the story of early Rome, not so much in opposition to the conclusions of modern criticism, but because, in order to understand a people's history, we must know its own idea of it, and must give a just weight to fables, not as truths, but as forces. So much truth there is in the saying that a people would be in the power of the man who should have the making of its ballads.

The present derives its explanation from the past, as the past becomes intelligible from the present; causes must be examined in their effects, and effects understood in their causes. Neither is intelligible when considered alone.

> What is the present but the shadow cast,
> Part by the future, partly by the past?

Published in the *Rambler* n.s. 5 (July 1861): 190–213. *Wellesley* II: 782; Döllinger I: 216; Acton-Simpson II: 149.

There is a prophetic office in history, and our notions of the future are shaped according to our experience of the past. A people that has a consistent view of its career and of its position inevitably forms, in harmony with this view, some idea of the things that are to come. It discerns its ideal in the direction it has previously pursued, and its memories justify its anticipation. All these are part of the influences that form its character and spirit, and deeply modify its bearing. The past acts upon our conduct chiefly by the views of the future which it suggests, and the expectations it creates. It influences the present through the future. In their own glorious or mournful recollections nations found the hopes, the aspirations, and the fears which guide their course. Not because men act in unconscious conformity with their expectations, and bend their conduct according to their notions of fate, but forasmuch as history is not a result of human design, because there is something deeper than interest or conjecture in popular instinct, because patience and longanimity are attributes of the Providence which leads by long but sure preparation to great results, and conducts innumerable streams by the same current to the same goal, because intelligible warnings precede great catastrophes, and nations read as it were in their consciences the signs of the times; therefore there is a teaching in history which is equivalent to prophecy, and in which the historian recognizes both a power and a token.

Yet this is an element of their science which modern historians have altogether neglected. Many of the chapters of the famous history of human error have been written, and the imponderables and curiosities of history have been specially cultivated; but none have cared to trace the influence of prophecy on events, or rather of events on prophecy, and the reality of ideas of this kind has not been admitted. We have had writers who delight in portents and prodigies, and writers who believe in nothing but fixed laws; but none have adopted into their inquiry the influence of that sort of prescience and prediction which ought to have been attractive to both, because it is a great instance of divine mercy, and at the same time the highest effort of human wisdom. Marvel-mongers have discouraged sober men from inquiring for reasonable instances of a faculty which degenerates easily into the marvellous, and prophecies have been noted and remembered in proportion to their unreasonableness and incredibility. But they are really both instructive and characteristic when they are founded on the signs of the times, and are uttered by men capable of discerning and exhibiting in the circumstances and conditions of their own age the seeds and causes of impending change. And this foresight, the privilege at first of the highest minds, gradually extends, as the development of things converts the speculation of the few into the instinct of the many; that which was at first a prediction becomes a proverb and a commonplace, and the truth, which the wisest had divined, grows into a power when it is believed by the mass.

No instance of this can be found which is more remarkable than the gradual rise of an almost general expectation of the Revolution, which had almost a hundred years of preparatory growth, and which was ripened and announced in every sphere of society and in every region of thought, in France. For it proceeded from no isolated cause, but came as the result of the whole political, social, religious, and intellectual progress of the age; as a judgment on the Church and on the State, on the Court and the Parliament, on the administration of justice and on the administration of finance, on errors of philosophy and politics, ethics and literature; and in every department in which the great convulsion was prepared, we may discover, along with the germ, the anticipation of what was to come; in every step of that downward course, at each period of that century of decline, from the time of Leibnitz to the time of Burke, as the consequence became more inevitable, the prospect became more distinct, and the presentiment more positive.

"What must appear most strange," says Tocqueville, "to us who have before our eyes the wrecks of so many revolutions, is that even the notion of a violent revolution was absent from the thoughts of our fathers. It was not discussed, it was not even conceived. . . . In that French society of the eighteenth century which was about to fall into the abyss, nothing had yet given warning of decline."[1] It is surprising that so great a writer should have been betrayed into such a mistake. True it is that the blindness and ignorance of many was one of the marvels and one of the calamities of that age; but it is astonishing, not so much if we consider the danger that was really approaching, as the alarm with which it was expected.

> A thousand horrid prophecies foretold it:
> A feeble government, eluded laws,
> A factious populace, luxurious nobles,
> And all the maladies of sinking states—

[1] L'ancien Régime et la Révolution, p. 219.

> When public villany, too strong for justice,
> Shows his bold front, the harbinger of ruin.

At the time of the greatest prosperity of Lewis XIV, when the French monarchy had reached the moment of its utmost splendour, the consequences of absolutism began to be foreseen. It made itself felt at the close of the seventeenth century in every way, and every where it created instruments by which retribution was to come. The Church was oppressed, the Protestants persecuted or exiled, Jansenism converted by severity from a party into a sect, from an adversary into a disease; the aristocracy was degraded, the people exhausted by taxes and wars, society corrupted, literature rendered unproductive by a selfish and haughty patronage. In all these things men saw omens of ruin. Racine, in 1698, lost the favour of the king by a memoir which he presented to Madame de Maintenon, on the state of the nation. "Does he think," cried Lewis, "that he knows every thing because he knows how to make admirable verses? and because he is a great poet, does he want to be minister?" A hundred years later, Napoleon, who was no patron of literature, declared that if Corneille were living, he would make him minister; but Lewis was accustomed to see in poets only an object of patronage. Duclos relates that the Bishop of Limoges (Charpin) wrote to the king with so much power on the sufferings of the people, that Lewis was touched to such a degree that his health suffered. Soon after another appeal for the nation was made by a man who was the foremost in another line. In 1707 Vauban published his *Dîme Royale,* in which he describes the misery of the people, and demands a total revolution in the system of government. Ten per cent of the population lived by alms; fifty per cent were too poor to give alms; thirty per cent were *fort malaisées, embarrassées de dettes et de procès;* about one per cent he reckoned *fort à leur aise.* Yet at that time there were no signs of communism, or even of sedition, among the poor. The revolutionary ideas had not gone down from the palace and the study to the cottage, so that it did not occur to men to question the right by which they suffered. Next to Vauban the loftiest character in the French army was a Huguenot, Marshal Catinat, and he was the first to perceive that the evils of the State were leading to a revolution. "France," he said, "is rotten from head to foot; it must and will happen that she will be thrown upside down."

But the most earnest and prophetic protest against the system of Lewis XIV was that of Fénelon. In the war of the Spanish Succession the ambition of the king had involved him in an enterprise far beyond the resources of the country, and which raised to a tyrannical pitch the requirements and the authority of the State. After nine years of unsuccessful war, the defeat of Malplaquet brought the State to the verge of ruin, and Lewis opened negotiations for peace at Gertruyden-berg. He offered Alsace and Spain as the condition of a treaty; he even agreed to pay subsidies to the allies for the purpose of expelling his grandson from his Spanish throne; and the conferences were only broken off when his enemies insisted that he should also send his armies to fight against the cause which he had upheld for so many years. In this extremity the disgraced Archbishop of Cambray wrote a memoir on the state of the country, and on the means of saving it.

"For my part, if I were to undertake to judge of the state of France by the traces of government which I see on this frontier, I should conclude that it exists only by a miracle; that it is an old broken-down machine, which continues by the force of the impetus it formerly received, and which will be destroyed utterly at the first shock. . . . The people no longer live the life of human beings, and their patience is so hardly tried that it can no longer be relied on. . . . As they have nothing to hope for, they have nothing to fear. . . . The nation is falling into contempt, and is becoming the object of public scorn. There is no longer in the people, in our soldiers, or in our officers, either affection, or esteem, or confidence, or hope of recovery, or awe for authority."

The remedy which he proposed was the restoration of constitutional government by the convocation of Notables; the remedy which was resorted to after eighty years, when it was too late. "I would have it left to the wisest and most considerable men in the nation to seek the resources necessary to save the nation itself. . . . It would be necessary that every body should know how the funds are applied, so that all might be convinced that nothing should be employed on the expenses of the Court. I admit that such a change might disturb the minds of men, and carry them suddenly from an extreme dependence to a dangerous excess of liberty. It is from fear of this drawback that I do not propose that the States-General be convoked, which would other-wise be very necessary, and which it would be most important to restore." But two years later Fénelon insisted on the absolute necessity of triennial sessions of the States-General.

Taking a wider survey than that which his great contemporary confined to his own country, Leibnitz considered the preference which was already given to the natural and the exact sciences over historical studies as the commencement of a vast revolution. He is speaking of historical criticism, and goes on to say, "I believe that if this art, which was so long forgotten, has reappeared with brilliant effect, and has been so carefully cultivated in the last two centuries, . . . it is an act of Divine Providence which had chiefly in view to spread more light on the truth of the Christian religion. . . . History and criticism are really necessary only to establish the truth of Christianity. For I cannot doubt that if the art of criticism were ever totally to perish, the human instruments of divine faith, that is, the motives of credibility, will perish at the same time. . . . I believe that the great obstacle to Christianity in the East is that these nations are completely ignorant of universal history, and do not therefore feel the force of those demonstrations by which the truth of our religion is established. . . . I see with regret the class of critical scholars daily diminishing, so that it may be expected to disappear altogether. . . . The disputes on religion encouraged and excited this sort of study, for there is no evil that does not give birth to some good. . . . But at length, these disputes having degenerated into open war, and wise men seeing that after such long discussions and great bloodshed nothing had been gained, it happened that they began to make peace, and many persons grew disgusted with these questions, and in general with the study of former ages. Then ensued a revolution which was a new epoch in learning. Writers celebrated for splendid discoveries and successful systems turned men's minds to the study of nature, giving them the hope that with the help of mathematics they might succeed in knowing her. . . . Since that time ancient learning and solid erudition have fallen into a sort of contempt; so that some authors affect to employ no quotations in their writings, either to hint at their genius, or to disguise their indolence. . . . It is in the interest of religion that sound learning should be preserved. Casaubonus gave a warning in his English writings, where he says with reason that he has great fears for piety, if the study of antiquity and classical literature is neglected for the sake of natural science." Elsewhere he speaks of "the general revolution which menaces Europe with the destruction of all that remains in the world of the generous sentiments of the ancients."

These opinions were amply confirmed by the events of later times. La Harpe, one of the few conspicuous infidels whom the Revolution converted, once said in his lectures at the Lycée, "Atheism is a pernicious doctrine, the enemy of social order and of all government." He was denounced by Lalande, the great geometrician, who declared that he hoped this abomination had been uttered, not "par scélératesse, mais par imbécillité." Condorcet says of algebra, "It includes the principles of a universal instrument applicable to every combination of ideas." And in another passage he shows in a striking way the truth of what Leibnitz said concerning the social and political influence of mathematics and natural philosophy: "All errors in politics and morals are based on philosophic errors, which, again, are allied to physical errors. There exists neither a religious system, nor a supernatural extravagance, which is not founded on ignorance of the laws of nature."[2]

It was in reference to the same class of phenomena that Du Bos wrote in 1719: "The philosophic spirit will soon do with great part of Europe what was formerly done to it by the Goths and Vandals, provided it continues to advance at the same rate as for the last seventy years." But there were few who could distinguish at that early period the dangerous tendencies of a species of literature which was but just beginning, and which was still overshadowed by the reputation of the Augustan age, and many years went by before the ideas of the 18th century manifested to the world their destructive character. During the Regency other fears predominated, and the general discontent displayed itself by an address to the King of Spain, praying him to deliver France from the evils that threatened her from a despotism exercised by Dubois on behalf of the Duke of Orleans.

The conspiracy, which was discovered and suppressed, aimed at the union of the French and Spanish crowns. The States-General were to be summoned; and in their memorial to Philip V it was intended that they should express themselves in the following terms: "We do not vainly flatter ourselves, sire, in feeling persuaded that we shall hear from your mouth these consoling words—'I feel for your sufferings; but what remedy can I apply?' . . . You will see, sire, that union which is so necessary to both crowns accomplished in a manner which would render them irresistible. By this means you will restore tranquillity to a people who look on you as their father, and who cannot be indifferent to you. By this means you will prevent misfortunes which we dare not contemplate, and which you are compelled to foresee. How your majesty would reproach yourself, if that should happen which we have

---

[2] Esquisse d'un Tableau historique des Progrès de l'Esprit humain, pp. 285, 313.

so much reason to apprehend!" The long and peaceful administration of Fleury postponed the evil day, and the alarm subsided; whilst Marshal Saxe even gave a transient lustre to the reign by the victory of Fontenoy. But while there was an apparent interruption in the decline of the State, the decline of religion was evident; and from time to time the clergy drew attention to it, and pointed out the danger which would ensue to the whole fabric of society from the increase of unbelief. For fifty years before the revolution their warnings were incessant.

In a panegyric on St. Augustine, pronounced 1736, Father Neuville said: "Let these detestable systems continue to extend and to strengthen themselves, and their devouring poison will end by consuming the principles, the props, and supports which are necessary to the State. . . . Then, however flourishing the empire, it must all fall asunder, sink down, and perish. To destroy it there will be no need of the thunders of God; Heaven may trust to the earth for the accomplishment of its revenge. Carried away by the frenzy of the nation, the State will be plunged into an abyss of anarchy, confusion, slumber, inaction, decline and decrepitude." Twenty years later, Caveirac wrote: "The revolution of which I speak has already made great progress, and I pray the reader's attention to it. . . . The enemy is at our gates, and nobody sees him. He has confederates in the place, and all men are asleep. Bishops and magistrates, what will your astonishment be, when, at your waking, you will see the revolution accomplished!" A few years before this was published Lord Chesterfield had made the same remark. "All the symptoms which I have ever met with in history previous to great changes and revolutions in government now exist and daily increase in France." This was in 1753. In 1763 Labat preached a sermon at Paris, in which he spoke of the decline of religion and the progress of philosophy, in consequence of the character of the government, from which, he said, "a revolution must sooner or later ensue, and it is not far distant."

On many occasions, but especially at the Conference of 1770, the clergy invoked the protection of the government against the progress of unbelief; and they showed, with great justice, that the Church was not free while there was no restraint upon the publication of the most dangerous books. "It is this fatal liberty," they said, "which has introduced among our island neighbours that confused multitude of sects, opinions, and parties, that spirit of independence and rebellion, which has so often shaken the throne or stained it with blood. Amongst ourselves it may produce still more fatal consequences; for it would find, in the inconstancy of the nation, in its activity, its love of change, its impetuous and inconsiderate ardour, additional means for causing the most strange revolutions, and for precipitating it into all the horrors of anarchy." It was at the instance of the Bishops that Séguier, the Attorney-General, delivered his celebrated discourse to the Parliament demanding the condemnation of certain books. In several parts it resembles, almost literally, the paper we have just quoted. But he cited so many of the most powerful passages from the works he was assailing, and met them with such feeble replies, that it was supposed the whole thing was an act of perfidious irony. The following sentences show how clearly the position was understood. "A sort of confederacy unites a number of writers against religion and the government. . . . With one hand they have tried to shake the throne, with the other they have sought to overturn the altar. . . . The government ought to tremble at the toleration of a sect of ardent unbelievers, who seem to wish to excite the people to sedition, under pretence of enlightening them. . . . Their desires will be satisfied only when they have placed the executive and the legislative power in the hands of the multitude; when they have destroyed the necessary inequality of ranks and conditions; when they have degraded the majesty of kings, made their authority precarious, and subordinate to the caprice of an ignorant crowd; and when, finally, by means of these strange alterations, they have thrown the whole world into anarchy, and the evils that are inseparable from it. Perhaps, in the troubles and confusion into which they have brought the nations, these pretended philosophers and independent spirits intend to raise themselves above the common level, and to tell the people that those by whom they have been enlightened are alone fit to govern them." Séguier lived to witness the 17th July 1789, when Lewis XVI was brought to the Hôtel de Ville, and he said, "Those are his first steps towards the scaffold."

When the great school of pulpit eloquence had died out in France with Mascaron, the Abbé Poulle became the most popular preacher in the South. Preaching on the duties of civil life, he said: "Suffer patiently that decency and morality shall be outraged, and you will introduce a boundless license which will destroy society. Those who boldly break the laws of God do not fear to break human laws; and bad Christians will always be bad citizens." In his last sermon he said: "All is lost, religion, morality, civil society. You deemed formerly that our prophecies were the exaggerations of an excessive zeal. We ourselves did not imagine that they would be so soon fulfilled."[3] The Abbé de Boulogne, who became a Bishop under the Restoration, said in the *Éloge du Dauphin,* which he published in 1779, "He saw the fatal revolution preparing; the invasion of the impious, more fatal than that of the barbarians; and, as a consequence, the national spirit spoilt and degraded."

The Bishop of Lescar published a Pastoral in the year 1783, in which he rebuked both the clergy and the nobles, and foretold the approaching retribution. "Do you wish that, armed with the law, and led by the magistrates who are its depositaries, the poor should demand of you, rich men of the world, the portion of the inheritance of which you deprive them? Do you wish that they should enter into our temples—for the temple is made for man, not for God, who needs it not—and strip the sanctuary of its most precious ornaments, whilst the ministers of the altar have no right to prevent it or to complain? Do you wish that they should pass from the house of the Lord to that of the priest and the Levite, and that, finding them plunged in abundance and luxury, they should grow indignant at the sight, break out in reproaches, and summon them to judgment as ravishers of the goods intrusted to them for a worthier use? . . . I see the reformers bear a sacrilegious hand on the ornaments of the sanctuary, load themselves eagerly with its spoils, close the doors of the house of God, or change its destination; throw down our temples and drag from them the priests employed in the sacrifice; pursue outside its walls their impious victory; insult our grief by their triumphs and feasting; and desecrate by their impure libations vessels consecrated for the celebration of our most awful mysteries. . . . And will you ask for signs and portents of the revolution which the Holy Spirit desires you to fear? Do you want more than the revolution itself, which, long prepared, advances with rapid strides, and accomplishes itself before your eyes?"

The abominations of the reign of Lewis XV were such that men

---

[3] La Harpe quotes the following sentences with just praise (*Cours de Littérature,* xiv. 86, 112, 113): "La piété est si méprisée qu'il n'y a plus d'hypocrites." "Nous savons que toute ignorance volontaire et affectée, loin d'être une excuse, est elle-même un crime de plus." "Nos instructions ont dégénéré; elles se ressentent de la corruption des mœurs qu'elles combattent; elles ont perdu de leur première onction en perdant de leur ancienne simplicité. Nous nous le reprochons en gémissant, vous nous le reprochez peut-être avec malignité; mais ne vous en prenez qu'à vous-mêmes."

marvelled less at the general consciousness of danger than at the duration of the State. "I know not," said Benedict XIV, "what can be the power that sustains France over the precipice into which she is ever ready to fall." And Clement XIV said: "Can any other proof of the existence of a Providence be required than to see France flourishing under Lewis XV?"

There was one who did not fear to give expression before the King himself to the universal indignation and hatred. This was the Abbé de Beauvais, afterwards Bishop of Sénez, who preached at Versailles during the Lent of 1774. The boldness and severity of his first sermon astonished and offended the court; but Lewis *a déclaré qu'il faisait son métier.* He spoke, say the *Mémoires Secrets,* which we are quoting, of the misfortunes of the State, of the ruin of the finances, and of the abuse of authority.[4] On Maundy Thursday his sermon terrified the king. He spoke of the troubles of the poor, of the corruption of the rich, of the love which the people had shown the king when he was in danger thirty years before; and he told him that that love had grown cold; that the people, oppressed with imposts, could do nothing but groan under its own trials. This made a deep impression on Lewis XV; he spoke graciously to the preacher, and reminded him of his engagement to preach at court in the Lent of 1776. A few weeks later he was dead, and Beauvais had to preach at his funeral. He had obtained, by his courage at Versailles, the right to speak without disguise at St. Denis; and he declared that the day of punishment for the nation was at hand. "There will be no more superstition, because there will be no more religion; no false heroism, because there will be no honour; no prejudices, because there will be no principles; no hypocrisy, because there will be no virtues! Audacious spirits, behold the devastation caused by your systems, and tremble at your success! Revolution more fatal than the heresies which have changed around us the face of several states! They have left at least a worship and morals, but our unhappy children are to have neither worship nor God."

The Pastoral of the Bishop of Alais on this occasion contains a striking picture of the misery of France. "Let the monarch love God, and he will love his people; and from the foot of his throne he will carry his beneficent view into the provinces, where the miserable inhabitants are sometimes without bread, or often wet it with their

---

[4] vi. 293.

tears. . . . And we shall no longer see the kingdom divided as it were into two classes, in one of which the spoils of the provinces serve as a trophy to the luxury and splendour of a few families, as contemptible by their origin as by their lives, who never see any superfluity in their opulence; whilst in the other thousands of families hardly obtain what is necessary from painful toil, and seem to reproach Providence with this humiliating iniquity." Meantime, La Luzerne, the Bishop of Langres, delivered a panegyric of the dead king at Notre Dame, in which he compared the various reigns of French kings, and concluded that the people had never been so happy as under Lewis XV.

In the reign of Lewis XVI no preacher was more renowned than Beauregard, who seems beyond all others to have been gifted with a presentiment of definite calamities. "The axe and the hammer," he said on one occasion, "are in the hands of the philosophers; they await only the favourable moment to destroy the altar and the throne." A passage in one of his sermons at Notre Dame became famous by the literal fulfilment, in the same place, a few years later, of the prophecy it contained: "Yes, O Lord, Thy temples will be pillaged and destroyed, Thy festivals abolished, Thy name blasphemed, Thy worship proscribed. But what do I hear? Great God! what do I behold? The holy hymns which made the sacred arches resound in Thy honour are succeeded by profane and licentious songs! And thou, infamous divinity of paganism, obscene Venus, comest here to take audaciously the place of the living God, to seat thyself on the throne of the Holy of Holies, and to receive the guilty incense of thy new adorers." On Passion Sunday 1789 he preached before the king, when, interrupting his sermon for a moment, he suddenly exclaimed, "France! France! thy hour is at hand; thou shalt be convulsed and confounded!"

Parallel with these vaticinations of the clergy of France, and abundantly justifying them, we find in the writings of the infidels similar expectations, and a constant desire to accomplish that which their adversaries so much dreaded. It has been much questioned whether they really desired such a revolution as ultimately ensued. Many of them became its victims; and Rousseau, the master of the Jacobins, had a horror of bloodshed: the establishment of liberty, he said, would be too dearly purchased if it cost a single human life. It has been said with some truth that if Voltaire had lived to behold the effect of his writings, he would have taken a cross in his hand, and preached against himself; yet he well knew, and rejoiced to know, that in pulling down the Church of France he was destroying the State. In 1764, April 2, he writes: "All that I see is sowing the seeds of a revolution, which will inevitably ensue, and which I shall not have the happiness to behold. The French arrive slowly at every thing, but at least they do arrive. The light has been so widely spread, that there will be an explosion at the first opportunity, and then there will be a famous row." In the following year, April 5th, he writes to D'Alembert, "The world is growing less green at a furious pace. A great revolution in men's minds announces itself on every side." And, 15th October 1766, he writes to the same correspondent, "Can you not tell me what will be the result in thirty years of the revolution going on in the minds of men from Naples to Moscow?"

Rousseau had not the same ferocity of temper; he was animated by ideals, not by passion; and when he wrote, "We are approaching a state of crisis, and the age of revolution," he did not know that it would be the fruit of his own doctrines. The *Contrat Social* had an immediate success in France. The entry in the Journal of Bachaumont is as follows: "3 September 1762. The *Contrat Social* is gradually becoming known: it is highly important that a book of this kind should not ferment in heads easily excited; it would lead to very serious disorders. . . . However, he merely develops the maxims which all men have graven in their hearts." At the beginning of the same year he says, that the *Gazette de France* owed its popularity, not to its veracity, but to its republican tone. It is easy, therefore, to understand the success of Rousseau's book in France. At Geneva the secular authorities condemned it, and a great disturbance ensued. The ministers of the Reformed Church declared that the government had acted from party spirit, because the *Contrat Social* maintains the real democratic principles in opposition to the aristocratic system, which they were seeking to introduce. We are told that the French Dauphin censured the *Émile* because it attacks religion, disturbs society, and the civil order; and can only serve to make men miserable. Somebody said that the *Contrat Social* had also been considered very dangerous. "That is a different thing," said the prince; "it attacks only the authority of sovereigns; that is a thing that will bear discussion. There is much to be said; it is more open to controversy."

Raynal expressed the sentiments of Rousseau, with the cynicism which was peculiar to him, in his History of the Indies: "When will that exterminating angel come who will cut down every thing that lifts

its head, and will reduce all to a common level?" Helvetius, disgusted
at finding his country so hopelessly remote from his ideal state, augurs
as follows in the preface to his work *De l'Homme:* "This degraded
nation is the scorn of Europe. No salutary crisis will restore its liberty;
it will perish by consumption; conquest is the only remedy of its
misfortunes." Condorcet, who may have changed his opinion before
he destroyed himself in the midst of the Revolution, whose advent had
filled him with joy, was more sanguine than Helvetius: "Is not this
nation destined by the very nature of things to give the first impulse
to that revolution which the friends of humanity expected with so
much hope and impatience? It could not fail to begin with France."[5]
In another place he describes the influence and position of the infidel
philosophers in France. "Often the government rewarded them with
one hand, whilst it paid their calumniators with the other; proscribed
them, and was proud that fate had put their birthplace on its territory;
punished them for their opinions, and would have been ashamed to
be suspected of not sharing them."[6]

The *Système Social* of Mustel, published in 1773, is an elaborate satire
on France, and a plea for revolution: "The condition of a people that
is beginning to be instructed, to desire enlightenment, to occupy itself
with great and useful things, is by no means desperate. Whilst tyranny
makes continual efforts to divert men's minds from reflection, its strokes
lead back to it at every moment; and this reflection, aided by
circumstances, must sooner or later succeed in destroying the tyranny.
It cannot long survive among a people that reasons. . . . If a people is
wholly degenerate, oppression incites it to fury; its ignorance prevents
it from reasoning; and as soon as it loses patience, it destroys without
reasoning those whom it considers the instruments of its sorrows.
Slaves without enlightenment exterminate without foresight or reflection the blind tyrants who oppress them."[7] In another book,[8] which
was condemned by the Parliament in 1773, he says: "A people that
undertakes to throw off the yoke of despotism risks nothing, for slavery
is assuredly the last degree of misery. It has not only the right of
refusing to receive that form of government, but the right to throw it
off."

[5] Esquisse, p. 279.
[6] Ibid. p. 263.
[7] Pp. 60, 61.
[8] Réflexions philosophiques sur le Système de la Nature.

The fanatical opinions of Diderot are well known. He not only desired the destruction of Church and State, but believed that it was not far distant. Broglie seeing him in mourning, asked him whether he wore it for his friends the Russians. "If I had to wear mourning for a nation," said Diderot, "I should not go so far to find one." D'Alembert was less of a politician, and understood only the changes that occurred in science and literature. "It is difficult," he says, "not to perceive that a remarkable change has taken place in many respects in our ideas; a change which seems by its rapidity to promise a still greater. Time will fix the object, the nature, and the limits of this revolution, of which posterity will know better than we do the drawbacks and the advantages."

Next to the partition of Poland, there was no event which gratified the infidel party, and prepared men for the Revolution, so much as the suppression of the Jesuits. When the news came from Spain, Frederic the Great wrote to Voltaire: "Cruel revolution! What may not the age which is to succeed our own expect? The wedge is put to the root of the tree. . . . That edifice, sapped at its base, is about to fall; and the nations will inscribe in their annals, that Voltaire was the author of this revolution." There was a real bond of union and amity between the despotic king and the revolutionary writers. The object of Voltaire and his friends was not the destruction of all monarchy, but of all authority connected with divine law. They were aristocrats and courtiers, and hated the old *régime* because of its alliance with the Church. The democratic school of Rousseau withstood the blandishments of Frederic, Joseph, and Catherine, and affected a republican austerity. Yet the horrors of later years were due less to the speculations of Rousseau than to the ribaldry of Voltaire. There were others of the infidel school who saw the approach of great public disasters without desiring it.

Condillac, the only metaphysical genius among them, published in 1775 his *Cours d'Étude pour l'Instruction du Prince de Parme*, in which we find passages which prove that he saw the coming storm: "Revolutions never happen suddenly, because we do not change in one day our mode of thought and feeling. . . . If a people seems suddenly to alter its habits, its genius, and its laws, be sure that this revolution has been prepared long before, by a long series of events and by a long fermentation of passions. . . . The discomfort we feel in society is a warning to inform us of our faults, and to invite us to repair them. . . .

When the government falls into decay because morals have become corrupt; when the new passions can no longer tolerate the old laws; when the commonwealth is infected with avarice, prodigality, and luxury; when minds are occupied in seeking enjoyments; when wealth is more precious than virtue and freedom—reform is impracticable." His vision extended beyond the outburst of the Revolution, and embraced its consequences: "The troubles of a people generally excite the ambition of its neighbours, who despise it, insult it, and at last declare war, because they hope to conquer and to subdue it. If the strangers spare it, it will fall beneath a domestic enemy. The success of intriguers, who obtain offices of which they will not discharge the duties, will soon call into existence ambitious men who will openly aspire to sovereign power. There is no tyrant yet, and yet tyranny is already established. Exhausted by the movement, the agitation, the difficulties, and the disquiet that accompany an expiring liberty, men desire repose; and in order to escape the caprice and the violence of an agitated and tumultuous oligarchy, they will give themselves a master."[9]

What was announced by the clergy and foreseen by philosophers was present also to the minds of statesmen who watched the course of public affairs from the middle of the century. In the year 1757 the Archbishop of Paris issued a Pastoral on the crime of Damiens. A reply appeared to it in which the following words occur: "Let us open our eyes to the present condition of the kingdom. Do we not see in every part an unsteadiness which betrays a plan of subversion on the point of being executed?"[10] Four years later, in 1761, an anonymous letter reached the king, and left a deep impression. "Your finances, sire, are in the greatest disorder, and the great majority of States have perished through this cause. . . . A seditious flame has sprung up in the very bosom of your parliament; you seek to corrupt them, and the remedy is worse than the disease. . . . All the different kinds of liberty are connected: the philosophers and the Protestants tend towards republicanism, as well as the Jansenists: the philosophers strike at the root, the others lop the branches; and their efforts, without being concerted, will one day lay the tree low. Add to this the Economists, whose object is political liberty, as that of the others is liberty of

---

[9] Vol. xvi. pp. 272, 284, 304, 305.
[10] Lettre d'un Solitaire, in Recueil de Pièces sur Damiens, 1760, p. 146

worship, and the government may find itself in twenty or thirty years undermined in every direction, and will then fall with a crash."[11]

Choiseul, who for several years exercised an unlimited power in France, wrote a character of the Dauphin, in which he said: "If this prince remains what he is, it is to be feared that his imbecility, and the ridicule and the contempt which are the consequence, will naturally produce in this empire a decline which might deprive your majesty's posterity of the throne."[12] When Choiseul was dismissed, the Duke of Chartres called on him, and expressed his regret at what had occurred, declaring that the monarchy was lost. After the disgrace of Choiseul, his successor Maupeou banished the Parliament of Paris, and destroyed the only remnant of independent authority and of freedom in France. The effect on the public mind was immense. A war of pamphlets followed, and in a few months ninety-five were published in defence of the minister. One of the arguments in favour of the *coup d'état* was, that the jurists were the authors of the despotism of the French government: "Tous les jurisconsultes français avaient érigé la monarchie en despotisme." We read in one of the numerous writings on the other side, called *Le Maire du Palais:* "This is a barbarous flattery, which will cost France many tears, and perhaps blood. For all men are not equally submissive to the decrees of Providence. The seditious teaching of the infidels raises up in the State serpents, who will be easily irritated by hunger, and the standard of revolt will soon be unfurled. . . . Thousands have already succumbed beneath the horrors of famine. . . . When the people believes itself strongest, it rises in revolt; if it is not, it murmurs and curses the tyrant. Hence so many revolutions in despotic states."[13]

This act of tyranny added to the execration which was heaped on the last years of the reign of Lewis XV. In the year in which it occurred the unpopularity of the king was so great, that when he appeared at Neuilly nobody cheered him, and a wit said, "When the king is deaf, the people are dumb." The effect of Maupeou's measure was to convert the magistracy from an instrument of despotism into an instrument of revolution; for, when they were recalled in the next reign, they had become the enemies of the throne. This was understood by the Count

[11] Mémoires de Mme. Hausset, p. 37.

[12] Soulavie, Mémoires de Louis XVI, i. 95.

[13] See the collection: *Les Efforts de la Liberté contre le Despotisme de Maupeou,* 1772, pp. 70, 75, 83.

of Provence, the most intelligent member of the royal family; and he addressed a memoir to Lewis XVI against the proposed recall. "When they have recovered their places," he said, "they will be lions instead of lambs; they will use as a pretext the interests of the State, of the people, and of our lord the king. In the act of disobedience they will declare that they do not disobey; the populace will come to their assistance, and the royal authority will one day fall, crushed by the weight of their resistance."[14]

The first minister of Lewis XVI was Maurepas, who had been Secretary of State under Lewis XIV, but had been in disgrace under his successor. In the first year of his administration he received an anonymous letter on the state of the nation, in which he was told: "You know that the whole kingdom is in a flame, that the administration of justice is almost suspended every where, . . . that the minds of men are embittered beyond the possibility of reconciliation, and that civil war is in the hearts of all."

Maurepas was asked whether he or the Foreign Secretary, Vergennes, had formed the project of the American war. His answer shows how little prudence there was in the ministers of that school, and how little they endeavoured to provide against the evils they foresaw. "Neither of us," he said; "at my age no plans are made, one is occupied only with the present, because one cannot reckon on the future. . . . Vergennes and I lived from day to day, and but for Franklin's threats we should still be amusing England, and should have concluded no treaty with the United States. . . . I hope to live long enough to see the independence of America recognised, and England humbled; that is all I promised the king."[15]

Turgot considered that the war would be the ruin of France. He wrote to the king in April 1776: "We must confess that it ought to be avoided as the greatest of misfortunes, as it would render impossible for a long time, and perhaps for ever, a reform which is absolutely necessary for the prosperity of the State and the relief of the people."[16] The dismissal of Turgot at the end of two years was considered by many a great misfortune. Lacretelle says: "Le parti philosophique s'alarme, et prédit une révolution; la guerre en retarda l'explosion."[17]

---

[14] Soulavie, ii. 208.
[15] Moniteur, i. 45.
[16] Oeuvres de Turgot, iii. 195.
[17] Art de vérifier les Dates depuis 1770, 1821, i. 18.

No speech of that day is more characteristic than what was written by Vergennes to the king after the American war, in 1786: "There is no longer a clergy, or a nobility, or a third estate in France; the distinction is fictitious, purely representative, and without real consequence. The monarch speaks; all the rest is the people, and all obey. Is not France, in this position, arbiter of her rights abroad and flourishing at home? What can she desire more?"[18] These were the ideas of government which guided one of the most influential ministers in the last years before the fall of the monarchy. They are not a prediction of the Revolution, but an anticipation of that state of things which it was to introduce—absolute sovereignty on the one hand, and on the other equality in submission.

Lewis XV had said: "It is I who name the ministers of finance, but the public sends them away." Necker was twice raised to office by public opinion against the wishes of the king and court. When he was first proposed to Maurepas, the minister said: "He is a republican; *il voudra nous républicaniser.*" The freedom of his manners, and his ignorance of etiquette, first revealed to the queen the imminence of some dreadful change. At his first audience he took her hand and kissed it without asking leave. This, we learn, was deemed a more significant and alarming circumstance than the attacks on the royal authority.[19] And the Maréchale de B. made the same discovery when the advocate T. took snuff in her presence, "*sans aucune politesse préalable.*" The recall of Necker after his first disgrace was extremely distasteful to the king. "Then," he said, "I must surrender my throne to him." When he had yielded, he said to his family, "They have compelled me to recall Necker, which I was unwilling to do; but it will not be long before they repent. I shall do all he tells me, and you will see the consequences."[20] He was still more reluctant to appoint Brienne. At length he gave way, saying: "You are determined; but it may happen that you will be sorry for it." That frivolous minister had an uneasy foreboding of evil ludicrously inadequate to the event. At the death of the Cardinal de Luynes he obtained as much as he could of the benefices which had belonged to him. "I take my precautions," he

---

[18] Montgaillard, Histoire de France, 1827, i. 345.

[19] "Cette familiarité impertinente du Genevois fit sentir à cette princesse, plus que les infractions des droits du roi, que le trône était ébranlé." *Observations sur les Ministres des Finances,* 1812, p. 216.

[20] Sallier, Annales Françaises, 1813, p. 199.

said; "for I fear that before long the clergy will pay the penalty of all that is going on, and I shall deem myself fortunate if I retain half of what I am taking."[21] He wrote to the Archbishop of Lyons: "I have never been a partisan of the States-General; this resolution will be the occasion of a discussion in the three orders, and of troubles without remedy throughout the State. . . . I should not be surprised if disorder and anarchy were to ensue, rather than settlement and union." His friend the Abbé de Vermond saw deeper when he wrote to him: "For the clergy the rods are preparing, and they may expect a bloody scourge."[22]

Malesherbes said to the king, in September 1787: "It is not a question of appeasing a momentary crisis, but of extinguishing a spark which may produce a great conflagration."[23] About the same time, Lamoignon said: "The parliament, the nobles, and the clergy have dared to resist the king; in two years there will be neither parliament, nor nobles, nor clergy."[24] On the 22d December 1788, the first President of the Parliament, D'Ormesson, pronounced an address to the king, in which he spoke of the state of the nation. "Already the partisans of opposite ideas take umbrage at each other; they seem to fear and to avoid each other, and to prepare for open discord; they throw themselves inconsiderately into the commencement of associations more dangerous than they imagine; they think that they are conducting the State towards reform, and they are only leading it to its ruin. . . . What they are determined to destroy they can no longer respect. . . . Where can be found the obedience which your majesty has a right to expect? A fatal shock makes it totter on all sides. The consequences make themselves felt from the foundations to the summit of the State. This general commotion is increased by ideas of equality, which men endeavour to erect into a system, as if it were possible for equality really to subsist. These speculations, however vain they may be, sow amongst the citizens the germs of anarchy; they are the destruction of the royal authority, and at the same time the destruction of the civil and monarchical order. It is this, sire, that alarms your Parliament." These representations, we are told, were received with an indifference which filled the Parliament with consternation.

[21] Montgaillard, i. 424.
[22] Ibid. p. 428.
[23] Montgaillard, p. 373.
[24] Sallier, p. 186.

As the plot thickened, the alarm became more general, and foresight ceased to be the dismal privilege of far-seeing men. At the assembly of the Notables, the Prince de Conti spoke in these terms to the Count of Provence: "The monarchy is attacked; men desire its destruction, and the fatal moment is at hand. . . . Whatever happens, I shall not have to reproach myself with having left you in ignorance of the excessive evils with which we are overwhelmed, and the still greater evils with which we are threatened." In December 1788, he joined D'Artois, Condé, and Bourbon, in signing a memoir, in which the king was told, "Sire, the State is in danger; your person is respected, the virtues of the monarch secure to him the homage of the nation; but a revolution is preparing in the principles of government." From the Travels of Arthur Young we know that the same sort of language was common in French society. "One opinion pervaded the whole company, that they are on the eve of some great revolution in the government; that every thing points to it; . . . a great ferment among all ranks of men, who are eager for some change, without knowing what to look to or what to hope for."[25]

Soon after his dismissal, Calonne wrote to his brother: "I look upon France as a body festering in almost every part, on which it is feared to operate, because too many amputations are required; the disease increases, and the body dies while the remedy is discussed. Be sure that this will be the result of the States-General. . . . The State, without obtaining a useful change, will only be convulsed."[26]

Marmontel relates a conversation with Chamfort, some time before the meeting of the States-General, from which it is clear that what happened was not only foreseen, but prepared, by the popular party. "Repairs," said Chamfort, "often cause ruins: if we strike an old wall, we cannot be certain that it will not crumble beneath the hammer; and assuredly here the edifice is so decayed that I should not wonder if it became necessary to demolish it altogether. . . . And why not rebuild it on another plan, less Gothic and more regular? Would it be, for instance, so great a misfortune if there were not so many stories, and every thing were on the ground floor? . . . The nation is a great herd, that thinks only of feeding, and which, with good dogs, the shepherds drive as they please. . . . All this is a shame and a pity in an age like our own; and in order to trace a new plan, it is quite right

[25] Travels in France in 1787, p. 66.
[26] Montgaillard, i. p. 358.

to clear the place. . . . And the throne and the altar will fall together; they are two buttresses supporting each other; and when one is broken, the other will give way. . . . There are in the clergy some virtues without talents, and some talents degraded and dishonoured by vice. . . . The advantage on the side of the people in revolution is, that it has no morality. How can you resist men to whom all means are good?"[27] Marmontel repeated this remarkable speech the same evening to Maury: "It is but too true," he replied, "that in their speculations they are not far wrong, and that the faction has chosen its time well to meet with few obstacles. . . . I am resolved to perish in the breach; but I have at the same time the melancholy conviction that they will take the place by assault, and that it will be pillaged." The most significant saying of all is that of a Bishop to whom Maury communicated what he had heard: "We are not so far gone as is supposed; and, with the sword in one hand and the crucifix in the other, the clergy will defend its rights." Marmontel himself went to the minister Montmorin, spoke of the danger, and urged him to put the king in safety in one of the fortresses. Montmorin objected that there was no money, that the State was bankrupt, and could not incur the chance of civil war. "You think," he said, "that the danger is very pressing, to go at once to extremities?" "So pressing," was the answer, "that in a months' time from now I would not answer for the liberty of the king, nor for his head, nor for yours." The writer remarks very justly, that although the state of affairs and the general excitement had long threatened an approaching crisis, it is nevertheless true that it occurred only through the imprudence of those who were obstinately determined to think it impossible. Pitt wrote on the 6th September 1788: "The state of France, whatever else it may produce, seems to promise us more than ever a considerable respite from any dangerous projects."

Omens had cast their shadow on the unfortunate king from his birth. He was born at Versailles while the court was at Choisy, and none of the princes of the blood were present. This did not look well, in the ideas which then pervailed; but, worse than this, the courier who was sent to carry the news to court fell from his horse and was killed on the way. The great disaster which occurred at the festivities of his accession was still more ominous. "I saw," said a contemporary, "this sinister event disturb all the imaginations of men with the notion

---

[27] Marmontel, Mémoires, iv. p. 77 sqq.

of an awful future."[28] In a remarkable military work, written early in his reign, there are some very impressive reflections on the state of the country. "The discomfort and anxiety of the nations under most governments are such that they live with disgust and mechanically; and that, if they had the power to break the bonds that hold them, they would give themselves other laws and other men to administer them. . . . Suppose there were to arise in Europe a vigorous people, with genius, resources, and a government—a people combining with austere virtues and a national militia a fixed plan of aggrandisement, which should not lose sight of that system, and knowing how to make war at little cost, and how to subsist by its victories, should not be compelled to lay down its arms by calculations of finance—we should see it subjugate its neighbours, and overturn our feeble governments, as the north wind bends the reed. . . . France is now the country that is most rapidly declining. The government does not sustain it; and the vices which every where else are spread only by imitation are born there, are more inveterate, more destructive, and must destroy her first. . . . The monstrous and complicated system of our laws, our finances, and our military power, will fall to pieces."[29]

No writer of that age seems to have possessed greater foresight, or to have formed his opinions on a larger induction than Linguet, a pamphleteer of great activity, but of no great authority while he lived. In the first volume of his *Annales Politiques*, published in the year 1777, he writes as follows: "It is a tendency common to all, from the princes to the lowest of their subjects, to consider success as a right, and to

---

[28] Fantin Desodoards, Histoire de France, xxiii, 224. In the same year, 1775, Delille circulated a rhyming prophecy of the good times that were coming. We will quote a few verses:

> Des biens on fera des lots
> Qui rendront les gens égaux. . . .
> Du même pas marcheront
> Noblesse et roture;
> Les Français retourneront
> Au droit de nature.
> Adieu parlemens et lois,
> Ducs et princes et rois! . . .

> Les Français auront des dieux à leur fantaisie.

[29] Guibert, Essai général de Tactique, tome i., Discours préliminare, pp. ix, xiii, xix, xliv.

deem oneself innocent when one has not failed.[30] . . . Unjust conquests had been seen before, but hitherto usurpers had been scrupulous to conceal their sword behind manifestoes. . . . But now it is in the lifetime of the owner, in the midst of peace, without a grievance, with a pretext even in appearance, the crown of Sarmatia has been shattered to pieces by the hands of friends. The weakness of the one, the power of the others, have been the only reasons invoked or recognised. The terrible principle that force is the best argument of kings, so often put in practice, but always so sedulously disguised, has been for the first time produced, and practised openly and without concealment. . . . It cannot be but that something should filter imperceptibly from this into general habits. . . . Never perhaps, in the midst of an apparent prosperity, has Europe been so near a total subversion, the more terrible because despair will be its cause. . . . We have arrived by a directly contrary road precisely to the point where Italy stood when the servile war inundated her with blood, and carried carnage and conflagration to the gates of the mistress of the world."[31]

In the importance which this able writer attributes to the partition of Poland he is supported by Burke, who called it "the very first great breach in the modern political system of Europe." It did more than any other event, except the suppression of the Jesuits, to obscure the political conscience of mankind, and to prepare men to despise the obligations of right, in obedience to the example set them by their kings. The consequences were inevitable, and they were foretold, and the Revolution was heralded and announced at each step of its approach by all the most competent observers. The feeling of its approaching end was strong in the old society, and both the party of those who were the authors of the great catastrophe, and of those who were to be its victims, agreed in those expectations which were the hopes of the first and the fears of the other. "Revolutions," says Bonald, "have immediate material causes which strike the least attentive eye. These are in reality only the occasions. The real causes, the deep and efficient causes, are moral causes, which small minds and corrupt men do not understand. . . . You think that a financial deficit was the cause of the

---

[30] The elder Mirabeau says, in the *Ami des Hommes* (iii. 33), "La loi des plus forts fait de la révolte le droit des gens."

[31] pp. 76, 78, 80, 85.

Revolution: seek deeper, and you will find a deficit in the very principles of the social order." One of the ablest of those who saw the Revolution mingles perhaps some vanity with much truth when he says: "I know nothing of importance that has happened in Church or State since I grew up which I did not foresee. God does not permit that men should allow a principle, and restrain that which flows naturally from it."

[5]
Review of Carlyle's
Friedrich II

Most of the reviews of this book that have appeared are depre-
catory of criticism rather than actually laudatory. There are so few
among the writers of the day who have not experienced more or less
the influence of Mr. Carlyle's former writings, that almost all are
interested in the preservation of his fame. Yet there is no English
historian who has a right to be judged by a higher or severer test, for
no one has spoken more deeply and truly on the character and dignity
of history. "All history," he writes, in one of the lucid intervals of his
Latter-Day Pamphlets, "is an inarticulate Bible, and in a dim intricate
manner reveals the Divine Appearances in this lower world. . . . There
is no biography of a man, much less any history or biography of a
nation, but wraps in it a message out of heaven, addressed to the
hearing ear or to the not hearing." Of this conception of history *Past
and Present* and *The French Revolution* were not entirely unworthy. The
disgust which Mr. Carlyle feels for the men and things of his own time
seemed to give him a clearer eye for the past than most of those possess
whose vision is distorted by the prejudices of their age. He showed an
intelligence of things which no other English historian has understood.
He dwelt upon the invisible impersonal forces that act in history, and
appreciated, often with rare sagacity, the true significance and sequence
of events. But he was unable to follow the course he had pointed out,
and failed even to maintain himself on the high ground he had reached.
He could not distinguish in history what was unknown to him in
religion: thus he fell to the exclusive contemplation of certain typical

Thomas Carlyle, *History of Friedrich II of Prussia, called Frederick the Great*, vols. 1 and 2
(London: Chapman and Hall, 1858). This review was published in the *Rambler* 10
(December 1858): 429–431. *Wellesley* II: 776; Döllinger I: 159; Acton-Simpson I: 80.

individuals, whose greatness appeared to supply what he wanted, an object of worship, and personified invisible elements in visible men. And now the belongings of his hero possess so great an importance that they distract his attention from him; he invests with an absurd dignity not only his relations, but their goods and chattels, and allows merely material things to eclipse the human interest of his subject. It is a history made up of eccentricities. This is the way that Mr. Dickens writes novels; for whom the spectacles of an elderly gentleman, a pair of mulberry-coloured hose, or a wandering American pig, have greater attractions than any psychological problem. Mr. Carlyle told us long ago, "I have to speak in crude language, the wretched times being dumb and deaf." But if the history of the house of Brandenburg was worth relating, as a prologue to the life of Frederick, in two volumes almost equal in bulk to Hume's *History of England,* it was worth giving in its natural colours. Instead of that, however, events and persons the least suggestive of humorous ideas are converted into a list of extravagant oddities. We have an agreeable episode concerning a "thrice-memorable shoe-buckle," swallowed by the father of Frederick "31 December 1692"; and are informed with pharmaceutical accuracy that "a few grains of rhubarb restored it safely to the light of day." The prince who so narrowly escaped an untimely end was "an unruly fellow, and dangerous to trust among crockery"; "a solid, honest, somewhat explosive bear," to whom Leibniz, "with his big black periwig and large patient nose" and "bandy legs," was not likely to teach much metaphysics. The pendant to this flattering sketch of the philosopher is "Prince Eugenio," with a "nose not unprovided with snuff, and lips in consequence rather open." In Albert the Bear's time "the Wends are finally reduced to silence; their anarchy well buried, and wholesome Dutch cabbage planted over it." There is a succession of pleasing pictures of "a poor old anatomy, or lean human nailrod"; "a mere betitled, betasselled, elderly military gentlemen, of no special qualities, . . . behung with titles, and no doubt a stomach in the inside"; "a solid dull man, capable of liquor among other things, not wiser than he should be"; and "an ugly dragoon-major of a woman." We are told how "simple Orson of a Prussian majesty" falls in with "a bepainted, beribboned, insulting playactor majesty," and how he subsequently "looks down like a rhinoceros on all these cobwebberies." In this wise Mr. Carlyle beguiles the prodigious tedium of his subject, and refreshes himself after the study of "watery quartos." He abuses at every turn, in sentences as humorous and epigrammatic as they are unjust, the German historians, who will be rather surprised at the way he has done their work for them. What most provokes him in their books is the absence of curiosities. He makes much of a certain old gun called *Lazy Peg,* and distinguishes it above all other old guns: "I have often inquired after Lazy Peg's fate in subsequent times; but could never learn any thing distinct. The German Dryasdust is a dull dog, and seldom carries any thing human in those big wallets of his." Judged by such canons, what a dull dog he must deem the Attic Dryasdust Thucydides! There is, however, very little pretence of going to the real authorities for the purpose of mitigating the insipidity of the early part of the history. These absurdities are sometimes relieved by bits of the old rugged eloquence, and by felicitous passages, such as the description of the Emperor Charles IV: "He kept mainly at Prag, ready for receipt of cash, and holding well out of harm's way; . . . much blown to and fro, poor light wretch, on the chaotic winds of his Time—steering towards no star." His judgment of Bayle's philosophy is worthy of his better time: "Let us admit that it was profitable, at least that it was inevitable; let us pity it and be thankful for it, and rejoice that we are well out of it. Scepticism, which is there beginning at the very top of the world-tree, and has to descend through all the boughs, with terrible results to mankind, is as yet pleasant, tinting the leaves with fine autumnal red."

In such a book it seems hardly fair to take note of errors in matters of fact; but in one place Mr. Carlyle, contrary to his wont, makes a clumsy show of quoting an authority to establish the truth of a story which it has long been disreputable to repeat. He judiciously confines his research to a writer who has been dead a hundred years. The Emperor Henry VII, he says, "died on a sudden, poisoned in sacramental wine" by a "rat-eyed Dominican"; . . . "one of the crowning summits of human scoundrelism which painfully stick in the mind." "Ptolemy of Lucca, himself a Dominican, is one of the *accusing* spirits." So far from it, Ptolemy says in one place merely, "viam universae carnis ingressus est" (Muratori Scriptores, xi. 1208); and elsewhere, with the addition "a fide dignis accepi qui fuerunt presentes," "Moritur autem xxiii Augusti morte naturali, quamquam aliqui malevoli dixerunt quod fuit datum sibi venenum in eucharistia" (Ibid. 1240). Now long before Ptolemy was printed, he was quoted, on the authority of manuscripts, as one of the accusers of his order. When the text was published, first of all in an extract by Bzovius, then completely by Muratori, it was found that the accusation was contained in an interpolation, with the heading "additio." Whereupon, of course, the Catholic historians were accused of fraud; and about the time of Mr. Carlyle's chief authority, Köhler, the Protestants triumphed more loudly than ever. At last the original work was found from which the interpolated passage was taken. It proved to be by Henry, canon of Constance, from whom most of the German chroniclers afterwards borrowed the tale of poison. The origin of the calumny is easy to find; but here we have only wished to expose Mr. Carlyle's way of adopting it.

[6]
Mr. Goldwin Smith's
Irish History

When Macaulay republished his Essays from the *Edinburgh Review*, he had already commenced the great work by which his name will be remembered; and he had the prudence to exclude from the collection his early paper on the art of historical writing. In the maturity of his powers, he was rightly unwilling to bring into notice the theories of his youth. At a time when he was about to claim a place among the first historians, it would have been injudicious to remind men of the manner in which he had described the objects of his emulation or of his rivalry—how in his judgment the speeches of Thucydides violate the decencies of fiction, and give to his book something of the character of the Chinese pleasure-grounds, whilst his political observations are very superficial; how Polybius has no other merit than that of a faithful narrator of facts; and how in the nineteenth century, from the practice of distorting narrative in conformity with theory, "history proper is disappearing." But in that essay, although the judgments are puerile, the ideal at which the writer afterwards aimed is distinctly drawn, and his own character is prefigured in the description of the author of a history of England as it ought to be, who "gives to truth those attractions which have been usurped by fiction," "intersperses the details which are the charm of historical romances," and "reclaims those materials which the novelist has appropriated."

Mr. Goldwin Smith, like Macaulay, has written on the study of history, and he has been a keen critic of other historians before becoming one himself. It is a bold thing for a man to bring theory so near to execution, and, amidst dispute on his principles and resentment

Published in the *Rambler* n.s. 6 (January 1862): 190–220. *Wellesley* II: 783; Döllinger I: 244; Acton-Simpson II: 191. Reprinted in Acton, *History of Freedom*, pp. 232–269.

at his criticism, to give an opportunity of testing his theories by his own practice, and of applying his own canons to his performance. It reminds us of the professor of Cologne, who wrote the best Latin poem of modern times, as a model for his pupils; and of the author of an attack on Dryden's *Virgil*, who is styled by Pope the "fairest of critics," "because," says Johnson, "he exhibited his own version to be compared with that which he condemned." The work in which the professor of history and critic of historians teaches by example is not unworthy of his theory, whilst some of its defects may be explained by it.

The point which most closely connects Mr. Goldwin Smith's previous writings with his *Irish History* is his vindication of a moral code against those who identify moral with physical laws, who consider the outward regularity with which actions are done to be the inward reason why they must be done, and who conceive that all laws are opposed to freedom. In his opposition to this materialism, he goes in one respect too far, in another not far enough.

On the one hand, whilst defending liberty and morality, he has not sufficient perception of the spiritual element; and on the other, he seems to fear that it would be a concession to his antagonists to dwell on the constant laws by which nature asserts herself, and on the regularity with which like causes produce like effects. Yet it is on the observation of these laws that political, social, and economical science rests; and it is by the knowledge of them that a scientific historian is guided in grouping his matter. In this he differs from the artist, whose principle of arrangement is drawn from himself, not from external nature; and from the annalist, who has no arrangement, since he sees, not the connection, but the succession of events. Facts are intelligible and instructive—or, in other words, history exhibits truths as well as facts—when they are seen not merely as they follow, but as they correspond; not merely as they have happened, but as they are paralleled. The fate of Ireland is to be understood not simply from the light of English and Irish history, but by the general history of other conquests, colonies, dependencies, and establishments. In this sort of illustration by analogy and contrast Mr. Goldwin Smith is particularly infelicitous. Nor does Providence gain what science loses by his treatment of history. He rejects materialism, but he confines his view to motives and forces which are purely human.

The Catholic Church receives, therefore, very imperfect measure at his hands. Her spiritual character and purpose he cannot discern behind the temporal instruments and appendages of her existence; he confounds authority with influence, devotion with bigotry, power with force of arms, and estimates the vigour and durability of Catholicism by criterions as material as those of the philosophers he has so vehemently and so ably refuted. Most Protestant writers fail in approbation; he fails in appreciation. It is not so much a religious feeling that makes him unjust, as a way of thinking which, in great measure, ignores the supernatural, and therefore precludes a just estimate of religion in general, and of Catholicism in particular. Hence he is unjust rather to the nature than to the actions of the Church. He caricatures more than he libels her. He is much less given to misrepresentation and calumny than Macaulay, but he has a less exalted idea of the history and character of Catholicism. As he underrates what is divine, so he has no very high standard for the actions of men, and he is liberal in admitting extenuating circumstances. Though he never suspends the severity of his moral judgment in consideration of the purpose or the result, yet he is induced by a variety of arguments to mitigate its rigour. In accordance with the theory he has formerly developed, he is constantly sitting in judgment; and he discusses the morality of men and actions far oftener than history—which has very different problems to solve—either requires or tolerates. De Maistre says that in our time compassion is reserved for the guilty. Mr. Goldwin Smith is a merciful judge, whose compassion generally increases in proportion to the greatness of the culprit; and he has a sympathy for what is done in the grand style, which balances his hatred of what is wrongly done.

It would not be fair to judge of an author's notion and powers of research by a hasty and popular production. Mr. Goldwin Smith has collected quite enough information for the purpose for which he has used it, and he has not failed through want of industry. The test of solidity is not the quantity read, but the mode in which the knowledge has been collected and used. Method, not genius, or eloquence, or erudition, makes the historian. He may be discovered most easily by his use of authorities. The first question is, whether the writer understands the comparative value of sources of information, and has the habit of giving precedence to the most trustworthy informant. There are some vague indications that Mr. Goldwin Smith does not understand the importance of this fundamental rule. In his Inaugural Lecture, published two years ago, the following extravagant sentence occurs: "Before the Revolution, the fervour and the austerity of Rousseau had cast out from good society the levity and sensuality of Voltaire" (p. 15). This view—which he appears to have abandoned, for in his *Irish History* he tells us that France "has now become the eldest daughter of Voltaire"—he supports by a reference to an abridgment of French history, much and justly esteemed in French schools, but, like all abridgments, not founded on original knowledge, and disfigured by exaggeration in the colouring. Moreover, the passage he refers to has been misinterpreted. In the *Irish History* Mr. Goldwin Smith quotes, for the character of the early Celts, without any sufficient reason, another French historian, Martin, who has no great authority, and the younger Thierry, who has none at all. This is a point of very little weight by itself; but until our author vindicates his research by other writings, it is not in his favour.

The defects of Mr. Goldwin Smith's historic art, his lax criticism, his superficial acquaintance with foreign countries, his occasional proneness to sacrifice accuracy for the sake of rhetorical effect, his aversion for spiritual things, are all covered by one transcendent merit, which, in a man of so much ability, promises great results.

Writers the most learned, the most accurate in details, and the soundest in tendency, frequently fall into a habit which can neither be cured nor pardoned—the habit of making history into the proof of their theories. The absence of a definite didactic purpose is the only security for the good faith of a historian. This most rare virtue Mr. Goldwin Smith possesses in a high degree. He writes to tell the truths he finds, not to prove the truths which he believes. In character and design he is eminently truthful and fair, though not equally so in execution. His candour never fails him, and he is never betrayed by his temper; yet his defective knowledge of general history, and his crude notions of the Church, have made him write many things which are untrue, and some which are unjust. Prejudice is in all men of such early growth, and so difficult to eradicate, that it becomes a misfortune rather than a reproach, especially if it is due to ignorance and not to passion, and if it has not its seat in the will. In the case of Mr. Goldwin Smith it is of the curable and harmless kind. The fairness of his intention is far beyond his knowledge. When he is unjust, it is not from hatred; where he is impartial, it is not always from the copiousness of his information. His prejudices are of a nature which his ability and honesty will in time inevitably overcome.

The general result and moral of his book is excellent. He shows that the land-question has been from the beginning the great difficulty in Ireland; and he concludes with a condemnation of the Established Church, and a prophecy of its approaching fall. The weakness of Ireland and the guilt of England are not disguised; and the author has not written to stimulate the anger of one nation or to attenuate the remorse of the other. To both he gives wise and statesman-like advice, that may soon be very opportune. The first American war was the commencement of the deliverance of Ireland, and it may be that a new American war will complete the work of regeneration which the first began. Agreeing as we do with the policy of the author, and admiring the spirit of his book, we shall not attempt either to enforce or to dispute his conclusions, and we shall confine our remarks to less essential points on which he appears to us in the wrong.

There are several instances of inaccuracy and negligence which, however trivial in themselves, tend to prove that the author is not always very scrupulous in speaking of things he has not studied. A purist so severe as to write "Kelt" for "Celt" ought not to call Mercury, originally a very different personage from Hermes, one of "the legendary authors of Greek civilisation" (p. 43); and we do not believe that anybody who had read the writings of the two primates could call Bramhall "an inferior counterpart of Laud" (p. 105). In a loftier mood, and therefore apparently with still greater license, Mr. Goldwin Smith declares that "the glorious blood of Orange could scarcely have run in a low persecutor's veins" (p. 123). The blood of Orange ran in the veins of William the Silent, the threefold hypocrite, who confessed Catholicism whilst he hoped to retain his influence at court, Lutheranism when there was a chance of obtaining assistance from the German princes, Calvinism when he was forced to resort to religion in order to excite the people against the crown, and who persecuted the Protestants in Orange and the Catholics in Holland. These, however, are matters of no consequence whatever in a political history of Ireland; but we find ourselves at issue with the author on the important question of political freedom. "Even the highly civilised Kelt of France, familiar as he is with theories of political liberty, seems almost incapable of sustaining free institutions. After a moment of constitutional government, he reverts, with a bias which the fatalist might call irresistible, to despotism in some form" (p. 18). The warning so frequently uttered by Burke in his last years, to fly from the liberty of France, is still

more needful now that French liberty has exhibited itself in a far more
seductive light. The danger is more subtle, when able men confound
political forms with popular rights. France has never been governed
by a Constitution since 1792, if by a Constitution is meant a definite
rule and limitation of the governing power. It is not that the French
failed to preserve the forms of parliamentary government, but that
those forms no more implied freedom than the glory which the Empire
has twice given in their stead. It is a serious fault in our author that
he has not understood so essential a distinction. Has he not read the
Rights of Man, by Tom Paine?

"It is not because a part of the government is elective that makes it
less a despotism, if the persons so elected possess afterwards, as a
parliament, unlimited powers. Election, in this case, becomes separated
from representation, and the candidates are candidates for despotism."[1]

Napoleon once consulted the cleverest among the politicians who
served him, respecting the durability of some of his institutions. "Ask
yourself," was the answer, "what it would cost you to destroy them.
If the destruction would cost no effort, you have created nothing; for
politically, as well as physically, only that which resists endures." In
the year 1802 the same great writer said: "Nothing is more pernicious
in a monarchy than the principles and the forms of democracy, for
they allow no alternative, but despotism and revolutions." With the
additional experience of half a century, a writer not inferior to the last
repeats exactly the same idea:

"Of all societies in the world, those which will always have most
difficulty in permanently escaping absolute government will be precisely
those societies in which aristocracy is no more, and can no more be."[2]

French constitutionalism was but a form by which the absence of
self-government was concealed. The State was as despotic under Villèle
or Guizot as under either of the Bonapartes. The Restoration fenced
itself round with artificial creations, having no root in the condition
or in the sympathies of the people; these creations simply weakened it
by making it unpopular. The hereditary peerage was an anomaly in a
country unused to primogeniture, and so was the revival, in a nation
of sceptics, of the Gallican union between Church and State. The
monarchy of July, which was more suited to the nature of French

---

[1] *Works,* ii. 47. This is one of the passages which, seventy years ago, were declared to
be treasonable. We trust we run no risk in confessing that we entirely agree with it.

[2] Tocqueville, *L'Ancien Régime et la Révolution,* Préface, p. xvi.

society, and was thus enabled to crush a series of insurrections, was at last forced, by its position and by the necessity of self-preservation, to assume a very despotic character. After the fortifications of Paris were begun, a tendency set in which, under a younger sovereign, would have led to a system hardly distinguishable from that which now prevails; and there are princes in the House of Orleans whose government would develop the principle of democracy in a manner not very remote from the institutions of the second Empire. It is liberalism more than despotism that is opposed to liberty in France; and it is a most dangerous error to imagine that the Governments of the French Charter really resemble ours. There are States without any parliament at all, whose principles and fundamental institutions are in much closer harmony with our system of autonomy. Mr. Goldwin Smith sees half the truth, that there is something in the French nation which incapacitates it for liberty; but he does not see that what they have always sought, and sometimes enjoyed, is not freedom; that their liberty must diminish in proportion as their ideal is attained; and that they are not yet familiar with the theory of political rights. With this false notion of what constitutes liberty, it is not surprising that he should repeatedly dwell on its connection with Protestantism, and talk of "the political liberty which Protestantism brought in its train" (p. 120). Such phrases may console a Protestant reader of a book fatal to the Protestant ascendency in Ireland; but as there are no arguments in support of them, and as they are strangely contradicted by the facts in the context, Mr. Goldwin Smith resorts to the ingenious artifice of calling to mind as many ugly stories about Catholics as he can. The notion constantly recurs that, though the Protestants were very wicked in Ireland, it was against their principles and general practice, and is due to the Catholics, whose system naturally led them to be tyrannical and cruel, and thus provoked retaliation. Mr. Smith might have been reminded by Peter Plymley that when Protestantism has had its own way it has uniformly been averse to freedom: "What has Protestantism done for liberty in Denmark, in Sweden, throughout the north of Germany, and in Prussia?"—not much less than democracy has done in France. An admirer of the constitutions of 1791, 1814, or 1830 may be excused if he is not very severe on the absolutism of Protestant countries.

Mr. Goldwin Smith mistakes the character of the invasion of Ireland because he has not understood the relative position of the civilisation of the two countries at the time when it occurred. That of the Celts was in many respects more refined than that of the Normans. The Celts are not among the progressive, initiative races, but among those which supply the materials rather than the impulse of history, and are either stationary or retrogressive. The Persians, the Greeks, the Romans, and the Teutons are the only makers of history, the only authors of advancement. Other races possessing a highly developed language, a copious literature, a speculative religion, enjoying luxury and art, attain to a certain pitch of cultivation which they are unable either to communicate or to increase. They are a negative element in the world; sometimes the barrier, sometimes the instrument, sometimes the material of those races to whom it is given to originate and to advance. Their existence is either passive, or reactionary and destructive, when, after intervening like the blind forces of nature, they speedily exhibit their uncreative character, and leave others to pursue the course to which they have pointed. The Chinese are a people of this kind. They have long remained stationary, and succeeded in excluding the influences of general history. So the Hindoos; being Pantheists, they have no history of their own, but supply objects for commerce and for conquest. So the Huns, whose appearance gave a sudden impetus to a stagnant world. So the Slavonians, who tell only in the mass, and whose influence is ascertainable sometimes by adding to the momentum of active forces, sometimes by impeding through inertness the progress of mankind.

To this class of nations also belong the Celts of Gaul. The Roman and the German conquerors have not altered their character as it was drawn two thousand years ago. They have a history, but it is not theirs; their nature remains unchanged, their history is the history of the invaders. The revolution was the revival of the conquered race, and their reaction against the creations of their masters. But it has been cunning only to destroy; it has not given life to one constructive idea, or durability to one new institution; and it has exhibited to the world an unparalleled political incapacity, which was announced by Burke, and analysed by Tocqueville, in works which are the crowning pieces of two great literatures.

The Celts of these islands, in like manner, waited for a foreign influence to set in action the rich treasure which in their own hands could be of no avail. Their language was more flexible, their poetry and music more copious, than those of the Anglo-Normans. Their laws, if we may judge from those of Wales, display a society in some respects highly cultivated. But, like the rest of that group of nations to which they belong, there was not in them the incentive to action and progress which is given by the consciousness of a part in human destiny, by the inspiration of a high idea, or even by the natural development of institutions. Their life and literature were aimless and wasteful. Without combination or concentration, they had no star to guide them in an onward course; and the progress of dawn into day was no more to them than to the flocks and to the forests.

Before the Danish wars, and the decay, which is described by St. Bernard in terms which must not be taken quite literally, had led to the English invasion, there was probably as much material, certainly as much spiritual, culture in Ireland as in any country in the West; but there was not that by whose sustaining force alone these things endure, by which alone the place of nations in history is determined— there was no political civilisation. The State did not keep pace with the progress of society. This is the essential and decisive inferiority of the Celtic race, as conspicuous among the Irish in the twelfth century as among the French in our own. They gave way before the higher political aptitude of the English.

The issue of an invasion is generally decided by this political aptitude, and the consequences of a conquest always depend on it. Subjection to a people of a higher capacity for government is of itself no misfortune; and it is to most countries the condition of their political advancement. The Greeks were more highly cultivated than the Romans, the Gauls than the Franks; yet in both cases the higher political intelligence prevailed. For a long time the English had, perhaps, no other superiority over the Irish; yet this alone would have made the conquest a great blessing to Ireland, but for the separation of the races. Conquering races necessarily bring with them their own system of government, and there is no other way of introducing it. A nation can obtain political education only by dependence on another. Art, literature, and science may be communicated by the conquered to the conqueror; but government can be taught only by governing, therefore only by the governors; politics can only be learnt in this school. The most uncivilised of the barbarians, whilst they slowly and imperfectly learned the arts of Rome, at once remodelled its laws. The two kinds of civilisation, social and political, are wholly unconnected with each other. Either may subsist, in high perfection, alone. Polity grows like language, and is part of a people's nature, not dependent on its will. One or the other can be developed, modified, corrected; but they cannot be subverted or changed by the people itself without an act of suicide. Organic change, if it comes at all, must come from abroad. Revolution is a malady, a frenzy, an interruption of the nation's growth, sometimes fatal to its existence, often to its independence. In this case revolution, by making the nation subject to others, may be the occasion of a new development. But it is not conceivable that a nation should arbitrarily and spontaneously cast off its history, reject its traditions, abrogate its law and government, and commence a new political existence.

Nothing in the experience of ages, or in the nature of man, allows us to believe that the attempt of France to establish a durable edifice on the ruins of 1789, without using the old materials, can ever succeed, or that she can ever emerge from the vicious circle of the last seventy years, except by returning to the principle which she then repudiated, and by admitting, that if States would live, they must preserve their organic connection with their origin and history, which are their root and their stem; that they are not voluntary creations of human wisdom; and that men labour in vain who would construct them without acknowledging God as the artificer.

Theorists who hold it to be a wrong that a nation should belong to a foreign State are therefore in contradiction with the law of civil progress. This law, or rather necessity, which is as absolute as the law that binds society together, is the force which makes us need one another, and only enables us to obtain what we need on terms, not of equality, but of dominion and subjection, in domestic, economic, or political relations. The political theory of nationality is in contradiction with the historic nation. Since a nation derives its ideas and instincts of government, as much as its temperament and its language, from God, acting through the influences of nature and of history, these ideas and instincts are originally and essentially peculiar to it, and not separable from it; they have no practical value in themselves when divided from the capacity which corresponds to them. National qualities are the incarnations of political ideas. No people can receive its government from another without receiving at the same time the ministers of government. The workman must travel with the work. Such changes can only be accomplished by submission to a foreign State, or to another race. Europe has seen two great instances of such conquests, extending over centuries—the Roman Empire, and the settlement of the barbarians in the West. This it is which gives unity to the history of the Middle Ages. The Romans established a universal empire by subjecting all countries to the authority of a single power. The barbarians introduced into all a single system of law, and thus became the instrument of a universal Church. The same spirit of freedom, the same notions of the State, pervade all the *Leges Barbarorum,* and all the polities they founded in Europe and Asia. They differ widely in the surrounding conditions, in the state of society, in the degree of advancement, in almost all external things. The principle common to them all is to acknowledge the freedom of the Church as a corporation and a proprietor, and in virtue of the principle of self-government to allow religion to develop her influence in the State. The great migration which terminated in the Norman conquests and in the Crusades gave the dominion of the Latin world to the Teutonic chivalry, and to the Church her proper place. All other countries sank into despotism, into schism, and at last into barbarism, under the Tartars or the Turks. The union between the Teutonic races and the Holy See was founded on their political qualities more than on their religious fervour. In modern times, the most pious Catholics have often tyrannised over the Church. In the Middle Ages her liberty was often secured and respected where her spiritual injunctions were least obeyed.

The growth of the feudal system coinciding with the general decay of morals led, in the eleventh century, to new efforts of the Church to preserve her freedom. The Holy See was delivered from the Roman factions by the most illustrious of the emperors, and a series of German Popes commenced the great reform. Other princes were unwilling to submit to the authority of the imperial nominees, and the kings of France and Castile showed symptoms of resistance, in which they were supported by the heresy of Berengarius. The conduct of Henry IV delivered the Church from the patronage of the Empire, whilst the Normans defended her against the Gallican tendencies and the feudal tyranny. In Sicily, the Normans consented to hold their power from the Pope; and in Normandy, Berengarius found a successful adversary, and the King of France a vassal who compelled him to abandon his designs. The chaplain of the Conqueror describes his government in terms which show how singularly it fulfilled the conditions which the Church requires. He tells us that William established in Normandy a truly Christian order; that every village, town, and castle enjoyed its own privileges; and that, while other princes either forbade the erection of churches or seized their endowments, he left his subjects free to make pious gifts. In his reign and by his conduct the word "bigot" ceased to be a term of reproach, and came to signify what we now should call "ultramontane." He was the foremost of those Normans who were called by the Holy See to reclaim what was degenerate, and to renovate the declining States of the North.

Where the Church addressed herself to the conversion of races of purely Teutonic origin, as in Scandinavia, her missionaries achieved the work. In other countries, as in Poland and Hungary, political dependence on the Empire was the channel and safeguard of her influence. The Norman conquest of England and of Ireland differs from all of these. In both islands the faith had been freely preached, adopted, and preserved. The rulers and the people were Catholic. The last Saxon king who died before the Conquest was a saint. The last archbishop of Dublin appointed before the invasion was a saint. Neither of the invasions can be explained simply by the demoralisation of the clergy, or by the spiritual destitution of the people.

Catholicism spreads among the nations, not only as a doctrine, but as an institution. "The Church," says Mr. Goldwin Smith, "is not a disembodied spirit, but a spirit embodied in human society." Her teaching is directed to the inner man, and is confined to the social order; but her discipline touches on the political. She cannot permanently ignore the acts and character of the State, or escape its notice. Whilst she preaches submission to authorities ordained by God, her nature, not her interest, compels her to exert an involuntary influence upon them. The jealousy so often exhibited by governments is not without reason, for the free action of the Church is the test of the free constitution of the State; and without such free constitution there must necessarily ensue either persecution or revolution. Between the settled organisation of Catholicism and every form of arbitrary power, there is an incompatibility which must terminate in conflict. In a State which possesses no security for authority or freedom, the Church must either fight or succumb. Now, as authority and freedom, the conditions of her existence, can only be obtained through the instrumentality of certain nations, she depends on the aid of these nations. Religion alone cannot civilise men, or secure its own conquest. It promotes civilisation where it has power; but it has not power where its way is not prepared. Its civilising influence is chiefly indirect, and acts by its needs and wants as much as by the fulness of its ideas. So Christianity extends itself by the aid of the secular power, relying, not on the victories of Christian arms, but on the progress of institutions and ideas that harmonise with ecclesiastical freedom. Hence, those who have most actively served the interests of the Church are not always those who have been most faithful to her doctrines. The work which the Goth and the Frank had done on the continent of Europe the Normans came to do in England, where it had been done before but had failed, and in Ireland, where neither Roman nor German influences had entered.

Thus the theory of nationality, unknown to Catholic ages, is inconsistent both with political reason and with Christianity, which requires the dominion of race over race, and whose path was made straight by two universal empires. The missionary may outstrip, in his devoted zeal, the progress of trade or of arms; but the seed that he plants will not take root, unprotected by those ideas of right and duty which first came into the world with the tribes who destroyed the civilisation of antiquity, and whose descendants are in our day carrying those ideas to every quarter of the world. It was as impossible to realise in Ireland the mediaeval notions of ecclesiastical liberty without a great political reform, as to put an end to the dissolution of society and the feuds of princes without the authority of a supreme lord.

There is one institution of those days to which Mr. Goldwin Smith has not done entire justice.

"It is needless to say that the Eric, or pecuniary composition for blood, in place of capital or other punishment, which the Brehon law sanctioned, is the reproach of all primitive codes, and of none. It is the first step from the license of savage revenge to the ordered justice of a regular law" (p. 41).

Pecuniary composition for blood belongs to an advanced period of defined and regular criminal jurisprudence. In the lowest form of civil society, when the State is not yet distinct from the family, the family is compelled to defend itself; and the only protection of society is the vendetta. It is the private right of self-defence combined with the public office of punishment, and therefore not only a privilege but an obligation. The whole family is bound to avenge the injury; but the duty rests first of all with the heir. Precedency in the office of avenger is naturally connected with a first claim in inheritance; and the succession to property is determined by the law of revenge. This leads both to primogeniture, because the eldest son is most likely to be capable of punishing the culprit; and, for the same reason, to modifications of primogeniture, by the preference of the brother before the grandson, and of the male line before the female. A practice which appears barbarous is, therefore, one of the foundations of civilisation, and the origin of some of the refinements of law. In this state of society there is no distinction between civil and criminal law; an injury is looked upon as a private wrong, not, as religion considers it, a sin, or, as the State considers it, a crime.

Something very similar occurs in feudal society. Here all the barons were virtually equal to each other, and without any superior to punish their crimes or to avenge their wrongs. They were, therefore, compelled to obtain safety or reparation, like sovereigns, by force of arms. What war is among States, the feud is in feudal society, and the vengeance of blood in societies not yet matured into States—a substitute for the fixed administration of justice.

The assumption of this duty by the State begins with the recognisance of acts done against the State itself. At first, political crimes alone are visited with a public penalty; private injuries demand no public expiation, but only satisfaction of the injured party. This appears in its most rudimentary form in the *lex talionis*. Society requires that punishment should be inflicted by the State, in order to prevent continual disorders. If the injured party could be satisfied, and his duty fulfilled without inflicting on the criminal an injury corresponding to that which he had done, society was obviously the gainer. At first it was optional to accept or to refuse satisfaction; afterwards it was made obligatory.

Where property was so valuable that its loss was visited on the life or limb of the robber, and injuries against property were made a question of life and death, it soon followed that injury to life could be made a question of payment. To expiate robbery by death, and to expiate murder by the payment of a fine, are correlative ideas. Practically this custom often told with a barbarous inequality against those who were too poor to purchase forgiveness; but it was otherwise both just and humane in principle, and it was generally encouraged by the Church. For in her eyes the criminal was guilty of an act of which it was necessary that he should repent; this made her desire, not his destruction, but his conversion. She tried, therefore, to save his life, and to put an end to revenge, mutilation, and servitude; and for all this the alternative was compensation. This purpose was served by the right of asylum. The Church surrendered the fugitive only on condition that his life and person should be spared in consideration of a lawful fine, which she often paid for him herself. "Concedatur ei vita et omnia membra. Emendat autem causam in quantum potuerit," says a law of Charlemagne, given in the year 785, when the influence of religion on legislation was most powerful in Europe.

No idea occurs more frequently in the work we are reviewing than that of the persecuting character of the Catholic Church; it is used as a perpetual apology for the penal laws in Ireland:

"When the Catholics writhe under this wrong, let them turn their eyes to the history of Catholic countries, and remember that, while the Catholic Church was stripped of her endowments and doomed to political degradation by Protestant persecutors in Ireland, the Protestant churches were exterminated with fire and sword by Catholic persecutors in France, Austria, Flanders, Italy, and Spain" (p. 92). He speaks of Catholicism as "a religion which all Protestants believed to be idolatrous, and knew by fearful experience to be persecuting" (p. 113). "It would not be difficult to point to persecuting laws more sanguinary than these. Spain, France, and Austria will at once supply signal examples. . . . That persecution was the vice of an age and not only of a particular religion, that it disgraced Protestantism as well as Catholicism, is true. But no one who reads the religious history of Europe with an open mind can fail to perceive that the persecutions carried on by Protestants were far less bloody and less extensive than those carried on by Catholics; that they were more frequently excusable as acts of retaliation; that they arose more from political alarm, and less from the spirit of the religion; and that the temper of their authors yielded more rapidly to the advancing influence of humanity and civilisation" (pp. 127, 129).

All these arguments are fallacies; but as the statements at the same time are full of error, we believe that the author is wrong because he has not studied the question, not because he has designed to misrepresent it. The fact that he does not distinguish from each other the various kinds and occasions of persecution, proves that he is wholly ignorant of the things with which it is connected.

Persecution is the vice of particular religions, and the misfortune of particular stages of political society. It is the resource by which States that would be subverted by religious liberty escape the more dangerous alternative of imposing religious disabilities. The exclusion of a part of the community by reason of its faith from the full benefit of the law is a danger and disadvantage to every State, however highly organised its constitution may otherwise be. But the actual existence of a religious party differing in faith from the majority is dangerous only to a State very imperfectly organised. Disabilities are always a danger. Multiplicity of religions is only dangerous to States of an inferior type. By persecution they rid themselves of the peculiar danger which threatens them, without involving themselves in a system universally bad. Persecution comes naturally in a certain period of the progress of society, before a more flexible and comprehensive system has been introduced by that advance of religion and civilisation whereby Catholicism gradually penetrates into hostile countries, and Christian powers acquire dominion over infidel populations. Thus it is the token of an epoch in the political, religious, and intellectual life of mankind, and it disappears with its epoch, and with the advance of the Church militant in her Catholic vocation. Intolerance of dissent and impatience of contradiction are a characteristic of youth. Those that have no knowledge of the truth that underlies opposite opinions, and no experience of their consequent force, cannot believe that men are sincere in holding them. At a certain point of mental growth, tolerance implies indifference, and intolerance is inseparable from sincerity. Thus intolerance, in itself a defect, becomes in this case a merit. Again, although the political conditions of intolerance belong to the youth and immaturity of nations, the motives of intolerance may at any time be just and the principle high. For the theory of religious unity is founded on the most elevated and truest view of the character and function of the State, on the perception that its ultimate purpose is not distinct from that of the Church. In the pagan State they were identified; in the Christian world the end remains the same, but the means are different.

The State aims at the things of another life but indirectly. Its course runs parallel to that of the Church; they do not converge. The direct subservience of the State to religious ends would imply despotism and persecution just as much as the pagan supremacy of civil over religious authority. The similarity of the end demands harmony in the principles, and creates a decided antagonism between the State and a religious community whose character is in total contradiction with it. With such religions there is no possibility of reconciliation. A State must be at open war with any system which it sees would prevent it from fulfilling its legitimate duties. The danger, therefore, lies not in the doctrine, but in the practice. But to the pagan and to the mediaeval State, the danger was in the doctrine. The Christians were the best subjects of the emperor, but Christianity was really subversive of the fundamental institutions of the Roman Empire. In the infancy of the modern States, the civil power required all the help that religion could give in order to establish itself against the lawlessness of barbarism and feudal dissolution. The existence of the State at that time depended on the power of the Church. When, in the thirteenth century, the Empire renounced this support, and made war on the Church, it fell at once into a number of small sovereignties. In those cases persecution was self-defence. It was wrongly defended as an absolute, not as a conditional principle; but such a principle was false only as the modern theory of religious liberty is false. One was a wrong generalisation from the true character of the State; the other is a true conclusion from a false notion of the State. To say that because of the union between Church and State it is right to persecute, would condemn all toleration; and to say that the objects of the State have nothing to do with religion, would condemn all persecution. But persecution and toleration are equally true in principle, considered politically; only one belongs to a more highly developed civilisation than the other. At one period toleration would destroy society; at another, persecution is fatal to liberty. The theory of intolerance is wrong only if founded absolutely upon religious motives; but even then the practice of it is not necessarily censurable. It is opposed to the Christian spirit, in the same manner as slavery is opposed to it. The Church prohibits neither intolerance nor slavery, though in proportion as her influence extends, and civilisation advances, both gradually disappear.

Unity and liberty are the only legitimate principles on which the position of a Church in a State can be regulated, but the distance between them is immeasurable, and the transition extremely difficult. To pass from religious unity to religious liberty is to effect a complete inversion in the character of the State, a change in the whole spirit of legislation, and a still greater revolution in the minds and habits of men. So great a change seldom happens all at once. The law naturally follows the condition of society, which does not suddenly change. An intervening stage from unity to liberty, a compromise between toleration and persecution, is a common but irrational, tyrannical, and impolitic arrangement. It is idle to talk of the guilt of persecution, if we do not distinguish the various principles on which religious dissent can be treated by the State. The exclusion of other religions—the system of Spain, of Sweden, of Mecklenburg, Holstein, and Tyrol—is reasonable in principle, though practically untenable in the present state of European society. The system of expulsion or compulsory conformity, adopted by Lewis XIV and the Emperor Nicholas, is defensible neither on religious nor political grounds. But the system applied to Ireland, which uses religious disabilities for the purpose of political oppression,[3] stands alone in solitary infamy among the crimes and follies of the rulers of men.

The acquisition of real definite freedom is a very slow and tardy process. The great social independence enjoyed in the early periods of national history is not yet political freedom. The State has not yet developed its authority, or assumed the functions of government. A period follows when all the action of society is absorbed by the ruling power, when the license of early times is gone, and the liberties of a riper age are not yet acquired. These liberties are the product of a long conflict with absolutism, and of a gradual development, which, by establishing definite rights revives in positive form the negative liberty of an unformed society. The object and the result of this process is the organisation of self-government, the substitution of right for force, of authority for power, of duty for necessity, and of a moral for a physical relation between government and people. Until this point is reached, religious liberty is an anomaly. In a State which possesses all power and all authority there is no room for the autonomy of religious communities. Those States, therefore, not only refuse liberty of conscience, but deprive the favoured Church of ecclesiastical freedom. The principles of religious unity and liberty are so opposed that no

---

[3] "From what I have observed, it is pride, arrogance, and a spirit of domination, and not a bigoted spirit of religion, that has caused and kept up those oppressive statutes. I am sure I have known those who have oppressed Papists in their civil rights exceedingly indulgent to them in their religious ceremonies, and who really wished them to continue Catholics, in order to furnish pretences for oppression. These persons never saw a man (by converting) escape out of their power but with grudging and regret" (Burke, "On the Penal Laws against Irish Catholics," *Works*, iv. 505).

"I vow to God, I would sooner bring myself to put a man to immediate death for opinions I disliked, and so to get rid of the man and his opinions at once, than to fret him into a feverish being tainted with the jail-distemper of a contagious servitude, to keep him above ground, an animated mass of putrefaction, corrupted himself, and corrupting all about him" (Speech at Bristol, *ibid.* iii. 427).

modern State has at once denied toleration and allowed freedom to its established Church. Both of these are unnatural in a State which rejects self-government, the only secure basis of all freedom, whether religious or political. For religious freedom is based on political liberty; intolerance, therefore, is a political necessity against all religions which threaten the unity of faith in a State that is not free, and in every State against those religions which threaten its existence. Absolute intolerance belongs to the absolute State; special persecution may be justified by special causes in any State. All mediaeval persecution is of the latter kind, for the sects against which it was directed were revolutionary parties. The State really defended, not its religious unity, but its political existence.

If the Catholic Church was naturally inclined to persecute, she would persecute in all cases alike, when there was no interest to serve but her own. Instead of adapting her conduct to circumstances, and accepting theories according to the character of the time, she would have developed a consistent theory out of her own system, and would have been most severe when she was most free from external influences, from political objects, or from temporary or national prejudices. She would have imposed a common rule of conduct in different countries in different ages, instead of submitting to the exigencies of each time and place. Her own rule of conduct never changed. She treats it as a crime to abandon her, not to be outside her. An apostate who returns to her has a penance for his apostasy; a heretic who is converted has no penance for his heresy. Severity against those who are outside her fold is against her principles. Persecution is contrary to the nature of a universal Church; it is peculiar to the national Churches.

While the Catholic Church by her progress in freedom naturally tends to push the development of States beyond the sphere where they are still obliged to preserve the unity of religion, and whilst she extends over States in all degrees of advancement, Protestantism, which belongs to a particular age and state of society, which makes no claim to universality, and which is dependent on political connection, regards persecution, not as an accident, but as a duty.

Wherever Protestantism prevailed, intolerance became a principle of State, and was proclaimed in theory even where the Protestants were in a minority, and where the theory supplied a weapon against themselves. The Reformation made it a general law, not only against Catholics by way of self-defence or retaliation, but against all who dissented from the reformed doctrines, whom it treated, not as enemies, but as criminals—against the Protestant sects, against Socinians, and against atheists. It was not a right, but a duty; its object was to avenge God, not to preserve order. There is no analogy between the persecution which preserves and the persecution which attacks; or between intolerance as a religious duty, and intolerance as a necessity of State. The Reformers unanimously declared persecution to be incumbent on the civil power; and the Protestant Governments universally acted upon their injunctions, until scepticism escaped the infliction of penal laws and condemned their spirit.

Doubtless, in the interest of their religion, they acted wisely. Freedom is not more decidedly the natural condition of Catholicism than intolerance is of Protestantism; which by the help of persecution succeeded in establishing itself in countries where it had no root in the affections of the people, and in preserving itself from the internal divisions which follow free inquiry. Toleration has been at once a cause and an effect of its decline. The Catholic Church, on the other hand, supported the mediaeval State by religious unity, and has saved herself in the modern State by religious freedom. No longer compelled to devise theories in justification of a system imposed on her by the exigencies of half-organised societies, she is enabled to revert to a policy more suited to her nature and to her most venerable traditions; and the principle of liberty has already restored to her much of that which the principle of unity took away. It was not, as our author imagines (p. 119), by the protection of Lewis XIV that she was formidable; nor is it true that in consequence of the loss of temporalities, "the chill of death is gathering round the heart of the great theocracy" (p. 94); nor that "the visible decline of the papacy" is at hand because it no longer wields "the more efficacious arms of the great Catholic monarchies" (p. 190).

The same appeal to force, the same principles of intolerance which expelled Catholicism from Protestant countries, gave rise in Catholic countries to the growth of infidelity. The Revolutions of 1789 in France, and of 1859 in Italy, attest the danger of a practice which requires for its support the doctrines of another religion, or the circumstances of a different age. Not till the Church had lost those props in which Mr. Goldwin Smith sees the secret of her power, did she recover her elasticity and her expansive vigour. Catholics may have learnt this truth late, but Protestants, it appears, have yet to learn it.

In one point Mr. Goldwin Smith is not so very far from the views of the Orange party. He thinks, indeed, that the Church is no longer dangerous, and would not therefore have Catholics maltreated; but this is due, not to her merits, but to her weakness.

"Popes might now be as willing as ever, if they had the power, to step between a Protestant State and the allegiance of its subjects" (p. 190).

Mr. Smith seems to think that the Popes claim the same authority over the rulers of a Protestant State that they formerly possessed over the princes of Catholic countries. Yet this political power of the Holy See was never a universal right of jurisdiction over States, but a special and positive right, which it is as absurd to censure as to fear or to regret at the present time. Directly, it extended only over territories which were held by feudal tenure of the Pope, like the Sicilian monarchy. Elsewhere the authority was indirect, not political but religious, and its political consequences were due to the laws of the land. The Catholic countries would no more submit to a king not of their communion than Protestant countries, England for instance, or Denmark. This is as natural and inevitable in a country where the whole population is of one religion, as it is artificial and unjust in a country where no sort of religious unity prevails, and where such a law might compel the sovereign to be of the religion of the minority.

At any rate, nobody who thinks it reasonable that any prince abandoning the Established Church should forfeit the English throne, can complain of a law which compelled the sovereign to be of the religion, not of a majority, but of the whole of his subjects. The idea of the Pope stepping between a State and the allegiance of its subjects is a mere misapprehension. The instrument of his authority is the law, and the law resides in the State. The Pope could intervene, therefore, only between the State and the occupant of the throne; and his intervention suspended, not the duty of obeying, but the right of governing. The line on which his sentence ran separated, not the subjects from the State, but the sovereign from the other authorities. It was addressed to the nation politically organised against the head of the organism, not to the mass of individual subjects against the constituted authorities. That such a power was inconsistent with the modern notion of sovereignty is true; but it is also true that this notion is as much at variance with the nature of ecclesiastical authority as with civil liberty. The Roman maxim, *princeps legibus solutus*, could not be admitted by the Church; and an absolute prince could not properly be invested in her eyes with the sanctity of authority, or protected by the duty of submission. A moral and *a fortiori* a spiritual, authority moves and lives only in an atmosphere of freedom.

There are, however, two things to be considered in explanation of the error into which our author and so many others have fallen. Law follows life, but not with an equal pace. There is a time when it ceases to correspond to the existing order of things, and meets an invincible obstacle in a new society. The exercise of the mediaeval authority of the Popes was founded on the religious unity of the State, and had no basis in a divided community. It was not easy in the period of transition to tell when the change took place, and at what moment the old power lost its efficacy; no one could foresee its failure, and it still remained the legal and recognised means of preventing the change. Accordingly, it was twice tried during the wars of religion, in France with success, in England with disastrous effects. It is a universal rule that a right is not given up until the necessity of its surrender is proved. But the real difficulty arises, not from the mode in which the power was exercised, but from the way in which it was defended. The mediaeval writers were accustomed to generalise; they disregarded particular circumstances, and they were generally ignorant of the habits and ideas of their age. Living in the cloister, and writing for the school, they were unacquainted with the polity and institutions around them, and sought their authorities and examples in antiquity, in the speculations of Aristotle, and the maxims of the civil law. They gave to their political doctrines as abstract a form, and attributed to them as universal an application, as the modern absolutists or the more recent liberals. So regardless were they of the difference between ancient times and their own, that the Jewish chronicles, the Grecian legislators, and the Roman code supplied them indifferently with rules and instances; they could not imagine that a new state of things would one day arise in which their theories would be completely obsolete. Their definitions of right and law are absolute in the extreme, and seem often to admit of no qualification. Hence their character is essentially revolutionary, and they contradict both the authority of law and the security of freedom. It is on this contradiction that the common notion of the danger of ecclesiastical pretensions is founded. But the men who take alarm at the tone of the mediaeval claims judge them with a theory just as absolute and as excessive. No man can fairly denounce imaginary pretensions in the Church of the nineteenth century, who does not understand that rights which are now impossible may have been reasonable and legitimate in the days when they were actually exercised.

The zeal with which Mr. Goldwin Smith condemns the Irish establishment and the policy of the ascendency is all the more meritorious because he has no conception of the amount of iniquity involved in them.

"The State Church of Ireland, however anomalous and even scandalous its position may be as the Church of a dominant minority upheld by force in the midst of a hostile people, does not, in truth, rest on a principle different from that of other State Churches. To justify the existence of any State Church, it must be assumed as an axiom that the State is the judge of religious truth; and that it is bound to impose upon its subjects, or at least to require them as a community to maintain, the religion which it judges to be true" (p. 91).

No such analogy in reality subsists as is here assumed. There is a great difference between the Irish and the English establishment; but even the latter has no similarity of principle with the Catholic establishments of the continent.

The fundamental distinction is, that in one case the religion of the people is adopted by the State, whilst in the other the State imposes a religion on the people. For the political justification of Catholic establishments, no more is required than the theory that it is just that the religion of a country should be represented in, and protected by, its government. This is evidently and universally true; for the moral basis which human laws require can only be derived from an influence which was originally religious as well as moral. The unity of moral consciousness must be founded on a precedent unity of spiritual belief. According to this theory, the character of the nation determines the forms of the State. Consequently it is a theory consistent with freedom. But Protestant establishments, according to our author's definition, which applies to them, and to them alone, rest on the opposite theory, that the will of the State is independent of the condition of the community; and that it may, or indeed must, impose on the nation a faith which may be that of a minority, and which in some cases has been that of the sovereign alone. According to the Catholic view, government may preserve in its laws, and by its authority, the religion of the community; according to the Protestant view it may be bound to change it. A government which has power to change the faith of its subjects must be absolute in other things; so that one theory is as favourable to tyranny as the other is opposed to it. The safeguard of the Catholic system of Church and State, as contrasted with the Protestant, was that very authority which the Holy See used to prevent the sovereign from changing the religion of the people, by deposing him if he departed from it himself. In most Catholic countries the Church preceded the State; some she assisted to form; all she contributed to sustain. Throughout Western Europe Catholicism was the religion of the inhabitants before the new monarchies were founded. The invaders, who became the dominant race and the architects of a new system of States, were sooner or later compelled, in order to preserve their dominion, to abandon their pagan or their Arian religion, and to adopt the common faith of the immense majority of the people. The connection between Church and State was therefore a natural, not an arbitrary, institution; the result of the submisison of the Government to popular influence, and the means by which that influence was perpetuated. No Catholic Government ever imposed a Catholic estab-lishment on a Protestant community, or destroyed a Protestant estab-lishment. Even the revocation of the Edict of Nantes, the greatest wrong ever inflicted on the Protestant subjects of a Catholic State, will bear no comparison with the establishment of the religion of a minority. It is a far greater wrong than the most severe persecution, because persecution may be necessary for the preservation of an existing society, as in the case of the early Christians and of the Albigenses; but a State Church can only be justified by the acquiescence of the nation. In every other case it is a great social danger, and is inseparable from political oppression.

Mr. Goldwin Smith's vision is bounded by the Protestant horizon. The Irish establishment has one great mark in common with the other Protestant establishments—that it is the creature of the State, and an instrument of political influence. They were all imposed on the nation by the State power, sometimes against the will of the people, sometimes against that of the Crown. By the help of military power and of penal laws, the State strove to provide that the Established Church should not be the religion of the minority. But in Ireland the establishment was introduced too late—when Protestantism had spent its expansive force, and the attraction of its doctrine no longer aided the efforts of the civil power. Its position was false from the beginning, and obliged it to resort to persecution and official proselytism in order to put an end to the anomaly. Whilst, therefore, in all cases, Protestantism became the Established Church by an exercise of authority tyrannical in itself, and possible only from the absolutism of the ruling power, in Ireland the tyranny of its institution was perpetuated in the system by which it was upheld, and in the violence with which it was introduced; and this tyranny continues through all its existence. It is the religion of the minority, the church of an alien State, the cause of suffering and of disturbance, an instrument, a creature, and a monument of conquest and of tyranny. It has nothing in common with Catholic establishments, and none of those qualities which, in the Anglican Church, redeem in part the guilt of its origin. This is not, however, the only point on which our author has mistaken the peculiar and enormous character of the evils of Ireland.

With the injustice which generally attends his historical parallels, he compares the policy of the Orange faction to that of the Jacobins in France:

"The ferocity of the Jacobins was in a slight degree redeemed by their fanaticism. Their objects were not entirely selfish. They murdered aristocrats, not only because they hated and feared them, but because they wildly imagined them to stand in the way of the social and political millennium, which, according to Rousseau, awaited the acceptance of mankind" (p. 175).

No comparison can be more unfair than one which places the pitiless fanaticism of an idea in the same line with the cruelty inspired by a selfish interest. The Reign of Terror is one of the most portentous events in history, because it was the consistent result of the simplest and most acceptable principle of the Revolution; it saved France from the coalition, and it was the greatest attempt ever made to mould the form of a society by force into harmony with a speculative form of Government. An explanation which treats self-interest as its primary motive, and judges other elements as merely qualifying it, is ludicrously inadequate.

The Terrorism of Robespierre was produced by the theory of equality, which was not a mere passion, but a political doctrine, and at the same time a national necessity. Political philosophers who, since the time of Hobbes, derive the State from a social compact, necessarily assume that the contracting parties were equal among themselves. By nature, therefore, all men possess equal rights, and a right to equality. The introduction of the civil power and of private property brought inequality into the world. This is opposed to the condition and to the rights of the natural state. The writers of the eighteenth century attributed to this circumstance the evils and sufferings of society. In France, the ruin of the public finances and the misery of the lower orders were both laid at the door of the classes whose property was exempt from taxation. The endeavours of successive ministers—of Turgot, Necker, and Calonne—to break down the privileges of the aristocracy and of the clergy were defeated by the resistance of the old society. The Government attempted to save itself by obtaining concessions from the Notables, but without success, and then the great reform which the State was impotent to carry into execution was effected by the people. The destruction of the aristocratic society, which the absolute monarchy had failed to reform, was the object and the triumph of the Revolution; and the Constitution of 1791 declared all men equal, and withdrew the sanction of the law from every privilege.

This system gave only an equality in civil rights, a political equality such as already subsisted in America; but it did not provide against the existence or the growth of those social inequalities by which the distribution of political power might be affected. But the theory of the natural equality of mankind understands equal rights as rights to equal things in the State, and requires not only an abstract equality of rights, but a positive equality of power. The varieties of condition caused by civilisation were so objectionable in the eyes of this school, that Rousseau wrote earnest vindications of natural society, and condemned the whole social fabric of Europe as artificial, unnatural, and monstrous. His followers laboured to destroy the work of history and the influence of the past, and to institute a natural, reasonable order of things which should dispose all men on an equal level, which no disparity of wealth or education should be permitted to disturb. There were, therefore, two opinions in the revolutionary party. Those who overthrew the monarchy, established the republic, and commenced the war, were content with having secured political and legal equality, and wished to leave the nation in the enjoyment of those advantages which fortune distributes unequally. But the consistent partisans of equality required that nothing should be allowed to raise one man above another. The Girondists wished to preserve liberty, education, and property; but the Jacobins, who held that an absolute equality should be maintained by the despotism of the government over the people, interpreted more justly the democratic principles which were common to both parties;

and, fortunately for their country, they triumphed over their illogical and irresolute adversaries. "When the revolutionary movement was once established," says De Maistre, "nothing but Jacobinism could save France."

Three weeks after the fall of the Gironde, the Constitution of 1793, by which a purely ideal democracy was instituted, was presented to the French people. Its adoption exactly coincides with the supremacy of Robespierre in the Committee of Public Safety, and with the inauguration of the Reign of Terror. The danger of invasion made the new tyranny possible, but the political doctrine of the Jacobins made it necessary. Robespierre explains the system in his report on the principles of political morality, presented to the Convention at the moment of his greatest power:

"If the principle of a popular government in time of peace is virtue, its principle during revolution is virtue and terror combined: virtue, without which terror is pernicious; terror, without which virtue is powerless. Terror is nothing but rapid, severe, inflexible justice; therefore a product of virtue. It is not so much a principle in itself, as a consequence of the universal principle of democracy in its application to the urgent necessities of the country."

This is perfectly true. Envy, revenge, fear, were motives by which individuals were induced or enabled to take part in the administration of such a system; but its introduction was not the work of passion, but the inevitable result of a doctrine. The democratic Constitution required to be upheld by violence, not only against foreign arms, but against the state of society and the nature of things. The army could not be made its instrument, because the rulers were civilians, and feared, beyond all things, the influence of military officers in the State. Officers were frequently arrested and condemned as traitors, compelled to seek safety in treason, watched and controlled by members of the Convention. In the absence of a military despotism, the revolutionary tribunal was the only resource.

The same theory of an original state of nature, from which the principle of equality was deduced, also taught men where they might find the standard of equality; as civilisation, by means of civil power, education, and wealth, was the source of corruption, the purity of virtue was to be found in the classes which had been least exposed to those disturbing causes. Those who were least tainted by the temptations of civilised society remained in the natural state. This was the definition of the new notion of the people, which became the measure of virtue and of equality. The democratic theory required that the whole nation should be reduced to the level of the lower orders in all those things in which society creates disparity, in order to be raised to the level of that republican virtue which resides among those who have retained a primitive simplicity by escaping the influence of civilisation.

The form of government and the condition of society must always correspond. Social equality is therefore a postulate of pure democracy. It was necessary that it should exist if the Constitution was to stand, and if the great ideal of popular enthusiasm was ever to be realised. The Revolution had begun by altering the social condition of the country; the correction of society by the State had already commenced. It did not, therefore, seem impossible to continue it until the nation should be completely remodelled in conformity with the new principles. The system before which the ancient monarchy had fallen, which was so fruitful of marvels, which was victorious over a more formidable coalition than that which had humbled Lewis XIV, was deemed equal to the task of completing the social changes which had been so extensively begun, and of moulding France according to the new and simple pattern. The equality which was essential to the existence of the new form of government did not in fact exist. Privilege was abolished, but influence remained. All the inequality founded on wealth, education, ability, reputation, even on the virtues of a code different from that of republican morality, presented obstacles to the establishment of the new *régime,* and those who were thus distinguished were necessarily enemies of the State. With perfect reason, all that rose above the common level, or did not conform to the universal rule, was deemed treasonable. The difference between the actual society and the ideal equality was so great that it could be removed only by violence. The great mass of those who perished were really, either by attachment or by their condition, in antagonism with the State. They were condemned, not for particular acts, but for their position, or for acts which denoted, not so much a hostile design, as an incompatible habit. By the *loi des suspects,* which was provoked by this conflict between the form of government and the real state of the country, whole classes, rather than ill-disposed individuals, were declared objects of alarm. Hence the proscription was wholesale. Criminals were judged and executed in categories; and the merits of individual cases were, therefore, of little account. For this reason, leading men of ability, bitterly hostile to the new system, were saved by Danton; for it was often indifferent who were the victims, provided the group to which they belonged was struck down. The question was not, what crimes has the prisoner committed? but, does he belong to one of those classes whose existence the Republic cannot tolerate? From this point of view, there were not so many unjust judgments pronounced, at least in Paris, as is generally believed. It was necessary to be prodigal of blood, or to abandon the theory of liberty and equality, which had commanded, for a whole generation, the enthusiastic devotion of educated men, and for the truth of which thousands of its believers were ready to die. The truth of that doctrine was tested by a terrible alternative; but the fault lay with those who believed it, not exclusively with those who practised it. There were few who could administer such a system without any other motive but devotion to the idea, or who could retain the coolness and indifference of which St. Just is an extraordinary example. Most of the Terrorists were swayed by fear for themselves, or by the frenzy which is produced by familiarity with slaughter. But this is of small account. The significance of that sanguinary drama lies in the fact, that a political abstraction was powerful enough to make men think themselves right in destroying masses of their countrymen in the attempt to impose it on their country. The horror of that system and its failure have given vitality to the communistic theory. It was unreasonable to attack the effect instead of the cause, and cruel to destroy the proprietor, while the danger lay in the property. For private property necessarily produces that inequality which the Jacobin theory condemned; and the Constitution of 1793 could not be maintained by Terrorism without Communism, by proscribing the rich while riches were tolerated. The Jacobins were guilty of inconsistency in omitting to attack inequality in its source. Yet no man who admits their theory has a right to complain of their acts. The one proceeded from the other with the inflexible logic of history. The Reign of Terror was nothing else than the reign of those who conceive that liberty and equality can co-exist.

One more quotation will sufficiently justify what we have said of the sincerity and ignorance which Mr. Goldwin Smith shows in his remarks on Catholic subjects. After calling the Bull of Adrian IV "the stumbling-block and the despair of Catholic historians," he proceeded to say:

"Are Catholics filled with perplexity at the sight of infallibility sanctioning rapine? They can scarcely be less perplexed by the title which infallibility puts forward to the dominion of Ireland. . . . But this perplexity arises entirely from the assumption, which may be an article of faith, but is not an article of history, that the infallible morality of the Pope has never changed" (pp. 46, 47).

It is hard to understand how a man of honour and ability can entertain such notions of the character of the Papacy as these words imply, or where he can have found authorities for so monstrous a caricature. We will only say that infallibility is no attribute of the political system of the Popes, and that the Bulls of Adrian and Alexander are not instances of infallible morality.

Great as the errors which we have pointed out undoubtedly are, the book itself is of real value, and encourages us to form sanguine hopes of the future services of its author to historical science, and ultimately to religion. We are hardly just in complaining of Protestant writers who fail to do justice to the Church. There are not very many amongst ourselves who take the trouble to ascertain her real character as a visible institution, or to know how her nature has been shown in her history. We know the doctrine which she teaches; we are familiar with the outlines of her discipline. We know that sanctity is one of her marks, and that beneficence has characterised her influence. In a general way we are confident that historical accusations are as false as dogmatic attacks, and most of us have some notion of the way in which the current imputations are to be met. But as to her principles of action in many important things, how they have varied in course of time, what changes have been effected by circumstances, and what rules have never been broken—few are at the pains to inquire. As adversaries imagine that in exposing a Catholic they strike Catholicism, and that the defects of the men are imperfections in the institution and a proof that it is not divine, so we grow accustomed to confound in our defence that which is defective and that which is indefectible, and to discover in the Church merits as self-contradictory as are the accusations of her different foes. At one moment we are told that Catholicism teaches contempt, and therefore neglect of wealth; at another, that it is false to say that the Church does not promote temporal prosperity. If a great point is made against persecution, it will be denied that she is intolerant, whilst at another time it will be argued that heresy and unbelief deserve to be punished.

We cannot be surprised that Protestants do not know the Church better than we do ourselves, or that, while we allow no evil to be spoken of her human elements, those who deem her altogether human should discover in her the defects of human institutions. It is intensely difficult to enter into the spirit of a system not our own. Particular principles and doctrines are easily mastered; but a system answering all the spiritual cravings, all the intellectual capabilities of man, demands more than a mere mental effort—a submission of the intellect, an act of faith, a temporary suspension of the critical faculty. This applies not merely to the Christian religion, with its unfathomable mysteries and its inexhaustible fund of truth, but to the fruits of human speculation. Nobody has ever succeeded in writing a history of philosophy without incurring either the reproach that he is a mere historian, incapable of entering into the genius of any system, or a mere metaphysician, who can discern in all other philosophies only the relation they bear to his own. In religion the difficulty is greater still, and greatest of all with Catholicism. For the Church is to be seen, not in books, but in life. No divine can put together the whole body of her doctrine; no canonist the whole fabric of her law; no historian the infinite vicissitudes of her career. The Protestant who wishes to be informed on all these things can be advised to rely on no one manual, on no encyclopaedia of her deeds and of her ideas; if he seeks to know what these have been, he must be told to look around. And to one who surveys her teaching and her fortunes through all ages and all lands, ignorant or careless of that which is essential, changeless, and immortal in her, it will not be easy to discern through so much outward change a regular development, amid such variety of forms the unchanging substance, in so many modifications fidelity to constant laws; or to recognise, in a career so chequered with failure, disaster, and suffering, with the apostasy of heroes, the weakness of rulers, and the errors of doctors, the unfailing hand of a heavenly Guide.

[7]
The Protestant Theory
of Persecution

The manner in which Religion influences State policy is more easily ascertained in the case of Protestantism than in that of the Catholic Church: for whilst the expression of Catholic doctrines is authoritative and unvarying, the great social problems did not all arise at once, and have at various times received different solutions. The reformers failed to construct a complete and harmonious code of doctrine; but they were compelled to supplement the new theology by a body of new rules for the guidance of their followers in those innumerable questions with regard to which the practice of the Church had grown out of the experience of ages. And although the dogmatic system of Protestantism was not completed in their time, yet the Protestant spirit animated them in greater purity and force than it did any later generation. Now, when a religion is applied to the social and political sphere, its general spirit must be considered, rather than its particular precepts. So that in studying the points of this application in the case of Protestantism, we may consult the writings of the reformers with greater confidence than we could do for an exposition of Protestant theology; and accept them as a greater authority, because they agree more entirely among themselves. We can be more sure that we have the true Protestant opinion in a political or social question on which all the reformers are agreed, than in a theological question on which they differ; for the concurrent opinion must be founded on an element common to all, and therefore essential. If it should further appear that this opinion was injurious to their actual interests, and maintained at a sacrifice to

Published in the *Rambler* n.s. 6 (March 1862): 318–351. *Wellesley* II: 784; Döllinger I: 237; Acton-Simpson II: 266. Reprinted in Acton, *History of Freedom*, pp. 150–187; Acton, *Freedom and Power*, pp. 88–127.

themselves, we should then have an additional security for its necessary connection with their fundamental views.

The most important example of this law is the Protestant theory of toleration. The views of the reformers on religious liberty are not fragmentary, accidental opinions, unconnected with their doctrines, or suggested by the circumstances amidst which they lived; but the product of their theological system, and of their ideas of political and ecclesiastical government. Civil and religious liberty are so commonly associated in people's mouths, and are so rare in fact, that their definition is evidently as little understood as the principle of their connection. The point at which they unite, the common root from which they derive their sustenance, is the right of self-government. The modern theory, which has swept away every authority except that of the State, and has made the sovereign power irresistible by multiplying those who share it, is the enemy of that common freedom in which religious freedom is included. It condemns, as a State within the State, every inner group and community, class or corporation, administering its own affairs; and, by proclaiming the abolition of privileges, it emancipates the subjects of every such authority in order to transfer them exclusively to its own. It recognises liberty only in the individual, because it is only in the individual that liberty can be separated from authority, and the right of conditional obedience deprived of the security of a limited command. Under its sway, therefore, every man may profess his own religion more or less freely; but his religion is not free to administer its own laws. In other words, religious profession is free, but Church government is controlled. And where ecclesiastical authority is restricted, religious liberty is virtually denied.

For religious liberty is not the negative right of being without any particular religion, just as self-government is not anarchy. It is the right of religious communities to the practice of their own duties, the enjoyment of their own constitution, and the protection of the law, which equally secures to all the possession of their own independence. Far from implying a general toleration, it is best secured by a limited one. In an indifferent State, that is, in a State without any definite religious character (if such a thing is conceivable), no ecclesiastical authority could exist. A hierarchical organisation would not be tolerated by the sects that have none, or by the enemies of all definite religion; for it would be in contradiction to the prevailing theory of atomic freedom. Nor can a religion be free when it is alone, unless it makes the State subject to it. For governments restrict the liberty of the favoured Church, by way of remunerating themselves for their service in preserving her unity. The most violent and prolonged conflicts for religious freedom occurred in the Middle Ages between a Church which was not threatened by rivals and States which were most attentive to preserve her exclusive predominance. Frederic II, the most tyrannical oppressor of the Church among the German emperors, was the author of those sanguinary laws against heresy which prevailed so long in many parts of Europe. The Inquisition, which upheld the religious unity of the Spanish nation, imposed the severest restrictions on the Spanish Church; and in England conformity has been most rigorously exacted by those sovereigns who have most completely tyrannised over the Established Church. Religious liberty, therefore, is possible only where the coexistence of different religions is admitted, with an equal right to govern themselves according to their own several principles. Tolerance of error is requisite for freedom; but freedom will be most complete where there is no actual diversity to be resisted, and no theoretical unity to be maintained, but where unity exists as the triumph of truth, not of force, through the victory of the Church, not through the enactment of the State.

This freedom is attainable only in communities where rights are sacred, and where law is supreme. If the first duty is held to be obedience to authority and the preservation of order, as in the case of aristocracies and monarchies of the patriarchal type, there is no safety for the liberties either of individuals or of religion. Where the highest consideration is the public good and the popular will, as in democracies, and in constitutional monarchies after the French pattern, majority takes the place of authority; an irresistible power is substituted for an idolatrous principle, and all private rights are equally insecure. The true theory of freedom excludes all absolute power and arbitrary action, and requires that a tyrannical or revolutionary government shall be coerced by the people; but it teaches that insurrection is criminal, except as a corrective of revolution and tyranny. In order to understand the views of the Protestant reformers on toleration, they must be considered with reference to these points.

While the Reformation was an act of individual resistance and not a system, and when the secular Powers were engaged in supporting the authority of the Church, the authors of the movement were compelled to claim impunity for their opinions, and they held language regarding the right of governments to interfere with religious belief which resembles that of friends of toleration. Every religious party, however exclusive or servile its theory may be, if it is in contradiction with a system generally accepted and protected by law, must necessarily, at its first appearance, assume the protection of the idea that the conscience is free.[1] Before a new authority can be set up in the place of one that exists, there is an interval when the right of dissent must be proclaimed. At the beginning of Luther's contest with the Holy See there was no rival authority for him to appeal to. No ecclesiastical organism existed, the civil power was not on his side, and not even a definite system had yet been evolved by controversy out of his original doctrine of justification. His first efforts were acts of hostility, his exhortations were entirely aggressive, and his appeal was to the masses. When the prohibition of his New Testament confirmed him in the belief that no favour was to be expected from the princes, he published his book on the Civil Power, which he judged superior to everything that had been written on government since the days of the Apostles, and in which he asserts that authority is given to the State only against the wicked, and that it cannot coerce the godly. "Princes," he says, "are not to be obeyed when they command submission to superstitious errors, but their aid is not to be invoked in support of the Word of God."[2] Heretics must be converted by the Scriptures, and not by fire, otherwise the hangman would be the greatest doctor.[3] At the time

---

[1] "Le vrai principe de Luther est celui-ci: La volonté est esclave par nature. . . . Le libre examen a été pour Luther un moyen et non un principe. Il s'en est servi, et était contraint de s'en servir pour établir son vrai principe, qui était la toute-puissance de la foi et de la grâce. . . . C'est ainsi que le libre examen s'imposa au Protestantisme. L'accessoire devint le principal, et la forme dévora plus ou moins le fond" (Janet, *Histoire de la Philosophie Morale,* ii. 38, 39).

[2] "If they prohibit true doctrine, and punish their subjects for receiving the entire sacrament, as Christ ordained it, compel the people to idolatrous practices, with masses for the dead, indulgences, invocation of saints, and the like, in these things they exceed their office, and seek to deprive God of the obedience due to Him. For God requires from us this above all, that we hear His Word, and follow it; but where the Government desires to prevent this, the subjects must know that they are not bound to obey it" (Luther's *Werke,* xiii. 2244). "Non est, mi Spalatine, principum et istius saeculi Pontificum tueri verbum Dei, nec ea gratia ullorum peto praesidium" (Luther's *Briefe,* ed. De Wette, i. 521, Nov. 4, 1520). "I will compel and urge by force no man; for the faith must be voluntary and not compulsory, and must be adopted without violence" ("Sermonen an Carlstadt," *Werke,* xx. 24, 1522).

[3] "Schrift an den christlichen Adel" *(Werke,* x. 574, June 1520). His proposition,

when this was written Luther was expecting the bull of excommunication and the ban of the empire, and for several years it appeared
doubtful whether he would escape the treatment he condemned. He
lived in constant fear of assassination, and his friends amused themselves
with his terrors. At one time he believed that a Jew had been hired
by the Polish bishops to despatch him; that an invisible physician was
on his way to Wittenberg to murder him; that the pulpit from which
he preached was impregnated with a subtle poison.[4] These alarms
dictated his language during those early years. It was not the true
expression of his views, which he was not yet strong enough openly to
put forth.[5]

The Zwinglian schism, the rise of the Anabaptists, and the Peasants'
War altered the aspect of affairs. Luther recognised in them the fruits
of his theory of the right of private judgment and of dissent,[6] and the
moment had arrived to secure his Church against the application of
the same dissolving principles which had served him to break off from
his allegiance to Rome.[7] The excesses of the social war threatened to

---

Haereticos comburi esse contra voluntatem spiritus, was one of those condemned by Leo X as
pestilent, scandalous, and contrary to Christian charity.

[4] "Nihil non tentabunt Romanenses, nec potest satis Huttenus me monere, adeo mihi
de veneno timet" (De Wette, i. 487). "Etiam inimici mei quidam miserti per amicos ex
Halberstadio fecerunt moneri me: esse quemdam doctorem medicinae, qui arte magica
factus pro libito invisibilis, quemdam occidit. mandatum habentem et occidendi Lutheri,
venturumque ad futuram Dominicam ostensionis reliquiarum: valde hoc constanter
narratur" (De Wette, i. 441). "Est hic apud nos Judaeus Polonus, missus sub pretio
2000 aureorum, ut me veneno perdat, ab amicis per litteras mihi proditus. Doctor est
medicinae, et nihil non audere et facere paratus incredibili astutia et agilitate" (De
Wette ii. 616). See also Jarcke, *Studien zur Geschichte der Reformation*, p. 176.

[5] "Multa ego premo et causa principis et universitatis nostrae cohibeo, quae (si alibi
essem) evomerem in vastatricem Scripturae et Ecclesiae Romanae. . . . Timeo miser, ne
forte non sim dignus pati et occidi pro tali causa: erit ista felicitas meliorum hominum,
non tam foedi peccatoris. Dixi tibi semper me paratum esse cedere loco, si qua ego
principi illi. viderer periculo hic vivere. Aliquando certe moriendum est, quanquam jam
edita vernacula quadam apologia satis aduler Romanae Ecclesiae et Pontifici, si quid
forte id prosit" (De Wette, i. 260, 261). "Ubi periculum est, ne iis protectoribus tutus
saevius in Romanenses sim grassaturus, quam si sub principis imperio publicis militarem
officiis docendi. . . . Ego vicissim, nisi ignem habere nequeam damnabo, publiceque
concremabo jus pontificium totum, id est, lernam illam haeresium; et finem habebit
humilitatis exhibitae hactenusque frustratae observantia qua nolo amplius inflari hostes
Evangelii" (*Ibid.* pp. 465, 466, July 10, 1520).

[6] "Out of the Gospel and divine truth come devilish lies; . . . from the blood in our
body comes corruption; out of Luther come Müntzer, and rebels, Anabaptists, Sacra-
mentarians, and false brethren" (*Werke*, i. 75).

[7] "Habemus," wrote Erasmus, "fructum tui spiritus. . . . Non agnoscis hosce seditiosos,

deprive the movement of the sympathy of the higher classes, especially of the governments; and with the defeat of the peasants the popular phase of the Reformation came to an end on the Continent. "The devil," Luther said, "having failed to put him down by the help of the Pope, was seeking his destruction through the preachers of treason and blood."[8] He instantly turned from the people to the princes;[9] impressed on his party that character of political dependence, and that habit of passive obedience to the State, which it has ever since retained, and gave it a stability it could never otherwise have acquired. In thus taking refuge in the arms of the civil power, purchasing the safety of his doctrine by the sacrifice of its freedom, and conferring on the State, together with the right of control, the duty of imposing it at the point of the sword, Luther in reality reverted to his original teaching.[10] The notion of liberty, whether civil or religious, was hateful to his despotic nature, and contrary to his interpretation of Scripture. As early as 1519 he had said that even the Turk was to be reverenced as an authority.[11] The demoralising servitude and lawless oppression which the peasants endured, gave them, in his eyes, no right to relief; and when they rushed to arms, invoking his name as their deliverer, he exhorted the nobles to take a merciless revenge.[12] Their crime was,

---

opinor, sed illi te agnoscunt . . . nec tamen efficis quominus credant homines per tuos libellos . . . pro libertate evangelica, contra tyrannidem humanam, hisce tumultibus fuisse datam occasionem." "And who will deny," adds a Protestant classic, "that the fault was partly owing to them?" (Planck, *Geschichte der protestantischen Kirche*, ii. 183).

[8] "Ich sehe das wohl, dass der Teufel, so er mich bisher nicht hat mögen umbringen durch den Pabst, sucht er mich durch die blutdürstigen Mordpropheten und Rottengeisten, so unter euch sind, zu vertilgen und auffressen" (*Werke*, xvi. 77).

[9] Schenkel, *Wesen des Protestantismus*, iii. 348, 351; Hagen, *Geist der Reformation*, ii. 146, 151; Menzel, *Neuere Geschichte der Deutschen*, i. 115.

[10] See the best of his biographies, Jürgens, *Luther's Leben*, iii. 601.

[11] "Quid hoc ad me? qui sciam etiam Turcam honorandum et ferendum potestatis gratia. Quia certus sum non nisi volente Deo ullam potestatem consistere" (De Wette, i. 236).

[12] "I beg first of all that you will not help to mollify Count Albert in these matters, but let him go on as he has begun. . . . Encourage him to go on briskly, to leave things in the hands of God, and obey His divine command to wield the sword as long as he can." "Do not allow yourselves to be much disturbed, for it will redound to the advantage of many souls that will be terrified by it, and preserved." "If there are innocent persons amongst them, God will surely save and preserve them, as He did with Lot and Jeremiah. If He does not, then they are certainly not innocent. . . . We must pray for them that they obey, otherwise this is no time for compassion; just let the guns deal with them." "Sentio melius esse omnes rusticos caedi quam principes et magistratus, eo quod rustici sine auctoritate Dei gladium accipiunt. Quam nequitiam

that they were animated by the sectarian spirit, which it was the most important interest of Luther to suppress.

The Protestant authorities throughout Southern Germany were perplexed by their victory over the Anabaptists. It was not easy to show that their political tenets were revolutionary, and the only subversive portion of their doctrine was that they held, with the Catholics, that the State is not responsible for religion.[13] They were punished, therefore, because they taught that no man ought to suffer for his faith. At Nuremberg the magistrates did not know how to proceed against them. They seemed no worse than the Catholics, whom there was no question at that time of exterminating. The celebrated Osiander deemed these scruples inconsistent. The Papists, he said, ought also to be suppressed; and so long as this was not done, it was impossible to proceed to extremities against the Anabaptists, who were no worse than they. Luther also was consulted, and he decided that they ought not to be punished unless they refused to conform at the command of the Government.[14] The Margrave of Brandenburg was also advised by the divines that a heretic who could not be converted out of Scripture might be condemned; but that in his sentence nothing should be said about heresy, but only about sedition and murderous intent, though he should be guiltless of these.[15] With the aid of this artifice great numbers were put to death.

Luther's proud and ardent spirit despised such pretences. He had cast off all reserve, and spoke his mind openly on the rights and duties

---

Satanae sequi non potest nisi mera Satanica vastitas regni Dei, et mundi principes etsi excedunt, tamen gladium auctoritate Dei gerunt. Ibi utrumque regnum consistere potest, quare nulla misericordia, nulla patientia rusticis debetur, sed ira et indignatio Dei et hominum" (De Wette, ii. 653, 655, 666, 669, 671).

[13] "Wir lehren die christliche Obrigkeit möge nicht nur, sondern solle auch sich der Religion und Glaubenssachen mit Ernst annehmen; davon halten die Wiedertäufer steif das Widerspiel, welches sie auch zum Theil gemein haben mit den Prälaten der römischen Kirche" (Declaration of the Protestants, quoted in Jörg, *Deutschland von* 1522 *bis* 1526, p. 709).

[14] "As to your question, how they are to be punished, I do not consider them blasphemers, but regard them in the light of the Turks, or deluded Christians, whom the civil power has not to punish, at least bodily. But if they refuse to acknowledge and to obey the civil authority, then they forfeit all they have and are, for then sedition and murder are certainly in their hearts" (De Wette, ii. 622; Osiander's opinion in Jörg, p. 706).

[15] "Dass in dem Urtheil und desselben öffentlicher Verkündigung keines Irrthums oder Ketzereien . . . sondern allein der Aufruhr und fürgenommenen Mörderei, die ihm doch laut seiner Ursicht nie lieb gewesen, gedacht werde" (Jörg, p. 708).

of the State towards the Church and the people. His first step was to proclaim it the office of the civil power to prevent abominations.[16] He provided no security that, in discharging this duty, the sovereign should be guided by the advice of orthodox divines;[17] but he held the duty itself to be imperative. In obedience to the fundamental principle, that the Bible is the sole guide in all things, he defined the office and justified it by scriptural precedents. The Mosaic code, he argued, awarded to false prophets the punishment of death, and the majesty of God is not to be less deeply reverenced or less rigorously vindicated under the New Testament than under the Old; in a more perfect revelation the obligation is stronger. Those who will not hear the Church must be excluded from the communion; but the civil power is to intervene when the ecclesiastical excommunication has been pronounced, and men must be compelled to come in. For, according to the more accurate definition of the Church which is given in the Confession of Schmalkald, and in the Apology of the Confession of Augsburg, excommunication involves damnation. There is no salvation to be hoped for out of the Church, and the test of orthodoxy against the Pope, the devil, and all the world, is the dogma of justification by faith.[18]

The defence of religion became, on this theory, not only the duty of the civil power, but the object of its institution. Its business was solely the coercion of those who were out of the Church. The faithful could not be the objects of its action; they did of their own accord more than any laws required. "A good tree," says Luther, "brings forth good fruit by nature, without compulsion; is it not madness to prescribe laws to an apple-tree that it shall bear apples and not thorns?"[19] This view naturally proceeded from the axiom of the certainty of the salvation of all who believe in the Confession of Augsburg.[20] It is the most important element in Luther's political system, because, while it

---

[16] "Principes nostri non cogunt ad fidem et Evangelion, sed cohibent externas abominationes" (De Wette, iii. 50). "Wenn die weltliche Obrigkeit die Verbrechen wider die zweite Gesetzestafel bestrafen, und aus der menschlichen Gesellschaft tilgen solle, wie vielmehr denn die Verbrechen wider die erste?" (Luther, *apud* Bucholtz, *Geschichte Ferdinands I*, iii. 571).

[17] Planck, iv. 61, explains why this was not thought of.

[18] Linde, *Staatskirche*, p. 23. "Der Papst sammt seinem Haufen glaubt nicht; darum bekennen wir, er werde nicht selig, das ist verdammt werden" (*Table-Talk*, ii. 350).

[19] Kaltenborn, *Vorläufer des Grotius*, 208.

[20] Möhler, *Symbolik*, 428.

made all Protestant governments despotic, it led to the rejection of the
authority of Catholic governments. This is the point where Protestant
and Catholic intolerance meet. If the State were instituted to promote
the faith, no obedience could be due to a State of a different faith.
Protestants could not conscientiously be faithful subjects of Catholic
Powers, and they could not therefore be tolerated. Misbelievers would
have no rights under an orthodox State, and a misbelieving prince
would have no authority over orthodox subjects. The more, therefore,
Luther expounded the guilt of resistance and the Divine sanction of
authority, the more subversive his influence became in Catholic
countries. His system was alike revolutionary, whether he defied the
Catholic powers or promoted a Protestant tyranny. He had no notion
of political right. He found no authority for such a claim in the New
Testament, and he held that righteousness does not need to exhibit
itself in works.

It was the same helpless dependence on the letter of Scripture which
led the reformers to consequences more subversive of Christian morality
than their views on questions of polity. When Carlstadt cited the
Mosaic law in defence of polygamy, Luther was indignant. If the
Mosaic law is to govern everything, he said, we should be compelled
to adopt circumcision.[21] Nevertheless, as there is no prohibition of
polygamy in the New Testament, the reformers were unable to condemn
it. They did not forbid it as a matter of Divine law, and referred it
entirely to the decision of the civil legislator.[22] This, accordingly, was
the view which guided Luther and Melanchthon in treating the problem,
the ultimate solution of which was the separation of England from the

---

[21] "Quodsi unam legem Mosi cogimur servare, eadem ratione et circumcidemur, et
totam legem servare oportebit. . . . Nunc vero non sumus amplius sub lege Mosi, sed
subjecti legibus civilibus in talibus rebus" (Luther to Barnes, Sept. 5, 1531; De Wette,
iv. 296).

[22] "All things that we find done by the patriarchs in the Old Testament ought to be
free and not forbidden. Circumcision is abolished, but not so that it would be a sin to
perform it, but optional, neither sinful nor acceptable. . . . In like manner it is not
forbidden that a man should have more than one wife. Even at the present day I could
not prohibit it; but I would not recommend it" (Commentary on Genesis, 1528; see
Jarcke, *Studien*, p. 108). "Ego sane fateor, me non posse prohibere, siquis plures velit
uxores ducere, nec repugnat sacris literis: verum tamen apud Christianos id exempli
nollem primo introduci, apud quos decet etiam ea intermittere, quae licita sunt, pro
vitando scandalo, et pro honestate vitae" (De Wette, ii. 459, Jan. 13, 1524). "From
these instances of bigamy (Lamech, Jacob) no rule can be drawn for our times; and
such examples have no power with us Christians, for we live under our authorities, and
are subject to our civil laws" (*Table-Talk*, v. 64).

Church.[23] When the Landgrave Philip afterwards appealed to this opinion, and to the earlier commentaries of Luther, the reformers were compelled to approve his having two wives. Melanchthon was a witness at the wedding of the second, and the only reservation was a request that the matter should not be allowed to get abroad.[24] It was the same portion of Luther's theology, and the same opposition to the spirit of the Church in the treatment of Scripture, that induced him to believe in astrology and to ridicule the Copernican system.[25]

His view of the authority of Scripture and his theory of justification both precluded him from appreciating freedom. "Christian freedom," he said, "consists in the belief that we require no works to attain piety and salvation."[26] Thus he became the inventor of the theory of passive

[23] "Antequam tale repudium, probarem potius regi permitterem alteram reginam quoque ducere, et exemplo patrum et regum duas simul uxores seu reginas habere. . . . Si peccavit ducendo uxorem fratris mortui, peccavit in legem humanam seu civilem; si autem repudiaverit, peccabit in legem mere divinam" (De Wette, iv. 296). "Haud dubio rex Angliae uxorem fratris mortui ductam retinere potest . . . docendus quod has res politicas commiserit Deus magistratibus, neque nos alligaverit ad Moisen. . . . Si vult rex successioni prospicere, quanto satius est, id facere sine infamia prioris conjugii. Ac potest id fieri sine ullo periculo conscientiae cujuscunque aut famae per polygamiam. Etsi enim non velim concedere polygamiam vulgo, dixi enim supra, nos non ferre leges, tamen in hoc casu propter magnam utilitatem regni, fortassis etiam propter conscientiam regis, ita pronuncio: tutissimum esse regi, si ducat secundam uxorem, priore non abjecta, quia certum est polygamiam non esse prohibitam jure divino, nec res est omnino inusitata" (*Melanchthonis Opera*, ed. Bretschneider, ii. 524, 526). "Nolumus esse auctores divortii, cum conjugium cum jure divino non pugnet. Hi, qui diversum pronunciant, terribiliter exaggerant et exasperant jus divinum. Nos contra exaggeramus in rebus politicis auctoritatem magistratus, quae profecto non est levis, multaque justa sunt propter magistratus auctoritatem, quae alioqui in dubium vocantur" (Melanchthon to Bucer, Bretschneider, ii. 552).

[24] "Suadere non possumus ut introducatur publice et velut lege sanciatur permissio, plures quam unam uxores ducendi. . . . Primum ante omnia cavendum, ne haec res inducatur in orbem ad modum legis, quam sequendi libera omnibus sit potestas. Deinde considerare dignetur vestra celsitudo scandalum, nimirum quod Evangelio hostes exclamaturi sint, nos similes esse Anabaptistis, qui plures simul duxerunt uxores" (De Wette, v. 236. Signed by Luther, Melanchthon, and Bucer).

[25] "He that would appear wise will not be satisfied with anything that others do; he must do something for himself, and that must be better than anything. This fool (Copernicus) wants to overturn the whole science of astronomy. But, as the holy Scriptures tell us, Joshua told the sun to stand still, and not the earth" (*Table-Talk*, iv. 575).

[26] "Das ist die christliche Freiheit, der einige Glaube, der da macht, nicht dass wir müssig gehen oder übel thun mögen, sondern dass wir keines Werks bedürfen, die Frömmigkeit und Seligkeit zu erlangen" (*Sermon von der Freiheit*). A Protestant historian, who quotes this passage, goes on to say: "On the other hand, the body must be brought

obedience, according to which no motives or provocation can justify a revolt; and the party against whom the revolt is directed, whatever its guilt may be, is to be preferred to the party revolting, however just its cause.[27] In 1530 he therefore declared that the German princes had no right to resist the Emperor in defence of their religion. "It was the duty of a Christian," he said, "to suffer wrong, and no breach of oath or of duty could deprive the Emperor of his right to the unconditional obedience of his subjects."[28] Even the empire seemed to him a despotism, from his scriptural belief that it was a continuation of the last of the four monarchies.[29] He preferred submission, in the hope of seeing a future Protestant Emperor, to a resistance which might have dismembered the empire if it had succeeded, and in which failure would have been fatal to the Protestants; and he was always afraid to draw the logical consequences of his theory of the duty of Protestants towards Catholic sovereigns. In consequence of this fact, Ranke affirms that the great reformer was also one of the greatest conservatives that ever lived; and his biographer, Jürgens, makes the more discriminating remark that history knows of no man who was at once so great an insurgent and so great an upholder of order as he.[30] Neither of these writers understood that the same principle lies at the root both of revolution and of passive obedience, and that the difference is only in the temper of the person who applies it, and in the outward circumstances.

Luther's theory is apparently in opposition to Protestant interests, for it entitles Catholicism to the protection of Catholic Powers. He disguised from himself this inconsistency, and reconciled theory with expediency by the calculation that the immense advantages which his system offered to the princes would induce them all to adopt it. For,

---

under discipline by every means, in order that it may obey and not burden the inner man. Outward servitude, therefore, assists the progress towards internal freedom" (Bensen, *Geschichte des Bauernkriegs,* 269.)

[27] *Werke,* x. 413.

[28] "According to Scripture, it is by no means proper that one who would be a Christian should set himself against his superiors, whether by God's permission they act justly or unjustly. But a Christian must suffer violence and wrong, especially from his superiors. . . . As the emperor continues emperor, and princes princes, though they transgress all God's commandments, yea, even if they be heathen, so they do even when they do not observe their oath and duty. . . . Sin does not suspend authority and allegiance" (De Wette, iii. 560).

[29] Ranke, *Reformation,* iii. 183.

[30] Ranke, iv. 7; Jürgens, iii. 601.

besides the consolatory doctrine of justification—"a doctrine original, specious, persuasive, powerful against Rome, and wonderfully adapted, as if prophetically, to the genius of the times which were to follow"[31]— he bribed the princes with the wealth of the Church, independence of ecclesiastical authority, facilities for polygamy, and absolute power. He told the peasants not to take arms against the Church unless they could persuade the Government to give the order; but thinking it probable, in 1522, that the Catholic clergy would, in spite of his advice, be exterminated by the fury of the people, he urged the Government to suppress them, because what was done by the constituted authority could not be wrong.[32] Persuaded that the sovereign power would be on his side, he allowed no limits to its extent. It is absurd, he says, to imagine that, even with the best intentions, kings can avoid committing occasional injustice; they stand, therefore, particularly in need—not of safeguards against the abuse of power, but—of the forgiveness of sins.[33] The power thus concentrated in the hands of the rulers for the guardianship of the faith, he wished to be used with the utmost severity against unregenerate men, in whom there was neither moral virtue nor civil rights, and from whom no good could come until they were converted. He therefore required that all crimes should be most cruelly punished and that the secular arm should be employed to convert where it did not destroy. The idea of mercy tempering justice he denounced as a Popish superstition.[34]

The chief object of the severity thus recommended was, of course, efficaciously to promote the end for which Government itself was held to be instituted. The clergy had authority over the conscience, but it was thought necessary that they should be supported by the State with

[31] Newman, *Lectures on Justification,* p. 386.

[32] "Was durch ordentliche Gewalt geschieht, ist nicht für Aufruhr zu halten" (Bensen, p. 269; Jarcke, *Studien,* p. 312; Janet, ii. 40).

[33] "Princes, and all rulers and governments, however pious and God-fearing they may be, cannot be without sin in their office and temporal administration. . . . They cannot always be so exactly just and successful as some wiseacres suppose; therefore they are above all in need of the forgiveness of sins" (see Kaltenborn, p. 209).

[34] "Of old, under the Papacy, princes and lords, and all judges, were very timid in shedding blood, and punishing robbers, murderers, thieves, and all manner of evildoers; for they knew not how to distinguish a private individual who is not in office from one in office, charged with the duty of punishing. . . . The executioner had always to do penance, and to apologise beforehand to the convicted criminal for what he was going to do to him, just as if it was sinful and wrong." "Thus they were persuaded by monks to be gracious, indulgent, and peaceable. But authorities, princes and lords ought not to be merciful" (*Table-Talk,* iv. 159, 160).

the absolute penalties of outlawry, in order that error might be exterminated, although it was impossible to banish sin.[35] No Government, it was maintained, could tolerate heresy without being responsible for the souls that were seduced by it;[36] and as Ezechiel destroyed the brazen serpent to prevent idolatry, the mass must be suppressed, for the mass was the worst kind of idolatry.[37] In 1530, when it was proposed to leave the matters in dispute to the decision of the future Council, Luther declared that the mass and monastic life could not be tolerated in the meantime, because it was unlawful to connive at error.[38] "It will lie heavy on your conscience," he writes to the Duke of Saxony, "if you tolerate the Catholic worship; for no secular prince can permit his subjects to be divided by the preaching of opposite doctrines. The Catholics have no right to complain, for they do not prove the truth of their doctrine from Scripture, and therefore do not conscientiously believe it."[39] He would tolerate them only if they acknowledged themselves, like the Jews, enemies of Christ and of the Emperor, and consented to exist as outcasts of society.[40] "Heretics," he said, "are not to be disputed with, but to be condemned unheard, and whilst they perish by fire, the faithful ought to pursue the evil to its source, and bathe their hands in the blood of the Catholic bishops, and of the Pope, who is a devil in disguise."[41]

The persecuting principles which were involved in Luther's system, but which he cared neither to develop, to apply, nor to defend, were

[35] "Den weltlichen Bann sollten Könige und Kaiser wieder aufrichten, denn wir können ihn jetzt nicht anrichten. . . . Aber so wir nicht können die Sünde des Lebens bannen und strafen, so bannen wir doch die Sünde der Lehre" (Bruns, *Luthers Predigten*, 63).

[36] "Wo sie solche Rottengeister würden zulassen und leiden, so sie es doch wehren und vorkommen können, würden sie ihre Gewissen gräulich beschweren, und vielleicht nimmermehr wieder stillen können, nicht allein der Seelen halben, die dadurch verführt und verdammt werden . . . sondern auch der ganzen heiligen Kirchen halben" (De Wette, iv. 355).

[37] "Nu ist alle Abgötterey gegen die Messe ein geringes" (De Wette, v. 191; sec. iv. 307)

[38] Bucholtz, iii. 570.

[39] "Sie aber verachten die Schrift muthwilliglich, darum wären sie billig aus der einigen Ursach zu stillen, oder nicht zu leiden" (De Wette, iii. 90).

[40] "Wollen sie aber wie die Juden seyn, nicht Christen heissen, noch Kaisers Glieder, sondern sich lassen Christus und Kaisers Feinde nennen, wie die Juden; wohlan, so wollen wir's auch leiden, dass sie in ihren Synagogen, wie die Juden, verschlossen lästern, so lang sie wollen" (De Wette, iv. 94).

[41] Riffel, *Kirchengeschichte*, ii. 9; *Table-Talk*, iii. 175.

formed into a definite theory by the colder genius of Melanchthon. Destitute of Luther's confidence in his own strength, and in the infallible success of his doctrine, he clung more eagerly to the hope of achieving victory by the use of physical force. Like his master he too hesitated at first, and opposed the use of severe measures against the Zwickau prophets; but when he saw the development of that early germ of dissent, and the gradual dissolution of Lutheran unity, he repented of his ill-timed clemency.[42] He was not deterred from asserting the duty of persecution by the risk of putting arms into the hands of the enemies of the Reformation. He acknowledged the danger, but he denied the right. Catholic powers, he deemed, might justly persecute, but they could only persecute error. They must apply the same criterion which the Lutherans applied, and then they were justified in persecuting those whom the Lutherans also proscribed. For the civil power had no right to proscribe a religion in order to save itself from the dangers of a distracted and divided population. The judge of the fact and of the danger must be, not the magistrate, but the clergy.[43] The crime lay, not in dissent, but in error. Here, therefore, Melanchthon repudiated the theory and practice of the Catholics, whose aid he invoked; for all the intolerance in the Catholic times was founded on the combination of two ideas—the criminality of apostasy, and the inability of the State to maintain its authority where the moral sense of a part of the community was in opposition to it. The reformers, therefore, approved the Catholic practice of intolerance, and even encouraged it, although their own principles of persecution were destitute not only of connection, but even of analogy, with it. By simply accepting the inheritance of the mediaeval theory of the religious unity of the empire,

[42] "Ego ab initio, cum primum coepi nosse Ciconiam et Ciconiae factionem, unde hoc totum genus Anabaptistarum exortum est, fui stulte clemens. Sentiebant enim et alii haereticos non esse ferro opprimendos. Et tunc dux Fridericus vehementer iratus erat Ciconiae: ac nisi a nobis tectus esset, fuisset de homine furioso et perdite malo sumptum supplicium. Nunc me ejus clementiae non parum paenitet. . . . Brentius nimis clemens est" (Bretschneider, ii. 17. Feb. 1530).

[43] "Sed objiciunt exemplum nobis periculosum: si haec pertinent ad magistratus, quoties igitur magistratus judicabit aliquos errare, saeviet in eos. Caesar igitur debet nos opprimere, quoniam ita judicat nos errare. Respondeo: certe debet errores et prohibere et punire. . . . Non est enim solius Caesaris cognitio, sicut in urbibus haec cognitio non est tantum magistratus prophani, sed est doctorum. Viderit igitur magistratus ut recte judicet" (Bretschneider, ii. 712). "Deliberent igitur principes, non cum tyrannis, non cum pontificibus, non cum hypocritis, monachis aut aliis, sed cum ipsa Evangelii voce, cum probatis scriptoribus" (Bretschneider, iii. 254).

they would have been its victims. By asserting that persecution was justifiable only against error, that is, only when purely religious, they set up a shield for themselves, and a sword against those sects for whose destruction they were more eager than the Catholics. Whether we refer the origin of Protestant intolerance to the doctrines or to the interests of the Reformation, it appears totally unconnected with the tradition of Catholic ages, or the atmosphere of Catholicism. All severities exercised by Catholics before that time had a practical motive; but Protestant persecution was based on a purely speculative foundation, and was due partly to the influence of Scripture examples, partly to the supposed interests of the Protestant party. It never admitted the exclusion of dissent to be a political right of the State, but maintained the suppression of error to be its political duty. To say, therefore, that the Protestants learnt persecution from the Catholics, is as false as to say that they used it by way of revenge. For they founded it on very different and contradictory grounds, and they admitted the right of the Catholics to persecute even the Protestant sects.

Melanchthon taught that the sects ought to be put down by the sword, and that any individual who started new opinions ought to be punished with death.[44] He carefully laid down that these severities were requisite, not in consideration of the danger to the State, nor of

---

[44] "Quare ita sentias, magistratum debere uti summa severitate in coercendis hujusmodi spiritibus. . . . Sines igitur novis exemplis timorem incuti multitudini . . . ad haec notae tibi sint causae seditionum, quas gladio prohiberi oportet. . . . Propterea sentio de his qui etiamsi non defendunt seditiosos articulos, habent manifeste blasphemos, quod interfici a magistratu debeant" (ii. 17, 18). "De Anabaptistis tulimus hic in genere sententiam: quia constat sectam diabolicam esse, non esse tolerandam: dissipari enim ecclesias per eos, cum ipsi nullam habeant certam doctrinam. . . . Ideo in capita factionum in singulis locis ultima supplicia constituenda esse judicavimus" (ii. 549). "It is clear that it is the duty of secular government to punish blasphemy, false doctrine, and heresy, on the bodies of those who are guilty of them. . . . Since it is evident that there are gross errors in the articles of the Anabaptist sect, we conclude that in this case the obstinate ought to be punished with death" (iii. 199). "Propter hanc causam Deus ordinavit politias ut Evangelium propagari possit . . . nec revocamus politiam Moysi, sed lex moralis perpetua est omnium aetatum . . . quandocumque constat doctrinam esse impiam, nihil dubium est quin sanior pars Ecclesiae debeat malos pastores removere et abolere impios cultus. Et hanc emendationem praecipue adjuvare debent magistratus, tanquam potiora membra Ecclesiae" (iii. 242, 244). "Thammerus, qui Mahometicas seu Ethnicas opiniones spargit, vagatur in dioecesi Mindensi, quem publicis suppliciis adficere debebant. . . . Evomuit blasphemias, quae refutandae sunt non tantum disputatione aut scriptis, sed etiam justo officio pii magistratus" (ix. 125, 131).

immoral teaching, nor even of such differences as would weaken the authority or arrest the action of the ecclesiastical organization, but simply on account of a difference, however slight, in the theologumena of Protestantism.[45] Thamer, who held the possibility of salvation among the heathen; Schwenkfeld, who taught that not the written Word, but the internal illumination of grace in the soul was the channel of God's influence on man; the Zwinglians, with their error on the Eucharist, all these met with no more favour than the fanatical Anabaptists.[46] The State was held bound to vindicate the first table of the law with the same severity as those commandments on which civil society depends for its existence. The government of the Church being administered by the civil magistrates, it was their office also to enforce the ordinances of religion; and the same power whose voice proclaimed religious orthodoxy and law held in its hand the sword by which they were enforced. No religious authority existed except through the civil power.[47] The Church was merged in the State; but the laws of the State, in return, were identified with the commandments of religion.[48]

In accordance with these principles, the condemnation of Servetus

---

[45] "Voco autem blasphemos qui articulos habent, qui proprie non pertinent ad civilem statum, sed continent θεωρίας ut de divinitate Christi et similes. Etsi enim gradus quidam sunt, tamen huc etiam refero baptismum infantum. . . . Quia magistratui commissa est tutela totius legis, quod attinet ad externam disciplinam et externa facta. Quare delicta externa contra primam tabulam prohibere ac punire debet. . . . Quare non solum concessum est, sed etiam mandatum est magistratui, impias doctrinas abolere, et tueri pias in suis dictionibus" (ii. 711). "Ecclesiastica potestas tantum judicat et excommunicat haereticos, non occidit. Sed potestas civilis debet constituere poenas et supplicia in haereticos, sicut in blasphemos constituit supplicia. . . . Non enim plectitur fides, sed haeresis" (xii. 697).

[46] "Notum est etiam, quosdam tetra et δύσφημα dixisse de sanguine Christi, quos puniri oportuit, et propter gloriam Christi, et exempli causa" (viii. 553). "Argumentatur ille praestigiator (Schwenkfeld), verbum externum non esse medium, quo Deus est efficax. Talis sophistica principum severitate compescenda erat" (ix. 579).

[47] "The office of preacher is distinct from that of governor, yet both have to contribute to the praise of God. Princes are not only to protect the goods and bodily life of their subjects, but the principal function is to promote the honour of God, and to prevent idolatry and blasphemy" (iii. 199). "Errant igitur magistratus, qui divellunt guberna-tionem a fine, et se tantum pacis ac ventris custodes esse existimant. . . . At si tantum venter curandus esset, quid differrent principes ab armentariis? Nam longe aliter sentiendum est. Politias divinitus admirabili sapientia et bonitate constitutas esse, non tantum ad quaerenda et fruenda ventris bona, sed multo magis, ut Deus in societate innotescat, ut aeterna bona quaerantur" (iii. 246).

[48] "Neque illa barbarica excusatio audienda est, leges illas pertinere ad politiam Mosaicam, non ad nostram. Ut Decalogus ipse ad omnes pertinet, ita judex ubique omnia Decalogi officia in externa disciplina tueatur" (viii. 520).

by a civil tribunal, which had no authority over him, and no jurisdiction over his crime—the most aggressive and revolutionary act, therefore, that is conceivable in the casuistry of persecution—was highly approved by Melanchthon. He declared it a most useful example for all future ages, and could not understand that there should be any who did not regard it in the same favourable light.[49] It is true that Servetus, by denying the divinity of Christ, was open to the charge of blasphemy in a stricter sense than that in which the reformers generally applied it. But this was not the case with the Catholics. They did not represent, like the sects, an element of dissolution in Protestantism, and the bulk of their doctrine was admitted by the reformers. They were not in revolt against existing authority; they required no special innovations for their protection; they demanded only that the change of religion should not be compulsory. Yet Melanchthon held that they too were to be proscribed, because their worship was idolatrous.[50] In doing this he adopted the principle of aggressive intolerance, which was at that time new to the Christian world; and which the Popes and Councils of the Catholic Church had condemned when the zeal of laymen had gone beyond the lawful measure. In the Middle Ages there had been persecution far more sanguinary than any that has been inflicted by Protestants. Various motives had occasioned it and various arguments had been used in its defence. But the principle on which the Protestants oppressed the Catholics was new. The Catholics had never admitted the theory of absolute toleration, as it was defined at first by Luther, and afterwards by some of the sects. In principle, their tolerance differed from that of the Protestants as widely as their intolerance. They had exterminated sects which, like the Albigenses, threatened to

---

[49] "Legi scriptum tuum, in quo refutasti luculenter horrendas Serveti blasphemias, ac filio Dei gratias ago, qui fuit βραβευτής hujus tui agonis. Tibi quoque Ecclesia et nunc et ad posteros gratitudinem debet et debebit. Tuo judicio prorsus adsentior. Affirmo etiam, vestros magistratus juste fecisse, quod hominem blasphemum, re ordine judicata, interfecerunt" (Melanchthon to Calvin, Bretschneider, viii. 362). "Judico etiam Senatum Genevensem recte fecisse, quod hominem pertinacem et non omissurum blasphemias sustulit. Ac miratus sum, esse, qui severitatem illam improbent" (viii. 523). "Dedit vero et Genevensis reip. magistratus ante annos quatuor punitae insanabilis blasphemiae adversus filium Dei, sublato Serveto Arragone pium et memorabile ad omnem posteritatem exemplum" (ix. 133).

[50] "Abusus missae per magistratus debet tolli. Non aliter, atque sustulit aeneum serpentem Ezechias, aut excelsa demolitus est Josias" (i. 480). "Politicis magistratibus severissime mandatum est, ut suo quisque loco manibus et armis tollant statuas, ad quas fiunt hominum concursus et invocationes, et puniant suppliciis corporum insanabiles, qui idolorum cultum pertinaciter retinent, aut blasphemias serunt" (ix. 77).

overturn the fabric of Christian society. They had proscribed different religions where the State was founded on religious unity, and where this unity formed an integral part of its laws and administration. They had gone one step further, and punished those whom the Church condemned as apostates; thereby vindicating, not, as in the first case, the moral basis of society, nor, as in the second, the religious foundation of the State, but the authority of the Church and the purity of her doctrine, on which they relied as the pillar and bulwark of the social and political order. Where a portion of the inhabitants of any country preferred a different creed, Jew, Mohammedan, heathen, or schismatic, they had been generally tolerated, with enjoyment of property and personal freedom, but not with that of political power or autonomy. But political freedom had been denied them because they did not admit the common ideas of duty which were its basis. This position, however, was not tenable, and was the source of great disorders. The Protestants, in like manner, could give reasons for several kinds of persecution. They could bring the Socinians under the category of blasphemers; and blasphemy, like the ridicule of sacred things, detroys reverence and awe, and tends to the destruction of society. The Anabaptists, they might argue, were revolutionary fanatics, whose doctrines were subversive of the civil order; and the dogmatic sects threatened the ruin of ecclesiastical unity within the Protestant community itself. But by placing the necessity of intolerance on the simple ground of religious error, and in directing it against the Church which they themselves had abandoned, they introduced a purely subjective test, and a purely revolutionary system. It is on this account that the *tu quoque,* or retaliatory argument, is inadmissible between Catholics and Protestants. Catholic intolerance is handed down from an age when unity subsisted, and when its preservation, being essential for that of society, became a necessity of State as well as a result of circumstances. Protestant intolerance, on the contrary, was the peculiar fruit of a dogmatic system in contradiction with the facts and principles on which the intolerance actually existing among Catholics was founded. Spanish intolerance has been infinitely more sanguinary than Swedish; but in Spain, independently of the interests of religion, there were strong political and social reasons to justify persecution without seeking any theory to prop it up; whilst in Sweden all those practical considerations have either been wanting, or have been opposed to persecution, which has consequently had no justification except the theory of the Reformation. The only instance in which the Protestant theory has been adopted by Catholics is the revocation of the Edict of Nantes.

Towards the end of his life, Melanchthon, having ceased to be a strict Lutheran, receded somewhat from his former uncompromising position, and was adverse to a strict scrutiny into minor theological differences. He drew a distinction between errors that required punishment and variations that were not of practical importance.[51] The English Calvinists who took refuge in Germany in the reign of Mary Tudor were ungraciously received by those who were stricter Lutherans than Melanchthon. He was consulted concerning the course to be adopted towards the refugees, and he recommended toleration. But both at Wesel and at Frankfort his advice was, to his great disgust, overruled.[52]

The severities of the Protestants were chiefly provoked by the Anabaptists, who denied the lawfulness of civil government, and strove to realise the kingdom of God on earth by absorbing the State in the

---

[51] "If the French and English community at Frankfort shared the errors of Servetus or Thamer, or other enemies of the Symbols, or the errors of the Anabaptists on infant baptism, against the authority of the State, etc., I should faithfully advise and strongly recommend that they should be soon driven away; for the civil power is bound to prevent and to punish proved blasphemy and sedition. But I find that this community is orthodox in the symbolical articles on the Son of God, and in other articles of the Symbol. . . . If the faith of the citizens in every town were inquired into, what trouble and confusion would not arise in many countries and towns!" (ix. 179).

[52] Schmidt, *Philipp Melanchthon*, p. 640. His exhortations to the Landgrave to put down the Zwinglians are characteristic: "The Zwinglians, without waiting for the Council, persecute the Papists and the Anabaptists; why must it be wrong for others to prohibit their indefensible doctrine independent of the Council?" Philip replied: "Forcibly, to prohibit a doctrine which neither contradicts the articles of faith nor encourages sedition, I do not think right. . . . When Luther began to write and to preach, he admonished and instructed the Government that it had no right to forbid books or to prevent preaching, and that its office did not extend so far, but that it had only to govern the body and goods. . . . I had not heard before that the Zwinglians persecute the Papists; but if they abolish abuses, it is not unjust, for the Papists wish to deserve heaven by their works, and so blaspheme the Son of God. That they should persecute the Anabaptists is also not wrong, for their doctrine is in part seditious." The divines answered: "If by God's grace our true and necessary doctrine is tolerated as it has hitherto been by the emperor, though reluctantly, we think that we ought not to prevent it by undertaking the defence of the Zwinglian doctrine, if that should not be tolerated. . . . As to the argument that we ought to spare the people while persecuting the leaders, our answer is, that it is not a question of persons, but only of doctrine, whether it be true or false" (Correspondence of Brenz and Melanchthon with Landgrave Philip of Hesse, Bretschneider, ii. 95, 98, 101).

Church.[53] None protested more loudly than they against the Lutheran intolerance, or suffered from it more severely. But while denying the spiritual authority of the State, they claimed for their religious community a still more absolute right of punishing error by death. Though they sacrificed government to religion, the effect was the same as that of absorbing the Church in the State. In 1524 Münzer published a sermon, in which he besought the Lutheran princes to extirpate Catholicism. "Have no remorse," he says; "for He to whom all power is given in heaven and on earth means to govern alone."[54] He demanded the punishment of all heretics, the destruction of all who were not of his faith, and the institution of religious unity. "Do not pretend," he says, "that the power of God will accomplish it without the use of your sword, or it will grow rusty in the scabbard. The tree that bringeth not forth good fruit must be cut down and cast into the fire." And elsewhere, "the ungodly have no right to live, except so far as the elect choose to grant it them."[55] When the Anabaptists were supreme at Münster, they exhibited the same intolerance. At seven in the morning of Friday, 27th February 1534, they ran through the streets crying, "Away with the ungodly!" Breaking into the houses of those who refused their baptism, they drove the men out of the town, and forcibly rebaptized the women who remained behind.[56] Whilst, therefore, the Anabaptists were punished for questioning the authority of the Lutherans in religious matters, they practically justified their persecution by their own intolerant doctrines. In fact, they carried the Protestant principles of persecution to an extreme. For whereas the Lutherans regarded the defence of truth and punishment of error as being, in part, the object of the institution of civil government, they recognised it as an advantage by which the State was rewarded for its pains; but the Anabaptists repudiated the political element altogether, and held that error should be exterminated solely for the sake of truth, and at the expense of all existing States.

Bucer, whose position in the history of the Reformation is so peculiar, and who differed in important points from the Saxon leaders, agreed with them on the necessity of persecuting. He was so anxious for the success of Protestantism, that he was ready to sacrifice and renounce

[53] Hardwicke, *Reformation*, p. 274.

[54] Seidemann, *Thomas Münzer*, p. 35.

[55] Schenkel, iii. 381.

[56] Heinrich Grosbeck's *Bericht*, ed. Cornelius, 19.

important doctrines, in order to save the appearance of unity;[57] but those opinions in which he took so little dogmatic interest, he was resolved to defend by force. He was very much dissatisfied with the reluctance of the Senate of Strasburg to adopt severe measures against the Catholics. His colleague Capito was singularly tolerant; for the feeling of the inhabitants was not decidedly in favour of the change.[58] But Bucer, his biographer tells us, was, in spite of his inclination to mediate, not friendly to this temporising system; partly because he had an organising intellect, which relied greatly on practical discipline to preserve what had been conquered, and on restriction of liberty to be the most certain security for its preservation; partly because he had a deep insight into the nature of various religious tendencies, and was justly alarmed at their consequences for Church and State.[59] This point in the character of Bucer provoked a powerful resistance to his system of ecclesiastical discipline, for it was feared that he would give to the clergy a tyrannical power.[60] It is true that the demoralisation which ensued on the destruction of the old ecclesiastical authority rendered a strict attention on the part of the State to the affairs of religion highly necessary.[61] The private and confidential communications of the German reformers give a more hideous picture of the moral condition of the generation which followed the Reformation than they draw in their published writings of that which preceded it. It is on this account that Bucer so strongly insisted on the necessity of the interference of the civil power in support of the discipline of the Church.

The Swiss reformers, between whom and the Saxons Bucer forms a connecting link, differ from them in one respect, which greatly influenced their notions of government. Luther lived under a monarchy which was almost absolute, and in which the common people, who were of Slavonic origin, were in the position of the most abject servitude; but the divines of Zürich and Bern were republicans. They

---

[57] Herzog, *Encyclopädie für protestantische Theologie*, ii. 418.

[58] Bussierre, *Establissement du Protestantisme en Alsace*, p. 429.

[59] Baum, *Capito und Butzer*, p. 489.

[60] Baum, p. 492; Erbkam, *Protestantische Sekten*, p. 581.

[61] Ursinus writes to Bullinger: "Liberavit nos Deus ab idolatria: succedit licentia infinita et horribilis divini nominis, ecclesiae doctrinae purioris et sacramentorum prophanatio et sub pedibus porcorum et canum, conniventibus atque utinam non defendentibus iis qui prohibere suo loco debebant, conculcatio" (Sudhoff, *Oleviannus und Ursinus*, p. 340).

did not therefore entertain his exalted views as to the irresistible might of the State; and instead of requiring as absolute a theory of the indefectibility of the civil power as he did, they were satisfied with obtaining a preponderating influence for themselves. Where the power was in hands less favourable to their cause, they had less inducement to exaggerate its rights.

Zwingli abolishes both the distinction between Church and State and the notion of ecclesiastical authority. In his system the civil rulers possess the spiritual functions; and, as their foremost duty is the preservation and promotion of the true religion, it is their business to preach. As magistrates are too much occupied with other things, they must delegate the ministry of the word to preachers, for whose orthodoxy they have to provide. They are bound to establish uniformity of doctrine, and to defend it against Papists and heretics. This is not only their right, but their duty; and not only their duty, but the condition on which they retain office.[62] Rulers who do not act in accordance with it are to be dismissed. Thus Zwingli combined persecution and revolution in the same doctrine. But he was not a fanatical persecutor, and his severity was directed less against the Catholics than against the Anabaptists,[63] whose prohibition of all civil offices was more subversive of order in a republic than in a monarchy. Even, however, in the case of the Anabaptists the special provocation was—not the peril to the State, nor the scandal of their errors, but—the schism which weakened the Church.[64] The punishment of heresy for the glory of God was almost inconsistent with the theory that there is no ecclesiastical power. It was not so much provoked in Zürich as elsewhere, because in a small republican community, where the governing body was supreme over both civil and religious affairs, religious unity was a matter of course. The practical necessity of maintaining unity put out of sight the speculative question of the guilt and penalty of error.

Soon after Zwingli's death, Leo Jud called for severer measures against the Catholics, expressly stating, however, that they did not

---

[62] "Adserere audemus, neminem magistratum recte gerere ne posse quidem, nisi Christianus sit" (Zwingli, *Opera*, iii. 296). "If they shall proceed in an unbrotherly way, and against the ordinance of Christ, then let them be deposed, in God's name" (Schenkel, iii. 362).

[63] Christoffel, *Huldreich Zwingli*, p. 251.

[64] Zwingli's advice to the Protestants of St. Gall, in Pressel, *Joachim Vadian*, p. 45.

deserve death. "Excommunication," he said, "was too light a punishment to be inflicted by the State which wields the sword, and the faults in question were not great enough to involve the danger of death."[65] Afterwards he fell into doubts as to the propriety of severe measures against dissenters, but his friends Bullinger and Capito succeeded in removing his scruples, and in obtaining his acquiescence in that intolerance, which was, says his biographer, a question of life and death for the Protestant Church.[66] Bullinger took, like Zwingli, a more practical view of the question than was common in Germany. He thought it safer strictly to exclude religious differences than to put them down with fire and sword; "for in this case," he says, "the victims compare themselves to the early martyrs, and make their punishment a weapon of defence."[67] He did not, however, forbid capital punishment in cases of heresy. In the year 1535 he drew up an opinion on the treatment of religious error, which is written in a tone of great moderation. In this document he says "that all sects which introduce division into the Church must be put down, and not only such as, like the Anabaptists, threaten to subvert society, for the destruction of order and unity often begins in an apparently harmless or imperceptible way. The culprit should be examined with gentleness. If his disposition is good he will not refuse instruction; if not, still patience must be shown until there is no hope of converting him. Then he must be treated like other malefactors, and handed over to the torturer and the executioner."[68] After this time there were no executions for religion in Zürich, and the number, even in the lifetime of Zwingli, was less considerable than in many other places. But it was still understood that confirmed heretics would be put to death. In 1546, in answer to the Pope's invitation to the Council of Trent, Bullinger indignantly repudiates the insinuation that the Protestant cantons were heretical, "for, by the grace of God, we have always punished the vices of heresy and sodomy with fire, and have looked upon them, and still look upon them, with horror."[69] This accusation of heresy inflamed the zeal of the reformers against heretics, in order to prove to the Catholics that they had no sympathy with them. On these grounds Bullinger rec-

---

[65] Pestalozzi, *Heinrich Bullinger*, p. 95.
[66] *Ibid.*, *Leo Judä*, p. 50.
[67] Pestalozzi, *Heinrich Bullinger*, p. 146.
[68] *Ibid.* p. 149.
[69] *Ibid.* p. 270.

ommended the execution of Servetus. "If the high Council inflicts on him the fate due to a worthless blasphemer, all the world will see that the people of Geneva hate blasphemers, and that they punish with the sword of justice heretics who are obstinate in their heresy. . . . Strict fidelity and vigilance are needed, because our churches are in ill repute abroad, as if we were heretics and friends of heresy. Now God's holy providence has furnished an opportunity of clearing ourselves of this evil suspicion."[70] After the event he advised Calvin to justify it, as there were some who were taken aback. "Everywhere," he says, "there are excellent men who are convinced that godless and blaspheming men ought not only to be rebuked and imprisoned, but also to be put to death. . . . How Servetus could have been spared I cannot see."[71]

The position of Oecolampadius in reference to these questions was altogether singular and exceptional. He dreaded the absorption of the ecclesiastical functions by the State, and sought to avoid it by the introduction of a council of twelve elders, partly magistrates, partly clergy, to direct ecclesiastical affairs. "Many things," he said, "are punished by the secular power less severely than the dignity of the Church demands. On the other hand, it punishes the repentant, to whom the Church shows mercy. Either it blunts the edge of its sword by not punishing the guilty, or it brings some hatred on the Gospel by severity."[72] But the people of Basel were deaf to the arguments of the reformer, and here, as elsewhere, the civil power usurped the office of the Church. In harmony with this jealousy of political interference, Oecolampadius was very merciful to the Anabaptists. "Severe penalties," he said, "were likely to aggravate the evil; forgiveness would hasten the cure."[73] A few months later, however, he regretted this leniency. "We perceive," he writes to a friend, "that we have sometimes shown too much indulgence; but this is better than to proceed tyrannically, or to surrender the keys of the Church."[74] Whilst, on the

---

[70] Pestalozzi, *Heinrich Bullinger*, p. 426.

[71] In the year 1555 he writes to Socinus: "I too am of opinion that heretical men must be cut off with the spiritual sword. . . . The Lutherans at first did not understand that sectaries must be restrained and punished, but after the fall of Münster, when thousands of poor misguided men, many of them orthodox, had perished, they were compelled to admit that it is wiser and better for the Government not only to restrain wrong-headed men, but also, by putting to death a few that deserve it, to protect thousands of inhabitants" (*Ibid.* p. 428).

[72] Herzog, *Leben Oekolampads*, ii. 197.

[73] *Ibid.* p. 189.

[74] *Ibid.* p. 206.

other hand, he rejoiced at the expulsion of the Catholics, he ingeniously justified the practice of the Catholic persecutors. "In the early ages of the Church, when the divinity of Christ manifested itself to the world by miracles, God incited the Apostles to treat the ungodly with severity. When the miracles ceased, and the faith was universally adopted, He gained the hearts of princes and rulers, so that they undertook to protect with the sword the gentleness and patience of the Church. They rigorously resisted, in fulfilment of the duties of their office, the contemners of the Church."[75] "The clergy," he goes on to say, "became tyrannical because they usurped to themselves a power which they ought to have shared with others; and as the people dread the return of this tyranny of ecclesiastical authority, it is wiser for the Protestant clergy to make no use of the similar power of excommunication which is intrusted to them."

Calvin, as the subject of an absolute monarch, and the ruling spirit in a republic, differed both from the German and the Swiss reformers in his idea of the State both in its object and in its duty towards the Church. An exile from his own country, he had lost the associations and habits of monarchy, and his views of discipline as well as doctrine were matured before he took up his abode in Switzerland.[76] His system was not founded on existing facts; it had no roots in history, but was purely ideal, speculative, and therefore more consistent and inflexible than any other. Luther's political ideas were bounded by the horizon of the monarchical absolutism under which he lived. Zwingli's were influenced by the democratic forms of his native country, which gave to the whole community the right of appointing the governing body. Calvin, independent of all such considerations, studied only how his doctrine could best be realised, whether through the instrumentality of existing authorities, or at their expense. In his eyes its interests were paramount, their promotion the supreme duty, opposition to them an unpardonable crime. There was nothing in the institutions of men, no authority, no right, no liberty, that he cared to preserve, or towards which he entertained any feelings of reverence or obligation.

His theory made the support of religious truth the end and office of the State,[77] which was bound therefore to protect, and consequently

---

[75] Herzog, *Leben Oekolampads*, ii. 195. Herzog finds an excuse for the harsh treatment of the Lutherans at Basel in the still greater severity of the Lutheran Churches against the followers of the Swiss reformation (*Ibid.* 213).

[76] Hundeshagen, *Conflikte des Zwinglianismus und Calvinismus*, 41.

[77] "Huc spectat (politia) . . . ne idololatria, ne in Dei nomen sacrilegia, ne adversus

to obey, the Church, and had no control over it. In religion the first and highest thing was the dogma: the preservation of morals was one important office of government; but the maintenance of the purity of doctrine was the highest. The result of this theory is the institution of a pure theocracy. If the elect were alone upon the earth, Calvin taught, there would be no need of the political order, and the Anabaptists would be right in rejecting it;[78] but the elect are in a minority; and there is the mass of reprobates who must be coerced by the sword, in order that all the world may be made subject to the truth, by the conquerors imposing their faith upon the vanquished.[79] He wished to extend religion by the sword, but to reserve death as the punishment of apostasy; and as this law would include the Catholics, who were in Calvin's eyes apostates from the truth, he narrowed it further to those who were apostates from the community. In this way, he said, there was no pretext given to the Catholics to retaliate.[80] They, as well as the Jews and Mohammedans, must be allowed to live: death was only the penalty of Protestants who relapsed into error; but to them it applied equally whether they were converted to the Church or joined the sects and fell into unbelief. Only in cases where there was no danger of his words being used against the Protestants, and in letters not intended for publication, he required that Catholics should suffer the same penalties as those who were guilty of sedition, on the ground

---

ejus veritatem blasphemiae aliaeque religionis offensiones publice emergant ac in populum spargantur. . . . Politicam ordinationem probo, quae in hoc incumbit, ne vera religio, quae Dei lege continetur, palam, publicisque sacrilegiis impune violetur" (*Institutio Christianae Religionis*, ed. Tholuck, ii. 477). "Hoc ergo summopere requiritur a regibus, ut gladio quo praediti sunt utantur ad cultum Dei asserendum" (*Praelectiones in Prophetas, Opera*, v. 233, ed. 1667).

[78] "Huic etiam colligere promptum est, quam stulta fuerit imaginatio eorum qui volebant usum gladii tollere e mundo, Evangelii praetextu. Scimus Anabaptistas fuisse tumultuatos, quasi totus ordo politicus repugnaret Christi regno, quia regnum Christi continetur sola doctrina; deinde nulla futura sit vis. Hoc quidem verum esset, si essemus in hoc mundo angeli: sed quemadmodum jam dixi, exiguus est piorum numerus: ideo necesse est reliquam turbam cohiberi violento freno: quia permixti sunt filii Dei vel saevis belluis, vel vulpibus et fraudulentis hominibus" (*Pr. in Michaeam*, v. 310). "In quo non suam modo inscitiam, sed diabolicum fastum produnt, dum perfectionem sibi arrogant; cujus ne centesima quidem pars in illis conspicitur" (*Institutio*, ii. 478).

[79] "Tota igitur excellentia, tota dignitas, tota potentia Ecclesiae debet huc referri, ut omnia subjaceant Deo, et quicquid erit in gentibus hoc totum sit sacrum, ut scilicet cultus Dei tam apud victores quam apud victos vigeat" (*Pr. in Michaeam*, v. 317).

[80] "Ita tollitur offensio, quae multos imperitos fallit, dum metuunt ne hoc praetextu ad saeviendum armentur Papae carnifices." Calvin was warned by experience of the imprudence of Luther's language. "In Gallis proceres in excusanda saevitia immani allegant auctoritatem Lutheri" (Melanchthon, *Opera*, v. 176).

that the majesty of God must be as strictly avenged as the throne of the king.[81]

If the defence of the truth was the purpose for which power was intrusted to princes, it was natural that it should be also the condition on which they held it. Long before the revolution of 1688, Calvin had decided that princes who deny the true faith, "abdicate" their crowns, and are no longer to be obeyed;[82] and that no oaths are binding which are in contradiction to the interests of Protestantism.[83] He painted the princes of his age in the blackest colours,[84] and prayed to God for their destruction;[85] though at the same time he condemned all rebellion on the part of his friends, so long as there were great doubts of their

[81] "Vous avez deux espèces de mutins qui se sont eslevez entre le roy et l'estat du royaume: Les uns sont gens fantastiques, qui soubs couleur de l'évangile vouldroient mettre tout en confusion. Les aultres sont gens obstinés aux superstitions de l'Antéchrist de Rome. Tous ensemble méritent bien d'estre réprimés par le glayve qui vous est commis, veu qu'ils s'attaschent non seulement au roy, mais à Dieu qui l'a assis au siège royal" (Calvin to Somerset, Oct. 22, 1540; *Lettres de Calvin,* ed. Bonnet, i. 267. See also Henry, *Leben Calvins,* ii. Append. 30).

[82] "Abdicant enim se potestate terreni principes dum insurgunt contra Deum: imo indigni sunt qui censeantur in hominum numero. Potius ergo conspuere oportet in ipsorum capita, quam illis parere, ubi ita proterviunt ut velint etiam spoliare Deum jure suo, et quasi occupare solium ejus, acsi possent eum a coelo detrahere" (*Pr. in Danielem,* v. 91).

[83] "Quant au serment qu'on vous a contraincte de faire, comme vous avez failli et offensé Dieu en le faisant, aussi n'estes-vous tenue de le garder" (Calvin to the Duchess of Ferrara, *Bonnet,* ii. 338). She had taken an oath, at her husband's death, that she would not correspond with Calvin.

[84] "In aulis regum videmus primas teneri a bestiis. Nam hodie, ne repetamus veteres historias, ut reges fere omnes fatui sunt ac bruti, ita etiam sunt quasi equi et asini brutorum animalium. . . . Reges sunt hodie fere mancipia" (*Pr. in Danielem,* v. 82). "Videmus enim ut hodie quoque pro sua libidine commoveant totum orbem principes; quia produnt alii aliis innoxios populos, et exercent foedam nundinationem, dum quisque commodum suum venatur, et sine ullo pudore, tantum ut augeat suam potentiam, alios tradit in manum inimici" (*Pr. in Nahum,* v. 363). "Hodie pudet reges aliquid prae se ferre humanum, sed omnes gestus accommodant ad tyrannidem" (*Pr. in Jeremiam,* v. 257).

[85] "Sur ce que je vous avais allégué, que David nous instruict par son exemple de haïr les ennemis de Dieu, vous respondez que c'estoit pour ce temps-là duquel sous la loi de rigueur il estoit permis de haïr les ennemis. Or, madame, ceste glose seroit pour renverser toute l'Escriture, et partant il la fault fuir comme une peste mortelle. . . . Combien que j'aye tousjours prié Dieu de luy faire mercy, si est-ce que j'ay souvent désiré que Dieu mist la main sur luy (Guise) pour en deslivrer son Eglise, s'il ne le vouloit convertir" (Calvin to the Duchess of Ferrara, *Bonnet,* ii. 551). Luther was in this respect equally unscrupulous: "This year we must pray Duke Maurice to death, we must kill him with our prayers; for he will be an evil man" (MS. quoted in Döllinger, *Reformation,* iii. 266).

success.[86] His principles, however, were often stronger than his exhortations, and he had difficulty in preventing murders and seditious movements in France.[87] When he was dead, nobody prevented them, and it became clear that his system, by subjecting the civil power to the service of religion, was more dangerous to toleration than Luther's plan of giving to the State supremacy over the Church.

Calvin was as positive as Luther in asserting the duty of obedience to rulers irrespective of their mode of government.[88] He constantly declared that tyranny was not to be resisted on political grounds; that no civil rights could outweigh the divine sanction of government; except in cases where a special office was appointed for the purpose. Where there was no such office—where, for instance, the estates of the realm had lost their independence—there was no protection. This is one of the most important and essential characteristics of the politics of the reformers. By making the protection of their religion the principal business of government, they put out of sight its more immediate and universal duties, and made the political objects of the State disappear behind its religious end. A government was to be judged, in their eyes, only by its fidelity to the Protestant Church. If it fulfilled those requirements, no other complaints against it could be entertained. A tyrannical prince could not be resisted if he was orthodox; a just prince could be dethroned if he failed in the more essential condition of faith. In this way Protestantism became favourable at once to despotism and to revolution, and was ever ready to sacrifice good government to its own interests. It subverted monarchies, and, at the same time,

---

[86] "Quod de praepostero nostrorum fervore scribis, verissimum est, neque tamen ulla occurrit moderandi ratio, quia sanis consiliis non obtemperant. Passim denuntio, si judex essem, me non minus severe in rabiosos, istos impetus vindicaturum, quam rex suis edictis mandat. Pergendum nihilominus, quando nos Deus voluit stultis esse debitores" (Calvin to Beza; Henry, *Leben Calvins*, iii. Append. 164).

[87] "Il n'a tenu qu'à moi que, devant la guerre, gens de faict et d'exécution ne se soyent efforcez de l'exterminer du monde (Guise) lesquels ont esté retenus par ma seule exhortation."—*Bonnet*, ii. 553.

[88] "Hoc nobis si assidue ob animos et oculos obversetur, eodem decreto constitui etiam nequissimos reges, quo regum auctoritas statuitur; nunquam in animum nobis seditiosae illae cogitationes venient, tractandum esse pro meritis regem nec aequum esse, ut subditos ei nos praestemus, qui vicissim regem nobis se non praestet. . . . De privatis hominibus semper loquor. Nam si qui nunc sint populares magistratus ad moderandam regum libidinem constituti (quales olim erant . . . ephori . . . tribuni . . . demarchi: et qua etiam forte potestate, ut nunc res habent, funguntur in singulis regnis tres ordines, quum primarios conventus peragunt) . . . illos ferocienti regum licentiae pro officio intercedere non veto" (*Institutio*, ii. 493, 495).

denounced those who, for political causes, sought their subversion; but though the monarchies it subverted were sometimes tyrannical, and the seditions it prevented sometimes revolutionary, the order it defended or sought to establish was never legitimate and free, for it was always invested with the function of religious proselytism,[89] and with the obligation of removing every traditional, social, or political right or power which could oppose the discharge of that essential duty.

The part Calvin had taken in the death of Servetus obliged him to develop more fully his views on the punishment of heresy. He wrote a short account of the trial,[90] and argued that governments are bound to suppress heresy, and that those who deny the justice of the punishment, themselves deserve it.[91] The book was signed by all the clergy of Geneva, as Calvin's compurgators. It was generally considered a failure; and a refutation appeared, which was so skilful as to produce a great sensation in the Protestant world.[92] This famous tract, now of extreme rarity, did not, as has been said, "contain the pith of those arguments which have ultimately triumphed in almost every part of Europe;" nor did it preach an unconditional toleration.[93] But it struck

[89] "Quum ergo ita licentiose omnia sibi permittent (Donatistae), volebant tamen impune manere sua scelera: et in primis tenebant hoc principium: non esse poenas sumendas, si quis ab aliis dissideret in religionis doctrina: quemadmodum hodie videmus quosdam de hac re nimis cupide contendere. Certum est quid cupiant. Nam si quis ipsos respiciat, sunt impii Dei contemptores: saltem vellent nihil certum esse in religione; ideo labefactare, et quantum in se est etiam convellere nituntur omnia pietatis principia. Ut ergo liceat ipsis evomere virus suum, ideo tantopere litigant pro impunitate, et negant poenas de haereticis et blasphemis sumendas esse" (*Pr. in Danielem*, v. 51).

[90] "Defensio Orthodoxae Fidei . . . ubi ostenditur Haereticos jure gladii coercendos esse," 1554.

[91] "Non modo liberum esse magistratibus poenas sumere de coelestis doctrinae corruptoribus, sed divinitus esse mandatum, ut pestiferis erroribus impunitatem dare nequeant, quin desciscant ab officii sui fide. . . . Nunc vero quisquis haereticis et blasphemis injuste poenam infligi contenderet, sciens et volens se obstringet blasphemiae reatu. . . . Ubi a suis fundamentis convellitur religio, detestandae in Deum blasphemiae proferuntur, impiis et pestiferis dogmatibus in exitium rapiuntur animae; denique ubi palam defectio ab unico Deo puraque doctrina tentatur, ad extremum illud remedium descendere necesse" (see Schenkel, iii. 389; Dyer, *Life of Calvin*, p. 354; Henry, iii. 234).

[92] *De Haereticis an sint persequendi*, Magdeburgi, 1554. Chataillon, to whom it is generally attributed, was not the author (see Heppe, *Theodor Beza*, p. 37).

[93] Hallam, *Literature of Europe*, ii. 81; Schlosser, *Leben des Beza*, p. 55. This is proved by the following passage from the dedication: "This I say not to favour the heretics, whom I abhor, but because there are here two dangerous rocks to be avoided. In the first place, that no man should be deemed a heretic when he is not, . . . and that the real rebel be distinguished from the Christian who, by following the teaching and example of his Master, necessarily causes separation from the wicked and unbelieving. The other danger is, lest the real heretics be not more severely punished than the discipline of the Church requires" (Baum, *Theodor Beza*, i. 215).

hard at Calvin by quoting a passage from the first edition of his *Institutes*, afterwards omitted, in which he spoke for toleration. "Some of those," says the author, "whom we quote have subsequently written in a different spirit. Nevertheless, we have cited the earlier opinion as the true one, as it was expressed under the pressure of persecution."[94] The first edition, we are informed by Calvin himself, was written for the purpose of vindicating the Protestants who were put to death, and of putting a stop to the persecution. It was anonymous, and naturally dwelt on the principles of toleration.

Although this book did not denounce all intolerance, and although it was extremely moderate, Calvin and his friends were filled with horror. "What remains of Christianity," exclaimed Beza, "if we silently admit what this man has expectorated in his preface? . . . Since the beginning of Christianity no such blasphemy was ever heard."[95] Beza undertook to defend Calvin in an elaborate work,[96] in which it was easy for him to cite the authority of all the leading reformers in favour of the practice of putting heretics to death, and in which he reproduced all the arguments of those who had written on the subject before him. More systematic than Calvin, he first of all excludes those who are not Christians—the Jews, Turks, and heathen—whom his inquiry does not touch; "among Christians," he proceeds to say, "some are schismatics, who sin against the peace of the Church, or disbelievers, who reject her doctrine. Among these, some err in all simplicity; and if their error is not very grave, and if they do not seduce others, they need not be punished."[97] "But obstinate heretics are far worse than

---

[94] "Multis piis hominibus in Gallia exustis grave passim apud Germanos odium ignes illi excitaverant, sparsi sunt, ejus restinguendi causa, improbi ac mendaces libelli, non alios tam crudeliter tractari, quam Anabaptistas ac turbulentos homines, qui perversis deliriis non religionem modo sed totum ordinem politicum convellerent. . . . Haec mihi edendae Institutionis causa fuit, primum ut ab iniusta contumelia vindicarem fratres meos, quorum mors pretiosa erat in conspectu Domini; deinde quum multis miseris eadem visitarent supplicia, pro illis dolor saltem aliquis et sollicitudo exteras gentes tangeret" (*Praefatio in Psalmos.* See "Historia Litteraria de Calvini Institutione," in *Scrinium Antiquarium*, ii. 452).

[95] Baum, i. 206. "Telles gens," says Calvin, "seroient contents qu'il n'y eust ne loy, ne bride au monde. Voilà pourquoy ils ont basti ce beau libvre *De non comburendis Haereticis*, où ils ont falsifié les noms tant des villes que des personnes, non pour aultre cause sinon pource que le dit livre est farcy de blasphèmes insupportables" (Bonnet, ii. 18).

[96] *De Haereticis a civili Magistratu puniendis*, 1554.

[97] "Absit autem a nobis, ut in eos, qui vel simplicitate peccant, sine aliorum pernicie et insigni blasphemia, vel in explicando quopiam Scripturae loco dissident a recepta opinione, magistratum armemus" (*Tractatus Theologici*, i. 95).

parricides, and deserve death, even if they repent."[98] "It is the duty of the State to punish them, for the whole ecclesiastical order is upheld by the political."[99] In early ages this power was exercised by the temporal sovereigns; they convoked councils, punished heretics, promulgated dogmas. The Papacy afterwards arose, in evil times, and was a great calamity; but it was preferable a hundred times to the anarchy which was defended under the name of merciful toleration.

The circumstances of the condemnation of Servetus make it the most perfect and characteristic example of the abstract intolerance of the reformers. Servetus was guilty of no political crime; he was not an inhabitant of Geneva, and was on the point of leaving it, and nothing immoral could be attributed to him. He was not even an advocate of absolute toleration.[100] The occasion of his apprehension was a dispute between a Catholic and a Protestant, as to which party was most zealous in suppressing egregious errors. Calvin, who had long before declared that if Servetus came to Geneva he should never leave it alive,[101] did all he could to obtain his condemnation by the Inquisition at Vienne. At Geneva he was anxious that the sentence should be death,[102] and in this he was encouraged by the Swiss churches, but

---

[98] This was sometimes the practice in Catholic countries, where heresy was equivalent to treason. Duke William of Bavaria ordered obstinate Anabaptists to be burnt; those who recanted to be beheaded. "Welcher revocir, den soll man köpfen; welcher nicht revocir, den soll man brennen" (Jörg, p. 717).

[99] "Ex quibus omnibus una conjunctio efficitur, istos quibus haeretici videntur non esse puniendi, opinionem in Ecclesiam Dei conari longe omnium pestilentissimam invehere et ex diametro repugnantem doctrinae primum a Deo Patre proditae, deinde a Christo instauratae, ab universa denique Ecclesia orthodoxa perpetuo consensu usurpatae, ut mihi quidem magis absurde facere videantur quam si sacrilegas aut parricidas puniendos negarent, quum sint istis omnibus haeretici infinitis partibus deteriores" (*Tract. Theol.* i. 143).

[100] "Verum est quod correctione non exspectata Ananiam et Sapphiram occidit Petrus. Quia Spiritus Sanctus tunc maxime vigens, quem spreverant, docebat esse incorrigibiles, in malitia obstinatos. Hoc crimen est morte simpliciter dignum et apud Deum et apud homines. In aliis autem criminibus, ubi Spiritus Sanctus speciale quid non docet, ubi non est inveterata malitia, aut obstinatio certa non apparet aut atrocitas magna, correctionem per alias castigationes sperare potius debemus" (Servetus, *Restitutio Christianismi*, 656; Henry, iii. 235).

[101] "Nam si venerit, modo valeat mea authoritas, vivum exire nunquam patiar" (Calvin to Farel, in Henry, iii. Append 65; Audin, *Vie de Calvin*, ii. 314; Dyer, 544).

[102] "Spero capitale saltem fore judicium: poenae vero atrocitatem remitti cupio" (Calvin to Farel, Henry, iii. 189). Dr. Henry makes no attempt to clear Calvin of the imputation of having caused the death of Servetus. Nevertheless he proposed, some years later, that the three-hundredth anniversary of the execution should be celebrated

especially by Beza, Farel, Bullinger, and Peter Martyr.[103] All the Protestant authorities, therefore, agreed in the justice of putting a writer to death in whose case all the secondary motives of intolerance were wanting. Servetus was not a party leader. He had no followers who threatened to upset the peace and unity of the Church. His doctrine was speculative, without power or attraction for the masses, like Lutheranism; and without consequences subversive of morality, or affecting in any direct way the existence of society, like Anabaptism.[104] He had nothing to do with Geneva, and his persecutors would have rejoiced if he had been put to death elsewhere. "Bayle," says Hallam,[105]

in the Church of Geneva by a demonstration. "It ought to declare itself in a body, in a manner worthy of our principles, admitting that in past times the authorities of Geneva were mistaken, loudly proclaiming toleration, which is truly the crown of our Church, and paying due honour to Calvin, because he had no hand in the business (parce qu'il n'a pas trempé dans cette affaire), of which he has unjustly borne the whole burden." The impudence of this declaration is surpassed by the editor of the French periodical from which we extract it. He appends to the words in our parenthesis the following note: "We underline in order to call attention to this opinion of Dr. Henry, who is so thoroughly acquainted with the whole question" (*Bulletin de la Société de l'Histoire du Protestantisme Français*, ii. 114).

[103] "Qui scripserunt de non plectendis haereticis, semper mihi visi sunt non parum errare" (Farel to Blaarer, Henry, iii. 202). During the trial he wrote to Calvin: "If you desire to diminish the horrible punishment, you will act as a friend towards your most dangerous enemy. If I were to seduce anybody from the true faith, I should consider myself worthy of death; I cannot judge differently of another than of myself" (Schmidt, *Farel und Viret*, p. 33).

Before sentence was pronounced Bullinger wrote to Beza: "Quid vero amplissimus Senatus Genevensis ageret cum blasphemo illo nebulone Serveto. Si sapit et officium suum facit, caedit, ut totus orbis videat Genevam Christi gloriam cupere servatam" (Baum, i. 204). With reference to Socinus he wrote: "Sentio ego spirituali gladio abscindendos esse homines haerecticos" (Henry iii. 225).

Peter Martyr Vermili also gave in his adhesion to Calvin's policy: "De Serveto Hispano, quid aliud dicam non habeo, nisi eum fuisse genuinum Diaboli filium, cujus pestifera et detestanda doctrina undique profliganda est, neque magistratus, qui de illo supplicium extremum sumpsit, accusandus est, cum emendationis nulla indicia in eo possent deprehendi, illiusque blasphemiae omnino intolerabiles essent" (*Loci Communes*, 1114. See Schlosser, *Leben des Beza und des Peter Martyr Vermili*, 512).

Zanchi, who at the instigation of Bullinger also published a treatise, *De Haereticis Coercendis*, says of Beza's work: "Non poterit non probari summopere piis omnibus. Satis superque respondit quidem ille novis istis academicis, ita ut supervacanea et inutilis omnino videatur mea tractatio" (Baum, i. 232).

[104] "The trial of Servetus," says a very ardent Calvinist, "is illegal only in one point—the crime, if crime there be, had not been committed at Geneva; but long before the Councils had usurped the unjust privilege of judging strangers stopping at Geneva, although the crimes they were accused of had not been committed there" (Haag, *La France Protestante*, iii. 129).

[105] *Literature of Europe*, ii. 82.

"has an excellent remark on this controversy." Bayle's remark is as follows: "Whenever Protestants complain, they are answered by the right which Calvin and Beza recognised in magistrates; and to this day there has been nobody who has not failed pitiably against this *argumentum ad hominem.*"

No question of the merits of the Reformation or of persecution is involved in an inquiry as to the source and connection of the opinions on toleration held by the Protestant reformers. No man's sentiments on the rightfulness of religious persecution will be affected by the theories we have described, and they have no bearing whatever on doctrinal controversy. Those who—in agreement with the principle of the early Church, that men are free in matters of conscience—condemn all intolerance, will censure Catholics and Protestants alike. Those who pursue the same principle one step farther and practically invert it, by insisting on the right and duty not only of professing but of extending the truth, must, as it seems to us, approve the conduct both of Protestants and Catholics, unless they make the justice of the persecution depend on the truth of the doctrine defended, in which case they will divide on both sides. Such persons, again, as are more strongly impressed with the cruelty of actual executions than with the danger of false theories, may concentrate their indignation on the Catholics of Languedoc and Spain; while those who judge principles, not by the accidental details attending their practical realisation, but by the reasoning on which they are founded, will arrive at a verdict adverse to the Protestants. These comparative inquiries, however, have little serious interest. If we give our admiration to tolerance, we must remember that the Spanish Moors and the Turks in Europe have been more tolerant than the Christians; and if we admit the principle of intolerance, and judge its application by particular conditions, we are bound to acknowledge that the Romans had better reason for persecution than any modern State, since their empire was involved in the decline of the old religion, with which it was bound up, whereas no Christian polity has been subverted by the mere presence of religious dissent. The comparison is, moreover, entirely unreasonable, for there is nothing in common between Catholic and Protestant intolerance. The Church began with the principle of liberty, both as her claim and as her rule; and external circumstances forced intolerance upon her, after her spirit of unity had triumphed, in spite both of the freedom she proclaimed and of the persecutions she suffered. Protestantism set up intolerance as an imperative precept and as a part of its doctrine, and it was forced to admit toleration by the necessities of its position, after the rigorous penalties it imposed had failed to arrest the process of internal dissolution.[106]

At the time when this involuntary change occurred the sects that caused it were the bitterest enemies of the toleration they demanded. In the same age the Puritans and the Catholics sought a refuge beyond the Atlantic from the persecution which they suffered together under the Stuarts. Flying for the same reason, and from the same oppression, they were enabled respectively to carry out their own views in the colonies which they founded in Massachusetts and Maryland, and the history of those two States exhibits faithfully the contrast between the two Churches. The Catholic emigrants established, for the first time in modern history, a government in which religion was free, and with it the germ of that religious liberty which now prevails in America. The Puritans, on the other hand, revived with greater severity the penal laws of the mother country. In process of time the liberty of conscience in the Catholic colony was forcibly abolished by the neighbouring Protestants of Virginia; while on the borders of Massachusetts the new State of Rhode Island was formed by a party of fugitives from the intolerance of their fellow-colonists.

---

[106] This is the ground taken by two Dutch divines in answer to the consultation of John of Nassau in 1579: "Neque in imperio, neque in Galliis, neque in Belgio speranda esset unquam libertas in externo religionis exercitio nostri ... si non diversarum religionum exercitia in una eademque provincia toleranda.... Sic igitur gladio adversus nos armabimus Pontificios, si hanc hypothesin tuebimur, quod exercitium religionis alteri parti nullum prorsus relinqui debeat" (*Scrinium Antiquarium*, i. 335).

[8]
Secret History of
Charles II

In the register of the House of Novices of the Jesuits at Rome there is the following entry: *Jacobus de la Cloche ingressus II Aprilis* 1668. From another list, which is signed by the novice himself, we learn that he came from the island of Jersey, and was a subject of the King of England; that his age was about twenty-four; and that he presented himself for admission in the dress of an ecclesiastic, with scarcely any luggage but the clothes he wore. This youth, whose name occurs no more in the books of the Order, and has never yet been pronounced by history, was the eldest of the sons of Charles the Second, the elder brother of Monmouth, and destined to be for a moment his rival in the fanciful schemes of his father. So well was the secret of his birth preserved that throughout the long intrigue to save the Protestant succession, and to supplant the Duke of York by the son of Lucy Walters, no man ever discovered that there was another who, by his age and by his mother's rank, had a better claim than the popular favourite, and who had voluntarily renounced the dazzling fortunes which were once within his grasp. The obscurity which he preferred has endured for nearly two hundred years, and even now is not entirely dispelled; but the facts which I have to relate add a new and interesting episode to the chequered history of the Stuarts, and clear up whatever remained uncertain as to the attachment of Charles II to the Catholic Church.

This attachment, which excited so keenly the curiosity of the world, and influenced so many of the actions of his reign, has been admitted with greater unanimity by recent historians than by those who spoke

Published in the *Home and Foreign Review* 1 (July 1862):146–174. *Wellesley* I, p. 550; Döllinger I, p. 262; Acton-Simpson II, p. 278. Reprinted in Acton, *Historical Essays*, pp. 85–122; Acton, *Liberal Interpretation of History*, pp. 95–130.

from personal observation, and whom Charles succeeded in partially misleading. "It was not," says the ablest of the statesmen who approached him, "the least skilful part of his concealing himself to make the world think he leaned towards an indifference in religion."[1] That belief was long since found to be untenable. Mr. Fox, and the author of the *Annals of England,* believe that he had been actually reconciled to the Catholic Church; and Mackintosh fixes the date of that event in the year 1658. Hallam justly rejects this opinion, but is certain that the king had imbibed during the period of his banishment a persuasion that if any scheme of Christianity was true, it could only be found in the bosom of an infallible Church. Dr. Vaughan believes that, so far as he could be said to have any religion, he was a Catholic; and Macaulay exactly agrees with Dr. Vaughan. Lingard, who declares his early professions of regard for Catholicism a pretence, supplies no psychological explanation of the discrepancy between the scene at his death and his previous insincerity; while Dod more reasonably considers the reconciliation at the last moment a proof that he had inwardly espoused the Catholic doctrines before.

Many things contributed during the life of Charles to spread and to keep alive the report of his conversion. His mother's sincerity and zeal in religion were well known. She had attempted to instil the sentiments of her faith into her eldest daughter Mary, afterwards Princess of Orange, and although this was prevented by the king, she obtained his consent in her exile that their youngest child Henrietta should be educated a Catholic. At Paris Henrietta Maria exerted herself to induce the Duke of Gloucester to change his religion; and when the exhortations of Charles, the influence of Ormond, and the memory of the last solemn parting with his father prevailed against her efforts, she drove him from her presence. Charles I had feared that the religion of his queen would injure the cause of his son, and sent earnest warnings to both when the prince joined his mother in France. To the former he wrote from Oxford, 22nd March 1646: "I command you, upon my blessing, to be constant to your religion; neither hearkening to Roman superstitions, nor the seditious and schismatical doctrines of the Presbyterians and Independents; for know that a persecuted church is not thereby less pure, though less fortunate. For all other things I command you to be totally directed by your mother."[2] Shortly after,

[1] Halifax, *Character of Charles* II, p. 11.
[2] Clarendon, *History of the Rebellion,* x. 8.

he wrote to the queen from Newcastle: "In God's name, let him stay with thee till it is seen what ply my business will take; and, for my sake, let the world see that the queen seeks not to alter his conscience."[3] Clarendon entertained the same fears, and endeavoured to keep the prince at Jersey, away from his mother's influence. But he bears testimony that, for six years, down to 1652, when the fortunes of the Stuarts seemed desperate, and the motives for prudence had disappeared with the hope of success, Henrietta Maria was sensible of the impolicy of a step which, more than any other act, must have alienated the English people from their king.[4] That she recognised it at first we may conclude from the failure of the match between Charles and Mademoiselle de Montpensier, the cousin of Lewis XIV. That princess insisted that the difference of religion was an insurmountable obstacle; and Jermyn, who was conducting the business, and must have spoken the thoughts of the queen-mother, thereupon replied that the king could not change his religion for her sake without forfeiting for ever the crown of his kingdom.[5]

When, at length, it appeared certain that no chance of recovering the throne remained, except through the support of the Catholic Powers, the exiled courtiers began to debate whether some sacrifice might not be made for the purpose of obtaining their assistance. "The Protestant religion was found to be very unagreeable to their fortune, and very many exercised their thoughts most how to get handsomely from it. . . . Many made little doubt but that it would shortly be very manifest to the king that his restoration depended wholly upon a conjunction of Catholic princes, who could never be united but on the behalf of Catholic religion."[6] Digby, Clifford, and Bennet became Catholics, and proved their sincerity at their deaths; but they all agreed that it would be dangerous for Charles to imitate them. Clarendon, whose purpose it was to divert from his master the suspicion of popery, wished it to be believed that no religious scruples, no doubts in the orthodoxy of the Anglican Church, had ever invaded the exiled court, and that the Catholic inclinations or professions of some of its members were the effects of political design. He had argued with great force that even though Charles should give no cause for suspicion, the fact

---

[3] *Clarendon Papers*, ii. 239.
[4] *History*, xiii. 131.
[5] *Mémoires de Mademoiselle*, 57, ed. Michaud.
[6] *Clarendon*, xvi. 74.

of his residence in a Catholic country would be a pretext for his enemies to accuse him. It would not be hard, he wrote to Jermyn, to persuade them who believed the king a papist when he was seen every day at Church in England, to believe the prince a papist when he had no church in France to go to.[7] But the other advisers, who were less sturdy Protestants than the Chancellor, knew that nothing was to be expected for their cause from a change of religion. In the period of the administration of Mazarin and the peace of Westphalia, no reasonable man could believe that any State would incur the expense and the risk of war for the establishment of a Catholic dynasty in England; and even those who believed that Charles leaned from conviction towards Rome, and whose sympathies were on the same side, were careful to conceal the fact.[8]

A rumour reached their friends in England, and caused an extreme alarm. "There is a report," wrote Mordaunt to Ormond, in November 1659, "so hot of your master's being turned papist, that unless it be suddenly contradicted, and the world disabused by something coming expressly from him, it is likely, in this extraordinary conjuncture, to do him very great injury amongst his friends both in city and country, in both which his constancy all this while hath rendered him many considerable proselytes."[9] This letter justly represents the position of affairs, and the state of public feeling; and Clarendon took his measures to undeceive his party and to silence their enemies.

Yet, although political interest forbade a public declaration, there was truth in the reports circulated in England, and so stoutly contradicted by the royalists. It is certain that Charles had, during the last years of his exile, secretly adopted the Catholic faith, although the fear of detection prevented a formal abjuration of Protestantism. Burnet says he was received before he left Paris, and that Cardinal de Retz and Aubigny had a hand in it. This information he had obtained from two sources, and indirectly, he affirms, from Retz himself. When Charles was at Paris, after the flight from Worcester, he received instruction in religion from Olier, the celebrated founder of the seminary of St. Sulpice. His conferences were no secret, for Olier had informed

---

[7] Lister, *Life of Clarendon*, i. 284. He would not allow the prince to attend the service of the French Calvinists at Charenton (*History*, xiii. 133).

[8] The testimony of Ormond and Burnet, and the worthless reports to the same effect in Kennet and Echard, are collected in the *Biographia Britannica*, ii. 177D, 2nd ed.

[9] Carte's *Collection*, ii. 264.

his friends of his hopes, and entreated their prayers. They probably gave occasion to the exaggerated report of Burnet. Charles, it is true, wrote from Paris to the Pope to ask for assistance in recovering his dominions. Innocent would have been satisfied, under the circumstances, with a private abjuration; but this was refused, and the king could not even obtain an answer to his application.[10] But although he was not received into the Church, he had advanced so far in his opinions that he might, as Thurloe affirmed, in his communications with the Spanish Government have declared himself in private to them to be a Catholic.[11] Neither France nor Spain had any inducement to publish what would diminish the chances of monarchy in England, and strengthen a Government they feared and hated. The story that Ormond discovered Charles on his knees hearing mass in a church at Brussels comes to us through two independent channels, Carte and Echard. The latter supposes the ceremony of abjuration to have occurred when the king was at Fuentarabia, at the time of the treaty of the Pyrenees. There is much reason in a remark which is made by Welwood: "The truth is, King Charles was neither bigot enough to any religion, nor loved his ease so little, as to embark in a business that must at least have disturbed his quiet, if not hazarded his crown."[12]

Ludovick Stuart, Lord Aubigny, to whom Burnet attributes the conversion of Charles, appeared at Whitehall immediately after the Restoration. In France, where he was educated and ordained, he had joined the party of Cardinal de Retz and the Jansenists, and had been made a canon of Notre Dame. As a relative of the royal family, and at one time an inmate of St. Sulpice, he was probably aware of the conferences which Olier, and perhaps others,[13] held with Charles during his residence at Paris. In April 1661, he officiated at the private marriage of Charles with Catherine of Braganza, and became almoner to the queen. His royal descent, and the position he had already attained in the Church, pointed him out as a suitable person to conduct the projected intercourse between the English court and the Holy See. In order to obtain that office, he sought the aid of a more powerful negotiator.

His friend Cardinal de Retz had taken the foremost part in the

---

[10] *Vie de M. Olier*, ii. 489, from the French Archives.

[11] Carte, ii. 102.

[12] *Memoirs*, p. 131.

[13] Charles is reported to have said that though many persons had discoursed with him on religion, none had affected him so much as Olier (*Vie de M. Olier*, ii. 490).

troubles which distracted both Church and State in France in the days of the Fronde, and after balancing for a season the power of Mazarin, had been deserted by fortune, and suffered in banishment the disgrace both of the French and of the Roman court. Upon the death of Cromwell Ormond had recourse to him in the name of the king, who promised, if the Cardinal would obtain for him some assistance from the Pope, to protect the Catholics after his restoration. Retz, hoping that the merit of having secured a promise of indulgence for the Catholic subjects of the King of England would powerfully assist his own cause, undertook the negotiation, and sent one of his adherents, the Abbé Charier, to Rome. The envoy could not, however, obtain an audience of the Pope; and he was assured by one of the Cardinals that the promises of Charles had made no impression, and that the prospect of relief to the oppressed Catholics would never induce Alexander VII to furnish him with money.[14] The Restoration soon altered the position of affairs, and improved the prospects of the Cardinal. He came to London in 1660, and received not only promises of support from the king, but large sums of money, on condition that he would promote the objects which Charles was pursuing in the court of Rome. These objects were of such importance that the notion of a marriage with one of the nieces of Mazarin was entertained for a moment by Charles as a means of securing them,[15] and was eagerly adopted by Retz for the purpose of recovering his favour at Paris. Mazarin despatched a special envoy to England charged with the mission of promoting the match. He found an auxiliary in Aubigny, who represented to Charles the beauty of the Cardinal's nieces, but more particularly their virtue, of which, says the envoy, the king was much pleased to hear. Together with this futile intrigue, Retz was pleading at Whitehall for the Catholics, and at Rome for the settlement of that important affair to which the alliance with Mazarin and the elevation of Aubigny were expected to contribute. The first of these subsidiary negotiations was speedily abandoned; the other was pursued with a strange pertinacity for several years.

At first Charles desired a mitre for his kinsman,[16] but he soon raised

---

[14] *Mémoires de Guy Joly*, p. 140, ed. Michaud.

[15] "Aujourd'hui la reine a reçu une lettre du roy son fils, où il parle positivement, et dit qu'après avoir considéré toutes les raisons de son mariage, il se conformoit à son sentiment pour vostre nièce, en vue du grand dessein à quoi il estoit porté de jour en jour avec plus de faveur" (Lionne to Mazarin, 7th July 1660, in Champollion, *Complément des Mémoires de Retz*, p. 589, ed. Michaud).

[16] Dod, *Church History of England*, iii. 239.

his demands, and insisted on having him created a cardinal. Clarendon, who was ignorant of the real design of which this was to be the prelude, entered into the idea, and drew up the instructions with which, in October 1662, the queen's secretary, Sir Richard Bellings, was sent to Rome. In the following year the Chancellor's share in these transactions was made a part of the abortive charge preferred against him by Bristol; and it appears from the articles that the great importance which was given to this negotiation, and the correspondence with the Roman cardinals, were generally known at the time. Retz advised Charles to secure the compliance of the Pope by sending a squadron to cruise off Civita Vecchia, and then proceeded to Hamburg to obtain the powerful intervention of the Queen of Sweden. He was charged at the same time with the distribution of a sum of fifteen thousand pounds, which Charles had determined to devote to the interests of Aubigny.[17] Letters were written by both the Queens of England to Cardinal Orsini, Protector of Portugal, urging him to press the suit, and assuring him that if the promotion should be refused, lamentable consequences might be apprehended from the disappointment of the king. Orsini, after an interview with Bellings, warmly took up the cause, and declared in a letter to the famous Cardinal Pallavicini, that he might, by assisting him, render a great service to religion. They also wrote to the two most influential men in Rome, Cardinals Chigi and Azzolini, the latter of whom was an active promoter of the design. His letter to the king, of 8th April 1663, advising the continuation of his efforts, and that of Cardinal Chigi, written on the following day, are in the State Paper Office.[18]

The question was maturely debated at Rome, and an opinion was drawn up in favour of Aubigny, founded partly on the statements of Bellings, and partly on the elaborate memorials of Retz, in which the services of the king were set forth. This opinion was to the following effect: the Restoration had improved the condition of the Catholics, and whatever relief they enjoyed was due to the influence of Charles himself, and was disliked by the Parliament and the country. The abolition of the penal laws could not be expected, for the royal authority was competent only to suspend them. Indeed, it might be considered almost more advantageous, under the circumstances, that the laws should be suspended than toleration proclaimed. For the same disa-

---

[17] *Mémoires de Guy Joly,* p. 149.
[18] Italian States, Bundle No. 24.

bilities from which the Catholics suffered extended in great part to the Presbyterians, and the other sects who were hostile to the monarchy. They could not therefore be abrogated without depriving the king of the weapons the law gave him to defend the crown against the Nonconformists, while a partial abolition would excite fresh envy against the Catholics, and add to the number of their enemies. Legislative toleration, inasmuch as its benefits would be shared by the Dissenters, was not to be desired, even if it could be obtained. It was necessary to rely solely on the power and the favour of the king. For his authority might be trusted not only as a security against the heretics, but also against that portion of the Catholics who were in opposition to the Jesuits. To his salutary influence was to be attributed the suppression of the measure for Catholic relief which had been brought forward in July 1662, in answer to the petition presented by that party, who had offered to swear that they did not hold the doctrine of the temporal authority of the Holy See, and that they would "oppose with their lives and fortunes the Pontiff himself, if he should ever attempt to execute that pretended power."[19] Again, when the Irish protestation of allegiance, which many leading Catholics had signed, was found in like manner to be very far removed from the obedience due to the Apostolic See, Charles had refused to countenance it, and had exhibited an unvarying respect for the Pope. Queen Henrietta Maria, who was now supporting the cause of Aubigny, had formerly obtained the same dignity for Conne, and only his death had prevented him from enjoying it. The state of the Catholics was more satisfactory and more hopeful than when the favour now asked for had been granted before, and the new king had in several ways shown that he was favourably disposed. Before leaving the Low Countries to ascend his throne, he had sent a rich present to the English nuns at Ghent. He had given audience to several Jesuits, and among others to two successive provincials, to whom he had promised his protection in case of need. He had been seen in a posture of adoration at high mass in the queen's chapel.

These were the views at that time entertained at Rome concerning the religious character of Charles II, and the arguments advanced in support of the promotion of Aubigny. Nevertheless the demand was rejected. The Pope's answer was conveyed in such terms that Charles

---

[19] Lingard, ix. 35.

was not offended, and accepted the explanation. The refusal, indeed, was only temporary. The solicitations of the English Court were soon after renewed, and they were at last successful. In November 1665, Aubigny, who was then at Paris, received his nomination, and died almost immediately after.[20] His name does not appear in the list of the cardinals created by Alexander VII, but his elevation, and the influence by which it had been obtained, were known, and had excited hopes for the Catholic Church in this country, which caused his death to be regarded as a serious calamity. The general of the Jesuits, on hearing of it, wrote to one of his correspondents: "The clouds which are gathering over Holland, Poland, and Constantinople are so dense, that every prudent man must see reason to apprehend enormous catastrophes, and storms that will not be ended without irreparable disasters. But in my mind all these coming evils are overshadowed by the death of the Abbé Aubigny, which deprives the Church, for a time at least, of the joy of beholding an English cardinal of such illustrious blood, created at the public instances of two queens, and at the secret request of a king: a prodigy which would without doubt have confounded heresy, and inaugurated bright fortunes to the unhappy Catholics."

The affair of the cardinal's hat was not the principal object of the mission of Sir Richard Bellings. It was intended as a preliminary to that more important negotiation which the envoy was instructed to reserve if the first should fail, and inspired Queen Catherine with so much anxiety, and Cardinal Orsini with such sanguine hopes of the advancement of religion. The two queens knew that Charles was at heart a Catholic, and they pressed him to declare himself. He was now firmly seated on his throne; the Established Church had recovered its supremacy, and was not only profoundly loyal, but still strongly impregnated with those Catholic tendencies which had hastened its fall; the Puritans and Independents were yet prostrate beneath the ruins of their political system, and the great body that reverenced Baxter as their chief was comparatively tolerant. Charles, believing that the step which would have prevented his return might now be taken without involving the risk of a new revolution, resolved to feel his way towards a reconciliation with the Holy See. In addition to the instructions drawn up by Clarendon, Sir Richard Bellings carried to Rome proposals for the submission of the three kingdoms to the

[20] Moréri, *Dictionnaire Historique*, ix. 597; his epitaph in Douglas, *Peerage of Scotland*, ii. 101.

Church, and presented to Alexander VII the king's profession of faith.[21] Charles declared that he was willing to accept the creed of Pius IV, the decrees of the Council of Trent and of all general Councils on faith and morals, and the decisions of the two last Pontiffs in the affair of the Jansenists, saving the particular rights and customs of the nation, as is the practice in France and in other countries, and provided always no new laws should be imposed upon his realm, and he should be free to complete in his own way the work of reconciliation. He declared that he renounced and detested all the heresies which had involved his country in ecclesiastical and civil troubles, and made England the most distracted State in the world. He undertook to restore the hierarchy as it was under Henry VIII; and added that the Protestants should have toleration as long as they did not disturb the peace.

In this very remarkable document, Charles, who believed that many of his subjects would follow his example, gave one of the earliest instances of what has since been constantly witnessed—that princes who, as head of the Protestant Church in their dominions, enjoy an almost unlimited authority, cannot view without jealousy the ecclesiastical liberty which is claimed by Catholicism. He carefully restricted the papal jurisdiction both of doctrine and discipline, and reserved to himself the rights which the Gallican system attributed to the secular power. He even proposed that the Church should abandon her essential function of judging and defining matters of faith as occasion should arise. Although this is a condition contrary to the nature of the Catholic Church, the document proposing it, which is followed by twenty-four articles on particular points, exhibits so much familiarity with ecclesiastical forms that it must have been drawn up by a Catholic hand. It is not probable that many persons were admitted on this occasion into the confidence of Charles. The whole scheme was not discussed beyond the door of the royal closet. It betrays the hand of a layman, for no priest could have expected the Church to discontinue her dogmatic progress; and Aubigny, the only priest likely to be consulted, was not likely to introduce the clause against Jansenism. Now we know that the secret was imparted to one lay Catholic, the agent who was charged with the negotiation. No man was more likely to be chosen for that important mission than he to whom the affair had been

---

[21] Oblatio ex parte Caroli II Magnae Brittanniae Regis pro optatissima trium suorum Regnorum Angliae, Scotiae et Hiberniae cum Sede Apostolica Romana reunione.

confided from the first, or who could discuss the proposals better than he who had helped to devise them. Bellings was a man of note and distinction among the Catholics in both islands, and was often employed by the court in confidential missions. His father had been one of the leaders in the opposition to the nuncio Rinuccini, and was the author of that protestation of allegiance which had been adopted by a large party in Ireland, and which was so badly received at Rome. The son was, therefore, not unlikely to suggest those limitations of ecclesiastical authority which he undertook to defend, and which corresponded with the views of his father and of those who, in the language of Bristol, were Catholics of the Church of Rome, not of the court of Rome.

The answer of Alexander was probably not very encouraging, for the negotiation was broken off. A suspicion was awakened that the king was in correspondence with the Pope, and Charles, in his alarm, took measures to prove his aversion of Catholicism. He opened Parliament on the 18th of February 1663 with a demand for new laws to restrain the progress of popery, and gave his assent to a proclamation ordering all priests to quit the kingdom under pain of death. He explained, five years later, in a letter to which I shall presently return, the failure of his negotiation, and the inconsistency of his subsequent conduct: "Quoy qu'elle nous fust présentée avec touttes les circonstances necessaires, et par personne catholique, touttefois ce ne peut estre avec tant de prudence que nous ne fussions soupçonnés d'intelligence avec le pape par les plus clairvoyants de nostre cour; mais ayant trouvé le moyen d'étouffer le soubçon que l'on començoit d'avoir que nous fussions catholique, nous fusmes obligé, crainte de ne le faire renaistre dans les esprits, de consentir aux occasions à plusieurs choses tournant au desavantage de plusieurs catholiques de nostre royaume d'Hybernie, ce qui est cause encore que bien que nous eussions escry assez secrettement à sa saincteté pour nostre rangement à l'eglise catholique, au mesme temps que nous prions sa saincteté de faire cardinal nostre très cher cousin le Milord d'Aubigny, dont nous fumes refusés pour bonnes raisons, nous n'avons peu poursuyvre nostre pointe." The scheme was not resumed for several years. Times were not propitious. The Dutch war, the Plague, the Fire, the Triple Alliance, intervened. Public animosity was inflamed against the Catholics; and Charles had no confidential agent whom he could employ without danger to propose, if not the reconciliation of the country, for which he was not disposed to make great efforts or great sacrifices, at least his own submission to the Catholic Church. During this interval, Jacques de la Cloche made his appearance for the first time in England.

In the spring 1646, during his first residence in Jersey, Charles fell in love with a young lady of high rank, who became the mother of a child, who enjoyed the prerogative, denied to all the other natural children of the king, of bearing his father's name. He was called James Stuart, and was brought up in the Protestant religion on the Continent. "Il nous est né lorsque nous n'avions guères plus de seize ou 17 ans, d'une jeune dame des plus qualifiées de nos royaumes, plustost par fragilité de nostre première jeunesse que par malice." The last words appear to indicate Charles's respect for the mother and the care with which he protected her fame. Unlike the Clevelands and Portsmouths who afterwards disgraced his court, the lady who was the object of his earliest attachment obtained of her royal lover the concealment of her fault, and her name has never been divulged. She is nowhere mentioned in the correspondence relating to her son; and if she died before his arrival in England, the reputation of her family may have induced the king to conceal his birth. After the Restoration he allowed him to remain abroad unnoticed, and under the disguise of an assumed name, until the year 1665. In that year he sent for him to England, supplied him with money, and gave him a certificate in which he recognised him as his son, but which he commanded him to show to nobody whilst his father lived. This document, written and signed by Charles's own hand, and sealed with his private seal, is dated Whitehall, 27th September 1665—a time at which the plague was at its height, and the court was not in London. For greater security he obliged his son once more to change his name. That which he had borne till then is not known. He was now called James de la Cloche du Bourg. It is not easy to say whether the last of these names may afford some clue to the discovery of his mother's family among the three thousand royalists who took refuge in Jersey at the same time as the Prince of Wales.[22] The former name had been made popular in that island when Charles arrived there by the spirit with which Mr. de la Cloche, a clergyman, had resisted the authority of Government.[23] After lying nearly a year in prison, he was released upon the arrival of the Prince, and then left the island. Had his release anything to do with Charles's private

---

[22] R. Augier to the Speaker, in Cary, *Memorials of the Civil War*, i. 7.
[23] Le Quesne, *Constitutional History of Jersey*, p. 325.

affairs? Was the boy christened by him, or afterwards committed to his charge?

James was unwilling to remain in England. It was not his country; he did not speak the language; he had no career and no recognised station; and his position was not to his taste. He had made great proficiency in his studies abroad, and he desired to continue them in the Dutch universities. His father did not know what to do with him in England, and allowed him to go. Eighteen months later, on the 7th of February 1667, he sent him another document, recognising his birth, and directing his successor to give him £500 a year. A condition was attached to the grant of this pension, that it could be enjoyed only while the claimant resided in London, and remained faithful to the religion of his fathers and to the Anglican liturgy. Six months after receiving this letter, on the 29th of July 1667, James Stuart became a Catholic at Hamburg.

The Queen of Sweden, who filled Europe with the fame of her abdication, her abjuration, her talents, and her eccentricities, was for the second time residing at Hamburg, and appears again on the scene of the secret history of Charles. She signed a paper for his son, certifying that he had been received into the Church at that particular place and time, in order that he might be able, in case of need, to satisfy his confessor of the identity of the convert of Hamburg with the Protestant whom the King of Great Britain had privately recognised as his son. This was now necessary, because he had determined, immediately after his conversion, to enter the novitiate of the Jesuits. Christine knew who he was, probably because he had been compelled to apply to her chaplains, or at least for her protection, in order to be received. The Senate of Hamburg exercised with extreme severity the right which the Treaties of Westphalia gave to each Government of exacting religious conformity; and the neighbouring town of Altona, peopled by the Catholics, Anabaptists, and Jews whom the Lutherans had expelled, grew up a monument of the intolerance of the Free City. The queen had attempted, some years before, to obtain freedom of conscience for her own religion through the intervention of the Catholic Powers; but the Emperor, whose rights were derived from the same treaty by which the senate justified its rigour, and who was not disposed to surrender them, refused to disturb the settlement of Münster. At the very time when James was converted, the town had been thrown into confusion by the uproar caused by a fête which Christine gave, in the midst of a Protestant population, to celebrate the election of Clement IX. Charles was much annoyed to learn that she was in his son's confidence. "She is prudent and wise," he said; "but she is a woman, and that is enough to make us doubt whether she is able to keep a secret."

James de la Cloche was hardly settled at Rome when his father determined to have him about his court. That vast intrigue had just commenced which was to raise France to the pinnacle of power, and which, by a timely subservience, promised to emancipate the princes of the House of Stuart from the control of Parliament, and from the terrors which had postponed the king's design of reconciliation with Rome. In that conspiracy the motives of religious belief and political ambition were strangely blended. Turenne, who was destined to be the foremost actor in the execution of the design, was a sincere Calvinist. He had shortly before refused the great dignity of Constable of France, when it was tendered as the reward of his conversion. On the 23rd of October 1668 Turenne became a Catholic. He was shortly after followed by his old lieutenant, a confederate in the new scheme, the Duke of York. James had applied to the Provincial of the Jesuits, and then to the Pope, for permission to conceal his religion, and had been told that it was impossible. With this answer he caught the conscience of the king. On the feast of the conversion of St. Paul, 1669, Charles summoned his Catholic counsellors, declared with tears how uneasy he was not to profess the faith which he believed, and consulted them as to the best mode of carrying out his resolutions. They concluded that the only way was to do it in conjunction with France.[24] A few months before this resolution was finally taken, in August 1668, Charles had written to the General of the Jesuits to send him his son, whose presence he needed for the good of his soul.

He had long sought in vain, the king said to Oliva, for a person with whom he could confer on spiritual matters without creating suspicion. The priests who lived in London were so well known that no disguise could conceal them;[25] but the conversion of his son, and his entrance into Orders, at length gave him an opportunity of receiving the sacraments without alarming the Protestant zeal of his subjects. His son might remain unknown, as the queens alone were aware of

[24] Clarke, *Life of James II*, i. 441.
[25] We know, from the account of his death, that none of the Portuguese chaplains of the queen could speak either English or French.

his existence; but before long he should be publicly acknowledged. "Plusieurs raisons considérables, et concernantes la paix de nos royaumes, nous ont empesché jusques à présent de le reconnestre publiquement pour notre fils; mais ce sera pour peu de temps, parceque nous sommes maintenant en dessein de faire en sorte de le reconnestre publiquement devant peu d'années." In case he was not a priest, and could not be ordained before starting, Charles directed that he should go to Paris, and address himself either to the king or to the Duchess of Orleans, who knew of his own design, and would have James ordained without betraying his rank; or, if he preferred it, the two queens would find an opportunity for his ordination in England. As soon as he had received his father into the Church, he would be free either to return to Rome or to live in England, so as to be within call; but not in London, lest people should suspect that the king's son was a Jesuit. This was written on the 3rd of August. On the 29th, Charles, having heard that the Queen of Sweden was on her way to Rome, wrote again to hasten the departure of his son; for he feared that Christine, if she saw him, would discover the purpose of his intended journey. If that should become known in England, he said, it would infallibly cost him his life. He therefore desired that his son, instead of stopping at Paris, should come with all speed to London, and there make himself known to the queen-mother by delivering to her a sealed letter in the form of a petition. This letter was scarcely sealed, when he wrote a third time to the General. It had occurred to his mother and his wife that a novice is not allowed among the Jesuits to travel alone. Charles hoped that this regulation would be dispensed with, and that his son would be permitted to set out by himself in the dress of a layman. Secret warning had already been given at the southern ports that a foreign prince, whose appearance was described as near that of James as possible, was about to seek refuge in England, and would arrive without any companion. The presence of a Jesuit father would have spoilt this plan. The better to meet the arrangements which had been made, the novice was to call himself Henry de Rohan, a name well known as that of one of the great Huguenot families of France. Charles declared on his royal word, *en foy de roy,* that the sole object of his letters was the salvation of his soul, and the good of his son and of the Order, and that he would either induce the Pope to make him a cardinal, or allow him, if he should prefer it, to remain a simple religious.

In the middle of October 1668 the young ecclesiastic started for England, disguised as a French cavalier. Together with his letters to Oliva, Charles had written to him in terms of the warmest affection. The temper of Parliament, he said, had hitherto made it necessary to defer the public acknowledgment of his birth, but the time was approaching when it would be possible for him to assume the rank which belonged to him. It behoved him, therefore, to reflect maturely on his altered prospects before entering irrevocably into sacred orders. His title was better than that of the Duke of Monmouth, and he had a right of precedence over him, "par touttes raisons, et à cause de la qualité de votre mère." The queen was childless, and the children of the Duke of York were delicate; and if the Catholic religion should be restored in England he would have a claim to the crown: "Nous pouvons vous asseurer que si Dieu permet que nous et notre très honoré frère le duc d'Yorck mourons sans enfans, les royaumes vous apartient, et le parlement ne peut pas legitimement s'y opposer; si ce n'est qu'en matière d'estre catholique vous en soyez exclus. . . . Croyez que nous vous avons toujours eu une affection particulière non seulement à cause que vous nous este né dans nostre plus tendre ieunesse, lorsque nous n'avions guères plus de 16 ou 17 ans, que particulièrement à cause de l'excelent naturel que nous avons toujours remarqué en vous."

Prince James Stuart, as the king now calls him, remained scarcely a fortnight in England. On the 18th of November he was sent back to Rome on a secret mission to the General of the Jesuits, with directions to return as soon as he had obtained what the king desired. It does not appear what that was. It is probable that Charles wished, like his brother, to be allowed to keep his change of religion a secret; and the application which James says that he made to the Pope at this time may have been conveyed, on the part of both brothers, by the youth whom Charles had already selected to be the medium of communication with the Holy See. The Duke of York's letter to the Pope required secrecy, and we know that no messenger was trusted by Charles but the young Stuart himself. This was not, however, the only condition he desired to exact in making his submission to the Holy See. We have seen the tenor of his demands in 1662. In his letters to his sister, published by Dalrymple, he mentions other points, which on the former occasion were probably included in the clause allowing him to carry out the details of the restoration of Catholicism in his own way.

"He talks," says Hallam, who has investigated the history of this period more carefully than any other writer, "of a negotiation with the court of Rome to obtain the permission of having mass in the vulgar tongue, and communion in both kinds, as terms that would render his conversion agreeable to his subjects."[26] Before departing for Rome, James must have assured his father that his resolution was fixed, and that he would live and die a Jesuit. Charles, who had promised not to interfere with his vocation, gave him a large subsidy for the new novitiate at St. Andrea on the Quirinal, which Oliva was then erecting, in addition to the old building of St. Francis Borgia. He also desired that on this second journey his son should be accompanied by a Jesuit; for, as he was not a priest, he was unable to receive his father into the Church, or to administer the sacraments to him. With these instructions James left England. From that day he disappears from history; and after his arrival in Rome, in November or December 1668, the name of De la Cloche, by which he was known in the novitiate, figures no more in the books of the society.

Towards the close of the year a young gentleman, who passed for an Englishman, and travelled with a servant and a well-stored purse, took up his abode at a very humble inn at Naples. The host had a daughter, Teresa Corona, whose extraordinary beauty won the heart of the guest. After he had satisfied the ecclesiastical authorities that he was a Catholic, they were married on the 19th of February 1669. It was not long before the attention of the neighbours was roused by their manner of life. Gold was observed to be suspiciously plentiful in the household of the poor innkeeper, and it began to be whispered that his English son-in-law was related to the King of Great Britain. Rumours came to the ear of the Spanish viceroy, who, in his solicitude for the honour of royalty, caused the stranger to be arrested. Letters were found in his possession bearing the title of Highness, together with many jewels and heaps of pistoles. He declared that he was Prince James Stuart, a son of the King of England, born in Jersey; and he sent for the English consul in order to obtain his release. But he could neither speak English nor give any satisfactory evidence in support of his statement. The viceroy wrote to England to ascertain the truth of the story, and in the meantime treated his captive as a prisoner of State, and sent him to the fortress of Gaeta, whilst he shut up his wife

[26] *Constitutional History,* ii. 387.

in a convent. Nobody knew what to believe. "Which," writes the English agent, Kent, to Williamson, on the 30th of March, "whether will end in prince or cheat I shall endeavour to inform you hereafter." The bewildered governor allowed his prisoner fifty crowns a month for his maintenance, and permitted his wife's family to visit him. Early in June came the answer of King Charles to the viceroy, who thereupon proclaimed the mysterious personage an imposter, removed him from his honourable confinement at Gaeta to the dungeons for common malefactors at Naples, and condemned him to be whipped through the city. Teresa Corona was taken from her convent on the discovery of her husband's real character; and the story, which was believed at the time, goes on to say that instead of being punished he was released at her intercession, and allowed to go to France, on a visit, as he affirmed, to his mother. Two months later he was again at Naples, asserting that his mother was dead. He called her the Lady Mary Stuart, of the house of the Barons of St. Mars, as it is in the contemporary English translation, or of San Marzo, as it stands in the Italian copy of his will; and said that it was in consequence of her relationship with the royal family that the king was unwilling to acknowledge him. The will is dated 24th August 1669, and two days later the testator died, reiterating his statements in the same breath in which he recommended his soul to the mercy of God and the intercession of Our Lady, in terms of the deepest piety and resignation. He appointed his cousin, Lewis XIV, his executor; demanded of Charles, for his unborn child, either the principality of Wales or Monmouth, or a royal dukedom, with an income of a hundred thousand crowns, besides his mother's fortune, amounting to £16,000 a year; and left enormous legacies to his wife's relations and to the Church. "And this," says Kent, "is the end of that princely cheat, or whatever he was." The cautious agent did not venture to determine the adventurer's quality; and in the manuscript letter of news sent weekly to the English Government, called the *Gazzetta di Roma,* from which most of his information was derived, the Englishman is constantly called the English prince.

Yet none of these contemporaries knew that there was actually at that time a son of King Charles born at Jersey of a lady of high rank, privately addressed as Highness, provided with money, and speaking French as his native tongue. Had they known it, and could they have discovered that the illegitimate prince was really called James Stuart;

that though a novice he was not ordained; and that all authentic traces of him were at an end from the moment of his arrival in Italy, at the very time when the English traveller put up at the inn of Corona—if, in short, their knowledge had extended generally as far as ours, and had stopped where ours stops, it is probable that they would not have hesitated to believe in the claims of the prisoner at Gaeta. The king's denial, and what followed, would not have shaken their conviction. Charles was always careful to conceal the existence of his son, and he was particularly tender of the mother's name. When informed that the young Jesuit who had refused his favour, and had gone forth to prepare the way for his father's conversion, was the husband of a publican's daughter at Naples, and had been thrown into prison after apprising the people of his rank and wealth, he would certainly not have responded to the appeal of the viceroy by a public acknowledgment. It was necessary, in order to shield the father, that the son should be proclaimed an impostor, and sentenced to condign punishment. But it was not necessary that he should be actually punished. Charles's interests were satisfied by his removal to the felons' prison, his sentence, and his immediate pardon. If the accusation had been true, the pardon could not have followed instantly on the discovery; the culprit, after leaving the scene of his disgrace, would not voluntarily have returned so soon; and he would not have mingled with his dying prayers the solemn repetition of a lie, which could serve no further purpose but to bring down disappointment and notoriety on his widow. The claims which he prefers for his child, though inconsistent with his own disinterested conduct, might have proceeded from a natural anxiety to provide for his posterity.

This is the case for the prisoner. It falls to the ground in cross-examination. The tenor of the will itself is fatal to it. The real James Stuart, who was sure of being able to obtain every just demand, would not have compromised the reasonable prospects of his family by the falsehoods and the extravagance of this document. He had, moreover, in his possession papers which proved his claim, and would have delivered him from the rigours of the Spanish governor. There was no reason for his sudden appearance at Naples at the very moment when he was charged with a negotiation of the greatest moment to his father, his Church, and himself. Nor would he have called his mother by a name and title which are unquestionably fictitious. And yet in that imaginary name and title there may perhaps be found a key to the mystery of the birth of the young James Stuart. For though the Neapolitan adventurer was an impostor, he enjoyed good sources of information, and possessed, though imperfectly, the secrets of King Charles's son. He knew that he was born at Jersey, and that his birth had been recognised by his father, and he had secured some of his papers and some of his property. All the wealth he showed at Naples did not come from that source, for the young novice was not so rich, and the impostor must have robbed other people. But he had certainly either accompanied, as his servant, the man he represented, or stolen his letters. Whatever be the secret of this strange adventure, it is so certain that it was not the real James Stuart who died at Naples in August 1669, that it is worth while to institute a further inquiry as to the probable events of his subsequent career.[27]

He must have returned almost immediately to his father's court; but here too he was compelled to lay aside the name which he had borne on his former journey. The same Henry de Rohan could not twice in two months seek an asylum in England without awakening the suspicions of that suspicious age. The name which he finally assumed is unknown, and we are unable with certainty to trace him further. But it can hardly be doubted that among the French Jesuits of that period the eldest son of Charles II may yet be identified. He was by speech and education a Frenchman, and it is likely that he again took a French name, and completed his novitiate in France or in Flanders. Had he quitted the Order, he would have taken with him the grant of his pension, which lies at Rome. Had he returned to Rome, he would have resumed his former name. Had he remained in England, it is hard to believe that he could have escaped discovery at the time of the Popish Plot, or among the clergy who frequented the palace. He did not succeed in effecting the actual reconciliation of his father with the Church, for it is certain that that event did not occur before the eve of Charles's death. When Charles feared that his brother would expose himself to danger by bringing a priest, and when James declared he would do it at the risk of his life, they could only allude to the law which made it penal to receive a convert. The mere administration of the Sacrament to one already Catholic could get no one into trouble.

---

[27] The papers from which this account is given are in the State Paper Office, "Italian States," Bundle 32; *Letters of Kent,* March 30, 1669, June 16, August 31, and September 7; *News Letters,* or *Gazetta di Roma,* of March 23, April 6, April 13, April 20, June 11, September 7. The will is in the Domestic Papers, Bundle for August 1669.

Huddlestone says that the king declared "that he was most heartily sorry for all the sins of his past life, and particularly for that he had deferred his reconciliation so long." This is implicitly confirmed by what he told Aprice, another priest, who wrote ten days later: "As Mr. Huddlestone himself has told me, by a particular instance of God's grace, the king was as ready and apt in making his confession, and all other things, as if he had been brought up a Catholic all his lifetime."[28] If we had not these proofs that Charles had not been received into the Church before his last illness, still there could be no doubt upon the subject, as the application of James for leave to conceal his religion was rejected, and the publication would also, in the case of the king, have been the necessary condition of his admission into the Church.

James Stuart's ministrations to his father must therefore have been confined to the discussion of the Catholic doctrines. It is possible that a memorial of these discussions and exhortations may still be extant. Manuscript copies of the two papers on religion, in the handwriting of Charles, which were found in his cabinet and published by his brother, were sent to Rome by Father Giudici, the confessor of Mary Beatrice. These copies, attested by King James's own signature, are in French. That which was printed in England was a translation. It would have been useless to publish a French text in England, where an immediate and general effect was required. There could be no object in sending a copy of the translation to Rome, where the original could be understood and interpreted. The title of the copies in Rome proves that the publication had already taken place. If the originals were printed, it would have been enough to send a printed copy, which would have possessed greater authenticity than a manuscript translation. It is impossible to compare the French and the English versions without perceiving that the latter is a translation of the former— inelegant, somewhat abridged, and not entirely faithful. The word *apogrifes*, which occurs in the French for *apocryphes*, shows that the papers were in the writing of a person who did not know theology. Father Giudici would not have allowed it to stand in the copy if it were not in the original manuscript of the king; but in the English edition the word was altogether omitted, probably because it would not be understood by Protestants in the sense in which the writer used it.

---

[28] Harris, *Life of Charles II*, ii. 391.

These papers, though in the handwriting of Charles II, were not composed by him. They are in the form of an argument, addressed by one person to another. For this he had no occasion, and he had no reason to write them in French. On the same ground, they cannot have been written by Bristol or Aubigny, to whom Burnet is inclined to attribute them. Bristol did not converse with the king in French. Aubigny, it is true, had spent most of his life in France, but he had not forgotten his native language. Little is known concerning him, but it is on record that his knowledge of English once saved his life. He was attacked at night by two English bloodhounds, who were kept in the garden of the Jacobins, and he pacified them by speaking to them in English.[29] Tallemant, who tells the tale, adds, that a thief who, being a Frenchman, had no means of making himself intelligible to the foreign dogs, was seized by them in getting over the wall, and soon despatched.

An ecclesiastic who conferred with Charles concerning his conversion after he had ascended the throne, and who knew French better than English, must have been the author of these compositions. This would bring the evidence to bear on the French priests about the queen-mother or the Duke of York, such as Mansuète or La Colombière. But the tone of these writings is not that which would be adopted by a foreign priest addressing the king. They are written with confidence, frankness, and even familiarity, and they must have been written by one who, though he could not write in English, might consider himself an Englishman. England is more than once spoken of as "nostre Angleterre." There is reason, therefore, to suspect that we have in these letters a record of the religious earnestness and filial piety of the Stuart who preferred a cloister to the steps of his father's throne.

Two years after the day when we lose sight of James Stuart, the question of the reconciliation of Charles II with the Catholic Church had become a part of European politics, and an element in confederations and treaties. Lewis XIV proposed that D'Estrées, then Bishop of Laon, and afterwards cardinal, the most successful negotiator in his kingdom, should be employed to bring the matter before the Holy See. Charles received the proposal coldly. He told the French ambassador that he had already made choice of an English priest to treat with the Pope for his conversion, and that instructions were being prepared for him.[30] Arlington undertook to hasten his departure; but he was then

---

[29] *Historiettes de Tallemant des Réaux*, vii. 293.

[30] Mignet, *Négociations relatives à la Succession d'Espagne*, iii. 232.

at St. Omers, and the illness of Clement IX made the king anxious to
wait, as he did not wish, he said, to confide his secret to a dying man.
It is most probable that the English priest at St. Omers, whom Charles
had already arranged to send to Rome, was the same through whom
he had previously opened the business. On his return from Rome at
the end of the year 1668, Prince James Stuart found that the king had
resolved to discuss his design with the ministers, and that the great
interests involved, and the choice of the mode, and the time of declaring
himself, would necessarily postpone the event. The negotiation with
France for the dissolution of the Triple Alliance, on which it depended,
required time, both on account of the secrecy which had to be preserved,
and of the vast preparations which were made for the war, which was
to be the signal for the change. James must have perceived that his
time had not arrived, and he was doubtless anxious to finish his
novitiate and to receive ordination. It is natural to conclude that he
would retire to some house of the Society where he could satisfy this
desire, and still be at hand whenever his father's plans were ripe, and
he should be summoned to be the instrument for their accomplishment.
The college of St. Omers, or the neighbouring English novitiate at
Watten, would be the fittest and likeliest place for him to inhabit.

We have no other probable record of his life. Once more, in the
midst of the excitement of the Popish Plot, the mysterious figure of a
foreign priest crosses the life of Charles. A gentleman told Welwood
that he was employed to bring over privately a Romish priest, then
beyond sea, by whose means the king had some secret matters to
manage. The king and the priest were a considerable time together
alone in the closet. At last the priest came out, with all the marks of
fright and astonishment in his face. Charles had been seized with a
fit, and the priest would have called for help; but the king, who feared
that their interview should become known, had strength and resolution
to hold him till he had recovered his speech.[31] Was this priest, with
whom Charles was in correspondence, whom he caused to be fetched
secretly from foreign parts, and the discovery of whose presence he so
passionately dreaded, his own son?

Among the letters of Oliva there is one that bears no date, addressed
to a king who is not named, respecting a certain Jesuit, whose name
is also concealed. This father, it appears, had received from the king

---

[31] Welwood's *Memoirs*, p. 146.

an important office, which he used for the purpose of interfering in affairs of State, and had not only made enemies by his imprudence, but had injured the interests of the king, and had alienated, by the acrimony and disrespect of his language, persons who belonged to the royal party. He was accused of bearing himself more like a prince than a religious, and his superiors feared that when the king, who was the protector of the Society, should be no more, they would incur great dangers through the animosity he had provoked. The General, therefore, asked leave to summon the father to Rome, promising that he should be treated with kindness. Of the seven kings then living in Europe, two, those of Sweden and Denmark, could not have been in friendly communication with the Jesuits, and neither of them in any way deserved to be called their protector. In France, in Spain, and in Portugal, it is difficult to understand what could be meant by the royal party, or by the fear of great calamities on the death of the king. Poland and England alone remain. Now there are in the collection other letters of Oliva to the King of Poland, and no secret is made about his name. The position of this father must have been quite peculiar. It is clear that he was not the king's confessor, and that he was not, like Father Petre, officially employed in political affairs; yet he had received from the king such a position that he could not be recalled like an ordinary Jesuit, and that the General was obliged to use elaborate precautions in order to obtain the king's consent, and to make the measure appear in his eyes as gentle as possible. This suggests a suspicion of some mystery. The general of the Jesuits writes to a sovereign, whose name he does not venture to publish, for permission to summon to Rome a father of the Society, who, though neither the confessor of the king nor a member of the Council, possesses considerable influence, and enjoys so much of the royal favour that, although his imprudence has injured the court, a pledge must be given in removing him that he will be treated well. If we imagine the Jesuit James Stuart established in England exercising some influence over his father and the men of his confidence, and led astray, partly by zeal, partly by the presumption engendered by his royal descent, to commit some acts of imprudence, such as those which were so soon after so greatly exaggerated by popular rumour, and so cruelly punished by the popular fanaticism, it would exactly answer all the conditions of the case. These letters of Oliva were prepared for publication by himself. Everything that is omitted is therefore designedly omitted, and the same caution which obliged him to conceal the name of the sovereign whom he addressed would have prohibited any more distinct allusion by which the position of the offending Jesuit might be betrayed.

These grounds, however, are far from sufficient to justify us in believing that James Stuart, who began life with so much discretion and reserve, afterwards became an ambitious and intriguing politician, and put in jeopardy his father's crown and the fortunes of his Order. That Order occupied in Poland a position in which great influence at court was combined with great unpopularity with his party among the nobles. At the election of 1668, a cry was raised that the new king should be forbidden to have a Jesuit for his confessor; and, at the same time, the grand Hetman, Sobieski, was taking a Jesuit confessor with him to bless his arms in the Turkish war. To him, in the year 1673, Oliva sent his congratulations on his election. He tells him that the Jesuits whom he may place over his conscience or his chapel must be faithful to their rule, and abstain from politics; and in speaking of the new king's affection for the society he uses a word, *svisceratamente*, that occurs in the same connection in the letter which is not directed. It may therefore refer to a father to whom Sobieski had committed some important functions in his court, and the name of the patron may be omitted lest the name of the offender should be surmised. Long after the probable date of this letter, John sent a bitter complaint to Oliva of the faults of the brethren in Poland. "I feel bound," he said, "both by interest and affection, to advise you to seek a remedy for the growing evils, and to remove from the Jesuits in Poland the too visible contagion of ambition and cupidity."[32] Between his predecessor and Oliva there had also been a friendly correspondence. Michael Korybuth was afflicted with a fabulous voracity. The stories told of the classical gluttons of antiquity are eclipsed by his horrible achievements. Once, it is related, the burghers of Dantzig presented him with a thousand China apples, and before night he had devoured them all. Oliva, like a prudent general, attacked this monarch at his weak point. A quantity of the finest chocolate has been sent to him from Mexico, and he straightway despatches one of his fathers to lay it at the feet of the King of Poland, "impelled," he says, "by a reverent solicitude to minister as well as I can to the weakness of your stomach, which has already been fortified by drugs of this kind." On the whole, then, it is

[32] Salvandy, *Histoire de Jean Sobieski*, ii. 97.

most probable that James Stuart is not the subject of the General's letter to the nameless correspondent; and comparing his letters written to the two kings it is more likely to have been sent to John Sobieski than to his respected but inglorious predecessor.

The manuscripts I have quoted, most of which I owe to the industry and kindness of Father Boero, librarian of the Gesu,[33] by whose care they have been brought to light and transcribed, reveal the influence actually exerted by religious sentiment in those transactions between Charles and Lewis XIV, which, as the occasion of the Popish Plot, and the commencement of that policy which terminated in the Revolution of 1688, occupy so important a place in our history. The intention of declaring himself a Catholic manifested by the king in the early part of his reign, and checked by the attitude of Parliament, was revived, as we have seen, in the summer of 1668. In the month of April Charles first expressed to the ambassador of Lewis the wish to

---

[33] I subjoin a list of the documents for which I am indebted to Father Boero. They are manifestly too long to be published *in extenso* in a Review.

1. Lettre de la Reine Mère (Henrietta) au Card. Orsini. De Londres, October 30, 1662.
2. Lettre de la Reine Catherine au même. De Londres, October 25, 1662.
3. Voto in favore della promozione al Cardinalato del Signor d'Aubigny.
4. Favori e benefizi fatti ai cattolici d' Inghilterra dal Re presente (in sixteen articles).
5. Bellings to Father Thomas Courtenay, October 22, 1662.
6. Lettera dal Card. Orsini al Card. Sforza Pallavicino. 24 gennaio 1663.
7. Oblatio ex parte Caroli II Magnae Britanniae Regis pro optatissima trium suorum regnorum Angliae, Scotiae et Hiberniae cum Sede Apostolica Romana reunione.
8. Certificate of Charles II in favour of Sieur James Stuart, his natural son.
9. Another certificate of the king to the same.
10. Certificate of Christine Queen of Sweden concerning the same, on his conversion at Hamburg.
11. Letter of Charles II to the General of the Jesuits, Oliva, at Rome. Whitehall, August 3, 1668.
12. Letter of Charles II to his son James Stuart at Rome. Whitehall, August 4, 1668.
13. Letter of Charles II to Oliva, General of the Jesuits, at Rome. Whitehall, August 29, 1668.
14. Letter of the same to the same, without date.
15. Reply of Oliva to the king's three letters. Livorno, October 14, 1668.
16. Certificate of Charles that he will pay the expenses of his son's voyage. November 18, 1668.
17. Letter of Charles to Oliva. Whitehall, November 18, 1668.
18 and 19. Two Memoirs written by Charles II on the Catholic religion.

form an alliance with his master.[34] As he had lately joined a league of Protestant Powers, whose purpose it was to arrest the ambition of that monarch, he desired that the understanding between them might be private. He said that he wished to treat as between gentlemen, and that he preferred the word of Lewis to all the parchments in the world. At first Lewis received these advances with reserve, and Charles and his brother were unwilling to trust to the ambassador the secret object of their overtures. But early in 1669 Lord Arundel was sent to Paris, accompanied by Sir Richard Bellings,[35] who was instructed to draw up the articles of the treaty by which England was to join France against the Dutch; while Lewis undertook to support Charles with money, that he might be able to declare himself a Catholic without having a parliament to fear. Of the two leading ministers of the Cabal, the Catholic Arlington was friendly to the Dutch alliance, whilst Buckingham, a Protestant, was a partisan of France. Though the latter encouraged the notion of a French alliance, he knew nothing of his master's design relative to the Catholic religion. It was confided to Arlington, and at length overcame his political scruples, but he was never reconciled to the war with Holland, and he endeavoured to postpone hostilities until the change of religion had been declared. The French envoy suspected that he wished to delude Lewis into supplying the means by which the king's conversion could be published without danger, and when that was done, to avoid quarrelling with the Dutch. The confidential envoys of Charles at Paris evidently entertained the same idea,[36] and the scheme was near succeeding.

Charles opened his mind to the French ambassador, the brother of the great Colbert, on the 12th of November 1669. It was, he said, the most important secret of his life, and he would probably be considered mad, and all those with him who were undertaking to restore Catholicism in England. Nevertheless he hoped, with the help of Lewis, to succeed in that great work. The sects hated the Established Church more than the Catholic religion, and would make no resistance if they obtained the freedom they desired. The great fortresses were in the

---

[34] See the Despatches of the French ambassadors Colbert and Ruvigny in Mignet, iii. 10 sq, and iv. 42 sq.

[35] Clarke, i. 442.

[36] "Il m'a paru que l'affaire de religion étant ce qui tient le premier lieu dans l'esprit de M. le Comte d'Arondel, il n'y a que le retardement de la déclaration qui le touche; et comme il croit que la guerre contre les Hollandais produiroit cet effet-là, c'est la seule raison pour laquelle il s'y oppose" (Turenne to Ruvigny: *Mémoires de Turenne*, i. 669).

hands of trusty men, and the Irish army might be relied upon, for Lord Orrery, who was at heart a Catholic, would take the lead if Ormond should refuse. On this point Charles was mistaken, for Orrery was sent for, and had an interview with the king, in which he was informed of the design, and refused to take part in it.[37] "He ended by saying that he was urged by his conscience, and by the confusion he saw increasing daily in his kingdom, to the diminution of his authority, to declare himself a Catholic; and that, besides the spiritual advantage he would derive from it, he considered also that it was the only way of restoring the monarchy." Lewis applauded the intention, but advised that it should be postponed until after the war; for he feared that he might be deprived of the assistance of England by the internal dissensions which that measure would be sure to provoke. These two influences contended for a while in the mind of Charles, but he had not strength of purpose to resist the pressure that came from France.

Arlington said of him, that he saw at once what was to be done in every affair that was submitted to him, and supported his opinion with good reasons, but that he did not take the trouble to go into the objections that were made, and, if he was spoken to again, often allowed himself to be carried away by the opinions of others.[38] This description was now verified. Charles shrank from the incongruity of the life he was then leading with a conversion which would be an arduous political undertaking. "The danger," says Colbert, "greatly alarms all who are in the secret, yet it has no effect on the mind of the king. But his mode of life—un peu de libertinage, si j'ose parler ainsi—makes him put it off as long as he can." The famous journey of Henrietta, Duchess of Orleans, to Dover, in May 1670, settled the question in favour of France. The treaty which was then signed by the four Catholic counsellors of Charles was first published from the English copy by Lingard. Mignet gives it from the French archives, and the texts do not entirely correspond.

Henrietta was in the secret of the whole scheme from the beginning, and we learn through her that Charles was at that time in direct communication with the Holy See. There was a French prelate whom she patronised, Daniel de Cosnac, Bishop of Valence and afterwards Archbishop of Aix, a clever, witty, and extravagant man, highly ambitious of a cardinal's hat. A year before the treaty was signed she

[37] Morrice, *Life of Orrery*, p. 86.
[38] *Mémoires de Gourville*, p. 566, ed. Michaud.

wrote to him that, among a variety of affairs which were being treated between France and England, this country would soon have one with Rome of such consequence, and on account of which the Pope would be so happy to oblige the king her brother, that she was persuaded he would refuse him nothing. She had already taken her measures with him to make him ask for a cardinal's hat, without saying for whom; Charles had promised, and it was to be for Cosnac.[39] After her return from Dover, but a few days before that tragic death scene which Bossuet has made memorable by the most striking of his orations, she informed the Bishop that she had succeeded in her mission, and that her brother had given her his word once more. Cosnac was not satisfied with these assurances. The influence of a Protestant king appeared to him a poor security for his elevation. But the Duchess told him that she not only had her brother's promise, but that the Pope had already granted his request, and she informed him, he says, of all that had passed between Pope Clement IX and the Kings of France and England.[40] This statement is not, however, supported by any of her letters that have been preserved; and we must bear in mind the judgment of his biographer, the Abbé de Choisy, on the character of Cosnac: "He is a man of surprising vivacity, and of such eloquence that it is impossible to doubt his words, although their number is so great that they cannot all be true." The agent on this occasion appears to have been the Lady Diana Digby, daughter of the Earl of Bristol, who had been so eager, six years before, to bring home to Clarendon a charge of corresponding with the Pope and cardinals. In June 1669, she arrived at Rome, in the coach of Cardinal Rospigliosi, the Pope's nephew, and lived for a time in one of his palaces so privately that her own cousin, James Russell, was not allowed to see her. But she was in correspondence with the English priests, and it was believed in Rome that the nomination of Archbishop Plunket to the See of Armagh, which was much opposed by Spain, had been obtained by her influence.[41]

Before anything could be done, the design was again betrayed, and

---

[39] *Mémoires de Cosnac*, i. 383.

[40] *Ibid*. ii. 81. "Retardabant eum voluptates blandissimae dominae, et quaedam iners et pene somniculosa natura, quam tamen plura animi ingeniique bona comitabantur. Huic quidem stimulos admovisse suspicor Clementem per occultos homines" (Fabroni, *Vitae Italorum*, ii. 107).

[41] State Paper Office, "Italian States," Letters of Kent, June 29, July 6, August 10, 1669.

once more, and for the last time, Parliament intervened. It was generally believed that the object of the war against Holland was the establishment of the Catholic faith. It is said that Arlington divulged the secret, partly in order to ruin Clifford, and partly to dissolve the French alliance. Even Protestant statesmen, talking in private with the king, spoke of it as a thing about which there was neither doubt nor concealment. Temple, before returning to the Hague in 1674, had an interview with Charles. He went, as he expresses it, to the bottom of the matter, showing how difficult, if not impossible, it was to set up here the same religion and government that was in France, and assuring him that even those who were indifferent to religion would not consent to have it changed by force of an army.[42] Charles relinquished his design, and recalled the warning which his father on the scaffold had intended to impress on his son, as well as on Juxon, by the famous word "Remember"—that if ever he came to the crown, he should so govern his subjects as not to force them to extremities. He declared that he was too old to go abroad again, and that he left that to his brother, if he had a mind to try it. For the ten remaining years of that reign, James took the lead in all the schemes for the restoration of the Church. It was of him that Coleman wrote in his fatal letter to La Chaise: "If he could gain any considerable new addition of power, all would come over to him as the only centre of our government, and nobody could contend with him further. Then would Catholics be at ease, and His Most Christian Majesty's interest secured with us in England, beyond all apprehensions whatsoever." But the most Christian king, as he had prevented the declaration of religion before the Dutch war, endeavoured afterwards to have the design abandoned. He found that the English Parliament was not averse to the French alliance provided it was not used for the promotion of Popery and arbitrary power in England; and Lewis was quite willing that religion should be sacrified in order to save his popularity with the English Protestants. Finding that the supposed connection of the king's conversion with the French alliance had brought suspicion on his ambassador, he replaced him by Ruvigny, who was a Calvinist. The new laws which were made against the Catholics, for the purpose of diverting suspicion, received his approbation; and he acted upon the hint given him by Bristol, that the House of Commons would be

[42] Courtenay, *Memoirs of Sir W. Temple*, i. 425.

favourable to the French alliance if the belief in the existence of the secret treaty for the restoration of Catholicism could be removed. That unhappy scheme defiled all that it touched, and neither those who shared in it nor those who condemned it came out of the transaction with honour.

If in the seventeenth century, which achieved so much for civil liberty, freedom of conscience was not established in England, the fault lay with the oppressed communities as much as with the crown or the dominant church. The Catholics and the Protestant sects were alike intolerant. The latter deserved what they received, and justified by their theories and their acts the penal laws by which they suffered. They were ready to do to others what was done to them. No religious party in the country admitted the right of minorities to the protection of the law. Religious liberty grew up in England as the fruit of civil liberty, of which it is a part, and in conjunction with which it has yet much way to make. But if the Protestants were not sincere in arguing for toleration, the Catholics were not honest in the means by which they endeavoured to obtain it. They sought as a concession that which was a right; they wished for privilege instead of liberty; and they defended an exception and not a principle. The Catholics of that age had degenerated from the old mediaeval spirit, which stood by the right and respected the law, but did not stoop to power. In the great constitutional struggle they disregarded the impending absolutism and the outraged laws, and gave to the royal cause, when it was most in fault, a support which, by prolonging the contest, drove the parliamentary opposition into lawless extremes, and postponed for half a century the establishment of freedom. After the Restoration they again trusted their interests to the favour of the court, and were willing to purchase advantages for their religion by political guilt, and to gain private ends at the price of a common servitude. That criminal and short-sighted policy brought quick retribution upon them, and explains how the party which saved the constitution in 1688 imposed disabilities on those who, by similar inconsistency, had been the declared adversaries of that freedom which their church had helped to institute.

[9]
Review of Gardiner's
History of England,
1603–1616

Mr. Gardiner chooses the period between 1603 and 1616 for his history of England, because it was the time during which, he says, the Constitution put on that Stuartine development of the supremacy of the prerogative, with power to suspend the sittings of Parliament, and to remove judges at will, which was combated by the Rebellion and the Revolution of 1688. He begins his history with a brief review of the political and religious developments of England up to the death of Elizabeth; and from that period to 1616 he gives a careful narrative of events, drawn up with continual reference to the original documents in the State-Paper Office, recently catalogued by Mrs. Green. His conclusions he regards as still liable to be modified by papers possibly existing in the archives of Simancas, now being gradually examined, and in the Hatfield Library, which the jealousy of its proprietor still makes useless to every one. This part of Mr. Gardiner's book is worked out with great candour and consecutiveness. His faults do not arise from party-spirit, or want of conscience, or want of knowledge, or study of inferior materials, but from his general conception of the province of the historian.

In its general scope his history is not a narrative written to show the triumph of right, or what he conceives to be so, and viewing all events from the moral elevation of a strong antecedent bias; but neither is it a passionless exposition of the series of events in their mechanical

Samuel Rawson Gardiner, *History of England from the Accession of James I to the Disgrace of Chief Justice Coke. 1603–1616*, 2 vols. (London: Hurst and Blackett, 1863). This review was published in the *Home and Foreign Review* 3 (July 1863):296–297. *Wellesley* I, p. 552. Acton-Simpson III, pp. 104, 109, 112, and 113 seem to leave some doubt as to whether Acton or Simpson actually wrote the review, but the description of the school of Carlyle reads like pure Acton.

and metaphysical relation of cause and effect. He belongs to Mr. Carlyle's school—a school which seeks to unite the moral interest of the first kind of history with the veracity of the second, by making itself the partisan of the fact, by subjecting the right to the test of success, and by assuming that the conquering cause was the favourite of the gods. A historian of this school will select any great Power that exists or has existed in the world, and trace the steps by which it came to be. In the history of this individual Power, every man who contributed to consolidate it is set forth as a hero, and every one who opposed it, and was crushed by it, as an idiot. Whether the Power is the English Constitution, or the Reformation, or the Napoleonic Empire, or the Prussian Kingdom, or the English Commonwealth, or the great war that ended with Waterloo, its central figure is always the hero of its history, and his might measures right, while opposition to him is the universal form of evil. Every reader of Hegel can recognise the pantheistic principle which lurks in this treatment of history as a war of Forces, in which the greater Force is the more ample manifestation of the Universal Mind. However successful such a school may be in particular histories, it is clear that it is powerless to construct a universal history. For it has no one principle but to accept success as the justification of a policy; and since nearly all principles have had their successes, nearly all are justified by it. But the school is well able to write monographs and particular histories. For as it makes success the final test of right, there is no previous idea which the facts are forced to illustrate; and as in the eyes of the historian the event proves the balance of right to be on the winning side, he can afford to allow for minor mistakes and lesser wrongs, which may diminish the final total, but do not alter its sign. Thus Mr. Gardiner says, "Some, either real or apparent, Antinomian sentences in Luther's polemical opinions cannot for a moment weigh against the hearty morality of his life, and the general tendency of his doctrines."

It is therefore in the general views of his preliminary chapters that Mr. Gardiner shows the weakness of his school—warping the great principles of universal history to illustrate his particular issue, the growth of the British Constitution, and the failure of the Stuarts to impress their stamp permanently upon it. In general, this part of the book is an echo of the current prejudices of Englishmen, not corrected by any original investigation, as in the later chapters, but seasoned with a show of liberality and candour which can afford to praise every institution while it had vitality—that is, while it was victorious.

[10]
Ranke

Within an interval of very few months Ranke has published a fifth edition of his *Popes*, a large volume on William III, and the two first volumes of a revised collection of his works. All literature can show no historian whose fame rests on so many separate masterpieces. His earlier writings gave an impulse to the study of history, which has produced, in an abundance such as nobody dreamed of, information that was inaccessible when they appeared. To bring them up to the level of what is now expected would overtask the powers of a man who is past seventy. The late edition of the *Popes* was made with so little preparation that blemishes which the author's later studies must have revealed to him long ago, are left as they stood when the knowledge of the sixteenth century was in its infancy. Fifty years of unremitting labour have matured his mind, but without adding to the faculties by which the triumphs of his youth were won. Practice has taught him to rely more on his tact than on his rules; he divines much that he does not prove; and the weight of his own opinion makes him careless of his authorities. The *Popes* cannot be a classic for this age as it was for the last. Time makes its defects more glaring; and no assiduity can superadd the qualities which would now be looked for, to those original merits which gave it an influence in an important branch of learning such as no book has since acquired.

Much of the success was due to the happy choice of the subject. Definite and familiar topics cannot be profitably treated, unless the historian not only exhausts the existing knowledge, but adds to it. There are competitors to outbid; the heading of successive chapters, the authorities to be consulted, are already known to the public; and

Leopold von Ranke, *Englische Geschichte vornehmlich im sechszehnten und siebzehnten Jahrhundert,* vol. 6 (Leipzig: Duncker und Humblot, 1866). This review was published in the *Chronicle,* 20 (July 1867):392–394. Ryan, p. 389.

the writer has to struggle with the ballast accumulated by a hundred predecessors. The novelty which does not reside in the subject must be imported by the author. In the *Popes* the subject itself, as Ranke viewed it, was almost a discovery. The historian wandered through pleasant fields, crossing diagonally the beaten paths which others trod. It is not exactly a history of Rome, or of Italy, or of the Church, or of modern Europe; but just so much of each as there were materials at hand for. It does not give a presentable history of a single pontificate, but fragments and illustrations of very many. The great stream is not there, but its course is marked by a string of lakes. We see a line of skirmishers, but not the chief array. In a miscellaneous subject, the books used, though common enough in their own departments, do not seem obvious, and suggest vast research. The life of Palestrina is not very recondite; but Ranke's devious method leads him to consult it for the Council of Trent, and he exults at the farfetched prize. There is a sort of affectation with which, after a book has yielded a particular extract, it is ceremoniously dismissed as otherwise worthless. In this way Ranke treats Daru, Capefigue, and Van der Vynckt; and he has not got rid of the habit in his English history. In the second volume he uses that wonderful letter in which James I, rebuking the presumption of Somerset, lays down with force and earnestness, and almost with dignity, his theory of royal favourites. But he immediately adds that Mr. Halliwell's book, in which it appeared, has nothing else to recommend it. Compared with the later performances of the author, the *Popes* was not, in truth, a book of great power or research; but it taught by its example the critical use of printed, and the value of unprinted, sources. Before Ranke appeared modern history was in the hands of Robertson and Roscoe, Coxe and Sismondi, good easy men whose merit consisted chiefly in making things more accessible which were quite well known already. But it was beginning to be understood that historical writing requires complex and methodical literary preliminaries, of which the writers on modern history knew no more than Hooke, or Hume, or Mitford. When the text of a chronicler has been ascertained, there is much remaining to be done before his statements can be accepted. His character, position, and opportunities must be investigated; his design and motives enquired into; above all, it is necessary to examine the materials of which his narrative is constructed, and to resolve it into its component parts. These principles, after having effected a revolution in the study of antiquity, had been applied by Stenzel to the Middle Ages, when Ranke adopted them in modern history. He first made himself known as a critic of published histories; and it does not appear that he was induced to resort to archives by the insufficiency of printed materials. The celebrated John Müller, in his dreamy way, had called attention to a collection of Italian documents in the Berlin library, and there Ranke opened those investigations which he pursued at Vienna, and then more seriously at Venice and Rome. It was a new vein, and a little produce went a great way. The reports which the Venetian ambassadors made at the close of a three years' residence abroad were first brought into notice by him; but the time was not long in coming when no historian would be content without the whole of the ambassadors' correspondence, day by day. Thirty years ago the use of a few unconnected reports, or a few casual instructions, implied a miracle of research. At first, Ranke employed his manuscripts like his books, to give point rather than solidity to his narrative. When he came to a well-cultivated field, the German Reformation, he found so little new matter, that Eichhorn fell into the mistake of concluding, from the poverty of his harvest, that the soil was exhausted, and that our knowledge of that eventful period was destined to have no further accessions. Ranke was not willing to admit that modern history is buried in myriads of documents yet unseen, and that the composition of books fit to live must be preceded by the underground labour of another generation. The manuscripts served him rather as a magazine of curiosities than as the essential basis of a connected history; and he has been accused of indifference to the publication of further papers, at least when they were taken from archives which he had consulted. In his *Traité de Législation*, Mably prophesied a long duration to the Swedish Constitution of 1720: before the book appeared the Constitution had been upset. Mably exclaimed: "Le roi de Suède peut changer son pays, mais il ne changera pas mon livre." The stories told of Ranke's impatience of the gleaners who plod after him parody that speech. Nevertheless he set the example of that occasional miscellaneous use of unpublished materials as a subsidiary aid to history, which has been followed by the school now predominant in Belgium, Germany, and France, and which has diffused much light, but concentrated little. In the *Popes* there are even portions of the text which possess nearly the value of direct original authority: such, for instance, as the description of the occupation of Ferrara by Clement VIII, which is founded on the contemporary memoirs of the Venetian

Thuanus, Nicholas Contarini, which are to be found among the manuscripts of several European libraries. And the first volume of his History of the Reformation, which opens the series of his collected works, has gained notably by the researches made since its first appearance.

The new volume of the History of England is written in striking contrast to the *Popes*. The sparkle is gone, but there is much more body. The striving for effect has disappeared. Hallam's Constitutional History, or Guizot's Memoirs, are less solid and not more grave. This is not a history by glimpses and flashes, but a patient, consecutive narration, offering an unbroken chain of causes and effects, in which the relative importance of events is distinguished with a care and judgment that would be impossible in pictorial writing. Ranke has gone out of his way to avoid comparisons. The siege of Londonderry, the relief of Limerick, the victory and death of Dundee, scenes which Macaulay has made as vivid as anything in epic poetry, are described with elaborate dulness. The book suffers not only from the want of colour, but from the want of sympathy. Except William III it has hardly any living characters. Marlborough, Seymour, Somers, Montague, and Shrewsbury are expressions standing for a certain quantity of force or talent, or a certain kind of opinion. They are effigies, but they are not men. It is hard to imagine a more remarkable position than that of Russell at La Hogue. He wished that the French might escape him, and that James might be restored, and in that frame of mind it was his fortune to crush the French fleet. Ranke knows the minutest particulars; he sees the interest of the thing; he says that it is very curious, but his account is incredibly unreal and reflected. This want of interest in his personages contributes to make him so reserved in his moral judgments. His description of the massacre of Glencoe is most exact, and betrays not the least temptation to diminish the guilt of William. Perhaps the case against him has never been put in a more damaging way. But not a word of criticism is wasted upon it. It was an action (*eine Handlung*), an incident (*eine Begebenheit*), which posterity has made a subject of reproach to the memory of King William. But to say that it was a crime would not make it more intelligible, and would not help forward the narrative. The disregard for the question which amuses ingenious boys and idle men, whether people were good or bad, extends from persons to ideas, from the question of moral virtue to the question of intellectual truth.

The problems discussed in William's reign, as to the limitation of the royal power by Parliament, and the control of Parliament by the nation, are at the root of all the political agitation of modern Europe. The debates were the nursery of political philosophy, and are as interesting as the experiments which preceded the discoveries of natural science. Ranke shows faithfully the conflict of the systems, but he does not enquire whether either of them was the right one, and does not perceive in the midst of an apparent chaos, truth fighting its way against the resisting influences of habit and of profit. He describes the proceedings at the trial: he does not say that the verdict has long been pronounced. It is as though one should write a biography of Galileo or of Harvey without admitting that anything is definitely known about the hypothesis of the movement of the earth, or of the circulation of the blood. History, in Ranke's conception, is a science complete in itself, independent, and ancillary to none, borrowing no instruments, and supplying no instruction, beyond its own domain. This dignified isolation involves a certain poverty in the reflections, a certain inadequacy of generalization. The writer seldom illustrates his facts from the state of ancient or general learning, or by the investigation of legal and constitutional problems. He does not explain the phenomena by political laws, the teaching of observation and comparison; and he has no care for literature, or for the things, apart from politics, which manifest the life and thought of nations. He is more conversant with the shifting relations of cabinets and factions than with the convictions, errors, prejudices, and passions that urge the masses of mankind and sway their rulers. He keeps these things at a distance, lest they should impede the clearness of his vision. They touch him not, and he chooses not to contemplate them. Hence his later works especially are tame and frigid compared with the books of men who have not a tenth of his learning or any conception of the disciplined and inquisitive energy which has raised him to be the Niebuhr, almost the Columbus, of modern history.

Ranke has nowhere defined what he conceives to have been the real essence of the conflict between William and James, and the cause of its importance in general history. In one or two characteristic passages he invokes the goddess Necessity, fixed fate, and unrelenting, force with an awe worthy of Aeschylus. But there is a hidden under-current running counter to the assumptions on which men are used to judge the great struggle, and take their side in it. The account of home politics goes to prove that William was not a friend of popular liberties; the account of foreign affairs shows that he was not the champion of the Protestant religion. Of all foreign courts the one most interested in the success of his expedition was the Court of Vienna. The Emperor had the Turkish war on his hands, while Lewis XIV was intriguing to have his son elected King of the Romans, and to obtain the succession of the Spanish Crown. The Revolution which detached Great Britain from the French alliance was an immense relief for Leopold, and he answered James's petition for assistance by telling him that he had brought his disaster on himself by his untimely zeal. The Austrian and Spanish envoys are accordingly found at once on confidential terms with the Prince of Orange, and he assured Ronquillo that he might be trusted as a good Castilian. At that time the Habsburgs represented the Catholic cause. Lewis XIV was on the point of making war on the Pope, who refused money for the support of James on the plea that all his resources were needed to protect his dominions against the French. He spoke of France as an anti-Catholic power, and armed as for a religious war. It was the first occasion since the Reformation on which by common consent Europe abandoned even the pretence of guiding policy by religion. The aid of the prince who ruled over the two great maritime States was necessary to the Catholic Powers, and their friendship was essential to the stability of his throne. In his domestic policy he was not a liberal sovereign, and the best parts of Ranke's volume are those which describe his efforts to maintain intact the power which had belonged to the Stuart kings. His countrymen in the Netherlands accused him of arbitrary acts; and the meditated treason of men like Russell was provoked by the discovery that William was a more dexterous and more formidable adversary of popular liberties than James. It was a necessity of his position to observe the capitulation of Limerick, for, until Ireland was pacified, he was robbed of much of his military power. This was prevented by the violence of the Irish Parliament, which united zeal against the Catholics with ardour aganst the Prerogative. The situation suggested the famous argument of Molyneux—that Ireland, being a conquered country, was subject to the royal pleasure. All these things pointed in one direction. William required all the resources of his kingdom and of his crown to carry on the war which was the object and the passion of his life. The opposition and the intolerance of Parliament were both impediments to his action. Richard Temple, one of the popular spokesmen, was the first to move the revival of the old penal laws. William's authority was as closely linked with the cause of toleration as that of James had been with the dispensing Power. He did not belong to the Established Church, in whose behalf the penal enactments were made. His doctrines were as odious to Episcopalians, and at least as much dreaded by them, as those of James. It was to exclude successors of his faith that the clause limiting the Protestant succession was inserted in the Act of 1701. He called the Anglican ceremonial a comedy. When the Scots required him to promise that he would exterminate heretics, he replied that he would not be a persecutor. In the Irish Parliament the favour which he ventured to show to Catholics was violently denounced. Ranke affirms that events had made toleration a necessity of policy, and that William bore it aloft at all times on his banner. And if his volume has any loftier theme than intrigues of ambition and trials of strength, it is the establishment of religious freedom in the country which had become the stronghold of civil freedom.

It is true that the personal position of William III and his international policy required that Catholic and Presbyterian should alike remain unmolested. But Parliament thwarted the design, and religious oppression kept pace during his reign with the increase of parliamentary influence. The power of the crown was effectually restricted, and a parliamentary power was substituted for it, equally absolute, equally ambitious, and less easy to resist. The Revolution did not establish the principles of liberty; and it is liberty acknowledged as a principle, not liberties obtained by compromise and concession, that generates toleration. The inherent connection of civil and religious freedom was not understood in England until the extinction of the Jacobite party. Somers and Locke were men of a more enlightened liberality than William, and less jealous of maintaining the State power; and they were eminently fitted to pursue a principle to its consequences. Yet they were not friendly to the liberty of conscience. Something of the same confusion which deceived those illustrious men bewilders the keen, clear, cold intellect of the great Prussian historian. During the last years of his life James and not William represented the cause of toleration. On the throne he had been animated by the desire to achieve, not liberty, but victory, for his Church—that is, by a religious, not a political or philosophical motive. He raised an issue between two religious interests, not between two principles of government, and that error cost him his throne. Some years later, when his fortune was beginning to prosper, Middleton induced him to declare that he would maintain the Test; and Ranke is persuaded that this concession would have accomplished his restoration. At the last moment James revoked the promise, and the scheme at once broke down. Now, as between those who insisted on the Test, and James who rejected it, the cause of toleration is on the side of James. On that occasion the question of the royal authority caused no difficulty. The English finally refused to have James for their king, not because of his unpopularity, or of his faith, or of his arbitrary maxims, but because he would not preserve religious disabilities. Ranke pronounces that in this matter he acted the part of a bigot. In our judgment, it is the most honourable act in the public life of James II, and gives a dignity to his exile which was wanting in the days of his greatness, and at the moment of his fall.

In this volume, as in all the works of the author, there is much new matter. He has examined in the French archives the correspondence of Marshal Tallard during his embassy to London, and the despatches of Lauzun and D'Avaux on the expedition to Ireland. Holland supplies printed as well as unprinted documents, which it is not creditable to previous writers to have overlooked. The correspondence between William and Heinsius has been partially used; but the extracts recently made known by Noorden prove that there is much more than this in the Heinsius papers, and that a vast accession of important knowledge may be expected from their publication. The manuscripts of the British Museum have been, we suspect, rather hastily consulted. Melfort's despatches from Rome would have thrown additional light on the negotiations of the banished Court. The most valuable addition has been the discovery of the correspondence of the Brandenburg envoys, extending over many years. The Elector was represented by two Swiss brothers, named Bonnet. They were well-informed and impartial; and their letters give an uninterrupted narrative of events at court and in the parliament. They enable the historian to restore lost debates; and it is due to them that Ranke has surpassed his predecessors in domestic politics, and not only in international affairs, where he is always supreme.

[11]
The Rise and Fall of
the Mexican Empire

The scene of the tragedy which I will attempt to describe is a country on which Nature's fairest gifts have been lavished with an unsparing hand, but where man has done his utmost to thwart the designs of Providence. Its social condition is so far removed from our experience that I must ask you to forget this evening the maxims and even the political terms we use nearer home.

Mexico possesses a territory more than thrice as large as France, with the fertility of the tropics, and the climate of the temperate zone, seated between two oceans, in the future centre of the commerce of the world. Its wealth in precious metals is so enormous that the time will come when the market will be flooded with silver, and its price will not allow the mines to be worked with profit. The only drawbacks on its prosperity are the badness of the harbours, the excessive dryness of the plains, and the disappearance of the forest timber, a curse which almost always follows the footstep of the Spaniard.

When England recognised the independence of the Spanish colonies, Mr. Canning declared that he had called a new world into existence to redress the balance of the old. But it was long before the new States justified the boast, and it is still generally believed that in point of political and material success they contrast much to their disadvantage with the North American Republic. In the greater part of South America this is no longer true, for in several of those vast communities population and trade are growing at a rate that exceeds that of the Union.

Mexico is the saddest and most conspicuous exception in the midst

This lecture, delivered at the Literary and Scientific Institution, Bridgnorth, March 10, 1868, was published in the *Bridgnorth Journal*, March 14, 1868. Reprinted in Acton, *Historical Essays*, pp. 143–173; Acton, *Liberal Interpretation of History*, pp. 214–242.

of the general improvement. It is the pride of the colonial system of Spain, and the one merit in which it was superior to our own, that it succeeded in preserving and partially civilising the native race. The English settled in a region where the natives were hunters and wanderers, unskilled in the cultivation of the soil, who roamed into the West to elude the grasp of civilisation, or perished by its contact. The colonists retained their own congenial laws, the purity of European blood was maintained, and the portentous problem of race was happily averted. But in Mexico Cortez found a numerous and settled population, dwelling in cities, tilling the land, and brilliantly though superficially civilised. It was part of the Spanish system to protect, to preserve, and to convert the conquered heathens, whose number vastly exceeded that of their masters; a people of mixed blood sprang up between them, and thus there were three races separated by a very broad line, and isolated by the pride and the jealousy of colour. The Indian nobles were mostly exterminated, and the land was distributed among the families of a small group of conquerors. This arrangement of property remains unchanged. The natives are still without any interest in the land, and the immense estates have not been subdivided. In one of the richest districts on the Atlantic, the coast, for one hundred and fifty miles, is owned by one proprietor.

A society so constituted could not make a nation. There was no middle class, no impulse to industry, no common civilisation, no public spirit, no sense of patriotism. The Indians were not suffered to acquire wealth or knowledge, and every class was kept in ignorance and in rigorous seclusion; when, therefore, the Mexicans made themselves independent, the difficulty was to throw off, not the bondage, but the nonage in which they had been held, and to overcome the mental incapacity, the want of enterprise, the want of combination among themselves, and the want of the enlightenment which comes from intercourse with other nations. They formed a republic after the model of their more fortunate neighbours, and accepted those principles which are so inflexible in their consequences, and so unrelenting in their consistency. It soon appeared that there was not propelling power in the State equal to the heavy burden of a half-barbarous population. The intelligent minority was too undisciplined and too demoralised to elevate and to sway the degraded millions of the Indian race. The habits of authority and subordination departed with the Spaniards, and the faculty of organisation could not exist in a people that had never learned to help themselves. No man of very superior character and understanding arose. The leading men in the various provinces sought to maintain their own power by the continuance of anarchy; they combined against the central authority as fast as it changed hands, and overthrew thirty Presidents in thirty years. The requisite conditions of a Republican government did not exist. There was the greatest social inequality that can be conceived between the wealthy landowners and the Indian masses, who possessed neither the mental independence conferred by education nor the material independence which belongs to property. There was Democracy in the State, while society was intensely aristocratic.

The largest landowner in Mexico was the Church; and as there was no religious toleration, it was the Church of the whole nation, the only teacher of the moral law to the natives, the sole channel through which the majority of the people had access to the civilisation of Christendom. Therefore the clergy enjoyed an influence of which there has been no example in Europe for the last five hundred years, and formed a strong basis of aristocracy and the most serious barrier to the realisation of the Democratic principle that nominally prevailed. To establish a real Democracy the first thing to be done was to reduce this immense and artificial influence. For the last twelve years this has been the one constant object of the Democratic party. It was a war of principles, a struggle for existence, on either side, in which conciliation was impossible and which could only terminate by the ruin of one of the contending forces.

Now, as long as the conflict was confined to America, the Republicans could not be utterly defeated, for they could fall back on the unfailing sympathy and resources of the United States. Sooner or later the end would be the confiscation of the lands in mortmain, and the downfall of the Conservatives. Their only hope was in the assistance of Europe, and the establishment of a monarchy under foreign protection. Long before the antagonism became so definite and so extreme, the idea had begun to gain ground that a monarchy was the only form of government adapted to the character of Mexican society, and capable of arresting its decay; and the monarch, if he was not to be a party chief, must be a European prince. Negotiations for this object were opened as early as 1846; Mexican emissaries, acting in concert with the then President, addressed themselves to Prince Metternich, who received them coldly, to Bavaria, and then to France, where the plan was favourably entertained, when it was interrupted by the revolution of 1848. It was revived twelve years later by the progress of events in Mexico. In 1857 the Democratic party carried a new Constitution, abridging the privileges of the clergy, and including a law of mortmain which obliged them to convert their estates into money.

This was the signal for civil war. The Conservatives, led by a young man who, at the age of twenty-seven, had shown a remarkable capacity for war, Miguel Miramon, gained possession of the capital, and their President was recognised by Europe. The Constitutional President held the important seaport of Vera Cruz, and was recognised by the United States. His name, destined like that of his rival to a wide and melancholy celebrity, was Benito Juarez. He was an Indian of pure blood, nearly sixty years old. He had ascended to power by means of his eminence as a lawyer, and because, in the midst of almost universal corruption, he was deemed incorruptible. Unlike the intriguers and the soldiers of fortune who were his rivals, he had risen slowly, without perfidy and without violence—a patient, steadfast man, and, as we should say, a man of extreme opinions. It would seem that in this educated, ambitious, successful Indian, the pent-up hatred of the oppressed race for the oppressor had broken forth, and formed his strongest political motive; and that he was striving for the social and political emancipation of his people when he tore down the privileges and annihilated the power of the class that lorded over them. He professed the principles of 1789, principles which had triumphed in France by a civil war, a reign of terror, ten years of military despotism, and sixty years of intermittent revolution. There was no reason to think they would succeed more easily in a country so backward as Mexico, but Juarez was ready to abide the issue. As there was no system of regular taxation, and all manufactured articles were imported by sea, the customs were the chief source of revenue. It was an advantage to Juarez to possess the chief seaport of the country, and as he dwelt under the cannon of European men-of-war, he was careful not to make enemies by plundering the foreigners.

Miramon, up in the interior, had neither the same resources nor the same restraint. There was no money to be had but that of foreign residents, or of the Church. He could not rob his own party, so he determined to turn to the other source of supply. He had so used his power, and his lieutenant, Marquez, had acted so ferociously, that the English Minister had left Mexico, when Miramon seized a sum of

£130,000 belonging to British landholders, which was deposited at the Legation. He also contracted a loan with the Swiss banker, Jecker, on terms so exorbitant that it seems to have been a stratagem to embarrass those who were to come after him. These two measures were eventually fatal to Miramon, for they were the cause of the European intervention.

Juarez immediately obtained his recognition by England by promising to restore the stolen money, and to satisfy other British claims. He made the same promise to France. With this moral support, and by undertaking to grant away to his partisans the property of the Church, he obtained the means of expelling Miramon from Mexico, and in 1861 he was elected President for a term of four years. He at once dismissed the Spanish and the Papal envoys, decreed the absolute confiscation of the Church lands, and carried out with ruthless energy the triumph of his opinions. But he proved incapable as a ruler, and utterly unequal to the desperate task of restoring order in a country distracted by passion and ruined by anarchy.

The condition of affairs in the summer of 1861 is described by the English Minister in the following passages, which are important because they determined the policy of England:

"As long as the present dishonest and incapable administration remains in power, things will go from bad to worse; but with a government formed of respectable men, could such be found, the resources of the country are so great that it might easily fulfil its engagements, and increase threefold the amount of its exportations, not only of the precious metals, but of those productions for which they receive British manufactured goods in exchange. Mexico furnishes two-thirds of the silver now in circulation, and might be made one of the richest and most prosperous countries of the world; so that it becomes the interest of Great Britain to put a stop by force, if necessary, to its present state of anarchy, and insist on its government paying what it owes to British subjects. All the respectable classes look forward with hope to a foreign intervention as the sole means of saving them from ruin, and preventing a dissolution of the Confederation, as well as a general rising of the Indians against the white population. Every day's experience duly tends to prove the utter absurdity of attempting to govern the country with the limited powers granted to the Executive by the present ultra-liberal Constitution, and I see no hope of improvement unless it comes from a foreign intervention, or the formation of a rational government, composed of the leading men of the moderate party, who, at present, are void of moral courage and afraid to move, unless with some material support from abroad. If the question was, what form of government would most conduce to the welfare of Mexico, by the establishment of order and a permanent state of things, there can be no doubt that a Constitutional monarchy is the one most likely to have central power sufficient to enable it to consolidate the nation, perhaps the only form of government that would give much hope of such a result; but as the question is not what is best for Mexico, but what are the wishes of the Mexican people, I fear that the answer must be that the great mass of the intelligent population are in favour of Republican institutions. Many well-educated and intelligent individuals who stand well in society form a well-grounded desire for a strong government, but these people are unfortunately timid, and passive in action, ready to accept what is done for them, but incapable of doing anything to bring about what they desire."

As it turned out, these were prophetic words. The sale of the Church property was carried on in a very disorderly way, and the money was squandered. A scheme to satisfy the urgent European claims with money lent by the United States, though entertained by the American Government, was rejected by the Senate, and in July 1861 the Mexican Congress resolved that all payments on European agreements should be suspended for two years.

The Powers most concerned in this act of repudiation—France, Spain, and Great Britain—now determined to intervene jointly, and to obtain by force of arms some real security for the property of their subjects, and for the establishment, if necessary, of a more trustworthy government. The conjuncture was favourable, for the Civil War had just broken out in the United States, and from that quarter there was no immediate danger of interruption. Spain took the lead, her military establishment at Cuba enabling her to act promptly, with some suspicion of a desire to recover her ancient dominion. England followed warily, with an eye only to mercantile interests. France did not yet reveal her intentions, and probably had not yet matured them.

The allied forces, amounting to about 6000 men, without means of transport or materials for a campaign in the interior, were placed under the command of the Spanish general Prim, a clever, showy, and ambitious officer, but a capricious and unstable politician. On their arrival, the town and fort of Vera Cruz were evacuated by the Mexican troops. In this extremity Juarez strengthened himself by putting at the head of the Ministry General Doblado, the leader of the moderate party, a man whose reputation for caution and ability stood high, and whose acts in office prove that it was well-deserved. In January 1862, he issued a decree directing all those who should be taken in arms against the Republic to be tried by court-martial and put to death as traitors. This is the law by which the Emperor was to die, and which gave a legal character to his execution. Doblado had an interview with Prim, expatiated on the deplorable condition of the country, and undertook that the legitimate demands of the allies should be faithfully complied with, provided only they would recognise the existing government. These terms seemed acceptable to the allies, who were not equipped for a campaign, and they took Doblado at his word. But the agreement had to be sent to Europe for approval, and in the meantime it was arranged that the allies should move up from the pestilential swamp of Vera Cruz to healthier quarters on the first range of hills. This placed them within the outer line of the Mexican defences, and it was stipulated that if the preliminaries were not ratified, before commencing hostilities they should first withdraw to the plain below.

The claims of the three Powers had now to be specified. Those of Spain and England were clear, and easily ascertained. The French commissioners demanded, in addition to other large sums, three millions sterling for the banker Jecker. Their colleagues protested against this excessive demand. They affirmed that the sum advanced by the banker to Miramon was only £160,000, and they pointed out that he was not a Frenchman but a Swiss, and that the guardianship of Swiss interests in Mexico pertained to the American Legation. Jecker was immediately naturalised a Frenchman, and the French Government bought up his bonds. Agents were sent for this purpose with sealed instructions to America, two of whom, when they discovered the errand upon which they were employed, indignantly threw up the commission. Whilst this transaction was sowing discord in the allied camp, several Mexican exiles of the Conservative party made their appearance at Vera Cruz. One of these was Miramon. He was arrested and sent away by the British Commodore, on the ground that the expedition could not connect itself with one party while acknowledging the government of the other.

Miramon was speedily followed by General Almonte, for many years the chief agent of the Conservative party in Europe, and the secret councillor of the French Government, a man of high character and great influence. He stated that he came with a mission from France to establish a provisional government, to introduce a monarchy, and to procure the election of the Archduke Maximilian. The English and Spanish Commissioners demanded his expulsion, when General Lorencez arrived with French reinforcements, and announced that Napoleon had rejected the convention with Doblado, that he had sent Almonte to Mexico, and meant war. The alliance of the three Powers was at once dissolved; the Spaniards sailed for Cuba in English ships, and France was left alone, to accomplish the avowed design of erecting a throne beyond the Atlantic.

In the intention of the Emperor Napoleon, the Mexican expedition was the first step towards the execution of a bold and magnificent scheme, to which he gave the name of the regeneration of the Latin world. The ancient rivalry between France and England was expanded into the rivalry of the Latin with the Anglo-Saxon race. If we carry back our thoughts for a century, it will not be difficult to find in the history of the two nations the motives which suggested the idea. Scarcely one hundred years ago vast territories in Canada, on the Mississippi, and in the West Indies belonged to the Crown of France, and French adventurers of great daring and ability were laying the foundation of an Empire in Hindostan. One by one these possessions have gone, and France, watched by jealous neighbours, has nearly lost the power of expansion in Europe.

What has been, in the meantime, the progress of England? The colonies which France has lost have almost all been won by her. England, not France, wields the sceptre of the Great Mogul. Her people have encircled the globe with a girdle of British settlements. New continents, I may almost say, have arisen out of the Southern ocean to receive the incessant overflow of her population. Her colonial empire is a nursery of mighty nations, that carries to the distant places of the earth the language and the laws of home. George III inherited dominions peopled perhaps by ten million human beings. His granddaughter reigns over two hundred millions. In America the children of our race are waiting the time when the whole continent shall be theirs.

But on that continent there are thirty millions of men, not of French descent, but of a stock allied with the French, who derive their literary culture and intellectual impulse from Paris, whose traffic is carried on with French ports, who look up to France as their head, and turn to her to protect them from being absorbed by an alien race. The trade of France with South America is nearly equal to her trade with the United States, and is more profitable because it is carried in French ships. In the ten years before the expedition, it had grown from £6,000,000 to £20,000,000 a year. South America is the largest and safest opening that remains for the development of French commerce, the most increasing market for French industry. It was manifestly the interest of France to prevent it from falling under the control of the narrow mercantile policy of the United States, and to secure her own influence over nations with such a future. In the words of the Emperor: "It is not our interest that the United States should grasp the whole Gulf of Mexico, the Antilles, and South America, and become the sole dispensers of the produce of the New World. We have seen by sad experience how precarious is the fate of an industry which is forced to seek its raw material in a single market, under all the vicissitudes to which that market is liable." The establishment of a French dependency in Mexico would have checked the southward progress of the Union, and have cut the continent in two.

When Juarez repudiated his engagements with European creditors the Confederates had won their first victories, and the North was not able to repel the intervention upon its frontier. Shortly after, the Southern Commissioners were seized on board the *Trent*, and England began to arm. The French Emperor calculated that he would be able to do his work without interruption, and that England, in case of need, would help him to support the South. Therefore, from the end of 1861 he lent a willing ear to the Mexican exiles, who displayed the sufferings and the capabilities of their country, and allured him with the splendid vision of a nation to be regenerated by France. They persuaded him that the presence of his troops would be welcomed, that there would be no serious resistance, and that a powerful party would rally to his standard. In this belief, and with Almonte in their camp, the French advanced against Mexico, 6000 strong. On the 5th of May 1862, they appeared before Puebla, the second city in the land, on the road from Vera Cruz to the capital. They were received with so vigorous a cannonade that they were forced to retire to a position where they could await reinforcements without danger of being dislodged. After this military repulse, public opinion in France supported the Emperor in despatching an army of 30,000 men, provided with all the appliances of war. They landed in the autumn, and the winter was spent in preparations.

A whole year had been lost before Puebla fell, after an obstinate defence, and in June 1863 the French entered the city of Mexico. The early reverses and the long delays of the French greatly strengthened the position of Juarez. The invasion exalted the Indian leader of an extreme party into a champion of the dignity and the independence of the country, and his tenacity in upholding the cause did not allow this halo to depart from him even in the worst times. The capital was not fortified, and when the French appeared, Juarez carried the seat of his government to one of the Northern towns.

A new provisional government was instituted, in which Almonte was associated with the Archbishop of Mexico, and an assembly of notables, selected and convened by the French, met to decide on the future of the country. Many of the principal men in the capital who had been invited, refused to attend, and the assembly was composed of Conservatives who took their orders from Almonte and the French. The orders were to proclaim a monarchy, and to offer the Crown to the Archduke. They were obeyed on the 8th July 1863. The long-deferred hopes of the Mexican royalists seemed to be fulfilled, when a deputation proceeded to Europe to invite the Archduke to ascend the throne of Montezuma. Ferdinand Maximilian, the next brother of the Emperor of Austria, had long occupied a peculiar and exceptional position in his native country. There were circumstances which made him appear a possible rival to his brother, and the many errors of Francis Joseph, the waning confidence in his fortune and his judgment, kept alive the habit of looking to the Archduke, who was altogether excluded from the conduct of affairs, as a refuge in extremity. He possessed some of the best qualities of a ruler, honesty and firmness of purpose, a kind and true heart, and a mind fixed on high designs. In spite of much and various experience of mankind, he retained an unpractical imaginativeness, which is often connected with extreme cultivation, and a certain impetuous generosity frequently marred the effect of his sagacity. Though undoubtedly very intelligent, he was so often deceived that he must have lacked the faculty of judging men and choosing friends, without which there is no success in government. His ardent, lofty spirit, perpetually curbed and chafed by the prevailing dulness, selfishness, and incapacity in Austria, imparted something that was cold and sarcastic to his manner. His outspoken censure of his brother's unstable policy caused an estrangement between them, which was increased by his marriage with the daughter of the wise Leopold, a clever and accomplished woman, whose family has grown great by renouncing those principles of strict legitimacy which Austria specially represents. The Archduke was the last Austrian Governor of Lombardy. In that thankless office it was impossible to conciliate the Italians, and he could not permanently serve the interests of his country. But he made many friends, and men believed that he would willingly have been the Minister of a less unpopular system. It was even whispered that he had wished to set up a throne for himself in Lombardy and Venice, separate from the Austrian monarchy. At least he had so far deserted the ancient ways of his family as to fall under the ban of distrust and suspicion at Vienna. About the time of the marriage of the Princess Royal he visited the British Court, and made so favourable an impression that there were some who regretted that he could not have been a candidate for her hand. For who could then have dreamed that the reserved and unpretending Prussian was to be the spoilt darling of victory, while the genial, frank, and brilliant Austrian was destined to a traitor's death? He devoted his care to the navy, a department always neglected in Austria, and the virtue of his administration became apparent when the fleet which he had created won the greatest sea-fight of our time. The war of 1859 deprived him of his high position, and reproaches and recriminations followed, which separated him yet more from the Emperor. He dwelt in his castle of Miramar at the head of the Adriatic, mourning over wasted talents, a ruined career, and an unsatisfied ambition.

Very soon the prospect of a new adventure opened before him. By a strange fatality his wife, the daughter of a Princess of the House of Orléans, was an enthusiastic Bonapartist, and not only admired, but trusted the Emperor Napoleon. When, therefore, he proposed to hand over his conquest to the Archduke, hoping thereby to conciliate Austria, the Archduchess Charlotte urged her husband to accept it. Their unsettled position must have become very irksome to her, for when they left their home Maximilian wept bitterly, and she showed no emotions but hope and joy. His brother's government employed strong measures to dissuade him from accepting, and it was decided that he must renounce his place in the succession, and be counted last after all the princes of the line.

When the vote of the Assembly of Notables was made known to

him, he replied that he could not accept the crown unless he was assured of the support of the great Powers, or until it was offered to him by the free choice of the whole Mexican people. The French are skilled in managing the machinery of a spontaneous election; and in April 1864, a second deputation carried to Miramar a sceptre of Mexican gold, with the assurance that the whole nation had elected Maximilian Emperor. In reality the French were masters of a very small portion of the country, and the vast majority were not polled at all. Where the French were present there was no serious difficulty, though in some places the chief inhabitants were thrown into prison before they gave in their adhesion. Maximilian was fully informed that the pretended election was nothing but a ceremonious farce. A Mexican Republican made his way to Miramar, and warned him that the real feeling of the country was adverse to the invaders, and that the expedition would end in disaster.

But the promises of France were excessively enticing. The French army was to complete the pacification of the country, and a powerful corps was to be left for several years in the service of Maximilian. France negotiated a loan in his behalf, and seventeen chests filled with gold pieces found their way to Miramar. The Archduke was not in a position to disregard such inducements, for his private fortune was in disorder, and the first £300,000 of the Mexican loan went to clear his debts. Other points were raised which have been kept secret, and the friends of Maximilian still look for important revelations.

At his trial he instructed his counsel to say that Napoleon had required the cession of a portion of Mexican territory as large as Great Britain, and that he had indignantly refused to dismember the country which had given him a crown. He accepted it at a time when the tide of success had turned in the American War, and the prospects of the Confederacy were no longer hopeful. The Archduke demanded a pledge that he should be supported by a French alliance in case of war with the United States; and it is positively asserted that Napoleon gave the required pledge. He gave it believing that England would join him in recognising the South, if it was found that its resistance would be crushed without aid from Europe, and the time came when he made the proposal of a joint recognition to Lord Palmerston. It happened that the two foremost statesmen in the Ministry had made speeches in the provinces which appeared to show a disposition favourable to the Confederates; and the Emperor believed that they would carry their colleagues with them. This was the gravest miscalculation he made in the whole Mexican affair. The Cabinet, taking one of the most momentous resolutions ever adopted by a Ministry, rejected the proposal, and the Emperor shrank from a war single-handed with the United States.

Maximilian, on his part, undertook to pay a million a year while the French remained, and to liquidate all those accumulated claims which Juarez had rejected. In fact, he submitted to conditions impossible to meet, and commenced an undertaking predestined to financial ruin. He reached Mexico in June 1864, and was favourably if not warmly received. The French had ruled the country through the provisional government for a whole year, with almost uninterrupted military success. But they had encountered a difficulty of a formidable and unexpected kind. Juarez had had more than two years to accomplish the overthrow of the clergy, and their property had passed into the hands of speculators, chiefly foreigners, who, it was thought, would not easily be compelled to restore it. The Church party had called for intervention in the hope of recovering these losses, and when the French placed the leaders of the party at the head of the State, they preferred their claims with a sure expectation of success.

The Church in France is supported by the State, and owns no independent property. The French supposed that the practice of their own country could not be unsuitable to Mexico, where a revolution would be required to restore the ancient order, and where the clergy would not bear a comparison with the salaried priesthood of France. The demand was summarily refused. The Episcopate united to denounce the sacrilegious invaders, and the Archbishop ceased to be a member of the provisional government. The breach, for the moment, was complete; and the only hope of the clergy was in Maximilian. He knew that, for a Sovereign to be strong, he must be identified with no party. It was his mission to conciliate and blend together interests severed by years of antagonism. In declining the crown for the first time, he had signified that he would consent to receive it only as the gift of the entire nation. In accepting it afterwards, he made known that he looked upon himself as the elect of the nation, not as the nominee of a powerful interest. From the moment of his arrival he held out the olive branch to the Republicans, and sought their confidence by offering them place and power. Many accepted his offers, and he was surrounded by men who were hateful to those who had seated him on the throne. In adopting this policy it was impossible to draw a line, to examine antecedents, or to reject utterly any candidate for favour. The Emperor was often deceived, and lost on one side without gaining on the other.

After a long delay, which exasperated the trembling holders of Church property, as well as those whom they had despoiled, he decided that all legal purchases should be confirmed, and those which were fraudulent revised, but that nothing should be restored to the clergy, who were to be paid by the State. The Nuncio quarrelled with him upon this, and left the country. Maximilian, irritated by the hostile attitude of the clergy, went further, and restored what was called the *Exequatur,* a law forbidding any document to be published in ecclesiastical affairs without the consent of the civil power. This right has been abandoned by his brother, in Austria; by the Italian Government, last year; and even in Mexico, by Juarez, who adopted the voluntary principle. It could not be defended as a liberal law, and its revival seemed to be simply a blow at the independence of religion. The clergy protested that they had not borne the burden of civil war and brought foreign armies into the country, in order that a prince of their choosing should confirm decrees which had made their property the spoil of their enemies.

They declared that their position was worse under their friend than it had been under their persecutor Juarez. Thenceforth they withdrew their support, and observed a hostile neutrality, watching the time when the Emperor, driven to extremities, would be ready to purchase their assistance at any sacrifice they might demand. In some instances they even fomented the Republican opposition.

This was the first great and visible disaster that the Empire incurred. Another was soon known to be imminent. Financial capacity, rare in every country, was not to be found in Mexico; and Napoleon, who wished his creation to succeed, sent out a Chancellor of the Exchequer from France, with a staff of clerks. But the imported Minister died, and could not be replaced. The finances broke down so completely that Maximilian was obliged to ask for money from the military chest of the French army, and thus fell into the power of its commander. As he could not fulfil his engagements with the Emperor Napoleon, he was guilty of a breach of the treaty signed between them, and gave France an excuse, when her turn came, to justify her own breach of faith.

The year 1865 passed prosperously, on the whole. Maximilian visited many of the towns, saw what he could with his own eyes, and devoted his time to the fabrication of decrees by which he hoped to regenerate the country. These decrees are generally sensible and just; they incline in a good direction, but not always by the right road, and ornamental superfluities sometimes usurp the place of more difficult but more essential things. Maximilian was an anxious and determined educator, and his zeal was praiseworthy, for ninety per cent of the people could neither read or write. But it shows a want of practical capacity when in a community wanting the first necessaries of popular instruction the Sovereign founds an Academy of Sciences, and gravely inculcates on his Ministers the importance of encouraging the study of metaphysics. He found himself in the rare position of a lawgiver called to legislate in a country for which everything remained to be done, and he enjoyed the luxury of carrying out, at least on paper, systems nurtured in days of visionary retirement. He had not time or vigour to execute much of what he had projected.

There was one question that called for an act of high and generous statesmanship. The Indians had been reduced by their poverty and want of energy to the position of serfs. They were in debt to their landlords, and the whole hopeless labour of their lives, without the chance of profit or release, was due to their creditors. They had greeted the coming of Maximilian as the dawn of their deliverance, and he might have made them the willing prop of the imperial throne. In the 800,000 square miles of Mexico, peopled by 8,000,000 of men, but capable of sustaining 100,000,000, it would have been easy, without any spoliation, to distribute land among the countrymen of its ancient owners. Maximilian adopted a half measure. He abolished the debts of the Indians, and thus made them free; but he did no more, and left them to relapse, under pressure of the old causes, into the old degradation. The Indians were not satisfied, and the landowners were alienated.

Something, but not enough, was done for the creation of a native army to defend the crown and country when the French should depart. An Austrian and a Belgian corps were formed, but did not answer expectation. Next to the French, the most efficient body was the division of the Indian general Mejia, a man of a very pure fame. But the French were successful in all they undertook during the whole of 1865. The Republican bands were scattered, many of their generals made their submission, and Juarez, driven from place to place, disappeared at last at a point in the extreme north of Mexico, on the American frontier, more than a thousand miles from the capital. It was reported that he had escaped into the United States. At this time also the four years for which he had been elected expired, and it was impossible to convene a Congress for a new election. Many of his followers now held that he had ceased to govern, and the Vice-President Ortega, the defender of Puebla, claimed the vacant post. The strict legality which had been the strength of the position of Juarez was seriously impaired, and his authority was unquestionably shaken. The country was in a wretched state of insecurity and misery. Plunderers and assassins plied their trade under pretence of being real combatants. Mexican warfare is often scarcely distinguishable from armed robbery, and, as it was the plan of the Republicans to fight in small guerrilla bands, the line separating the soldier from the brigand was often indistinct. The Government thought the time had come to exterminate these bands, and to protect the inhabitants against their incursions. The victory over the regular army was complete, and it seemed that men who infested the roads, when organised resistance was over, did not deserve the treatment of prisoners of war.

On the 2nd of October Maximilian drew up a decree ordering all who should be taken with arms in their hands to be shot, and when he signed it he signed his own death-warrant. Immediately after its publication a Republican force, commanded by Arteaga, was defeated, and the leaders were captured. In obedience to the new order the Imperial General Mendez put them to death. But the Republicans, though dispersed and dispirited, were not destroyed. A report made to the Emperor in November 1865 estimates their force at 24,000 men, and Juarez had not abandoned the struggle. He remained on Mexican territory, in a town on the Rio del Norte, from which a boat could take him in a few minutes to the American bank, and he remained in communication with the generals of his party. There he waited for the deliverance which he knew was coming. For at that moment, near the close of 1865, his cause was taken up by an ally so powerful and so much feared as to be able, without firing a shot or wasting a single life, to expel the French from Mexico, and to lay the Empire in the dust.

The United States had watched the intervention and the erection of the Empire with anger and alarm. They knew that it had sprung from a desire to cripple their influence, and they could not be indifferent to the presence of an European army on their frontier while they were embarrassed by a civil war. They denied that the Empire was the free choice of the Mexicans, and they highly disapproved of an Emperor that was absolute, for he retained in his own hands all the powers of the State. They refused to recognise him, but they remained neutral, determined not to act until they could act decisively. They rejected various schemes for assisting Juarez with money in return for land, and they declined not only the overtures of Napoleon and of Juarez, but one which was still more tempting. During the siege of Richmond the Confederates proposed that they should unite their armies for the conquest of Mexico and of Canada, but the North refused.

When the war of Secession was over, the Government of Washington had to apply a little diplomatic pressure to the Emperor Napoleon to hasten the recall of his troops. The pressure quickly took the form of threats, and Napoleon very speedily gave way. Events were passing in Europe which made him impatient that Maximilian should restore his legions. In June 1866 war broke out in Italy and in Germany, and in the first week of July Prussia had struck a blow that made half Europe tremble, and menaced the military supremacy and the pride of France. In these circumstances it was certain that the offensive language of America could not be resented, and Mr. Seward used his advantage with cruel complacency. Napoleon informed Maximilian that he must provide for himself, and he informed the American Government that he would retire from Mexico in March 1867.

Rumors of this strange correspondence, and of its probable result, reached Mexico and gave new spirit to the Republicans. Maximilian had refused permission to 25,000 confederates to settle in his dominions; but stragglers found their way to the armies of Juarez, and in June 1866 the important town of Matamoros was surrendered to Escobedo by Mejia. From the moment of that reverse fortune began rapidly to change; and as the French retired from more distant posts, swarms of Republicans appeared in every direction.

When Maximilian learnt the altered intention of Napoleon, he foresaw the end, and spoke of abdication. The Empress persuaded him to remain, while she undertook a journey to Europe. She would compel the French Emperor to fulfil his promises. She would induce the Pope to reconcile the clergy with the Empire. She failed utterly in both endeavours, and in her last interview with Pius IX, perceiving that all hope was ended, she went out of her mind. Early in October the news reached her husband, and then his courage gave way. He had lately exchanged what was called a Liberal for a Conservative Ministry, and had offered the principal departments to two French generals. But they were forbidden by Napoleon to accept, and still no substantial help came from the clergy. Worn out with illness and sorrow, deserted on all sides, and knowing that his Empire was crumbling, Maximilian started for the coast with an undefined intention of sailing for Europe. His most trusted adviser, a Belgian, who had accompanied the Empress, attempted at this conjuncture to draw him away by an appeal to his ambition. He described the discontent of the humbled Austrians and assured him that they wished his brother to abdicate, while sympathy for himself was increasing throughout the country.

Francis Joseph was aware of this intrigue, but he made a last effort to save his brother by restoring to him, if he would return, his position at the head of the princes of the blood. An aide-de-camp of Napoleon arrived in Mexico to hasten the departure of the troops, and was instructed to use everything but force to induce Maximilian to abdicate. The French did not like the dishonour of leaving him to his fate, and they hoped, if he ceased to reign, to make their own terms with the Mexicans, and to leave behind them a government not utterly hostile to themselves. That the expedition was a gigantic failure, injurious to the reputation of the army and the stability of the throne, could not be disguised. But the blow would be more keenly felt if the man on whom they had made war for four years, and with whom they had refused to treat, remained unshaken in his office, victorious over the arms and arts of Napoleon III. So great was their urgency that Maximilian felt insulted, and at last believed himself betrayed.

Whilst he was wavering and lingering near the coast, an American frigate appeared at Vera Cruz, conveying General Sherman and Mr. Campbell, accredited as envoys to Juarez. They had sailed from New York on the 11th of November, when it was supposed that Maximilian had abdicated, leaving the French in the country. The Government at Washington were determined that in that case their candidate, and not that of Napoleon, should prevail. Mr. Campbell was charged to offer support and aid to the Republic, and the presence of the ablest soldier of the Union indicated ostentatiously of what nature that aid was to be. When these envoys found that Maximilian had not departed, they understood that their mission was a blunder and withdrew. The

Emperor did not believe that an American Minister, escorted by such a personage as Sherman, had come all the way to Vera Cruz and had gone away without doing anything. He persuaded himself that France and America had come to an understanding, and had made a bargain of which his crown was to be the price. The pressing invitations to depart with the French appeared to him perfidious, and he thought it would be disgraceful that his life should be rescued by those who had bartered his throne.

Meantime the Church party, which had so long coldly stood aloof, thought that the moment had arrived when it could impose its own conditions. It was represented to the Emperor that the disappearance of the invaders would remove the cause of his unpopularity, and that good patriots would support him now, who had refused to acknowledge the nominee of a foreign Power. Miramon arrived from Europe at the critical moment and offered his sword to Maximilian. The Prussian Minister also advised him to remain. The clergy promised their powerful aid, and he yielded. There was nothing for him to look forward to in Europe. No public career was open to the man who had failed so signally in an enterprise of his own seeking. His position in Austria, which was distressing before, would be intolerable now. He had quarrelled with his family, with his church, with the protector to whose temptations he had hearkened. And for him there was to be no more the happiness of the domestic hearth.

In Mexico there were no hopes to live for, but there was still a cause in which it would be glorious to die. There were friends whom he could not leave to perish in expiation of measures which had been his work. He knew what the vengeance of the victors would be. He knew that those who had been most faithful to him would be most surely slaughtered; and he deemed that he, who had never yet been seen on a field of battle, had no right to fly without fighting. Probably he felt that when a monarch cannot preserve his throne, nothing becomes him better than to make his grave beneath its ruins. He yielded, and returned, sullenly and slowly, to the capital. What concessions had been wrung from the party in whose hands he was, I do not know. But he addressed a letter to the Pope, expressing regret for the policy which had failed, and at Rome, where he was once regarded as a persecutor and almost an apostate, the letter was hailed as a solemn and complete retraction.

From that moment Maximilian was no longer the chief of a national government, but a partisan leader, who had not even the control of his party. He laid aside the pomp of Majesty, and lived in private houses, especially as the guest of the clergy. He declared that he was only provisionally the chief of the State, and held office only until a national assembly had decided what should be the future of Mexico. He invited Juarez to submit his claim to the same peaceful arbitration, and proposed that there should be a general amnesty, to stop the shedding of blood. The Republicans saw nothing in all this but the signs of weakness, and of their own approaching triumph. They opposed no obstacles in the way of the departing French, but they closed in overwhelming numbers upon the feeble army of the Empire.

The defeat of Miramon on the great North road in February compelled Maximilian to take the field. He put himself for the first time at the head of his troops, and joined Miramon at Queretaro. On this day last year he was surrounded and besieged by Escobedo with an army which rose speedily to more than 40,000 men. Marquez was sent to Mexico for reinforcements, but he never returned, and spent the short time that remained in wringing money from the inhabitants. The siege proceeded slowly, and on the 24th of April Miramon made a successful sally, and opened for a moment the road to the capital. But the men were worn out with fighting, and the Emperor refused to leave them. He declared he had not come to Queretaro to fly from danger. To those who saw him during those anxious days, haggard and aged, with a long beard flowing over his breast, and the fever of despair in his eyes, conducting the defence and constantly under fire, it seemed that he was longing for the glory of a soldier's death. At length the supplies were nearly exhausted, the certainty of the treason of Marquez removed all hope of relief, and it was resolved that the garrison should make an attempt to cut its way through the enemy on the 15th day of May. It was too late. For four days Lopez, the second in command, had been in communication with Escobedo, and had accepted a bribe of £1400. Late in the night of the 14th he saw the Emperor; and then, at two in the morning, he introduced a Republican general into the fort. This general was disguised, and carried concealed arms. He remained two hours, and examined the interior of the works. Then Lopez withdrew the Imperial sentries, and their posts were silently occupied by the soldiers of Riva Palacio, the only officer who had been excepted, by name, from the decree of October.

At daybreak the bells of the churches of Queretaro announced to the Republican camp that the place was won. The traitor went up to the Emperor's room, and told him that the enemy was in town. Maximilian rushed forth, and was stopped by Republican soldiers, who did not recognise him. Lopez whispered to the officer who it was. Then the generous Mexican allowed the Emperor to pass, pretending to take him for a civilian; and he escaped to a fortified position at some distance. Here he was joined by the faithful Mejia, and as many officers and men as could hew their way through the columns of Republicans that were now pouring into the town. Miramon alone attempted a forlorn resistance. A shot struck him in the face, and he fell, blinded with blood, into the hands of his enemies.

The position occupied by the Imperialists was swept by artillery and could not be defended, and at eight o'clock they surrendered. Among the prisoners was Mendez, who had caused the decree of October to be executed on Arteaga and his companions. He was shot the same day. The Emperor was shut up, with Miramon and Mejia, in a cell of the Capuchin convent, and it was announced to them that they would be tried by court-martial, under the decree of January. From that moment Maximilian retained no hope of life. He presented his war-horse to Riva Palacio, the most chivalrous of his enemies, and telegraphed to Mexico for the Prussian Minister, and for legal advice in preparing his defense.

Mexico was already besieged by a Republican army, and hollow shells were thrown into the town, stuffed with telegrams proclaiming the fall of Queretaro. But Marquez, the most detested of the Imperial generals, wished to gain time, and he suppressed the news. Maximilian had deposited his abdication in the hands of the President of Council, to be produced if he died or fell a prisoner; but Marquez compelled him to keep it secret, and prevented for several days the departure of the defenders who had been summoned. The most eminent of these was the advocate Riva Palacio, the father of the general, a leading Republican, who had refused all solicitations to serve the Emperor in the days of his power. The others seem to have been less distinguished, but they were all chosen among the Republicans. The Prussian Minister, Baron Magnus, had lived on intimate terms with the Emperor, and had been one of the advisers of the expedition which had ended so fatally. No European Power was less compromised in Mexican affairs, or less obnoxious to the dominant party than Prussia, and it was thought that Baron Magnus would be the best mediator.

The seat of Government was at San Luis, 200 miles beyond Queretaro, but connected with it by telegraph. Two lawyers remained with the Emperor, while Riva Palacio and the Prussian Minister repaired to San Luis to intercede with Juarez. The court-martial which was to try the prisoners met on the stage of the theatre of Queretaro on the morning of Friday, the 14th of June. The house was lighted up and full of spectators. Maximilian had been ill in bed for several days, and self-respect forbade him to appear on such a scene. The two generals were present. Their case was manifestly desperate; yet the defender of Mejia caused a deep impression when he claimed for his client the same mercy which, in spite of stern decrees, he had always shown to his captives, and appealed to Escobedo to say how he had fared when he was Mejia's prisoner. The defence of Miramon was less dignified and less loyal. He pleaded that he had had no command while the French were in the country, that he had been hostile to the Empire which had sent him on an idle mission to Europe, and that he had offered his services to the chief of the Republic. These facts were true; and at Paris Miramon had said openly that the end of the intervention would be to make him President again. Maximilian knew all this, and he knew the manner of his defence. This must not be forgotten when we come to the last scene of all, and see how the Emperor bore himself towards the brave but ambitious soldier, who had been ready to desert the cause in which he was to die.

The strongest points of the indictment against Maximilian were, that he had known the decree of January, which had been published long before he came; that the necessity of foreign support must have proved to him that he was not the legitimate, national Sovereign, and that he could not therefore justify the October decree, by which it was pretended, with great exaggeration, that 40,000 Mexicans had suffered death; that he was responsible for the continuance of civil war after the departure of the French, and for the introduction of Belgian and Austrian soldiers, whose Governments were not at war with the Republic, and who came therefore in the character of filibusters and assassins. The reply to these charges was narrow and technical, and not worthy of the occasion. It amounted in substance to that which the Emperor had said himself: "You may dispute the original probability of my success, but not the sincerity of my motives." As to the decree of October, his advocates defied the prosecution to name a single instance in which he had refused a pardon.

A little before midnight on the 15th the prisoners were found guilty, and their sentence having been confirmed by Escobedo on the Sunday morning, they were informed that they would be shot at three o'clock on the same day. Meanwhile the issue of the trial had been foreseen, and the friends of the Emperor were pleading with Juarez for his pardon. On the ground of political expediency their position was undoubtedly more favourable than that of men restricted to legal arguments. During the war in Mexico a yet deadlier struggle had raged beyond the American border. The author of Secession was not a foreigner, like Maximilian, but a citizen of the country in which he had conspired. He too had been defeated and captured, and then, while European monarchies suppressed revolution with atrocious cruelty, Jefferson Davis had been released by the great Republic. Therefore, they said, the honour of Republican institutions was in the keeping of Juarez, and required that Mexico should follow that example of triumphant clemency, and should betray neither hatred for the past nor alarm for the future.

The President and his minister, Lerdo, listened patiently but coldly. They said that Europe could give no guarantee that it would not renew the same attempt, that Maximilian would continue, even in spite of himself, to be a pretext and a rallying cry for faction, and an instrument by which foreign Powers, when complications arose, might gain a party in the country. The decree of October cried for expiation, and the death of its author would enable them to spare the rest. Many Mexicans had been put to death under the decree of January, and the punishment of inferiors could not be justified if that of the leader was remitted. They seem to have believed that if the doorposts of the Republic were marked with the blood of a prince, the angel of destruction would pass them by. They showed no inclination to cast on others the responsibility of their act, but it is difficult to believe that it was determined by reason of state dispassionately weighed.

Juarez possessed but a precarious authority over the army; and the army was infuriated by strife, and thirsted to avenge the comrades who had been executed like murderers. We can imagine what their feelings would be towards the foreigner whose title was a vote extracted by the bayonets of invaders, who had ordered their countrymen and themselves to be slaughtered, and who was now convicted of having been a pretender and a usurper, as he was the champion of the weaker party. It is probable that the real author of the Emperor's execution is Escobedo, and that Juarez was powerless to save him. When the news that he was to die in three hours reached San Luis at noon on the Sunday, the Prussian Minister prayed for a short delay. He knew that Maximilian had matters to settle before death, and there was some hope that foreign intercession would be in time to save his life. But the American Government, at the request of the Emperor of Austria, had already interceded for his brother, and had interceded in vain. A delay of three days was granted, but the order did not reach Queretaro till the last moment, when the prisoners had made themselves ready for immediate death. For himself, indeed, Maximilian had no hope, and was perfectly resigned. A report that his wife was dead made him meet his fate with joy. On the eve of his execution he telegraphed to Juarez requesting that he might be the only victim.

At six in the morning of Wednesday, the 19th of last June, he was led forth to the doom he had not deserved. His last act before going to the place of execution had been to write the following letter to his implacable conqueror: "I give up my life willingly, if the sacrifice can promote the welfare of my new country. But nothing healthy can grow upon a soil saturated with blood, and therefore, I entreat you, let mine be the last you shed. The fortitude with which you upheld the cause that triumphs now won my admiration in happier days, and I pray that it may not fail you in the peaceful work of conciliation that is to come." When they came to the appointed place, he gave money to the soldiers by whose hands he was to fall, asking them to aim at his heart, for he wished that his mother might look upon his face again. The officer who was to give the word assured him that he detested the duty, and implored him not to die with a feeling of resentment against him. Maximilian thanked him, and said that he must obey orders. Mejia was in great trouble and dejection. His wife had just borne him a son, and as he left his prison he had seen her rushing through the streets, raving mad, with the child in her arms. The Emperor bade him farewell affectionately, saying: "There is a reward in the next world for that which is not requited here." He was standing between the Mexicans, but out of humility, or magnanimity, or because a solemn and sacred memory was present to his mind at that last awful moment, he turned to Miramon and said that out of esteem for his courage he would yield to him the place of honour. His last words were: "I die for a just cause—the independence and the liberty of Mexico. May my death close the era of the misfortunes of my adopted country: God save Mexico!" Then he crossed his hands upon his breast and fell, pierced by nine balls.

He fell, and carried with him in his fall the independence of the people he had come to save. Nothing henceforth remains that can permanently arrest the United States in the annexation of Spanish America. If they have prudence to avoid European war, and wisdom to compose their own dissensions, they may grasp the most glorious inheritance the earth affords. The conquest of Spanish America would be easy and certain, but beset with dangers. A confederacy loses its true character when it rules over dependencies; and a Democracy lives a threatened life that admits millions of a strange and inferior race which it can neither assimilate nor absorb. It is more likely that the Americans will bind their neighbours by treaties, which will throw open the whole continent to their own influence and enterprise, without destroying their separate existence.

The memory of the fair-haired stranger, who devoted his life to the good of Mexico, and died for guilt which was not his own, will live in sorrow rather than in anger among the people for whom he strove in vain. Already we may pronounce the verdict of history upon his sad career—his worst crime was in accepting the treacherous gift of Empire, but his misfortune was greater than his fault. I think he was well-nigh the noblest of his race, and fulfilled the promise of his words: "The fame of my ancestors will not degenerate in me."

[12]

The Massacre of
St. Bartholomew

The way in which Coligny and his adherents met their death has been handed down by a crowd of trustworthy witnesses, and few things in history are known in more exact detail. But the origin and motives of the tragedy, and the manner of its reception by the opinion of Christian Europe, are still subject to controversy. Some of the evidence has been difficult of access, part is lost, and much has been deliberately destroyed. No letters written from Paris at the time have been found in the Austrian archives. In the correspondence of thirteen agents of the House of Este at the Court of Rome, every paper relating to the event has disappeared. All the documents of 1572, both from Rome and Paris, are wanting in the archives of Venice. In the Registers of many French towns the leaves which contained the records of August and September in that year have been torn out. The first reports sent to England by Walsingham and by the French Government have not been recovered. Three accounts printed at Rome, when the facts were new, speedily became so rare that they have been forgotten. The Bull of Gregory XIII was not admitted into the official collections; and the reply to Muretus has escaped notice until now. The letters of Charles IX to Rome, with the important exception of that which he wrote on the 24th of August, have been dispersed and lost. The letters of Gregory XIII to France have never been seen by persons willing to make them public. In the absence of these documents the most authentic information is that which is supplied by the French Ambassador and by the Nuncio. The despatches of Ferralz, describing the attitude of the Roman court, are extant, but have not been used. Those of Salviati

Published in the *North British Review* 51 (October 1869):30–70. *Wellesley* I, p. 693; Döllinger I, pp. 562, 564; Acton-Simpson III, pp. 276, 285. Reprinted in Acton, *History of Freedom*, pp. 101–149.

have long been known. Chateaubriand took a copy when the papal archives were at Paris and projected a work on the events with which they are concerned. Some extracts were published, with his consent, by the continuator of Mackintosh; and a larger selection, from the originals in the Vatican, appeared in Theiner's *Annals of Gregory XIII.* The letters written under Pius V are beyond the limits of that work; and Theiner, moreover, has omitted whatever seemed irrelevant to his purpose. The criterion of relevancy is uncertain; and we shall avail ourselves largely of the unpublished portions of Salviati's correspondence, which were transcribed by Chateaubriand. These manuscripts, with others of equal importance not previously consulted, determine several doubtful questions of policy and design.

The Protestants never occupied a more triumphant position, and their prospects were never brighter, than in the summer of 1572. For many years the progress of their religion had been incessant. The most valuable of the conquests it has retained were already made; and the period of its reverses had not begun. The great division which aided Catholicism afterwards to recover so much lost ground was not openly confessed; and the effectual unity of the Reformed Churches was not yet dissolved. In controversial theology the defence was weaker than the attack. The works to which the Reformation owed its popularity and system were in the hands of thousands, while the best authors of the Catholic restoration had not begun to write. The press continued to serve the new opinions better than the old; and in literature Protestantism was supreme. Persecuted in the South, and established by violence in the North, it had overcome the resistance of princes in Central Europe, and had won toleration without ceasing to be intolerant. In France and Poland, in the dominions of the Emperor and under the German prelates, the attempt to arrest its advance by physical force had been abandoned. In Germany it covered twice the area that remained to it in the next generation, and, except in Bavaria, Catholicism was fast dying out. The Polish Government had not strength to persecute, and Poland became the refuge of the sects. When the bishops found that they could not prevent toleration, they resolved that they would not restrict it. Trusting to the maxim, "Bellum Haereticorum pax est Ecclesiae," they insisted that liberty should extend to those whom the Reformers would have exterminated.[1] The

---

[1] Satius fore ducebam, si minus profligari possent omnes, ut ferrentur omnes, quo

Polish Protestants, in spite of their dissensions, formed themselves into one great party. When the death of the last of the Jagellons, on the 7th of July 1572, made the monarchy elective, they were strong enough to enforce their conditions on the candidates; and it was thought that they would be able to decide the election, and obtain a king of their own choosing. Alva's reign of Terror had failed to pacify the Low Countries, and he was about to resign the hopeless task to an incapable successor. The taking of the Brill in April was the first of those maritime victories which led to the independence of the Dutch. Mons fell in May; and in July the important province of Holland declared for the Prince of Orange. The Catholics believed that all was lost if Alva remained in command.[2]

The decisive struggle was in France. During the minority of Charles IX persecution had given way to civil war, and the Regent, his mother, had vainly striven, by submitting to neither party, to uphold the authority of the Crown. She checked the victorious Catholics, by granting to the Huguenots terms which constituted them, in spite of continual disaster in the field, a vast and organised power in the State. To escape their influence it would have been necessary to invoke the help of Philip II, and to accept protection which would have made France subordinate to Spain. Philip laboured to establish such an alliance; and it was to promote this scheme that he sent his queen, Elizabeth of Valois, to meet her mother at Bayonne. In 1568 Elizabeth died; and a rumour came to Catherine touching the manner of her death which made it hard to listen to friendly overtures from her husband. Antonio Perez, at that time an unscrupulous instrument of his master's will, afterwards accused him of having poisoned his wife. "On parle fort sinistrement de sa mort, pour avoir été advancée," says Brantôme. After the massacre of the Protestants, the ambassador at Venice, a man distinguished as a jurist and a statesman, reproached Catherine with having thrown France into the hands of him in whom the world recognised her daughter's murderer. Catherine did not deny the truth of the report. She replied that she was "bound to think of her sons in preference to her daughters, that the foul-play was not fully proved, and that if it were it could not be avenged so long as

---

mordentes et comedentes invicem, consumerentur ab invicem (Hosius to Karnkowsky, Feb. 26, 1568).

[2] The Secretary of Medina Celi to Çayas, June 24, 1572 *(Correspondance de Philippe II,* ii. 264).

France was weakened by religious discord."[3] She wrote as she could not have written if she had been convinced that the suspicion was unjust.

When Charles IX began to be his own master he seemed resolved to follow his father and grandfather in their hostility to the Spanish Power. He wrote to a trusted servant that all his thoughts were bent on thwarting Philip.[4] While the Christian navies were fighting at Lepanto, the King of France was treating with the Turks. His menacing attitude in the following year kept Don Juan in Sicilian waters, and made his victory barren for Christendom. Encouraged by French protection, Venice withdrew from the League. Even in Corsica there was a movement which men interpreted as a prelude to the storm that France was raising against the empire of Spain. Rome trembled in expectation of a Huguenot invasion of Italy; for Charles was active in conciliating the Protestants both abroad and at home. He married a daughter of the tolerant Emperor Maximilian II; and he carried on negotiations for the marriage of his brother with Queen Elizabeth, not with any hope of success, but in order to impress public opinion.[5] He made treaties of alliance, in quick succession, with England, with the German Protestants, and with the Prince of Orange. He determined that his brother Anjou, the champion of the Catholics, of whom it was said that he had vowed to root out the Protestants to a man,[6] should be banished to the throne of Poland. Disregarding the threats and

---

[3] Quant à ce qui me touche à moy en particulier, encores que j'ayme unicquement tous mes enffans, je veulx préférer, comme il est bien raysonnable, les filz aux filles; et pour le regard de ce que me mandez de celluy qui a faict mourir ma fille, c'est chose que l'on ne tient point pour certaine, et où elle le seroit, le roy monsieur mondit filz n'en pouvoit faire la vengence en l'estat que son royaulme estoit lors; mais à présent qu'il est tout uni, il aura assez de moien et de forces pour s'en ressentir quant l'occasion s'en présentera (Catherine to Du Ferrier, Oct. 1, 1572; Bib. Imp. F. Fr. 15,555). The despatches of Fourquevaulx from Madrid, published by the Marquis Du Prat in the *Histoire d'Elisabeth de Valois,* do not confirm the rumour.

[4] Toutes mes fantaisies sont bandées pour m'opposer à la grandeur des Espagnols, et je délibère m'y conduire le plus dextrement qu'il me sera possible (Charles IX to Noailles, May 2, 1572; Noailles, *Henri de Valois,* i. 8).

[5] Il fault, et je vous prie ne faillir, quand bien il seroit du tout rompu, et que verriés qu'il n'y auroit nulle espérance, de trouver moyen d'en entretenir toujours doucement le propos, d'ici à quelque temps; car cella ne peut que bien servir à establir mes affaires et aussy pour ma réputation (Charles IX to La Mothe, Aug. 9, 1572; *Corr. de La Mothe,* vii. 311).

[6] This is stated both by his mother and by the Cardinal of Lorraine (Michelet, *La Ligue,* p. 26).

entreaties of the Pope, he gave his sister in marriage to Navarre. By the peace of St. Germains the Huguenots had secured, within certain limits, freedom from persecution and the liberty of persecuting; so that Pius V declared that France had been made the slave of heretics. Coligny was now the most powerful man in the kingdom. His scheme for closing the civil wars by an expedition for the conquest of the Netherlands began to be put in motion. French auxiliaries followed Lewis of Nassau into Mons; an army of Huguenots had already gone to his assistance; another was being collected near the frontier, and Coligny was preparing to take the command in a war which might become a Protestant crusade, and which left the Catholics no hope of victory. Meanwhile many hundreds of his officers followed him to Paris, to attend the wedding which was to reconcile the factions, and cement the peace of religion.

In the midst of those lofty designs and hopes, Coligny was struck down. On the morning of the 22nd of August he was shot at and badly wounded. Two days later he was killed; and a general attack was made on the Huguenots of Paris. It lasted some weeks, and was imitated in about twenty places. The chief provincial towns of France were among them.

Judged by its immediate result, the massacre of St. Bartholomew was a measure weakly planned and irresolutely executed, which deprived Protestantism of its political leaders, and left it for a time to the control of zealots. There is no evidence to make it probable that more than seven thousand victims perished. Judged by later events, it was the beginning of a vast change in the conflict of the churches. At first it was believed that a hundred thousand Huguenots had fallen. It was said that the survivors were abjuring by thousands,[7] that the children of the slain were made Catholics, that those whom the priest had admitted to absolution and communion were nevertheless put to death.[8] Men who were far beyond the reach of the French Government lost their faith in a religion which Providence had visited with so tremendous a judgment;[9] and foreign princes took heart to employ severities which could excite no horror after the scenes in France.

---

[7] In reliqua Gallia fuit et est incredibilis defectio, quae tamen usque adeo non pacavit immanes illas feras, ut etiam eos qui defecerunt (qui pene sunt innumerabiles) semel ad internecionem una cum integris familiis trucidare prorsus decreverint (Beza, Dec. 3, 1572; *Ill. vir. Epp. Sel.*, p. 621, 1617).

[8] Languet to the Duke of Saxony, Nov. 30, 1572 *(Arcanca*, sec. xvi. 183).

[9] Vidi et cum dolore intellexi lanienam illam Gallicam perfidissimam et atrocissimam

Contemporaries were persuaded that the Huguenots had been flattered and their policy adopted only for their destruction, and that the murder of Coligny and his followers was a long premeditated crime. Catholics and Protestants vied with each other in detecting proofs of that which they variously esteemed a sign of supernatural inspiration or of diabolical depravity. In the last forty years a different opinion has prevailed. It has been deemed more probable, more consistent with testimony and with the position of affairs at the time, that Coligny succeeded in acquiring extraordinary influence over the mind of Charles, that his advice really predominated, and that the sanguinary resolution was suddenly embraced by his adversaries as the last means of regaining power. This opinion is made plausible by many facts. It is supported by several writers who were then living, and by the document known as the Confession of Anjou. The best authorities of the present day are nearly unanimous in rejecting premeditation.

The evidence on the opposite side is stronger than they suppose. The doom which awaited the Huguenots had been long expected and often foretold. People at a distance, Monluc in Languedoc, and the Protestant Mylius in Italy, drew the same inference from the news that came from the court. Strangers meeting on the road discussed the infatuation of the Admiral.[10] Letters brought from Rome to the Emperor the significant intimation that the birds were all caged, and now was the time to lay hands on them.[11] Duplessis-Mornay, the future chief of the Huguenots, was so oppressed with a sense of coming evil, that he hardly ventured into the streets on the wedding-day. He warned the Admiral of the general belief among their friends that the marriage concealed a plot for their ruin, and that the festivities would end in some horrible surprise.[12] Coligny was proof against suspicion. Several of his followers left Paris, but he remained unmoved. At one moment the excessive readiness to grant all his requests shook the confidence of his son-in-law Téligny; but the doubt vanished so completely that

---

plurimos per Germaniam ita offendisse, ut jam etiam de veritate nostrae Religionis et doctrinae dubitare incoeperint (Bullinger to Wittgenstein, Feb. 23, 1573; Friedländer, *Beiträge zur rel. Gesch.* p. 254).

[10] De Thou, *Mémoires*, p. 9.

[11] Il me dist qu'on luy avoist escript de Rome, n'avoit que trois semaines ou environ, sur le propos des noces du roy de Navarre en ces propres termes; Que à ceste heure que tous les oiseaux estoient en cage, on les pouvoit prendre tous ensemble (Vulcob to Charles IX, Sept. 26, 1572; Noailles, iii. 214).

[12] *Mémoires de Duplessis-Mornay*, i. 38; Ambert, *Duplessis-Mornay*, p. 38.

Téligny himself prevented the flight of his partisans after the attempt on the Admiral's life. On the morning of the fatal day, Montgomery sent word to Walsingham that Coligny was safe under protection of the King's Guards, and that no further stir was to be apprehended.[13]

For many years foreign advisers had urged Catherine to make away with these men. At first it was computed that half a dozen victims would be enough.[14] That was the original estimate of Alva, at Bayonne.[15] When the Duke of Ferrara was in France in 1564, he proposed a larger measure, and he repeated this advice by the mouth of every agent whom he sent to France.[16] After the event, both Alva and Alfonso reminded Catherine that she had done no more than follow their advice.[17] Alva's letter explicitly confirms the popular notion which connects the massacre with the conference of Bayonne; and it can no longer now be doubted that La Roche-sur-Yon, on his death-bed, informed Coligny that murderous resolutions had been taken on that occasion.[18] But the Nuncio, Santa Croce, who was present, wrote to Cardinal Borromeo that the Queen had indeed promised to punish the infraction of the Edict of Pacification, but that this was a very different thing from undertaking to extirpate heresy. Catherine affirmed that in this way the law could reach all the Huguenot ministers; and Alva professed to believe her.[19] Whatever studied ambiguity of language

[13] Digges, *Compleat Ambassador,* pp. 276, 255.

[14] Correr, *Relazione;* Tommaseo, ii. 116.

[15] He said to Catherine: Que quando quisiesen usar de otro y averlo, con no mas personas que con cinc o seys que son el cabo de todo esto, los tomasen a su mano y les cortasen las cabeças (Alva to Philip II, June 21, 1565; *Papiers de Granvelle.* ix. 298).

[16] Ci rallegriamo con la maestà sua con tutto l'affetto dell' animo, ch' ella habbia presa quella risolutione così opportunamente sopra la quale noi stesso l' ultima volta che fummo in Francia parlammo con la Regina Madre. . . . Dipoi per diversi gentilhuomini che in varie occorrenze habbiamo mandato in corte siamo instati nel suddetto ricordo (Alfonso II to Fogliani, Sept. 13, 1572; Modena Archives).

[17] Muchas vezes me ha accordado de aver dicho a Su Mag. esto mismo en Bayona, y de lo que mi offrecio, y veo que ha muy bien desempeñado su palabra (Alva to Zuñiga, Sept. 9, 1572; Coquerel, *La St. Barthélemy,* p. 12).

[18] Kluckhohn, *Zur Geschichte des angeblichen Bündnisses von Bayonne,* p. 36, 1868.

[19] Il signor duca di Alva . . . mi disse, che come in questo abboccamento negotio alcuno non havevano trattato, ne volevano trattare, altro che della religione, cosi la lor differenza era nata per questo, perchè non vedeva che la regina ci pigliasse risolutione a modo suo ne de altro, che di buone parole ben generali. . . . È stato risoluto che alla tornata in Parigi si farà una ricerca di quelli che hanno contravenuto all' editto, e si castigaranno; nel che dice S. M. che gli Ugonotti ci sono talmente compresi, che spera con questo mezzo solo cacciare i Ministri de Francia. . . . Il Signor Duca di Alva si satisfa più di questa deliberatione di me, perchè io non trovo che serva all' estirpation

she may have used, the action of 1572 was uninfluenced by deliberations which were seven years old.

During the spring and summer the Tuscan agents diligently prepared their master for what was to come. Petrucci wrote on the 19th of March that, for a reason which he could not trust to paper, the marriage would certainly take place, though not until the Huguenots had delivered up their strongholds. Four weeks later Alamanni announced that the Queen's pious design for restoring unity of faith would, by the grace of God, be speedily accomplished. On the 9th of August Petrucci was able to report that the plan arranged at Bayonne was near execution.[20] Yet he was not fully initiated. The Queen afterwards assured him that she had confided the secret to no foreign resident except the Nuncio,[21] and Petrucci resentfully complains that she had also consulted the Ambassador of Savoy. Venice, like Florence and Savoy, was not taken by surprise. In February the ambassador Contarini explained to the Senate the specious tranquillity in France, by saying that the Government reckoned on the death of the Admiral or the Queen of Navarre to work a momentous change.[22] Cavalli, his successor, judged that a business so grossly mismanaged showed no signs of deliberation.[23] There was another Venetian at Paris who was better informed. The Republic was seeking to withdraw from the league against the Turks; and her most illustrious statesman, Giovanni Michiel, was sent to solicit the help of France in negotiating peace.[24] The account which he gave of his mission has been pronounced by a consummate judge of Venetian State-Papers the most valuable report of the sixteenth century.[25] He was admitted almost daily to secret conference with Anjou, Nevers, and the group of Italians on whom the chief odium rests; and there was no counsellor to whom Catherine

---

dell' heresia il castigar quelli che hanno contravenuto all' editto (Santa Croce to Borromeo, Bayonne, July 1, 1565, MS.).

[20] Desjardins, *Négociations avec la Toscane*, iii. 756, 765, 802.

[21] Io non ho fatto intendere cosa alcuna a nessuno principe; ho ben parlato al nunzio solo (Desp. Aug. 31; Desjardins, iii. 828).

[22] Alberi, *Relazioni Venete*, xii. 250.

[23] Alberi, xii. 328.

[24] Son principal but et dessein estoit de sentir quelle espérance ilz pourroient avoir de parvenir à la paix avec le G. S. dont il s'est ouvert et a demandé ce qu'il en pouvoit espérer et attendre (Charles IX to Du Ferrier, Sept. 28, 1572; Charrière, *Négociations dans le Levant*, iii. 310).

[25] Ranke, *Französische Geschichte*, v. 76.

more willingly gave ear.[26] Michiel affirms that the intention had been long entertained, and that the Nuncio had been directed to reveal it privately to Pius V.[27]

Salviati was related to Catherine, and had gained her good opinion as Nuncio in the year 1570. The Pope had sent him back because nobody seemed more capable of diverting her and her son from the policy which caused so much uneasiness at Rome.[28] He died many years later, with the reputation of having been one of the most eminent Cardinals at a time when the Sacred College was unusually rich in talent. Personally, he had always favoured stern measures of repression. When the Countess of Entremont was married to Coligny, Salviati declared that she had made herself liable to severe penalties by entertaining proposals of marriage with so notorious a heretic, and demanded that the Duke of Savoy should, by all means in his power, cause that wicked bride to be put out of the way.[29] When the peace of St. Germains was concluded, he assured Charles and Catherine that their lives were in danger, as the Huguenots were seeking to pull down the throne as well as the altar. He believed that all intercourse with them was sinful, and that the sole remedy was utter extermination by the sword. "I am convinced," he wrote, "that it will come to this." "If they do the tenth part of what I have advised, it will be well for them."[30] After an audience of two hours, at which he had presented a letter from Pius V, prophesying the wrath of Heaven, Salviati perceived that his exhortations made some impression. The King and Queen whispered to him that they hoped to make the peace yield such fruit that the end would more than countervail the badness of the beginning; and the King added, in strict confidence, that his plan was one which, once told, could never be executed.[31] This might have been said to delude the Nuncio; but he was inclined on the whole to believe that it was sincerely meant. The impression was confirmed by the Archbishop of Sens, Cardinal Pellevé, who informed him that the Huguenot leaders were caressed at Court in order to detach them from their party, and that after the loss of their leaders it would not take more than three

[26] Digges, p. 258; Cosmi, *Memorie di Morosini*, p. 26.

[27] Alberi, xii. 294.

[28] Mittit eo Antonium Mariam Salviatum, reginae affinem, eique pergratum, qui eam in officio contineat (Cardinal of Vercelli, *Comment. de Rebus Gregorii XIII*; Ranke, *Päpste*, App. 85).

[29] Desp. Aug. 30, 1570.

[30] Oct. 14, 1570.

[31] Sept. 24, 1570.

days to deal with the rest.[32] Salviati on his return to France was made aware that his long-deferred hopes were about to be fulfilled. He shadowed it forth obscurely in his despatches. He reported that the Queen allowed the Huguenots to pass into Flanders, believing that the admiral would become more and more presumptuous until he gave her an opportunity of retribution; for she excelled in that kind of intrigue. Some days later he knew more, and wrote that he hoped soon to have good news for his Holiness.[33] At the last moment his heart misgave him. On the morning of the 21st of August the Duke of Montpensier and the Cardinal of Bourbon spoke with so much unconcern, in his presence, of what was then so near, that he thought it hardly possible the secret could be kept.[34]

The foremost of the French prelates was the Cardinal of Lorraine. He had held a prominent position at the council of Trent; and for many years he had wielded the influence of the House of Guise over the Catholics of France. In May 1572 he went to Rome; and he was still there when the news came from Paris in September. He at once made it known that the resolution had been taken before he left France, and that it was due to himself and his nephew, the Duke of Guise.[35] As the spokesman of the Gallican Church in the following year he delivered a harangue to Charles IX, in which he declared that Charles had eclipsed the glory of preceding kings by slaying the false prophets, and especially by the holy deceit and pious dissimulation with which he had laid his plans.[36]

---

[32] Nov. 28, 1570.

[33] Quando scrissi ai giorni passati alla S. V. Illma in cifra, che l' ammiraglio s' avanzava troppo et che gli darebbero su l' unge, già mi ero accorto, che non lo volevano più tollerare, et molto più mi confermai nell' opinione, quando con caratteri ordinarii glie scrivevo che speravo di dover haver occasione di dar qualche buona nova a Sua Beatitudine, benchè mai havrei creduto la X. parte di quello, che al presente veggo con gli occhi (Desp. Aug. 24; Theiner, *Annales*, i. 329).

[34] Che molti siano stati consapevoli del fatto è necessario, potendogli dizer che a 21 la mattina, essendo col Cardinal di Borbone et M. de Montpensier, viddi che ragionavano si domesticamente di quello che doveva seguire, che in me medesimo restando confuso, conobbi che la prattica andava gagliarda, e piutosto disperai di buon fine che altrimente (same Desp.; Mackintosh, *History of England*, ii. 355).

[35] Attribuisce a se, et al nipote, et a casa sua, la morte dell' ammiraglio, gloriandosene assai (Desp. Oct. 1; Theiner, p. 331). The Emperor told the French ambassador "que, depuis les choses avenues, on lui avoit mandé de Rome que Mr. le Cardinal de Lorraine avoit dit que tout le fait avoit esté délibéré avant qu'il partist de France" (Vulcob to Charles IX, Nov. 8; Groen van Prinsterer, *Archives de Nassau*, iv. App. 22).

[36] Marlot, *Histoire de Reims*, iv. 426. This language excited the surprise of Dale, Walsingham's successor (Mackintosh, iii. 226).

There was one man who did not get his knowledge from rumour, and who could not be deceived by lies. The King's confessor, Sorbin, afterwards Bishop of Nevers, published in 1574 a narrative of the life and death of Charles IX. He bears unequivocal testimony that that clement and magnanimous act, for so he terms it, was resolved upon beforehand, and he praises the secrecy as well as the justice of his hero.[37]

Early in the year a mission of extraordinary solemnity had appeared in France. Pius V, who was seriously alarmed at the conduct of Charles, had sent the Cardinal of Alessandria as Legate to the Kings of Spain and Portugal, and directed him, in returning, to visit the Court at Blois. The Legate was nephew to the Pope, and the man whom he most entirely trusted.[38] His character stood so high that the reproach of nepotism was never raised by his promotion. Several prelates destined to future eminence attended him. His chief adviser was Hippolyto Aldobrandini, who, twenty years later, ascended the papal chair as Clement VIII. The companion whose presence conferred the greatest lustre on the mission was the general of the Jesuits, Francis Borgia, the holiest of the successors of Ignatius, and the most venerated of men then living. Austerities had brought him to the last stage of weakness; and he was sinking under the malady of which he was soon to die. But it was believed that the words of such a man, pleading for the Church, would sway the mind of the King. The ostensible purpose of the Legate's journey was to break off the match with Navarre, and to bring France into the Holy League. He gained neither object. When he was summoned back to Rome it was understood in France that he had reaped nothing but refusals, and that he went away disappointed.[39] The jeers of the Protestants pursued him.[40] But it was sufficiently certain beforehand that France could not plunge into a Turkish war.[41]

---

[37] *Archives Curieuses*, viii. 305.

[38] Egli solo tra tutti gli altri è solito particolarmente di sostenere le nostre fatiche. . . . Essendo partecipe di tutti i nostri consigli, et consapevole de segreti dell' intimo animo nostro (Pius V to Philip II, June 20, 1571; Zucchi, *Idea del Segretario*, i. 544).

[39] Serranus, *Commentarii*, iv. 14; Davila, ii. 104.

[40] Digges, p. 193.

[41] Finis hujus legationis erat non tam suadere Regi ut foedus cum aliis Christianis principibus iniret (id nempe notum erat impossibile illi regno esse); sed ut rex ille praetermissus non videretur, et revera ut sciretur quo tenderent Gallorum cogitationes. Non longe nempe a Rocella naves quasdam praegrandes instruere et armare coeperat Philippus Strozza praetexens vela ad Indias a Gallis inventas navigare *(Relatio gestorum in Legatione Card. Alexandrini MS.).*

The real business of the Legate, besides proposing a Catholic husband for the Princess, was to ascertain the object of the expedition which was fitting out in the Western ports. On both points he had something favourable to report. In his last despatch, dated Lyons, the 6th of March, he wrote that he had failed to prevent the engagement with Navarre, but that he had something for the Pope's private ear, which made his journey not altogether unprofitable.[42] The secret was soon divulged in Italy. The King had met the earnest remonstrances of the Legate by assuring him that the marriage afforded the only prospect of wreaking vengeance on the Huguenots: the event would show; he could say no more, but desired his promise to be carried to the Pope. It was added that he had presented a ring to the Legate, as a pledge of sincerity, which the Legate refused. The first to publish this story was Capilupi, writing only seven months later. It was repeated by Folieta,[43] and is given with all details by the historians of Pius V— Catena and Gabuzzi. Catena was secretary to the Cardinal of Alessandria as early as July 1572, and submitted his work to him before publication.[44] Gabuzzi wrote at the instance of the same Cardinal, who supplied him with materials; and his book was examined and approved by Borghese, afterwards Paul V. Both the Cardinal of Alessandria and Paul V, therefore, were instrumental in causing it to be proclaimed that the Legate was acquainted in February 1572 with the intention which the King carried out in August.

The testimony of Aldobrandini was given still more distinctly, and with greater definiteness and authority. When he was required, as Pope, to pronounce upon the dissolution of the ill-omened marriage, he related to Borghese and other Cardinals what had passed in that interview between the Legate and the King, adding that, when the report of the massacre reached Rome, the Cardinal exclaimed: "God be praised! the King of France has kept his word." Clement referred D'Ossat to a narrative of the journey which he had written himself, and in which those things would be found.[45] The clue thus given has

---

[42] Con alcuni particulari che io porto, de' quali ragguaglierò N. Signore a bocca, posso dire di non partirmi affatto mal espedito (Ranke, *Zeitschrift*, iii. 598). Le temps et les effectz luy témoigneront encores d'advantage *(Mémoire baillé au légat Alexandrin*, Feb. 1572; Bib. Imp. F. Dupuy, 523).

[43] *De Sacro Foedere, Graevius Thesarus*, i. 1038.

[44] Catena, *Vita di Pio V*, p. 197; Gabutius, *Vita Pii V*, p. 150, and the Dedication.

[45] D'Ossat to Villeroy, Sept. 22, 1599; *Lettres*, iii. 503. An account of the Legate's

been unaccountably neglected, although the Report was known to exist. One copy is mentioned by Giorgi; and Mazzuchelli knew of another. Neither of them had read it; for they both ascribe it to Michele Bonelli, the Cardinal of Alessandria. The first page would have satisfied them that it was not his work. Clement VIII describes the result of the mission to Blois in these words: "Quae rationes eo impulerunt regem ut semel apprehensa manu Cardinalis in hanc vocem proruperit: Significate Pontifici illumque certum reddite me totum hoc quod circa id matrimonium feci et facturus sum, nulla alia de causa facere, quam ulciscendi inimicos Dei et hujus regni, et puniendi tam infidos rebelles, ut eventus ipse docebit, nec aliud vobis amplius significare possum. Quo non obstante semper Cardinalis eas subtexuit difficultates quas potuit, objiciens regi possetne contrahi matrimonium a fidele cum infidele, sitve dispensatio necessaria; quod si est nunquam Pontificem inductum iri ut illam concedat. Re ipsa ita in suspenso relicta discedendum esse putavit, cum jam rescivisset qua de causa naves parabantur, qui apparatus contra Rocellam tendebant."

The opinion that the massacre of St. Bartholomew was a sudden and unpremeditated act cannot be maintained; but it does not follow that the only alternative is to believe that it was the aim of every measure of the Government for two years before. Catherine had long contemplated it as her last expedient in extremity; but she had decided that she could not resort to it while her son was virtually a minor.[46] She suggested the idea to him in 1570. In that year he gave orders that the Huguenots should be slaughtered at Bourges. The letter is preserved in which La Chastre spurned the command: "If the people of Bourges learn that your Majesty takes pleasure in such tragedies, they will repeat them often. If these men die, let them first be tried; but do not reward my services and sully my reputation by such a stain."[47]

In the autumn of 1571 Coligny came to Blois. Walsingham suspected,

---

journey was found by Mendham among Lord Guildford's manuscripts, and is described in the Supplement to his life of Pius V, p. 13. It is written by the Master of Ceremonies, and possesses no interest. The *Relatio* already quoted, which corresponds to the description given by Clement VIII of his own work, is among the manuscripts of the Marquis Capponi, No. 164.

[46] Vuol andar con ogni quiete et dissimulatione, fin che il Rè suo figliolo sia in età (Santa Croce, Desp. June 27, 1563; *Lettres du Card. Santa Croce*, p. 243).

[47] La Chastre to Charles IX, Jan. 21, 1570; Raynal, *Histoire du Berry*, iv. 105; Lavallée, *Histoire des Français*, ii. 478. Both Raynal and Lavallée had access to the original.

and was afterwards convinced that the intention to kill him already existed. The Pope was much displeased by his presence at Court; but he received assurances from the ambassador which satisfied him. It was said at the time that he at first believed that Coligny was to be murdered, but that he soon found that there was no such praiseworthy design.[48]

In December the King knew that, when the moment came, the burghers of Paris would not fail him. Marcel, the Prévôt des Marchands, told him that the wealth was driven out of the country by the Huguenots: "The Catholics will bear it no longer. . . . Let your Majesty look to it. Your crown is at stake, Paris alone can save it."[49] By the month of February 1572 the plan had assumed a practical shape. The political idea before the mind of Charles was the same by which Richelieu afterwards made France the first Power in the world; to repress the Protestants at home, and to encourage them abroad. No means of effectual repression was left but murder. But the idea of raising up enemies to Spain by means of Protestantism was thoroughly understood. The Huguenots were allowed to make an expedition to aid William of Orange. Had they gained some substantial success, the Government would have followed it up, and the scheme of Coligny would have become for the moment the policy of France. But the Huguenot commander Genlis was defeated and taken. Coligny had had his chance. He had played and lost. It was useless now to propose his great venture against the King of Spain.[50]

Philip II perfectly understood that this event was decisive. When the news came from Hainaut, he sent to the Nuncio Castagna to say that the King of France would gain more than himself by the loss of so many brave Protestants, and that the time was come for him, with the aid of the people of Paris, to get rid of Coligny and the rest of his

[48] Il Papa credeva che la pace fatta, e l'aver consentito il Rè che l'Ammiraglio venisse in corte, fusse con disegno di ammazzarlo; ma accortosi come passa il fatto, non ha creduto che nel Rè Nostro sia quella brava resoluzione (Letter of Nov. 28, 1571; Desjardins, iii. 732). Pour le regard de M. l'Admiral, je n'ay failly de luy faire entendre ce que je devois, suyvant ce qu'il a pleu à V. M. me commander, dont il est demeuré fort satisfaict (Ferralz to Charles IX, Dec. 25, 1571; Bib. Imp. F. Fr. 16,039: Walsingham to Herbert, Oct. 10, 1571; to Smith, Nov. 26, 1572; Digges, p. 290).

[49] Marcel to Charles IX, December 20, 1571: *Cabinet Historique*, ii. 253.

[50] Le Roy estoit d'intelligence, ayant permis à ceux de la Religion de l'assister, et, cas advenant que leurs entreprises succédassent, qu'il les favoriserait ouvertement . . . Genlis, menant un secours dans Mons, fut défait par le duc d'Alve, qui avoit comme investi la ville. La journée de Saint-Barthélemi se résolut (Bouillon, *Mémoires*, p. 9).

enemies.[51] It appears from the letters of Salviati that he also regarded the resolution as having been finally taken after the defeat of Genlis.

The Court had determined to enforce unity of faith in France. An edict of toleration was issued for the purpose of lulling the Huguenots; but it was well known that it was only a pretence.[52] Strict injunctions were sent into the provinces that it should not be obeyed;[53] and Catherine said openly to the English envoy, "My son will have exercise but of one Religion in his Realm." On the 26th the King explained his plan to Mondoucet, his agent at Brussels: "Since it has pleased God to bring matters to the point they have now reached, I mean to use the opportunity to secure a perpetual repose in my kingdom, and to do something for the good of all Christendom. It is probable that the conflagration will spread to every town in France, and that they will follow the example of Paris, and lay hands on all the Protestants. . . . I have written to the governors to assemble forces in order to cut to pieces those who may resist."[54] The great object was to accomplish the extirpation of Protestantism in such a way as might leave intact the friendship with Protestant States. Every step was governed by this consideration; and the difficulty of the task caused the inconsistencies and the vacillation that ensued. By assassinating Coligny alone it was expected that such an agitation would be provoked among his partisans as would make it appear that they were killed by the Catholics in self-defence. Reports were circulated at once with that object. A letter written on the 23rd states that, after the Admiral was wounded on the day before, the Huguenots assembled at the gate of the Louvre, to avenge him on the Guises as they came out.[55] And the first explanation sent forth by the Government on the 24th was to the effect that the old feud between the Houses of Guise and of Chatillon had broken

---

[51] Si potria distruggere il resto, maxime che l' ammiraglio si trova in Parigi, populo Catholico et devoto del suo Rè, dove potria se volesse facilmente levarselo dinnanzi per sempre (Castagna, Desp. Aug. 5, 1572; Theiner, i. 327).

[52] *Mémoires de Claude Haton*, 687.

[53] En quelque sorte que ce soit ledict Seigneur est résollu faire vivre ses subjectz en sa religion, et ne permettre jamais ny tollérer, quelque chose qui puisse advenir, qu'il n'y ait aultre forme ny exercice de religion en son royaulme que de la catholique (Instruction for the Governors of Normandy, Nov. 3, 1572; La Mothe, vii. 390).

[54] Charles IX to Mondoucet, Aug. 26, 1572; *Compte Rendu de la Commission Royale d'Histoire*, 2ᵉ Série, iv. 327.

[55] Li Ugonotti si ridussero alla porta del Louvre, per aspettare che Mons. di Guisa e Mons. d'Aumale uscissero per ammazzarli (Borso Trotti, Desp. Aug. 23; Modena Archives).

out with a fury which it was impossible to quell. This fable lasted only for a single day. On the 25th Charles writes that he has begun to discover traces of a Huguenot conspiracy;[56] and on the following day this was publicly substituted for the original story. Neither the vendetta of the Guises nor the conspiracy at Paris could be made to explain the massacre in the provinces. It required to be so managed that the King could disown it; Salviati describes the plan of operations. It was intended that the Huguenots should be slaughtered successively by a series of spontaneous outbreaks in different parts of the country. While Rochelle held out, it was dangerous to proceed with a more sweeping method.[57] Accordingly, no written instructions from the King are in existence; and the governors were expressly informed that they were to expect none.[58] Messengers went into the provinces with letters requiring that the verbal orders which they brought should be obeyed.[59] Many governors refused to act upon directions so vague and so hard to verify. Burgundy was preserved in this way. Two gentlemen arrived with letters of recommendation from the King, and declared his commands. They were asked to put them on paper; but they refused to give in writing what they had received by word of mouth. Mandelot, the Governor of Lyons, the most ignoble of the instruments in this foul deed, complained that the intimation of the royal wishes sent to him was obscure and insufficient.[60] He did not do his work thoroughly, and incurred the displeasure of the King. The orders were complicated as well as obscure. The public authorities were required to collect the Huguenots in some prison or other safe place, where they could be got at by hired bands of volunteer assassins. To screen the King it was desirable that his officers should not superintend the work themselves. Mandelot, having locked the gates of Lyons, and shut up the Huguenots together, took himself out of the way while they were being butchered. Carouge, at Rouen, received a commission to visit the other towns in

[56] L'on a commencé à descouvrir la conspiration que ceux de la religion prétendue réformée avoient faicte contre moy mesmes, ma mère et mes frères (Charles IX to La Mothe, Aug. 25; La Mothe, vii. 325).

[57] Desp. Sept. 19, 1572.

[58] Il ne fault pas attendre d'en avoir d'autre commandement du Roy ne de Monseigneur, car ils ne vous en feront point (Puygaillard to Montsoreau, Aug. 26, 1572; Mourin, *La Réforme en Anjou*, p. 106).

[59] Vous croirez le présent porteur de ce que je luy ay donné charge de vous dire (Charles IX to Mandelot, Aug. 24, 1572; *Corr. de Charles IX avec Mandelot*, p. 42).

[60] Je n'en ay aucune coulpe, n'ayant sceu quelle estoit la volunté que par umbre, encores bien tard et à demy (Mandelot to Charles IX, Sept. 17, p. 73).

his province. The magistrates implored him to remain, as nobody, in his absence, could restrain the people. When the King had twice repeated his commands, Carouge obeyed; and five hundred Huguenots perished.[61]

It was thought unsafe even for the King's brother to give distinct orders under his own hand. He wrote to his lieutenant in Anjou that he had commissioned Puygaillard to communicate with him on a matter which concerned the King's service and his own, and desired that his orders should be received as if they came directly from himself. They were, that every Huguenot in Angers, Saumur, and the adjoining country should be put to death without delay and without exception.[62] The Duke of Montpensier himself sent the same order to Brittany; but it was indignantly rejected by the municipality of Nantes.

When reports came in of the manner in which the event had been received in foreign countries, the Government began to waver, and the sanguinary orders were recalled. Schomberg wrote from Germany that the Protestant allies were lost unless they could be satisfied that the King had not decreed the extermination of their brethren.[63] He was instructed to explain the tumult in the provinces by the animosity bequeathed by the wars of religion.[64] The Bishop of Valence was intriguing in Poland on behalf of Anjou. He wrote that his success had been made very doubtful, and that, if further cruelties were perpetrated, ten millions of gold pieces would not bribe the venal Poles. He advised that a counterfeit edict, at least, should be published.[65] Charles perceived that he would be compelled to abandon his enterprise, and set about appeasing the resentment of the Protestant Powers. He promised that an inquiry should be instituted, and the proofs of the conspiracy communicated to foreign Governments. To give a judicial aspect to the proceedings, two prominent Huguenots were ceremoniously hanged. When the new ambassador from Spain praised the long concealment of the plan, Charles became indignant.[66] It was repeated everywhere that the thing had been arranged with Rome and Spain;

---

[61] Floquet, *Histoire du Parlement de Normandie*, iii. 121.

[62] Anjou to Montsoreau, Aug. 26; Mourin, p. 107; Falloux, *Vie de Pie V*, i. 358; Port, *Archives de la Mairie d'Angers*, pp. 41, 42.

[63] Schomberg to Brulart, Oct. 10, 1572; Capefigue, *La Réforme*, iii. 264.

[64] Instructions for Schomberg, Feb. 15, 1573; Noailles, iii. 305.

[65] Monluc to Brulart, Nov. 20, 1572; Jan. 20, 1573: to Charles IX, Jan. 22, 1573; Noailles, iii. 218, 223, 220.

[66] Charles IX to St. Goard, Jan. 20, 1573; Groen, iv. App. 29.

and he was especially studious that there should be no symptoms of a private understanding with either power.[67] He was able to flatter himself that he had at least partially succeeded. If he had not exterminated his Protestant subjects, he had preserved his Protestant allies. William the Silent continued to solicit his aid; Elizabeth consented to stand godmother to the daughter who was born to him in October; he was allowed to raise mercenaries in Switzerland; and the Polish Protestants agreed to the election of his brother. The promised evidence of the Huguenot conspiracy was forgotten; and the King suppressed the materials which were to have served for an official history of the event.[68]

Zeal for religion was not the motive which inspired the chief authors of this extraordinary crime. They were trained to look on the safety of the monarchy as the sovereign law, and on the throne as an idol that justified sins committed in its worship. At all times there have been men, resolute and relentless in the pursuit of their aims, whose ardour was too strong to be restricted by moral barriers or the instinct of humanity. In the sixteenth century, beside the fanaticism of freedom, there was an abject idolatry of power; and laws both human and divine were made to yield to the intoxication of authority and the reign of will. It was laid down that kings have the right of disposing of the lives of their subjects, and may dispense with the forms of justice. The Church herself, whose supreme pontiff was now an absolute monarch, was infected with this superstition. Catholic writers found an opportune argument for their religion in the assertion that it makes the prince master of the consciences as well as the bodies of the people, and enjoins submission even to the vilest tyranny.[69] Men whose lives were precious to the Catholic cause could be murdered by royal command, without protest from Rome. When the Duke of Guise, with the Cardinal

---

[67] Letter from Paris in Strype's *Life of Parker*, iii. 110; "Tocsain contre les Massacreurs," *Archives Curieuses*, vii. 7.

[68] Afin que ce que vous avez dressé des choses passées à la Saint-Barthélemy ne puisse être publié parmi le peuple, et mêmement entre les étrangers, comme il y en a plusieurs qui se mêlent d'écrire et qui pourraient prendre occasion d'y répondre, je vous prie qu'il n'en soit rien imprimé ni en français ni en Latin, mais si vous en avez retenu quelque chose, le garder vers vous (Charles IX to the President de Cély, March 24, 1573; *Revue Rétrospective*, 2 Série, iii. 195).

[69] Botero, *Della Ragion di Stato*, 92. A contemporary says that the Protestants were cut to pieces out of economy, "pour afin d'éviter le coust des exécutions qu'il eust convenu payer pour les faire pendre"; and that this was done "par permission divine" *(Relation des troubles de Rouen par un témoin oculaire*, ed. Pottier, 36, 46).

his brother, was slain by Henry III, he was the most powerful and devoted upholder of Catholicism in France. Sixtus V thundered against the sacrilegious tyrant who was stained with the blood of a prince of the Church; but he let it be known very distinctly that the death of the Duke caused him little concern.[70]

Catherine was the daughter of that Medici to whom Machiavelli had dedicated his *Prince*. So little did religion actuate her conduct that she challenged Elizabeth to do to the Catholics of England what she herself had done to the Protestants of France, promising that if they were destroyed there would be no loss of her good will.[71] The levity of her religious feelings appears from her reply when asked by Gomicourt what message he should take to the Duke of Alva: "I must give you the answer of Christ to the disciples of St. John, 'Ite et nuntiate quae vidistis et audivistis; caeci vident, claudi ambulant, leprosi mundantur.' " And she added, "Beatus qui non fuerit in me scandalizatus."[72]

If mere fanaticism had been their motive, the men who were most active in the massacre would not have spared so many lives. While Guise was galloping after Ferrières and Montgomery, who had taken horse betimes, and made for the coast, his house at Paris was crowded with families belonging to the proscribed faith, and strangers to him. A young girl who was amongst them has described his return, when he sent for the children, spoke to them kindly, and gave orders that they should be well treated as long as his roof sheltered them.[73] Protestants even spoke of him as a humane and chivalrous enemy.[74] Nevers was considered to have disgraced himself by the number of those whom he enabled to escape.[75] The Nuncio was shocked at their ill-timed generosity. He reported to Rome that the only one who had acted in the spirit of a Christian, and had refrained from mercy, was the King; while the other princes, who pretended to be good Catholics, and to deserve the favour of the Pope, had striven, one and all, to save as many Huguenots as they could.[76]

[70] Del resto poco importerebbe a Roma (Card. Montalto to Card. Morosini; Tempesti, *Vita di Sisto V*, ii. 116).

[71] Quand ce seroit contre touts les Catholiques, que nous ne nous en empescherions, ny altérerions aucunement l'amitié d'entre elle et nous (Catherine to La Mothe, Sept. 13, 1572; La Mothe, vii. 349).

[72] Alva's Report; *Bulletins de l'Académie de Bruxelles*, ix. 564.

[73] Jean Diodati, *door Schotel*, 88.

[74] *Oeuvres de Brantôme*, ed. Lalanne, iv. 38.

[75] Otros que salvo el Duque de Nevers con harto vituperio suyo (Cabrera de Cordova, *Felipe Segundo*, p. 722).

[76] Il Re Christianissimo in tutti questi accidenti, in luogo di giudicio e di valore ha

The worst criminals were not the men who did the deed. The crime of mobs and courtiers, infuriated by the lust of vengeance and of power, is not so strange a portent as the exultation of peaceful men, influenced by no present injury or momentary rage, but by the permanent and incurable perversion of moral sense wrought by a distorted piety.

Philip II, who had long suspected the court of France, was at once relieved from the dread which had oppressed him, and betrayed an excess of joy foreign to his phlegmatic nature.[77] He immediately sent six thousand crowns to the murderer of Coligny.[78] He persuaded himself that the breach between France and her allies was irreparable, that Charles would now be driven to seek his friendship, and that the Netherlands were out of danger.[79] He listened readily to the French ambassador, who assured him that his court had never swerved from the line of Catholic policy, but had intended all along to effect this great change.[80] Ayamonte carried his congratulations to Paris, and pretended that his master had been in the secret. It suited Philip that this should be believed by Protestant princes, in order to estrange them still more from France; but he wrote on the margin of Ayamonte's instructions, that it was uncertain how long previously the purpose had subsisted.[81] Juan and Diego de Zuñiga, his ambassadors at Rome and at Paris, were convinced that the long display of enmity to Spain was genuine, that the death of Coligny had been decided at the last moment, and that the rest was not the effect of design.[82] This opinion found friends at first in Spain. The General of the Franciscans undertook

---

mostrato animo christiano, con tutto habbia salvato alcuno. Ma li altri principi che fanno gran professione di Cattolici et di meritar favori e gratie del papa hanno poi con estrema diligenza cercato a salvare quelli più di Ugonotti che hanno potuto, e se non gli nomino particolarmente, non si maravigli, per che indifferentemente tutti hanno fatto a un modo (Salviati, Desp. Sept. 2, 1572).

[77] Estque dictu mirum, quantopere Regem exhilaravit nova Gallica (Hopperus to Viglius, Madrid, Sept. 7, 1572; *Hopperi Epp.* 360).

[78] Ha avuto, con questa occasione, dal Rè di Spagna, sei mila scudi a conto della dote di sua moglie e a richiesta di casa di Guise (Petrucci, Desp. Sept. 16, 1572; Desjardins, iii. 838). On the 27th of December 1574, the Cardinal of Guise asks Philip for more money for the same man (Bouillé, *Histoire des Ducs de Guise,* ii. 505).

[79] Siendo cosa clara que, de hoy mas, ni los protestantes de Alemania, ni la reyna de Inglaterra se fiaran dél (Philip to Alva, Sept. 18, 1572; *Bulletins de Bruxelles,* xvi. 255).

[80] St. Goard to Charles IX, Sept. 12, 1572; Groen, iv. App. 12; Raumer, *Briefe aus Paris,* i. 191.

[81] *Archives de l'Empire,* K. 1530, B. 34, 299.

[82] Zuñiga to Alva. Aug. 31, 1572: No fue caso pensado sino repentino (*Archives de l'Empire,* K. 1530, B. 34, 66).

to explode it. He assured Philip that he had seen the King and the Queen-mother two years before, and had found them already so intent on the massacre that he wondered how anybody could have the courage to detract from their merit by denying it.[83] This view generally prevailed in Spain. Mendoça knows not which to admire more, the loyal and Catholic inhabitants of Paris, or Charles, who justified his title of the most Christian King by helping with his own hands to slaughter his subjects.[84] Mariana witnessed the carnage, and imagined that it must gladden every Catholic heart. Other Spaniards were gratified to think that it had been contrived with Alva at Bayonne.

Alva himself did not judge the event by the same light as Philip. He also had distrusted the French Government; but he had not feared it during the ascendency of the Huguenots. Their fall appeared to him to strengthen France. In public he rejoiced with the rest. He complimented Charles on his valour and his religion, and claimed his own share of merit. But he warned Philip that things had not changed favourably for Spain, and that the King of France was now a formidable neighbour.[85] For himself, he said, he never would have committed so base a deed.

The seven Catholic Cantons had their own reason for congratulation. Their countrymen had been busy actors on the scene; and three soldiers of the Swiss guard of Anjou were named as the slayers of the Admiral.[86] On the 2nd of October they agreed to raise 6000 men for the King's service. At the following Diet they demanded the expulsion of the fugitive Huguenots who had taken refuge in the Protestant parts of the Confederation. They made overtures to the Pope for a secret alliance against their Confederates.[87]

In Italy, where the life of a heretic was cheap, their wholesale destruction was confessed a highly politic and ingenious act. Even the sage Venetians were constrained to celebrate it with a procession. The Grand Duke Cosmo had pointed out two years before that an insidious peace would afford excellent opportunities of extinguishing Protes-

---

[83] St. Goard to Catherine, Jan. 6, 1573; Groen, iv. App. 28.

[84] *Comment. de B. de Mendoça*, i. 344.

[85] Alva to Philip, Oct. 13, 1572; *Corr. de Philippe II*, ii. 287. On the 23rd of August Zuñiga wrote to Philip that he hoped that Coligny would recover from his wound, because, if he should die, Charles would be able to obtain obedience from all men (*Archives de l'Empire*, K. 1530, B. 34, 65).

[86] *Bulletins de la Société pour l'Histoire du Protestantisme Français*, viii. 292.

[87] *Eidgenössische Abschiede*, iv. 2, 501, 503, 506, 510.

tantism; and he derived inexpressible consolation from the heroic enterprise.[88] The Viceroy of Naples, Cardinal Granvelle, received the tidings coldly. He was surprised that the event had been so long postponed, and he reproved the Cardinal of Lorraine for the unstatesmanlike delay.[89] The Italians generally were excited to warmer feelings. They saw nothing to regret but the death of certain Catholics who had been sacrificed to private revenge. Profane men approved the skill with which the trap was laid; and pious men acknowledged the presence of a genuine religious spirit in the French court.[90] The nobles and the Parisian populace were admired for their valour in obeying the sanctified commands of the good King. One fervent enthusiast praises God for the heavenly news, and also St. Bartholomew for having lent his extremely penetrating knife for the salutary sacrifice.[91] A month after the event the renowned preacher Panigarola delivered from the pulpit a panegyric on the monarch who had achieved what none had ever heard or read before, by banishing heresy in a single day, and by a single word, from the Christian land of France.[92]

The French churches had often resounded with furious declamations; and they afterwards rang with canticles of unholy joy. But the French clergy does not figure prominently in the inception or the execution of the sanguinary decree. Conti, a contemporary indeed, but too distant for accurate knowledge, relates that the parish priest went round, marking with a white cross the dwellings of the people who were doomed.[93] He is contradicted by the municipal Registers of Paris.[94] Morvilliers, Bishop of Orleans, though he had resigned the seals which he received from L'Hôpital, still occupied the first place at the royal council. He was consulted at the last moment, and it is said that he nearly fainted with horror. He recovered, and gave his opinion with the rest. He is the only French prelate, except the cardinals, whose complicity appears to be ascertained. But at Orleans, where the

[88] Cosmo to Camaiani, Oct. 6, 1570 (Cantù, *Gli Eretici d'Italia*, iii. 15); Cosmo to Charles IX, Sept. 4, 1572 (Gachard, *Rapport sur les Archives de Lille*, 199).

[89] Grappin, *Mémoire Historique sur le Card. de Granvelle*, 73.

[90] Bardi, *Età del Mondo*, 1581, iv. 2011; Campana, *Historie del Mondo*, 1599, i. 145; B. D. da Fano, *Aggiunte all' Historie di Mambrino Roseo*, 1583, v. 252; Pellini, *Storia di Perugia*, vol. iii. MS.

[91] Si è degnato di prestare alli suoi divoti il suo taglientissimo coltello in così salutifero sacrificio (Letter of Aug. 26; Alberi, *Vita di Caterina de' Medici*, 401).

[92] Labitte, *Démocratie chez les Prédicateurs de la Ligue*, 10.

[93] Natalis Comes, *Historiae sui temporis*, 512.

[94] Capefigue, iii. 150.

bloodshed was more dreadful in proportion than at Paris, the signal is said to have been given, not by the bishop, but by the King's preacher, Sorbin.

Sorbin is the only priest of the capital who is distinctly associated with the act of the Government. It was his opinion that God has ordained that no mercy shall be shown to heretics, that Charles was bound in conscience to do what he did, and that leniency would have been as censurable in his case as precipitation was in that of Theodosius. What the Calvinists called perfidy and cruelty seemed to him nothing but generosity and kindness.[95] These were the sentiments of the man from whose hands Charles IX received the last consolations of his religion. It has been related that he was tortured in his last moments with remorse for the blood he had shed. His spiritual adviser was fitted to dispel such scruples. He tells us that he heard the last confession of the dying King, and that his most grievous sorrow was that he left the work unfinished.[96] In all that blood-stained history there is nothing more tragic than the scene in which the last words preparing the soul for judgment were spoken by such a confessor as Sorbin to such a penitent as Charles.

Emond Auger, one of the most able and eloquent of the Jesuits, was at that time attracting multitudes by his sermons at Bordeaux. He denounced with so much violence the heretics and the people in authority who protected them, that the magistrates, fearing a cry for blood, proposed to silence or to moderate the preacher. Montpezat, Lieutenant of Guienne, arrived in time to prevent it. On the 30th of September he wrote to the King that he had done this, and that there were a score of the inhabitants who might be despatched with advantage. Three days later, when he was gone, more than two hundred Huguenots were murdered.[97]

[95] Pourront-ils arguer de trahison le feu roy, qu'ils blasphèment luy donnant le nom de tyran, veu qu'il n'a rien entrepris et exécuté que ce qu'il pouvoit faire par l'expresse parole de Dieu . . . Dieu commande qu'on ne pardonne en façon que ce soit aux inventeurs ou sectateurs de nouvelles opinions ou hérésies. . . . Ce que vous estimez cruauté estre plutôt vraye magnanimité et doulceur (Sorbin, *Le Vray resveille-matin des Calvinistes*, 1576, pp. 72, 74, 78).

[96] Il commanda à chacun de se retirer au cabinet et à moy de m'asseoir au chevet de son lict, tant pour ouyr sa confession, et luy donner ministérialement absolution de ses péchez, que aussi pour le consoler durant et après la messe (Sorbin, *Vie de Charles IX; Archives Curieuses*, viii. 287). Est très certain que le plus grand regret qu'il avoit à l'heure de sa mort estoit de ce qu'il voyoit l'idole Calvinesque n'estre encores du tout chassée (*Vray resveille-matin*, 88).

[97] The charge against the clergy of Bordeaux is brought by D'Aubigné (*Histoire*

Apart from these two instances it is not known that the clergy interfered in any part of France to encourage the assassins.

The belief was common at the time, and is not yet extinct, that the massacre had been promoted and sanctioned by the Court of Rome. No evidence of this complicity, prior to the event, has ever been produced; but it seemed consistent with what was supposed to have occurred in the affair of the dispensation. The marriage of Margaret of Valois with the King of Navarre was invalid and illicit in the eyes of the Church; and it was known that Pius V had sworn that he would never permit it. When it had been celebrated by a Cardinal, in the presence of a splendid court, and no more was heard of resistance on the part of Rome, the world concluded that the dispensation had been obtained. De Thou says, in a manuscript note, that it had been sent, and was afterwards suppressed by Salviati; and the French bishop, Spondanus, assigns the reasons which induced Gregory XIII to give way.[98] Others affirmed that he had yielded when he learned that the marriage was a snare, so that the massacre was the price of the dispensation.[99] The Cardinal of Lorraine gave currency to the story. As he caused it to be understood that he had been in the secret, it seemed probable that he had told the Pope; for they had been old friends.[100] In the commemorative inscription which he put up in the Church of St. Lewis he spoke of the King's gratitude to the Holy See

---

Universelle, ii. 27) and by De Thou. De Thou was very hostile to the Jesuits, and his language is not positive. D'Aubigné was a furious bigot. The truth of the charge would not be proved, without the letters of the President L'Agebaston and of the Lieutenant Montpezat: "Quelques prescheurs se sont par leurs sermons (ainsi que dernièrement j'ai escript plus amplement à votre majesté) estudié de tout leur pouvoir de troubler ciel et terre, et conciter le peuple à sédition, et en ce faisant à passer par le fil de l'espée tous ceulx de la prétendue religion réformée. . . . Après avoir dès le premier et deuxième de ceste mois fait courir un bruit sourd que vous. Sire, aviez envoyé nom par nom un rolle signé de votre propre main au Sieur de Montferaud, pour par voie de fait et sans aultre forme de justice, mettre à mort quarante des principaulx de cette ville . . ." (L'Agebaston to Charles IX, Oct. 7, 1572; Mackintosh, iii. 352). "J'ai trouvé que messieurs de la cour de parlement avoyent arresté que Monsieur Emond, prescheur, seroit appellé en ladicte court pour luy faire des remonstrances sur quelque langaige qu'il tenoit en ses sermons, tendant à sédition, à ce qu'ils disoyent. Ce que j'ay bien voullu empescher, craignant que s'il y eust esté appellé cella eust animé plusieurs des habitants et estre cause de quelque émotion, ce que j'eusse voluntiers souffert quant j'eusse pansé qu'il n'y en eust qu'une vingtaine de despéchés" (Montpezat to Charles IX, Sept. 30, 1572; *Archives de la Gironde,* viii. 337).

[98] *Annal. Baronii Contin.* ii. 734; Bossuet says: "La dispense vint telle qu'on la pouvoit désirer" (*Histoire de France,* p. 820).

[99] Ormegregny, *Réflexions sur la Politique de France,* p. 121.

[100] De Thou, iv. 537.

for its assistance and for its advice in the matter—"consiliorum ad eam rem datorum." It is probable that he inspired the narrative which has contributed most to sustain the imputation.

Among the Italians of the French faction who made it their duty to glorify the act of Charles IX, the Capilupi family was conspicuous. They came from Mantua, and appear to have been connected with the French interest through Lewis Gonzaga, who had become by marriage Duke of Nevers, and one of the foremost personages in France. Hippolyto Capilupi, Bishop of Fano, and formerly Nuncio at Venice, resided at Rome, busy with French politics and Latin poetry. When Charles refused to join the League, the Bishop of Fano vindicated his neutrality in a letter to the Duke of Urbino.[101] When he slew the Huguenots, the Bishop addressed him in verse:

> Fortunate puer, paret cui Gallica tellus,
>   Quique vafros ludis pervigil arte viros,
> Ille tibi debet, toti qui praesidet Orbi,
>   Cui nihil est cordi relligione prius. . . .
>
> Qui tibi saepe dolos struxit, qui vincla paravit,
>   Tu puer in laqueos induis arte senem. . . .
>
> Nunc florent, tolluntque caput tua lilia, et astris
>   Clarius hostili tincta cruore micant.[102]

Camillo Capilupi, a nephew of the Mantuan bard, held office about the person of the Pope, and was employed on missions of consequence.[103] As soon as the news from Paris reached Rome he drew up the account which became so famous under the title of *Lo Stratagemma di Carlo IX*. The dedication is dated the 18th of September 1572.[104] This tract was suppressed, and was soon so rare that its existence was unknown in 1574 to the French translator of the second edition. Capilupi republished his book with alterations, and a preface dated the 22nd of October. The substance and purpose of the two editions is the same. Capilupi is not the official organ of the Roman court: he was not allowed to see the letters of the Nuncio. He wrote to proclaim the praises of the King

---

[101] Charrière, iii. 154.

[102] *Carmina III. Poetarum Italorum*, iii. 212, 216.

[103] Tiepolo, Desp. Aug. 6, 1575; Mutinelli, *Storia Arcana*, i. III.

[104] Parendomi, che sia cosa, la quale possa apportar piacere, e utile al mondo, si per la qualità del soggetto istesso, come anco per l'eleganza, e bello ordine con che viene cosi leggiadramente descritto questo nobile, e glorioso fatto . . . a fine che una cosi egregia attione non resti defraudata dell' honor, che merita (The editor, Gianfrancesco Ferrari, to the reader).

of France and the Duke of Nevers. At that moment the French party in Rome was divided by the quarrel between the ambassador Ferralz and the Cardinal of Lorraine, who had contrived to get the management of French affairs into his own hands.[105] Capilupi was on the side of the Cardinal, and received information from those who were about him. The chief anxiety of these men was that the official version which attributed the massacre to a Huguenot conspiracy should obtain no credence at Rome. If the Cardinal's enemies were overthrown without his participation, it would confirm the report that he had become a cipher in the State. He desired to vindicate for himself and his family the authorship of the catastrophe. Catherine could not tolerate their claim to a merit which she had made her own; and there was competition between them for the first and largest share in the gratitude of the Holy See. Lorraine prevailed with the Pope, who not only loaded him with honours, but rewarded him with benefices worth 4000 crowns a year for his nephew, and a gift of 20,000 crowns for his son. But he found that he had fallen into disgrace at Paris, and feared for his position at Rome.[106] In these circumstances Capilupi's book appeared,

[105] Huc accedit, Oratorem Ser[mi] Regis Galliae, et impulsu inimicorum saepedicti Domini Cardinalis, et quia summopere illi displicuit, quod superioribus mensibus Illma Sua Dominatio operam dedisset, hoc sibi mandari, ut omnia Regis negotia secum communicaret, nullam praetermisisse occasionem ubi ei potuit adversari (Cardinal Delfino to the Emperor, Rome, Nov. 29, 1572; Vienna Archives).

[106] Fà ogni favor et gratia gli addimanda il Cardinale di Lorena, il consiglio del quale usa in tutte le più importanti negotiationi l' occorre di haver a trattar (Cusano to the Emperor, Rome, Sept. 27, 1572).—Conscia igitur Sua Dominatio Illma quorundam arcanorum Regni Galliae, creato Pontifice sibi in Concilio Tridentino cognito et amico, statuit huc se recipere, ut privatis suis rebus consuleret, et quia tunc foederati contra Thurcam, propter suspicionem Regi Catholico injectam de Orangio, et Gallis, non admodum videbantur concordes, et non multo post advenit nuncius mortis Domini de Colligni, et illius asseclarum; Pontifex justa de causa existimavit dictum Ill[mum] Cardinalem favore et gratia sua merito esse complectendum. Evenit postmodum, ut ad Serenissimam Reginam Galliarum deferretur, bonum hunc Dominum jactasse se, quod particeps fuerit consiliorum contra dictum Colligni; id quod illa Serenissima Domina iniquo animo tulit, quae neminem gloriae socium vult habere; sibi enim totam vendicat, quod sola talis facinoris auctor, et Dux exiterit. Idcirco commorationem ipsius Lotharingiae in hac aula improbare, ac reprehendere aggressa est. Haec cum ille Illustrissimus Cardinalis perceperit, oblata sibi occasione utens, exoravit a Sua Sanctitate gratuitam expeditionem quattuor millia scutorum reditus pro suo Nepote, et 20 millia pro filio praeter sollicitationem, quam prae se fert, ut dictus Nepos in Cardinalium numerum cooptetur. . . . Cum itaque his de causis authoritas hujus Domini in Gallia imminuta videatur, ipseque praevideat, quanto in Gallia minoris aestimabitur, tanto minori etiam loco hic se habitum iri, statuit optimo judicio, ac pro eo quod suae existimacioni magis conducit, in Galliam reverti (Delfino, *ut supra*, both in the Vienna Archives).

and enumerated a series of facts proving that the Cardinal was cognisant of the royal design. It adds little to the evidence of premeditation. Capilupi relates that Santa Croce, returning from France, had assured Pius V, in the name of Catherine, that she intended one day to entrap Coligny, and to make a signal butchery of him and his adherents, and that letters in which the Queen renewed this promise to the Pope had been read by credible witnesses. Santa Croce was living, and did not contradict the statement. The *Stratagemma* had originally stated that Lorraine had informed Sermoneta of the project soon after he arrived at Rome. In the reprint this passage was omitted. The book had, therefore, undergone a censorial revision, which enhances the authenticity of the final narrative.

Two other pieces are extant, which were printed at the Stamperia Camerale, and show what was believed at Rome. One is in the shape of a letter written at Lyons in the midst of scenes of death, and describing what the author had witnessed on the spot, and what he heard from Paris.[107] He reports that the King had positively commanded that not one Huguenot should escape, and was overjoyed at the accomplishment of his orders. He believes the thing to have been premeditated, and inspired by Divine justice. The other tract is remarkable because it strives to reconcile the pretended conspiracy with the hypothesis of premeditation.[108] There were two plots which went parallel for months. The King knew that Coligny was compassing his death, and deceived him by feigning to enter into his plan for the invasion of the Low Countries; and Coligny, allowing himself to be overreached, summoned his friends to Paris, for the purpose of killing Charles, on the 23rd of August. The writer expects that there will soon be no Huguenots in France. Capilupi at first borrowed several of his facts, which he afterwards corrected.

The real particulars relative to the marriage are set forth minutely in the correspondence of Ferralz; and they absolutely contradict the supposition of the complicity of Rome.[109] It was celebrated in flagrant defiance of the Pope, who persisted in refusing the dispensation, and therefore acted in a way which could only serve to mar the plot. The accusation has been kept alive by his conduct after the event. The

---

[107] *Intiera Relatione della Morte dell' Ammiraglio.*

[108] *Ragguaglio degli ordini et modi tenuti dalla Majestà Christianissima nella distruttione della setta degli Ugonotti Con la morte dell' Ammiraglio*, etc.

[109] Bib. Imp. F. Fr. 16, 139.

Jesuit who wrote his life by desire of his son, says that Gregory thanked God in private, but that in public he gave signs of a tempered joy.[110] But the illuminations and processions, the singing of Te Deum and the firing of the castle guns, the jubilee, the medal, and the paintings whose faded colours still vividly preserve to our age the passions of that day, nearly exhaust the modes by which a Pope could manifest delight.

Charles IX and Salviati both wrote to Rome on St. Bartholomew's Day; and the ambassador's nephew, Beauville, set off with the tidings. They were known before he arrived. On the 27th, Mandelot's secretary despatched a secret messenger from Lyons with orders to inform the Pope that the Huguenot leaders were slain, and that their adherents were to be secured all over France. The messenger reached Rome on the 2nd of September, and was immediately carried to the Pope by the Cardinal of Lorraine. Gregory rewarded him for the welcome intelligence with a present of a hundred crowns, and desired that Rome should be at once illuminated. This was prevented by Ferralz, who tried the patience of the Romans by declining their congratulations as long as he was not officially informed.[111] Beauville and the courier of the Nuncio arrived on the 5th. The King's letter, like all that he wrote on the first day, ascribed the outbreak to the old hatred between the rival Houses, and to the late attempt on the Admiral's life. He expressed a hope that the dispensation would not now be withheld,

---

[110] Maffei, *Annali di Gregorio XIII,* i. 34.

[111] La nouvelle qui arriva le deuxième jour du présent par ung courrier qui estoit depesché secrètement de Lyon par ung nommé Danes, secrétaire de M. de Mandelot . . . à ung commandeur de Sainct Anthoine, nommé Mr. de Gou, il luy manda qu'il allast advertir le Pape, pour en avoir quelque présant ou bienfaict, de la mort de tous les chefs de ceulx de la religion prétendue refformée, et de tous les Huguenotz de France, et que V. M. avoit mandé et commandé à tous les gouverneurs de se saisir de tous iceulx huguenotz en leurs gouvernemens; ceste nouvelle, Sire, apporta si grand contentement a S. S., que sans ce que je luy remonstray lors me trouvant sur le lieu, en présence de Monseigneur le C[1] de Lorraine, qu'elle devoit attendre ce que V. M. m'en manderoit et ce que son nonce luy en escriroit, elle en vouloit incontinent faire des feux de joye. . . . Et pour ce que je ne voulois faire ledict feu de joye la première nuict que ledict courrier envoyé par ledict Danes feust arrivé, ny en recevoir les congratulations que l'on m'en envoyoit faire, que premièrement je n'eusse eu novelles de V. M. pour sçavoir et sa voulanté et comme je m'avoys a conduire, aucuns commençoient desjà de m'en regarder de maulvais oeills (Ferralz to Charles IX, Rome, Sept. 11, 1572; Bib. Imp. F. Fr. 16,040). Al corriero che portò tal nuova Nostro Signore diede 100 Scudi oltre li 200 che hebbe dall' Illustrissimo Lorena, che con grandissima allegrezza se n'ando subito a dar tal nuova per allegrarsene con Sua Santita (Letter from Rome to the Emperor, Sept. 6, 1572; Vienna Archives).

but left all particulars to Beauville, whose own eyes had beheld the scene.[112] Beauville told his story, and repeated the King's request; but Gregory, though much gratified with what he heard, remained inflexible.[113]

Salviati had written on the afternoon of the 24th. He desired to fling himself at the Pope's feet to wish him joy. His fondest hopes had been surpassed. Although he had known what was in store for Coligny, he had not expected that there would be energy and prudence to seize the occasion for the destruction of the rest. A new era had commenced; a new compass was required for French affairs. It was a fair sight to see the Catholics in the streets wearing white crosses, and cutting down heretics; and it was thought that, as fast as the news spread, the same thing would be done in all the towns of France.[114] This letter was read before the assembled Cardinals at the Venetian palace, and they thereupon attended the Pope to a Te Deum in the nearest church.[115] The guns of St. Angelo were fired in the evening, and the

---

[112] Charles IX to Ferralz, Aug. 24, 1572; Mackintosh, iii. 348.

[113] Elle fust merveilheusement ayse d'entendre le discours que mondit neueu de Beauville luy en feist. Lequel, après luy avoir conté le susdit affayre, supplia sadicte Saincteté, suyvant la charge expresse qu'il avoit de V. M. de vouloir concéder, pour le fruict de ceste allegresse, la dispense du mariage du roy et royne de Navarre, datée de quelques jours avant que les nopces en feussent faictes, ensemble l'absolution pour Messeigneurs les Cardinaux de Bourbon et de Ramboilhet, et pour tous les aultres evesques et prélatz qui y avoient assisté. . . . Il nous feit pour fin response qu'il y adviseroit (Ferralz, *ut supra*).

[114] Pensaci che per tutte le città di Francia debba seguire il simile, subitoche arrivi la nuova dell' esecutione di Parigi. . . . A N. S. mi faccia gratia di basciar i piedi in nome mio, col quale mi rallegro con le viscere del cuore che sia piaciuto alla Dio. Mtà. d' incaminar nel principio del suo pontificato si felicemente e honoratamente le cose di questo regno, havendo talmente havuto in protettione il Rè e Regina Madre che hanno saputo e potuto sbarrare queste pestifere radici con tanta prudenza, in tempo tanto opportuno, che tutti lor ribelli erano sotto chiave in gabbia (Salviati, Desp. Aug. 24; Theiner, i. 329; Mackintosh, iii. 355).

[115] Sexta Septembris, mane, in Senatu Pontificis et Cardinalium lectae sunt literae a legato Pontificio e Gallia scriptae, admiralium et Huguenotos, destinata Regis voluntate atque consensu, trucidatos esse. Ea re in eodem Senatu decretum esse, ut inde recta Pontifex cum Cardinalibus in aedem D. Marci concederet, Deoque Opt. Max. pro tanto beneficio Sedi Romanae orbique Christiano collato gratias solemni more ageret (*Scriptum Roma missum* in Capilupi, 1574, p. 84). Quia Die 2ª praedicti mensis Septembris S^{mus} D. N. certior factus fuerat Colignium Franciae Ammiralium a populo Parisien, occisum fuisse et cum eo multos ex Ducibus et primoribus Ugonotarum haereticorum eius sequacibus Rege ipso Franciae approbante, ex quo spes erat tranquillitatem in dicto Regno redituram expulsis haereticis, idcirco S^{tas} Sua expleto concistorio descendit ad ecclesiam Sancti Marci, praecedente cruce et sequentibus Cardinalibus et genuflexus

city was illuminated for three nights. To disregard the Pope's will in this respect would have savoured of heresy. Gregory XIII exclaimed that the massacre was more agreeable to him than fifty victories of Lepanto. For some weeks the news from the French provinces sustained the rapture and excitement of the Court.[116] It was hoped that other countries would follow the example of France; the Emperor was informed that something of the same kind was expected of him.[117] On the 8th of September the Pope went in procession to the French Church of St. Lewis, where three-and-thirty Cardinals attended at a mass of thanksgiving. On the 11th he proclaimed a jubilee. In the Bull he said that forasmuch as God had armed the King of France to inflict vengeance on the heretics for the injuries done to religion, and to punish the leaders of the rebellion which had devastated his kingdom, Catholics should pray that he might have grace to pursue his auspicious enterprise to the end, and so complete what he had begun so well.[118] Before a month had passed Vasari was summoned from Florence to decorate the hall of kings with paintings of the massacre.[119] The work

---

ante altare maius, ubi positum fuerat sanctissimum Sacramentum, oravit gratias Deo agens, et inchoavit cantando hymnum Te Deum (*Fr. Mucantii Diaria*, B. M. Add. MSS. 26, 811).

[116] Après quelques autres discours qu'il me feist sur le contentement que luy et le collège des Cardinaux avoient receu de ladicte exécution faicte et des nouvelles qui journellement arrivoient en ceste court de semblables exécutions que l'on a faicte et font encore en plusieurs villes de vostre royaume, qui, à dire la vérité, sont les nouvelles les plus agréables que je pense qu'on eust sceu apporter en ceste ville, sadicte Saincteté pour fin me commanda de vous escrire que cest événement luy a esté cent fois plus agréable que cinquante victoires semblables à celle que ceulx de la ligue obtindrent l'année passée contre le Turcq, ne voulant oublier vous dire, Sire, les commandemens estroictz qu'il nous feist à tous, mesmement aux françois d'en faire feu de joye, et qui ne l'eust faict eust mal senty de la foy (Ferralz, *ut supra*).

[117] Tutta Roma stà in allegria di tal fatto et frà i più grandi si dice, che 'l Rè di Francia ha insegnato alli Principi christiani ch' hanno de simili vassalli ne' stati loro a liberarsene, et dicono che vostra Maestà Cesara dovrebbe castigare il conte Palatino tanto nemico della Serenissima casa d'Austria, et della Religione cattolica, come l'anni passati fece contra il Duca di Sassonia tiene tuttavia prigione, che a un tempo vendicarebbe le tante ingiurie ha fatto detto Palatino alla Chiesa di Dio, et poveri Christiani, et alla Maestà Vostra et sua Casa Serenissima sprezzando li suoi editti et commandamenti, et privarlo dell' elettione dell'Imperio et darlo al Duca di Baviera (Cusano to the Emperor, Rome, Sept. 6, 1572; Vienna Archives).

[118] The Bull, as published in Paris, is printed by Strype (*Life of Parker*, iii. 197). La prima occasione che a ciò lo mosse fù per lo stratagemma fatto da Carlo Nono Christianissimo Rè di Francia contra Coligno Ammiraglio, capo d' Ugonotti, et suoi seguaci, tagliati a pezzi in Parigi (Ciappi, *Vita di Gregorio XIII*, 1596, p. 63).

[119] Vasari to Borghini, Oct. 5, 1572; March 5, 1573; to Francesco Medici, Nov. 17, 1572; Gaye, *Carteggio d' Artisti*, iii. 328, 366, 341.

was pronounced his masterpiece; and the shameful scene may still be traced upon the wall, where, for three centuries, it has insulted every pontiff that entered the Sixtine Chapel.

The story that the Huguenots had perished because they were detected plotting the King's death was known at Rome on the 6th of September. While the sham edict and the imaginary trial served to confirm it in the eyes of Europe, Catherine and her son took care that it should not deceive the Pope. They assured him that they meant to disregard the edict. To excuse his sister's marriage, the King pleaded that it had been concluded for no object but vengeance; and he promised that there would soon be not a heretic in the country.[120] This was corroborated by Salviati. As to the proclaimed toleration, he knew that it was a device to disarm foreign enmity, and prevent a popular commotion. He testified that the Queen spoke truly when she said that she had confided to him, long before, the real purpose of her daughter's engagement.[121] He exposed the hollow pretence of the plot. He announced that its existence would be established by formalities of law, but added that it was so notoriously false that none but an idiot could believe in it.[122] Gregory gave no countenance to the official falsehood. At the reception of the French ambassador, Rambouillet, on the 23rd of December, Muretus made his famous speech. He said that there could not have been a happier beginning for a new pontificate, and alluded to the fabulous plot in the tone exacted of French officials. The Secretary, Boccapaduli, replying in behalf of the Pope, thanked the King for destroying the enemies of Christ; but strictly avoided the conventional fable.[123]

[120] Indubitatamente non si osservarà interamente, havendomi in questo modo, punto che torno dall' audienza promesso il Re, imponendomi di darne conto in suo nome a Nostro Signore, di volere in breve tempo liberare il Regno dalli Ugonotti. ... Mi ha parlato della dispensa, escusandosi non haver fatto il Parentado per ultro, che per liberarsi da suoi inimici (Salviati, Desp. Sept. 3, Sept. 2, Oct. 11, 1572).

[121] Si vede che l' editto non essendo osservato ne da' popoli, ne dal principe, non è per pigliar piede (Salviati, Desp. Sept. 4). Qual Regina in progresso di tempo intende pur non solo di revocare tal editto, ma per mezzo della giustitia di restituir la fede cattolica nell' antica osservanza, parendogli che nessuno ne debba dubitare adesso, che hanno fatto morire l'ammiraglio con tanti altri huomini di valore, conforme ai raggionamenti altre volte havuti con esso meco essendo a Bles, et trattando del parentado di Navarra, et dell' altre cose che correvano in quei tempi, il che essendo vero, ne posso rendere testimonianza, e a Nostro Signore e a tutto il mondo (Aug. 27; Theiner, i. 329, 330).

[122] Desp. Sept. 2, 1572.

[123] The reply of Boccapaduli is printed in French, with the translation of the oration of Muretus, Paris, 1573.

Cardinal Orsini went as Legate to France. He had been appointed in August, and he was to try to turn the King's course into that line of policy from which he had strayed under Protestant guidance. He had not left Rome when the events occurred which altered the whole situation. Orsini was now charged with felicitations, and was to urge Charles not to stop half-way.[124] An ancient and obsolete ceremonial was suddenly revived; and the Cardinals accompanied him to the Flaminian gate.[125] This journey of Orsini, and the pomp with which it was surrounded, were exceedingly unwelcome at Paris. It was likely to be taken as proof of that secret understanding with Rome which threatened to rend the delicate web in which Charles was striving to hold the confidence of the Protestant world.[126] He requested that the Legate might be recalled; and the Pope was willing that there should be some delay. While Orsini tarried on his way, Gregory's reply to the announcement of the massacre arrived at Paris. It was a great consolation to himself, he said, and an extraordinary grace vouchsafed to Christendom. But he desired, for the glory of God and the good of France, that the Huguenots should be extirpated utterly; and with that view he demanded the revocation of the edict. When Catherine knew that the Pope was not yet satisfied, and sought to direct the actions of the King, she could hardly restrain her rage. Salviati had never seen her so furious. The words had hardly passed his lips when she exclaimed that she wondered at such designs, and was resolved to tolerate no interference in the government of the kingdom. She and

---

[124] Troverà le cose cosi ben disposte, che durarà poca fattica in ottener quel tanto si desidera per Sua Beatitudine, anzi haverà più presto da ringratiar quella Maestà Christianissima di cosi buona et sant' opera, ha fatto far, che da durare molta fatica in persuaderli l' unione con la Santa Chiesa Romana (Cusano to the Emperor, Rome, Sept. 6). Sereno (*Comment. della guerra di Cipro*, p. 329) understands the mission in the same light.

[125] Omnes mulas ascendentes cappis et galeris pontificalibus induti associarunt R[mum] D. Cardinalem Ursinum Legatum usque ad portam Flaminiam et extra eam ubi factis multis reverentiis eum ibi reliquerunt, juxta ritum antiquum in ceremoniali libro descriptum qui longo tempore intermissus fuerat, ita Pontifice iubente in Concistorio hodierno (*Mucantii Diaria*). Ista associatio fuit determinata in Concistorio vocatis X. Cardinalibus et ex improviso exequuti fuimus (*C. Firmani Diaria*, B. M. Add. MSS. 8448).

[126] Mette in consideratione alla Santità Sua che havendo deputato un Legato apostolico sù la morte dell' ammiraglio, et altri capi Ugonotti, ha fatti ammazzare a Parigi, saria per metterla in molto sospetto et diffidenza delli Principi Protestanti, et della Regina d' Inghilterra, ch'ella fosse d' accordo con la sede Apostolica, et Principi Cattolici per farli guerra, i quali cerca d' acquettar con accertarli tutti, che non ha fatto ammazzar l' ammiraglio et suoi seguaci per conto della Religione (Cusano to the Emperor, Sept. 27).

her son were Catholics from conviction, and not through fear or influence. Let the Pope content himself with that.[127] The Nuncio had at once foreseen that the court, after crushing the Huguenots, would not become more amenable to the counsels of Rome. He wrote, on the very day of St. Bartholomew, that the King would be very jealous of his authority, and would exact obedience from both sides alike.

At this untoward juncture Orsini appeared at Court. To Charles, who had done so much, it seemed unreasonable that he should be asked for more. He represented to Orsini that it was impossible to eradicate all the remnants of a faction which had been so strong. He had put seventy thousand Huguenots to the sword; and, if he had shown compassion to the rest, it was in order that they might become good Catholics.[128]

The hidden thoughts which the Court of Rome betrayed by its conduct on this memorable occasion have brought upon the Pope himself an amount of hatred greater than he deserved. Gregory XIII appears as a pale figure between the two strongest of the modern Popes, without the intense zeal of the one and the ruthless volition of the other. He was not prone to large conceptions or violent resolutions. He had been converted late in life to the spirit of the Tridentine Reformation; and when he showed rigour it was thought to be not in his character, but in the counsels of those who influenced him.[129] He did not instigate the crime, nor the atrocious sentiments that hailed it. In the religious struggle a frenzy had been kindled which made weakness violent, and turned good men into prodigies of ferocity; and at Rome, where every loss inflicted on Catholicism and every wound was felt, the belief that, in dealing with heretics, murder is better than toleration prevailed for half a century. The predecessor of Gregory had been Inquisitor-General. In his eyes Protestants were worse than

---

[127] Salviati, Desp. Sept. 22, 1572.

[128] Charles IX to S. Goard, Oct. 5, 1572; Charrière, iii. 330. Ne poteva esser bastante segno l'haver egli doppo la morte dell' Ammiraglio fatto un editto, che in tutti i luoghi del suo regno fossero posti a fil di spada quanti heretici vi si trovassero, onde in pochi giorni n' erano stati ammazzati settanta milla e d' avantaggio (Cicarelli, *Vita di Gregorio XIII;* Platina, *Vite de' Pontefici,* 1715, 592).

[129] Il tengono quasiche in filo et il necessitano a far cose contra la sua natura e la sua volontà perche S. Sta è sempre stato di natura piacevole e dolce (*Relatione di Gregorio XIII;* Ranke, *Päpste,* App. 80). Faict Cardinal par le pape Pie IV, le 12e de Mars 1559, lequel en le créant, dit qu'il n'avoit créé un cardinal ains un pape (Ferralz to Charles IX, May 14, 1572).

Pagans, and Lutherans more dangerous than other Protestants.[130] The Capuchin preacher, Pistoja, bore witness that men were hanged and quartered almost daily at Rome;[131] and Pius declared that he would release a culprit guilty of a hundred murders rather than one obstinate heretic.[132] He seriously contemplated razing the town of Faenza because it was infested with religious error, and he recommended a similar expedient to the King of France.[133] He adjured him to hold no intercourse with the Huguenots, to make no terms with them, and not to observe the terms he had made. He required that they should be pursued to the death, that not one should be spared under any pretence, that all prisoners should suffer death.[134] He threatened Charles with the punishment of Saul when he forebore to exterminate the Amalekites.[135] He told them that it was his mission to avenge the injuries of the Lord, and that nothing is more cruel than mercy to the impious.[136] When he sanctioned the murder of Elizabeth he proposed that it should be done in execution of his sentence against her.[137] It became usual with those who meditated assassination or regicide on the plea of religion to look upon the representatives of Rome as their natural advisers. On the 21st of January 1591, a young Capuchin came, by permission of his superiors, to Sega, Bishop of Piacenza, then Nuncio at Paris. He said that he was inflamed with the desire of a martyr's death; and having been assured by divines that it would be meritorious to kill that heretic and tyrant, Henry of Navarre, he asked to be dispensed from the rule of his Order while he prepared his measures

---

[130] S^mus Dominus Noster dixit nullam concordiam vel pacem debere nec posse esse inter nos et hereticos, et cum eis nullum foedus ineundum et habendum . . . verissimum est deteriores esse haereticos gentilibus, eo quod sunt adeo perversi et obstinati, ut propemodum infideles sint (*Acta Concistorialia*, June 18, 1571; Bib. Imp. F. Lat. 12,561).

[131] Ogni giorno faceva impiccare e squartare ora uno, ora un altro (Cantù, ii. 410).

[132] *Legazioni di Serristori*, 436, 443.

[133] Elle désire infiniment que vostre Majesté face quelque ressentement plus qu'elle n'a faict jusques à ceste heure contre ceux qui lui font la guerre, comme de raser quelques-unes de leurs principales maisons pour une perpétuelle mémoyre (Rambouillet to Charles IX, Rome, Jan. 17, 1569; Bib. Imp. F. Fr. 17,989).

[134] Pius V to Catherine, April 13, 1569.

[135] Pius V to Charles IX, March 28, 1569.

[136] Sa Saincteté m'a dict que j'escrive à vostre majesté que icelle se souvienne qu'elle combat pour la querelle de Dieu, et que ceste à elle de faire ses vengeances (Rambouillet to Charles IX, Rome, March 14, 1569; Bib. Imp. F. Fr. 16,039). Nihil est enim ea pietate misericordiaque crudelius, quae in impios et ultima supplicia meritos confertur (Pius V to Charles IX, Oct. 20, 1569).

[137] *Correspondance de Philippe II*, ii. 185.

and watched his opportunity. The Nuncio would not do this without authority from Rome; but the prudence, courage, and humility which he discerned in the friar made him believe that the design was really inspired from above. To make this certain, and to remove all scruples, he submitted the matter to the Pope, and asked his blessing upon it, promising that whatever he decided should be executed with all discretion.[138]

The same ideas pervaded the Sacred College under Gregory. There are letters of profuse congratulation by the Cardinals of Lorraine, Este, and Pellevé. Bourbon was an accomplice before the fact. Granvelle condemned not the act but the delay. Delfino and Santorio approved. The Cardinal of Alessandria had refused the King's gift at Blois, and had opposed his wishes at the conclave. Circumstances were now so much altered that the ring was offered to him again, and this time it was accepted.[139] The one dissentient from the chorus of applause is said to have been Montalto. His conduct when he became Pope makes it very improbable; and there is no good authority for the story. But Leti has it, who is so far from a panegyrist that it deserves mention.

The theory which was framed to justify these practices has done more than plots and massacres to cast discredit on the Catholics. This theory was as follows: Confirmed heretics must be rigorously punished whenever it can be done without the probability of greater evil to religion. Where that is feared, the penalty may be suspended or delayed for a season, provided it be inflicted whenever the danger is past.[140]

---

[138] Inspirato più d' un anno fà di esporre la vita al martirio col procurare la liberatione della religione, et della patria per mezzo della morte del tiranno, et assicurato da Theologi che il fatto saria stato meritorio, non ne haveva con tutto ciò mai potuto ottenere da superiori suoi la licenza o dispensa. . . . Io quantunque mi sia parso di trovarlo pieno di tale humiltà, prudenza, spirito et core che arguiscono che questa sia inspiratione veramente piuttosto che temerità o legerezza, non cognoscendo tuttavia di potergliela concedere l' ho persuaso a tornarsene nel suo covento raccommandarsi a Dio et attendere all' obbedienza delli suoi superiori finchè io attendessi dallo assenso o ripulsa del Papa che haverei interpellato per la sua santa beneditione, se questo spirito sia veramente da Dio donde si potrà conjetturare che sia venendo approvato da Sua Sta, e perciò sarà più sicuro da essere eseguito. . . . Resta hora che V. S. Illma mi favorisca di communicare a S. B. il caso, et scrivermene come la supplico quanto prima per duplicate et triplicate lettere la sua santa determinatione assicurandosi che per quanto sarà in me il negotio sarà trattato con la debita circumspetione (Sega, Desp. Paris, Jan. 23, 1591; deciphered in Rome, March 26).

[139] Ferralz to Charles IX, Nov. 18, Dec. 23, 1572.

[140] De Castro, *De Justa Haeret. Punitione,* 1547, p. 119. Iure Divino obligantur eos extirpare, si absque maiori incommodo possint (Lancelottus, *Haereticum quare per Catholicum*

Treaties made with heretics, and promises given to them must not be kept, because sinful promises do not bind, and no agreement is lawful which may injure religion or ecclesiastical authority. No civil power may enter into engagements which impede the free scope of the Church's law.[141] It is part of the punishment of heretics that faith shall not be kept with them.[142] It is even mercy to kill them that they may sin no more.[143]

Such were the precepts and the examples by which the French Catholics learned to confound piety and ferocity, and were made ready to immolate their countrymen. During the civil war an association was formed in the South for the purpose of making war upon the Huguenots; and it was fortified by Pius V with blessings and indulgences. "We doubt not," it proclaimed, "that we shall be victorious over these enemies of God and of all humankind; and if we fall, our blood will be as a second baptism, by which, without impediment, we shall join the other martyrs straightway in heaven."[144] Monluc, who told Alva at Bayonne that he had never spared an enemy, was shot through the face at the siege of Rabasteins. Whilst he believed that he was dying, they came to tell him that the place was taken. "Thank God!" he said, "that I have lived long enough to behold our victory; and now I care not for death. Go back, I beseech you, and give me a last proof of friendship, by seeing that not one man of the garrison escapes alive."[145] When Alva had defeated and captured Genlis, and expected to make many more Huguenot prisoners in the garrison of Mons, Charles IX wrote to Mondoucet "that it would be for the service of God, and of

---

quia, 1615, p. 579). Ubi quid indulgendum sit, ratio semper exacta habeatur, an Religioni Ecclesiae, et Reipublicae quid vice mutua accedat quod majoris sit momenti, et plus prodesse possit (Pamelius, *De Relig. diversis non admittendis*, 1589, p. 159). Contagium istud sic grassatum est, ut corrupta massa non ferat antiquissimas leges, severitasque tantisper remittenda sit (Possevinus, *Animadv. in Thuanum;* Zachariae, *Iter Litterarium*, p. 321).

[141] Principi saeculari nulla ratione permissum est, haereticis licentiam tribuere haereses suas docendi, atque adeo contractus ille iniustus. . . . Si quid Princeps saecularis attentet in praeiudicium Ecclesiasticae potestatis, aut contra eam aliquid statuat et pacciscatur, pactum illud nullum futurum (R. Sweertii, *De Fide Haereticis servanda*, 1611, p. 36).

[142] Ad poenam quoque pertinet et odium haereticorum quod fides illis data servanda non sit (Simancha, *Inst. Cath.* pp. 46, 52).

[143] Si nolint converti, expedit eos citius tollere e medio, ne gravius postea damnentur, unde non militat contra mansuetudinem christianam, occidere Haereticos, quin potius est opus maximae misericordiae (Lancelottus, p. 579).

[144] De Rozoy, *Annales de Toulouse*, iii. 65.

[145] Alva to Philip, June 5, 1565; *Pap. de Granvelle*, ix. 288; *Comment. de Monluc*, iii. 425.

the King of Spain, that they should die. If the Duke of Alva answers that this is a tacit request to have all the prisoners cut to pieces, you will tell him that that is what he must do, and that he will injure both himself and all Christendom if he fails to do it."[146] This request also reached Alva through Spain. Philip wrote on the margin of the despatch that, if he had not yet put them out of the world, he must do so immediately, as there could be no reason for delay.[147] The same thought occurred to others. On the 22nd of July Salviati writes that it would be a serious blow to the faction if Alva would kill his prisoners; and Granvelle wrote that, as they were all Huguenots, it would be well to throw them all into the river.[148]

Where these sentiments prevailed, Gregory XIII was not alone in deploring that the work had been but half done. After the first explosion of gratified surprise men perceived that the thing was a failure, and began to call for more. The clergy of Rouen Cathedral instituted a procession of thanksgiving, and prayed that the King might continue what he had so virtuously begun, until all France should profess one faith.[149] There are signs that Charles was tempted at one moment, during the month of October, to follow up the blow.[150] But he died without pursuing the design; and the hopes were turned to his successor. When Henry III passed through Italy on his way to assume the crown, there were some who hoped that the Pope would induce him to set resolutely about the extinction of the Huguenots. A petition was addressed to Gregory for this purpose, in which the writer says that hitherto the French court has erred on the side of mercy, but that the new king might make good the error if rejecting that pernicious maxim that noble blood spilt weakens a kingdom, he would appoint an execution which would be cruel only in appearance, but in reality glorious and holy, and destroy the heretics totally, sparing neither life nor property.[151] Similar exhortations were addressed from Rome to Henry himself by Muzio, a layman who had gained repute, among

---

[146] Charles IX to Mondoucet, Aug. 31, 1572; *Compte Rendu,* iv. 349.

[147] *Bulletins de Bruxelles,* xvi, 256.

[148] Granvelle to Morillon, Sept. 11, 1572; Michelet, p. 475.

[149] Floquet, iii. 137.

[150] Walsingham to Smith, Nov. 1, 1572; Digges. p. 279. Ita enim statutum ab illis fuit die 27 Octobris (Beza, Dec. 3, 1572; *Ill. vir. Epp. Sel.* 621). La Mothe, v. 164; Faustino Tasso, *Historie de nostri tempi,* 1583, p. 343.

[151] *Discorso di Monsignor Terracina a Gregorio XIII; Thesauri Politici Contin.* 1618, pp. 73–76.

other things, by controversial writings, of which Pius V said that they had preserved the faith in whole districts, and who had been charged with the task of refuting the Centuriators. On the 17th of July 1574, Muzio wrote to the King that all Italy waited in reliance on his justice and valour, and besought him to spare neither old nor young, and to regard neither rank nor ties of blood.[152] These hopes also were doomed to disappointment; and a Frenchman, writing in the year of Henry's death, laments over the cruel clemency and inhuman mercy that reigned on St. Bartholomew's Day.[153]

This was not the general opinion of the Catholic world. In Spain and Italy, where hearts were hardened and consciences corrupted by the Inquisition; in Switzerland, where the Catholics lived in suspicion and dread of their Protestant neighbours; among ecclesiastical princes in Germany, whose authority waned as fast as their subjects abjured their faith, the massacre was welcomed as an act of Christian fortitude. But in France itself the great mass of the people was struck with consternation.[154] "Which maner of proceedings," writes Walsingham on the 13th of September, "is by the Catholiques themselves utterly condemned, who desire to depart hence out of this country, to quit themselves of this strange kind of government, for that they see here none can assure themselves of either goods or life." Even in places still steeped in mourning for the atrocities suffered at the hands of Huguenots during the civil war, at Nîmes, for instance, the King's orders produced no act of vengeance. At Carcassonne, the ancient seat of the Inquisition, the Catholics concealed the Protestants in their houses.[155] In Provence, the news from Lyons and the corpses that came down in the poisoned waters of the Rhone awakened nothing but horror and compassion.[156] Sir Thomas Smith wrote to Walsingham that in England "the minds of the most number are much alienated from that nation, even of the

[152] Infin che ne viverà grande, o picciolo di loro, mai non le mancheranno insidie (*Lettere del Mutio,* 1590, p. 232).

[153] Coupez, tronquez, cisaillez, ne pardonnez à parens ny amis, princes et subjets, ny à quelque personne de quelque condition qu'ils soient (D'Orléans, *Premier advertissement des Catholiques Anglois aux François Catholiques,* 1590, p. 13). The notion that Charles had displayed an extreme benignity recurs in many books: "Nostre Prince a surpassé toute mesure de clémence" (Le Frère de Laval, *Histoire des Troubles,* 1576, p. 527).

[154] Serranus, *Comment.* iv. 51.

[155] Bouges, *Histoire de Carcassonne,* p. 343.

[156] *Sommaire de la Félonie commise à Lyon.* A contemporary tract reprinted by Gonon, 1848, p. 221.

very Papists."[157] At Rome itself Zuñiga pronounced the treachery of which the French were boasting unjustifiable, even in the case of heretics and rebels;[158] and it was felt as an outrage to public opinion when the murderer of Coligny was presented to the Pope.[159] The Emperor was filled with grief and indignation. He said that the King and Queen-mother would live to learn that nothing could have been more iniquitously contrived or executed: his uncle Charles V, and his father Ferdinand, had made war on the Protestants, but they had never been guilty of so cruel an act.[160] At that moment Maximilian was seeking the crown of Poland for his son; and the events in France were a weapon in his hands against his rival, Anjou. Even the Czar of Muscovy, Ivan the Terrible, replying to his letters, protested that all Christian princes must lament the barbarous and needless shedding of so much innocent blood. It was not the rivalry of the moment that animated Maximilian. His whole life proves him to have been an enemy of violence and cruelty; and his celebrated letter to Schwendi, written long after, shows that his judgment remained unchanged. It was the Catholic Emperor who roused the Lutheran Elector of Saxony to something like resentment of the butchery in France.[161]

For the Lutherans were not disposed to recognise the victims of Charles IX as martyrs for the Protestant cause. During the wars of religion Lutheran auxiliaries were led by a Saxon prince, a margrave of Baden, and other German magnates, to aid the Catholic forces in putting down the heresy of Calvin. These feelings were so well known that the French Government demanded of the Duke of Wirtemberg the surrender of the Huguenots who had fled into his dominions.[162] Lutheran divines flattered themselves at first with the belief that it was the Calvinistic error, not the Protestant truth, that had invited

---

[157] On this point Smith may be trusted rather than Parker (*Correspondence*, p. 399).

[158] *Bulletins de Bruxelles*, xvi. 249.

[159] Qui è venuto quello che dette l' archibusata all' ammiraglio di Francia, et è stato condotto dal Cardinal di Lorena et dall' Ambasciator di Francia, al papa. A molti non è piaciuto che costui sia venuto in Roma (Prospero Count Arco to the Emperor, Rome, Nov. 15, 1572; Vienna Archives).

[160] Zuñiga to Philip, March 4, 1573; *Arch. de l'Empire*, K. 1531, B. 35, 70. Zuñiga heard it from Lorraine.

[161] Et est toute la dispute encores sur les derniers événemens de la France, contre lesquels l'Electeur est beaucoup plus aigre qu'il n'estoyt à mon aultre voyage, depuys qu'il a esté en l'escole à Vienne (Schomberg to Brulart, May 12, 1573; Groen, iv. App. 76).

[162] Sattler, *Geschichte von Wüttemberg*, v. 23.

and received the blow.[163] The most influential of them, Andreæ, declared that the Huguenots were not martyrs but rebels, who had died not for religion but sedition; and he bade the princes beware of the contagion of their spirit, which had deluged other lands with blood. When Elizabeth proposed a league for the defence of Protestantism, the North German divines protested against an alliance with men whose crime was not only religious error but blasphemous obstinacy, the root of many dreadful heresies. The very proposal, they said, argued a disposition to prefer human succour rather than the word of God.[164] When another invitation came from Henry of Navarre, the famous divine Chemnitz declared union with the disciples of Calvin a useless abomination.[165]

The very men whose own brethren had perished in France were not hearty or unanimous in execrating the deed.[166] There were Huguenots who thought that their party had brought ruin on itself, by provoking its enemies, and following the rash counsels of ambitious men.[167] This was the opinion of their chief, Theodore Beza, himself. Six weeks before, he wrote that they were gaining in numbers but losing in quality, and he feared lest, after destroying superstition, they should destroy religion: "Valde metuo ne superstitioni successerit impietas."[168] And afterwards he declared that nobody who had known the state of the French Protestants could deny that it was a most just judgment upon them.[169]

Beza held very stringent doctrines touching the duty of the civil

[163] Audio quosdam etiam nostrorum theologorum cruentam istam nuptiarum feralium celebrationem pertinaciae Gallorum in semel recepta de sacramentalibus mysteriis sententia acceptam referre et praeter illos pati neminem somniare (Steinberger to Crato, Nov. 23, 1572; Gillet, *Crato von Crafftheim*, ii. 519).

[164] Heppe, *Geschichte des deutschen Protestantismus*, iv. 37, 47, 49.

[165] Hachfeld, *Martin Chemnitz*, p. 137.

[166] Sunt tamen qui hoc factum et excusare et defendere tentant (Bullinger to Hotoman, Oct. 11, 1572; Hotoman, *Epis.* 35).

[167] Nec dubium est melius cum ipsis actum fuisse, si quemadmodum a principio instituerant, cum disciplinam ecclesiasticam introduxere, viros modestos et piae veraeque reformationis cupidos tantum in suos coetus admississent, reiectis petulantibus et fervidis ingeniis, quae eos in diros tumultus, et inextricabilia mala comecerunt (Dinothus, *De Bello Civili*, 1582, p. 243).

[168] Beza to Tilius, July 5, 1572; *Ill. vir. Epp. Sel.* 607.

[169] Quoties autem ego haec ipse praedixi! quoties praemonui! Sed sic Deo visum est, iustissimis de causis irato, et tamen servatori (Beza to Tilius, Sept. 10, 1572, 614). Nihil istorum non iustissimo iudicio accidere necesse est fateri, qui Galliarum statum norunt (Beza to Crato, Aug. 26, 1573; Gilliet, ii. 521).

magistrate to repress religious error. He thought that heresy is worse than murder, and that the good of society requires no crime to be more severely punished.[170] He declared toleration contrary to revealed religion and the constant tradition of the Church, and taught that lawful authority must be obeyed, even by those whom it persecutes. He expressly recognised this function in Catholic States, and urged Sigismund not to rest until he had got rid of the Socinians in Poland;[171] but he could not prevail against the vehement resistance of Cardinal Hosius. It was embarrassing to limit these principles when they were applied against his own Church. For a moment Beza doubted whether it had not received its death-blow in France. But he did not qualify the propositions which were open to be interpreted so fatally,[172] or deny that his people, by their vices, if not by their errors, had deserved what they had suffered.

The applause which greeted their fate came not from the Catholics generally, nor from the Catholics alone. While the Protestants were ready to palliate or excuse it, the majority of the Catholics who were not under the direct influence of Madrid or Rome recognised the inexpiable horror of the crime. But the desire to defend what the Pope approved survived sporadically, when the old fierceness of dogmatic hatred was extinct. A generation passed without any perceptible change in the judgment of Rome. It was a common charge against De Thou that he had condemned the blameless act of Charles IX. The blasphemies of the Huguenots, said one of his critics, were more abominable than their retribution.[173] His History was put on the Index; and Cardinal Barberini let him know that he was condemned because he not only favoured Protestants to the detriment of Catholics, but had even disapproved the Massacre of St. Bartholomew.[174] Eudæmon-

---

[170] Ut mihi quidem magis absurde facere videantur quam si sacrilegas parricidas puniendos negarent, quum sint istis omnibus haeretici infinitis partibus deteriores. . . . In nullos unquam homines severius quam in haereticos, blasphemos et impios debet animadvertere (*De Haereticis puniendis*, Tract. Theol. i. 143, 152).

[171] *Epist. Theolog.* 1575, p. 338.

[172] Beza to Wittgenstein, Pentecost, 1583; Friedlander, 143.

[173] Lobo de Silveis to De Thou, July 7, 1616; *Histoire*, xv. 371; J. B. Gallus, *Ibid.* p. 435.

[174] Le Cardinal Barberin, que je tiens pour Serviteur du Roy, a parlé franchement sur ceste affaire, et m'a dit qu'il croyoit presqu'impossible qu'il se trouve jamais remède, si vous ne la voulez recommencer; disant que depuis le commencement jusqu'à la fin vous vous estes monstré du tout passionné contre ce qui est de l'honneur et de la grandeur de l'Eglise, qu'il se trouvera dans vostre histoire que vous ne parlez jamais

Johannes, the friend of Bellarmine, pronounces it a pious and charitable act, which immortalised its author.[175] Another Jesuit, Bompiani, says that it was grateful to Gregory, because it was likely to relieve the Church.[176] The well-known apology for Charles IX by Naudé is based rather on political than religious grounds; but his contemporary Guyon, whose History of Orleans is pronounced by the censors full of sound doctrine and pious sentiment, deems it unworthy of Catholics to speak of the murder of heretics as if it were a crime, because when done under lawful authority, it is a blessed thing.[177] When Innocent XI refused to approve the Revocation of the Edict of Nantes, Frenchmen wondered that he should so far depart from the example which was kept before him by one of the most conspicuous ornaments of his palace.[178] The old spirit was decaying fast in France, and the superb indignation of Bossuet fairly expresses the general opinion of his time. Two works were published on the medals of the Popes, by a French and an Italian writer. The Frenchman awkwardly palliates the conduct of Gregory XIII; the Italian heartily defends it.[179] In Italy it was still dangerous ground. Muratori shrinks from pronouncing on the question,[180] while Cienfuegos, a Jesuit whom his Order esteemed one of the most distinguished Cardinals of the day, judges that Charles IX died too soon for his fame.[181] Tempesti, who lived under the enlightened rule of Benedict XIV, accuses Catherine of having arrested the slaughter, in order that some cause should remain to create a demand for her counsels.[182] The German Jesuit Biner and the Papal historian Piatti, just a century ago, are among the last downright apologists.[183]

---

des Catholiques qu'avec du mépris et de la louange de ceux de la religion; que mesme vous avez blasmé ce que feu Monsieur le président de Thou vostre père avoit approuvé, qui est la S. Barthélemy (De Brèves to De Thou, Rome, Feb. 18, 1610; Bib. Imp. F. Dupuy, 812).

[175] Crudelitatisne tu esse ac non clementiae potius, pietatisque putas? (*Resp. ad Ep. Casauboni*, 1612, p. 118).

[176] Quae res uti Catholicae Religioni sublevandae opportuna, ita maxime jucunda Gregorio accidit (*Hist. Pontif. Gregori XIII*, p. 30).

[177] *Histoire d'Orléans*, pp. 421, 424.

[178] Germain to Bretagne, Rome, Dec. 24, 1685; Valéry, *Corresp. de Mabillon*, i. 192.

[179] Du Molinet, *Hist. S. Pont. per Numismata*, 1679, 93; Buorranni, *Numismata Pontificum*, i. 336.

[180] *Annali d' Italia* ad ann. 1572.

[181] Si huviera respirado mas tiempo, huviera dado a entender al mundo, que avia Rey en la Francia, y Dios en Israel (*Vida de S. Francisco De Borja*, 446).

[182] *Vita di Sisto V*, i. 119.

[183] Quo demum res evaderent, si Regibus non esset integrum, in rebelles, subditos,

Then there was a change. A time came when the Catholics, having long relied on force, were compelled to appeal to opinion. That which had been defiantly acknowledged and defended required to be ingeniously explained away. The same motive which had justified the murder now prompted the lie. Men shrank from the conviction that the rulers and restorers of their Church had been murderers and abetters of murder, and that so much infamy had been coupled with so much zeal. They feared to say that the most monstrous of crimes had been solemnly approved at Rome, lest they should devote the Papacy to the execration of mankind. A swarm of facts were invented to meet the difficulty: The victims were insignificant in number; they were slain for no reason connected with religion; the Pope believed in the existence of the plot; the plot was a reality; the medal is fictitious; the massacre was a feint concerted with the Protestants themselves; the Pope rejoiced only when he heard that it was over.[184] These things were repeated so often that they have been sometimes believed; and men have fallen into this way of speaking whose sincerity was unimpeachable, and who were not shaken in their religion by the errors or the vices of Popes. Möhler was pre-eminently such a man. In his lectures on the history of the Church, which were published only last year,[185] he said that the Catholics, as such, took no part in the massacre; that no cardinal, bishop, or priest shared in the councils that prepared it; that Charles informed the Pope that a conspiracy had been discovered; and that Gregory made his thanksgiving only because the King's life was saved.[186] Such things will cease to be written when men perceive that truth is the only merit that gives dignity and worth to history.

---

quietisque publicae turbatores animadvertere? (*Apparatus Eruditionis*, vii. 503; Piatti, *Storia de' Pontefici XI*, p. 271).

[184] Per le notizie che ricevette della cessata strage (Moroni, *Dizionario di Erudizione Ecclesiastica*, xxxii. 298).

[185] [1868.]

[186] *Kirchengeschichte*, iii. 211.

[13]
The Borgias and Their Latest Historian

The Renaissance is the only epoch of history that has equal charms for idle and for thoughtful men, and stands in visibly intimate connection with the civilisation of the present time, yet beyond the range of its controversies. The interest it awakens is undisturbed by the contests that immediately followed it. Neither religious nor political differences affect the feelings with which men regard the age to which they owe the knowledge of Pagan, of Jewish, and of Christian antiquity, the formation of modern literature, and the perfection of art. The degradation which Italy suffered under native tyrants cannot prevent the pride with which she remembers the days of her national independence and her intellectual supremacy. Stores of new materials continue to be produced in uninterrupted profusion by patriotic scholars; and the way in which they modify the aspects of the fifteenth century is shown in several recent works. Zeller's *Italie et Renaissance* and Reumont's *Geschichte der Stadt Rom* mark the progress which has been made beyond the range of Roscoe and Sismondi. Both are well-written books, and the authors are perfectly familiar with the spirit of those brilliant times. Burckhardt's *Kultur der Renaissance in Italien* is the most penetrating and subtle treatise on the history of civilisation that exists in literature; but its merit lies in the originality with which the author uses common books, rather than in actually new investigations. The last traveller over the ground is Gregorovius.

The seventh volume of his *History of Mediaeval Rome* virtually completes his task, for it reaches the beginning of the sixteenth century. Another volume will include the age of Leo X and terminate with the siege

Published in the *North British Review* 53 (January 1871):351–367. *Wellesley* I, p. 695; Döllinger III, p. 14. Reprinted in Acton, *Historical Essays*, pp. 65–84.

and devastation of the city in 1527. The work gains in breadth and variety as it proceeds, and at times it is little less than a history of the Popes. The treatment is unequal. Pius II, the ablest and most interesting pontiff of the fifteenth century, receives but little attention, probably because a voluminous life of him appeared only a few years ago. But the pontificate of Alexander VI is described with elaborate care, and occupies great part of the volume. These chapters are amongst the best and most solid that Gregorovius has written. Continuous reports by the envoys of Florence, Venice, and Ferrara at the court of Rome enable him to emancipate himself from the trivial diarists on whom every writer since Raynaldus has been obliged to depend for the secret history of the Vatican. He is so well supplied with unpublished documents, and he employs them with so little regard for purposes of vulgar controversy, that his estimate of Alexander, which contradicts the unanimous judgment of all the contemporaries of the Pope, cannot be put aside at once, and without examination, amongst historical paradoxes. Alexander VI is described by his latest historian as a man whose everyday mediocrity reflects the sinfulness of a godless age, whose motives were the love of pleasure and the advancement of his family, who had neither political capacity nor serious design, and whose nature was too frivolous and too passive even for ambition.[1]

This excessive depreciation of a man whose talents and success were the admiration of Europe in his time is not due to an irrelevant indignation at his depravity, but to the historian's habit of avoiding the ecclesiastical part of his subject. Looking at secular and profane things only, he does not see that Alexander fills a great space in history, because he so blended his spiritual and temporal authority as to apply the resources of the one to the purposes of the other. The strain which his policy as an Italian sovereign laid on his power in the Church was fruitful of consequences in the next generation, and for all later times. His energy in making the prerogative of the Holy See profitable and exchangeable in the political market was an almost immediate cause of the revolt of Northern Europe. The system which Luther assailed was the system which Alexander VI had completed

---

[1] In Wahrheit zeigt es sich, wie gewöhnlich und klein dieser Mensch gewesen ist. . . . Sein ganzer Pontifikat zeigt keine einzige grosse Idee weder in Kirche noch Staat. . . . Nichts von jenem rastlosen Thatendrange und Herrschersinn eines Sixtus IV oder Julius II erscheint in der wollüstigen und passiven Natur dieses kleinen Genussmenschen (pp. 500–502).

and bequeathed to his successors. It was his work and example that Adrian meant to repudiate when he attributed the corruption of the Church to the recent usurpation and immorality of the papacy.[2] And Julius II attempted to liberate the Church from the responsibility of his acts by declaring that a Pope elected by simony could never become legitimate.[3]

The leading fact that governs his whole pontificate is the notorious invalidity of his election. There had been no hypocrisy in the transaction; and all Europe was able to learn the exact sums that he had paid or promised to his supporters, and even to their attendants. His seat never became secure. His right was permanently threatened. The shadow of an impending Council darkened his life, and ruined his authority. He was obliged to create for himself the power which belonged in theory to his See. He could not have held his position without perpetual activity and effort.

He was hailed at first with flattery so general and excessive that it must have been more than conventional. Men said that he was more than human, that he surpassed all mankind in righteousness, that the splendour of Christ Himself shone forth when he ascended the throne.[4]

---

[2] Scimus in hac sancta sede aliquot jam annis multa abominanda fuisse, abusus in spiritualibus, excessus in mandatis, et omnia denique in perversum mutata (Indicat hic optimus Pontifex ea, quae nos in Alexandro VI deploravimus); nec mirum si aegritudo a capite in membra, a summis Pontificibus in alios inferiores praelatos descenderit (Raynaldus, *Annales Ecclesiastici*, 1522, p. 70).

[3] Contra dictum sic electum vel assumptum de simoniaca labe a quocumque Cardinali, qui eidem electioni interfuerit, opponi et excipi possit, sicut de vera et indubitata haeresi (Raynaldus, 1506, p. 1).

[4] Politian, speaking in the name of Siena, said: "Praestans animi magnitudo, qua mortales crederes omnes antecellere—Magna quaedam de te nobis rara, ardua, singularia, incredibilia, inaudita pollicentur." The Orator of Lucca: "Quid est tuus divinus et majestate plenus aspectus?" The Genoese: "Adeo virtutum gloria et disciplinarum laude, et vitae sanctimonia decoraris, et adeo singularum, ac omnium rerum ornamento dotaris, quae talem summam ac venerandam dignitatem praebeant, ut valde ab omnibus ambigendum sit, tu ne magis pontificatui, an illa tibi sacratissima et gloriosissima Papatus dignitas offerenda fuerit" (Ciaconius, *Vitae Pont.*, iii. 152, 159). The Venetian Senate rejoiced: "Propter divinas virtutes et dotes quibus ipsum insignitum et ornatum conspiciebamus, videbatur a divina providentia talem pastorem gregi, dominio et sacrosanctae romanae ecclesiae vicarium suum fuisse delectum et praeordinatum" (Romanin, *Storia di Venezia*, v. 10). The Archbishop of Colocza wrote: "Omnes id satis exploratum habent, mitiorem Pontificem nec optari, nec creari potuisse, cui tantum sapientiae, probitatis, experientiae, ac integritatis est, quantum in quovis alio unquam audiverimus" (Petrus de Warda, *Epistolae*, 33). A priest of Parma wrote: "Hominem non dicam, sed divinum hominem, magnanimum pietate gravem ac meritis sapientis-

His very countenance was divine. The golden age came back again; Astraea returned to earth at his accession. It was really believed that he would be a glorious pontiff.[5] Ferrante of Naples and Ferdinand of Aragon were hostile to him from the beginning; but in many countries the illusion was not dispelled until the cardinals who had refused his bribes published his iniquity. Julian della Rovere, afterwards Pope Julius II, insisted that a Council should be summoned in order to judge him.[6]

The idea was taken up by the Court of France, when the Pope appointed one of his kinsmen to the archbishopric of Rouen, whilst the Chapter elected George d'Amboise.[7] The ministers boasted that the king possessed an infallible means of subjugating Alexander by calling a Council.[8] Charles VIII claimed the crown of Naples, and threatened, if investiture should be refused, to depose the Pope, not by force, but by canonical proof that he was a heretic and an intruder.[9] When Alexander took the side of the house of Aragon, and the French invaded Italy, his prospects seemed hopeless. He expected to be deposed.[10] The Cardinal of Siena, whom he sent to mollify the King of France, could not obtain an audience, and wrote to warn his master of the approaching danger.[11] The French intended to summon a

---

simum, ingenio praestantem, consiliis et sententiis probatissimum, omnibus denique virtutibus ornatissimum."

[5] Dicesi che sarà glorioso pontefice (Manfredi to the Duchess of Ferrara, Aug. 17, 1492; *Atti e Memorie,* iv. 323).

[6] Quid enim felicis recordationis Alexandro VI. Romano Pontifici praedecessori nostro magis nos odiosos fecit, nisi studium et cura generalis concilii celebrandi? Quid nos terra marique jactavit, cum nobis idem Alexander praedecessor esset infensus? quid toties Alpes transcendere transalpinas, Gallias peragrare per aestus, nives et glacies compulit, nisi quod nitebamur, ut a Romano Pontifice concilium indiceretur, convocaretur et celebraretur? (Raynaldus, 1511, 10).

[7] Sdegnato di questa collazione contro del Papa, il Rè tenne il dì medesimo gran consiglio, dove furono proposte e trattate più cose contro del Papa, in riformazione della chiesa (Desp. of Aug. 31, 1493; Canestrini, *Négociations avec la Toscane,* i. 249).

[8] Venetian despatches of the same month of August, in Romanin, v. 33.

[9] Soggiungeva che rifiutando le cose che ricercava, considerasse bene essere a Carlo cosa libera, poichè adjutato dall' imperatore de' Romani il quale da pochi giorni s' era seco lui confederato, era per privarlo dalla dignità apostolica, non solo colle armi colle quali superava tutti gli altri, ma per diritto, radunando un concilio de' prelati, i quali potevano giustamente pronunziare avere egli comperato la pontificia dignità, di maniera che non si poteva chiamare vero pastore di Santa Chiesa (Corio, *Storia de Milano,* iii. 525).

[10] Dubitava che il rè lo dimitesse del Papato (Marin Sanuto, in Cherrier, *Hist. de Charles VIII,* ii. 61).

[11] Aiunt etiam multo vulgo inter illos iactari, regem Romam venturum et statum Romanae Ecclesiae reformaturum (Piccolomini to Alexander, Lucca, Nov. 4, 1494).

Council at Ferrara to sit in judgment on the Pope,[12] and they believed that the consciousness of his guilt would make him pliable.[13] They occupied Rome without resistance. Alexander shut himself up in St. Angelo, with a small group of faithful prelates; but the majority of the Cardinals were urging the king to depose him.[14] The instrument pronouncing his deposition was drawn up:[15] French cannon were pointed against the fort; and part of the walls suddenly gave way. When it seemed that nothing could save Alexander, Charles relented and made terms with him. The reforming cardinals quitted Rome, indignant at the failure of their design. As the Pope instantly broke the treaty that had been forced upon him, Briçonnet himself thought that the king could proceed to extremities against him on his return from Naples.[16] Alexander escaped by flight. He afterwards said that Charles had been restrained from acts of violence by the piety of his

[12] Le quali cose sono di qualità, secondo che me concluse dicto oratore (the French envoy at Florence), che daranno materia al prefato Rè Christ., de fare praticha con qualche Cardinale, come già se fece, de chiamare Sua Santità a Concilio, dicendomi che el credeva che non passariano molti giorni che 'l se ordinaria dicto Concilio, et di farlo a Ferrara, dove pare che se debba fare per omni rispecto. Et a questo gli è molto inclinata prefata Regia M[ta] (Manfredi to Duke of Ferrara, Feb. 16, 1495; *Atti e Memorie,* iv. 341).

[13] Crediamo che la Santità di nostro Signore, il quale di sua natura è vile e è conscius criminis sui, ancora de facili si potrebbe ridurre alle cose oneste, per dubio delle cose di qua (Florentine Desp., Lyons, June 6, 1494: Canestrini, i. 399). Eulx deux (Borgia and Sforza) estoient a l'envy qui seroit Pape. Toutesfois je croy qu'ilz eussent consenty tous deux d'en faire ung nouveau au plaisir du Roy, et encores d'en faire ung françois (Comines, *Mémoires,* ii. 386).

[14] Nostre Saint Père est plus tenu au roy qu'on ne pense, car si ledit seigneur eust voulu obtemperer à la plupart de Messeigneurs les Cardinaulx, ilz eussent fait ung autre pappa en intention de refformer l'église ainsi qu'ilz disaient (Briçonnet to Queen of France, Rome, Jan. 13, 1495; De la Pilorgerie, *Campagne d'Italie,* 135).

[15] This was stated by Paul IV: "Sua Santità entrò a deplorar le miserie de' Italia et narrò l' historia dal principio che fù chiamato Re Carlo in Italia da Ludovico Moro et Alfonso d' Aragona, con li particolari del parentado fra questi due, la causa dell' inimicitia, il passar Re Carlo per Roma, la paura di Papa Alessandro di esser deposto, come publicamente dicevano li Cardinali che vennero co 'l Rè tra quali erano S. Pietro in Vincola, che fù poi Giulio Secondo: che furno fatti li capitoli della privatione da un Vicentino Vescovo di (illegible), all' hora auditor della Camera" (Desp. of B. Navagero, Rome, May 21, 1577; MS. Foscarini, 6255).

[16] Divinendo in ragionamento col Card. de S. Malo (Briçonnet) del facto del Papa, sua Rev[ma] Sig[ria] me disse che il Re ch[mo] non ne remaneva cum quella bona satisfactione che 'l sperava, havendose portato non troppo bene in queste pratiche de Spagne, etc., concludendo dicto Card[e] che 'l dubitava assai, che, finita che fosse questa impresa del Reame de Napoli, la M[tà] del Re non se desponesse a pigliare qualche expediente per reformare la chiesa, parendogli che 'l sia molto necessario, vedendosi come sono gubernate le cose della chiesa et sede apostolica (Manfredi to Duke of Ferrara, Feb. 25, 1495; *Atti e Memorie,* iv. 342).

courtiers;[17] but the language of Briçonnet and Comines proves that the opinion of the French camp was in favour of a bolder policy, and the king had not courage to attempt it. When he was gone and the danger was over Alexander excommunicated him. Shortly before he died the Sorbonne exhorted him to convoke a Council, and accomplish the reforms which the Pope persisted in refusing.

Under his successor, Lewis XII, the plan was revived. The Cardinal d'Amboise opened negotiations with Ferdinand and Maximilian with a view to a new election.[18] In the summer of the year 1501, Piccolomini, Cardinal of Siena, who became Alexander's successor, proposed to him to call together a Council and undertake reforms himself, lest the thing should be done in spite of him, to the detriment of the papacy, by the cardinals who were living abroad. Alexander entertained the idea for a moment, and then gave it up when he was reminded that Piccolomini was a nephew of Pius II, "un concilionista," whose advice in these matters was open to suspicion.[19] In the following year it was reported in Rome that the French were resolved to depose him. There is a celebrated medal bearing the effigy of Lewis XII, with the lilies, and the words "Perdam Babylonis nomen," which is ascribed to the time of the deadly quarrel between Lewis and Julius II. It belongs to the times of Alexander VI. Constabili speaks of it, and describes the sensation which it made at Rome, in a letter to the Duke of Ferrara, on the 11th of August 1502.

The aspiration of the Councils of Constance and Basel, the hope of honest reforms, had remained unsatisfied, and was kept up by the condition of the Roman Court during several pontificates. It was scarcely worse under Alexander than under his predecessors, and the zeal of the French Government was not attributable exclusively to disinterested motives of conscience. The flaw in his election was too tempting an instrument to be neglected. There was more to gain by practising on his fears than by deposing him. Neither Germany nor Spain was willing to accept a Pope created by the King of France.[20]

[17] Adducendo su questo proposito quello che accadette al Christianissimo Re Carlo quando andava in lo reame: che avendo pur contra sua santità malo animo, non solo fù consentito per li Sig.ri francesi che ageret contra eam, ma fù necessitato ad inclinarseli et basarli lo pede, et tenerli la staffa in mezo lo fango (Desp. of Saracini to Duke of Ferrara, Rome, Oct. 27, 1501).

[18] Le Gendre, *Vie du Cardinal d'Amboise*, i. 245.

[19] Constabili to Duke of Ferrara, Rome, Feb. 23, 1502.

[20] Cardinal Perrauld said to the Venetian Ambassador at the Court of Maximilian:

King Ferdinand continually impressed on Alexander that he heartily despised him. Gonzalvo of Cordova came to Rome and spoke out the indignation and horror of Europe.[21] A joint embassy was despatched by the Kings of Spain and Portugal to protest against the scandals of the papacy.[22] Alexander received the envoys in the presence of five cardinals. They represented the immediate necessity of a thorough reformation; they demanded that a Council should be assembled at the Lateran; they informed the Pope that all Italy could bear witness that his election was void.[23] He replied that their king was excommunicated, and that it was well for them that Caesar Borgia did not hear them. Later on he made one concession. He promised that the Duchy of Benevento should not be alienated from the See of Rome. He had conferred it on his son, the Duke of Gandia, who was almost immediately murdered; and the Spanish Ambassador had resisted, and declared that it should not be done.

Grief for the loss of his son roused the conscience of the Pope, and he spoke of abdicating the throne and changing his life. He would send Caesar to reside in his diocese of Valencia. He would resign the Government into the hands of the cardinals. A commission of six was appointed on the 17th of June 1497, and drew up in the following month a scheme of reform which has not been noticed by Gregorovius.[24] Their proposals were quickly forgotten; but two months later they were still acting as advisers of the Pope in the affair of Savonarola.[25]

During the short interregnum over which the promise of improvement lasted, Cardinal Borgia was sent with the powers of a papal legate

---

"Non se parla de deporre el Pontifice; ma se vol provvedere che el stato della chiesa non sia tirannizzato, ovviar alla simonia, coreger la vita dei prelati et levare le estorsioni che se fano nela cancelaria" (De Leva, *Storia di Carlo V*, i. 73).

[21] Zurita, *Historia del Rey Don Hernando*, i. 117.

[22] Mores esse profligatos, pietatis studium restinctum, flagitiorum licentiam solutam, res sanctissimas pretio indignissimis addici—remque esse in extremum paene discrimen adductam (Osorius, "De rebus gestis Emanuelis," *Opera*, i. 595).

[23] Italia tutta avrebbe dimostrato lui non esser vero Pontefice (Marin Sanuto, in *De Leva*, 61). Que eran notorias las formas que se tuvieron en su eleccion, y quan graves cosas se intentaron, y quan escandalosos (Zurita, 159).

[24] Raynaldus, who is his sole authority here, depends upon Zurita, and Zurita gives no particulars. The plan is in Malipiero (*Annali Veneti*, 494).

[25] Se era deliberato per el Papa et per li sei Cardinali deputati pro reformatione, che ullo pacto non se dasse la absolutione che addimandava questa Signoria per fra Hieronimo nostro, nisi prius pararet mandatis del suo generale et del Papa, non se attendendo alli ragionamenti facti per li antedicte Cardinali de suspendere le censure per duos menses (Manfredi to Duke of Ferrara, Aug. 16, 1497; *Atti e Memorie*, iv. 585).

into Umbria. His letters to Alexander VI, written in the summer of
1497, are the most eloquent testimony we possess touching the state
of society which the Borgias set themselves to abolish in the dominions
of the Church, and the influences which determined their unrelenting
policy.[26] It was a pacific mission. The legate went unarmed to try the
force of persuasion, and to test the moral authority of the papacy in a
district where the idea of the State was quenched in feudal strife, and
each man's safety consisted in the terror he was able to inspire. In his
first letter, on the day of his arrival at Narni, he announced that he
could accomplish nothing without troops, as the demons he had to
deal with were not to be frightened with holy water.[27] The presence
of a legate was so little heeded that Alviano, the same who afterwards
commanded the Venetians when their power was broken at Agnadello,
seized a town belonging to the Pope and sacked it almost before his
face. Borgia sent for him, and summoned him to keep the peace.
Alviano replied that he would gladly help the Pope to subdue his
neighbours, but that he would destroy the town rather than give it
up.[28] It was soon discovered that the legate was not followed by an
army; and things grew worse.[29] The country was without police or
law. The inhabitants of Todi, finding that there was no government
to protect them, deserted the town in despair.[30] Brigands held unmolested sway, and were only checked by rival bands. At Perugia the
legate caused a murderer to be put to death.[31] It was an immense

[26] The originals are among the manuscripts in St. Mark's Library (Lat. Cl. x. 176).

[27] È molto necessaria la provvisione de le genti d' arme contro questi demonii che
non fugono per acqua sancta (July 16, 1497).

[28] Intendendo che quando l' antique sue rasoni non li siano sopra de quella da la Sta
vostra instaurate, spianarla per modo che dire sepossa, qui fù Lugnano (July 17).

[29] Solo in la mia prima ionta in provintia cessarono un poco per timore dele gente d'
arme, fo dicto me seguitavano, ma hormai reassicurati comensano nel primo modo
offenderse et non dare loco ad mei commandamenti (July 27).

[30] Ricevo ad ogni hora da quelli poveri loro castelli querele miserabili che le prede et
occisioni se le fanno tutta via maiuri. Per la qual cosa la Sa Va po ben comprendere che
tucto lo remedio de questi mali consiste in la venuta de la gente d' arme, le quali
tardando più forniscese el paese de Tode da desolare, essendo da la partita mia in qua
la cita totalmente derelicta et lassata vacua (July 30).

[31] In questa cita hieri si fecero li bannamenti et con maraviglioso consenso sonno da
tucti posti in observantia, et procedono le cose qui con tanta obedientia et quiete che
meglio non si potriano desiderare (July 30). Dopo li Bandimenti, dui becharini homicidi
ho facti pigliar, et son stati senza tumulto et placer del popolo menati in presione. Cosa
da bon tempo in qua insolita in questa città, et questa matina ne è stato appichato uno
(Aug. 2).

achievement. Murder was common, but legal punishment was a thing almost unknown. Perugia, in consternation, became an altered city. Borgia was proud of his success. He assured the Pope that the rest of the country could be reduced to order and peace by measures of exceeding rigour.

Reigning over subjects unaccustomed to obey, befriended by no Power in Europe except the Turk, surrounded by hostile cardinals, with a flaw in his title which invited defiance and contempt, Alexander found himself in a position of the utmost danger. In the natural course of things, a power so wrongfully acquired, and so ill secured would have fallen speedily; and the Papacy bearing the penalty of its corruption would have been subjugated. It was only by resorting to extraordinary artifice of policy, by persisting in the unlimited use of immoral means, and creating resources he did not lawfully possess, that Alexander could supply the total want of moral authority and material force. He was compelled to continue as he had begun, with the arts of a usurper, and to practise the maxim by which his contemporaries Lewis XI, Ferrante of Naples, and Ferdinand of Aragon prevailed over the disorganised and dissolving society of feudalism, that violence and fraud are sometimes the only way to build up a State.[32] He depended on two things—on the exchange of services done in his spiritual capacity for gold, troops, and political support; and on the establishment of principalities for his own family. The same arts had been employed by his predecessors with less energy and profit. It was an unavoidable temptation, almost a necessity of his position, to carry them to the furthest excess.

The theory of the Papal prerogative was already equal to the demands he made on it. Flatterers told him that he was invested with the power of Almighty God on earth, that he was supreme in the temporal as well as the spiritual order, that no laws or canons could bind him, for he himself was the animated law and the rightful judge over the princes of the world.[33] He made the most of this doctrine,

---

[32] Uno in una città disordinata merita laude, se, non potendo riordinarla altrimenti, lo fa con la violenza e con la fraude, e modi estraordinarii (Guicciardini, in *Opere Inedite*, i. 22).

[33] Tibi supremi rerum omnium opificis potestas in terris concessa est. Pontifex est, qui Lege, Canone, et propria constitutione Papali solutus, ea tamen vivere non dedignatur; qui Canon in terris animatus vocatur: qui denique omnium Principum, Regum et Imperatorum Judex legitimus appellatur. Negabit ergo quispiam, quod gladii potestatem utriusque a vero Deo demandatam non obtineas? (Ciaconius, 155, 158).

and resolutely applied it in practice. He declared that his authority was unlimited, that it extended over all men and all things.[34] In virtue of this claim he bestowed Africa and America on the kings of Spain, excommunicating beforehand all who would presume to trespass on these regions without licence.[35] The plenitude of power thus exercised was justified by an enlargement of the mediaeval theory, which adapted it to the enlarged horizon of the Church. It is the Pope's office, it was argued, to teach the Gospel to all nations, and to compel observance of natural law. But the heathen will not hear the Gospel, and will not keep the law, unless they are made subject to Christians. Conquest, said one of the best writers of the next generation, makes more converts in a few days than mere preaching in three hundred years. Civil rights and authorities cannot lawfully obstruct the propagation of the faith.[36] The Spanish Government profited by this sweeping grant, but attached no religious value to it, for they soon after agreed with Portugal to shift the line of partition which the Pope had drawn across the earth.

Alexander VI employed the terrors of excommunication with a sparing hand. The risk was great and the weapon blunted. His censures against the King of France were effectually suppressed by Cardinal

[34] Altissimus, sicut in Beato Petro, Apostolorum Principe, aeternae vitae clavigero, omnes atque omnia, nullo prorsus excepto, ligandi atque solvendi plenariam tribuit potestatem, ita Nos, super gentes et regna constitutos . . . in Prophetam mandavit (to Charles VIII, Aug. 5, 1495).

[35] Auctoritate omnipotentis Dei nobis in Beato Petro concessa, ac vicariatus Jesu Christi qua fungimur in terris. Ac quibuscunque personis cujuscumque dignitatis, etiam imperialis et regalis status gradus ordinis vel conditionis sub excomunicationis latae sententiae poena, quam eo ipso, si contra fecerint, incurrant districtius inhibemus ne ad insulas et terras firmas inventas et inveniendas . . . accedere praesumant.—Auctoritate nobis in B. Petro concessa, de ipsa Africa omnibusque regnis, terris et dominiis illius sine alicujus Christiani principis praejudicio, auctoritate, apostolica tenore praesentium . . . plene investimus (Raynaldus, 1493, p. 22; 1494, p. 36).

[36] Habet igitur Papa potestatem ubique gentium, non solum ad praedicandum Evangelium, sed etiam ut gentes si facultas adsit, cogat, legem naturae cui omnes homines subjecti sunt, servare. . . . Ut autem infideles Evangelicam praedicationem audire et legem naturae servare cogantur, necesse est ut Christianorum imperio subjiciantur. . . . Hac ratione paucis diebus plures et tutius ad Christi fidem convertuntur, quam fortasse trecentis annis sola predicatione converterentur. . . . Quanquam enim Ecclesiastica potestas, quam Christus tradidit Vicario suo, in iis potissimum rebus versatur, quae religionem attingunt, patet tamen latissime in omni terrarum orbe, pertinetque etiam ad imperia civilia et omne genus, si hoc religionis moderandae vel propagandae ratio postulare videatur. . . . Belli parandi classisque mitendae gravissimus auctor fuit Alexander VI Pontifex Max. cujus Pontificis auctoritas ea est ut ejus legibus atque decretis publice factis obsistere vel contradicere nefas sit, et sacrorum interdicto haereticorumque poenis sancitum (Sepulveda, *Opera*, iv. 334, 335, 340; iii. 12, 15).

Julian. The Sorbonne declared that his threats might be disregarded with a safe conscience. They were of no avail when unsupported by material force. But in Italy, where they were backed by carnal weapons, men thought of them with awe, and the Venetians dreaded them even when unjust.[37] Accordingly, the Pope used excommunication as a way of declaring war on those whom he was about to attack. The rebellious vassals were assailed with spiritual arms on account of their impiety as a prelude to the arrival of Caesar's army.[38]

It was by squandering ecclesiastical privileges, by the profusion of graces and dispensations, that he disarmed enemies, made friends, and got money. The Venetians accused him of abetting the Turks against them,[39] and they dreaded extremely the progress of Caesar Borgia in Romagna. Yet they feared to oppose him, for they required the Pope's aid in taxing the clergy, and in raising money from the people. They gained 120,000 ducats by the Jubilee in 1501.

Marriage dispensations became, by careful management, productive sources of revenue and of political influence. Charles VIII wished to marry the betrothed bride of the King of the Romans, and the Pope was solicited on either side to permit or to prevent the match. He informed Valori that he meant to decide in favour of France, as the stronger and more useful power.[40] But he said the thing was too scandalous to be done publicly, and afterwards spoke of the marriage as invalid.[41] Divorce served him better even than dispensations. Lewis XII wished to marry the widow of his predecessor, whose dower was the duchy of Brittany. He was already married; but Caesar was despatched to France with the permission for the king to put away his wife. He was rewarded by a French principality, a French wife, and a

[37] Perchè giusta vale, ingiusta timenda est. . . . Con veritate il favor d' un Papa è più grande di quello che cadauno può considerare. . . . Perchè l' auttorità sua vale assai, edico grandemente apud Deum et homines (Priuli, May 25, June 10, Aug. 23, 1501).

[38] Alexander to the Magistrates of Bologna, Jan. 28, 1501, in Gozzadini, *Memorie di Bentivoglio,* Doc. 75.

[39] Se la stessa Santità Vostra persuade altrui ci si lasci punire e battere dagli infedeli, convien pur dire si voglia e si desideri che prima noi, e poco dopo l' universa religione cristiana vada in ruina (Council of Ten to the Pope, June 30, 1500; De Leva, i. 69).

[40] Lo ricercammo, qual era in secreto la intenzione sua. Rispose che in ultimo satisfarebbe al Re di Francia, e terrebbe più conto di lui che del Re de' Romani; non solo perchè la Francia è più potente, ma anco perchè quella casa è stata sempre amica e difensora di Santa Chiesa (Desp. Rome, March 31, 1493; Canestrini, i. 486).

[41] Publicava que la dispensacion que el Rey Carlos tenia, con la qual casò con la duquesa de Bretaña, era de ningun efecto . . . y dezia, que en publico no queria concenderla, por el escandalo (Zurita, 27).

French army wherewith to conquer Romagna. Ladislaus of Hungary desired to put away his wife, the widow of Mathias Corvinus. The Pope gave him leave, and earned 25,000 ducats by the transaction. He twice dissolved the marriage of Lucretia. The King of Poland had married a princess of the Greek Church, and had bound himself by oath not to compel her to change her religion. The Pope informed him that the oath was illegal, and not only absolved him from it, but required that compulsion should be used, if necessary, in order to convert her. But if neither ecclesiastical nor secular weapons should avail to subdue her obstinacy, then he commanded that she should be punished by having her goods confiscated, and by being turned out of her husband's house.[42]

In order to make money by Indulgences, Alexander claimed jurisdiction over the other world. When the Jubilee of 1500 was celebrated, he was advised that it would produce far more if it were made applicable to the dead. Divines reported that this power was included in the Pope's prerogative.[43] Sixtus IV had attempted to restrain this superstition, but Alexander allowed it to prevail, and the idea that the release of a soul could be insured by a mass at a particular altar became in his time the recognised belief in Rome.[44] It was supposed that the two last kings of Portugal had died under sentence of excommunication. The Pope gave them posthumous absolution, on condition that their successor discharged their debts to the Church.[45]

---

[42] Pollicitus es, quod eciam iuramento forte dictorum oratorum sub nomine tuo confirmatum extitit, nunquam eandem compulsurum ad ritum Romane ecclesie suscipiendum: sed si sponte sua ad eandem Romanam ecclesiam venire vellet, libertati sue in hoc eam dimitteres, que tua Nobilitas, quamvis perniciosa satis et iuri contraria fuerint, per quinquennium observare curavit. . . . Volumus, teque oneramus, ut non obstantibus promissionibus et iuramentis predictis, quibus te nullatenus teneri tenore presentium declaramus, denuo tentes, ac ea omnia agas, que tibi necessaria videbuntur quo eadem uxor tua, relicta pessima Ruthenorum secta, tandem resipiscat (to Alexander of Lithuania, June 8, 1501). Per censuras ecclesiasticas et alia iuris remedia, etiam cum invocacione, si opus fuerit, brachii secularis, cogas et compellas, . . . Concedens licentiam eidem Alexandro ipsam Helenam auctoritate nostra apostolica ex lecto, domo et omni maritali consorcio penitus excludendi, illamque pro meritis errorum suorum, etiam dotem et omnia alia bona eiusdem confiscata declarando, punias. . . . Non obstantibus quibus vis promissionibus eciam iuramento firmatis (to Bishop of Wilna; Theiner, *Monumenta Poloniae*, ii. 288–90).

[43] Duke of Ferrara to Cardinal of Modena, Jan. 1, 1501.

[44] It was officially affirmed by the legate Raymundus at the Jubilee of 1500.

[45] Tibi per presentes committimus et mandamus ut Alfonsum et Joannem, si in eorum obitu manifesta penitentie signa apparuerunt, ab excommunicationis sententia necnon

It was he who simplified and cheapened the deliverance of souls in purgatory, and instituted the practices which Arcimboldus and Prierias, in an evil hour, set themselves to defend. The mass was not held necessary; to visit the churches did as well.[46] Neither confession nor contrition was required, but only money.[47] It came to be the official doctrine that a soul flew up to heaven as fast as the money chinked in the box.[48] Whoso questioned the rightfulness of the system was declared a heretic.[49]

By these measures in the spiritual order Alexander exercised vast influence over the future of the Catholic Church, whilst by his nepotism he caused the Papacy to become a political power in Italy. His nepotism is commonly explained by his desire to enrich his kindred. But there was more than this. There was the desire to put in the place of almost independent feudatories a prince who represented the person, and could be trusted to do the will, of the Pope, and to strengthen and sustain the Papacy by the introduction of an hereditary element. It is a wise saying of Guicciardini, that the Popes were badly served because their reigns were short, but that the Borgias proved what could be accomplished by a well-served Pope.[50] It was a substitute for the security derived from dynastic interests and influence. There was a vulgar nepotism in the solicitude of Alexander to heap wealth and

---

aliis censuris et penis ecclesiasticis si quas propterea incurrerunt . . . absolvas (to Bishop of Oporto, July 3, 1502; *Corpo Diplomatico Portugues,* i. 39).

[46] Quam Ecclesiam (St. Laurentii) si quis visitaverit in omnibus diebus Mercurii per totum annum, habet a Deo et Sanctis Laurentio et Stephano istam gratiam extrahendi unam animam de purgatorio (Raymundus, in Amort, *De Origine Indulgentiarum,* ii. 283).

[47] Valde iniquum est quod pauper defunctus gravissimis peccatorum penis tamdiu affligatur, qui liberari posset pro modica substantie parte, quam post se reliquit. . . . Neque in hoc casu erit opus contribuentibus esse corde contritos et ore confessos, cum talis gratia charitati, in qua defunctus decesserit, et contributioni viventis duntaxat innitatur (Instructiones Arcimboldi, 1514; Kapp, *Urkunden,* iii. 190, 191).

[48] Praedicator, animam quae in Purgatorio detinetur, adstruens evolare in eo instanti, in quo plene factum est illud, gratia cujus plena venia datur, puta dejectus est aureus in pelvim, non hominem, sed meram et catholicam veritatem praedicat (Prierias, "Dialogus," in Luther, *Opera Latina,* i. 357).

[49] Qui circa indulgentias dicit, ecclesiam Romanam non posse facere id quod de facto facit, haereticus est (Prierias, *Ibid.*).

[50] Essendo communemente di brieve vita, non hanno molto tempo a fare uomini nuovi; non concorrono le ragioni medesime di potersi fidare de quelli che sono stati appresso allo antecessore . . . in modo che è periculo non siano più infedeli e manco affezionati al servizio del padrone, che quelli che servono uno principe seculare. Dimostro quanto fussi grande la potenza di un pontefice, quando ha uno valente capitano e di chi si possa fidare (Guicciardini, *Opere Inedite,* i. 87; iii. 304).

titles on his obscurer sons and kinsmen. But Caesar's career of conquest, the great reproach of the Borgias, was not a mere pursuit of mean and sordid objects; it belonged to a system of policy founded on reason and design, and pregnant with consequences not yet extinct.

The secret of Caesar's power over his father was not love but fear. Machiavelli saw that he really controlled the action of the pontiff, and advised the Florentines that they would obtain more by keeping an agent at Cesena than by their embassy at Rome;[51] but he did not discover the nature of the relations that existed between the father and the son. There was complicity, mutual dependence, even confidence, but not affection. The immense value which Alexander set on the advancement of his son, the perils and sacrifices he incurred to promote it, were not caused by family feelings. He justified his resignation of the Cardinal's hat, and his marriage, by saying that his presence among the clergy was enough to prevent their reformation.[52] He spoke of Caesar with the bitterness of aversion. When the Spanish and Portuguese ambassadors boldly reproached him with his nepotism, he answered helplessly that Caesar was terrible, and that he would give a quarter of his dominions to keep him from Rome.[53] At other times he complained that he could not be made to reside there,[54] and that, when he did, he allowed ambassadors to wait an audience for months, and turned night into day, so that it was doubtful whether after his own death his son would be found capable of keeping what he had got.[55] The year before his death he said to an envoy who was trusted with his secret plans, that he hoped Caesar's character would change, and that he would learn to tolerate advice.[56] Twelve months later, when he was at the height of his fortunes, Alexander was still lamenting that he would listen to nobody, that he made enemies everywhere, and

---

[51] Se ne ha contentare costui, e non il Papa, e per questo le cose che si concludessino dal Papa possono bene essere ritrattate da costui, ma quelle che si concludessino da costui non saranno gia ritrattate dal Papa (Desp. Cesena, Dec. 14, 1502; *Opere*, v. 354).

[52] Una de las mas principales causas que dava, para que el Cardenal de Valencia dexasse el capelo era, porque siendo aquel Cardenal, mientras en la Iglesia estuviesse, era bastante para impedir que no se hiziesse la reformacion (Zurita, 126).

[53] Que bien conocia que era muy terrible: y que èl daria la quarta parte del Pontificado, porque no bolviesse a Roma (*Ibid.* 160).

[54] Saraceni to Duke of Ferrara, Sept. 22, 1501.

[55] The same, Oct. 6.

[56] Dicendomi Sua Santità che epso Il[mo] Sig[r] Duca era uno bello Signore, et che sperava mutaria natura, et se lasaria parlare (the same, April 6, 1502).

all Italy cried out against him as a bastard and a traitor.[57] At last, when nothing else would restrain him from attacking Siena, the Pope threatened him with excommunication.[58]

When Alexander was dead, Caesar Borgia attempted to excuse himself by attributing his own acts to his father's will. He wrote to Ferdinand that he had sought the French alliance against his own wishes, in obedience to the Pope. He tried to conciliate the Duke of Urbino, the most tame and patient vassal of the Church, whom he had twice driven into exile. Caesar knelt before him, pleaded his own youth, and cursed his father's soul, whose baseness had led him astray.[59]

One point of contrast between the two, which the Pope was in the habit of urging, is curious, for it does not turn quite to Caesar's disadvantage. The Pope used to represent him as implacably cruel in punishing his enemies, and loved to dwell on his own generosity towards those who had injured or insulted him. In Rome he said speech was free, and he cared not for the things which were published against himself.[60] This praise was not quite hollow. That he was not excessively sensitive, that he could bear with adversaries, appears from the fact that he sent Ludovico di Ferrara to offer a cardinal's hat to Savonarola.[61] He did not proceed to extremities against him until Savonarola had written to the monarchs of Europe bidding them make a new Pope. Caesar was capable of equal self-restraint, less from temperament than his father, and more from calculation. When, by an act of consummate treachery, he made himself master of Urbino, he published a general amnesty, and observed it even against his worst enemies.[62] But he caused all those to be seized and punished who had betrayed their former master to him, showing, says the chronicler, that he hated the traitor though he loved the treason.[63]

It was said with truth that Alexander VI succeeded beyond his

---

[57] Constabili to Duke of Ferrara, Jan. 23, 1503.

[58] The same, March 1, 1503.

[59] Incolpando la giovintù sua, li mali consigli soi, le triste pratiche, la pessima natura del Pontifice, et qualche uno altro che 'l haveva spirito a tale impresa; dilatandosi sopra el Pontefice, et maledicendo l' anima sua (Letter from Rome in Ugolini, *Duchi d' Urbino*, ii. 524).

[60] Constabili to Duke of Ferrara, Feb. 1, 1502.

[61] Quétif et Echard, *Script. O. P.*, i. 883.

[62] Ugolini, ii. 111.

[63] Per dar ad intender a tutti, che 'l Signor over Signori hanno appiacer del tradimento, ma non del traditore (Priuli, July 6, 1502).

designs.[64] When Caesar stood at the head of a victorious army, the only Italian army in existence, the ambition of the Borgias soared to great heights. They were absolute in Central Italy, where no Pope had exercised real direct authority for ages.[65] The kingdom of Naples was the Pope's to grant, to take away, or to distribute. Lucretia was married to the heir of Ferrara. A marriage was proposed between an infant Borgia and the Duke of Mantua. Caesar possessed Piombino; he threatened Florence, Siena, Bologna, Ravenna, even Venice. He received tribute as *condottiere* from the chief independent States of Italy. The King of France offered Naples to the Pope.[66] The King of Aragon proposed that Caesar should receive Tuscany with the title of king.[67] Men spoke of him as the future emperor, and dreamed of Italy united and independent, under the sceptre of a papal dynasty.[68] Public expectation went at least as far as the secret hopes of Borgia. And it is certain that Caesar, hateful as he was, and hated by the great families he had overthrown, was not disliked by the masses of the people whom he governed.[69]

It is not just to condemn the establishment of a powerful dynasty in Romagna as an act of treason against the rights of the Church. Though not done for her sake, it was not done at her expense. Caesar was more powerful than Malatesta or Varano, but not practically more independent. Rome had derived little benefit from her suzerainty over the petty tyrants whose dominions were merged in the new duchy of Romagna, and incurred no positive loss by the change. In reality there was closer connection with Caesar than with the vassals he had deposed, and more reliance to be placed in him. His fidelity was

---

[64] Furono i successi sua più volte maggiori che i disegni (Guicciardini, *Opere Inedite*, iii. 304).

[65] Fu più assoluto Signore di Roma che mai fusse stato Papa alcuno (*Ibid.*). Donde viene che la Chiesa nel temporale sia venuta a tanta grandezza, conciossiachè da Alessandro indietro i potentati Italiani, e non solamente quelli che si chiamono potentati, ma ogni Barone e Signore, benchè minimo, quanto al temporale, la stimaba poco; e ora un Rè di Francia ne trema (Machiavelli, "Principe," *Opere*, i. 55).

[66] Constabili to Duke of Ferrara, Aug. 3, 1503.

[67] Zurita, 242.

[68] Nobody execrated the Borgias more than the Venetian chronicler Priuli. After the destruction of the Condottieri at Sinigaglia, he writes: "Alcuni lo volevano far Re dell' Italia, e coronarlo, altri lo volevano far Imperator, perche 'l prosperava talmente, che non era alcuno li bastasse l' animo d' impedirlo in cosa alcuna" (Jan. 11, 1503).

[69] Aveva il Duca gittati assai buoni fondamenti alla potenza sua, avendo tutta la Romagna con il ducato di Urbino, e guadagnatosi tutti quei popoli, per avere incominciato a gustare il ben essere loro (Machiavelli, "Principe," *Opere*, i. 35).

secured, for he could not maintain himself in opposition to the Pope. He had no friends in the other Italian States. Supported by the inexhaustible wealth of the Church, he could keep up an army which no power in Italy could resist; and the Papacy, assured of his fidelity, obtained for the first time a real material basis of independence. Before the French invasion of 1494, the Italians had so little habit of serious warfare that the various States enjoyed a sort of inert immunity from attack.[70] The expedition of Charles VIII showed how little there was of real security in the general proneness to inaction. By the aid of Caesar Borgia the Papacy became a military power. That aid was purchased at a great price, but it was sure to be efficient.

The danger was not that the provinces would be alienated, but that the Papacy would fall under the sway of its formidable vassal. Alexander not only foresaw this result, but anxiously contrived to make it certain. It meant that his family should not relax their hold on the Church, to which they owed their elevation. He did not wish to weaken the staff on which they were obliged to lean. His purpose was not to dismember the State, but to consolidate part of it in such a way that his descendants should be the servants and yet the masters of his successors, and that a dynasty of Borgias should protect and should control the Papacy. There was ruin in the scheme, but not the obvious ruin commonly supposed. It was not inspired by religion or restrained by morality, but it was full of intelligent policy of a worldly sort. Caesar's principality fell to pieces, but the materials enabled Julius II to build up the Roman State, which was destined to last so long. The Borgias had laid so firmly the foundations of their power, that the death of the Pope would not have shaken its stability if Caesar had not been disabled for action at the moment when he was left to his own resources.[71]

Gregorovius, like Ranke, accepts the story that Alexander perished by poison which had been prepared for others. It was the common rumour. Two other guests at the fatal supper, Caesar and Cardinal Adrian, were seized with illness at the same time, and the latter assured Giovio that he had been poisoned. This statement, recorded by Giovio, is the only evidence that positively supports the suspicion. The report

---

[70] Chi aveva uno Stato era quasi impossibile lo perdesse (Guicciardini, *Opere Inedite*, i. 109).

[71] Se nella morte di Alessandro fusse stato sano, ogni cosa gli era facile (Machiavelli, "Principe," *Opere*, i. 39).

arose before the Pope was dead, as soon as the sudden illness of the others became known.[72] But it was founded entirely on conjecture. Guicciardini, who did much to spread it, possessed no proof. He says that the story is confirmed by the fact that the Pope died within twenty-four hours.[73] In reality he died on the seventh day after his attack. The witness who has been hitherto the principal authority proves, therefore, to have no evidence. There are almost daily accounts of the Pope's state between the 12th and the 18th August from Giustinian to Constabili. They suggest nothing more unusual than a violent Roman fever.

[72] Per la qual infermità si giudicava fosse stato avoelenato, e questo perchè etiam il giorno sequente il prefato Duca Valentino et il Card' s' erano buttati al letto con la febre (Priuli, Aug. 16, 1503).

[73] Guicciardini, *Istoria d' Italia,* iii. 162. E che questa sia la verità, ne fà fede che lui morì o la notte medesima o il dì seguente (*Opere Inedite,* iii. 302).

[14]
Wolsey and the Divorce of Henry VIII

Half a century ago a writer of great authority delivered the opinion that few things in history were better known than the divorce of Catharine of Aragon. Since that time the archives have been explored, and the old story which satisfied Hallam will never be told again. Mr. Brewer has done more than any other man to dispel the dark tradition, and to pour light upon an epoch which will always interest every description of educated men. After all that has been already gathered from Rome and Venice and Simancas, from Brussels and Vienna, his volume on the last and most momentous years of Wolsey's ministry embraces seven thousand letters, of which a large proportion are important and new. The most competent of his foreign critics, Dr. Pauli, reviewing the earlier part of the Calendar, declared that no other country possesses a work so satisfactory and complete; and this is not exaggerated praise, although even Mr. Brewer's analysis cannot be accepted as a substitute for the full text of documents. He has not aimed so high; and his readers will not seldom find that there is something still to learn in earlier and humbler publications.

If the Calendar does not utterly supersede all previous collections, the introduction in which Mr. Brewer has gathered up the innumerable threads, and has woven them into a consistent picture, so far surpasses all former narratives of the same events as to cause regret that he has not chosen rather to write a life of Wolsey, which everybody would have read, than to bury the fruit of so much study in prefaces to bulky and not very accessible volumes. With little additional labour he would

Published as a review of J. S. Brewer, *Letters and Papers, Foreign and Domestic, of the Reign of Henry VIII,* in the *Quarterly Review* 143 (January 1877):1–51. *Wellesley* I, p. 759; Döllinger III, pp. 162, 170. Reprinted with the title "Wolsey and the Divorce of Henry VIII" in Acton, *Historical Essays,* pp. 1–64.

have enjoyed greater freedom in the management of materials and in the use of colour, and literature would have been endowed with a popular masterpiece. Mr. Brewer has thought it a duty to devote the whole of his accumulated knowledge and power to the public work which has occupied so large a portion of his life. So few men are capable of extracting for themselves and digesting all the information his Calendar contains, that the elaborate introductions by the editor add immeasurably to its permanent utility and value. But it is impossible not to feel and to regret the generosity of so great a sacrifice.

Many of the problems that have agitated and perplexed ten generations of men are still unsolved. Yet, although we have not reached the fulness of knowledge that sates curiosity, it is not likely that much more will be learnt. Some progress may be looked for in biography; for the early lives of Gardiner, Tunstall, and Cromwell have not been studied; nobody has taken the pains to restore the true text of the original Life of Fisher; and not one of More's fifteen biographers has worked from manuscripts. The Vatican continues to yield priceless additions to the works of Raynaldus, of Theiner, and of Lämmer; part of the correspondence of Charles V lies unused at Brussels; and the papers of Campeggio may yet, perhaps, be found in the place where Sigonius saw them. But whatever the future may reveal, we now possess, in Mr. Brewer's pages, an account of the Divorce, to the fall of Wolsey, which is eminently trustworthy and intelligible.

That which distinguishes the whole reign of Henry VIII, both in Wolsey's happier days and during the riotous tyranny of later years, the idea of treating ecclesiastical authority not as an obstruction, but as a convenient auxiliary to the Crown, was anticipated by the example of his father-in-law Ferdinand. The Norman conquerors of Sicily established a form of government in which the spiritual power was more completely subdued by the civil than in any other place beyond the Byzantine boundary. In the struggle for the inheritance of the Suabian emperors, the Sicilians resisted for centuries the anathemas and the arms of Rome, and the kings of the House of Aragon maintained themselves in defiance of excommunications which were almost perpetual, and of an interdict which lasted seventy years. In a country which had endured ecclesiastical isolation so long, the Papacy could not recover its influence when the dynastic strife was ended. The Kings of Sicily acknowledged no superior, but exercised all jurisdiction themselves, allowing no appeals, and holding under strict control the intercourse between Rome and the Church within the island. This system of undivided power, consolidated and codified under Fedinand the Catholic, became known by the significant designation of the Sicilian Monarchy. It was established without a conflict, and without ostensibly derogating from the papal dignity, by the instrumentality of the fiction that the King was, in his own dominions, hereditary Legate of the Pope. The combination of legatine authority with the highest political office in the person of Wolsey was an expedient that bore close practical resemblance to this institution.

It was in 1515 that Ferdinand proclaimed himself the virtual head both of Church and State in Sicily—*cujus tam in spiritualibus quam in temporalibus curam gerimus*. In the following year Henry VIII demanded that Leo X would appoint his favourite minister Legate *a latere*. For three years he made the demand in vain. It was granted at length, and the appointment was justly described as the keystone of the Cardinal's position. Henry had too much of the instinct and of the passion of power to surrender willingly the advantage which it gave him. That advantage could be preserved only by close union with Rome, or by the exclusion of its authority. The intimate alliance with the Papacy through every vicissitude of political fortune which is characteristic of Wolsey's administration, actually prepared the way for separation after his disgrace. It was so essential an element in his scheme of government that it was not disturbed when Henry imputed to Leo, and bitterly resented, his failure to obtain the Imperial crown.

The elevation of his rival, the King of Spain, suddenly raised England to an important position in the politics of Europe. An auction began, at which Francis I sought to purchase her friendship with gold; whilst Charles V not only offered the same sums as his competitor, but increase of territory at his competitor's expense. France was still our hereditary enemy. England remembered that an English King had been crowned in the French capital; and Calais was an irritating memorial of the lost inheritance, and of conquests that had ended in defeat. The nation adopted with joy the alliance with the House of Burgundy, and Parliament voted supplies for war against France.

To make sure of Wolsey, Charles promised that he should be made Pope; and the compact was scarcely concluded when the See of Rome fell vacant. The Cardinal summoned the Emperor to employ his army in securing his election. Charles assured him that he would not shrink from force if it was needed; but the choice of the conclave fell so speedily on Adrian VI that his sincerity was not tested. Wolsey waited, without discouragement, for another chance. In less than two years Adrian died, and Wolsey was again a candidate. His ambition was not unreasonable. He was the foremost of ecclesiastics and of statesmen; and it had been said of him long since that he was seven times greater than the Pope. In the conclave of 1522 six cardinals had paid him the compliment of inscribing his name on their votes.[1] The traditional aversion of the College for men from the barbarous North had been put aside in favour of one who, in point of public service and political reputation, bore no comparison with the Cardinal of York; and when it was first reported that a foreigner was elected, people supposed that it must be Wolsey. He now tempted his colleagues with enormous bribes, and he appealed once more to the Emperor. Charles acknowledged his engagements, and even exhibited a copy of the orders sent to his ambassador to procure Wolsey's election. But he caused the original to be detained, and took care that no effort should be spared to ensure the elevation of Medici; or, failing Medici, of Colonna or Farnese.

This time the disappointment was final, and no hope remained. It could not escape the sagacity of the Cardinal that the new Pontiff, who was younger than himself, had been raised to the throne by him whose support he had so painfully striven to secure, that his own claim had not been seriously put forward, and that he had been fooled with false professions. He at once prepared to withdraw from the warlike alliance against France.

In the year 1523, while Suffolk ingloriously harried Picardy, Wolsey already manifested his disbelief in the project for recovering the lost dominions of the English Crown, and opposed the attempt to push the frontier beyond the Somme. His moderate counsels were encouraged by the new Pope, Clement VII, whose minister, the famous *Datario* Giberti, revolving vast schemes for the expulsion of foreigners from Italy, solicited in secret the co-operation of England, and began by proposing a suspension of arms. Just then the French were expelled from Lombardy; and Bourbon, on the point of invading France, bound

---

[1] They were probably split votes, involving little more than a compliment or a warning; for a voting paper sometimes contained six or eight names. On the 3rd of January 1522 thirty-nine Cardinals gave more than sixty votes. Volterra had twelve, De Monte seven, Ancona seven, Medici, Santa Croce, Della Valle, Aegidius of Viterbo, Wolsey, six each; Adrian of Utrecht, eight.

himself by the most sacred oaths to depose Francis, and to acknowledge no King but Henry. Richard Pace, the successor of Colet at the Deanery of St. Paul's, a respectable scholar, but a negotiator of unsound judgment, who was destined, in the imagination of the Imperialists, to supplant Wolsey, followed the invaders over the Maritime Alps, and witnessed the easy conquest of Provence. He persuaded himself that the whole kingdom would speedily be overrun, and that Bourbon would be faithful to his oath. The Constable was a traitor and a deserter, yet Pace declared that it would be folly to doubt his word, and that it would be Wolsey's fault if he did not seat his master on the throne of the Valois. The prospect that dazzled Pace, and attracted the ambitious King, did not disturb the Cardinal's clearer vision. He supplied the Imperial generals with some money and much advice, reminding them of the first axiom of military science, that the object of war is the destruction of the enemy's forces in the field. When Pescara turned aside from the campaign to besiege Marseilles, he refused to send a single English soldier into France. That Bourbon and Pescara should employ their victorious troops in making the Emperor master of the coast that connected his Spanish dominions with his Italian conquests, was reasonable. But it was not to be believed that they would risk destruction by plunging into the heart of France, from a chivalrous desire that a foreign potentate, who refused to help them, should be made, in spite of himself, as powerful as their master. Wolsey warned Pace that he had allowed himself to be made a dupe; and Pace protested that the ruin of the expedition was due to the malice of Wolsey.

For many months a discreet agent of the French King had been concealed at Blackfriars, and he was followed, before the end of 1524, by an envoy of great distinction. As the tide of fortune turned, and the besiegers of Marseilles were shut up in Lodi and Pavia, Wolsey drew nearer to France, without renouncing his claims on Spain. The rivalry that subsisted like a permanent force of nature between the two Powers, gave him hope that he would be able, by his skill in negotiation, to derive profit, and to incur no risk, from the success of either. Whilst the issue was undecided, he would not commit England irrevocably. But the spirit of the Burgundian alliance gradually changed to resentment, and in February 1525 the seizure of the Imperial agent's papers disclosed the secret animosity that was parting the allies. The French envoys were on the way to their first audience, when they were met by the news from Italy that their King was taken, and his army destroyed. The calculations founded on the balance of power were overthrown. No advantage could be extracted from the keenness of a competition which had come to an end. The men who in the previous year had denounced the backwardness of Wolsey, were triumphant; and in Spain, in Italy, in the Low Countries, the English agents clamoured for the immediate partition of France.

If the policy of the last four years was worth anything, the time had come to prove it. The allies were victorious; Charles had gained the object for which he had associated himself with England; it was now to be shown what English purpose that association had served. Henry sent Tunstall to Madrid to demand the Crown of France. At the same time he attempted to raise money for the French war by a method of coercion which was termed an Amicable Grant.

Charles V refused everything. He would fulfil no engagement. He would not keep his promise to marry Henry's daughter, unless she was sent to be educated in Spain. Instead of paying his debts, he asked for more money. At the same time the Amicable Grant was met by a general and indignant resistance. Henry could obtain no help at home or abroad towards the conquests which had formed so long the ruling purpose of his actions. The political system which had been constructed on the friendship and the pledges of Charles V had ended in disastrous and dishonourable failure. England had spent much, and had acquired nothing. The Emperor, who had undertaken to continue the payments and pensions formerly made by France, had repudiated his obligation, and had solicited the Pope to release him from it. When he wanted the help of England, he had obtained it for nothing. He contemptuously refused to pay for it now that he required it no more.

Wolsey had long prepared for this. Whilst, with seeming confidence, he invited Charles to redeem his bond, he was making his bargain out of the extreme necessity of France. The Regent, Louise of Savoy, could cede no territory; but she was willing to pay a heavy price for the only succour that could avail, and Wolsey exacted a sum of money equal to the ransom for which Charles afterwards released his captive. Gold was in his eyes a surer gain than the expensive chances of conquest; but it was hard for Henry to content himself with a sordid equivalent for glory. The Emperor Maximilian, whose capricious and ingenious fancy was so little satisfied with things as they were that he wanted to be Pope, and talked of making Henry Emperor in his stead, had also suggested that he should be King of France. Down to the battle of

Pavia Henry pursued this idea. What Henry V had done with the slender resources of his time seemed not impossible now, with the aid of the most powerful of the French vassals, and of those alliances which displayed Wolsey's imperial art. To relinquish so hopeful an enterprise without a shadow of political or military success, whilst the hearts of his people were hardened against him, and his confederate defied him at the division of the spoil, was an impotent and ignominious end of Henry's aspiring schemes. The author of all this humiliation was Wolsey. It was his policy that had been brought to ruin by the subtler art of the Imperial Chancellor Gattinara. His enemies at home had their opportunity, and they were the whole nation. Detested by the nobles for his influence over Henry, by the clergy for his use of the powers delegated by Rome, and, in spite of his profuse beneficence, by the people of England, as the oppressor of the nobility, he had hardly a friend except the King, whose pride he had brought so low.

Yet Wolsey withstood the shock, and his credit remained unshaken. Henry adopted his inglorious policy, bowed his own imperious will before the resistance of London citizens and Kentish monks, and, at the moment when the crown of France seemed near his grasp, abandoned without a struggle the cherished hope of rivalling the Plantagenets. Wolsey was able to bring these things about because of an important change that had come over the domestic life of the King.

Catharine of Aragon was little past forty; but the infirmities of age had befallen her prematurely, and her husband, though he betrayed it by no outward sign, had become estranged from her since the end of the year 1524.[2] As long as she was fair and had hope of children, and as long as the Austrian alliance subsisted, her position was unassailed. But when her eldest children died, people had already begun to predict that her marriage would not hold good;[3] and now that she had lost the expectations and the attractiveness of youth, a crisis came in which England ceased to depend on the friendship of her family, and was protected against their enmity by a close union with France and Rome.

The motives that impelled Wolsey to take advantage of the change

---

[2] That is the date given by Henry himself to Grynaeus. His secretary, 4th December 1527, calls the divorce a thing he "hath long tyme desyred." Wolsey writes 5th December, "longo jam tempore." Campeggio writes, 17th October 1529, "piu di due anni." But on the 28th, after hearing the Queen's confession, he says, on her authority, "già molti anni." There is no reason to doubt the report of Grynaeus.

[3] Rawdon Brown, 1st September 1514.

were plausible. For a quarter of a century the strength of the Tudors had been the safety with which the succession was provided for; but when it became certain that Catharine would have no son to inherit the crown, the old insecurity revived, and men called to mind the havoc of the civil war, and the murders in the Royal House, which in the seven preceding reigns had seven times determined the succession. To preserve the Tudor dynasty, the first of the English nobles had suffered death; but nothing was yet secure. If a Queen could reign in England, Henry VII, who had no hereditary claim except through his mother, who survived him, was not the rightful king. Until the birth of Elizabeth no law enabled a woman to wear the crown; no example justified it; and Catharine's marriage contract, which provided that her sons should succeed, made no such provision for her daughters. It was uncertain whether Mary would be allowed to reign unchallenged by the Scots or by adherents of the House of York. The White Rose had perished, in the main line, amid the rout of Pavia; yet Catharine tortured herself with misgivings as to her daughter's claim. The Earl of Warwick, a helpless and unoffending prisoner, had been put to death, that her wedding might be auspicious. His sister Margaret, the Countess of Salisbury, was living, and directed the Princess's education. Catharine vowed that she could not die in peace unless the crimes of her husband's family against the House of York had been atoned by the marriage of Mary with the Countess of Salisbury's son.

It was not unreasonable to apprehend that Henry, who had been unfaithful to the Queen in earlier years, would not be true to her now; that he would fall under the dominion of favourites put forward and prompted by the Cardinal's enemies, and that his inheritance would be disputed by bastards. The King's soul, the monarchy, and Wolsey's own position were in jeopardy. It might well be difficult to distinguish the influence of politics, interest, and conscience on his choice of the expedient by which he hoped to avert the peril.

To a man who understood policy better than religion, the public reasons for dissolving the King's marriage were better than those which had recommended it to his father; and there was a strong inducement, therefore, to ponder the words of Leviticus, and to regard the almost immediate death of the King's three sons as the penalty of his transgression. In the arbitrary and uncertain condition of the law, it was seldom difficult to find excuses for the dissolution of a Royal marriage. Henry could expect that nothing would be denied to him that favour or influence could procure for others. No man's marriage was exposed to more obvious objection.

The battle of Pavia had placed Rome at the mercy of the Emperor. Giberti appealed to Wolsey to unite with France in a league for the protection of Italy and of the Church. A breach between Spain and Rome was essential to the success of that which he meditated; and nothing could be more welcome than the appearance of the Pope striving to combine in one confederacy all the enemies of Spain. Having embarked in so perilous a venture, he could assuredly be made to give a heavy price for English aid. Wolsey received his proposals with the promise of hearty assistance. The Queen, the Court, every influence in the State and in the nation was against him. But he persuaded the King to enter into the scheme of Clement VII, with the assurance that he would be rewarded by spiritual favours more than sufficient to repay all that he gave up to obtain them. From that moment may be discerned the faint but suggestive trace of a secret that required the intervention of the Pope and threatened disturbance at home.

On Easter Sunday, two months after the great turn of fortune at Pavia, Wolsey first caused it to be known that he had renounced the expectation of benefit from the friendship of Charles V.[4] Just at this time the Primate Warham reminded him that it was unwise to broach too many causes of displeasure at once, and advised that the Amicable Grant be dropped "till this great matter of the King's grace be ended."[5] On the 21st of April Wolsey wrote to Clement a solemn and mysterious letter, entreating him to listen favourably to a certain matter which would be submitted to him by Clerk, the Bishop of Bath, who was the Cardinal's most trusted confidant. But the secret was one which the Bishop thought it an unpropitious moment to reveal. He was recalled in the summer, and Casale and Ghinucci, the two men whom Wolsey selected to take charge of the divorce in 1527, were sent in his place to expose business of great moment to the Pope.

Clement and his allies did not dare to defy the Emperor while the King of France remained his prisoner, for they justly feared that Francis would seek his own freedom by betraying them. He proposed to Charles that they should subjugate Italy together, and should reduce the Pope to the position occupied by the Patriarch of Constantinople

---

[4] Gayangos, *Spanish Calendar*, 20th April 1525.

[5] Brewer, iv. 1263. A misprint makes it uncertain whether Warham wrote on the 12th or 19th of April. Easter fell on the 16th.

at the Court of the Macedonian Emperors. But the chief Minister of Charles V, Gattinara, was a Piedmontese, who preserved the love of his country in the service of its oppressor. He distrusted and opposed the plans of Francis. He even imagined a scheme by which his countrymen, having been rescued from the French by the Spaniards, should buy off the Spaniards by a tribute large enough to avert the financial ruin of Spain. Before attempting war, the Italians tried what could be done by treachery. They offered the crown of Naples to Pescara, the ablest of the Imperial Commanders, as a bribe to desert the Emperor. Pescara threw his tempter into prison; and a year passed without an effort to mend the fortune of Italy. At length Francis was released, and the Italian patriots took heart to avow their warlike purpose. Clement put himself at the head of a Sacred League, which was joined by France, and protected by England. Giberti called upon his countrymen to cast out the invader; and Sadolet, in State papers, which are perhaps the noblest compositions of the Renaissance, proclaimed the liberty and the independence of Italy.

The moment for which Henry waited had come. Clement had burnt his ships, had refused fair terms of peace, and could not venture to deny the allies who sheltered him from manifest ruin. The secret matter which had slumbered for a year revived. Giberti assured Wolsey that the Pope would do for him all that was within his power.[6] But Clerk, who was again at Rome, reported that all else would be well but for the inauspicious business of the divorce. Henry paid a large sum into the Papal treasury: but his cause made no progress during the autumn of 1526. Six months later the difficulties were overcome, and matters were arranged in a way so satisfactory to Wolsey that he boasted of it as a triumph of skill.[7]

The Pope soon repented of the temerity with which he had challenged the supremacy of Spain. The stronger confederates held back, while the weaker stood exposed to the calculated vengeance of Charles V. Imperial partisans made their way into the Leonine City and plundered the Vatican. The Emperor appealed before the assembled Cardinals to a General Council against the acts of the Pontiff. This threat had

---

[6] "In iis secretioribus ac majoris momenti tantum sibi polliceri potest D. V. R. de S. D. N. voluntate quantum progredi potest auctoritas S. S." (Brewer, iv. 2579).

[7] "Wherin such good and substancial ordre and processe hathe hitherto been made and used, as the like, I suppose, hath not been seen in any time hertofore" (*State Papers*, i, 189).

power over Clement. He could not, without danger, allow his claim to be disputed before a hostile audience. His right to enjoy the higher honours of the Church had been questioned by reason of his birth, and his election to the Papacy had been accomplished under conditions which gave ground for cavil. He was elected in consequence of a private agreement with Cardinal Colonna, who was his enemy through life, who had tried to exclude him from the conclave, who attempted afterwards to expel him from the throne. Men suspected the secret method which had wrought that surprising change. It was reported that the rivals had made a simoniacal compact by which Medici obtained the tiara, while Colonna received the richest office and the finest palace in the gift of the Pope. But by a recent law of Julius II an election won by bribes or promises was for ever invalid. The Pope's courage gave way; even Sadolet declared that resistance was unavailing; and Giberti, boiling with indignation and resentment, and bewailing that it was his fate to serve the subtle and vacillating Florentine instead of the resolute English Cardinal, confessed that, without encouragement from France or hope from England, it was necessary to submit to terms dictated by Spanish generals. In a condition so precarious, the Pope could take no active share in a transaction which was an outrage to the Royal family of Spain. But the *Datario's* animosity against the Imperialists was such as to incline him towards measures which would injure them without compromising the Papacy.

Giberti had applied for an English pension, and he long continued to be trusted as a supporter of Henry's cause. After the fall of Rome he withdrew to his diocese of Verona, where the fame which he won as the model of a perfect bishop has obscured the memory of his political career. He confided to the English agents the fact that he had left the Court because Clement was ungrateful to those who deserved well of him.[8] They understood that Giberti had advised him to concede what Henry asked for in his matrimonial affairs; and they induced him to return to Rome, under a promise that he would use all his influence in the King's behalf. What was the measure of encouragement

---

[8] "He promises, however, to use all efforts in the King's behalf. He says the only cause of his leaving the Pope's palace was that the Pope did not attend to good advice, and was not grateful to those that deserved well of him; but Wolsey must take care not to tell this to Campeggio" (Vannes to Wolsey, Brewer, iv. 5344). "Praecepit etiam Dominus Veronensis Vicario suo non modo favere Maj. tuae causae, sed etiam in absentia sua convocare et hortari Theologos ut pro Maj. tua scribant; sed et se quoque subscripturum pollicitus est" (Croke to Henry, *Pocock's Records*, i. 531).

he gave during the last days of his ministry, in the spring of 1527, cannot be ascertained. It probably amounted to no more than this, that the marriage might be tried in England without the interference of the Pope. As things then stood, such an understanding would be sufficient to justify the exultation of Wolsey.

Up to this time the idea of divorce had occupied the thoughts of Henry in a vague and languid way. Neither aversion for the Queen, nor desire of an heir, nor religious scruple caused him to pursue it with a fixed determination. Whilst it was uncertain who was to be his future Queen, the King displayed no eagerness. The only power whose aid was worth seeking, or that could venture to affront Charles by taking advantage of his kinswoman's disgrace, was France. In the House of Valois there were two princesses. Renée, the Queen's sister, was ill-favoured and all but deformed. Henry was not likely to incur such risk for such a bride. On his last journey to France Wolsey met an envoy from Hungary, who had been sent to ask the hand of Renée for his master. He wrote to the King that the envoy when he saw her had forthwith renounced his purpose. He wrote in terms he would not have thought prudent if he had lately designed that she should be Catharine's successor.

The King's sister, Margaret Duchess of Alençon, was richly endowed with talent and beauty, and she became a widow in April 1525, at the moment when England forsook her Burgundian ally. At first it was imagined that she would marry the Emperor; and she visited Spain, hoping, perhaps, in that way to effect her brother's deliverance. In the year 1526 Margaret was again in France: and a widely spread tradition, doubted but not discussed by Mr. Brewer, points to her as the wife intended for the King. The Venetian Falier, the only diplomatist who showed a disposition to accept the Cardinal's account of the divorce, says that he had made proposals for her hand. The testimony of other writers is vitiated by an anachronism; for they assign the divorce to the year 1527, when Margaret was already married to a second husband. Guicciardini and Harpsfield speak of Renée, as if either name was a guess suggested by obvious probability. Du Bellay, the shrewdest of courtiers, conjectured that Renée had been thought of. He cannot have heard that it was Margaret. She herself once reminded Henry, in after-years, that she was to have been his wife. This speech, which would have been ungracious if she had refused him, was an allusion to proposals made by Lewis XII, immediately after Prince

Arthur's death, and renewed in vain until 1507. Francis I was willing to encourage a measure which would perpetuate enmity between his powerful neighbours; but he would have lost his advantage by implicating himself irrevocably on one side of the quarrel. Intermarriage with the House of Tudor was an object of his policy; but before concluding it he gave his sister in marriage to the King of Navarre, and planned a match between Renée and Hercules, Prince of Este.[9] In the spring of 1527 no princess was left who could have taken the place of Catharine. The repudiation of his Spanish wife would not enable Henry to compensate himself by closer ties with France. The divorce, promising no political advantage, could only make way for the elevation of an English bride. But though purposeless now as an affair of State, it became an object of passion.

After long preliminaries a treaty of alliance with France was signed in April 1527; and Henry betrothed his daughter Mary to the son of his ally. The event was celebrated on the 4th of May by a ball, at which the French ambassador, Turenne, danced with the Princess. King Henry's partner was Anne Boleyn. At that time she had lived at Court four years, and Henry, though not dissolute according to the standard of contemporary monarchs, had long regarded her with feelings which contributed to make him indifferent to a foreign match. She repelled his suit; and for more than a year he could obtain no sign of requited love. At length he made her an offer of marriage, which was accepted. His letter is undated; but it must have been written about the time when Anne Boleyn first became conspicuous: not later, because the intrigue which was designed to make her Queen stood revealed before the end of May. There is cogent reason to believe that it was not written earlier. Lord Rochford deposed before the Legates at Blackfriars that the conjugal estrangement between the King and Queen had begun in 1527.[10] His evidence is worthless regarding the date of the desertion of Catharine; but it goes far to determine the date of the engagement of Anne, which he must have known. For in the interest of the Boleyns it was essential that the scruples of Henry should have preceded the proposals of marriage to

---

[9] Margaret was betrothed to Navarre at Christmas, 1526. The proposed match between Renée and the son of the Duke of Ferrara was known 4th April 1527 (Desjardins, *Négoc. avec la Toscane,* ii. 935).

[10] Speaking on the 15th of July 1529, he said, "about two years since" (*Herbert's Life,* 114).

their daughter. If the offer had been made earlier than 1527, it would have ruined their cause to assign to that year the awakening of the King's conscience.

As soon as the Queen had an appointed rival, and the pleas of policy and religion were absorbed in the stronger influences of passion, the divorce was pressed forward with desperate and unrelenting energy. The friendship of France was secured, and there was nothing to be feared from Rome. On the 17th of May, the Archbishops, Warham and Wolsey, responsible in their character of Legates for the observance of public morality and ecclesiastical law, called Henry to justify himself before them, forasmuch as he was living, in defiance of the Levitical prohibition, in wedlock with his brother's widow. The proceedings were secret. Proctors appeared to accuse and to defend the marriage. Both accuser and defender were officers in the household of the King.

The effect of this collusive suit was to put Henry in the position of defendant. He took charge of the Queen's interests as well as his own. He was not a persecutor, but a victim; the protector, not the assailant, of her happiness and honour. It was in his power so to conduct the defence as to ensure his condemnation, and so to contrive his appeal as to ensure its rejection. Instead of putting forward his own suspicious scruples, he would appear to yield, with grief and remorse, to the solemn voice of the Church, reproaching him with involuntary sin, and dividing those whom God had not joined. It was intended that Catharine should know nothing until sentence was given.

At the end of a fortnight Wolsey adjourned the court. So grave an issue required, he said, that he should consult with the most learned prelates. In truth, the plot was marred by the fall of Rome. The Pope was shut up in the castle of St. Angelo. There was no hope that the Emperor's prisoner would confirm a sentence against the Emperor's aunt. There was danger that he might be induced, by fear or calculation, to revoke the Legate's authority, or to visit the fraudulent intrigue with the censures which were never better employed than in protecting the weak, and upholding the sanctity of marriage. That danger neither Henry nor Wolsey had the hardihood to face. No more was heard of the abortive suit until, in our day, Mr. Brewer dragged it into the light.

Wolsey had already sounded the opinion of the divines. The first consultation was unfavourable. The Bishop of London, the Dean of St. Paul's, Wakefield, the first Hebrew scholar in the country, six learned men sent up to Lambeth by the University of Cambridge, pronounced that the marriage was valid. Pace and Wakefield promptly retracted. Cambridge was partially brought round by Cranmer. It was generally believed in England that Catharine, in her brief union with Prince Arthur, had not, in fact, contracted affinity with her husband's kindred. It was difficult otherwise to understand how Henry VII could have spoken seriously of making her his Queen. Such things might be in Portugal, where the King could scarcely be prevented from marrying his step-mother. But in England stricter notions prevailed. Tunstall afterwards declared that he had defended the marriage only until he was convinced that the popular belief on this point was wrong.

No English divine enjoyed so high a reputation as John Fisher, the Bishop of Rochester. Of all the works written against Luther in the beginning of the Reformation, his were the most important; and he was eminent not only in controversy, but as a promoter of that new learning which theologians who were weaker in the faith looked on with detestation and dismay. Fisher's support would have been worth having; for he was neither subservient to Wolsey, like the Bishops of Lincoln and Bath, nor afraid of him, like the Primate; and he would have carried with him the whole weight of the school of Erasmus, which constituted the best portion of the English Church. As Wolsey deemed him an enemy, the question was submitted to him in terms so general that Fisher appears to have made answer without suspecting that he was taking the first step on a road ending at the scaffold.

Catharine had been apprised, very early, of all that was done. In the month of March she had taken alarm. She was not allowed to see the Spanish ambassador alone; but she warned him that she had need of his protection.[11] On the 22nd of June Henry informed her that he could regard her no longer as his lawful wife. In spite of the vigilance of the Government, Catharine despatched her physician and one of her attendants to Spain, to instruct the Emperor of the outrage inflicted on his blood. The remedy she desired was that he should cause the Pope to revoke the powers which had been delegated to the Cardinal for life. The ambassador, Mendoza, reported at the same time that public animosity was rising against him; that his enemies were forcing upon him measures by which he would inevitably work out his own destruction; and that Tunstall would soon be Chancellor in his stead.

---

[11] "Esta muy sospechosa que en ninguna cosa se hablen verdad" (Mendoza to Charles, 10th March 1527).

The French alliance afforded Wolsey the means of recovering his influence, and of becoming once more, for a short space, the principal personage in Europe. At the head of the most splendid embassy that ever crossed the Channel, he went to concert with Francis the measures to be taken in common defence against their triumphant enemy. It was necessary to provide, during the abeyance of the Papacy, for the government of the national Churches. Wolsey agreed with Francis that they should administer the ecclesiastical interests of both countries without reference to the Pope while his captivity lasted, and should be free to accept his acts or to reject them at pleasure. A still larger scheme for the government of the entire Church was proposed by the French. The suspension of the Papal authority was not so formidable as the uses to which it might be put by the ambition of Charles. If he could not compel his prisoner to serve him as the instrument of his vengeance against France and England, it was in his power to put a more pliant and trusty cardinal in his place. This was no visionary apprehension. Ferdinand of Austria was entreating his brother not to relax his grasp until the Pope had accomplished all that was wanted for the settlement of Europe; and Mendoza, seeking to tempt Wolsey away from the connection with France, whispered to him that the Emperor now united the spiritual and temporal power, and was in a position to fulfil his ancient promise, by deposing Clement. Wolsey was proof against such solicitation. The Divorce parted him irrevocably from Charles; and when the Emperor, seriously alarmed by the report that Wolsey was to be made Patriarch of Gaul, and meant to detach the Gallican and Anglican Churches from the See of Rome, offered him a sum which would be now £160,000, even that stupendous bribe was tendered in vain.

Francis I offered passports to the Italian cardinals, inviting them to assemble at Avignon to consult with Wolsey and with their French colleagues for the welfare of religion. Wolsey urged them to come, in the expectation that he would, at their head, possess a virtual supremacy. The cardinals who were in France joined with him to inform Clement that they held themselves absolved from their obedience, and intended, if he should die in captivity, to elect a Pontiff for themselves. Among the signatures to this momentous declaration are the names not only of the French and English Chancellors, but of the Legate Salviati, who was nearly related to the Pope. It was not entirely unwelcome to Clement himself,[12] as it made it less likely that the Emperor would coerce him. But he refused to permit his cardinals to accept the ominous invitation to Avignon, for Gattinara met it by threatening him with a council to be summoned by Colonna. To meet the resistance of the Italian cardinals, Wolsey devised the boldest of all his manoeuvres. He proposed that Clement should sign a protest nullifying all the acts he might perform under pressure of captivity; and should appoint Wolsey his Vicar-General until the moment of his deliverance. He charged Gambara, the Nuncio in England, to obtain these powers by persuading the Pope that Charles would never set him free, and that his Vicar would do his will in all things. He was carefully to conceal from him the purpose to which the required authority was to be applied. It would have settled the question of Divorce, by enabling Wolsey to appoint the judges and to hear the appeal. To strengthen his envoy's hands, he proposed to the French Chancellor, Duprat, that Francis should pledge himself to Wolsey to employ all the resources of France in the Pope's service, and not to sheathe the sword until he was delivered. The engagement was to be seen before starting by Gambara. Then Wolsey undertook, by virtue of his special powers, to release the French King from his bond. After it had been described in fitting terms to Clement, and had exalted his confidence and admiration for the Cardinal, it was to become waste paper.

It was the opinion of Henry's advisers that the question of his marriage might still have been settled, as it was begun, within the realm; and Wolsey's elaborate and demonstrative arrangements for a separation from Rome that might endure indefinitely, confirmed their advice. It was unreasonable that grave ecclesiastical causes should wait the pleasure of the hostile soldiery that guarded the Pontiff; or that an issue of vital consequence to the English crown and nation should be left to the judgment of men who were the helpless prisoners of an interested and adverse party. But on this point Wolsey was resolved to bear down all opposition. Rome supplied the qualification that made him indispensable. To preserve that supply, to maintain

---

[12] "Gaudeoque nostra in S. D. N. ecclesiasticaeque authoritatis gratiam suscepta consilia, ex his indiciis ab ejus Sanctitate probari, quae exhibuit per nuncium illum clandestinum quem ad Dom Lautrec ab ea nuper missum V. R. D. scribit" (Wolsey to Duprat, 5th October 1527).

his position as Legate against the influence of Charles V, he upheld with a firm and jealous hand the prerogatives of the Papacy; and he succeeded, with some difficulty, in convincing his master that it would be unsafe to proceed with no better warrant than they possessed already.

The Cardinal was absent during the whole summer; the ablest men who were engaged in public affairs, Tunstall, More, and Gardiner, were in his retinue, and those who envied his greatness and denied his capacity possessed the King's ear. They disbelieved that the Pope would be willing now to help them against the Emperor, or would assent to Wolsey's audacious plans for assuming his place. He might succeed, without any profit to the King. He might effect his own exaltation, and might then be intimidated from employing it for the desired end. It was plain that he was using the Divorce for his own aggrandisement. His aggrandisement might, after all, do nothing for the Divorce. When his vast designs were unfolded, a sense that they were outwitted fell upon the cabal that were pushing the fortunes of Anne Boleyn. Wolsey had been ready in May to go all lengths, and he now declined to go further without the cognisance of Rome, or to question the plentitude of the dispensing power. It seemed that he was betraying the King to the Pope. He defended himself in a remarkable letter, and fancied that he had dispersed the gathering storm. When Henry expressed a wish to see Gardiner, he replied that he could not spare him.

Then, for a season, his adversaries prevailed. They persuaded Henry that he could reach his end by a shorter road; and he sent his Secretary Knight to Rome, with instructions which were unknown to Wolsey. For the delicate mission of inducing the Pope to abdicate his supreme functions in Wolsey's hands, he had chosen to employ none but Italians. The Nuncio Gambara, supported by letters from Cardinal Salviati, was to open the matter. Gambara was to be followed by Casale and Ghinucci. Stafileo, Bishop of Sebenico and Dean of the Rota, promised his assistance; for Wolsey had found him in France, and had no difficulty in moulding his opinion. Ghinucci and Casale were the most respectable of all the agents engaged in these transactions. But Gambara was a man steeped in Italian intrigue; and Stafileo obtained the promise of a French bishopric and a Cardinal's hat, and died in the following summer, claiming his reward with a vigour injurious to the credit of his legal advice. Clement afterwards accused

Stafileo of having been the author of the mischief. His adhesion was a notable event, for he presided over the supreme tribunal by which, in the last instance, the validity of marriages was decided; and it was a significant circumstance that the King's cause was at once taken up and pleaded by the official agents of the Papacy.

But the artful machinery which Wolsey had contrived was thrust aside, the management was wrested from his hands, and he was obliged to recall his instructions; while Knight proceeded to execute orders which were studiously concealed from his knowledge. During the interval in which his adversaries pursued the matter in their own way, and laboured to rob him of the merit of success, Clement made terms with his conquerors. The Protest and the Vicariate became words without a meaning, and Wolsey's dream of superseding the Pope was dissolved.

The substance of Knight's mission was to procure a dispensation for bigamy. The original intention was only to seek a dispensation for marriage within the forbidden degrees when the first should be dissolved. It could be requisite only because the King had been the lover of the mother or sister of Anne Boleyn. He declared that it was not the mother. The dispensation demanded would, in some measure, have confirmed the right to try the cause in London. But the Nuncio advised that it should be unconditional, and should not be made to depend on the divorce of Catharine. This petition was not brought before the Pope. Knight was overtaken on the way by Lord Rochford's chaplain, bringing an altered draft. Cranmer was chaplain to Lord Rochford. He was so much averse to the theories that were undermining the marriage-law, that he protested vehemently against the later practice of his Lutheran friends, calling them Mohammedans for their encouragement of polygamy. It would appear that he was the author of the altered counsels.

When Wolsey on his return reported himself to Henry, the answer came to him in the shape of an order from Anne Boleyn. He could measure the ground he had lost by his prolonged absence. He regained it in the following winter by his inexhaustible energy and resource; and the importunities of Anne for some token of attention, were it even a basket of shrimps, confirmed him in the assurance of recovered power. Knight's negotiations with Roman and Tuscan masters of refined diplomacy ended in quick discomfiture. Long before his complacent incompetence was exposed, Wolsey had taken back into his own hands the conduct of affairs. The sharp lesson just administered had taught him caution. His services in promoting the Divorce were certain to increase the exasperation of the people, and could never disarm the hatred or the vengeance of the magnates whom he had humbled. Success was not less dangerous than failure. It became the object of his efforts to transfer from himself the formidable burden of responsibility, and to take shelter behind a higher authority. He applied first for powers for himself, or for Stafileo, to try the validity of the marriage; but he required that their commission should be couched in terms which implicitly ruled the decision. When he knew that the Pope was about to be released, he tried to give him a larger share of action, by proposing that a Cardinal should be sent over as Legate, in the hope that his Commission would enable him to control the Legate's course, and to dictate the sentence. In a passage which was omitted from the fair copy of this despatch, Wolsey confessed that the dissolution of a marriage which had lasted so long would give too great a shock to public feeling for him to take it upon himself.

Before the day came on which the Imperialists had covenanted to release the Pope, he was allowed to escape, and he made his way to Orvieto, where the emissaries of Henry, bringing to his feet the humble but fervent prayer of their King, taught him that he possessed, as Bishop of Rome, resources more than sufficient to restore the lost sovereignty of Central Italy. He was without the semblance of a Court. Few of the prelates, and not the best of them, had joined him in his flight. His chief adviser in this most arduous conjuncture of his stormy Pontificate was Lorenzo Pucci, Cardinal of Santi Quattro, a Florentine, and an adherent of his house, who, after the death of Leo, had attempted to raise him, by surprise and acclamation, to the vacant throne. To many sordid vices Pucci added the qualities of energy and intrepidity, which his master wanted. At the storming of Rome he was the only Cardinal seen upon the walls. He was struck down whilst, with his voice and his example, he strove to rally the defenders, and climbed into the Castle through a window after the gates had been closed. He had been Minister under Julius, and, for his extortions under Leo, men said that no punishment was too bad for him. Wolsey had given orders that money must not be spared; but Pucci, who was noted for cupidity, refused a present of two thousand crowns, and could never be made to swerve in his resistance to the English petitions. He drew up the Commission which Knight asked for, with alterations that made it of no effect; and he baffled the English envoys with such address that the winter passed away before Henry had obtained any concession that he could use, or that the Pope could reasonably regret.

The dominant purpose was to gain time. The Emperor, on receiving the messages of Catharine and Mendoza, immediately insisted, through his Viceroy at Naples, that Wolsey should be forbidden to act in the matter, and this demand reached Clement whilst still surrounded by the soldiery that had sacked Rome before his face. He had now become free; but it was the freedom of an exile and a fugitive, without a refuge or a protector from an enemy who was supreme in the Peninsula. The instrument which the skill of Pucci had made innocuous and unavailing, appeared to him charged with dreadful consequences. He begged that it might be suppressed. His dejection made him slow to perceive how much Henry's intense need of his spiritual services improved his political position. He strove to exclude the cause from his own direct jurisdiction. Having consulted with Pucci, and with Simonetta, the ablest canonist in Rome, he exhorted Henry to obey the dictates of his own conscience, and to dismiss the Queen and take another wife, if he was convinced that he could lawfully do it. Wolsey's Legatine powers, or the Commission lately issued, were ample for the purpose. Once married to Anne Boleyn, Henry had nothing to fear. But if he waited the slow process of law, and gave time for protests and appeals, the Emperor might compel them to give sentence in Rome. Clement deemed that it would be a less exorbitant strain of his prerogative, and less offensive to Charles V, to tolerate the second marriage, than to annul the first.

Henry VIII consented to be guided by Wolsey against the judgment of his Council, but he had inclined at first to more summary and rapid methods, and the mission of Knight in the autumn of 1527 showed that he was slow to abandon that alternative. That he should, nevertheless, have rejected an expedient which was in the interest of those to whom he habitually listened, which was recommended by his own strong passions, and which the confidential counsel of the Pope invested with exceptional security, is the strangest incident in the history of the Divorce. Wolsey's influence is insufficient to explain it; for Clement repeated his advice after Wolsey's fall, and yet three years passed before Henry's tenacity yielded. In March 1530, the Pope was at Bologna, holding conference with the newly crowned and reconciled Emperor. Charles V required him to threaten Henry with anathema and interdict if he should contract a second marriage pending judgment on the first. Clement could not resist the demand, but he yielded reluctantly. He put forth a Bull in the terms which the Emperor required. But in private he expressed a wish that his menace might be vain, and that the King's purpose might be accomplished without involving him in complicity. These words were spoken in secret; and at Orvieto also Clement had desired that his advice should be attributed to the prelates who were about him. Henry may well have feared that, after taking an irrevocable step, he might be compelled to purchase indemnity by some exorbitant sacrifice; or he may have apprehended in 1528 what happened five years later, that the Pope, compelled by the Emperor, would excommunicate him for disobeying his injunctions. Having taken his stand, and resolved to seek his end on the safer ground of submission and authority, he refused to abandon it.

All the auspices at first favoured Henry, and every prejudice told against the Emperor, whose crafty policy, while it enabled Lutheranism to establish itself in Germany, had inflicted irreparable injury on the See of Rome. The sympathies of the Roman Court were as decided on one side as they might be now in a dispute between the head of the House of Bourbon and the head of the House of Savoy. Henry VIII had given, during a reign of eighteen years, proofs of such fidelity and attachment as had never been seen on any European throne. No monarch since Saint Lewis had stood so high in the confidence and the gratitude of the Church. He had varied his alliances between Austria, France, and Spain; but during four warlike pontificates Rome had always found him at its side. He had stood with Julius against Maximilian and Lewis, with Leo against Francis, with Clement against Charles. He had welcomed a Legate in his kingdom, where none had been admitted even by the House of Lancaster. He was the only inexorable repressor of heresy among the potentates of Europe; and he permitted the man to whom the Pope had delegated his own authority to govern almost alone the councils of the State.

No testimony of admiration and good will by which Popes acknowledge the services of kings was wanting to his character as the chosen champion of religion. The hat, the sword, and the golden rose had repeatedly been sent to him. Julius, in depriving Lewis XII of his designation of the Most Christian King, had conferred it upon Henry; and he bore, before Luther was heard of, the title of Defender of the

Faith.[13] His book was not yet written when Leo X convoked the cardinals in order that they might select a title of honour worthy of such services and such fame; and it was suggested in the Consistory that Henry deserved to be called the Angelic King.[14] His bitterest enemy, Pole, averred that no man had done more for Rome, or had been so much beloved. Such was his reputation in Christendom that when he talked of putting away a wife who was stricken in years to marry a bride in the early bloom of her beauty, the world was prepared to admire his scruples rather than to doubt his sincerity. Clement, though not without suspicions, suffered them to be allayed. He spoke of the case as one which was beyond his skill, but which no divine was more competent to decide than Henry himself. Campeggio declared, even at the Imperial Court, his belief that Henry's doubts were real. Cajetan wrote of him in 1534, Cochlaeus in 1535, with the full assurance that he had been deceived by others, and that his own religious knowledge was teaching him to discover and to repair the error of his advisers. After the final condemnation had been pronounced, a prelate engaged in the affair wrote to him in terms implying that in Rome it was understood that he had been led astray, not by passion but by designing men. Even Paul III protested that he had made Fisher a Cardinal in the belief that Henry would esteem the elevation of his subject a compliment to himself.

The good faith of Henry was attested by an imposing array of supporters. The Nuncio came to Rome to plead his cause. Stafileo and Simonetta, the foremost judges of the Rota, admitted that it was just. Two French bishops who had visited England, and who afterwards became cardinals, Du Bellay and Grammont, persistently supported it. Cardinal Salviati entreated Clement to satisfy the English demands. Wolsey, on whom the Pope had lavished every token of his confidence;

---

[13] "Regia etiam Majestas aegre fert quod de titulo defensoris sanctae Fidei nihil adhuc acceperit, quasi ejus sanctitas ea re timuerit Gallos offendere" (Wolsey, Desp., 22nd May 1517. Martene, *Amplissima Collectio*, iii. 1274).

[14] "Cardinalis de Flisio tunc primus in ordine Card. in Consistorio existentium, dixit sibi videri quod posset scribi et denominari pius, seu pientissimus. Papa dicebat quod forsitan posset denominari Rex Apostolicus. Nonnulli ex Cardinalibus dicebant velle scire causam propter quam dicto regi hujusmodi titulus concederetur, ut melius discuti posset qui titulus ei concedendus foret. Alius dicebat denominandum regem Fidelem, alius Angelicum, tanquam ab Anglia, alius Orthodoxum, alius Ecclesiasticum, alius Protectorem" (Acta Consistorialia, 10th June 1521). A slightly different report of this curious debate may be found in Lämmer's *Meletematum Mantissa*, 199.

Warham, the sullen and jealous opponent of Wolsey, who had been primate for a quarter of a century, and who was now an old man drawing near the grave; Longland, the Bishop of Lincoln,[15] the King's confessor, and a bulwark against heresy—all believed that the marriage was void. The English bishops, with one memorable exception, confirmed the King's doubts. The Queen's advisers, Clerk, Standish, Ridley, successively deserted her. Lee, the adversary of Erasmus, who followed Wolsey at York, and Tunstall, the Bishop of London, who followed him at Durham, went against her. The most serious defection was that of Tunstall; for the school of Erasmus were known to oppose the Divorce, and of the friends of Erasmus among the English clergy, Cuthbert Tunstall was the most eminent. He is the only Englishman whose public life extended through all the changes of religion, from the publication of the Theses to the Act of Uniformity. The love and admiration of his greatest contemporaries, the persecution which he endured under Edward, his tolerance under Mary, have preserved his name in honour. Yet we may suspect that a want of generous and definite conviction had something to do with the moderation which is the mark of his career. He reproved[16] Erasmus for his imprudence in making accessible the writings of the early Fathers; and in the deliberations touching the separation from Rome, in the most important Session of the Parliament of England, when he was, by his position, his character, and his learning, the first man in the House of Lords, he allowed himself to be silenced by an order from the King. Tunstall informed Catharine that he had abandoned her cause because he believed that she had sworn a false oath.

Nor did the conduct of the most distinguished English laymen confirm the reported unpopularity of the Divorce. It is certain that Sir Thomas More and Reginald Pole were conscientiously persuaded that the Queen was a lawful wife. Pole had, moreover, an almost personal interest to preserve inviolate Mary's right to the Crown;[17] and he wrote

---

[15] Chapuys calls him: "Principal Promoteur et brasseur de ce Divorce" (Legrand, *Lettres à Burnet*, 141).

[16] "Cui etiam si germana sit Origenis, et non ab aemulis addita, veteres omnes refragantur. Quare optassem magis delituisse non versam" (Tunstall to Erasmus, 24th October 1529. Burscher, *Spicilegium*, xviii. 13).

[17] "Caterina . . . sentiva rimorso nell' animo, et hebbe a dir che non moriva contenta, se nel sangue della Signora Margarita non ritornava la speranza della successione di quel Regno, significando di volere maritar la figliola con uno delli figlioli di detta Signora, alli quali mostrava grande amore" (Beccadelli, *Vita del Polo*, 280).

in its defence with such ability and persuasiveness, that Cranmer thought he would carry the whole country with him if his book became known. Yet Pole allowed himself to be employed in obtaining the assent of the University of Paris, and accepted his share of merit and responsibility in a success which cost Henry more than a million of francs.

Sir Thomas More had defended divorce in the most famous work that England had produced since the invention of printing. The most daring innovator of the age, he had allowed his sentiments to be moulded by the official theology of the Court. Under that sinister influence, More, the apostle of Toleration, who had rivalled Tertullian and Lactantius in asserting the liberty of conscience, now wrote of the Lutherans such words as these: "For heretykes as they be, the clergy dothe denounce them. And as they be well worthy, the temporaltie dothe burne them. And after the fyre of Smythfelde, hell dothe receyve them, where the wretches burne for ever." Henry supposed that a man whose dogmatic opinions he had been able to modify would not resist pressure on a subject on which he had already shown a favourable bias. More was steadfast in upholding the marriage, but never permitted his views to be known. He represented to Henry that he was open to conviction; that he was incompetent to pronounce and willing to receive instruction. He promised to read nothing that was written in favour of the Queen. So reticent and discreet a supporter could not be counted on her side; and More consented, as Chancellor, to act ministerially against her. He assured the House of Commons that Henry was not urging the Divorce for his own pleasure, but solely to satisfy his conscience and to preserve the succession; that the opinions of the Universities had been honestly given, and that those of Oxford and Cambridge alone were enough to settle the question. Whilst he remained in power he left the Queen to her fate, and did his best to put off the hour of trial that was to prove the heroic temper of his soul.

The Bishop of Rochester, indeed, was faithful and outspoken to the end; but his judgment was not safe to trust. Death for the sake of conscience has surrounded the memory of Fisher with imperishable praise; but at that time he was the one writer among our countrymen who had crudely avowed the conviction that there is no remedy for religious error but fire and steel; and the sanction of his fame was already given to the Bloody Statute, and to a century of persecution and of suffering more cruel than his own. Fisher suspected the attack on the Dispensation of concealing a design against the Church; and he therefore based the Queen's defence on the loftiest assertion of prerogative. His examination of the authorities was able and convincing. He admitted that they were not all on his side; but he held that even if the balance had leaned heavily against him it would not have injured his client. The interpretation of law, the solution of doubts pertained to the Pope; and the Pope had decided this dispute by the undeniable act of dispensation. The question might have been difficult on its merits; but there was, in reality, no question at all.

The value of the maxim, that the fact proves the right, had just then been seriously impaired. The divine whom Leo X appointed to encounter Luther had invoked that principle. It was absurd, he contended, to try the existing sytem of indulgences by the rule of tradition, when it was plainly justified by the daily practice of the Church. But the argument of Prierias was discredited by Adrian VI, who readily avowed that there had of late been grievous abuse of power, and that dispensations only hold good if they are granted for sufficient cause. It was a source of weakness in dealing with the first signs of Protestantism in England to adopt a position which had been so recently discarded in the conflict with the Reformation in Germany. But Fisher went still farther. The strength of the argument for the Queen was that a prohibition could not be absolute from which the contingency of a brother dying childless had been specially excepted. But her advisers would not trust that plea. The law was clearer than the exception. No brother, in the history of Christianity, had felt bound to obey the injunction of Deuteronomy. The prohibition of Leviticus had been almost universally observed. This objection was felt so strongly, that Fisher and the advocates of Catharine contended that even if the Divine law forbade the marriage, the Divine law must yield to the law of the Church.[18] Clement, however, admitted that the right to dispense against the law of God was not generally assigned to him by divines,[19] and, being so little versed in books himself that he took

[18] The Belgian canonists employed for Catharine said: "Concedantur omnia Regi, quod auctoritas praedicta sit juris divini, et quod factum de quo est quaestio, sit in terminis affinitatis, nullatenus tamen illi concedendum est, quod Pont. non licuerit etiam hoc casu dispensare. . . . Cum maximo consensu et canonum consulta et prudentum responsa pontifici juris divini declarandi, interpretandi, limitandi, et contra illud dispensandi potestatem concedant." Fisher, *De Causa Matrimonii*, p. 42, writes: "Nullis argumentationibus diffiniri potest, sed solius Pont. interpretatione."

[19] The Pope said to Casale on Christmas Day, 1529, that all the divines are against

no offence when men spoke of his want of learning, he did not insist on it. The claim was an unsafe ground for sustaining the marriage; for the marriage was the most effective precedent by which papal Canonists sustained the claim.[20] The argument was set aside by the more cautious disputants, both in Rome and in England; but it had done the work of a signal of distress, to indicate the insecurity of the cause, and it had deepened the consciousness of division in the English Church.

The shifts by which several writers defended the marriage betray much perplexity. One divine attributed the matrimonial troubles of Jupiter and Saturn to the want of a Papal dispensation. Another explained that the prohibition to marry a brother's wife had crept into the Pentateuch by the fault of a transcriber. It was commonly believed, by a mistaken application of a pronoun in the works of St. Antoninus, that Martin V, with a view to avoid scandal, had permitted a man to marry his own sister. And there were some who maintained that a man might marry not only his sister, but his grandmother, and even his own mother or daughter.

The reasons submitted on the part of Henry VIII for suspecting the validity of his marriage were presented with such moderation, and such solicitude to avoid disparaging the Papal power, that they explain, apart from the weighty considerations of interest, the long hesitation of Rome. The maxim that a dispensation, to be good, must be warranted by sufficient reason, was generally admitted by canonists; and Julius, in excusing his delay, had said that a dispensation opposed to law and good morals can be justified only by necessity. Assuming, therefore, in principle, his right to perform the act, the question raised was, whether necessity had been shown, and whether the motives alleged by the petitioners were adequate and true. The English argued that Henry VII and Ferdinand V had deceived the Pope with false statements. Henry had pretended that without the marriage there was danger of war; yet he made it manifest that no such urgent purpose of public welfare existed. The dispensation had no sooner reached his

the power of the Pope to dispense in such a case (Brewer, iv. 6103). Gardiner wrote on the 21st of April: "The Pope will hear no disputation as to his power of dispensing. He seems not to care himself whether the cause be decided by that article or no, so he did it not" (5476).

[20] "Quod Papa possit, ex gestis Rom. Pont. patet. . . . Moderna quoque Regina Angliae consummaverat prius matrimonium cum olim fratre istius Regis Angliae sui mariti" (Cajetan, *in Summam, Sec. Secundae*, 154, 9).

hands than he confessed that it was not wanted, by causing his son to make a solemn protest that he did not mean to use it. Henry VII survived four years longer, persisting in his determination to prevent the match. It was said that he was troubled in conscience;[21] and Erasmus affirms that extraordinary pressure was afterwards required to induce Henry VIII to recant his protest and to marry Catharine.

Her father, though more deeply interested than Henry VII in securing her marriage, refused for many years to pay the money, without which, according to the agreement, there was to be no wedding. The plea of political necessity for a dispensation, which was repudiated as soon as received, and was not employed during six years from the date of the first demand, was nothing but a transparent pretence.

To this was added another argument, calculated immeasurably to facilitate the task of the Pope. Ferdinand assured him that Prince Arthur had been too young for marriage, and that Catharine, during her short union with a failing invalid, had not contracted the supposed affinity.[22] The dispensation might therefore be granted easily without the presence of those cogent reasons which, in ordinary circumstances, would be required to make it valid. He was willing, to satisfy English scruples, that the Bull should provide for the opposite conditions; but he insisted that no such provision was necessary for the security of his daughter's conscience or of her legal position. The Bull was drawn to meet the wishes of the English, but in terms which significantly indicated the influence of the Spanish representations.

Julius had promised it at the eve of his election, and he granted it by word of mouth immediately after. Nevertheless, the Bull was wrung from him with great difficulty after a year's delay, by accident rather than consent. When Isabella the Catholic was dying, she implored him to comfort her last days with the sight of the dispensation which was to secure her daughter's happiness. It was impossible to refuse her prayer. Against the wish of Julius, a copy was sent from Spain to Henry VII, and the authentic instrument could not be withheld. But for this, the Pope would not have yielded. To the Cardinal Adrian, who was one of those whom he had appointed to advise him in the

---

[21] Lopez to Emanuel, Gardiner, *Letters of Henry VII*, ii. 147.

[22] "Ahunque en el dicho capitulo dize quel matrimonio de la dicha princesa nuestra hija con el principe de Gales Arthur ya deffunto, que gloria haya, fue consumado, pero la verdad es que no fue consumado. . . . y esto es muy cierto y muy sabido donde ella sta" (Ferdinand to Rojas, 23rd August 1503).

matter, he expressed a doubt whether such an act lay within his power. The Cardinal assured him that the thing had been done repeatedly by recent Pontiffs.

The contention was that these statements had misled the Pope into the belief that he was doing no more than the facts amply justified, whilst he was in reality exceeding the limits which all his predecessors had observed, on the strength of facts which were untrue. Unless it was certain that neither the imaginary precedents of Adrian, nor the pretended motives of Henry, nor the improbable allegations of Ferdinand, had influenced the decision of Julius II, there was serious ground to question its validity.

It was an issue charged with genuine doubt, and not necessarily invidious in the sight of Rome. Nothing had yet occurred to fix men's minds on the problem, and opinion honestly differed. In the French and English Universities, responses favourable to Henry were obtained with some difficulty, and against strong minorities. Although jurists in Italy could not earn his fee without risk of life, famous teachers of Bologna, Padua, and Sienna, whose names were cited with reverence in the Roman Courts, approved of his cause. The judgments of men in this controversy were not swayed by the position they occupied towards the Papacy. Luther strenuously upheld the rights of Catharine. Sixtus V declared that Clement had deserved the sorrows that befell his Pontificate by permitting so iniquitous a marriage to endure so long. For the action of Julius was challenged as a judge of fact, not as a judge of law. The English disputed not the plenitude of his authority, but the information which had determined its use; and it was the opinion of Clement VII that Julius had not taken due pains to ascertain the truth.[23] The gloss of almost ostentatious respect wore off in the friction of conflict. But it was essential at first to the position and the tactics of Wolsey. Henry appeared in the character of an affectionate husband, bewildered in conscience by scruples he was anxious to remove. Nobody could bind him under deeper obligation than by enabling him to live with Catharine undisturbed. As late as the month of May 1529, long after this fiction had become contemptible, Gardiner had the effrontery to say that Henry still lived with the Queen on

---

[23] Clement said to Charles V at Bologna: "The Pope's function is to judge whether such a cause has arisen; but no such inquiry was made, or judgment given, when the dispensation by Julius was granted" (Brewer, iv. 6103).

unaltered terms.[24] But Wolsey soon put off this pretence; for if the only difficulty arose from a defect in the dispensation, the Pope could have afforded relief, as the Emperor proposed, by an act in more ample form.

After the failure of Knight, and of his Italian colleagues, Wolsey's tone became peremptory, and he resolved to make his strong hand felt. He despatched the King's almoner, Fox, with his own secretary, Gardiner, a man who had been engaged in the hidden work of the preceding May, and who was fitted to encounter the Roman jurists on their own ground, unswayed by shame or fear. He charged them to make Clement understand that Henry's determination to put away Catharine was founded on secret causes lying deeper than love for Anne Boleyn, causes which neither the removal of his scruples nor any other remedy could touch; and that it would be executed, if necessary, independently of Rome. That course would imperil the succession, would overthrow Wolsey, and, in the presence of advancing Lutheranism, would ruin the Church of England. It was the Pope's interest, therefore, as much as his own, that the thing which could not be prevented should be done with full religious sanction; that an act of deference on one side should be met on the other by an act of grace. He wrote at the same time to Orvieto that the instruments granted to Knight were little better than a mockery, and that he regarded the hostile influence of the Emperor as the only obstacle he had to overcome.

Gardiner was charged to obtain a Bull for Wolsey, in conjunction with a Roman Cardinal, directing them to try the cause, and if they should be satisfied of certain facts, which he thought it not difficult to establish, to declare the marriage null and void. Next to this joint commission, he preferred one for a Roman Legate alone. In the last extremity he would accept one for the two English Archbishops; but he would not act by himself. The Bull, as Wolsey drafted it, made a defence impossible, made the trial a mere formality, and virtually dissolved the marriage. Both Fox and Gardiner declared that it would be hazardous to rely on powers obtained in so disgraceful a manner. They nevertheless attempted to obtain the Bull, hoping that it might be useful at least for the purposes of intimidation and coercion.

The English envoys found the Pope in the dwelling of Cardinal

---

[24] Brewer, iv. 5529.

Ridolfi, Bishop of Orvieto, beneath the shadow of the gorgeous cathedral, but surrounded by solitude and desolation, occupying a bare unfurnished chamber, and eating out of earthenware. At his first step Gardiner fell into an ambush. Clement inquired after Wolsey, touching a report that he was against the Divorce. Gardiner eagerly testified to his zeal in its favour. The Pope replied that, in that case, he would not be accepted as an impartial judge. During two long interviews he met the strenuous exertions of the Englishman with imperturbable temper and dexterity. He was ready to appoint Legates, and to confirm their sentence; but it was impossible to induce him to favour one party to the detriment of the other, in the manner of the proposed Bull. Gardiner plied his arguments with extreme vigour. Addressing the Pope, and the small group gathered round him, he protested that the King of England asked only for light to clear his conscience, and would obey the word of the Church, whatever it might be. He implored them not to repulse the wanderer who came as a suppliant to a guide. If he should appeal in vain to the Holy See, the world would say that they were deprived of wisdom, and that the Canons which were unintelligible to the Pope were only fit for the flames. Pucci and the other prelates listened without emotion, for they were persuaded that Henry had other wishes than to clear up doubts. Clement confessed that he was not a scholar, and that, if it was true, as men averred, that all law was locked in the breast of the Pope, it was a lock to which, unfortunately, he had no key. When Gardiner declared that Henry would help himself, if Rome refused to help him, Clement replied that he heartily wished he had done it. Finding that it was useless to ask for the Bull that Wolsey wanted, Gardiner proposed that an act defining the law as desired should be given privately, for fear of Spain, never to be produced unless Clement refused to confirm the sentence. To this the Pope replied that if the thing was just it should be done openly; and if unjust, not at all.

At length, when the final conference had lasted during many weary hours, Gardiner, believing that he had lost his cause, kindled into anger. Gambara and Stafileo were present, and he exclaimed that they had made themselves tools to deceive and to betray the King. Then he turned fiercely against Clement, and denounced him. It was well, he said, that men should know how Rome treats those who serve her, that she may find no succour in her own extremity, and may fall with the consent and the applause of all the world. At these words the Pope sprang to his feet, and strode about the room, waving his arms, and crying that they might have the Commission as they wished. It was past midnight, on Maundy Thursday morning, when he yielded. The clauses agreed upon were not what Gardiner wished for, but he thought them sufficient. They did not satisfy Wolsey. He feared that the cause might be taken out of his hands, that the rule of law by which he tried it might be rejected, that his judgment might be reversed, by Clement or by his successor.

When the English solicitations reached Clement, in the last days of his captivity and the first of his deliverance, he was weighed down by terror of the Spaniards, and he promised to do more for Henry whenever the approach of his allies made it a safer task. Lord Rochford's priest was sent to accelerate the movements of Marshal Lautrec, who, leaving the Pope to his fate, had wasted precious months in struggling with De Leyva for the possession of Lombardy. At length, by the roads that skirt the Adriatic, Lautrec marched south, and for the last time during many generations the French flag was welcomed in the ancient dominions of the house of Anjou. On the 18th of February the Imperialists evacuated Rome. They were speedily shut up in Naples and Gaeta, and up to the gates of the fortresses the French were masters of the country. In the bloodiest sea-fight of that age, the younger Doria, arming his galley-slaves, destroyed the Spanish fleet in the waters of Salerno. Naples was blockaded. The stream that turned the mills of the garrison was cut off, and it was expected that the city would be starved out before midsummer. It was in the midst of these changes that Clement held anxious conference with the energetic Englishman whose speech was so significant of diminished reverence, who, as Wolsey's successor at Winchester, was soon to lend his powerful aid to the separation of England, and who lived to undo his own work, and to supply history with the solitary example of a nation once separated returning voluntarily to union with Rome. Wolsey had already spoken of going over to Luther when the Papacy obstructed his designs; but Giberti had received the threat with scornful incredulity. Gardiner's warnings were less impressive than the vast change that was just then occurring in the condition of the Peninsula. From April to July French ascendency seemed to be established; and the Spanish commanders informed Charles V that, unless Naples was relieved before the end of August, his dominion over Italy was lost for ever. During those four months Wolsey was able to wring from Clement's unsteady hand every concession he required.

A Commission, dated 13th April 1528, gave him power, in conjunction with any English Bishop he might select, to try the cause, to
dissolve the marriage if the dispensation was not proved to be valid,
and to do all things that could be done by the Pope himself. A second
document of the same tenour was directed to Wolsey alone; but, as it
has not been found in this country, was probably never sent. The first
was not employed, as both Henry and his Chancellor felt that they
would not be safe without the intervention of an Italian cardinal. A
third Commission, enabling them to decide jointly or severally, was
therefore issued to Wolsey and Campeggio. Lest these immense
concessions should be neutralised by Spanish influence, they were
further secured by a written promise. Clement declared, on the solemn
word of a Roman Pontiff, that, considering the justice of the King's
cause, whose marriage transgressed divine and human law,[25] he would
never revoke the powers he had granted, or interfere with their
execution; and that if he should do anything inconsistent with that
promise, the act should be null and void. He went still further. He
entrusted to Campeggio a Decretal similar to that which he had
formerly refused, declaring the dispensation valid only in the event
that the assurance given to Pope Julius by Ferdinand of Aragon was
true. This important document was never to leave the Legate's hands,
and was to be seen by none but Wolsey and the King. At the end of
July, when the fortunes of Spain were at the darkest, Campeggio, thus
provided, set out for England.

Wolsey, relying on their own friendship and on the benefits of Henry,
made choice of Campeggio as early as December 1527. Gardiner was
persuaded that the cause would be safe in his hands, and Clement
encouraged the belief. But Casale, who knew the ground better than
Gardiner or Wolsey, remonstrated against the choice. The Spaniards
reported that the Pope had given Henry leave to have two wives; and
as it was commonly supposed that the Cardinal was sent to enable
him to gain his purpose, he was compelled to travel by roads that
were safe from the incursions of Imperialists. Charles V, convinced
that the cause was lost if tried in England, wrote that it must be
prevented at all costs, and lodged a protest against Campeggio's
mission. Contarini, the wisest and best of the Italian public men, saw
the Legate at Viterbo, and judged from his conversation that the
Emperor's fears were groundless. Another eminent Venetian, Navagero,

---

[25] Gardiner thought the first words of this document, "justiciam eius cause perpen-
dentes," the most decisive of all the concessions made by Clement (Brewer, iv. 5476).

who met him at Lyons, found that it was not his intention to content
the King. The Pope himself wrote to the Emperor that the legates
were not to pronounce sentence without referring to Rome; and Charles
thereupon assured Catharine that she had nothing to apprehend from
Campeggio.[26]

The origin of his elevation had been a successful mission to Austria,
to detach Maximilian from the schism of Pisa; and it was by that
emperor's influence that Campeggio obtained his mitre and his hat.
His conduct in two conclaves caused him to be ranked among the
most decided Imperialists, and Clement informed Contarini that he
belonged to the Imperial interest. In 1529, when a vacancy was
expected, during his absence in England, he was to have been one of
the Austrian candidates. After his return he was zealous in the Queen's
cause: he was one of the three cardinals who countersigned the Bull
threatening Henry with excommunication; and it was he who, in
conjunction with Cajetan, procured his final condemnation.

Campeggio foresaw the difficulties awaiting him. He was not eager
for the encounter with Henry and Wolsey, and he spent two months
on his way. Long before he reached England great changes had
occurred. Doria had gone over to the Emperor. Lautrec was dead.
The blockade of Naples was raised; and the besiegers had, on the 28th
of August, capitulated to the garrison. Five messengers pursued
Campeggio, warning him to adjust his conduct to the altered aspect
of things, and imploring him to do nothing that could excite the
displeasure of the victor. Clement had resolved to submit, at any
sacrifice, to the Imperialists.

When the Emperor learnt how vigorously the English envoys were
labouring to extort the Pope's assent to the Divorce, he resolved to
tempt him by splendid offers. He would restore his dominions; he
would release his hostages; and he proposed an alliance by marriage
between their houses. Musetola, who brought these proposals early in
June, was well received; and it soon appeared that the Pope was
willing to abandon the League. It had done nothing for him. There
was no hope for the Papacy in Italy, no prospect of resisting Lutheranism
in Germany, except through Charles V. No reliance could be placed

---

[26] Gayangos, 537: "I am certain, because the Pope writes me so, that nothing will be
done to your detriment, and that the whole case will be referred to him at Rome, the
Cardinal's secret mission being to advise the King, your husband, to do his duty." This
was written on the margin in the Emperor's own hand.

now in the French, or could ever have been placed with reason in the Italian confederates. The people for whom Clement had raised the cry of national independence, in whose cause, identified with his own, he had exposed the Church and himself to incalculable risk, and had suffered the extremity of humiliation and ruin, were making profit out of his disasters. Venice, his intimate ally, had laid its grasp on Cervia and Ravenna. The Duke of Ferrara, a papal vassal, occupied the papal cities of Modena and Reggio. Florence, his own inheritance, had cast off the dominion of his family, and restored the Republic. One way of recovering all things remained to him. He must put away the ambition of Giberti and Sadolet; he must accept Charles as the inevitable master of Italy, and stipulate with him for restitution and revenge. Early in September Clement's resolution was taken. In October he returned to Rome. At Christmas he bestowed the hat and sword on Philibert, Prince of Orange, the general who took the command of the Imperialists when Bourbon was struck down at the foot of the Janiculum, and on whom rested the responsibility for the unutterable horror of the sack of Rome. When Campeggio arrived in London, things had gone so far that a sentence dissolving the marriage was not to be thought of. The problem that taxed his ingenuity was to avoid the necessity of pronouncing sentence either way, at least until the Pope should be sufficiently assured of friendship from his detested enemy, to be able to defy the resentment of his ally.

Campeggio's instructions were to elude the difficulty by inducing Henry to desist, or by prevailing on Catharine to retire to a convent. If these resources failed, the Pope relied on his experience to find means to protract the business, and put off the evil day. With Henry there could be no hope. During the summer he was separated from Anne by the sweating sickness. She was taken ill. The King, in great alarm, made ready for the prospect of immediate death. He resorted with fervour to works of religion. He confessed frequently, and practised constant penance for his sins. But his treatment of Catharine was not among the sins of which he was taught to repent. He hailed the Legate's arrival as the signal of his approaching deliverance, and made open preparation for an early marriage. At Campeggio's endeavours to change his purpose by urging the danger of offending Caesar, he became indignant and vociferous; and the Legate could do nothing, for his hands were tied by the secret Bull.

When the King and Wolsey saw that document, they insisted that it should be shown to the Council. In their hands it would have served to settle the controversy. It decided the point of law in the manner desired by Henry. The Pope having declared the law, they could judge of the fact without him. They had got from Rome all that they absolutely required; and the object of Wolsey's policy was attained. To apply to the case in dispute the principle laid down by the supreme ecclesiastical authority, an inferior authority might suffice. Protected by the Bull, they would incur little danger in following Clement's unwelcome counsel to help themselves. The credit of Julius, the consistency of the See of Rome, were sufficiently guarded, when Clement determined under what conditions his predecessor's act was legal, and Wolsey determined, on evidence unattainable at Rome, whether the conditions of legality were fulfilled.

Wolsey sent to Rome to require that Campeggio should give up the Decretal. If it had been produced and acted on, the Pope could expect nothing but ruin. The responsibility of the Divorce and the wrath of the dreaded Spaniard would have fallen not on those who applied the law and were inaccessible, but on him who had laid down the law, and who was within his reach. Clement understood his danger. He lost the self-command which had not deserted him in the most distressing emergencies. Laying his hand on Casale's arm, he told him to be silent, and then burst forth in reproaches against the perfidy of Wolsey, at whose urgent prayer and for whose sake alone he had granted the secret Bull. He detected their object. With the Bull before them, even those who thought the marriage valid would give it up on the Pope's responsibility. Let them dismiss Campeggio, on the plea that he was slow to act, and accomplish their purpose themselves, without involving Rome. The Bull ought to have been destroyed, and he would cut off a finger to be able to recall it.

Clement at once despatched an envoy to make sure that the perilous document should remain no longer exposed to accident or treachery. For this important mission he selected Francesco Campana, a man who long enjoyed the confidence of his family, who, after the fall of Florence, proclaimed to the people the will of the conqueror, that the Medici should reign over the republican city, and who, as Secretary of State, gave efficient aid in building up the intelligent despotism of Cosmo. Campana travelled slowly; and when he reached London, with the order to burn the Decretal, Clement was reported to be dying. To destroy such a document in obedience to a pontiff who was probably dead, on the eve of a conclave, would have been the height of folly. Campeggio resolved to disobey. In the spring, when Clement had recovered, Campana brought the news that the Legate had yielded,[27] and the most memorable writing in the history of the Divorce disappeared for ever.

But Henry had seen, under the Pope's sign and seal, that he had never been Catharine's lawful husband. For it was now admitted that, if Julius was deceived, the dispensation was void. No attainable evidence could demonstrate that he was not deceived or could resist the strong presumption in favour of the allegation on which Henry's scruple rested. The uncertainty lay in the legal element of the case, and that uncertainty was now removed. The Pope had been consulted, and the answer he had given was against the Queen. Henry might be right in his facts, or honestly mistaken, or altogether insincere; but right or wrong, true or false, he could not, consistently with his previous conduct, hold himself free to live with Catharine. The nullity of his marriage still required to be publicly declared; but in strictness he was unmarried. It followed that he must consider himself free to marry Anne. Apart from the public sentence, the religious obstacle to the second marriage was removed when Campeggio exhibited the secret Bull.

Mr. Brewer signifies his disbelief in the improbable story which began to be told in Mary's reign, that Rowland Lee solemnised the marriage of Henry with Anne Boleyn at dead of night, in November 1532, in a secret chamber at Whitehall, on being assured that a permission, which could not be fetched at that hour, had arrived from Rome. We trust that, in his next volume, he will determine the true date, and the influence of the Decretal on the event. At Campeggio's coming Anne Boleyn was kept out of the way. She now came to Court, and was treated in public as if she had been Henry's wife. Charles V afterwards said to Campeggio that even the death of Catharine would be no deliverance, as the harm was done when Henry got possession of his Divorce. Elizabeth assured Parker that her mother's marriage

---

[27] Varchi, who had means of informing himself abut Campana's journey, says that he brought the Decretal back with him to Rome. But Mr. Stevenson has discovered, and Mr. Gardiner has deciphered, two very curious letters of Campeggio, in one of which he says: "Per questo fu mandato il Campano, il quale, ultra alia, quanto a questo proposito mi disse due cose; l'una fu de la decretale, di che è seguito quanto vostra Signoria da lui havrà inteso" (Brewer, Introduction, dclxxi).

had received the papal approbation. Three Popes offered to acknowledge her title if she would profess Catholicism, at least, in secret. The
secret Bull of Clement VII made it optional to disregard the claims of
Mary Stuart.

Failing to make an impression on Henry, Campeggio addressed
himself to the Queen. The Roman divines were, he told her, dubious
as to the merits of her cause; the future was uncertain; and the Pope
consequently desired that she would close her life in a convent. The
English bishops recommended the same easy solution. Henry eagerly
adopted it, affirming with gross exaggeration, that the Pope had already
pronounced against her. Then Catharine tasted the bitterness of the
trial that was to come. Had she yielded, as the injured Queen of France
had done, she might have averted the schism, until the genuine wave
of Protestant thought struck England, when the daughter of her rival
had sat for a generation on the throne. But she had no thought of
yielding, and displayed, in the evil days that remained to her, the stern
and tranquil courage of Isabella. She was alone, for she could not trust
her council, and a watch was set on her intercourse with Mendoza.
No Spaniard was allowed to approach her. The Belgian lawyers were
sent out of the country. The messenger who had apprised Charles of
her trouble was dismissed. Vives was put under arrest. Fisher refused
to advise her without the King's command. Warham and Tunstall
called on her to confess whether she had not practised against her
husband's life. In all her solitude and misery she never doubted that
her cause was just; she neglected no chance; and relied with signal
composure on the Emperor alone. Her friends among the common
people murmured loudly, and attended her in such crowds that the
gates of the palace were closed against them. She acknowledged their
cheers with a graciousness she had never shown, and asked for their
prayers. Her evident popularity led Catharine into her only serious
error. She believed that the Catholic spirit of the country could be
roused in her favour, and she forced the Pope, by her importunity and
her reproaches, to resort to those extreme measures which, in the end,
were fatal to her church.

To gain Campeggio she took the bold step of asking him to hear
her confession, when, relieving him of the obligation of secrecy, she
declared that her first marriage had never been consummated. Campeggio could not disbelieve her, and the judgment of history, differing
somewhat in the estimate of evidence from the judgment of law, must,

we think, accept her word.[28] Wolsey was so apprehensive of the effect of such a declaration made upon oath, that he proposed to assail the dispensation on totally different grounds. But Mendoza deemed it a dangerous plea, and difficult to sustain at law. He recommended a safer defence, and he possessed a weapon keen enough to defeat all the art of Wolsey and his master.

Early in the year he had received from Spain a copy of a dispensation in the form of a brief, which expressly excluded the doubt as to the nature of the first marriage. Soon after Campeggio's arrival Catharine sent this paper to the Legates. It contradicted her own statement, and she protested that she had had nothing to do with obtaining it. But it avoided the reproach which had been so damaging to the Bull. Wolsey was taken by surprise. The plan on which he had pursued his operations so long was overthrown in an instant. He could not abandon his system and attack the dispensing power itself. He confessed that the objections taken to the former document did not here apply; but he declared that the Brief was spurious, and set about procuring evidence to prove it. Yet for many months Wolsey remained in doubt whether the paper which frustrated the great undertaking of his life was false or genuine. The reasons for suspecting forgery were stronger than he supposed.

The Brief was unheard of until the need for it became apparent. It was unknown to Charles V when, on the 31st of July 1527, he suggested that the Pope should supply the defects of the Bull.[29] It was uncertain whether Clement would consent, when, towards the end of the year, the Brief made his consent unnecessary. Its existence was unexplained. It was said to have been obtained about the time of the marriage, in 1509;[30] but it was dated 1503. It was obtained by Ferdinand; yet Ferdinand did not possess a copy. It was sent to England; but it was admitted that it had left England before the marriage for which it was

---

[28] To the excellent summary of the evidence in Maurenbrecher's Lectures on the English Reformation, and to the ingenious inquiries of Lorentz, must be added the significant fact that Henry did not persistently deny that he had formerly admitted the truth of the Queen's affirmation. In the *Articuli in Causa Matrimonii Regii* this point is virtually given up: "Quarto nititur probare virginitatem ex confessione Henrici Octavi; circa eandem confessionem possint eadem dici quae dicta sunt circa confessionem Catharinae, videlicet quod testes quod testes sunt singulares, et quod confessio omnino est extrajudicialis et parte absente."

[29] In a Despatch to Lannoy, Bucholtz, iii. 95.

[30] "In brevi vero quod circiter tempus nuptiarum ut conficeretur ab Ferdinando Rege Catholico procuratum est" (*Philalethae Hyperborei Parasceue*, 1533, p. 30).

required. Ferdinand did not want it, for, on his theory, it was quite unnecessary. If he had asked for it, the Brief would have been addressed to him, and a copy would have been treasured up in Spain. It was addressed to Henry VII. But Henry did not want it; for he was more than content with the original Bull, which he never intended to use, and could never wish to amplify. The Brief was discovered among the papers of the Ambassador De Puebla, who had left England before the marriage, and who was now dead. A list of all his papers relating to the marriage is still extant, and the Brief is not among them.[31] Two men were living who could have given valuable testimony. De Puebla's heir, Fernandez, had possession of his papers. He was reputed an honest man, and it was desirable to have him examined. It appeared, however, that he had just been sent to one of the few places in Europe which were beyond the reach of Henry and the jurisdiction of Charles—to the dominions of the Earl of Desmond. Accolti, the Cardinal who in the name of Julius had drawn up the dispensation a quarter of a century earlier, was now the most zealous opponent of the Divorce in the Court of Rome. He could have settled the doubt whether a second dispensation had, in fact, been given. Accolti remained impenetrably silent. Though addressed to Henry VII, the Brief was unknown in England. It formed the strongest security for the honour and the legal position of a Spanish Princess: yet it did not exist in the archives of Spain. It constituted the most extreme exertion of the Pope's prerogative known till then: yet Rome preserved no record of its existence. In April 1529, Charles was in doubt as to the value of the Brief.[32] He was willing to submit it to the Pope. His mind would not, he said, be at rest until he knew whether it had been found in the Roman Registers. His doubts were soon satisfied. The Registers were subjected to the scrutiny of Spanish and English agents. They found no trace of the Brief.[33] Errors were detected in the text. A vital flaw was detected in the date. Charles never sent it to Rome for judgment; it was no longer necessary. The Brief had served to delay action in the Legate's Court until the Pope was reconciled with Spain.

---

[31] Bergenroth, i. 471.

[32] "He said also that his mind was not quiet until he knew whether the Brief was found in the Registry at Rome" (Ghinucci and Lee to Wolsey, 5th April 1529. Brewer, 5423).

[33] "Has done all he could to discover in the register books a copy of the Brief, but in vain. Has found instead two other briefs alluding to the affair" (Mai to Charles, 23rd March 1529. Gayangos, 659).

Wolsey knew that delay was ruin. To strengthen himself at Rome he despatched four new ambassadors. He offered to surround the Pope with a guard of two thousand—or even of twelve thousand—men; and he resorted to expedients which showed that he was desperate. He would resign his Commission and leave judgment to the Pope, with a pledge that judgment would be favourable. He inquired whether, if Henry should take monastic vows to induce the Queen to enter a nunnery, he could be dispensed from them and allowed to marry. Lastly, he desired to know whether the King might have two wives. These proposals were soon dropped, and exerted no influence on the event; but they show the condition of Henry's mind, and the extremity to which, at the end of 1528, Wolsey was reduced. By the first he surrendered his original position, and actually invited that which he afterwards described as the cause of an inevitable rupture with Rome. The scheme to inveigle the Queen into a convent by simulated vows might possibly be entertained without horror; for it was supposed to be no sin to take an oath intending to be dispensed from it. Francis I swore to observe the Treaty of Madrid, and bound himself, moreover, on his knightly honour. On the same day he had already declared before a notary that he was resolved to break the oath he was about to take; and his perjury was generally applauded. Cranmer, on becoming Archbishop, closely followed his example. If the desire of liberty excused Francis in deceiving Charles, Henry might plead that he, too, had a justifiable purpose in deceiving Catharine. The right to dispense from vows was not disputed.

It would appear that the proposal of bigamy, which was now made for the second time, never reached the Pope. The idea that the trouble might be healed in that way arose spontaneously in many quarters. The Secretary of Erasmus, writing from his house, made the suggestion that, inasmuch as polygamy was common in the Old Testament, and was nowhere forbidden in the New, Henry might take a new wife without dismissing the first. To Luther and Melanchthon this solution appeared most easy and desirable. They had fought hard to preserve monogamy among their own followers, and had prevailed upon the Landgrave Philip of Hesse to abstain from bigamy. But they found themselves unable to make the prohibition absolute. In Henry's case they thought the marriage originally wrong, but they objected still more to the Divorce. Luther advised that the king should take a second wife rather than put away the first; and Melanchthon thought that the double marriage would be good, and that the Pope would dispense for it. The Landgrave, having discovered this correspondence, renewed his demand, and the Reformers were compelled to sanction his crime. The agony of shame with which they yielded their consent suggests a doubt whether their advice to Henry might not have been prompted by an idea of embarrassing the Catholics. Twelve months earlier Clement had informed the English agents that one of the cardinals, doubtless Cajetan, had told him that it was in his power to grant a dispensation such as Melanchthon recommended. But he was afterwards advised that it could not be done. Wolsey's proposal was in reality borrowed from the theories put forward in the Queen's behalf, asserting an unlimited power of dispensing.

These extraordinary measures for resisting the Spanish Brief were interrupted, in January 1529, by the dangerous illness of Clement. Once more the early ambition of Wolsey revived; and he caused the Cardinals to be overwhelmed with offers of troops, of money, of political and spiritual benefits. The hand of the spoiler and the oppressor had not departed from the territory of the Church. The Spaniards still detained three Cardinals as hostages, still occupied the papal fortresses, and by their control of the sea, commanded the sources from which Rome drew its supplies. The situation was one to which the French and English protest against an election held under Spanish influence continued applicable. Wolsey urged his friends to leave Rome, to hold the conclave in some city of refuge, and there to make him Pope. One half of the college shrank from the prospect of a Spanish Conclave, and made ready to depart as soon as the Pope should be dead. The imperial agents met the threatening schism with excellent judgment. They released the hostages; they gave up the fortresses, which, indeed, they could have retaken in a week; and they sent to the Tiber vessels laden with grain. They soon received their reward. Clement, in making his farewell to the Cardinals, exhorted them, if he died, to recall Campeggio. He declared that, should he recover, he would visit the Emperor beyond the Mediterranean. He assured the French agent that the fee simple of France would not bribe him now to desert the Spaniards. When at the end of two months he resumed the management of affairs, the reconciliation was accomplished. Charles was supreme in the court of Rome, by the vivid memory of his irresistible power, and by the immediate sense of the priceless value of his friendship. The Cardinals had not forgotten the awful time of the siege and the sack of the city. In February they were still hostile to the Emperor. In

March the Austrian agents at Rome write that they have 448,000 ducats to dispose of; and the resistance of the hostile Cardinals melted away rapidly.

Clement now regarded Wolsey as a sort of antipope, and as a personal enemy who was seeking to bring instant ruin upon him by employing a writing wrung from his good nature by false promises. The situation of the year before was reversed. He had relied on England to rescue him from the clutches of the Imperialists. The Emperor was now his protector against the machinations of Wolsey. Gardiner, when he saw him in March, became aware that all his pleas were in vain. The English had lost as much ground in point of reason and justice, as of influence. Contrasted with their extravagant demands, the petitions of the Emperor were moderate and just. Wolsey now required that the Brief should be delivered up to him; that sentence should be given, if the original was not sent to England; that the Pope, of his absolute authority, and without inquiry, should declare it a forgery. He ordered Gardiner to pretend that the paper containing the promises of the Pope had suffered damage, and to procure his signature to a new copy, to be drawn up in stronger terms, by representing that it was unchanged.

The Emperor Charles V, and Catharine herself, in letters conveyed secretly to the hands of the Pope, insisted with unquestionable truth, that a tribunal on which this man sat as judge could not be deemed impartial. They demanded that the cause should be decided at Rome, where Wolsey himself had so lately proposed to carry it. Clement doubted no longer what he ought to do. One course was both safe and just. He did not indeed believe in the Spanish dispensation; but he refused to condemn it on an *ex parte* argument, if every Spaniard had vanished out of Italy. He would rather abdicate, he would rather die, than do what Wolsey asked of him. He made no further attempt to resist the appeals of the Spaniards. But he was oppressed, at intervals, with a definite expectation of losing the allegiance of England. His only expedient was delay. Clement was unconvinced by Campeggio's testimony to the innocence of Anne Boleyn. The King, whose passion had endured for three years, might become inconstant; or Catharine might be persuaded, as the King had ceased to live with her, to consent that the favourite should occupy her place. Her health was breaking, and he would have given the riches of Christendom that she should be in her grave.

In April the envoys of the two branches of the House of Austria formally called on him to revoke the powers of the Legates, and to bring the cause before the judgment seat of Rome. Gardiner thought that it would have been madness to resist. Clement consented. On the 9th of May he despatched a nuncio to Barcelona, with full and final powers to conclude a treaty with the Emperor. Until it should be ratified, and the imperial alliance firmly secured, he wished to postpone the inevitable shock which Henry's disappointment would inflict on their long friendship. An agreement was made between Clement and Casale, that the Commission should not be cancelled, but that the Legates should not proceed to execute it.

When it became certain, in the beginning of May, that there was no more hope from Rome, Wolsey's fall could not be distant. His obstinate determination, in spite of the general feeling both in Rome and in England, that there should be no divorce without papal sanction, had ended by making the divorce impossible, had brought upon the country the affront of seeing the King's cause removed to a hostile tribunal, and had afforded the Emperor a conspicuous triumph over the influence of England in a matter chiefly of English concern. At the moment when he was defeated by Spain, he was deserted by France. The dissolution of the League, and the ruin of his armies compelled Francis to give up the struggle for supremacy with Charles, and to submit to a dishonourable peace. Wolsey had traded on their rivalry. It was the obvious and superficial secret of his policy to sell the help of England to each, as necessity induced one to outbid the other. Neither of the Powers had an interest to maintain the statesman who had alternately betrayed them, and they made peace at his expense. Francis accused him of having intrigued on his own account with Rome. His treacherous reports, sent home by Suffolk, and aided by the certainty that Wolsey had misled the King, strengthened the constant asseveration of his enemies that he did not sincerely promote the Divorce. In truth he had striven for it with incessant care. But Du Bellay, Mendoza, and Campeggio had long perceived that his zeal was stimulated only by the desire to save himself; and he had implored Henry on his knees to give up his will. When it was announced that the Commission would be revoked, and that France was suing for a separate peace, his power was gone. He besought the King to allow him to attend the Congress at Cambray. The two men who were thought worthy to succeed him, More and Tunstall, were sent in his stead; and an indictment was prepared against him.

It was impossible to doubt that the revocation would be fatal to

Henry's wishes. That which Clement dared not allow his Legates to do in England, he would not do himself at Rome, when the Emperor had disarmed all his enemies, and was coming in triumph to visit his Italian conquests and to assume the imperial crown. At first Henry talked of appealing from Clement to the true Vicar of Christ, to be raised up in his place. But he was soon made to understand that the potentate who was feared, having power to coerce and to degrade, was the Emperor. He resolved to dissemble his anger. Intercepted letters exposed the Pope's intentions, and taught that nothing would be gained by waiting until Clement felt himself stronger. Something might, however, be gained by prompt and strenuous action. Henry resolved to take advantage of the delay in revoking the Commission to force on an immediate decision, and summoned Gardiner in all haste to conduct the case.

The Imperialists had consented that the revocation should be postponed in consequence of the pledge obtained by Clement that nothing should meanwhile be done in England. When it was found that the pledge was broken, and that Henry employed the respite to urge on the trial, every voice in Rome called on the Pope to satisfy the just claims of Spain. The English agents confessed that no choice was left him, and bore witness to his good will. Clement protested to them in pathetic terms that the Emperor had him utterly in his power. He made one effort more to get the Imperialists to assent to further delay, but they repulsed him with indignation. They believed that he was seeking an opportunity to deceive them. Even in the following year Charles half expected that Clement would pass over to the English side.

Campeggio had been instructed to create delay by telling Henry that, if he must give judgment, he must give it against him. He replied by asking what he should do in the not improbable event of the judgment being in Henry's favour. Clement's final orders were to proceed with the trial to the last stage preceding sentence, and then to adjourn for the purpose of consulting Rome. Campeggio combined both methods. On the 22nd of July Clement's irrevocable determination was known in London. The pleadings were completed. The parties awaited judgment. Campeggio suddenly adjourned the Court for the vacation, announcing that he must consult the Pope. He strove to comfort Henry by assuring him that the interruption was to his advantage, as the sentence would have been for the Queen.

When the vessel in which the Legate sailed from Dover was boarded by the custom-house officers, he believed that his last hour had come, and called for his confessor. The officers treated him with respect, but they examined his luggage, in the hope either of recovering the secret Bull, or of finding evidence that he had been paid by Catharine. Campeggio returned to Rome with the renown of a successful mission. Men were not blind to the effects which were to follow. But they followed too remotely to disturb the present joy at an immense deliverance. It was observed for the first time after years of anxiety and depression, that Clement VII held up his head and walked erect.

We have not allowed ourselves space to follow Mr. Brewer's vivid and powerful narrative over another year to the death of Wolsey, with which the volume ends. Before we conclude it is necessary that we should advert to one topic on which we have been unable to accept him for our guide. Touching the great question of the origin of the Divorce, Mr. Brewer wavers between three explanations: King Henry's scruples grew up in the recesses of his own conscience. They were awakened by his inclination for Anne Boleyn. They were suggested by her friends. Mr. Brewer, who adopts the first of these solutions at page 222, prefers the second at page 258, and, forty pages farther, is ready to accept the third.

The idea that the Divorce was instigated by divines of Anne Boleyn's faction was put forward by Pole, apparently with a view to connect Cranmer and the Lutheran influence with the beginning of the troubles. It is supported by no evidence; and it is in the highest degree improbable that the Boleyns conceived a design which could not have been accomplished without violently subverting the whole system of European politics. The theory which represents the scruple arising involuntarily, almost unconsciously, in the King's mind, is confirmed, no doubt, by his own public declarations; but it is difficult to reconcile with the coarse and candid admission which he made privately of the causes which estranged him from the Queen. Before the Court, at Blackfriars, he spoke only of scruples; in secret he urged motives of a less spiritual kind. It is quite natural that personal repulsion may have paved the way for scruples. It is much less likely that the idea of separation can have come first, and the unconquerable aversion followed. In the hypothesis that the whole business took its rise in the King's passion for Anne Boleyn, there is not the same inherent improbability. It leaves much unexplained, and suggests many difficulties; but it depends mainly on a question of chronology. If it should ever be possible to trace the idea of marrying Anne Boleyn farther back than we can trace the idea of repudiating Catharine of Aragon, the case would be proved. But with the materials now available the priority is decidedly with the Divorce. The latest date to which we can possibly assign the first steps towards the dissolution of the marriage is the summer of 1526. We have shown that we are unable to put the proposal to Anne earlier than 1527. There is an interval therefore during which the scheme of divorce is pursued, and is fully accounted for, whilst no trace of a rival can be detected. We are unable to accept either of Mr. Brewer's alternative solutions.

There is a fourth explanation to which he shows no mercy. He absolutely rejects the idea that Wolsey was the author of the Divorce. Such a report was, he says, put about by Tyndall and Roper; but it was contradicted by all those who knew best; by Henry, by Bishop Longland, and by the Cardinal himself—while Cavendish says that when the King first disclosed his intentions to Wolsey, the latter fell upon his knees and endeavoured to dissuade him. We regret that Mr. Brewer has not entered more fully into the evidence which has determined his judgment on this fundamental point. We will indicate as briefly as we can the reasons which induce us to attribute the Divorce of Queen Catharine, with all its momentous consequences, to the cause he has so pointedly rejected.

Longland never denied that Wolsey was the author of the King's doubts. It is true that Longland, a persecutor of Lutherans, and an eager and overbearing promoter of the Divorce, when he saw England drifting towards Lutheranism, in consequence, indirectly, of what he had helped to do, regretted his share in the transaction, and denied that he was primarily responsible. His Chancellor, Draycott, conveyed his denial to the historian Harpsfield, who records it in his Life of Sir Thomas More. But Harpsfield himself was not convinced. In the following year he wrote that Wolsey, "first by himselfe, or by John Longland, bishopp of Lincolne, and the King's confessor, putt this scruple and doubte into his head." Even if Longland's denial exonerates himself it does not exonerate Wolsey, whom he indicates when he speaks of "others, that weare the cheife setters forth of the divorce beetweene the Kinge and the Queene Catharine."

No serious import belongs to the testimony of Henry and Wolsey, given in open court, to silence just objections to Wolsey's presence there. It was necessary that he should be represented as impartial to justify his appearance on the judgment seat. It would certainly seem that Cavendish meant to say what Mr. Brewer imputes to him, that Wolsey dissuaded Henry from the beginning. But in reality he says no more than he would be justified in saying by the fact that Wolsey did, at various times, dissuade him; which is all that Wolsey himself has said. Nobody, however, knows better than Mr. Brewer that Cavendish is the author of much of the confusion that has, until the appearance of his work, obscured the history of the Divorce. We cannot allow decisive authority to one ambiguous sentence in an author who, though doubtless sincere, is both partial and inaccurate.

The weight of contemporary testimony is overwhelming against Wolsey. We will say nothing of Polydore Vergil, who was an enemy, or of the Belgian Macqueriau, and the Paris diarist, because they wrote only from rumour. But Jovius was a prelate of the Court of Clement. Guicciardini was connected with Casale, and was the only contemporary writer who knew the secret of Campana's mission. Both Guicciardini and Jovius lay the responsibility on Wolsey. Valdes, who was better informed than either of the Italians, does the same. For in Spain no doubt could subsist. Catharine had written to Charles that Wolsey was the author of her sorrows, and the Emperor never ceased to proclaim the fact.

The tradition of the English Catholics inclined strongly to assign to Wolsey the origin of their misfortunes. If they had any bias it would naturally have been to represent the Reformation in England as springing from an unclean passion. Pole, who was a great authority amongst them, had given the example of this controversial use of Anne Boleyn. But they departed from the example he had set, and preferred an explanation which could serve no polemical purpose. Pole himself once indicated the belief that Wolsey was the author of the King's design. It is firmly maintained by his archdeacon, Nicholas Harpsfield, who was a friend of the Warhams, who had lived with Roper, Rastall, Buonvisi, and the family of More, and in whom were concentrated the best Catholic traditions of that age.

Sir Richard Shelley wrote a history of the Divorce, which is still extant. He was the son of the well-known judge, and was employed both by Mary and Elizabeth in important embassies. He was the English Prior of St. John, and after 1559, swam in the full tide of the Catholic reaction. When the news of the Northern Rising reached Rome, Shelley was one of those whom the Pope consulted before issuing his Bull against the Queen. He attributes all the blame to Wolsey. If any man was more deeply involved than Shelley in the struggle against Elizabeth, it was Nicholas Sanders. Writing history for political effect, he had no scruple about inventing a scene or a fact that served his purpose; and he had read the works of Rastall and Hiliard, which we possess only in fragments. The evidence which was before him must have implicated Wolsey with a force that was irresistible. Richard Hall, a man who seems to have given proof of sincerity, as he was a Protestant under Mary, and a Catholic under Elizabeth, wrote a life of Fisher, about the year 1580. He had his information from Phillips, the last Prior of the Benedictines at Rochester, who had sat in the Convocation of 1529, and from Thomas Harding, who had been chaplain to Stokesley. Hall is, like the rest, among the Cardinal's accusers. William Forrest, who was a contemporary, and became chaplain to Queen Mary, agrees with Harpsfield and Shelley, Sanders and Hall.

Indeed, without resorting to contemporary foreigners, or to English writers of a later generation, the evidence that Wolsey first moved the idea of divorce appears to us conclusive. The Cardinal himself admitted it to Du Bellay, not speaking under pressing need of deception and excuse, but privately, to one who was his friend, who powerfully supported his policy, who needed no convincing, and had evidently not heard the contrary on any authority worthy of belief. A statement made in these circumstances is not necessarily credible, but it far outweighs a public declaration demanded by the stress of popular suspicion. Wolsey's communication to Du Bellay, confirming what he wrote to Casale,[34] connects the Divorce with the great change in the system of alliances which was made in the spring of 1525, and perfectly explains the tenacious grasp with which he then retained his power in spite of all the sacrifices which the failures of his policy imposed on the King. We cannot reject it without stronger reason than has been yet produced.

After his disgrace, Wolsey constantly declared himself innocent of crime, yet worthy of the royal displeasure. The Divorce, he said, was the cause of his fall, yet he denied that, in that, he had offended. This would be consistent and intelligible language if he was the author of counsels that had proved so pernicious. On his deathbed he delivered

---

[34] 6th December 1527.

to Kingston the lesson of his experience of Henry. He warned him to be cautious what matter he put into his head, as he would never put it out again. He was alluding to what had passed in the affair of Queen Catharine; and his words had a pregnant as well as a literal significance if he was thinking of a matter which he had himself incautiously put into the King's head.

We are at a loss to find a valid reason for doubting, except the authority of Mr. Brewer. We acknowledge the force of that objection. It is impossible to differ, without uneasiness and regret, from a historian who has supplied so large and so rich a part of the knowledge attainable on this subject, and who is unsurpassed for accuracy and penetration. But Mr. Brewer's words, in speaking of Wolsey, must be taken with a slight allowance. It is not only because of the dignified liberality, the ceremonious self-restraint, which is due from a divine of the English Church towards a Roman Cardinal, and from an illustrious scholar who is willing to think nobly and generously of the Church of Rome, towards a prelate by whose fault that Church was dishonoured and cast down. For as many years as Wolsey's administration lasted, Mr. Brewer has been employed in investigating his actions. He has hewn him out of the block. He has found much that is new and different from the character which Protestant and Catholic have had so much reason to blacken; and he has felt the influence not only of disgust for ignorant detractors, but of admiration for the strong man who, when the population of all England did not exceed that of a modern city, when the annual revenue was no more than that which is now received in a single day, when Scotland and Ireland were drains upon her power, when she was without dependencies and without a fleet, raised the kingdom by the force of his solitary genius, to a position among the European nations not inferior to that which it now enjoys.

For Wolsey as a Minister of tyranny, as a pensioner of foreign potentates, as a priest of immoral life, he has an extreme indulgence. The Cardinal attempted to obtain from Parliament a declaration that all things in the land belonged to the Crown—a doctrine which, from the day on which Frederic Barbarossa consulted the jurists of Bologna, until Lewis XIV caused it to be sanctioned by the divines of the Sorbonne, has been the symbol of despotic power. At the moment when he broke off the alliance with the House of Burgundy and sought the friendship of France, he had for four years been denied his pensions by the Power that he abandoned, whilst he required from the Power that he joined a sum equal in our money to £285,000. When he exchanged Durham for Winchester, he asked that the see which he vacated should be transferred to his son, a youth then studying in Paris. Mr. Brewer will not admit a doubt as to Wolsey's integrity. If we remember rightly, he nowhere mentions the proposed transfer of the great see of Durham. He is almost unwilling to believe that Wolsey had a son. That he had a daughter Mr. Brewer does not dispute. But he thinks that such transgressions did not necessarily involve any greater impropriety than the marriage of an English clergyman at the present day.[35] This view of the age of the Reformation leaves a great feature in its history unexplained. No influence then at work contributed more than the private lives of ecclesiastics such as Wolsey to undermine Catholicism, and to incline men towards a Church which renounced the hazards of an enforced celibacy. We would undertake, if necessary, to justify our words by proof which Mr. Brewer will accept, by the writings of the most eminent and the most impartial men of the sixteenth century, by the decrees of twenty synods, by the constitutions of York itself.

Mr. Brewer's abounding charity defends the Cardinal as a persecutor. Wolsey had caused Protestants to be burnt in the day of his power, and in the last hour of his life, when his speech faltered and his eyes grew dim, he uttered an exhortation that Henry would not spare the Lutherans, because they would prove a danger to the State. Yet even that appalling vision of the dying Prelate, who, having clothed himself in sackcloth, and made his peace with God, gathered his last breath to fan the flames of Smithfield, has no terrors for Mr. Brewer. No man, he says, was less disposed to persecute; and he excuses him by the examples of his age, and by the greater cruelty of More.

The argument which excuses Wolsey by the times he lived in, is a serious fallacy. Christians must be judged by a moral code which is not an invention of the eighteenth century, but is as old as the Apostles.

---

[35] "Here, as in other Catholic countries at the present day, or at least until recently, the marriage of the parochial clergy had to be tolerated more generally than is supposed. . . . In many instances such offences involved no greater transgression of the moral law than . . . such marriages, for instance, as are now contracted by the English prelates and clergy" (pp. 639, 640).

We are no wiser than the contemporaries of Wolsey regarding the rights of conscience. Persecution has indeed become more difficult to carry out; and the conditions of modern society make toleration easy. But there are, in our day, many educated men who think it right to persecute; and there were, in the days of Wolsey, many who were as enlightened on that point as Burke or Jefferson. There was a humane and liberal current, both in government and in literature, which the religious conflict that followed checked for generations. Whilst Lollards and Lutherans were burning, in the Chancellorship of Wolsey, the Greeks lived unmolested in Venice, and the Waldenses enjoyed a respite in Savoy; the Inquisition was forbidden to interfere with the Moriscoes of Granada; and in Portugal the later laws of Emanuel the Great protected the Judaising heretics from popular fanaticism. No country had suffered so much from religious strife as Bohemia; but in 1512 Catholics and Utraquists made an agreement in perpetuity that rich and poor of both churches should enjoy freedom unrestrained. In Denmark equal rights were assigned to Catholics and Protestants at the Diet of 1527. Before the close of the fifteenth century the French Inquisition had been shorn of its might; the bishops refused to prosecute those who were accused of heresy; the Parliament rescued them; and Lutheranism was allowed to spread with the connivance of the court, until the long absence and captivity of the King. Many years even then elapsed before the Protestants ceased to regard Francis as their defender. Beneath the sceptre of the Hapsburgs persecution reigned; yet in 1526 Ferdinand conceded territorial toleration, and Charles himself, in 1532, proclaimed the rights of conscience in language worthy of a better time.

There was a strong body of opinion on the other side, but authorities equally strong may be quoted in favour of murder, not merely among men entangled in the habits of a darker age, but among those who had struggled to emancipate their minds from tradition, and who made it the pride and the business of their lives to resist the vices of the vulgar. It was no reason for an assassin to escape the gallows that Melanchthon had prayed for a brave man to despatch Henry VIII; that the brave man who despatched the Duke of Guise was praised by Beza to the skies; that Knox wished the doom of Rizzio to be inflicted on every Catholic; that the Swedish bishops recommended that a dose of poison should be mixed with the King's food. Nor can we admit that the intolerance of Wolsey is excused by comparison with the greater intolerance of More. The Cardinal, in his last hours, asked for measures of repression, the nature of which his own example and the statute of Henry IV left in no kind of doubt. Sir Thomas More protested before his death, in terms which have satisfied the impartial judgment of one of his latest successors on the woolsack, that no Protestant had perished by his act.

[15]
Review of Döllinger's
Geschichte des Concils
von Trent

The author of the *Conciliengeschichte* breaks off his work at the Reformation, pleading that it would be idle to write on the Council of Trent without access to its authentic records. Great part of the desired documents has since been printed; but the difficulties which deterred Hefele are as great as before. The *Acta Authentica* contain, indeed, a brief summary of what was spoken, officially drawn up for publication in 1564; but many of the speeches are preserved in fuller reports, which discredit the official version, and many more are disfigured by the inability to estimate authorities, and to distinguish the spurious from the genuine, which casts a tinge of unreality over so much of the religious discussions in the sixteenth century. A writer who should define what was accurately known and what was fancifully believed at that time concerning the ancient literature of Christianity, the decrees of synods, and the Ecclesiastical Law, would do much to explain the hopelessness of controversy in the first age of the Reformation. The Council of Trent was, on at least two critical occasions, the centre of both civil and religious interest for the whole of Europe; and the great variety of forces that met in its arena have more significance than the scanty record of individual arguments. Theiner has relieved the bareness of the *Acta* with extracts from the more copious and confidential narratives out of which they were compiled; and it is apparent that private diaries kept by the officers of the Council, and by others in various positions, carry farther than the

Ignaz von Döllinger, *Ungedruckte Berichte und Tagebücher zur Geschichte des Concils von Trent* (Nördlingen: Beck, 1876). This review was published in *The Academy* 20 (May 1876):473–474.

superficial abridgment of debates, the best part of which was made known by Pallavicini.

Ten diaries had been printed down to the present time; and six more have now been published with a few pages of introduction by Dr. Döllinger. Half of the volume is devoted to the notes taken during the first, and theologically the most interesting, year of the assembly, by the secretary, Massarelli. Even in its broken and defective state this is a fragment of singular importance, written for private use, from day to day, and containing those matters which the Legates communicated to their trusty and indefatigable agent. To this has been added the little that deserves attention in the journals of Massarelli's assistant, Servanzio, a man who never rose above a subordinate position, whose vision is narrow and obscure, and whose work is in every respect inferior to that of his chief. A memoir, by Seripando, on the beginning of the Council, and another, by Musotti, on the later period, were composed after the event, from notes taken at the time. Seripando, the General of the Augustinians, occupied a position which was eminently favourable for observation and testimony. He lived on terms of intimacy with the ablest of the Legates, Cervini; he possessed the esteem of every party; he was honourably anxious to preserve the authority and to promote the reform of the Church; and his character gives a personal interest to his work beyond all others of the kind. He was one of the presiding Cardinals at his death in 1563, and the events of that time are described by his secretary, Musotti, in a Memoir which three or four authors have seen, but which was never printed before. Musotti enjoyed the confidence both of Seripando and Lorraine; the correspondence of the Legates passed through his hands; and although he gives fewer facts than Massarelli, he gives better information, for he had wit to discern the meaning of the things he saw. Besides these narratives, written at headquarters, the French and Spanish groups are represented by the diaries of the Bishops of Verdun and Salamanca, parts of which were already known.

In the preface the editor enumerates the principal publications on the Council which have preceded his own. He points out that the confidential letters of Visconti, published first by Aymon, are confined to the year 1563. It should be added that the letters of the preceding year, which are of greater consequence, were partially made known by Le Courayer in a review of Aymon's book, which is inserted in the *Europe Savante* for 1719. The correspondence was preserved in the

French king's library, in two manuscript volumes. Aymon stole one of them, and afterwards sold it, by the intervention of Toland, to the Earl of Oxford, in whose collection it may still be seen, covered with the handwriting of the dishonest editor. Sala's *Documenti di San Carlo,* to which Dr. Döllinger refers for the letters of the Cardinal d'Este, includes only three that had not been more correctly printed by Mansi; and the Venetian despatches, which he justly says are unavailable in the *Sommaire* of Baschet, have been lately published by Cecchetti, in his curious work on the ecclesiastical policy of the Republic. Dr. Döllinger has accepted without correction Le Plat's statement that he was the first to make known the *Epilogus* of the Belgian divine, Del Pré, which had appeared in 1725, in the fifth volume of the *Bibliothèque Françoise.* The only work of the sort which we owe to Le Plat's voluminous collection is a diary which Fickler, a layman, prepared from his notes, and meant to publish in 1605, but was prevented by the Archbishop of Salzburg. Fickler's manuscripts are still extant, and would supply matter more worthy of publicity than the greater part of his printed journals.

Dr. Döllinger makes generous allowance for the defects of Le Plat and the earlier writers, on the score of the censorship. As the volume of Raynaldus was kept back for some years, and parts of Pallavicini's History did not see the light until our day, the plea holds good for the seventeenth century. But it barely covers the delinquency of Le Plat, who lived in the reign of Joseph II, and omitted, not only the letters of Vargas, which were unknown to him except in a translation, and of Visconti, which had got into print under circumstances so suspicious as to raise doubts as to the integrity of the text, but even the invaluable reports of the Archbishop of Zara, which an Italian prelate had recently published without difficulty or scruple. He can hardly be acquitted of having selected his materials according to his bias, and of having left out what told against the episcopate. When Theiner was obliged to interrupt the publication of Massarelli's *Acta,* it was alleged that they had never been seen except by Pallavicini. Dr. Döllinger quotes the allegation without comment, probably supposing that contradiction is superfluous. In reality the secret was not impenetrable, and the seven mysterious volumes were frequently brought out. Duperron and Raynaldus saw them. They were known of course to Benedict XIV. They are quoted by Marini. While the archives of the Vatican were at Paris, the manuscript was inspected and minutely described by Agier; and in 1869 it was submitted to Hefele. Even the order of procedure, which was supposed to be the chief *arcanum*, was made known, in substance, by Reginaldus, on the very first pages of a work which has been widely read.

When Father Paul's History was originally published, in England, it was supposed that it had compromised the author, and had appeared without his sanction. As he never acknowledged it, and as the printed text differs often, though not materially, from the original, the story obtained credit, and survives in Dr. Döllinger's preface. The facts concerning this curious event of literary history were published as early as 1705, in a rare tract entitled *Some Letters relating to the History of the Council of Trent*. From these it appears that Archbishop Abbot, being informed that the book was finished, sent Nathaniel Brent to Venice to obtain it. Brent forwarded the manuscript to the Archbishop during the summer of 1618, in 197 instalments, and under various directions. Nobody except De Dominis was in the secret.

In the enquiry into the credibility of Sarpi and Pallavicini which is one of the gems of Ranke's *Popes,* the great critic pronounces that neither is impartial, but that Sarpi errs generally from ignorance. Dr. Döllinger's judgment on the two historians is nearly the same. He is more impressed than Ranke by their defects; but he assigns considerable authority to both, and thinks Sarpi the more trustworthy of the two. There is this great difference between them, that Pallavicini is the first modern historian who was diligent in stating his authorities, and that the better part of all he quotes is now within reach, either in print, or in libraries open to scholars, so that we can track his footsteps and detect almost every error; whereas Sarpi has scarcely acknowledged his sources more than half-a-dozen times, and it is often impossible to discover where he got his information. When a writer's veracity cannot be thoroughly brought to the proof, much will depend on his character. But few historians will stand the test, and it is questionable whether Sarpi is one of them. He assured his Protestant friends that he shared their creed, that he strove stealthily to convert his countrymen to the doctrines of Geneva, that he continued to say mass only because, being excommunicated, he was bound to defy the Pope. Whether these statements are true or false, there is no escape from the dilemma that he set himself to deceive either the Catholic neighbours who revered in him a saint after the model of the cloister, or the correspondents who took him for a convinced but undeveloped Calvinist. He was the obsequious and admiring servant of a Government which became, in his time, and before his eyes, the most systematically immoral tyranny in Christendom; and his political instincts were offended, not only by the constituted forms and authorities of the Church, but by that which is essentially the spirit of the Christian religion. In public he struggled against the privileges, the immunities, the competing powers which embarrassed the State: in private he was an unfriendly critic of a system which, by regarding the inward more than the outward life of men, and fixing their minds on the supernatural world, weakened, as he thought, the influence of earthly motives and the power of society over its members:

"Per haver levato la sollecitudine dell' honore et fama, et la sollecitudine delle virtù, che ha per impossibili; et in loro luoco sostituito la fede, non come virtù, ma per succedaneo. . . . Dona gran speranza, confidenza, et allegrezza. Leva la politica, dovendo immediate finir il mondo. Fa insociabili, havendo gl' altri per impii. Contraria al viver civile, sprezzando il tutto come abominabile o vano."

His sympathy with the Reformed Churches consisted in little more than aversion for the Papacy, and it is natural that he should have gradually lost ground in the estimation of Protestants, at the very time when his literary fame stood highest, and after he had put forth a work against Rome which has ever since continued to be more extensively read and more deeply studied than the writings of Erasmus, of Luther, or of Calvin. Men will differ in their judgments on his theology; but it should hardly be disputed that his ethics were injurious to his credit as a writer of history, and especially of religious history, for he held that it is lawful, by common consent, to employ falsehood in the promotion of truth: "Ogn' huomo ha opinione che il mendacio sia buono in ragion di medicina, et di far bene a far creder il vero et utile con premesse false."

By attributing to these renowned controversialists even a limited measure of authority, Dr. Döllinger somewhat disparages works like his own, which are destined ultimately to supersede them. The axiom that historic certainty depends on the substitution of documents for historians is nowhere nearer the truth than when applied to the Council of Trent. As long as men can plausibly support opposing views by appealing to Sarpi or to Pallavicini, the subject cannot be rescued from controversy. So much of the materials which those writers used has become accessible, so much is known that was unknown to them, that it will be possible at no distant day, not, indeed, to dispense with their writings, but to extinguish their influence. We have still to wait for a complete and critical edition of Massarelli's journals, of which Dr. Döllinger has revealed the value; for a memorandum written by Seripando in the summer of 1562; and for other writings by Musotti, Campeggio, and a Portuguese Bishop, which are not yet recovered. But if all the private diaries which were kept at Trent were set in type, they would not clear away doubt or close discussion. The last appeal will always lie to an authority necessarily recognised as decisive—that is, to the private and the official letters that passed between the Court of Rome and the Legates and agents at Trent. Portions of this correspondence may be found in every great library; but it is useless to hope for a complete collection until it is undertaken at Rome.

It has been often supposed that the breach opened in 1517 might have been healed until it was made irreparable at Trent; and that a party of reforming prelates would have disarmed and reconciled the Protestants but for the guile of those who wielded the majority. Dr. Döllinger's volume will go far to dispel this illusion. A door had been left partially open to the disciples of Luther during a quarter of a century, but it was finally closed three years before the Council met. There had been a strong desire at Rome to take advantage of the Confession of Augsburg to obtain the basis of an understanding; and conciliation was seriously attempted ten years later at Ratisbon. Moderate men there contrived terms of agreement on the main points of the original dispute; and Cardinal Contarini amazed Calvin by his anxiety to do justice to the other side. He composed a paper on Justification, in which he said: "Ex operibus qui dicunt nos justificari, verum dicunt; et qui dicunt nos justificari non ex operibus, sed per fidem, verum etiam dicunt." Pole congratulated him on having made manifest a half-hidden truth, on having been the instrument of a new revelation. It was afterwards said that the strange doctrine had spread so far that the Catholic faith was extinct in a considerable part of Italy. There was a sudden alarm followed by swift reaction. It was resolved that the Protestants should be overcome by force, as there was danger in attempting now to win them by concessions, and in 1542 the Inquisition was revived, and armed with increased powers. Thenceforward the policy pursued towards the Lutherans and the Huguenots was consistent, and allowed no hope of conciliation. The breach was complete without the intervention of the Council, and, apart from this, no concessions it could make would have availed with Luther, who repudiated the agreement accepted by Melanchthon, or with Calvin, who would not hear of making terms with Rome.

The belief that Trent was thronged with followers of Gerson and of Erasmus, earnest to obviate a Reformation like that of Wittenberg by reforms like those of Constance, is wholly imaginary. The most serious symptom of such a spirit is the scheme which the Emperor Ferdinand submitted to the Council. But the Emperor's advisers willingly took the money of Cardinal Morone, and their scheme was allowed to drop. The attitude of France was more energetic. Three ambassadors disturbed the Council by their unflinching Gallicanism. But their zeal for religion was so poor in quality that one of them, Du Ferrier, was silenced by an offer of gold; another, Birago, became the chief agent in the massacre of Paris, of which the third, Pibrac, was the most eloquent apologist. And the Cardinal of Lorraine, who was the leader of this party, had just prepared to exterminate heresy by a method more sure and unrelenting than that which was afterwards executed by feebler hands. The French Government having put in its demands, lost all interest in the proceedings, and contented itself with obtaining enormous subsidies from the Pope. The Spanish prelates and divines were individually superior to the French. Although they were suspicious of the concessions by which Catholicism sought to maintain itself in France and Germany, they were stern believers in the rights and duties of the episcopate. But they were men who had been chosen and sent by a prince whose motives were never really religious, and they were bound to do his will. When their advocacy of the prerogatives of their order became troublesome, the Pope invoked the authority of Philip. At a word from the Ambassador the Spaniards gave way, and wished to apologise; and Mendoza, the Bishop of Salamanca, who had been separated from his countrymen by the simplest of arts, sneered at their alacrity in obeying man rather than God. If there had been a genuine survival of the spirit which prevailed at Constance, the organisation for the control of the Council could not have borne the strain. The Legates were much divided among themselves, and sometimes agreed in contending against the Pope's commands. Gonzaga fell into disgrace, and asked permission to resign. Simonetta denounced his colleagues. Seripando entered a solemn declaration against the acts of Simonetta. Hosius was hopelessly inactive. Altemps was notoriously inefficient. There was so little reality or substance in the opposition these Legates encountered that, although they reported that the Council was all but unanimous in demanding to be described as representing the whole Church, they dismissed the claim without resistance. Their chief complaint, indeed, is not of their opponents, but of the anxiety caused by the intemperate zeal, the obstinacy and incapacity of their constant supporters. It was the conscious want of power in those who presided, rather than the unruly vigour of party feeling, that hampered the Council, and brought it to an abrupt termination.

[16]
Review of the Spanish Calendar

The second volume of the Spanish Calendar, prepared by Don Pascual de Gayangos, embraces two eventful years, from Bourbon's march against Rome to the reconciliation of the Pope with Spain; or, in English equivalents, from the opening of the Divorce question down to the beginning of the breach with the Papacy. It was the Divorce that healed the quarrel between Charles V and the Pope, and rescued Clement from a position of the utmost peril; and it was his reconciliation with Charles that determined the issue of Henry's matrimonial cause. The two series of events react on each other so continuously that they are not separately intelligible; and the inclusion in this Calendar of much matter that lies beyond the authentic sphere of insular politics is more than justified. Mr. Gayangos never strays from the great central range of fact into the byways of recondite history. He gives scarcely anything that is not worthy to be given entire; and there is little that is superfluous in his volume. Few men living can boast that they have discovered anything equal to Mendoza's plain account of the treatment and the conduct of Catharine, or to the astonishing miniatures in which the Catalonian jurist Mai depicts the Court of Rome during the illness of Clement VII. In 1873, I had an opportunity of examining that portion of the Vienna archives from which Mendoza's despatches have been taken, and, although it seemed worth while to take copies of some papers which Mr. Gayangos has omitted, I am able to testify that those which he has selected appear with all the completeness they deserve.

According to Mendoza, who was not allowed free access to the queen, she became aware of impending mischief in March, 1527, and

Calendar of State Papers relating to Negotiations between England and Spain, preserved at Simancas and elsewhere, 1527–1529, ed. Pascual de Gayangos (London: Longmans, 1877). This review was published in *The Academy* 7 (July 1877):1–2.

had already fixed upon the messenger who, in the following July, carried her secret to the Emperor. She generally obtained earlier information of what was being done against her than the ambassador; she rarely consulted him, and, in his judgment, she was swayed by bad advice. Mendoza attributes to Wolsey the project of Divorce, and regards it, together with the scheme for running Richmond against the Princess Mary, as a move in the game of the enemies of Spain. He is slow to recognise the influence of Anne Boleyn; and he shows Wolsey repenting very early, declining to act as judge, and laying the load on Campeggio. He almost gives countenance to Henry's complaint that Wolsey got him into the scrape, and then deserted him. But the ambassador was not a man of penetration. He seems not to have mastered the controversy; and his perpetual assurances that the king and the cardinal were detested, and the people ripe for rebellion, must have misled his employers.

In Italy the Emperor was better served; and the Italian portions of the volume contain more that is new than the English. It appears that Campeggio, whom Wolsey chose for his colleague, was known, throughout, to be an Imperialist; that the escape of Clement from St. Angelo was concerted with the Spanish commanders, to rescue him from their followers; and that Wolsey had, at one time, gained over a majority of the cardinals in Rome to his plan of a conclave at Avignon.

In his Introduction Mr. Gayangos indicates disagreement with Ranke and Mignet on one or two points without giving sufficient evidence. He is persuaded that the march to Rome was undertaken in defiance of orders. Charles V was much addicted to the vexatious practice of giving contradictory instructions, and he sometimes perplexed his own agents as much as his historians. It is, no doubt, possible to produce letters in which he recommended peace; but there are others, quite as definite, which prove that he was determined to make Clement harmless, and that he permitted the expedition. The mutiny of his army in Lombardy was quelled by a sum of money, and by promising the "law of Mahomet." Mr. Gayangos explains that the infantry was recruited among the Moriscos of Valencia, and that the prospect that pacified them was the promise of religious liberty at home. I would prefer the less ingenious interpretation of Mignet, that it was a licence of another kind, such as better men have sometimes granted to soldiers about to storm the walls of a fortified town.

The Calendar comes so soon after Mr. Gayangos' valuable *Catalogue of Spanish Manuscripts at the British Museum,* which was issued only last year, that readers will be prepared to find some signs of haste. The Protest of the Cardinals (195) has been centuries in print; and the Instructions to Farnese (280), which occupy nine pages, may be found in a book which is quoted elsewhere in this volume. A curious Memorandum on English affairs, apparently by De Praet, which Mr. Gayangos says he does not hesitate to assign to the month of December, 1527, refers to the expected assistance of Bourbon, who had died on May 6. Queen Catherine's letter to the Emperor and Empress, inserted under date of October 19, 1528, belongs to 1527, and was enclosed in Mendoza's despatch of October 26 in that year. A petition of Mai and De Burgo to the Pope, which bears some important annotations by a Roman lawyer, is placed in April, 1529, although it alludes to an act done in the following March. The Instructions prepared for Mai when it was intended that he should come to England as Catharine's adviser cannot belong to October 1, 1528, where we find them. At that time he was the Spanish envoy to the Pope; and it was at Christmas, 1527, that the English embassy was in contemplation. The month is therefore as doubtful as the year. The date is of some significance, for if the Instructions were written in the beginning of October, 1527, they would contain the earliest mention of the Brief of Dispensation. It was by the production of that document that the Spaniards prevailed against Henry, and men of great authority—Mr. Brewer, Mr. Pocock, and Mr. Gairdner—believe that it is genuine, and that the Spanish triumph was obtained by fair means. When Charles V first heard of the design to impugn the validity of the marriage, at the end of July, 1527, he knew nothing of that second dispensation which covered the assailable point of the first. Its first appearance, so far as we know, is on December 26. If reasons can be found for fixing the earliest mention in October, the probability of forgery would be diminished.

Some titles of books cited in the Introduction, such as *Annales Reginaldi,* Rome, 1646, and the *Codice Diplomatico Italiano* of Lünig, are unknown to the most expert bibliographers; and *"6 Calendas Augusti"* is not the 1st of August. We have Balore for Batori, Foligno for Forli, the Order of St. George for the Bank of St. George, a Duke of Hesse when no such personage existed, and a defective copy described as an original. *Plectuntur archivi* looks like an emendation suggested by long study at Simancas. By discarding the obvious meaning of the word *el Reyno,* Parliament is described as unanimous when no Parliament had sat for four years; a majority of at least two-thirds is given as "the two parties and more," and *foro* is called a privilege where it means a tribunal. In fact, the translator's licence is the most serious blot in a volume which is, undoubtedly, the most important contribution ever made by a Spaniard to the history of this country. Mendoza is made to say (224):

"The Legate, fearing lest by promoting the Divorce he should make an opening for the King to marry in France, and that instead of a Queen like the present, incapable of doing him any injury, there might come one who disliked him (perhaps this very lady whom he had so much offended), is not likely to favour any such alliance."

It would be strange if Wolsey dreaded a French match, or thought of Anne Boleyn with "perhaps" at the end of October, 1527. There is not a word about France, or the least uncertainty about Anne, in the Spanish sentence. In the following passage every word in italics is the unprovoked invention of the translator:

"He has *lately* offered me, *through his ambassador (Mendoça),* a large pension *in his kingdom,* and a considerable sum of money *besides,* if I will *only* serve his interest. These, *of course,* I have refused, *to prove* the Emperor's unfairness, and my own freedom from avarice."

The words *alegar el lugar sospechoso,* meaning that there was no chance of a fair trial in England, are rendered to "state whom she suspected of this suggestion." The Spanish saying, that honest men go to the wall, *el hombre honrado siempre va a menos,* is translated, "honest men were on the decrease." Mr. Brewer (iv., 2,393) gives the meaning better; but then there is the disturbing fact that these eminent authorities, with the same copy before them, read the words differently. Mr. Brewer writes, *"va en diminution."*

In every passage on which I have questioned the accuracy of the translation the original words have been scrupulously appended; and the doubts I have raised are not to detract from the imperishable merit of the work, but to promote caution in using it, and to lay the basis of a practical suggestion which, I hope, does not come too late. It is plain that Mr. Gayangos has struck a vein of extraordinary richness for the history of the Reformation. Abreast with him, Mr. Brewer is approaching the great religious struggle; and it is well known that the French correspondence, which is scarce in the lifetime of Wolsey, henceforth abounds. In those anxious and contentious years much will sometimes depend on the exact terms of a passage; and history cannot do its appointed work of rectifying the errors and reconciling the differences of men, if there is nothing better to depend on than despatches written originally in dog Latin, in barbarous German, or in arbitrary Venetian, which have to be deciphered, translated, summarised, and lose something of their flavour at every stage, even in the most practised and most faithful hands. Thus, in the Instructions for Mai, Gattinara affirms that the Brief of Dispensation was subsequent to the Bull, and his words bear on the question of its authenticity, as it afterwards appeared with the same date as the Bull. It would be hazardous to employ the statement for critical purposes, had not Mr. Gayangos, perceiving its importance, added the original words. Even the English Calendar, if I remember rightly, inadvertently omits a short paragraph in which Wolsey avowed himself the author of that change of policy of which the Divorce was an important part. And if historians who have diligently studied the entire Calendar know that they can trust the editor, and feel authorised to build upon his statements, they will be unable to impart the same confidence to their own readers; and there will be nothing solid to pass from hand to hand. The difficulty might be met in a way which is already prepared in the proceedings of the Master of the Rolls. Masses of authentic transcripts have been collected at the Rolls House; Bergenroth published a volume of documents in the original; and Mr. Brewer gives the Latin or Italian text of papers mutilated in the fire that damaged so many of the Cottonian manuscripts. Thus there are some papers which are printed in the original; others in ample translations; and others are abridged. The three methods might be fitly applied, not only to distinct papers, but to separate portions of the same, for the times of Henry VIII. Whatever possesses crucial or controversial significance, whether a letter or a paragraph, should be printed *verbatim*. Wherever verbal accuracy is needless, a translation or an abridgment would do, and the contents of each paper should be described in a couple of lines at the top. In this way the working value of these publications, for the turning-point of our history, would gain; and there would be no increase of bulk or of expense, unless it is thought that every piece of Latin or French must be put into English. Desjardins' compilation from the Tuscan despatches, and especially the works of Druffel on the later years of Charles V, and of Ritter on the epoch preceding the Thirty Years' War, are conspicuously successful examples of this method.

[17]
German Schools of History

Macaulay once lamented that there were no German historians in his time worthy of the name; and now M. Darmesteter tells us that they are ahead of other nations by twenty years. A perplexed person might read Professor Wegele's *Deutsche Historiographie*[1] without being quite sure which is right. Nine-tenths of his volume are devoted to the brave men who lived before Agamemnon, and the chapter on the rise of historical science, the only one which is meant for mankind, begins at page 975, and is the last. Before this century the Germans had scarcely reached the common level even in the storage of erudition. Their provincial histories could not be compared with those of Burgundy, of Brittany, or of Languedoc; they had nothing equal to the Annals of Bologna or of Milan, to Mamachi's *Life of Saint Dominic,* or even to Secousse's *Charles of Navarre.* History was subordinate to other things, to divinity, philosophy, and law; and the story worth telling would be the process of emancipation by which the servant of many masters rose to be a master over them, and having become a law to itself imposed it on others. The beginning was made by Niebuhr, and none of those who followed and strengthened the powerful impulse which he gave rival the best of their countrymen in perspicuity and grace.

When Germans assert that their real supremacy rests with their historians, they mean it in the sense of Bentley and Colebrooke, not of Machiavelli and Saint-Simon, in the sense in which the Bishop of Durham[2] and Sir Henry Maine take the lead in England, the sense in which M. Fustel de Coulanges calls history the most arduous of the

Published in the *English Historical Review* 1 (1886):7–42. Reprinted in Acton, *Historical Essays*, pp. 344–392.

[1] *Geschichte der deutschen Historiographie.* Von Dr. Franz X. von Wegele. Munich: Oldenbourg, 1885.

[2] Dr. Lightfoot.

sciences. A famous scholar, enumerating the models of historical excellence, named Humboldt, Savigny, Grimm, and Ritter, not one of whom had ever written history proper, in the common, classical, literary use of the term.

The better part of the ground has been occupied already by those who have celebrated German achievement in other branches of literature. Neander, Böckh, Baur, Schwegler, Lassen have their record elsewhere. Excepting Niebuhr and Ranke, Professor Wegele has had to deprive himself of his best materials. The division of labour removes almost every man who was an historian and something more.

Historical writing was old, but historical thinking was new in Germany when it sprang from the shock of the French Revolution. Condemnation of history had been the strongest plank in the platform of 1789. The evils exposed in the *cahiers* were not accidents of the age, but the bequest of malignant forces at work for centuries. Irresponsible power, the caprice of war, slavery, intolerance, arbitrary arrest, the deadly prison, the inhuman aggravation of the pains of death, had been the steady produce of elaborate design. The men who struck at the misery inflicted by traditional authority believed no dogma so firmly as that of the folly of their ancestors. The supreme object of their striving was to depose and to degrade a tyrant who, at his best, was blind and ignorant and cruel, and who, moreover, was dead. Their sternest resolve was that generations of astrologers, sorcerers, and torturers, of legislators unable to read, of sovereigns only able to kill, that the wisdom of the *code noir* and the statute book of George II should not be suffered to reign over Watt and Hunter, over Lavoisier and Laplace, Smith and Kant; and the most vigorous of the revolutionary thinkers, Jefferson and Sieyès, studied both to banish the past and to prevent the present from again overshadowing the future. It was under this flag that the armies conquered Germany, destroying and transforming, and left no institution standing but the monarchy of Frederic the Great.

The romantic reaction which began with the invasion of 1794 was the revolt of outraged history. The nation fortified itself against the new ideas by calling up the old, and made the ages of faith and of imagination a defence from the age of reason. Whereas the pagan Renaissance was the artificial resurrection of a world long buried, the romantic Renaissance revived the natural order and restored the broken links from end to end. It inculcated sympathy with what is past, unlovable, indefensible, especially with the age of twilight and scenes favourable to the faculties which the calculators despised. The romantic writers relieved present need with all the abounding treasure of other times, subjecting thereby the will and the conscience of the living to the will and conscience of the dead. Their lasting influence was out of proportion to their immediate performance. They were weak because they wanted strictness and accuracy, and never perceived that the Revolution was itself historic, having roots that could be profitably traced far back in the ages. But they were strong by the recovery of lost knowledge, and by making it possible to understand, to appreciate, and even to admire things which the judgment of rationalism condemned in the mass of worthless and indiscriminate error. They trifled for a time with fancy, but they doubled the horizon of Europe. They admitted India to an equality with Greece, mediaeval Rome with classical; and the thoughts they set in motion produced Creuzer's *Comparative Mythology* and Bopp's *Conjugations,* Grimm's enthusiasm for the liberty and belief of Odin's worshippers, and Otfried Müller's zeal for the factor of race.

As long as the romantics were a literary school, running aesthetical canons in opposition to Goethe, they remained unconscious of the active principle within. Dante and Calderon, Nibelungen and Sakuntala, were not so near the core as Burke's maxim that wisdom and religion dictate that we should follow events, and not attempt to lead, much less to force them. When their ideas came to be taken up by reasoners, they were found to involve a system of scientific definitions charged with interminable consequences. Their philosopher was Schelling, who married Schlegel's wife, and who, condensing the vapour of the school into something like solid propositions, taught that the State does not exist for purposes of men, and is not governed by laws of their devising, but by the cosmic force above.

Upon this aphorism, Savigny, the jurist of the party, developed the historic method of jurisprudence. The sovereign legislator is not the government, but the nation. Law, like language, proceeds from its primitive nature and its experience and is part of its identity. The deliberations of lawgiving consist in ascertaining not what is best, but what is consistent with usage. Laws are found, not made, for the treatment adapted to successive emergencies is already latent in the public conscience, and must be evolved from precedent. Laws and constitutions expand by sustenance drawn from the constant and original spring; the force preparing the future is the same that made the past, and the function of the jurist is to trace and to obey it faithfully, without attempting to explain it away.

Learning and eloquence long effectually concealed the logical effect of this doctrine. It assorted so well with the spirit of the age that it predominated for half a century against Bentham, and Hegel, and the year 1848, and is yielding slowly to the keener dialectics and deeper philosophy of Ihering. It is the strongest of all the agencies that have directed German effort towards history, viewed as a remedy for the eighteenth century and the malady of vain speculation. When Laboulaye described it as a school that had no masters in France and only one disciple, who was himself, it was controlling Germany.

In the mind of Savigny and his followers their doctrine made for progress and independence, but not for liberty. The notion that each generation of men is powerless over its own fortunes, and receives them subject to inherited conditions, combined well with the rooted conservatism of the country. But it possessed that property of the works of genius, that it could be carried out in opposite directions. If the nation is the source of law, it is reasonable to infer that national consent is a normal element in legislation, and that the State ought legitimately to take its limits from the nation. Niebuhr, in unguarded moments, drew one of these inferences, and Dahlmann the other. And it came to pass that the historical school, having abolished the law of nature which was the motive of 1789, instituted the law of nationality, which became the motive of 1848.

Bishop Stubbs informs us that history is likely to make men wise, and is sure to make them sad. In the long chapter of the melancholy historians no figure is more tragic than Niebuhr, the politician, as Savigny was the civilian, of the school. He had flashes of admiration for the English Government as it appeared under Eldonian auspices; but when the world went off the ancient ways, he lost his temper and his spirits, and his end was a warning to weaker men to keep their studies apart from the hopes and fears of life. Had he survived, he would have been what Radowitz became, the king's intimate adviser. The inflexible qualities which repelled his colleagues and spoilt him for a statesman fitted him for a critical historian. His passion for truthfulness was such that he defied Stein to show that he had ever subscribed himself the obedient servant of a man he did not respect. With his high notions there was no writer whom he could trust, and neither ancient nor modern veracity could stand before him.

The first edition of his *Roman History*, afterwards repudiated, began the evolution of historic science. It exhibited the theory that truth is not buried underneath tradition—that, although the Romans had forgotten the early state of their institutions, the processes of history are so well defined that it is possible to work back from the known to the unknown, from effect to cause, and so to recover the unrecorded past. This was the visible sign of the new doctrine of fixed lines, invariable laws, and overruled action of men. It indicated a mode of certainty which did not depend on the credit of historians. When they have been tested to the breaking-point, the critic comes in and begins his proper work. The right sphere of these operations is the primitive obscurity. They could not flourish in the daylight, and Niebuhr never showed that he knew how to apply them to events and characters told by contemporaries. When he filled the meagre outline of Manlius by transferring to him the character of Mirabeau, he gave the example which Stanley followed when he put Lord Shaftesbury into the Reformation, and Mr. Golightly into the Jewish monarchy. The weighty volumes, crowded with doubtful but suggestive matter, won so little popular success that he laid them by for many years. When he rewrote them, under the spur of contradiction, and in the midst of a vigorous intellectual movement which was partly his work, they found less favour than the finished productions of Savigny. The historical school penetrated everywhere and remodelled every branch of legal study excepting ecclesiastical and comparative law, which resisted the national principle. But the work of Niebuhr's life stood still. There was a temporary reaction in favour of Roman views of Roman history; and he had been dead for twenty years before he began to be superseded by innovators bolder and better appointed than himself. Schwegler's early death deprived Germany of the one man who combined real philosophic talent with the rarest critical faculty. Mommsen, whose book was begun at the same time as Schwegler's, realised that union of qualities which Macaulay described when he said that Niebuhr would have been the first writer of his time if his talent for communicating truths had borne any proportion to his talent for investigating them.

The fruit of the *Roman History* ripened for Greece. The men who made it known in this country were Thirlwall and Grote; it sent Otfried Müller to historical studies; and Böckh dedicated to Niebuhr a work which has stood the test of time better than his own. Under the powerful sway which Böckh exercised in Prussia for fifty years, Hellenic studies obtained the lead. A deeper scholar than Niebuhr, an historian, which the Saxon philologists disdained to be, he abandoned Rome to jurists and politicians, and primitive times to romantic theorists. His own taste was for the hardest possible facts and the clearest proofs. Like Niebuhr, he believed that antiquity is covered over with error, which will shrivel like a parched scroll, and that hidden truth will be brought to light. But instead of the incommunicable genius of conjecture he set to work with a new organon, and substituted improved evidence for dazzling guesswork.

Inscriptions had been always a source of dire confusion, for it paid local antiquaries to forge them, and two hundred consuls were invented by a single impostor. Niebuhr dismissed this branch of inquiry wholesale, saying that nobody could be expected to master it. Böckh showed that it could be made an instrument of discovery as efficacious as the boldest ingenuity, and it became, in his firm and patient hands, the corner-stone of the building. Besides showing the way of reaching truth even beyond Thucydides, he was an illustrious example of the historian who puts himself out of sight and displays what is certain, suppressing rigidly his personal sentiments. The tone of elegiac and cathartic poetry is one thing: the epic tone is another. After hearing his course on ancient philosophy, I asked him why his lectures were more interesting than his books. Böckh answered benignly, "Because I give my finished researches to the public, and keep my own views *(die ideale Anschauung)* for the students."

The *Public Economy of the Athenians* is almost the only history produced before the critical epoch which still stands, unshaken and erect. The critical epoch lies between 1824 and 1828. To mark the distinction between what was planted in those five years and the wild growth that preceded them, is half the work that Professor Wegele had to do.

In natural gifts and in acquirements the earlier writers were not, upon the whole, inferior to those who, with better opportunities, have made them a prey to dumb forgetfulness. It is a matter of legendary notoriety that Schlosser consumed so many thousand volumes in a given time. The *Symbolik* of his colleague Creuzer is a mine of learning animated with ideas. Voigt was among the first who, either from the easy indifference of rationalism or from the manifold interest of romanticism, released the mediaeval Papacy from the dilemma of good or bad. Few of those who have come since Luden can write so well. Raumer earned the praise of having written readably on the Middle

Ages, and made it known that there was much to be learnt from the Italians. Many writers of this epoch had qualities not cultivated afterwards by men of sterner stuff, and addressed their style to readers less learned than themselves, who preferred a clean text to perpetual dissertation. All the works of Schlosser deserve the malediction which Mr. Morley pronounced on one of them; yet there was a blunt integrity about him, and his influence upon men so superior to himself as Gervinus, Rothe, and Bernhardi proves, what his writings do not, that he possessed some higher quality. Luden made a name for patriotism; and Raumer was a liberal, often in tepid water for his opinions. Of the three periods into which the attitude of Germans towards the Middle Ages has been distributed—the contemptuous, the admiring, and the intelligent, these men generally represent the second. In point of trustworthiness they are near the level of their French contemporaries; of Thierry amplifying *Ivanhoe*, Barante transcribing Monstrelet, and Michaud flogging all the dead horses of the First Crusade. Waitz and Leo said of them that they could read texts but never studied them; and they stand condemned as men who did not know how to distinguish authentic knowledge from second-hand, and were at the mercy of their informants. They are gathered to the geographers who made charts before Columbus.

A new art of employing authorities came in with Ranke in 1824: Müller's *Introduction to the Science of Mythology* quickly followed; Gieseler and Neander began their histories of the Church; and Menzel, after an inferior book on the Middle Ages, published the first volume of what was long the best modern history of Germany. Niebuhr prepared the new edition, which is the pillar of his fame, in 1827; and in 1828 Stenzel adapted to the Gregorian epoch the canons of criticism which Ranke had made obligatory on every serious writer. These seven or eight works were the symptom of a great transition.

Ranke has not only written a larger number of mostly excellent books than any man that ever lived, but he has taken pains from the first to explain how the thing is done. He attained a position unparalleled in literature, less by the display of extraordinary faculties than by perfect mastery of the secret of his craft, and that secret he has always made it his business to impart. For his most eminent predecessors, history was applied politics, fluid law, religion exemplified, or the school of patriotism. Ranke was the first German to pursue it for no purpose but its own. He tried to make the generality of educated men understand how it came about that the world of the fifteenth century was changed into the Europe of the nineteenth. His own definite persuasions regarding church and king were not suffered to permeate his books. It was meritorious in Böckh, but not heroic, to contain his feelings about the Attic treasure and the setting of Arcturus; but Ranke was concerned with all the materials of abiding conflict, with every cause for which he cared and men are willing to kill or die.

He expects no professional knowledge in his readers, and never writes for specialists. He seldom probes to the bottom the problems of public life and the characters of men, and passes dryshod over much that is in dispute. As he writes history, not biography, he abstains from the secrets of private life; and as he writes history, not dogma, he never sorts men into black and white according to their bearing in vital controversies. His evil-doers escape the just rigour of the law, and he avoids hero-worship as the last ditch of prehistoric prejudice. He touches lightly on matters pertaining to the jurist and divine, but he has not their exclusiveness. His surface is more level than theirs, but his horizon is wider. The cup is not drained; part of the story is left untold; and the world is much better and very much worse than he chooses to say.

Ranke was profoundly influenced by Niebuhr; and the example of so wise a man sinking under the load of political disappointment impressed him with the belief that it is well for people generally to disconnect their scientific and their practical life. Niebuhr's treatment of history required men as able as himself, and as familiar with the play of institutions, but boded disaster in weaker hands. Ranke brought his art down to a lower capacity. In the preliminary measure of testing authorities, he showed that it is possible, by careful analysis, to learn whence a writer obtains his facts; and this part of the work is often almost mechanical. It depresses the study of history to a level with the collation of texts, and admits a large and useful body of workers who would make a mess of the three first Muses, or the first decade of Livy.

The task of analysing character is more complicated. There is a peculiarity about the revision of historians that excludes them from the benefit of the common law that innocence must be assumed until guilt is proved. The presumption which is favourable to makers of history is adverse to writers of history. For history deals considerably with hanging matter, and nobody ought to hang on damaged testimony.

The life of the witness must be subjected to closer scrutiny than the life of the culprit. He is condemned when he is suspected; doubt is decisive against him. When Father Paul relates that Luther's arguments were thought to be unanswerable at the court of Rome, but were resisted in order that authority might be upheld, he appeals to the diary of Chieregato, which has not been produced. The story, therefore, stands and falls with his own credibility. Nobody has a right to adopt it who is not able to vindicate the character of Sarpi. There is a test of credibility, and consequently a rule of right and wrong, which everybody must acknowledge, because without it there is no such thing as evidence, and the code which is applied to books applies to events. The maxims by which we judge the statements of Caesar or of Clarendon enable us to judge their actions. The principles are the same, though the rigour in employing them is unequal.

True impartiality is no respecter of persons, and judges resolutely regardless of the judgment of others. Ranke's merciful abstinence from strong language, his reserve in passing sentence, correspond to two governing facts in the movement to which he belongs. Germans, like other people, have certain hereditary landmarks not good to disturb, certain names too closely associated with national glory to be exposed to profanation. Luther is one of them, and Frederic, and Goethe. Döllinger's double-edged saying, that the nation recognises its own nature in Luther *(ihr potenzirtes Selbst)*, became popular; and the passionate temper of the Reformation tracts no more repels his countrymen than the violence of More, of Milton, or of Grattan interferes with their credit here. Gratitude to the king, pride in the poet, tell in the same way to exclude the vulgar standard and to check unruly speech touching such matters as divine right, arbitrary power, and ethical neutrality. There is, if not depreciation of the moral currency, impatience of the language men utter in censuring equals. The public feels a shock of incongruity when the President of the Bavarian Academy accuses an emperor of the murder of a Bavarian prince, or when Dahlmann crudely says that the sovereigns who divided Poland were as guilty as the Terrorists.

The infallible conscience, the universal and unwritten law, the principles of eternal justice, are precisely those eighteenth-century phantoms against which the romantic and historical school rose in defiance. The belief that men carry about them the knowledge of good and evil is the very root of revolution. Those who, in the words of De

Maistre and the Prussian conservatives, desired, not the counter-Revolution, but the contrary of revolution, decreed that the mighty past shall not be measured by present rules and the categorical imperative. Mankind varies and advances in ethical insight; the virtue of to-day was once a crime, and the code changes with the latitude. If King James burnt witches, if Machiavelli taught assassination as an art, if pious crusaders slaughtered peaceful Jews, if Ulysses played fast and loose, we are exhorted to remember the times they lived in, and leave them to the judgment of their peers. Mobility in the moral code, subjection of man to environment, indefinite allowance for date and race, are standing formulas from Schlegel to the realistic philosophy.

Although Ranke practises moderation and restraint, and speaks of transactions and occurrences when it would be safe to speak of turpitude and crime, he kept himself above the indifference and the incapable neutrality of those who held, with Gerard Hamilton, that there are few questions on which one may not vote conscientiously either way. This was the infant shape of impartiality. The Italians, said Raumer, justify the cities of Lombardy; the Germans justify their emperors: both are right and both are wrong. Raumer was not a strong man; but there were many in his day who admired such abdication as the triumph of fairness, and discarded human responsibility. On a solemn occasion Ranke declared that the modern to whom, after Niebuhr, he was most in debt, was Fichte. Of Fichte's philosophy there is little either in Ranke's sixty volumes or elsewhere now. But as the most advanced apostle, since Butler, of the efficacy of conscience, he opposed submission to impersonal forces, and no doubt strengthened Ranke in his resistance to more than one of his most famous colleagues.

Ranke acquired very early an unrivalled knowledge of historical literature, but towards 1840 he began to say that the last five centuries cannot be understood from printed books only. He did not lead the way to the archives. When an Englishman or Scotsman took a side in the revolution of 1688, he was accustomed to support himself with new documents. Austria was before the rest of Germany; and Mignet's incomparable fragment on the foreign policy of Lewis XIV surpassed all that the rest of Europe was doing. At first the narrow opening of archives was not an unmixed boon. The partial use of manuscripts was as misleading as the partial use of books. When Stein planned the *Monumenta,* Gentz avowed the opinion that truth is not always a desirable thing, and a Würzburg professor denounced the undertaking as a scheme of obscuration. 'Tis sixty years since, and now every state reveals its inner life: the Vatican and the *Affaires Étrangères* are as easy of access as the Frari, or the Hofburg under the generous management of Arneth; the chief archivist of Prussia, after declaring that his country has nothing to conceal, proves his sincerity by the publication of twenty-six volumes; and Treitschke adds the subtantial reason that the enemies of Prussia have told the worst, making concealment at once needless and impossible. Ranke has gone along with the progress which has so vastly extended the range and influence of historians. After starting without manuscripts, and then lightly skimming them, he ended by holding that it is not science to extract modern history from anything less than the entire body of written evidence. Touching which, there are two opinions. One is, that history would be all right but for historians; that nothing is certain but what is secret and official; and that no man is so safe to punish as he that is condemned out of his own mouth. Others deem that we cannot realise events without knowing how they seemed to those who saw them; that letters deceive as much as memoirs or chronicles; that rulers of men, not uncommonly, are rogues, provided with a set of false bottoms as a precaution against curious impertinence.

Ranke was at once acknowledged by Niebuhr as the first of historians, but he did not storm the position. At the university he was outshone by Gans, the mouthpiece of Hegel, and afterwards by Droysen, the mouthpiece of Imperialism. Böhmer, who so much disliked Berlin exports that he could read neither Duncker nor the *Life of Stein,* delighted to quote the description given by satirical students of Ranke lecturing, with his jerky manner, his chin pointing upwards, his fingers catching the air. There was a conspiracy in high quarters to raise up a rival to him in the person of Raumer, whom even Jaffé at first pronounced perfection; whilst Humboldt declared in favour of the Dryasdust grotesquely treated by Carlyle, and abetted the sneers of Varnhagen. Leo used to call Ranke a vase-painter, and denied that truth is hidden in the correspondence of envoys. Gervinus preferred Schlosser; and Droysen, his only rival in influence, derided his flexibility and kinship with the variable romantics. Eichhorn deplored that there was so little to learn from his *Reformation;* Wuttke published a tract against the *Servian History,* and Ritter against his ways generally. Rehm, dimly remembered by the light that shone from his Arabic studies on the Middle Ages, considered his books unfit for a place in the library of Marburg University. Sybel thought him too lenient to Austria; and Reimann accuses him of partiality in the affairs of Poland. Whilst a Prussian conservative complained that he was neither fish nor flesh, a liberal Saxon declared that he was too good a legitimist to master the problems of parliamentary states. His *Memoirs of Hardenberg* have not satisfied critics who knew the inside of the Berlin archives. The *English History* was received with cold but decent respect; and the *Grenzboten* published a hostile article on the first and weakest volume, by Bergenroth, then a new man, unfurnished with a horoscope. It has been a grievance with Villari that Ranke said, and misled Sybel's *Zeitschrift* into repeating, that he had overlooked manuscripts in his own town of Florence, which he, in fact, had cited scores of times. Panizzi objected that one of his books was not original; Green, that another was dull. Macaulay ended by resenting the threatened invasion of his prerogative, and was less favourably disposed than in the glowing days of the purple New Zealander. There was a brief opposition from the Catholics. Höfler attacked the *Popes;* a garbled manuscript of the sixteenth century was sent to press for the diminution of his credit; and Theiner assured the King of Bavaria that he had done less than justice to Gregory XIII. *Grand talent, petit esprit,* was the adverse verdict of the *Correspondant.* The Frenchman might have defended his point if it was a distant allusion to stature. When Lord John Russell was on his way to Vienna, it was reported that Frederic William IV, by a refinement of flattery, invited four eminent men to meet him who were all smaller than himself; and Ranke was one of them.

He outlived all rivalry, and well-nigh all antagonism. He lived to hear Arneth declare, before the assembled historians of the South, that he alone among writers of prose had furnished a masterpiece to every country. He was hailed by Döllinger as *praeceptor Germaniae.* In his own home the dissent of militant patriotism was expressed in the words of Dove, that pure history cannot satisfy the need of a struggling and travailing nation; and when Mommsen says that the only ascertained maxim of research is that hearsay evidence is as good as the source it comes from, I understand him to mean that genius is better than schooling.

In very early days it seemed that philosophy possessed an adept who would surpass Ranke, and bridge the afflicting chasm between fact and law. Leo had belonged to the most turbulent set of students in the time of Sand, when he came to Berlin, obtained the friendship of Hegel, and disparaged Ranke by reviews, and by encroaching on his domain. With other men the question is, how they came to succeed: the wonder in the case of Leo is, how such abilities contrived to miss not only the first place but the first rank. He scorned the tame spirit, the obscure labours, the negative results of fleshless scholars whose cares are bounded by scholarship, who aim at no target, and are incurious of things to come. He was always combative, homiletic, clamorous for quick returns, and, like men too eager, verbose and violent. He shed his Hegelian skin in the Middle Ages, and emerged from them detesting the three last centuries as an epoch of selfishness and decay. History became subservient to politics, to a policy of reaction against economists, humanitarians, and all men seeking happiness before authority. Having written too many books not destined to live, he made up his mind to abandon a hemisphere that was going wrong, and set about reducing his baggage and packing all he knew in a traveller's kit. This was the origin of Leo's *Universal History,* still, after half a century, the most thoughtful of the books that bear that ambitious title. What more he did during the restless remainder of his life for royalism and religious union is written in water. He is the most remarkable of all the men who, being partisans where partiality is discredit, failed through the want of discipline. Gfrörer, who was superior to him and perhaps to all men in historic grasp, is equally destitute of authority. But Gfrörer, though the most reckless and unsafe of guides, is as vigorous a stimulant in mediaeval study as Germany has possessed, and of the fourteen or fifteen volumes which he wrote from Charlemagne to Hildebrand, not one can be spared.

Without the training and habits of the new school even the learning of Neander fared not much better than the talent of Gfrörer and Leo. He was probably the best-read man living towards 1830; and he introduced into the permanent literature of his country a serious spiritual element that was wanting. For the romantic scholars were still incurably tainted with the vice which, outside of morals, bears no harsher name than inaccuracy; while the church historians in possession considered religion with a professional eye and were more secularly minded than professors of profane arts, such as Lachmann or Carl Ritter. He not only tried to bring within reasonable compass and under the control of ideas what used to straggle through forty-five and even eighty-five volumes, but he was profoundly in earnest; and it was of him that Tholuck said that the orthodox are generally the most pious. He had more heart for the interior life of saints than for the border history of Church and State. His knowledge, deep and massive as that of a later Benedictine, was seldom new, and with his traditional habits he was like a ghost in the company of Böckh and Ranke. Among books which he took faithfully as he found them, deeming with Mr. Freeman that manuscripts begin to be useful after they are printed, many were interpolated, incorrect, assigned to the wrong men. Schweighäuser's saying that for centuries no real care had been taken of classical texts was almost equally true of ecclesiastical; and the work of Wolf and Bekker scarcely began for them until Neander was dead. When the *Annals* of Baronius were reprinted, De Rossi reminded the editor that the primitive church presented no longer the same outlines as in 1567, or in the days of Pagi, and offered, unfortunately in vain, his aid as an annotator. Since Neander a deeper spirit of inquiry has possessed itself of his topic and is working changes as considerable as in all the time since Baronius. He spent his last days in a forlorn endeavour to trace the Bohemian revolution to Bohemian causes, telling much that nobody knew about a very obscure time. For, like all men before Shirley, he entirely mistook Wyclif. In our day Lechler and Arnold, Matthews, Buddensieg, and Loserth have published a new Wyclif, and a new pedigree of Hus, and the same transforming effect of the scientific approaches has befallen or yet awaits every chapter of Neander.

The tendency of the nineteenth-century German to subject all things to the government of intelligible law, and to prefer the simplicity of resistless cause to the confused conflict of free wills, the tendency which Savigny defined and the comparative linguists encouraged, was completed in his own way by Hegel. He displayed all history by the light of scientific unity, as the manifestation of a single force, whose works are all wise, and whose latest work is best. The *Volksgeist* of the new jurisprudence was less dazzling than the *Weltgeist* of the new philosophy, with the smallest allowance of hypothesis for the largest quantity of phenomena. Science was propitiated with visions of unity and continuity; religion, by the assurance of incessant progress; politics, by the ratification of the past. Liberty and morality were less well provided; but it was the epoch of the Restoration.

An ambiguous use of terms concealed the breach between pantheism and Christianity so well that the most learned catholic layman of the time rejoiced at the coming of a new era for religion. The breach with experimental science betrayed itself by the contempt for Newton in which Hegel was of one mind with Goethe and Schelling and Schopenhauer; but there were scientific men who, to the disgust of Humboldt, accepted the *Naturphilosophie*. Its defects were visible when Hegel's lectures appeared after his death, and the system went down under the assault of inductive science. But his influence on historical study has not gone down, and it is the one thing on which he retains his grasp. The *lex continui* was a central idea with Leibnitz, who discovered it, for it was the point in common between his anticipation of Darwin and his anticipation of Hegel. In the same double sense it was renewed by Haller, and obtained some superficial acceptance through Herder, until it came to govern entirely the Hegelian notion of history.

Hegel did not shine in expounding public transactions, excepting cases like the French Revolution, where the individual is swallowed up in the logic of events. He moved awkwardly in the presence of human agents, and was unskilled in playing his pawns. The quest of the *vera causa* failed with men, but it was beyond measure successful, away from the world of sense, in explaining the action and succession of ideas.

The history of philosophy had taken rise before Hegel was born, and was secreted in books not destitute of plodding merit, but unreasonably dead and dull. Under the magic wand systems fell into an appointed and harmonious order: λαμπάδα ἔχοντες διαδώσουσιν ἀλλήλοις. The progress of speculative thought has been made, by less systematic and coercive successors, one of the luminous spots in literature, to the damage and exclusion of more essential things. For the marrow of civilised history is ethical not metaphysical, and the deep underlying cause of action passes through the shape of right and wrong. Hegel did not promote the study of morals, and Germany fell behind the French eclectics, until, in the revolt of the last ten years against utilitarians and materialists, the growth of ethical knowledge has become, for the first time, the supreme object of history.

The main line of the Hegelian succession passed to the divines. It was of the essence of pantheism to transcend national limits and the conditions dear to jurists. Where one considers the British constitution as a plant of Teutonic growth, drawing life from ideas common to all the conquerors of Rome, or traceable to hazy customs on the Elbe, the other accounts it a phase of monarchy, a fragment from a sphere that is above race. In the same way, Hegel regarded Christianity as an episode in a natural process that began before the Christian era, and continued beyond the uttermost boundaries assignable to churches, as one step among many to be taken by mankind. The propositions issuing from this view of religion supply the work of the Tübingen school. They teach that the origin of the Christian faith is in the gradual action of antecedent causes; that it has been substantially true to itself in the formation of dogma, and has accomplished its mission of providing fuel for the flame of a higher philosophy.

On his first acquaintance with Hegel's writings, Strauss ceased to believe, and the motive of his book was to justify his disbelief with arguments derived from the scholarship of the day. But the soil that reared him was philosophic not historic. His reason for rejecting the gospel was metaphysical, though his argument was historical. The newest discovery was that certainty may be attained behind the back of historians, after finding whence they get their facts and with what mind they state them. Strauss renounced the attempt, and denied the possibility.

But the critical phase, if it did not prompt the *Leben Jesu,* contributed to its success by encumbering the business of reply. In those days the Nepaul transcripts were bewildering Europe with the spectacle of a lasting and widely spread religion sprung from an obscure and legendary, if not a mythical origin. Stapfer, the Swiss apologist, levying an argument from the lake and the fell, likened Strauss to the inventor of paradox, who presumed to doubt the story of William Tell, and was confounded by the indignant scholarship of Uri. Just then, that vivacious ghost was for ever laid by the reverent hand of a zealous conservative, ultramontane, and patriot, who exposed the fable and restored the real history of Swiss independence in a manner which showed that the lessons of Bonn and Berlin had penetrated to the forest cantons. A greater man than Stapfer objected to Strauss that the first century of the Church was too enlightened for mythology; but the study of the New Testament apocrypha, still in its infancy, showed that the apostolic age was rich in poetic and theological fiction.

The credulity of the last generation was put to a severe strain. The clearances went on at a pace that drove people to despair, and it appeared that the crop of falsehood grew too fast for the reapers. One is tempted to suppose that the conspicuous fabrications like those of Shapira, of Simonides, of the deft deceiver of Chasles, are exceptional. It is a new revelation to learn that a crust of designing fiction covers the truth in every region of European history. The most curious of the twenty-two thousand letters in the correspondence of Napoleon, that of 28th March 1808, on his Spanish policy, by which Thiers was taken in, proves to be a forgery, and the forger is Napoleon. Whole volumes of spurious letters of Joseph II, Marie Antoinette, and Ganganelli are still circulated. Prince Eugene should be well known to us through his autobiography, the collection of six hundred of his letters, and the *Life* by Kausler. But the letters are forged, the *Life* is founded upon them, and the autobiography is by the Prince de Ligne. The letter from the Pruth, which deceived the ablest of the historians of Peter the Great, is as fabulous as his political testament. So too are the *Monita Secreta*, the Life of the Almirante by his son, one of the trials of Savonarola, Daru's acts of the Venetian inquisitors, the most famous of the early Italian chronicles, the most famous of the early privileges and charters of almost every European country. The ancient monuments of Bohemian literature, edited in 1840 by the two best scholars of the Slavonic world, were a very recent imposture; and Saint Cyril, the apostle of the Slavonians, is credited with an account of his own life, a confession of faith, and an introduction to the gospels, none of which are authentic. At his first step in epigraphic science, Mommsen rejected one thousand and three Neapolitan inscriptions.

In the fervour of detection men were tempted to conclude with Goethe that poetry is the only form of truth, and that all history might with advantage go the way of Raleigh's book. The doctrine of the hopeless uncertainty of human testimony recommended the study of ideas instead of events, for we can follow the ideas of Abelard or Descartes under their own undisputed hand, with less risk than the secret councils of kings. A disposition to run riot, not only to doubt where doubt means safety, but to reject where there is only ground for doubting, appeared in several directions: the *Laws* and the *Parmenides* were written by the second Plato; many of the *Odes* were not composed by Horace; and Saint Patrick became an imaginary personage.

This excess prevailed in Germany less widely than is supposed. The restoring purpose, the craving for positive results, grew strong amid the devastation; exaggerated doubt was succeeded by activity in preserving, and the fictions unduly spared outnumber the truths unduly questioned. Methodical doubt had no affinity with a universal scepticism. Niebuhr, unlike Sir George Lewis, who represents him to us, passionately believed in the resources of his art, accepted the discoveries of Champollion when many hesitated, and looked forward to like results in Assyria, six years before Lassen appeared. Wolf wished his treatment of Homer to be applied to the Bible, but he stopped far short of the hypothesis of Graf. In spite of his weighty advocacy, Markland's attack on the *Epistles to Brutus* and the *Four Orations* did not prevail. Many things which the French reject are accepted by Germans who uphold Buddha against the solar interpretation of Senart, the Pragmatic Sanction of Saint Lewis against the doubts of Paul Viollet, the tables of Malaga and Salpensa against objections which Laboulaye would not abandon until the close of his life. There is a state paper on the Juliers succession in 1609 which was admitted by Ranke, Droysen, Treitschke, and never disputed until it went to pieces in 1883. Not very many years ago a monument was erected at Pforzheim by the Baden legislature in commemoration of an event that never occurred; and the purchase of the Moabite antiquities in 1873, advised by Schlottmann in spite of Ganneau's warning, exhibits the softer side of Prussian criticism and economy. The eagerness of juniors in urging every element of improbability has been rebuked by the master, Waitz; and Giesebrecht, the only critical historian of the Middle Ages who is a popular classic, who occupies a moderating position between extremes, is peculiarly cautious against the solicitations of doubt. His rare mistakes have come from conservative leanings, and he has rescued letters of Sylvester II denounced by his French editor, has reinstated Lambert as a main authority for Gregory VII against a host of detractors, and has maintained in the midst of much opposition the *Dictatus* of the pope himself. The severest repressor of overmuch doubting is Sickel, the prince of critics, who has been able to demonstrate that the skill of the forgers is less than was imagined, and that many pieces suspected thirty years ago were suspected wrongly. In earlier stages of the progress of knowledge the proper attitude is suspense, and when Maurenbrecher failed to establish the authenticity of Charles V's *Commentaries*, he rightly laid them aside until Ranke satisfied him.

While open questions of criticism diminish, new documents raise new problems, and nobody gets the last word. Much has come lately to light touching the partition of Poland. Who proposed it? The answer is continually shifting, and the truth goes farther off. It was Catharine or Prince Henry in 1771, Bibikoff at Christmas 1770, Joseph II in July, Wolkonsky in March. It was Count Lynar in 1769, or a mightier personage wearing his mask. Or it was Kaunitz in 1768, if not Choiseul in the same year. Panin started the idea in 1766, Czernitcheff or the electress of Saxony in 1763, Lord Stair in 1742, the King of Poland himself in 1732, or the crown prince of Prussia one year earlier. There is the same difficulty as to the man who shattered the empire of Napoleon by advising the retreat to Moscow. The idea is claimed for Alexander and Count Lieven, for five German officers at least, for the lesson of Torres Vedras, for Barclay, by whom it was executed. Or again, who was it that induced the allies, in March 1814, to advance on Paris? For that there are five competitors, a Russian, a Livonian, an Austrian, a Prussian, and a Corsican. Where we now stand, in the year 60 of renovated history, it does not seem impossible to settle some of these matters. But things were less clear during the procession of rival witnesses; and this is one of the elements which made the science of historians seem a solace for the imagination, a gallery of dissolving views, a museum of illusions in which a man of strong convictions was free to take or to leave. It was under this empire of instability that a group of Wirtemberg divines obtained the lead in critical research and kept it for twenty years.

A theologian who trod the paths of Hegel had lately introduced the study and the name of symbolism. Men who were not passionately addicted to the solutions of the sixteenth century were the better for knowing, as a matter of fact, without ulterior purpose, what it was all about, and why Erasmus, Luther, Calvin, and Socinus differed. Marheineke explained it to readers more curious of historic than dogmatic truth, who could enter heartily into every system not their own. Peace had been concluded between Lutheran and Calvinist, and a suspension of hostilities between Catholic and Protestant; and it was the time when a Protestant publisher circulated Stolberg's *Church History,* and Schlegel wrote to him: "Let us shake hands like Christians across the narrow stream between us." The first object of the new science was to explain the division of Christendom, not to justify, and not to heal it. The usefulness of this necessary chapter of history depended on the fidelity of the writer in refusing favour to his own side; and when Möhler took care, like Johnson, that the Whigs should have the worst of it, Marheineke called his book a treatise of controversy under the name of symbolism. The absence of the purely historical spirit gave Möhler his six editions and his immediate celebrity. Men came after him who restored the former tone, indifferent to peace or war. Koellner, being a Protestant, wrote an exposition of Catholicism, and, being a Calvinist, an exposition of Lutheranism, on the plan of describing them from within; but the public interest languished. The steps that had led up to the religious crisis of the present century were of more vital significance than the distant and inelastic formulas of the sixteenth. History, which already occupied other domains, was laying its hand on theology, and history is the knowledge of things that live and move. The process attracted more than the definition. Comparative dogmatics took the place which had been filled by the narrower treatment, and the history of Protestant theology was discussed in a series of books by Dorner and Gass in Germany, and by Schweizer and Schneckenburger in Switzerland, that carry matters a good deal beyond the point reached when the conflict raged round the *Symbolik*.

While the Protestants were interested in tracing dogmas down to their own day, it was the object of the Catholics to trace them upwards to the seed-time of the Church, in order that what was imputed to them as genuine might be tested by time. The generation of 1830, which in a variety of converging ways assigned the property of growth undetermined by will or wit of man, of development without forfeiture of identity, to the civil law, the academic philosophy, and the Aryan grammar, was not tempted to deny an analogous prerogative to Christianity. The principle had already found a home in the Church, and received new vigour from the mental revolution effected by the anti-revolutionary Germans. When Möhler, moved by the asperities of controversy, left Tübingen to teach ecclesiastical history at Munich, Döllinger made way for him and lectured on divinity. He directed his own historical method on theological system, and exhibited the faith of Christendom at successive stages, so that a man should stand at all the crossways, realise each problem as seen at its rising, and pass in his own mind through the experience of the Church.

The men who, at Munich, were working out the law of development within their communion, lived in acute and unappreciating hostility to the Suabian divine who was digging a theological bed for the teaching of the Suabian philosopher. The real importer of pantheism with its consequences into history, the man who grafted Hegel on Ranke, was Strauss's master, Baur, the colleague whose sarcasms drove Möhler from Tübingen. He was a convert from Creuzer's nebulous method, which looks for analogy and resemblance, and he adopted with uncommon energy the view which denies the supernatural, suspects marvels and coincidences, and adjusts spiritual life to the prosaic level of daily experience. Baur would give no opinion on the *Leben Jesu* until that which had been for ten years the law of profane history was thoroughly applied to sacred. He undertook the work and accomplished it himself, with the aid of those whom he called the critical school, implying that all others are uncritical, and, if they admit dogmatic motives, insincere. His postulates were that the gospels must be examined as profane books are, without presumption of truth, and that space must be given for Christianity to evolve itself from the combination of exceedingly dissimilar elements. According to Baur the business of history is not so much with facts as with ideas; and the idea, not the fact, of the Resurrection is the basis of the Christian faith. Doctrines are developed out of notions, not out of events. Whether or no the belief is true, he refuses to inquire. In the most characteristic passage ever written by a German historian, he declares that it is a question beyond the scope of history.

The view of the New Testament which the critics of Tübingen built up with an expenditure of intellectual force greater than Strauss had applied to demolition, was too deeply influenced by the specific negations of pantheism to live apart from their esoteric tenets. What was speculative in their system not only isolated them from the bulk of European science, but brought about divisions, and at last the dispersion of the school. Wherever their purpose was exclusively historical, they threw much light on matters which have been discussed for centuries; and their sagacity in the investigation of details has been fruitful for all men.

Their permanent action is less acknowledged in the foundation than in the development of Christianity. Baur's mastery in tracing the march of ideas through the ages, over the heads of men, was a thing new to literature. He maintained that the formation and growth of doctrine is consistent and normal, not accidental or arbitrary; and the impression made by his histories of the central dogmas appeared in many directions. Nearly half the books that have been written on dogmatic history came out in a space of six or seven years, under his impulse, and were often the work of men far from sharing his opinions. The inner circle of Lutheran orthodoxy has adopted from Tübingen the term—the Formation of truth (*das Werden der Wahrheit*), a notion which would have astonished Luther.

Baur's bitterest adversary was Ewald, whose competence in Old Testament studies was not then contested. But it is the last and most original of his disciples, a man better known amongst us than most German writers, who has set in motion that Mosaic controversy which has so much analogy with the views of Tübingen. From the days when he mingled imprecations against Gesenius with his prayers until he denounced the *Culturkampf,* Ewald had been steeped in dissent, and his fame had suffered diminution before the treason of Wellhausen.

The low political vitality of the Thirty Years' Peace was favourable to calm studies. It was the time when Goethe was amazed that any sane person should think the revolution of July a topic of interest, and when William Humboldt, the most central figure in Germany, the confidant of Schiller and Goethe, of Wolf and Niebuhr, who had fought Talleyrand at Vienna on the memorable day on which legitimacy was born, who had forged the link between science and force by organising a university at Berlin, and who, until the murder of Kotzebue, had been the pride and the hope of intelligent Prussia, devoted the maturity of his powers to Malay roots. Those were the days in which the familiar type of the German scholar was generated, of the man who complained that the public library allowed him only thirteen hours a day to read, the man who spent thirty years on one volume, the man who wrote upon Homer in 1806 and who still wrote upon Homer in 1870, the man who discovered the 358 passages in which Dictys has imitated Sallust, the man who carried an electric telegraph from his house to the church and carried it no farther.

Primarily, he was a Greek scholar, bounded by ancient horizons, and his mind was not seldom shaped by some favourite classic, as were Böckh by Plato, Creuzer by Plotinus, Trendelenburg by Aristotle, and Roscher by Thucydides. More rarely he carried the dry powder of philology into the early Christian conflicts, or the chaos of the first, the Teutonic, Middle Ages. On the modern world, with its unsettled and unsettling questions, and its inaccessible information, he sternly turned his back. He loved to settle on a space he could hope to exhaust by giving his life to it, unmindful of Godfrey Hermann and his dictum: "Est quaedam etiam nesciendi ars et scientia." Like Hegel, who comfortably finished his book at Jena during the battle, and, starting for the publisher's in the morning, was surprised to observe that the streets were full of Frenchmen, he did not allow the voices of the striving world to distract him. Often he had risen, by mere energy and conduct, from crushing poverty, had gone barefoot to school, or had begged his way like Hase across the Fatherland; and he remained frugal and austere, cultivating humble obscurity and the golden gift of silence, and marrying, as Feuerbach did, upon an income of forty pounds. With that genius for taking trouble which Ritschl called the way to everything, he was not sensitive to genius of any other sort. The extreme subdivision of labour narrowed his view, and gave an unusual scope and value to diligent mediocrity. Dull men built themselves an everlasting name at which we wonder as we wonder at the glory of Grant; and the excessive talent of Stahl and Lassalle was suspected, as a Jewish glitter, wanting substance. Walter, standing still on the old ground of Niebuhr, scoffed at that marvel of ability, the *Geist des römischen Rechts;* and W. Sickel's *Verfassungsgeschichte,* the most brilliant account of early institutions ever written, is scorned by the accepted teachers. "Too clever to make a good administrator" is a judgment of Napoleon's; and Metternich invokes the international epigram, "L'esprit sert à tout et ne mène à rien."

The scholar of the old school was an open adversary and a candid friend. Aristotelian Brandis, who was remarkable for social amenity, writes of his early fellowship with Bunsen that they disputed "without effeminate sensibility" (*ohne wehleidige Schonung*); and the Breslau students were gratified with the sight of Passow in the *Professorencarcer* for insulting Menzel. Thiers said to Senior: "I may call my opponent a villain, though I know him to be honest." Not so in Saxony, where the courts have decided that it is lawful to call a book foolish, but not to call the author a fool.

The leaders of the movement that sprang up in the second quarter of the century were animated by the conviction that the genius and learning of the modern world went to work the wrong way, and missed its aim, not from incapacity, but from interest, influence, and prejudice. It was their belief that literature had long been an arduous and comprehensive conspiracy against truth, and that much envenomed controversy could be set at rest by exposing the manifold arts that veil substantial falsehood—suppression, distortion, interpolation, forgery, legend, myth. The Germans came late upon the scene, and did not claim to be better than those who went before them; but they would begin their work over again—"expurgata jam et abrasa et aequata mentis area"—warned by example to escape the sources of error. By extreme patience and self-control, by seeking neither premature result nor personal reward, by sacrificing the present to the far-off future, by the obscure heroism of many devoted lives, they looked to prepare the foundation of the kingdom of knowledge. "Plurimi transibunt et multiplex erit scientia." They trained themselves to resist the temptations by which others had suffered, and stood to win by moral qualities. There was so much rough material to hew, so much time to recover, that they renounced making points and drawing conclusions. The politic Briton, with a practical object in view, avoids needless provocation to dissent; and the studious German tried to exclude contentious matter, and to adjust theory to fact, on the maxim; "On s'arrange plus facilement sur un fait que sur un principe."

Their literary dogma, that truth is worth living for, and honesty, in fact, is the best policy, yields to nobody now the fresh emotion of discovery. Lanfrey writes that the only patriotism of historians is sincerity; and the best of the French reviews has said the same thing in its prospectus. "Nous ne prétendons servir qu'une cause, celle de la science—Le livre seul est l'objet de la critique; l'auteur pour elle n'existe pas." A clever fellow assured Lasker that he lied no more, having observed that it is less profitable than it used to be, and that truth, on the whole, answers better. Half a century ago, when every member of an election committee was understood to vote with his party, when a cry of derision went up at the hyperbole that property has duties as well as rights, when one prime minister considered that rich men ought to know how poor men vote, and another said, "On ne trompe personne quand on trompe tout le monde," such principles were not yet trivial, and were enjoying the short span which Schopenhauer assigns to truth, between the paradox of yesterday and the commonplace of to-morrow.

Late in his life Thiers said of Napoleon, "Il faut convenir que c'était un scélérat et un fou." He had concealed his opinion in twenty volumes. Guizot having discovered certain scandal about a queen (who was not Queen Elizabeth), by the advice of the Duchess de Broglie suppressed it. Quite lately, the president of a great assembly avowed that impartiality is a merit only in presidents. When Tocqueville spent a lifetime in declaring the advent and the natural history of democracy, without betraying the intensity of his fears, and kept his religious opinions so well out of sight that the suppression of one or two letters has been enough to conceal them altogether; or when the Bishop of Chester[3] mentions, with becoming pride, that a man may read his

---

[3] Dr. Stubbs.

books and take him for a radical, they illustrate a phase of literary character which was specially developed by the Germans in the studious and pacific days before 1848. And Mr. Freeman's proposition, that historic criticism and historic fairness are hardly possible when a man writes simply as a partisan of the Papacy, would be accepted by them without the implied restriction. By what secret channels error filters into the mind, most people have read in Bacon, and may read much better in Spencer. The ideal historian adumbrated by Rothe, Kampschulte, Roscher, Dümmler, Löning, Gierke, Gass, is a man armed at all these points, and the discipline that makes him opens further visions of penetrating ethics, not obvious on the beaten track.

Among the historians of that epoch the most eminent, though he never wrote a page of history, was Böhmer, the librarian of Frankfort. Dumas's enthusiasm for the author of the *Girondins* broke out in the words: "Il a élevé l'histoire à la hauteur du roman"; and of Böhmer it can be said that he raised drudgery to the rank of a fine art. For the centuries to which he confined himself, from the eighth to the fourteenth, he made it a precept that truth dwells in documents, and not in chronicles or lives. The author of a grant or a state paper knows what he is doing; the author of a book does not. In one case history is told by those who make it; in the other, by those who hear of it from other people. The chronicle is a mixture of memory, imagination, and design. The charter is reality itself. When Thierry was overworked, he refreshed his mind with the glossary of Ducange; and there is no better reading in German than the prefaces of Böhmer, and his *Regesta* as completed by the Innsbruck professors. He makes all mediaeval literature subsidiary to the charters, and relieves his terse and telling abstract with illustrations from the historians as well as with points of his own. As the citizen of a republic, whose mental life was spent among the records of mediaeval empire, as a Protestant who sought the society of Catholics, he had the advantage of a central and independent position. But his warmest sympathies were with the institutions which had vanished in his lifetime, with the church whose tenets he rejected, and he delivered his sentiments with a petulance and malice which no other reputation could have withstood. Waitz, and the northern scholars whose modes of thought he flouted, voted him a prize, as the foremost historian of the day; and Ficker, who has carried forward his work with better training and at least equal solidity, devised a theory for his benefit, which maintains that prejudice is consistent with veracity. Like Stälin, who had his *Wirtembergische Geschichte*, the best of provincial histories, corrected by a priest, Böhmer gravitated towards the Catholic south, and was the chief of a scattered party of Guelphic scholars which has not survived. When he died, in 1863, the romantic school to which he had imparted the dignity of exact learning went below the horizon.

The chief promoter of mediaeval studies was the modern Ranke. He had been famous for ten years before his influence was established, for the strongest men who came up were carried away by Hegel. In 1834, when the lieutenants were dividing the empire, Ranke set the reign of Henry I, the imaginary Fowler, as a subject for an essay. Giesebrecht and Köpke competed, and were defeated by Waitz, who has just revised the third edition of his biography, fifty years after it gained the prize. This was the foundation of what has been for so long incomparably the first school of history in the world, not for ideas or eloquence, but for solid and methodical work. Ranke discouraged men from approaching the passionate discussions and buried materials which were his own domain, and directed them to the times before the thirteenth century, the sources of which occupy a limited compass, and were just then in process of being threshed out for Pertz. It was a time that could be studied in the same cool temper as the weights and measures of Babylon, and had some analogy with the things taught by Böckh. But no philologist had Ranke's mastery of the detective arts. Even Drumann, when he came to Boniface VIII, proved ignorant of technical rules, while, on the other hand, the canons which Nitzsch and Nissen applied to Rome were formed in the mediaeval school. It supplied the best editors of the *Monumenta,* eclipsing Pertz and his legal coadjutors, beat up all the libraries of Europe, and gradually obtained the control of the historical reviews. The Annals of the mediaeval empire are the most perfect achievement of these men. They were slow to quit the libraries for the archives; but a younger generation, working at Munich on the sixteenth and seventeenth centuries, and laying half of Europe under contribution, has solved the harder problem of making state papers the backbone of modern history.

The weak place was the nineteenth century until the revolution of 1848 compelled attention to the problems of the day. Droysen had already proposed a series of books on recent times, to be laid down on the lines of Dahlmann, which should fuse past and present, and treat politics and history as one. In connection with this plan, which was not carried out, Häusser produced the first serious work on the fall and the rise of Germany, between the death of Frederic and the overthrow of Napoleon, a work which hardly justifies the considerable influence which the author exercised without his pen, but which marks a new era as a plea for Prussia from a southern and avowedly liberal hand.

The next Heidelberg writer prophesied a democratic, not a Prussian future. Gervinus personates the average German, the average middle-class German from the smaller towns of the smaller States, crowded with indisputable information, sceptical and doctrinaire, more robust than elastic or alert, instructive but not persuasive, with a taste for broad paths and the judicious forcing of open locks. He began his *History of the Nineteenth Century* at the lowest ebb of national sentiment, and he left it, a fragment in eight volumes, when reviving nationality discarded his dogmas. Schlosser, the master in whom he persistently believed, confessed that the world moved away and left him superfluous and obsolete. The same experience darkened the last days of Gervinus, who thought that Cavour must fail, that Bismarck was a new Polignac, who kept his place among the vanquished of 1866, and died disowning the results of 1870. He had been a power in the land before 1848, when he applied the reigning theory to literature, and exhibited every writer limited and bound to fixed surroundings, and every poem a barometer. He rescued the realm of imagination from the wild will of poets and the incalculable sceptre, and brought a new region under scientific cultivation. Julian Schmidt and other vigorous men have enlarged his notions. The better part of the nation's mind works in pursuit of truth, and its thought, its knowledge, its errors, constitute the object of literary history as well as those things which may be lawfully told in verse. The flowery empire of aesthetics did not flourish under this amalgamation as it had done in less practical days. The best work is a history of Italian literature; but of the greatest living critics—Haym, Bernays, and Scherer—not one is great alike in the tracing of ideas, in perfect knowledge of biographical and bibliograph-ical fact, and in taste.

Gervinus and Sybel exhibit the contrast between north and south, and between the time before and after 1848. Sybel had learnt to make war on confusion and fiction in the strict mediaeval school; but his mind was essentially modern, his interest lay in practical directions, and he opened the way to the later, inexhaustible, and almost unattempted centuries. He studies the Revolution in the light of a vast disturbance of the permanent policy of cabinets, without mercy on its picturesque and passionate element. The Reformation was in fact a blow struck at reforming Catholicism, more than at the supine advocacy of things as they were; and this historian, without unction or sympathy, deplores the Revolution as a catastrophe that threw back intelligent progress for half a century. He began these studies forty years ago with two essays on Burke, whose letter to Mercer embodies much of his philosophy. Both in his history and in his review, Sybel adopts the dogmatic terms of Burke and Savigny; but he is never lost in theory. Although his introductory chapter anticipated the *Ancien Régime* with no better help than Tocqueville's article in the *Westminster Review,* the depth and soundness of his work was not perceived until his gradual discoveries in many archives awakened controversy and provoked a flood of answering matter.

The year 1848, which sent more than one hundred professors to Frankfort, had been detrimental to the British and Baconian maxim, that knowledge is power. In Sybel they were united; for he was learned in the wisdom of universities, and eminently conversant with the working of political forces; a man of life and action, an expert such as had not been seen. He became the first classic of imperialism, and helped to form that garrison of distinguished historians that prepared the Prussian supremacy together with their own, and now hold Berlin like a fortress. If any one will make a list of their names, he will see that such a phalanx was never arrayed before, and will also detect one of the *arcana imperii,* by which the rude strength centred in a region more ungenial than Latium was employed to absorb and to stiffen the diffused, sentimental, and strangely impolitic talent of the studious Germans.

Things were different heretofore, when history, not yet woven into the web of national greatness, was carried on by private enterprise. Men living in a small way, with a dim political background, were not often practical, but were generally disinterested. Göttingen, Tübingen, and Heidelberg had some advantages for historical teaching over Berlin, where "William Tell" was a forbidden play. Among their leisurely professors were men who found, like Dahlmann, that the great Frederic stuck in their throats; like Gervinus and Ewald, who repudiated Dahlmann's precept, that what their country wanted was force before freedom. The disconcerting verdict of events ruined their credit as readers of the signs of the times. Apart from the convenient popularity of the maxim, "Die Weltgeschichte ist das Weltgericht," it was apparent that the past had not revealed to them its inmost secret, and they were disparaged, as investigators of irreclaimable dry bones. The men who took betimes the side of the big battalions, showed superior penetration into the things beneath the sun. They brought history into touch with the nation's life, and gave it an influence it had never possessed out of France; and they won for themselves the making of opinions, mightier than laws. The most clear-sighted of those who resolved, after the failure of the Revolution, that the future of Germany belonged to Prussia, was Droysen.

Ten years before the fire-and-sword despatch revealed Count Ferro, while intelligent adherents of Greater Germany argued that without Austria there could be nothing but a magnified Prussia, Droysen affirmed that unity could never come from liberty and the vote of parliaments, that it required a power strong enough to crush resistance at home and abroad. The rest of his life was devoted to Prussian politics and the imperial arts; and he was one of that central band of writers and statesmen and soldiers who turned the tide that had run for six hundred years, and conquered the centrifugal forces that had reigned in Germany longer than the commons have sat at Westminster. He had learnt classical scholarship in the school of Böckh, and had acquired from Hegel the habit of abstract thought and that preference for the Hellenic empire which is adversely noted in the *History of Federal Government*. In spite of his Macedonian proclivity, his earliest pupil testifies that he was always a liberal, meaning a promoter of secondary liberties. Whatever element of the kind was in him, was fostered by his residence at Kiel, in a land flowing with political excitement, the early home of gratuitous education. To sustain the faith and the practice of patriotism, he published his lectures on the time between the Stamp Act and Waterloo, a book full of views and turbid cleverness. He passed on to his own domain with the biography of the grim warrior whose defection prepared the ruin of Napoleon, and whose son fell in the last action of the revolutionary war, refusing quarter, and exclaiming that his name was Yorck. The long *History of Prussian Policy* followed, and brought popularity and power. Being asked by what subtle charm he and the intimate advisers had changed the plain soldier of the last generation into the mightiest of conquerors, Droysen replied that it was nothing but the stern sense of duty (*die verfluchte*

Schuldigkeit). He made this the note of Hohenzollern history. Their success lay in diplomacy and war, and the narrative is international, not domestic. The affairs of Europe from the Great Elector to the eve of the Seven Years' War have never been told with so large a knowledge of politics; and the later volumes are more effective than the parallel work of his illustrious rival. Ranke, who discards the teleological argument of history, whose feelings are so well under control that he dilates on the disasters of 1806 more than on the triumphs of 1757, had neither his popular fibre nor his official sanction. Fastidious readers doubt at last the swiftness of Achilles and the piety of Aeneas; but to those who do not require conviction, the sagacious advocate of Prussian monarchy is as persuasive as the avowed defenders of other causes, of parliamentary government or federal democracy.

The one writer of history who is more brilliant and powerful than Droysen is Treitschke. Droysen's grasp of his materials began to relax when he came to Frederic; but Treitschke never flags, and is always vehement, certain, and overwhelming. As a political essayist, long ago he broke the spell of superiority which, until the death of Stahl, belonged to the religious and the strict conservative world. He was predestined for Berlin by his first conspicuous act; for he had attacked, and it was thought had refuted, the notion of a separate science of society, as the sphere of religion, morality, economy, and knowledge, as a vast community, organically distinct from the State, and able to control it. The idea, which comes from Harrington, and was pronounced by John Adams the greatest discovery in politics, had been made by Lorenz von Stein the key to the Revolution, in a work exposing the economic cause of political science, with Hegelian formalities which contrast unhappily with Treitschke's gleaming style. For he writes, with the force and the fire of Mommsen, of a time remembered by living men, and pregnant with the problems that are still open. He marshals his forces on a broader front than any other man, and accounts for the motives that stir the nation, as well as for the councils that govern it.

Treitschke's *History of Germany* belongs to a series that has made up for the long delay in approaching the present century, in which England, from the regency to Victoria, was allotted to Pauli. Reluctance to compete with Ranke had led him to abandon his former work, and in the stronger currents of his own country he drifted from his English moorings. In the last year of his life he was thinking of a compendium embracing his thirty years' study of every part of the history of England in one or two volumes. His book on the nineteenth century suffers by comparison with the powerful mixture prepared by Mr. Cory for the patient Asiatic, and is not equal to the Spanish or Russian histories in the same collection.

Bernhardi's *Russia* carries us from the unrealities of scholastic history, from the complacency of satisfied philosophers and the adoration of *Bonus Eventus,* to the most penetrating and relentless censure of the thoughts and deeds of men. The author combines what was never combined before by a writer of history, long and intimate initiation in secrets of state, with military science and the knowledge of an original and profound economist. He represses the inclination to think that what is explained is excused, that all ideas are reasonable and all events opportune, and gives a prominence, suggesting early contact with the dissatisfied Heidelbergers, to the imponderable and unaccountable elements of human weakness and folly. His principal work is oddly diversified with episodes on the British constitution and on Adam Smith, besides a slight sketch of universal history; and it is time that his account of 1815, composed without the papers of Talleyrand and Metternich for the congress, or of Gneisenau and Grouchy for the campaign, should be rewritten. Bernhardi is the ablest of the German writers on Napoleon. The affinity that may be discovered between the first consul in the plenitude of his own ideas, before the peace of Amiens, and much that is peculiarly Prussian, does not disarm this admirer of Frederic and friend of Moltke, and he dispels even the illusion of the war in Champagne. He also gives literary expression to the judgment of the Prussian staff on Wellington. At Vienna the duke departed from the policy of Castlereagh, joined Talleyrand in pleading the Saxon cause, and assured Metternich that Prussia was likely to become the most dangerous Power in Europe. Talleyrand recorded the scene twenty years later with satisfaction tempered with surprise at so gross a mistake. This was the feeling which Wellington took with him to Belgium; and Gneisenau informed the officer sent to attend him that he was an excellent commander, but as false as the wiliest Hindoo. From that day until his administration in 1830, it was a standing maxim at the Berlin foreign office that the duke might always be counted upon to desert a friend.

Probably there is no considerable group less in harmony with our sentiments in approaching the study of history than that which is mainly represented by Sybel, Droysen, and Treitschke, with Mommsen and Gneist, Bernhardi and Duncker on the flank. Up to this moment it is the best found and the most energetic of all; and as there is no symptom of declining favour and authority, it is important to understand along what lines of reasoning men so eminent, so quick to inquire into every new thing, have adhered to maxims which it has cost the world much effort to reverse. The theory of the political historian is distinct from the plea of the partisan. The historian displays the laws governing human life: it is not his duty to expound a private view, or to explain, like the wise Castilian, how much better the universe would be contrived if he had been consulted in time. He attends to the ship's course, not to the passengers. The forces to be reckoned are those which, in the long-run, prevail. The historian justifies only that which is just by the judgment of experience. It is the heresy of history to choose a side that seems good in our eyes, to reject the appointed course and the dominion of law, in order to degrade the life of nations under the anarchy of casual and disconnected causes. Consistency in the powers that direct the world is the supreme acquisition of all German thought. It is not partiality, but renunciation of party feeling and personal preference, to hold that the world works well, that what lives permanently in the light and strife of civilisation lives rightfully, that whatever perishes has earned its fate. Wyclif revived a very ancient saying when he wrote: "Ponat talis fidelis spem et causam suam in adiutorio altissimi, et non est compossibile quod vel persona vel causa pereat." It is the philosophy of Emerson proclaiming "the skill with which the great All maketh clean work as it goes along, leaves no rag, consumes its smoke." And does not a living classic write: "Somehow or other it is always the Eternal's wisdom which at last carries the day"?

There is no escape from the dogma that history is the conscience of mankind unless for those who reject the collective growth, the canons that rivet the future to the past, and take their stand aloof with Archimedes. All the successions of thought during three generations constitute the shaft whose shining point is made by the Berlin interpreters of enlightened and triumphant Germany. They are the legitimate dynasty, reigning by right as well as by force, inheritors of the line that comes down from Burke to the last stage of evolution and selection, who have set up the reign of imperishable moral forces for an intermittent Providence, the play of passion, and the blind will of man. Their doctrine proceeds as logically from the scientific as from the political experience of the country. And it is held, practically, even by men who do not stand with both feet within the charmed ring that binds history to politics; by Mommsen, when he scouts the idea of explaining Roman conquests by Roman perfidy; by Waitz, when he said that a censor of the Reformation had no right to pit himself against his nation; by Kurtz, who establishes a presumption in favour of the Church against the sects because the sects came to unspeakable grief, and in favour of the Reformation against Rome because the reformers were successful.

To be without party is to be without principle, according to that saying of an English statesman, that a man who denies party belongs to a party he is ashamed of. To be impartial is to follow a very wide induction, to acknowledge the manifest destiny of monarchy, with a mind prepared, if it must be, to follow "the tramp of democracy's earthquake feet."

There is no palliation of inaccuracy; but there are no men more accurate than these, and few more watchful of the springs of error within. Renan has said that hardly any one but Littré could confess a blunder without loss of dignity. If that Napoleonic sentiment prevails in France, it is a point of inferiority to the neighbouring rival. The puerile temptation of consistency, the weak reluctance to contradict what disciples are repeating on their authority, is inevitable among the chiefs of the many schools into which German scholarship is apt to crumble. Stronger still is the assurance that historical science is moving with the vigour and rapidity of a natural law, and that its teachers can no more stand still than chemists or biologists.

Ranke read before the French Institute his retractation of a mistake about the memoirs of Richelieu. Treitschke elaborately corrects an error into which Arndt had led him, an error concerning the disappearance of spoons, which had been exposed with insult. Gervinus used to call the *Philosophie der Griechen* a singular instance of a faultless book; hundreds of improvements in the last edition show that Zeller is himself of a different opinion. When Berghaus said that Humboldt had "invariably fixed" the longitude of Callao, the philosopher required him to strike out the word. There are, he said, no invariable fixtures. Albrecht, the jurist, was a man of one book, and his literary position depended on a treatise concerning a difficult point of early law. In 1858, 1869, and 1872 his conclusions were successively demolished by three different writers. To the first he wrote that the ruin of essential portions of his structure did not in the least interfere with his satisfaction. The next time he said that he did not mind even if it was to be the death-blow of his book. At last he admitted his defeat, and added that he had long expected it. So pleasant a temper has not been granted to every German. When Reinhold said that a philosopher should bear in mind that he may err and be ready to learn from others, Fichte told him that he spoke like a man who had never been convinced in his life.

The last twenty years have made the Germans careful in the economy of force, and they waste less powder in salutes. Their soldiers were on the Loire when they began to say that their scholars were to be no more the humble servants of the foreigner. Nothing, said Mommsen, is so hollow as the pretence of humility. "We are not modest by any means, and do not wish it to be thought of us." The *National-Zeitung* confessed that its countrymen, though not envious, are slow to acknowledge merit, and added that hundreds of Germans remain unknown, who in France would lead science and society. Würtz's exaltation of Lavoisier, and Schérer's highly discriminating estimate of Goethe, were received with indignation; and Rümelin's able but unceremonious book is one among many signs of rising impatience at the old enthusiasm for Shakespeare.

As early as 1849, Prince Albert said to Brunsen that self-sufficiency was the German rock ahead. The historians generally escaped this peril and welcomed every proof of superiority. During many years Pauli regularly introduced the Rolls publications which were undermining the work of his life, and admitted that there were points on which the *History of the Norman Conquest* surpasses everything yet written on the Middle Ages. Ewald preferred Selden to all his followers in Syriac. Lehrs declared that he could make nothing of the political life of Greece until he read Grote. The Prolegomena to Tischendorf's last text have, I believe, been committed to an English hand; and Bailleu says that the best lives of the greatest modern Germans, of Frederic, Stein, and Goethe, are those which have been written in England. Rosenkranz thought Damiron superior to the German historians of philosophy; Böhmer rated Delisle's *Philippe Auguste* above every German book of the same kind; and Böckh, irritated just then by the absurdities of Gerlach and the temerities of Mommsen, said that Wallon's *Histoire de l'Esclavage dans l'Antiquité* was better than what his own countrymen were doing in philology. A reviewer of Guerry declares him at least the equal of Roscher in learning; and Roscher places the *Réforme Sociale* of Le Play at the head of books on social science. The best Frenchmen— Rénier, Rougé, Le Blant, Molinier, Riant, A. Rambaud—stood or stand just as well on one side of the Vosges as on the other, although Bekker never forgave Cobet's utterance that Germans were *doctiores quam saniores*. Madvig's supremacy among Latinists was admitted by Halm, in spite of the Danish depreciation of Mommsen. Harnack, writing in the principal theological review, judges that his country possesses no history of early Christianity as good as that of Renan, nothing equal to Hatch on the primitive constitution of the Church, or to the *Introduction to Ecclesiastical History* of a Flemish Jesuit. A less perfect courtier than Bunsen would perhaps have made a better fight.

When the euthanasia of metaphysic anticipated by Carlyle was setting in about 1850, physical science came forward as its rival, and history as its heir. The philosophers themselves turned into historians, and beat their speculations into facts. Their lecture-rooms were empty, and Schelling confessed to a traveller that the end had come: "La pensée allemande est aujourd'hui dans un cul-de-sac, et je ne vois pas qui pourra l'en tirer." Braniss conceived that religion, which had been brought low by the negations of thinkers, would be restored by the affirmations of scholars; and others said that history is the only unassailable revelation. Belief and unbelief both led to the same conclusion: Kuno Fischer opened his great work on modern metaphysics by defining philosophy as the self-knowledge of history; and Schaar-schmidt, on the opposite side, calls philosophy and history one and the same thing. One of the philosophical reviews declared that the history of the systems was a substitute for the systems themselves; and even the laggards of *a priori* science were won by the assurance that the philosophical idea is the substance of all history. The historic mind had always glowed beneath the metaphysical ice cap. Goethe described it as one of his last steps in mental progress to have the unseen past always present; and he had approved the fine piece of idealism, since copied by Renan, in which Humboldt denounced the prosaic improve-ments which would make Rome a place unfitted for the spectres who are its worthiest inhabitants. Gerlach, the leader of the Prussian conservatives, used to say that what he had admired most in England was Mr. Speaker's wig. For when he spoke of it as a time-honoured relic, an historical-minded Englishman told him that it was nothing of the sort, but quite a modern institution, not two centuries old. At Göttingen one day a Protestant was defending the celibacy of the clergy, and saying that without it Catholicism would lose its identity. A Catholic replied: "We were used to married priests so long that it is the law of celibacy which we feel as an innovation."

The scientific era had its own lesson for historians. The world proceeded on its new path with increasing velocity, there was no stopping, and no step backward; and the law of progress, which had been a crude and vague speculation, became a manifest reality. With this new aspect of the life of men and of societies, a conception of history arose of which Du Bois Reymond is the prophet. The future depends on truths and forces being, and to be, discovered. The past survives only by supplying available material that may be a guide for science and an equivalent of power. The function of history is to reveal its own futility, to display the conquest of the ancient realm of uncertainty, probability, inheritance, by irresistible demonstration. Bourbons and Habsburgs go over to the Egyptian kings, and make room on earth for the monuments of a dynasty that begins with Copernicus and will never pass away. All else is ballast to be discharged, and the Greek exercise must surrender to conic sections. As mere denial of history, the new conception is an old one. But by promoting the neglected history of scientific ideas, it promises greatly to enrich both historians and philosophers.

Forty years after Savigny's *Vocation* made Germany a nation of historically thinking men, every branch of knowledge had felt its influence. It had penetrated jurisprudence by the end of the French war; language, with the first volume of Grimm's *Grammar* in the edition of 1822; geography, when Ritter drew the spark from Humboldt; philosophy, when Hegel lectured at Berlin; art, with Schnaase's *Letters from the Netherlands;* theology, with Baur's work on the Atonement; and canon law when Richter was made, instead of Stahl, the adviser of the Prussian government in Church and State. Until 1840, political economy was almost the only science in which Germany followed, with unequal steps, the lead of France and England. The change came when Roscher, who had been the ripest of Ranke's scholars, a man more perfectly endowed with historic instinct than Niebuhr or Baur, was set to train practical economists for the kingdom of Hanover. He united in an eminently receptive mind the better strains of the German character—the wide and not absorbing sympathy, the impartial attentiveness to the several sides of questions, the notion that error is not done with until it has been made to yield a residue of truth, confidence in the general reasonableness of things, regulation of private opinion by universal experience. Abstraction was already losing its strong grip, and experimental methods were obtaining sway. "The history of a science," said Goethe, "is the science itself"; Trendelenburg spoke of definitions as the end, not the beginning, of knowledge; and Say told de Candolle that he had acquired the art of observing social physiology from the naturalists. These fluid notions were much in the air. Hermann, the strictest of dogmatists, being asked what to read, advised men to learn the making of the science in the economic articles which appeared from the beginning in the *Edinburgh* and *Quarterly Reviews*. The prodigy of Roscher's reading and his historic bent of mind urged him to detach propositions from their place in the system, in order to trace their career in literature and the experience of nations. He required that the inductive argument shall meet and justify the deductive. He turned from the solid conclusion to the process which led up to it, from the discovered law to the law of discovery, the ineffectual anticipation, the simultaneous attainment, the contested reception, the disputed priority. If the full-blown precepts of developed science which accompany the mature, the normal, and therefore industrial epoch of national life were not clear formerly, Roscher explains the defect not by the fault of men groping in the dark, but by the fact that political economy, which exists for mankind, varies with the progress of events, and is subject to the conditions of youth and age. He distinguishes physiology from pathology, insists on the phenomena proper to epochs of decline, and notes with especial care the teaching of nations that have carried the experiment of existence to its conclusion. Starting with the idea that the ancients understood distribution better than we do, and that truth is often older than error, he has expanded and enriched professional literature with the study of all the economic notions in the civil and the ecclesiastical code, in Erasmus and Luther, Bacon and Burke. The worst use of theory is to make men insensible to fact; and facts, as they existed before Salmasius vindicated 5 per cent, or Gournay spoke the winged words, are nearly as good for instruction as the things that have been since the discoveries of 1776, 1798, 1815, and 1835.

With little less than Buckle's appreciation of Adam Smith, Roscher's memory, crowded with instances of the power of self-sacrifice, disinclines him from the doctrine which refers economic facts to the simplest and most universal of human motives, and he derives laws and theories from causes deep in the entire structure of society, and from combinations of human and spiritual influence. He came at a time when several candid generalisations of primitive liberalism were withering under the mathematical touch of comparative statistics, and is always ready to find a grain of wisdom in the oddities of our ancestors; and the saying of ancient practitioners that the lancet produced much the same results upon the generation that is past as its disuse upon the generation that is passing, is Roscher all over. Though he deems protection a mark of weakness, and its prolongation a mark of incapacity, he admits the use of temporary sacrifices in the training of resources. With Adam Smith he rejoices at the enactment of the navigation laws, and with Cobden at their repeal; he feels with Garrison about emancipation, but is vividly conscious of conditions in which slavery is an instrument of civilisation. He expounds with intelligent admiration the colonial system by which this country has changed the face of the world, but he studies with equal care, he admires in another way the system by which Spain preserved where we destroyed. Absolute monarchy is the note of first or second childhood, but absolute monarchy rescued the peasants. Monopolies are a mistake; but the monopoly of the Oporto Company saved port wine.

The best of the economists who last preceded Roscher admitted that in dealing with poverty their science failed. Mill thought that want in any sense implying suffering may be completely extinguished; and Roscher added that precept must be modified by fact. His disciples went on to argue that the principles of the classic teachers on the theory of population, of rent, of the source of wealth, lead beyond their conclusions. With Roscher's doctrine of relative truth, the impregnable stronghold was hard to keep against the assault of sympathy and the prickings of that delicate conscience which is defined, a conscience unequal to the struggle of life. He dwells complacently on the immeasurable progress of this age, on the enlarged sphere and accepted duties of the State in respect of misery, education, overwork, health, and help to the weak, and judges that the social advance cancels the socialist programme. "Socialism," said Dunoyer, "is merely the present system logically carried out." On the other side, if it is right that the State should do so much, the reign of the log was usurpation and the ancient ways were wrong. Then the indictment brought by Considérant and Engels against the society of 1840 is just, and the order of things which produced so much sorrow was criminal. So vast a change is not development but subversion, the departure of one principle, the development of another. In all that pertains to the past, the party now dominant in the universities, and destined, after calculable intervals, to dominate in literature and law, pursues the ideas of Roscher, and completes his work. In practical things it does not accept, as he does, the Frenchman's saying, "Je n'impose rien; je ne propose même pas: j'expose." His contemplative, retrospective spirit, borne backward by sheer weight of knowledge, is not easily roused by the spectacle of error, suffering, and wrong, and is slow to admit the guilt of omitted acts and the responsibility of States for all they might prevent or cure. He has attended as much to problems and their solution in other times as to the problems and solutions of his own; and the service done by his enormous influence to political economy, which Mr. Cliffe Leslie and Mr. Ingram have described, is far less than his services to the cause of intelligible history. A large number of the most valuable works on England proceed from the movement he has promoted. The academic socialists are proceeding to reconstrue history, making property and the social condition the determining factor, above the acts of government or the changes of opinion; and this is by many degrees the most important addition made of late years to historic science.

The successive schemes have been less a modification than an enlargement of the definition, and the best would be one that should complete and combine them all. The idea that the fine arts are a result of all that is at work in nations led to an attempt to focus their entire life, and the design of a history of civilisation grew out of the history of art. Burckhardt's *Renaissance* and Friedländer's *Sittengeschichte* are the only works in which the intellectual view of the subject has been adequately studied; and in both, the political, and therefore the practical, element is weakest. One man is living who has an equal grasp of the moving and the abiding forces of society. More than thirty years ago, before Burckhardt or Friedländer, Buckle or Symonds, Riehl, a scholar quickened by journalism, a student of art, an original political writer and teacher of social sciences, began to lecture on the history of civilisation, revealing to his fortunate audience new views of history deeper than any existing in literature. There is always much going on in lecture rooms beyond what is yet deposited in books; and if Professor Riehl has gone on as he began in 1854, there are materials for a new and curious chapter of German historiography. The newest chapter, and one of the most curious, should concern the histories which the Germans have not written, the threads they have dropped, and the points on which they yield to the superiority of other nations. My object has been to show neither their infirmity nor their strength, but the ways in which they break new ground and add to the notion and the work of history.

[18]
Review of Creighton's
History of the Papacy

Mr. Creighton's new volumes tell the story of the Papacy as an Italian power during the last half-century that preceded and prepared the rise of Protestantism. Next to the merits of moderation and sobriety which the preface rightly claims, their first characteristic is the economy of evidence, and the severity with which the raw material is repressed and so kept out of sight as not to divert the reader's attention or turn his pleasure into toil. The author prefers the larger public that takes history in the shape of literature, to scholars whose souls are vexed with the insolubility of problems and who get their meals in the kitchen. The extent of his research appears whenever there is a favourite point to illustrate; but he generally resembles a writer on the Long Parliament who should treat Rushworth and Clarendon as too trite for quotation, or Mr. Walpole if he were to strike out several hundred references to *Hansard* and the *Annual Register*. There is some risk in attempting a smooth narrative of transactions belonging to an age so rich in disputed matter and dispersed material, and quick with the causes of the Reformation. As the author rarely takes stock or shows the limit of his lore, the grateful student, on whom proofs are not obtruded, cannot tell whether they abound, and may be led wrongly and injuriously to doubt whether the sources of information and suggestion have been fully explored. Nobody should stand better with Mr. Creighton than Ranke. The late John Richard Green used to complain that it was from him that he had learnt to be so dispassionate and inattentive to everything but the chain of uncoloured fact. In

Mandell Creighton, *A History of the Papacy during the Period of the Reformation*, vols. 3 and 4, *The Italian Princes, 1464–1518* (London: Longmans, 1887). Published in the *English Historical Review* 2 (1877):571–581. Reprinted in Acton, *Historical Essays*, pp. 426–441.

reserve of language, exclusion of all that is not history, dislike of purple patchwork and emotional effect, their ways are one. At the same time, the chapter on Savonarola has been more distinctly a labour of love than any other part of these volumes. Yet the essay on Savonarola, which is among Ranke's later writings, has not been suffered to influence the account of the friar's constitution and of the challenge. Burckhardt, the most instructive of all writers on the Renaissance, is missed where he is wanted, though there is a trace of him in the description of Caterina Sforza. The sketch of Gemistus Pletho is founded on Alexandre's edition of his *Laws*, irrespective of Schulze's later and more comprehensive treatise. Schulze is as well known to Mr. Creighton as Ranke or Burckhardt, and his studious exclusion needlessly raises a question as to whether this book is written up to date. It relates from the usual authorities the story of the ancient Roman corpse that was discovered in 1485, carried to the Capitol, and tumultuously admired by the enthusiasts of the revival. Another account, written by an eye-witness, at the time, has been published by Janitschek, and reproduced by Geiger in works only second to those of Voigt and Burckhardt. The *Regesta Leonis X* should be an indispensable aid in the study of his pontificate, and should have roused a suspicion that the act confirming the legitimacy of Clement VII has long been known, and that the page of Balan's *Monumenta* to which we are referred for it is misprinted. They also prove (p. 323) that the *Bullarium Magnum* cannot be trusted by critical scholars. In the character of Paul II there is no notice of a statement made by Gregorovius (vol. vii. p. 212), whom Mr. Creighton has studied carefully, though not, I think, in the last edition.

To make this good and to strengthen confidence, we have many valuable extracts from unpublished works, such as the history of the Augustinian, Cardinal Egidius of Viterbo, one of the least inefficient among the Italian priesthood of that age, and the diaries of the master of the ceremonies and Bishop of Pesaro, whose manuscripts have been the mainstay of papal historians from Panvini and Raynaldus to Hergenröther. But the desire to reject superfluous notes and paraded erudition has influenced the author's manner in another way. No scrupulous and self-respecting writer will speak his mind or say things that challenge inquiry unless the proof is prompt. To relieve his text of the burden of incessant quotation, he must understate his meaning and lose in definiteness and precision what he gains in lightness. His chisel is necessarily blunted, and he cannot work in high relief. It has cost Mr. Creighton but little to accept this drawback on his method. He is not striving to prove a case, or burrowing towards a conclusion, but wishes to pass through scenes of raging controversy and passion with a serene curiosity, a suspended judgment, a divided jury, and a pair of white gloves. Avoiding both alternatives of the prophet's mission, he will neither bless nor curse, and seldom invites his readers to execrate or to admire. His tints are sometimes pale, and his tones indecisive. I do not refer to such ambiguous sayings as that Matilda left all her lands to St. Peter, or that the sudden death of Paul II was regarded as a judgment upon him for his want of faith, or that Julius II felt the calls of nature strong at the last. But there are places where, in the author's solicitude to be within the mark, the reader misses the point. There was a time when the schemes of ecclesiastical reform found a last refuge in the sacred college itself. In letters written from Rome on 23rd and 28th September 1503, we read: "Li Signori Cardinali essendo in Conclavi, hano ordinati multi Capituli tendenti a proponere de la Sede apostolica, et del Collegio, et creato el Pontefice, li hano facto giurare de observarli. . . . Tutti li Signori Cardinali furno chiamati per N. S. in Congregatione a Palatio, et per farse mentione de Concilio et de reformatione de la Corte neli Capituli del Conclavi, La Santità Sua propose et conclude, se habi a fare el Concilio, et se habi ad intimare ali Principi Christiani. Ma circa el loco et lo tempo de esso Concilio se reservò a deliberare un altra volta. Fu bene ragionato che lo ultimo Concilio fu facto in Basilea, et per Monsignor de Rohano fu ricordato, quando se tractarà del loco, se habi a chiamare lo Procuratore del Christianissimo Re, dimonstrando che essendo stato facto lo ultimo in Allamagna, seria conveniente questo farse in Franza. La Santità Sua anchora propose la reformatione dela Corte, et conclude se havesse a riformare." Mr. Creighton, who has no faith in the conciliar and spiritual movement, and is satisfied with the printed edition of Giustinian, merely says that Pius III "spoke of reforming the church." The flavour has evaporated. A patriotic Florentine, Boscoli, compassed the death of the Medicean monopolist of power, and suffered, reasonably, for his crime. We are told that the great question for his friends was the opinion of Aquinas on the sinfulness of tyrannicide; and that his confessor declared afterwards that his soul was in peace. The difficulty for his friends was to make him believe that St. Thomas condemned tyrannicide utterly, and what his confessor afterwards said

was that they had contrived to deceive him. There is a report that
Alexander objected to the ordeal of fire, because he feared it might
succeed. We are only told, in a note, that it would have been very
awkward for him if by any chance Savonarola had been successful.
Caesar Borgia "awakened the mingled terror and admiration of
bystanders." This is true of others, besides Machiavelli. When the
news of Caesar's most conspicuous crime reached Venice, a citizen
who hated him, and who kept in secret a diary which has not seen the
light, made this entry: "Tutto il mondo cridava contro di lui; tamen
per questo li morti non resusciteranno, e dimostrava haver un gran
coraggio, e di farsi signor di tutta l' Italia." And somewhat later: "Di
quanta riputatione, e fausto, e gloria s' attrovava all' hora il Signor
Duca Valentino in Italia, non lo posso per hora dichiarire, perche l'
effetto delli suoi successi, delle sue vittorie, e del stato acquistato, lo
dimostrava. Onde di lui si parlava variamente: alcuni lo volevano far
Re dell' Italia, e coronarlo; altri lo volevano far Imperator." The
picture of Julius at the Lateran council, when "he had forgotten to
prepare a speech," and when he "could only stammer through a few
sentences," is less vivid than the account of his oratory given by Paris
de Grassis: "Non facio mentionem de Julio, qui cum oraturus esset
semper per triduum ante actus occupatus erat in studio memorandi
sermonis; et tamen cum in consistorio publico dicere vellet semper
semimori videbatur, ita ut mihi esset necesse occurrere et excitare eum
in stupore membrorum occupatum et exanimatum, sicut omnes vide-
runt, et Sua Sanctitas saepe mihi hoc idem dixit."

Mr. Creighton has a decided opinion on the question whether
Alexander VI died a natural death, but the arguments on either side
might be strengthened. "Contemporaries saw a proof of the effects of
poison in the rapid decomposition of the pope's body, which grew
black and swollen. . . . It was evidence only of the state of the
atmosphere." Compared with the report in Sanuto, this is a tame
description: "El sangue ge abondava da le rechie, da la bocha e dal
naso, adeo che non potevano tanto sugar quanto l' abondava: i labri
erano più grossi che 'l pugno di un homo: era con la bocha aperta, e
ne la bocha ge bogliva il sangue, come faria una pignata che boglisse
al focho, e per la bocha ge saltava el sangue a modo de una spina, e
sempre abondava: e questo è de visu." Alexander fell ill on the 12th,
not on the 13th, of August. The error may be due to the omission, by
Villari, of the first sentence in a despatch of 14th August. In the

original it begins with the following words: "Sabato passato, dovendo andare N. S. in signatura, secondo el consueto, la signatura fu' destinata. Et de la causa non se ne intese altro per quella sera. Ma fù ascripto ad uno pocho de indispositione che havea havuto el Signor Duca, el dì inante." The despised Leonetti has the right date. "It is not surprising that two men, living under the same conditions and in the same place, should suffer from fever at the same time." It is a case, not of two men, but of three; for Cardinal Hadrian afterwards assured Jovius that he had been poisoned. When three men who have dined together are seized with such illness that the oldest dies, and the youngest is prostrated during the most critical week of his life, we even now suspect verdigris in the saucepan or a toadstool in the mushrooms. Villari, whose authority stands high, maintains that the suspicion of poison arose when the pope was dead. But on 18th August Sanuto writes: "Si divulga per Roma sia stà atosegado"; and Priuli has the following entry on the 16th: "Furono lettere da Roma volantissime, per le qual s' intendeva come il Sommo Pontifice essendo stato a solazzo a cena del R^{mo} Cardinale chiamato Adriano, insieme col Duca Valentino et alcuni altri Cardinali, havendo crapulato ad sobrietatem, essendo ritornato al Pontificale Palazzo, s' era buttato al letto con la febre molto grave, per la qual infermità si giudicava fosse stato avvelenato, e questo perchè etiam il giorno seguente il prefato Duca Valentino et il Cardinal s' erano buttati al letto con la febre." On the other hand, the only direct authorities available—Giustinian, Costabili, and Burchard—report that Alexander died a natural death, and it would appear that the famous supper took place nearly a week before the guests were taken ill. Giustinian writes on 13th August: "Uno di questi zorni, e fo ozi otto di, andorno a cena ad una vigna del R^{mo} Adriano, e stettero fin a notte; dove intravennero etiam altre persone, e tutti se ne hanno risentito."

Mr. Creighton warns us against the credulous malignity of the writers he is compelled to use. It must be appraised, he says, as carefully as the credulity of earlier chroniclers in believing miraculous stories. It will not do to press the analogy between Caesarius or the *Liber Conformitatum*, and Infessura or Burchard. Mr. Creighton accepts the most scandalous of the scenes recorded by the latter; he assuredly would not accept what is gravely testified in the Beatification of Ximenes, that he stopped the sun at Oran, so that several Moors, seeing the prodigy, asked to be baptized. But his reluctance to rely on common gossip is justified by the rank growth of myths in the journals of the *cinque cento* Grevilles. On the death of the Venetian Cardinal Michiel in April 1503, Priuli writes: "Fù discoperto, come qui sotto appar, che 'l detto Cardinal fù attossicato per intelligenza del Duca Valentino per haver li danari, e fù squartato et abbruciato questo tale, che era Cameriere del detto Cardinale." In August the same story is repeated: "Morse da morte repentina un Cardinale nepote del Pontefice, chiamato il Cardinale Monreale, huomo di grandissima auttorità, in due giorni, al qual fu trovato tra argenti e denari 120 M. ducati, e si diceva, e giudicavasi per certo, il detto povero Cardinale esser stato avvelenato dal Duca Valentino per li suoi danari, che all' hora era consueto ammazzare le persone c' havevano danari a Roma da questo Duca." The news of the pope's illness suggests the following reflections: "Si dubitava assai che 'l detto Pontefice non dovesse da questa infermità morire, perche, ut vulgo dicebatur, questo Pontefice havea dato l' anima et il corpo al gran Diavolo dell' Inferno; e però che non potesse morire ancora per far delli altri mali." Another relates that an ape was caught in the apartments of Alexander, who exclaimed, "Lasolo, lasolo, ch'è il diavolo." Sanuto has a detailed account of the supper party, according to which there was no mistake; but Hadrian, knowing his danger, gave the butler a heavy bribe to make the exchange. "El Cardinal, che pur havia paura, se medicinò e vomitò, et non have mal alcuno." A ghastly tale is told in the life of a man who, fifty years later, rose to the summit of power and dignity and historic fame, but who was then an obscure prelate about the court. When Alexander came to the villa of Cardinal Hadrian, it was found that the box containing a consecrated host, which he wore as a protection, had been forgotten. The prelate, who was sent for it, on arriving at the Vatican, beheld the pontiff lying dead in his chamber.

No authority is more often cited for the early part of the sixteenth century than the diary of Marin Sanuto. Mr. Creighton quotes sometimes from the printed edition, sometimes apparently from the Vienna transcript, which does not always agree with the original. In the conspiracy of the cardinals in 1517 his reliance on the fidelity of Marin Sanuto's *précis* of despatches raises an interesting problem of historical criticism. The statement of Pope Leo, as quoted vol. iv. p. 245, is inaccurate. There is no question of a letter written by Sauli, or of a promise made by him, or of a prisoner having confessed that the cardinal had actually plotted the death of the pope. The text of the despatch, which, upon all these points, has been distorted, is as follows:

"Sapiate che za alchuni giorni io feci retenir uno de i suo, apresso dil qual furono ritrovate alchune scritture, et tandem alchune lettere che lui scriveva al Cardinal, per che 'l non si havea potuto exeguir quanto lui li havea commesso cum molte altre parole; per modo che si poteva judicar ditto Cardinal haver trattato di voler avenenar Sua Bne. et posto de tormento confessò la verità, et etiam che 'l Cardinal de Sauli era conscio di tal ribaldaria." This prisoner, who was in the service of Petrucci, not of Sauli, confessed under torture; but the words *auto corda assai* do not apply to him, as Mr. Creighton supposes. They describe the fate of the physician whom he denounced. Marin Sanuto writes in the passage which seems to have been misunderstood: "Quel Zuan Baptista di Verzei a confessato il tutto, qual a auto corda assai." On the next page Leo is made to say: "4 zorni poi fussemo fatti Papa tramono questi di darmi la morte." The Venetian copy of the diary has: "4 zorni poi fossimo Papa tramono questi darne la morte." The words actually reported by the envoy are: "Quatro giorni da poi la nostra creatione questi Cardinali tractorono de far un altro Pontefice, da poi la nostra morte." Of Riario, whom the Venetians call the cardinal of St. George, Mr. Creighton writes: "Riario denied all knowledge of the matter till the confessions of the others were read to him; then he said, 'Since they have said so, it must be true.' He added that he had spoken about it to Soderini and Hadrian, who laughed and said they would make him pope." Marco Minio says: "Per le depositione del Sauli et etiam de qualche uno de li altri si vede come etiam haveano communicato questa cum li R^mi Cardinali Voltera et Adriano, et quel Adriano, intesa la cosa, si messe a rider stringendosi nelle spalle, che è uno atto solito per lui farsi molte volte, et il R^mo Volterra disse, 'Faciate pur presto.' Si che tutti loro dimostrar haver grandissimo odio al Pontefice. Ma San Zorzi dimostra haver havuto più presto grande desiderio al papato che altro; et loro promettevano di farlo papa." It does not appear that Riario admitted having sounded Soderini and Hadrian, nor that it was proved by the evidence of others, nor that the two cardinals implicated made any promise to elect him. All this is taken from Sanuto's summary: "Quando fo letto al Cardinal San Zorzi quello havia detto Siena e Sauli, qual primo negava, disse, za che lhoro hanno dito cussi el dia esser el vero, et chel comunichoe con Voltera et Hadriano Cardinali quali se la riseno come solito è a far Hadriano, et Voltera disse, 'Faziate pur presto,' e che li prometteva far esso San Zorzi Papa."

Mr. Creighton judges his half-century as an epoch of religious decline, during which the Papacy came down from the elevation at which it was left by Pius to the degeneracy in which it was found by Luther. With Paul II it starts well. Then the temptations of politics, the victorious creation of the temporal state, bring his successors into degrading and contaminating rivalry with wicked statesmen, and they learn to expend spiritual authority in exchange for worldly gains, until at last, when they have to face new antagonists, their dignity is tarnished and their credit gone. At each pontificate the judgment becomes more severe. Sixtus is worse than Paul, and Alexander than Sixtus. But worst of all are those prosperous pontiffs who, in their ambition to become great monarchs, sacrificed their country and their church. The reformers rose up in opposition to a vast political machine, to a faggot of secular motives, which had usurped the seat of Gregory VII and Innocent IV. The Papacy to which they were untrue had become untrue to itself.

This increasing rigour and occasional indignation, as the plot thickens, is assuredly in no wise due to the irrelevant detail that Cambridge does not elect its Dixie professor among the adherents of Rome. Religious differences do not tinge his judgment or obstruct the emollient influence of ingenuous arts. If Mr. Creighton, as a theologian, does not accept the claims of the pre-reformation popes, as an historian he prefers them to their adversaries. The members of the Council of Pisa are renegades and schismatics. When Paul II refused to be bound by the compact he had signed with the other cardinals, he was not to blame. "The attempt to bind the pope was a legacy of the schism, and rested upon the principles laid down by the conciliar movement. Such a proceeding was entirely contrary to the canonical conception of the plenitude of the papal power." The character of Pius III "stood high in all men's estimation, though he was the father of a large family of children." Mr. Creighton insists on the liberality of the popes, not only at the time of which he treats, but generally. "Fanaticism had no place in Rome, nor did the papal court trouble itself about trifles. It allowed free thought beyond the extremest limits of ecclesiastical prudence. The Papacy in the Middle Ages always showed a tolerant spirit in matters of opinion. We cannot think that Roman inquisitors were likely to err on the side of severity." The last sentence shows that in varying disinterested history with passages which might be taken from the polemics of Cardinal Newman, Mr. Creighton is not unmindful of the Inquisition. But he shows no strong feeling for the liberty of conscience. He speaks coldly of "writers who themselves regard toleration as a virtue," and say that Pomponatius "was judged in the papal court with a judicial calmness and impartiality which the modern advocates of religious tolerance might well admire." When speaking of Gemistus, the last original thinker of the tolerant eastern church, he passes unheeded the most curious passage of the *Laws:* οὐ καὶ σοφιστῶν, ἤν τις παρὰ τὰς ἡμετέρας ταύτας δόξας σοφιζόήμενος ἅλῶ, ζῶν καὶ οὗτος κεκαύσεται. He declares that it is unjust to brand Sixtus IV as a persecutor because he granted the powers asked for in the shape of the Spanish Inquisition. And this is prompted by no tenderness for the memory of Sixtus; for we find elsewhere that "he allowed himself to become an accomplice in a scheme for assassination which shocked even the blunted conscience of Italy." It may be safely said that Mr. Creighton esteems Ximenes a better specimen of the Christian priest than Julius or Leo, with all their religious liberality.

The spirit of retrospective indulgence and reverence for the operation of authority, whether it be due to want of certitude or to definite theory, is an advantage in writing on this portion of history. From a less conservative point of view the scenery is more gloomy, and the contending parties, tarred with the same brush, are apt to prove less interesting. Mr. Creighton is able to be considerate and appreciative both to popes and reformers. He has no love for the Italian humanists, and may reserve his harshest censures for the pseudonymous liberalism of More and Socinus. It is not necessary, he says, to moralise at every turn; and he neither worries and vilipends his culprits, like Carlyle and Taine, nor adapts his judgments to dogma, like Hook and Mozley. He goes farther, and declares that it is not becoming to adopt an attitude of lofty superiority over any one who ever played a prominent part in European affairs, or charitable to lavish undiscriminating censure. Of course this does not imply that justice has one law for the mighty and another for the fallen. If it means that every age ought to be tried by its own canons, the application of that sliding scale is a branch of ethical and historical inquiry that is yet in its teens, and practically of no avail. Or it may mean that power goes where power is due, that the will of Providence is made manifest by success, that the judgment of history is the judgment of heaven. That is undoubtedly a theory of singular interest and influence as the groundwork of historic conservatism; but it has never been brought to the test of exact definition. Mr. Creighton perceives the sunken rock of moral scepticism, and promises that he will not lower the standard of moral judgment. In this transition stage of struggling and straggling ethical science, the familiar tendency to employ mesology in history, to judge a man by his cause and the cause by its result, to obviate criticism by assuming the unity and wholeness of character, to conjure with great names and restore damaged reputations, not only serves to debase the moral standard, but aims at excluding it. And it is the office of historical science to maintain morality as the sole impartial criterion of men and things, and the only one on which honest minds can be made to agree.

I dwell on the spirit and method and *morale* of the *History of the Papacy,* not only because it is difficult to contend in detail with such a master of solid fact, but because it is by the spirit and not the letter that his book will live. Studious men who have examined the hidden treasures of many Italian libraries, and have grown grey with the dust of papal archives, are on the track behind him. Pastor's history has only just reached Pius II, but it is dense with new knowledge, and announces a worthy competitor to Ranke, Gregorovius, and Creighton. But not a hole must be left unpicked; and there are several particulars on which reader and writer may join issue. The account of the conclave of 1471 seems scarcely just to Bessarion. According to Panvini, he lost the tiara not from national or political jealousy, but because he refused an uncanonical compact: "Res ad Bessarionem, tum senatus principem senem doctrina et vitae integritate clarissimum, spectare videbatur. Quem Ursinus obtinendi pontificatus spe deposita, Mantuanus, Cancellarius convenientes certis sub conditionibus pontificatum se ei daturos polliciti sunt. Quumque ille se ea ratione pontificem creari velle pernegasset, ut scilicet pacto aliquo intercedente papatum obtineret, illi, intempestivam senis severitatem stomachati, ad Cardinalem Sancti Petri ad Vincula, Magistrum Franciscum Savonensem, sunt conversi, virum doctrina praestantissimum." In a passage apparently inspired by aversion for the irreligious renaissance, Savonarola is called "the most sincere man amongst the Italians of the time." It is invidious to disparage a man whose faith was strong enough to resist authority both in Church and State, and who impressed a doctrine which was newer if not more true then than now, that an awakened conscience must be traced and proved in public as much as in private life, so that a zealous priest is, normally, a zealous politician. And it may be that the shrill utterance of opportune prophecy is not always inconsistent with integrity. But the man who described in the pulpit his mission from Florence to heaven, and what he heard there, and afterwards explained that this was all a trope, cannot well be pronounced perfectly sincere on any hypothesis of sanity. How far the plea of partial insanity, which is gaining ground in society, may serve for the interpretation of history, is a problem which should commend itself to a writer so slow to use hard words and to associate *dolus* and *culpa*. Mr. Creighton describes the constitution of Julius against simony as a bold measure, showing a strong sense of the need of amendment. But he speaks of it as an incident in the annals of the year, a feature in the portrait of a pope, a plant sprung from no buried root. The prohibition of bribery at conclaves was old in the law of the Church. Four hundred and sixty years before, one of the popes wrote that he had been raised to the papal throne in place of three others, deposed for bribery—"explosis tribus illis, quibus nomen papatus rapina dederat." The rising against Alexander VI, the coalition between Julian and Savonarola to eject him, would hardly be intelligible if the law against simony had been no more than an abrupt innovation. It is not quite accurate to say that the first care of the cardinals on the death of Julius was to lay hands on the treasure which he left behind. The Venetian envoy wrote, 25th February: "Alcuni Cardinali voleano partir questo tesoro tra tutti li Cardinali, tamen li altri non hanno voluto, et si riserverà al novo Pontefice." On 2nd March he adds: "Hanno tratto li Cardinali di Castello ducati 30,000; et perche li Cardinali che non hanno intrada ducati 600 per uno, Julio fo una constitution di darli di danari del Papato fin a quella somma, perhòse li darà perlio se." The letter of the protonotary Marcello from which the dubious words are cited— "siche partivano duc. 120,000 tra lhoro"—goes on to say that they got less than this. The election of Leo X is told with the aid of extracts from Paris de Grassis; but neither text nor note speaks of the capitulations in which the future pope pledged himself to revoke, under pain of excommunication, the sale of indulgences for the fabric of St. Peter's. "Promittet, iurabit, et vovebit, statim post assumptionem suam omnes et singulas indulgentias revocare fratribus Sancti Francisci ordinis minorum, pro fabrica Sancti Petri concessas, sub quibusvis verborum formis, eisque mandabit, sub excommunicationis latae sententiae poena, ne illis ullo modo utantur." The terms of this covenant are not very comprehensive, yet they should possess some significance for one who thinks that a pope weak enough to keep an oath taken in conclave would betray his trust. They show that Rome was in some measure aware of present evil and impending danger; and that the refusal of remedy and precaution was not due to the corruption of courtiers, but to the plenitude of sovereignty.

Although it is not easy to detect a wrong quotation, a false inference, or an unjust judgment in these records of discredited popes, whoever consults them for the key to the coming Reformation will go away conscious of things left out and replenished with more political than religious secrets. He will know by what means the Papacy, borne on the stormy tide of absolutism which opens modern history, established an independent state on the subjugation of Italy. But the marrow of things does not lie in the making of a distinct principality, or in the price paid for it, or in the means by which its makers wrought. Other causes changed the axis of the world. Within the folds of temporal monarchy an ecclesiastical process was going on of more concern to us than the possession or the partition of Italy. De Maistre's argument that those who deem absolutism legitimate in the State have no foothold to resist it in the Church, had been proclaimed already by a writer favourably known to Mr. Creighton: "Nemo est tam parvae urbis dominus, qui a se appellari ferat: et nos Papam appellationi subiectum dicemus? At si me, ais, Pontifex indigne premit, quid agam? Redi ad eum supplex; ora, onus levet. At si rogatus, interpellatus nolit subvenire misero, quid agam? Quid agis, ubi tuus te princeps saecularis urget? Feram, dices, nam aliud nullum est remedium. Et hic ergo feras!" The miscarriage of reform left the Holy See on a solitary height never reached before. It was followed by indifference and despair, by patient watching for a new departure, by helpless schemes to push philosophy across the margin exposed by the religious ebb. We are familiar with the antipathy of Machiavelli and the banter of Erasmus; but the primary fact in the papal economy of that age is not the manifold and ineffective opposition, but the positive strengthening of authority and its claims. The change is marked by the extremity of adulation which came in about the time of Alexander. He is *semideus, deus alter in terris*, and, in poetry, simply *deus*. The belief that a soul might be rescued from purgatory for a few coppers, and the sudden expansion of the dispensing power, facts that alienated Germany and England, throve naturally in this atmosphere; and between the parallel and contemporaneous growth of the twin monarchies a close and constant connection prevails. From that last phase of mediaeval society to modern, there could be no evolution. But Mr. Creighton's second title is *The Italian Princes*. He describes the things that vary rather than the things that endure. We see the successive acts, the passing figures, the transitory forms, to which the spiritual element imparts an occasional relish; but we see little of the impersonal force behind. The system, the idea, is masked by a crowd of ingenious, picturesque, and unedifying characters, who exhibit the springs of Italian politics more truly than the solemn realities of the Church. We are seldom face to face with the institution. Very rarely, indeed, we are sent to the *Bullarium Magnum;* but that work, unwieldy as it is, contains an infinitesimal proportion of the acts of the mediaeval pontiffs. The inner mind of the Papacy has to be perused through many other collections pertaining to the several countries, churches, and religious orders; and these are so voluminous that three large folios are filled with the bulls that belong to St. Peter's alone. By giving us life and action for thought and law, Mr. Creighton lifts an enormous burden. The issues which he has so far deliberately avoided will force their way to the front when he reaches the commission given by Leo to the master of the sacred palace, Cajetan's expedition into Germany, and the pilgrimage of Eck to Rome. Without reversing his views, or modifying any statement, he has yet to disclose the reason, deeper and more interior than the worldliness, ignorance, and corruption of ecclesiastics, which compelled the new life of nations to begin by a convulsion.

[19]
Acton-Creighton Correspondence

Cannes, April 5, 1887

Dear Mr. Creighton,

I thank you very sincerely for your letter, which, though dated April 1, is as frank as my review was artful and reserved. The postponement gives me time to correct several errors besides those you point out, if you will let me have my manuscript out here. The other will also be the better for leisurely revision. Forgive me if I answer you with a diffuseness degenerating into garrulity.

The criticism of those who complained that I attacked the Germans without suggesting a better method seems to me undeserved. I was trying to indicate the progress and—partial—improvement of their historical writing; and when I disagreed I seldom said so, but rather tried to make out a possible case in favour of views I don't share. Nobody can be more remote than I am from the Berlin and the Tübingen schools; but I tried to mark my disagreement by the lightest touch. From the Heidelberg school I think there is nothing to learn, and I said so. Perhaps I have been ambiguous sometimes, for you say that appreciation such as yours for the essentials of the Roman system is no recommendation in my eyes. If that conclusion is drawn from my own words I am much in fault. But that has nothing of importance to do with a critique in the H. R. [*English Historical Review*].

And when you say that I am desirous to show how the disruption might have been avoided, I only half recognise myself. The disruption took place over one particular, well-defined point of controversy; and when they went asunder upon that, the logic of things followed. But they needed not to part company on that particular. It was a new view that Luther attacked. Theological authority in its favour there

Add. Mss. 6871. Published for the first time in their entirety in Acton, *Freedom and Power*, pp. 358–373.

was very little. It was not approved by Hadrian VI, or by many Tridentine divines, or by many later divines, even among the Jesuits. Supposing, therefore, there had been men of influence at Rome such as certain fathers of Constance formerly, or such as Erasmus or Gropper, it might well have been that they would have preferred the opinion of Luther to the opinion of Tetzel, and would have effected straightway the desired reform of the indulgences for the Dead.

But that is what set the stone rolling, and the consequences were derived from that one special doctrine or practice. *Cessante causa cessat effectus*. Introduce, in 1517, the reforms desired six years later, by the next Pope, demanded by many later divines, adopt, a century and a half before it was written, the Exposition de la Foi, and then the particular series of events which ensued would have been cut off.

For the Reformation is not like the Renaissance or the Revolution, a spontaneous movement springing up in many places, produced by similar though not identical causes. It all derives, more or less directly, from Luther, from the consequences he gradually drew from the resistance of Rome on that one disputed point.

I must, therefore, cast the responsibility on those who refused to say, in 1517, what everybody had said two centuries before, and many said a century later. And the motive of these people was not a religious idea, one system of salvation set up against another; but an ecclesiastical one. They said, Prierias says quite distinctly, that the whole fabric of authority would crumble if a thing permitted, indirectly or implicitly sanctioned by the supreme authority responsible for souls should be given up.

(The English disruption proceeded along other lines, but nearly parallel. Nearly the same argument applies to it, and it is not just now the question.)

Of course, an adversary, a philosophical historian, a *Dogmengeschichtslehrer*, may say that, even admitting that things arose and went on as I say, yet there was so much gunpowder about that any spark would have produced much the same explosion. I cannot disprove it. I do not wish to disprove it. But I know nothing about it. We must take things as they really occurred. What occurred is that Luther raised a just objection, that the authority of tradition and the spiritual interest of man were on his side, and that the Catholic divines refused to yield to him for a reason not founded on tradition or on charity.

Therefore I lay the burden of separation on the shoulders of two sets of men—those who, during the Vice chancellorship and the pontificate of Borgia, promoted the theory of the Privileged Altars (and indirectly the theory of the Dispensing Power); and those who, from 1517 to 1520, sacrificed the tradition of the Church to the credit of the Papacy.

Whether the many reforming rills, partly springing in different regions—Wyclif, the Bohemians before Hus, Hus, the Bohemians after him, the Fratres Communis Vitae, the divines described by Ullmann, and more than twenty other symptoms of somewhat like kind, would have gathered into one vast torrent, even if Luther had been silenced by knife or pen, is a speculative question not to be confounded with the one here discussed. Perhaps America would have gone, without the help of Grenville or North.

My object is not to show how disruption might have been avoided, but how it was brought on. It was brought on, *secundo me,* by the higher view of the papal monarchy in spirituals that grew with the papal monarchy in temporals (and with much other monarchy). The root, I think, is there, while the Italian prince is the branch. To the growth of those ideas after the fall of the Councils I attribute what followed, and into that workshop or nursery I want to pry. If Rovere or Borgia had never sought or won territorial sovereignty, the breach must have come just the same, with the Saxons if not with the English.

I was disappointed at not learning from you what I never could find out, how that peculiar discipline established itself at Rome between the days of Kempis and of Erasmus. It would not have appeared mysterious or esoteric to your readers if I had said a little more about it. Nor is this a point of serious difference. When you come to talk of the crisis I do not doubt you will say how it came about. Probably you will not give quite the same reasons that occur to me, because you are more sure than I am that the breach was inevitable. But I did think myself justified in saying that these two volumes do not contain an account of some of the principal things pertaining to the Papacy during the Reformation, and in indicating the sort of explanation I desiderate in Vol. V.

What is not at all a question of opportunity or degree is our difference about the Inquisition. Here again I do not admit that there is anything esoteric in my objection. The point is not whether you like the Inquisition—I mean that is a point which the H.R. may mark, but ought not to discuss—but whether you can, without reproach to historical accuracy, speak of the later mediaeval papacy as having been tolerant and enlightened. What you say on that point struck me exactly as it would strike me to read that the French Terrorists were tolerant and enlightened, and avoided the guilt of blood. Bear with me whilst I try to make my meaning quite clear.

We are not speaking of the Papacy towards the end of the fifteenth or early sixteenth century, when, for a couple of generations, and down to 1542, there was a decided lull in the persecuting spirit. Nor are we speaking of the Spanish Inquisition, which is as distinct from the Roman as the Portuguese, the Maltese, or the Venetian. I mean the Popes of the thirteenth and fourteenth centuries, from Innocent III down to the time of Hus. These men instituted a system of Persecution, with a special tribunal, special functionaries, special laws. They carefully elaborated, and developed, and applied it. They protected it with every sanction, spiritual and temporal. They inflicted, as far as they could, the penalties of death and damnation on everybody who resisted it. They constructed quite a new system of procedure, with unheard of cruelties, for its maintenance. They devoted to it a whole code of legislation, pursued for several generations, and not to be found in [ ].

But although not to be found there it is to be found in books just as common; it is perfectly familiar to every Roman Catholic student initiated in canon law and papal affairs; it has been worn threadbare in a thousand controversies; it has been constantly attacked, constantly defended, and never disputed or denied, by any Catholic authority. There are some dozens of books, some of them official, containing the particulars.

Indeed it is the most conspicuous fact in the history of the mediaeval papacy, just as the later Inquisition, with what followed, is the most conspicuous and characteristic fact in the history and record of the modern papacy. A man is hanged not because he can or cannot prove his claim to virtues, but because it can be proved that he has committed a particular crime. That one action overshadows the rest of his career. It is useless to argue that he is a good husband or a good poet. The one crime swells out of proportion to the rest. We all agree that Calvin was one of the greatest writers, many think him the best religious teacher, in the world. But that one affair of Servetus outweighs the nine folios, and settles, by itself, the reputation he deserves. So with the mediaeval Inquisition and the Popes that founded it and worked it. That is the breaking point, the article of their system by which they stand or fall.

Therefore it is better known than any other part of their government, and not only determines the judgment but fills the imagination, and rouses the passions of mankind. I do not complain that it does not influence your judgment. Indeed I see clearly how a mild and conciliatory view of Persecution will enable you to speak pleasantly and inoffensively of almost all the performers in your list, except More and Socinius; whilst a man with a good word for More and Socinius would have to treat the other actors in the drama of the Reformation as we treat the successive figures on the inclined plane of the French Revolution, from Dumouriez to Barras. But what amazes and disables me is that you speak of the Papacy not as exercising a just severity, but as not exercising any severity. You do not say, these misbelievers deserved to fall into the hands of these torturers and Fire-the-faggots; but you ignore, you even deny, at least implicitly, the existence of the torture-chamber and the stake.

I cannot imagine a more inexplicable error, and I thought I had contrived the gentlest formula of disagreement in coupling you with Cardinal Newman.

The same thing is the case with Sixtus IV and the Spanish Inquisition. What you say has been said by Hefele and Gams and others. They, at least, were in a sort, avowed defenders of the Spanish Inquisition. Hefele speaks of Ximenes as one might speak of Andrewes or Taylor or Leighton. But in what sense is the Pope not responsible for the constitution by which he established the new tribunal? If we passed a law giving Dufferin powers of that sort, when asked for, we should surely be responsible. No doubt, the responsibility in such a case is shared by those who ask for a thing. But if the thing is criminal, if, for instance, it is a license to commit adultery, the person who authorises the act shares the guilt of the person who commits it. Now the Liberals think Persecution a crime of a worse order than adultery, and the acts done by Ximenes considerably worse than the entertainment of Roman courtesans by Alexander VI. The responsibility exists whether the thing permitted be good or bad. If the thing be criminal, then the authority permitting it bears the guilt. Whether Sixtus is infamous or not depends on our view of persecution and absolutism. Whether he is responsible or not depends simply on the ordinary evidence of history.

Here, again, what I said is not in any way mysterious or esoteric. It appeals to no hidden code. It aims at no secret moral. It supposes nothing and implies nothing but what is universally current and familiar. It is the common, even the vulgar, code I appeal to.

Upon these two points we differ widely; still more widely with regard to the principle by which you undertake to judge men. You say that people in authority are not [to] be snubbed or sneezed at from our pinnacle of conscious rectitude. I really don't know whether you exempt them because of their rank, or of their success and power, or of their date. The chronological plea may have some little value in a limited sphere of instances. It does not allow of our saying that such a man did not know right from wrong, unless we are able to say that he lived before Columbus, before Copernicus, and could not know right from wrong. It can scarcely apply to the centre of Christendom, 1500 after the birth of our Lord. That would imply that Christianity is a mere system of metaphysics, which borrowed some ethics from elsewhere. It is rather a system of ethics which borrowed its metaphysics elsewhere. Progress in ethics means a constant turning of white into black and burning what one has adored. There is little of that between St. John and the Victorian era.

But if we might discuss this point until we found that we nearly agreed, and if we do argue thoroughly about the impropriety of Carlylese denunciations, and Pharisaism in history, I cannot accept your canon that we are to judge Pope and King unlike other men, with a favourable presumption that they did no wrong. If there is any presumption it is the other way against holders of power, increasing as the power increases. Historic responsibility has to make up for the want of legal responsibility. Power tends to corrupt and absolute power corrupts absolutely. Great men are almost always bad men, even when they exercise influence and not authority: still more when you superadd the tendency or the certainty of corruption by authority. There is no worse heresy than that the office sanctifies the holder of it. That is the point at which the negation of Catholicism and the negation of Liberalism meet and keep high festival, and the end learns to justify the means. You would hang a man of no position, like Ravaillac; but if what one hears is true, then Elizabeth asked the gaoler to murder Mary, and William III ordered his Scots minister to extirpate a clan. Here are the greater names coupled with the greater crimes. You would spare these criminals, for some mysterious reason. I would hang them, higher than Haman, for reasons of quite obvious justice; still more, still higher, for the sake of historical science.

The standard having been lowered in consideration of date, is to be still further lowered out of deference to station. Whilst the heroes of history become examples of morality, the historians who praise them, Froude, Macaulay, Carlyle, become teachers of morality and honest men. Quite frankly, I think there is no greater error. The inflexible integrity of the moral code is, to me, the secret of the authority, the dignity, the utility of history. If we may debase the currency for the sake of genius, or success, or rank, or reputation, we may debase it for the sake of a man's influence, of his religion, of his party, of the good cause which prospers by his credit and suffers by his disgrace. Then history ceases to be a science, an arbiter of controversy, a guide of the wanderer, the upholder of that moral standard which the powers of earth, and religion itself, tend constantly to depress. It serves where it ought to reign; and it serves the worst better than the purest.

Let me propose a crux whereby to part apologetic history from what I should like to call conscientious history: an Italian government was induced by the Pope to set a good round price on the heads of certain of its subjects, presumably Protestants, who had got away. Nobody came to claim the reward. A papal minister wrote to the government in question to say that the Holy Father was getting impatient, and hoped to hear soon of some brave deed of authentic and remunerated homicide. The writer of that letter lies in the most splendid mausoleum that exists on earth; he has been canonized by the lawful, the grateful, the congenial authority of Rome; his statue, in the attitude of blessing, looks down from the Alps upon the plain of Lombardy; his likeness is in our churches; his name is upon our altars; his works are in our schools. His editor specially commends the letter I have quoted; and Newman celebrates him as a glorious Saint.

Here is all you want, and more. He lived many a year ago; he occupied the highest stations, with success and honour; he is held in high, in enthusiastic reverence by the most intelligent Catholics, by converts, by men who, in their time, have drunk in the convictions, haply the prejudices, of Protestant England; the Church that holds him up as a mirror of sanctity stands and falls with his good name; thousands of devout men and women would be wounded and pained if you call him an infamous assassin.

What shall we call him? *In foro conscientiae*, what do you think of the man or of his admirers? What should you think of Charlotte Corday if, instead of Marat, she had stabbed Borromeo? At what stage of Dante's pilgrimage should you expect to meet him?

And whereas you say that it is no recommendation in my eyes to have sympathy with the Roman system in its essentials, though you did not choose those terms quite seriously, one might wonder what these essentials are. Is it essential—for salvation within the communion of Rome—that we should accept what the canonization of such a saint implies, or that we should reject it? Does Newman or Manning, when he invokes St. Charles [Borromeo], act in the essential spirit of the Roman system, or in direct contradiction with it? To put it in a walnutshell: could a man be saved who allowed himself to be persuaded by such a chain of argument, by such a cloud of witnesses, by such a concourse of authorities, to live up to the example of St. Charles?

Of course I know that you do sometimes censure great men severely. But the doctrine I am contesting appears in your preface, and in such places as where you can hardly think that a pope can be a poisoner. This is a far larger question of method in history than what you mean when you say that I think you are afraid to be impartial; as if you were writing with purposes of conciliation and in oppostion to somebody who thinks that the old man of the Seven Mountains is worse than the old man of one. I do not mean that, because your language about the Inquisition really baffles and bewilders me. Moreover, you are far more severe on Sixtus about the Pazzi than others; more, for instance, than Capponi or Reumont. And my dogma is not the special wickedness of my own spiritual superiors, but the general wickedness of men in authority—of Luther and Zwingli and Calvin and Cranmer and Knox, of Mary Stuart and Henry VIII, of Philip II and Elizabeth, of Cromwell and Louis XIV, James and Charles and William, Bossuet and Ken. Before this, it is a mere detail that imperfect sincerity is a greater reproach in divines than in laymen, and that, in our Church, priests are generally sacrilegious; and sacrilege is a serious thing. Let me add one word to explain my objection to your use of materials. Here is Pastor, boasting that he knows much that you do not. He does not stand on a very high level, and even his religion seems to be chiefly ecclesiastical. But I do apprehend that his massive information will give him an advantage over you when he gets farther. In that light I regret whatever does not tend to increase the authority of a work written on such *Culturstufe* as yours. I did not mean to overlook what may be urged *per contra*. When you began there was no rival more jealous than Gregorovius. That is not the case now. I should have wished your fortification to be strengthened against a new danger.

I am sure you will take this long and contentious letter more as a testimony of heart confidence and respect than of hostility—although as far as I grasp your method I don't agree with it. Mine seems to me plainer and safer; but it has never been enough to make me try to write a history, from mere want of knowledge. I will put it into canons, leaving their explanation and development to you.

I remain, yours most sincerely

Acton

Advice to persons about to write History: Don't. Visit the Monte Purgatorio, as Austin called the Magnesian rock that yields Epsom Salts; or: Get rid of Hole and Corner Buffery.

In the Moral Sciences Prejudice is Dishonesty.

A Historian has to fight against temptations special to his mode of life, temptations from Country, Class, Church, College, Party, authority of talents, solicitation of friends.

The most respectable of these influences are the most dangerous.

The historian who neglects to root them out is exactly like a juror who votes according to his personal likes or dislikes.

In judging men and things, Ethics go before Dogma, Politics or Nationality.

The Ethics of History cannot be denominational.

Judge not according to the orthodox standard of a system, religious, philosophical, political, but according as things promote or fail to promote the delicacy, integrity and authority of Conscience.

Put Conscience above both System and Success.

History provides neither compensation for suffering nor penalties for wrong.

The moral code, in its main lines, is not new; it has long been known; it is not universally accepted in Europe, even now. The difference in moral insight between past and present is not very large.

But the notion and analysis of Conscience is scarely older than 1700; and the notion and analysis of veracity is scarely older than our time—barring Sacred Writings of East and West.

In Christendom, time and place do not excuse—if the Apostle's Code sufficed for Salvation.

Strong minds think things out, complete the circle of their thinking, and must not be interpreted by types.

Good men and great men are *ex vi termini,* aloof from the action of surroundings.

But goodness generally appeared in unison with authority, sustained by environment, and rarely manifested the force and sufficiency of the isolated will and conscience.

The Reign of Sin is more universal, the influence of unconscious error is less, than historians tell us. Good and evil lie close together. Seek no artistic unity in character.

History teaches a Psychology which is not that of private experience and domestic biography.

The principles of public morality are as definite as those of the morality of private life; but they are not identical.

A good cause proves less in a man's favour than a bad cause against him.

The final judgment depends on the worst action.

Character is tested by true sentiments more than by conduct. A man is seldom better than his word.

History is better written from letters than from histories: let a man criminate himself.

No public character has ever stood the revelation of private utterance and correspondence.

Be prepared to find that the best repute gives way under closer scrutiny.

In public life, the domain of History, vice is less than crime.

Active, transitive sins count for more than others.

The greatest crime is Homicide.

The accomplice is no better than the assassin; the theorist is worse.

Of killing from private motives or from public, from political or from religious, *eadem est ratio.* Morally, the worst is the last. The source of crime is *pars melior nostri.* What ought to save, destroys. The sinner is hardened and proof against Repentance.

Faith must be sincere. When defended by sin it is not sincere; theologically, it is not Faith. God's grace does not operate by sin.

Transpose the nominative and the accusative and see how things look then.

History deals with Life; Religion with Death. Much of its work and spirit escapes our ken.

The systems of Barrow, Baxter, Bossuet higher, spiritually, construc-
tively, scientifically, than Penn's. In our scales his high morality
outweighs them.

Crimes by constituted authorities worse than crimes by Madame
Tussaud's private malefactors. Murder may be done by legal means,
by plausible and profitable war, by calumny, as well as by dose or
dagger.

The College,
Worcester
[April 9, 1887]

My dear Lord Acton,

Your letter is an act of true friendliness, and I am very grateful to
you for it, more grateful than I can say. It is a rare encouragement to
have such a standard set up as you have put before me. Judged by it
I have nothing to say except to submit: *efficaci do manus scientiae*. Before
such an ideal I can only confess that I am shallow and frivolous,
limited alike in my views and in my knowledge. You conceive of
History as an Architectonic, for the writing of which a man needs the
severest and largest training. And it is impossible not to agree with
you: so it ought to be.

I can only admit that I fall far short of the equipment necessary for
the task that I have undertaken. I was engaged in reading quietly for
the purpose, and the beginning of writing lay in the remote distance
in my mind, when I received a letter asking me to look through the
papers of an old gentleman whom I slightly knew, who on his deathbed
had made me his literary executor. I came across him at Oxford in
the Bodleian, where he came to read for a history of the rise of
Universities. He died at the age of seventy-four, possessor of a vast
number of notes, out of which all that I could piece together was an
article on Wyclif's Oxford life. This filled me with a horror of notebooks
and urged me to begin definitely to write. I thought that I had best
frankly do what I could; anything would serve as a step for my
successors. So I wrote.

I entirely agree with your principles of historical judgments: but
apparently I admit casuistry to a larger extent than you approve. I
remember that in 1880 I met John Bright at dinner: he was very cross,
apparently a cabinet meeting had disagreed with him. Amongst other
things he said: "If the people knew what sort of men statesmen were,

they would rise and hang the whole lot of them." Next day I met a young man who had been talking to Gladstone, who urged him to parliamentary life, saying: "Statesmanship is the noblest way to serve mankind."

I am sufficient of a Hegelian to be able to combine both judgments; but the results of my combination cannot be expressed in the terms of the logic of Aristotle. In studying history the question of the salvability of an archdeacon becomes indefinitely extended to all officials, kings and popes included. What I meant in my offending sentence in my preface was that anyone engaged in great affairs occupied a representative position, which required special consideration. Selfishness, even wrongdoing, for an idea, an institution, the maintenance of an accepted view of the basis of society, does not cease to be wrongdoing: but it is not quite the same as personal wrongdoing. It is more difficult to prove, and it does not equally shock the moral sense of others or disturb the moral sense of the doer. The acts of men in power are determined by the effective force behind them of which they are the exponents: their morality is almost always lower than the morality of the mass of men: but there is generally a point fixed below which they cannot sink with impunity. Homicide is always homicide: but there is a difference between that of a murderer for his own gain, and that of a careless doctor called in to see a patient who would probably have died anyhow; and the carelessness of the doctor is a difficult thing to prove.

What is tolerance nowadays? Is it a moral virtue in the possessor, or is it a recognition of a necessity arising from an equilibrium of parties? It often seems to me that we speak as if it was the first, when actually it is the second. My liberalism admits to everyone the right to his own opinion and imposes on me the duty of teaching him what is best; but I am by no means sure that that is the genuine conviction of all my liberal friends. French liberalism does not convince me that it is universal. I am not quite sure how Frederick Harrison or Cotter Morrison would deal with me if they were in a majority. The possession of a clear and definite ideal of society seems to me dangerous to its possessors. The Mediaeval Church had such an ideal: the result was the Inquisition, which was generally approved by the common consciousness. In the period of the end of the fifteenth century the Papacy seemed to me to have wearied of the Inquisition which was not much supported. The Popes were comparatively tolerant to Jews, Marrani, Turks; they did not attack the humanists; they did not furbish up the old weapons and apply them to new cases—except in the recognition of the Spanish Inquisition by Sixtus IV, about whom I have probably expressed myself loosely, but I have not my volumes here and I do not exactly [recall] what I said. What I meant was that to Sixtus IV this recognition was a matter of official routine. To have refused it he would have had to enunciate a new principle and make a new departure in ecclesiastical jurisdiction. I should have honoured him if he had done so; but I do not think him exceptionally persecuting because he did not do so. He accepted what he found. My purpose was not to justify him, but to put him in rank with the rest. I think, however, that I was wrong, and that you are right: his responsibility was graver than I have admitted. I think he knew better.

You judge the whole question of persecution more rigorously than I do. Society is an organism and its laws are an expression of the conditions which it considers necessary for its own preservation. When men were hanged in England for sheep stealing it was because people thought that sheep stealing was a crime and ought to be severely put down. We still think it a crime, but we think it can be checked more effectively by less stringent punishments. Nowadays people are not agreed about what heresy is; they do not think it a menace to society; hence they do not ask for its punishment. But the men who conscientiously thought heresy a crime may be accused of an intellectual mistake, not necessarily of a moral crime. The immediate results of the Reformation were not to favour free thought, and the error of Calvin, who knew that ecclesiastical unity was abolished, was a far greater one than that of Innocent III who struggled to maintain it. I am hopelessly tempted to admit degrees of criminality, otherwise history becomes a dreary record of wickedness.

I go so far with you that it supplies me with few heroes, and records few good actions; but the actors were men like myself, sorely tempted by the possession of power, trammeled by holding a representative position (none were more trammeled than popes), and in the sixteenth century especially looking at things in a very abstract way. I suppose statesmen rarely regard questions in the concrete. I cannot follow the actions of contemporary statesmen with much moral satisfaction. In the past I find myself regarding them with pity—who am I that I should condemn them? Surely they knew not what they did.

This is no reason for not saying what they did; but what they did was not always what they tried to do or thought that they were doing.

Moral progress has indeed been slow; it still is powerless to affect international relations. If Bright's remedy were adopted and every statesman in Europe were hanged, would that mend matters?

In return for your wisdom I have written enough to show my foolishness. Your letter will give me much food for meditation, and may in time lead to an amendment of my ways. That you should have written shows that you think me capable of doing better. I will only promise that if I can I will; but the labours of practical life multiply, and I have less time for work at my subject now than I had in the country. For a period coming on I ought to spend years in Archives: which is impossible. . . .

My jottings bear traces of the incoherence of one who has preached five sermons this week, and has two more to preach tomorrow. I have not had time to think over your letter: but I wanted to thank you. Perhaps the effort to rid myself of prejudice has left me cold and abstract in my mode of expression and thinking. If so it is an error to be amended and corrected.

Will you not someday write an article in the *Historical Review* on the Ethics of History? I have no objection to find my place among the shocking examples. Believe me that I am genuinely grateful to you.

Yours most sincerely

M. Creighton

[20]
Review of Lea's
History of the
Inquisition

A good many years ago, when Bishop Wilberforce was at Winchester, and the Earl of Beaconsfield was a character in fiction, the bishop was interested in the proposal to bring over the Utrecht Psalter. Mr. Disraeli thought the scheme absurd. "Of course," he said, "you won't get it." He was told that, nevertheless, such things are, that public manuscripts had even been sent across the Atlantic in order that Mr. Lea might write a history of the Inquisition. "Yes," he replied, "but they never came back again." The work which has been awaited so long has come over at last, and will assuredly be accepted as the most important contribution of the new world to the religious history of the old. Other books have shown the author as a thoughtful inquirer in the remunerative but perilous region where religion and politics conflict, where ideas and institutions are as much considered as persons and events, and history is charged with all the elements of fixity, development, and change. It is little to say, now, that he equals Buckle in the extent, and surpasses him in the intelligent choice and regulation, of his reading. He is armed at all points. His information is comprehensive, minute, exact, and everywhere sufficient, if not everywhere complete. In this astonishing press of digested facts there is barely space to discuss the ideals which they exhibit and the law which they obey. M. Molinier lately wrote that a work with this scope and title "serait, à notre sens, une entreprise à peu près chimérique."

Henry Charles Lea, *A History of the Inquisition of the Middle Ages* (London: Sampson Low, 1888). This review was published in the *English Historical Review* 3 (1888):773–788. Reprinted in Acton, *History of Freedom*, pp. 551–574.

It will be interesting to learn whether the opinion of so good a judge has been altered or confirmed.

The book begins with a survey of all that led to the growth of heresy, and to the creation, in the thirteenth century, of exceptional tribunals for its suppression. There can be no doubt that this is the least satisfactory portion of the whole. It is followed by a singularly careful account of the steps, legislative and administrative, by which Church and State combined to organise the intermediate institution, and of the manner in which its methods were formed by practice. Nothing in European literature can compete with this, the centre and substance of Mr. Lea's great history. In the remaining volumes he summons his witnesses, calls on the nations to declare their experience, and tells how the new force acted upon society to the end of the Middle Ages. History of this undefined and international cast, which shows the same wave breaking upon many shores, is always difficult, from the want of visible unity and progression, and has seldom succeeded so well as in this rich but unequal and disjointed narrative. On the most significant of all the trials, those of the Templars and of Hus, the author spends his best research; and the strife between Avignon and the Franciscans, thanks to the propitious aid of Father Ehrle, is better still. Joan of Arc prospers less than the disciples of Perfect Poverty; and after Joan of Arc many pages are allotted, rather profusely, to her companion in arms, who survives in the disguise of Bluebeard. The series of dissolving scenes ends, in order of time, at Savonarola; and with that limit the work is complete. The later Inquisition, starting with the Spanish and developing into the Roman, is not so much a prolongation or a revival as a new creation. The mediaeval Inquisition strove to control states, and was an engine of government. The modern strove to coerce the Protestants, and was an engine of war. One was subordinate, local, having a kind of headquarters in the house of Saint Dominic at Toulouse. The other was sovereign, universal, centred in the Pope, and exercising its domination, not against obscure men without a literature, but against bishop and archbishop, nuncio and legate, primate and professor; against the general of the Capuchins and the imperial preacher; against the first candidate in the conclave, and the president of the ecumenical council. Under altered conditions, the rules varied and even principles were modified. Mr. Lea is slow to take counsel of the voluminous moderns, fearing the confusion of dates. When he says that the laws he is describing are technically still in force, he makes too little of a fundamental distinction. In the eye of the polemic, the modern Inquisition eclipses its predecessor, and stops the way.

The origin of the Inquisition is the topic of a lasting controversy. According to common report, Innocent III founded it, and made Saint Dominic the first inquisitor; and this belief has been maintained by the Dominicans against the Cistercians, and by the Jesuits against the Dominicans themselves. They affirm that the saint, having done his work in Languedoc, pursued it in Lombardy: "Per civitates et castella Lombardiae circuibat, praedicans et evangelizans regnum Dei, atque contra haereticos inquirens, quos ex odore et aspectu dignoscens, condignis suppliciis puniebat" (Fontana, *Monumenta Dominicana*, 16). He transferred his powers to Fra Moneta, the brother in whose bed he died, and who is notable as having studied more seriously than any other divine the system which he assailed: "Vicarium suum in munere inquisitionis delegerat dilectissimum sibi B. Monetam, qui spiritu illius loricatus, tanquam leo rugiens contra haereticos surrexit. . . . Iniquos cum haereticos ex corde insectaretur, illisque nullo modo parceret, sed igne ac ferro consumeret." Moneta is succeeded by Guala, who brings us down to historic times, when the Inquisition flourished undisputed: "Facta promotione Guallae constitutus est in eius locum generalis inquisitor P. F. Guidottus de Sexto, a Gregorio Papa IX, qui innumeros propemodum haereticos igne consumpsit" (Fontana, *Sacrum Theatrum Dominicanum*, 595). Sicilian inquisitors produce an imperial privilege of December 1224, which shows the tribunal in full action under Honorius III: "Sub nostrae indignationis fulmine praesenti edicto districtius praecipiendo mandamus, quatenus inquisitoribus haereticae pravitatis, ut suum libere officium prosequi et exercere valeant, prout decet, omne quod potestis impendatis auxilium" (Franchina, *Inquisizione di Sicilia*, 1774, 8). This document may be a forgery of the fifteenth century; but the whole of the Dominican version is dismissed by Mr. Lea with contempt. He has heard that their founder once rescued a heretic from the flames; "but Dominic's project only looked to their peaceful conversion, and to performing the duties of instruction and exhortation." Nothing is better authenticated in the life of the saint than the fact that he condemned heretics and exercised the right of deciding which of them should suffer and which should be spared. "Contigit quosdam haereticos captos et per eum convictos, cum redire nollent ad fidem catholicam, tradi judicio saeculari. Cumque essent incendio deputati, aspiciens inter alios quemdam Raymundum de Grossi nomine, ac si aliquem re divinae praedestinationis radium fuisset intuitus, istum, inquit officialibus curiae, reservate, nec aliquo modo cum caeteris comburatur" (Constantinus, *Vita S. Dominici;* Echard, *Scriptores O.P.,* 1. 33). The transaction is memorable in Dominican annals as the one link distinctly connecting Saint Dominic with the system of executions, and the only security possessed by the order that the most conspicuous of its actions is sanctioned by the spirit and example of the founder. The original authorities record it, and it is commemorated by Bzovius and Malvenda, by Fontana and Percin, by Echard and Mamachi, as well as in the *Acta Sanctorum.* Those are exactly the authors to whom in the first instance a man betakes himself who desires to understand the inception and early growth of the Inquisition. I cannot remember that any one of them appears in Mr. Lea's notes. He says indeed that Saint Dominic's inquisitorial activity "is affirmed by all the historians of the order," and he is a workman who knows his tools so well that we may hesitate to impute this grave omission to inacquaintance with necessary literature. It is one of his characteristics to be suspicious of the *Histoire Intime* as the seat of fable and proper domain of those problems in psychology against which the certitude of history is always going to pieces. Where motives are obscure, he prefers to contemplate causes in their effects, and to look abroad over his vast horizon of unquestioned reality. The difference between outward and interior history will be felt by any one who compares the story of Dolcino here given with the account in Neander. Mr. Lea knows more about him and has better materials than the ponderous professor of pectoral theology. But he has not all Neander's patience and power to read significance and sense in the musings of a reckless erratic mind.

He believes that Pope Gregory IX is the intellectual originator, as well as the legislative imponent, of the terrific system which ripened gradually and experimentally in his pontificate. It does not appear whether he has read, or knows through Havet the investigations which conducted Ficker to a different hypothesis. The transition of 1231 from the saving of life to the taking of life by fire was nearly the sharpest that men can conceive, and in pursuance of it the subsequent legal forms are mere detail. The spirit and practice of centuries were renounced for the opposite extreme; and between the mercy of 1230 and the severity of 1231 there was no intervening stage of graduated rigour. Therefore it is probable that the new idea of duty, foreign to Italian and specifically to Roman ways, was conveyed by a new man, that a new influence just then got possession of the Pope. Professor Ficker signals Guala as the real contriver of the *régime* of terror, and the man who acquired the influence imported the idea and directed the policy. Guala was a Dominican prior whom the Pope trusted in emergencies. In the year 1230 he negotiated the treaty of San Germano between Frederic II and the Church, and was made Bishop of Brescia. In that year Brescia, first among Italian cities, inserted in its statutes the emperor's Lombard law of 1224, which sent the heretic to the stake. The inference is that the Dominican prelate caused its insertion, and that nobody is so likely to have expounded its available purport to the pontiff as the man who had so lately caused it to be adopted in his own see, and who stood high just then in merit and in favour. That Guala was bishop-elect on 28th August, half a year before the first burnings at Rome, we know; that he caused the adoption of Frederic's law at Brescia or at Rome is not in evidence. Of that abrupt and unexplained enactment little is told us, but this we are told, that it was inspired by Honorius: "Leges quoque imperiales per quondam Fredericum olim Romanorum imperatorem, tunc in devotione Romane sedis persistentem, procurante eadem sede, fuerunt edite et Padue promulgate" (Bern. Guidonis, *Practica Inquisitionis*, 173). At any rate, Gregory, who had seen most things since the elevation of Innocent, knew how Montfort dealt with Albigensian prisoners at Minerve and Lavaur, what penalties were in store at Toulouse, and on what principles Master Conrad administered in Germany the powers received from Rome. The Papacy which inspired the coronation laws of 1220, in which there is no mention of capital punishment, could not have been unobservant of the way in which its own provisions were transformed; and Gregory, whom Honorius had already called "magnum et speciale ecclesie Romane membrum," who had required the university of Bologna to adopt and to expound the new legislation, and who knew the Archbishop of Magdeburg, had little to learn from Guala about the formidable weapon supplied to that prelate for the government of Lombardy. There is room for further conjecture.

In those days it was discovered that Aragon was infested with heresy; and the king's confessor proposed that the Holy See be applied to for means of active suppression. With that object, in 1230 he was sent to Rome. The envoy's name was Raymond, and his home was on the coast of Catalonia in the town of Pennaforte. He was a Bolognese jurist, a Dominican, and the author of the most celebrated treatise on morals made public in the generation preceding the scholastic theology. The five years of his abode in Rome changed the face of the Church. He won the confidence of Gregory, became penitentiary, and was employed to codify the acts of the popes militant since the publication of Gratian. Very soon after Saint Raymond appeared at the papal court, the use of the stake became law, the inquisitorial machinery had been devised, and the management given to the priors of the order. When he departed he left behind him instructions for the treatment of heresy, which the pope adopted and sent out where they were wanted. He refused a mitre, rose to be general, it is said in opposition to Albertus Magnus, and retired early, to become, in his own country, the oracle of councils on the watch for heterodoxy. Until he came, in spite of much violence and many laws, the popes had imagined no permanent security against religious error, and were not formally committed to death by burning. Gregory himself, excelling all the priesthood in vigour and experience, had for four years laboured, vaguely and in vain, with the transmitted implements. Of a sudden, in three successive measures, he finds his way, and builds up the institution which is to last for centuries. That this mighty change in the conditions of religious thought and life and in the functions of the order was suggested by Dominicans is probable. And it is reasonable to suppose that it was the work of the foremost Dominican then living, who at that very moment had risen to power and predominance at Rome.

No sane observer will allow himself to overdraw the influence of national character on events. Yet there was that in the energetic race that dwell with the Pyrenees above them and the Ebro below that suited a leading part in the business of organised persecution. They are among the nations that have been inventors in politics, and both the constitution of Aragon and that of the society of Jesus prove their constructive science. While people in other lands were feeling their way, doubtful and debonair, Aragon went straight to the end. Before the first persecuting pope was elected, before the Child of Apulia, who was to be the first persecuting emperor, was born, Alfonso proscribed the heretics. King and clergy were in such accord that three years later the council of Girona decreed that they might be beaten while they remained, and should be burnt if they came back. It was under

this government, amid these surroundings, that Saint Dominic grew
up, whom Sixtus V, speaking on authority which we do not possess,
entitled the First Inquisitor. Saint Raymond, who had more to do with
it than Saint Dominic, was his countryman. Eymerici, whose *Directorium*
was the best authority until the *Practica* of Guidonis appeared, presided
during forty years over the Aragonese tribunal; and his commentator
Pegna, the Coke upon Littleton of inquisitorial jurisprudence, came
from the same stern region.

The *Histoire Générale de Languedoc* in its new shape has supplied Mr.
Lea with so good a basis that his obligations to the present editors
bring him into something like dependence on French scholarship. He
designates monarchs by the names they bear in France—Louis le
Germanique, Charles le Sage, Philippe le Bon, and even Philippe; and
this habit, with Foulques and Berenger of Tours, with Aretino for
Arezzo, Oldenburg for Altenburg, Torgau for Zürich, imparts an exotic
flavour which would be harmless but for a surviving preference for
French books. Compared with Bouquet and Vaissète, he is unfamiliar
with Böhmer and Pertz. For Matthew Paris he gets little or no help
from Coxe, or Madden, or Luard, or Liebermann, or Huillard. In
France few things of importance have escaped him. His account of
Marguerite Porrette differs from that given by Hauréau in the *Histoire
Littéraire,* and the difference is left unexplained. No man can write
about Joan of Arc without suspicion who discards the publications of
Quicherat, and even of Wallon, Beaucourt, and Luce. Etienne de
Bourbon was an inquisitor of long experience, who knew the original
comrade and assistant of Waldus. Fragments of him scattered up and
down in the works of learned men have caught the author's eye; but
it is uncertain how much he knows of the fifty pages from Stephanus
printed in Echard's book on Saint Thomas, or of the volume in which
Lecoy de la Marche has collected all, and more than all, that deserves
to live of his writings. The "Historia Pontificalis," attributed to John
of Salisbury, in the twentieth volume of the *Monumenta,* should affect
the account of Arnold of Brescia. The analogy with the Waldenses,
amongst whom his party seems to have merged, might be more strongly
marked. "Hominum sectam fecit que adhuc dicitur heresis Lumbar-
dorum. . . . Episcopis non parcebat ob avaritiam et turpem quaestum,
et plerumque propter maculam vite, et quia ecclesiam Dei in sangui-
nibus edificare nituntur." He was excommunicated and declared a
heretic. He was reconciled and forgiven. Therefore, when he resumed

his agitation his portion was with the obstinate and relapsed. "Ei populus Romanus vicissim auxilium et consilium contra omnes homines et nominatim contra domnum papam repromisit, eum namque excommunicaverat ecclesia Romana. . . . Post mortem domni Innocentii reversus est in Italiam, et promissa satisfactione et obediencia Romane ecclesie, a domno Eugenio receptus est apud Viterbum." And it is more likely that the fear of relics caused them to reduce his body to ashes than merely to throw the ashes into the Tiber.

The energy with which Mr. Lea beats up information is extraordinary even when imperfectly economised. He justly makes ample use of the *Vitae Paparum Avenionensium,* which he takes apparently from the papal volume of Muratori. These biographies were edited by Baluze, with notes and documents of such value that Avignon without him is like Athenaeus without Casaubon, or the Theodosian Code without Godefroy. But if he neglects him in print, he constantly quotes a certain Paris manuscript in which I think I recognise the very one which Baluze employed. Together with Guidonis and Eymerici, the leading authority of the fourteenth century is Zanchini, who became an inquisitor at Rimini in 1300, and died in 1340. His book was published with a commentary by Campeggio, one of the Tridentine fathers; and Campeggio was further annotated by Simancas, who exposes the disparity between Italian and Spanish usage. It was reprinted, with other treatises of the same kind, in the eleventh volume of the *Tractatus.* Some of these treatises, and the notes of Campeggio and Simancas, are passed over by Mr. Lea without notice. But he appreciates Zanchini so well that he has had him copied from a manuscript in France. Very much against his habit, he prints one entire sentence, from which it appears that his copy does not agree to the letter with the published text. It is not clear in every case whether he is using print or manuscript. One of the most interesting directions for inquisitors, and one of the earliest, was written by Cardinal Fulcodius, better known as Clement IV. Mr. Lea cites him a dozen times, always accurately, always telling us scrupulously which of the fifteen chapters to consult. The treatise of Fulcodius occupies a few pages in Carena, *De Officio S.S. Inquisitionis,* in which, besides other valuable matter, there are notes by Carena himself, and a tract by Pegna, the perpetual commentator of the Inquisition. This is one of the first eight or ten books which occur to any one whose duty it is to lay in an inquisitor's library. Not only we are never told where to find Fulcodius, but when Carena is mentioned it is so done as to defy verification. Inartistic references are not, in this instance, a token of inadequate study. But a book designed only for readers who know at a glance where to lay their finger on *S. Francis. Collat. Monasticae, Collat.* 20, or *Post constt. IV. XIX. Cod. I. v.* will be slow in recovering outlay.

Not his acquaintance with rare books only, which might be the curiosity of an epicurean, but with the right and appropriate book, amazes the reader. Like most things attributed to Abbot Joachim, the *Vaticinia Pontificum* is a volume not in common use, and decent people may be found who never saw a copy. Mr. Lea says: "I have met with editions of Venice issued in 1589, 1600, 1605, and 1646, of Ferrara in 1591, of Frankfort in 1608, of Padua in 1625, and of Naples in 1660, and there are doubtless numerous others." This is the general level throughout; the rare failures disappear in the imposing supererogation of knowledge. It could not be exceeded by the pupils of the Göttingen seminary or the École des Chartes. They have sometimes a vicious practice of overtopping sufficient proof with irrelevant testimony: but they transcribe all deciding words in full, and for the rest, quicken and abridge our toil by sending us, not to chapter and verse, but to volume and page, of the physical and concrete book. We would gladly give Bluebeard and his wife—he had but one after all—in exchange for the best quotations from sources hard of access which Mr. Lea must have hoarded in the course of labours such as no man ever achieved before him, or will ever attempt hereafter. It would increase the usefulness of his volumes, and double their authority. There are indeed fifty pages of documentary matter not entirely new or very closely connected with the text. Portions of this, besides, are derived from manuscripts explored in France and Italy, but not it seems in Rome, and in this way much curious and valuable material underlies the pages; but it is buried without opportunity of display or scrutiny. Line upon line of references to the Neapolitan archives only bewilder and exasperate. Mr. Lea, who dealt more generously with the readers of *Sacerdotal Celibacy,* has refused himself in these overcrowded volumes that protection against overstatement. The want of verifiable indication of authorities is annoying, especially at first; and it may be possible to find one or two references to Saint Bonaventure or to Wattenbach which are incorrect. But he is exceedingly careful in rendering the sense of his informants, and neither strains the tether nor outsteps his guide. The original words in very many cases would add definiteness and a touch of surprise to his narrative.

If there is anywhere the least infidelity in the statement of an author's meaning, it is in the denial that Marsilius, the imperial theorist, and the creator with Ockam of the Ghibelline philosophy that has ruled the world, was a friend of religious liberty. Marsilius assuredly was not a Whig. Quite as much as any Guelph, he desired to concentrate power, not to limit or divide it. Of the sacred immunities of conscience he had no clearer vision than Dante. But he opposed persecution in the shape in which he knew it, and the patriarchs of European emancipation have not done more. He never says that there is no case in which a religion may be proscribed; but he speaks of none in which a religion may be imposed. He discusses, not intolerance, but the divine authority to persecute, and pleads for a secular law. It does not appear how he would deal with a Thug. "Nemo quantumcumque peccans contra disciplinas speculativas aut operativas quascumque punitur vel arcetur in hoc saeculo praecise in quantum huiusmodi, sed in quantum peccat contra praeceptum humanae legis. . . . Si humana lege prohibitum fuerit haereticum aut aliter infidelem in regione manere, qui talis in ipsa repertus fuerit, tanquam legis humanae transgressor, poena vel supplicio huic transgressioni eadem lege statutis, in hoc saeculo debet arceri." The difference is slight between the two readings. One asserts that Marsilius was tolerant in effect; the other denies that he was tolerant in principle.

Mr. Lea does not love to recognise the existence of much traditional toleration. Few lights are allowed to deepen his shadows. If a stream of tolerant thought descended from the early ages to the time when the companion of Vespucci brought his improbable tale from Utopia, then the views of Bacon, of Dante, of Gerson cannot be accounted for by the ascendency of a unanimous persuasion. It is because all men were born to the same inheritance of enforced conformity that we glide so easily towards the studied increase of pain. If some men were able to perceive what lay in the other scale, if they made a free choice, after deliberation, between well-defined and well-argued opinions, then what happened is not assignable to invincible causes, and history must turn from general and easy explanation to track the sinuosities of a tangled thread. In Mr. Lea's acceptation of ecclesiastical history intolerance was handed down as a rule of life from the days of St. Cyprian, and the few who shrank half-hearted from the gallows and the flames were exceptions, were men navigating craft of their own away from the track of St. Peter. Even in his own age he is not careful to show that the Waldenses opposed persecution, not in self-defence, but in the necessary sequence of thought. And when he describes Eutychius as an obscure man, who made a point at the fifth general council, for which he was rewarded with the patriarchate of Constantinople— Eutychius, who was already patriarch when the council assembled; and when he twice tears Formosus from his grave to parade him in his vestments about Rome—we may suspect that the perfect grasp of documentary history from the twelfth century does not reach backwards in a like degree.

If Mr. Lea stands aloft, in his own domain, as an accumulator, his credit as a judge of testimony is nearly as high. The deciding test of his critical sagacity is the masterly treatment of the case against the Templars. They were condemned without mercy, by Church and State, by priest and jurist, and down to the present day cautious examiners of evidence, like Prutz and Lavocat, give a faltering verdict. In the face of many credulous forerunners and of much concurrent testimony Mr. Lea pronounces positively that the monster trial was a conspiracy to murder, and every adverse proof a lie. His immediate predecessor, Schottmüller, the first writer who ever knew the facts, has made this conclusion easy. But the American does not move in the retinue of the Prussian scholar. He searches and judges for himself; and in his estimate of the chief actor in the tragedy, Clement V, he judges differently. He rejects, as forgeries, a whole batch of unpublished confessions, and he points out that a bull disliked by inquisitors is not reproduced entire in the *Bullarium Dominicanum*. But he fails to give the collation, and is generally jealous about admitting readers to his confidence, taking them into consultation and producing the scales. In the case of Delicieux, which nearly closes the drama of Languedoc, he consults his own sources, independently of Hauréau, and in the end adopts the marginal statement in Limborch, that the pope aggravated the punishment. In other places, he puts his trust in the *Historia Tribulationum,* and he shows no reason for dismissing the different account there given of the death of Delicieux: "Ipsum fratrem Bernardum sibi dari a summo pontifice petierunt. Et videns summus pontifex quod secundum accusationes quas de eo fecerant fratres minores justitiam postularent, tradidit eis eum. Qui, quum suscepissent eum in sua potestate, sicut canes, cum vehementer furiunt, lacerant quam capiunt bestiam, ita ipsi diversis afflictionibus et cruciatibus laniaverunt eum. Et videntes quod neque inquisitionibus nec tormentis poterant pompam de eo facere in populo, quam quaerebant, in arctissimo carcere eum reduxerunt, ibidem eum taliter tractantes, quod infra paucos menses, quasi per ignem et aquam transiens, de carcere corporis et minorum et praedicatorum liberatus gloriose triumphans de mundi principe, migravit ad coelos."

We obtain only a general assurance that the fate of Cecco d' Ascoli is related on the strength of unpublished documents at Florence. It is not stated what they are. There is no mention of the epitaph pronounced by the pope who had made him his physician: "Cucullati Minores recentiorum Peripateticorum principem perdiderunt." We do not learn that Cecco reproached Dante with the same fatalistic leaning for which he himself was to die: "Non è fortuna cui ragion non vinca." Or how they disputed: "An ars natura fortior ac potentior existeret," and argument was supplanted by experiment: "Aligherius, qui opinionem oppositam mordicus tuebatur, felem domesticam Stabili objiciebat, quam ea arte instituerat, ut ungulis candelabrum teneret, dum is noctu legeret, vel coenaret. Cicchius igitur, ut in sententiam suam Aligherium pertraheret, scutula assumpta, ubi duo musculi asservabantur inclusi, illos in conspectu felis dimisit; quae naturae ingenio inemendabili obsequens, muribus vix inspectis, illico in terram candelabrum abjecit, et ultro citroque cursare ac vestigiis praedam persequi instituit." Either Appiani's defence of Cecco d' Ascoli has escaped Mr. Lea, who nowhere mentions Bernino's *Historia di tutte l' Heresie* where it is printed; or he may distrust Bernino for calling Dante a schismatic; or it may be that he rejects all this as legend, beneath the certainty of history. But he does not disdain the legendary narrative of the execution: "Tradition relates that he had learned by his art that he should die between Africa and Campo Fiore, and so sure was he of this that on the way to the stake he mocked and ridiculed his guards; but when the pile was about to be lighted he asked whether there was any place named Africa in the vicinage, and was told that that was the name of a neighbouring brook flowing from Fiesole to the Arno. Then he recognised that Florence was the Field of Flowers, and that he had been miserably deceived." The Florentine document before me, whether the same or another I know not, says nothing about untimely mockery or miserable deception: "Aveva inteso dal demonio dover lui morire di morte accidentale infra l' Affrica e campo di fiore; per lo che cercando di conservare la reputazione sua, ordinò di non andar mai nelle parti d' Affrica; e credendo tal fallacia è di potere sbeffare la gente, pubblicamente in Italia esecutava l'arte della negromanzia, et essendo per questo preso in Firenze e per la sua confessione essendo già giudicato al fuoco e legato al palo, nè vedendo alcun segno della sua liberazione, avendo prima fatto i soliti scongiuri, domandò alle persone che erano all' intorno, se quivi vicino era alcun luogo che si chiamasse Affrica, et essendogli risposto di si, cioè un fiumicello che correva ivi presso, il quale discende da Fiesole ed è chiamato Affrica, considerando che il demonio per lo campo de' fiori aveva inteso Fiorenza, e per l' Affrica quel fiumicello, ostinato nella sua perfidia, disse al manigoldo che quanto prima attaccasse il fuoco."

Mr. Lea thinks that the untenable conditions offered to the count of Toulouse by the council of Arles in 1211 are spurious. M. Paul Meyer has assigned reasons on the other side in his notes to the translation of the *Chanson de la Croisade*, pp. 75–77; and the editors of Vaissète (vi. 347) are of the same opinion as M. Paul Meyer. It happens that Mr. Lea reads the *Chanson* in the *editio princeps* of Fauriel; and in this particular place he cites the *Histoire du Languedoc* in the old and superseded edition. From a letter lately brought to light in the *Archiv für Geschichte des Mittelalters,* he infers that the decree of Clement V affecting the privilege of inquisitors was tampered with before publication. A Franciscan writes from Avignon when the new canons were ready: "Inquisitores etiam heretice pravitatis restinguuntur et supponuntur episcopis"—which he thinks would argue something much more decisive than the regulations as they finally appeared. Ehrle, who publishes the letter, remarks that the writer exaggerated the import of the intended change; but he says it not of this sentence, but of the next preceding. Mr. Lea has acknowledged elsewhere the gravity of this Clementine reform. As it stands, it was considered injurious by inquisitors, and elicited repeated protests from Bernardus Guidonis: "Ex predicta autem ordinatione seu restrictione nonnulla inconvenientia consecuntur, que liberum et expeditum cursum officii inquisitoris tam in manibus dyocesanorum quam etiam inquisitorum diminuunt seu retardant. . . . Que apostolice sedis circumspecta provisione ac provida circumspectione indigent, ut remedientur, aut moderentur in melius, seu pocius totaliter suspendantur propter nonnulla inconvenientia que consecuntur ex ipsis circa liberum et expeditum cursum officii inquisitoris."

The feudal custom which supplied Beaumarchais with the argument of his play recruits a stout believer in the historian of the Inquisition, who assures us that the authorities may be found on a certain page of his *Sacerdotal Celibacy*. There, however, they may be sought in vain. Some dubious instances are mentioned, and the dissatisfied inquirer is passed on to the Fors de Béarn, and to Lagrèze, and is informed that M. Louis Veuillot raised an unprofitable dust upon the subject. I remember that M. Veuillot, in his boastful scorn for book learning, made no secret that he took up the cause because the Church was attacked, but got his facts from somebody else. Graver men than Veuillot have shared his conclusion. Sir Henry Maine, having looked into the matter in his quick, decisive way, declared that an instance of the *droit du seigneur* was as rare as the Wandering Jew. In resting his case on the Pyrenees, Mr. Lea shows his usual judgment. But his very confident note is a too easy and contemptuous way of settling a controversy which is still wearily extant from Spain to Silesia, in which some new fact comes to light every year, and drops into obscurity, riddled with the shafts of critics.

An instance of too facile use of authorities occurs at the siege of Béziers. "A fervent Cistercian contemporary informs us that when Arnaud was asked whether the Catholics should be spared, he feared the heretics would escape by feigning orthodoxy, and fiercely replied, 'Kill them all, for God knows his own.' " Caesarius, to whom we owe the *locus classicus*, was a Cistercian and a contemporary, but he was not so fervent as that, for he tells it as a report, not as a fact, with a caution which ought not to have evaporated. "Fertur dixisse: Caedite eos. Novit enim Dominus qui sunt eius!" The Catholic defenders had been summoned to separate from the Cathari, and had replied that they were determined to share their fate. It was then resolved to make an example, which we are assured bore fruit afterwards. The hasty zeal of Citeaux adopted the speech of the abbot and gave it currency. But its rejection by the French scholars, Tamizey de Larroque and Auguste Molinier, was a warning against presenting it with a smooth surface, as a thing tested and ascertained. Mr. Lea, in other passages, has shown his disbelief in Caesarius of Heisterbach, and knows that history written in reliance upon him would be history fit for the moon. Words as ferocious are recorded of another legate at a different siege (Langlois, *Règne de Philippe le Hardi*, p. 156). Their tragic significance for history is not in the mouth of an angry crusader at the storming of a fortress, but in the pen of an inoffensive monk, watching and praying under the peaceful summit of the Seven Mountains.

Mr. Lea undertakes to dispute no doctrine and to propose no moral.

He starts with an avowed desire not to say what may be construed injuriously to the character or feelings of men. He writes pure history, and is methodically oblivious of applied history. The broad and sufficient realm of fact is divided by a scientific frontier from the outer world of interested argument. Beyond the frontier he has no cognisance, and neither aspires to inflame passions nor to compose the great eirenikon. Those who approach with love or hatred are to go empty away; if indeed he does not try by turns to fill them both. He seeks his object not by standing aloof, as if the name that perplexed Polyphemus was the proper name for historians, but by running successively on opposing lines. He conceives that civilised Europe owes its preservation to the radiant centre of religious power at Rome, and is grateful to Innocent III for the vigour with which he recognised that force was the only cure for the pestiferous opinions of misguided zealots. One of his authorities is the inquisitor Bernardus Guidonis, and there is no writer whom, in various shapes, he quotes so often. But when Guidonis says that Dolcino and Margarita suffered *per juditium ecclesie,* Mr. Lea is careful to vindicate the clergy from the blame of their sufferings.

From a distinction which he draws between despotism and its abuse, and from a phrase, disparaging to elections, about rivers that cannot rise above the level of their source, it would appear that Mr. Lea is not under compulsion to that rigid liberalism which, by repressing the time-test and applying the main rules of morality all round, converts history into a frightful monument of sin. Yet, in the wake of passages which push the praises of authority to the verge of irony, dire denunciations follow. When the author looks back upon his labours, he discerns "a scene of almost unrelieved blackness." He avers that "the deliberate burning alive of a human being simply for difference of belief, is an atrocity," and speaks of a "fiendish legislation," "an infernal curiosity," a "seemingly causeless ferocity which appears to persecute for the mere pleasure of persecuting." The Inquisition is "energetic only in evil"; it is "a standing mockery of justice, perhaps the most iniquitous that the arbitrary cruelty of man has ever devised."

This is not the protest of wounded humanity. The righteous resolve to beware of doctrine has not been strictly kept. In the private judgment of the writer, the thinking of the Middle Ages was sophistry and their belief superstition. For the erring and suffering mass of mankind he has an enlightened sympathy; for the intricacies of speculation he has none. He cherishes a disbelief, theological or inductive it matters not, in sinners rescued by repentence and in blessings obtained by prayer. Between remitted guilt and remitted punishment he draws a vanishing line that makes it doubtful whether Luther started from the limits of purgatory or the limits of hell. He finds that it was a universal precept to break faith with heretics, that it was no arbitrary or artificial innovation to destroy them, but the faithful outcome of the traditional spirit of the Church. He hints that the horror of sensuality may be easily carried too far, and that Saint Francis of Assisi was in truth not very much removed from a worshipper of the devil. Prescott, I think, conceived a resemblance between the god of Montezuma and the god of Torquemada; but he saw and suspected less than his more learned countryman. If any life was left in the Strappado and the Samarra, no book would deserve better than this description of their vicissitudes to go the way of its author, and to fare with the flagrant volume, snatched from the burning at Champel, which is still exhibited to Unitarian pilgrims in the Rue de Richelieu.

In other characteristic places we are taught to observe the agency of human passion, ambition, avarice, and pride; and wade through oceans of unvaried evil with that sense of dejection which comes from Digby's *Mores Catholici* or the *Origines de la France Contemporaine*, books which affect the mind by the pressure of repeated instances. The Inquisition is not merely "the monstrous offspring of mistaken zeal," but it is "utilised by selfish greed and lust of power." No piling of secondary motives will confront us with the true cause. Some of those who fleshed their swords with preliminary bloodshed on their way to the holy war may have owed their victims money; some who in 1348 shared the worst crime that Christian nations have committed perhaps believed that Jews spread the plague. But the problem is not there. Neither credulity nor cupidity is equal to the burden. It needs no weighty scholar, pressed down and running over with the produce of immense research, to demonstrate how common men in a barbarous age were tempted and demoralised by the tremendous power over pain, and death, and hell. We have to learn by what reasoning process, by what ethical motive, men trained to charity and mercy came to forsake the ancient ways and made themselves cheerfully familiar with the mysteries of the torture-chamber, the perpetual prison, and the stake. And this cleared away, when it has been explained why the gentlest of women chose that the keeper of her conscience should be

Conrad of Marburg, and, inversely, how that relentless slaughterer directed so pure a penitent as Saint Elizabeth, a larger problem follows. After the first generation, we find that the strongest, the most original, the most independent minds in Europe—men born for opposition, who were neither awed nor dazzled by canon law and scholastic theology, by the master of sentences, the philosopher and the gloss—fully agreed with Guala and Raymond. And we ask how it came about that, as the rigour of official zeal relaxed, and there was no compulsion, the fallen cause was taken up by the Council of Constance, the University of Paris, the States-General, the House of Commons, and the first reformers; that Ximenes outdid the early Dominicans, while Vives was teaching toleration; that Fisher, with his friend's handy book of revolutionary liberalism in his pocket, declared that violence is the best argument with Protestants; that Luther, excommunicated for condemning persecution, became a persecutor? Force of habit will not help us, nor love and fear of authority, nor the unperceived absorption of circumambient fumes.

Somewhere Mr. Lea, perhaps remembering Maryland, Rhode Island, and Pennsylvania, speaks of "what was universal public opinion from the thirteenth to the seventeenth century." The obstacle to this theory, as of a ship labouring on the Bank, or an orb in the tail of a comet, is that the opinion is associated with no area of time, and remains unshaken. The Dominican democrat who took his seat with the Mountain in 1848 never swerved from the principles of his order. More often, and, I think, more deliberately, Mr. Lea urges that intolerance is implied in the definition of the mediaeval Church, that it sprang from the root and grew with "the very law of its being." It is no desperate expedient of authority at bay, for "the people were as eager as their pastors to send the heretic to the stake." Therefore he does not blame the perpetrator, but his inherited creed. "No firm believer in the doctrine of exclusive salvation could doubt that the truest mercy lay in sweeping away the emissaries of Satan with fire and sword." What we have here is the logic of history, constraining every system to utter its last word, to empty its wallets, and work its consequences out to the end. But this radical doctrine misguides its author to the anachronism that as early as the first Leo "the final step had been taken, and the Church was definitely pledged to the suppression of heresy at whatever cost."

We do not demand that historians shall compose our opinions or

relieve us from the purifying pains of thought. It is well if they discard
dogmatising, if they defer judgment, or judge, with the philosopher,
by precepts capable of being a guide for all. We may be content that
they should deny themselves, and repress their sentiments and wishes.
When these are contradictory, or such as evidently to tinge the medium,
an unholy curiosity is engendered to learn distinctly not only what the
writer knows, but what he thinks. Mr. Lea has a malicious pleasure
in baffling inquiry into the principle of his judgments. Having found,
in the Catechism of Saint Sulpice, that devout Catholics are much on
a par with the fanatics whose sympathy with Satan made the holy
office a requisite of civilisation, and having, by his exuberant censure,
prepared us to hear that this requisite of civilisation "might well seem
the invention of demons," he arrives at the inharmonious conclusion
that it was wrought and worked, with benefit to their souls, by sincere
and godly men. The condemnation of Hus is the proper test, because
it was the extreme case of all. The council was master of the situation,
and was crowded with men accustomed to disparage the authority of
the Holy See and to denounce its acts. Practically, there was no pope
either of Rome or Avignon. The Inquisition languished. There was
the plausible plea of deference to the emperor and his passport; there
was the imperative consideration for the religious future of Bohemia.
The reforming divines were free to pursue their own scheme of justice,
of mercy, and of policy. The scheme they pursued has found an
assiduous apologist in their new historian. "To accuse the good fathers
of Constance of conscious bad faith" is impossible. To observe the
safe-conduct would have seemed absurd "to the most conscientious
jurists of the council." In a nutshell, "if the result was inevitable, it
was the fault of the system and not of the judges, and their conscience
might well feel satisfied."

There may be more in this than the oratorical precaution of a scholar
wanting nothing, who chooses to be discreet rather than explicit, or
the wavering utterance of a mind not always strung to the same pitch.
It is not the craving to rescue a favourite or to clear a record, but a
fusion of unsettled doctrines of retrospective contempt. There is a
demonstration of progress in looking back without looking up, in
finding that the old world was wrong in the grain, that the kosmos
which is inexorable to folly is indifferent to sin. Man is not an
abstraction, but a manufactured product of the society with which he
stands or falls, which is answerable for crimes that are the shadow

and the echo of its own nobler vices, and has no right to hang the rogue it rears. Before you lash the detected class, mulct the undetected. Crime without a culprit, the unavenged victim who perishes by no man's fault, law without responsibility, the virtuous agent of a vicious cause—all these are the signs and pennons of a philosophy not recent, but rather inarticulate still and inchoate, which awaits analysis by Professor Flint.

No propositions are simpler or more comprehensive than the two, that an incorrigible misbeliever ought to burn, or that the man who burns him ought to hang. The world as expanded on the liberal and on the hegemonic projection is patent to all men, and the alternatives, that Lacordaire was bad and Conrad good, are clear in all their bearings. They are too gross and palpable for Mr. Lea. He steers a subtler course. He does not sentence the heretic, but he will not protect him from his doom. He does not care for the inquisitor, but he will not resist him in the discharge of his duty. To establish a tenable footing on that narrow but needful platform is the epilogue these painful volumes want, that we may not be found with the traveller who discovered a precipice to the right of him, another to the left, and nothing between. Their profound and admirable erudition leads up, like Hellwald's *Culturgeschichte*, to a great note of interrogation. When we find the Carolina and the savage justice of Tudor judges brought to bear on the exquisitely complex psychological revolution that proceeded, after the year 1200, about the Gulf of Lyons and the Tyrrhene Sea, we miss the historic question. When we learn that Priscillian was murdered (i. 214), but that Lechler has no business to call the sentence on John Hus "ein wahrer Justizmord" (ii. 494), and then again that the burning of a heretic is a judicial murder after all (i. 552), we feel bereft of the philosophic answer.

Although Mr. Lea gives little heed to Pani and Hefele, Gams and Du Boys, and the others who write for the Inquisition without pleading ignorance, he emphasises a Belgian who lately wrote that the Church never employed direct constraint against heretics. People who never heard of the Belgian will wonder that so much is made of this conventional figleaf. Nearly the same assertion may be found, with varieties of caution and of confidence, in a catena of divines, from Bergier to Newman. To appear unfamiliar with the defence exposes the writer to the thrust that you cannot know the strength or the weakness of a case until you have heard its advocates. The liberality of Leo XIII, which has yielded a splendid and impartial harvest to Ehrle, and Schottmüller, and the École Française, raises the question whether the Abbé Duchesne or Father Denifle supplied with all the resources of the archives which are no longer secret would produce a very different or more complete account. As a philosophy of religious persecution the book is inadequate. The derivation of sects, though resting always upon good supports, stands out from an indistinct background of dogmatic history. The intruding maxims, darkened by shadows of earth, fail to ensure at all times the objective and delicate handling of mediaeval theory. But the vital parts are protected by a panoply of mail. From the Albigensian crusade to the fall of the Templars and to that Franciscan movement wherein the key to Dante lies, the design and organisation, the activity and decline of the Inquisition constitute a sound and solid structure that will survive the censure of all critics. Apart from surprises still in store at Rome, and the manifest abundance of Philadelphia, the knowledge which is common property, within reach of men who seriously invoke history as the final remedy for untruth and the sovereign arbiter of opinion, can add little to the searching labours of the American.

[21]
Döllinger's Historical Work

When first seen, at Würzburg, in the diaries of Platen the poet, Dr. Döllinger was an eager student of general literature, and especially of Schlegel and the romantic philosophy. It was an epoch in which the layman and the *dilettante* prevailed. In other days a divine had half a dozen distinct schools of religious thought before him, each able to develop and to satisfy a receptive mind; but the best traditions of western scholarship had died away when the young Franconian obtained a chair in the reorganized university of Munich. His own country, Bavaria, his time, the third decade of the century, furnished no guide, no master, and no model to the new professor. Exempt, by date and position, from the discipline of a theological party, he so continued, and never turned elsewhere for the dependence he escaped at home. No German theologian, of his own or other churches, bent his course; and he derived nothing from the powerful writer then dominant in the North. To a friend describing Herder as the one unprofitable classic, he replied, "Did you ever learn anything from Schleiermacher?" And if it is doubtful which way this stroke was aimed, it is certain that he saw less than others in the Berlin teacher.

Very young he knew modern languages well, though with a defective ear, and having no local or contemporary attachments he devoted himself systematically to the study of foreign divines. The characteristic universality of his later years was not the mere result of untiring energy and an unlimited command of books. His international habit sprang from the inadequacy of the national supply, and the search for truth in every century naturally became a lecturer whose function it was to unfold from first to last the entire life of the Church, whose range extended over all Christian ages, and who felt the inferiority of his

Published in the *English Historical Review* 5 (1890):700–744. Reprinted in Acton, *History of Freedom*, pp. 375–435.

own. Döllinger's conception of the science which he was appointed to carry forward, in conformity with new requirements and new resources, differed from the average chiefly by being more thorough and comprehensive. At two points he was touched by currents of the day. Savigny, the legal expert of a school recruited from both denominations and gravitating towards Catholicism, had expounded law and society in that historic spirit which soon pervaded other sciences, and restored the significance of national custom and character. By his writings Protestant literature overlapped. The example of the conspicuous jurist served as a suggestion for divines to realise the patient process of history; and Döllinger continued to recognise him as a master and originator of true scientific methods when his influence on jurisprudence was on the wane. On the same track, Drey, in 1819, defended the theory of development as the vital prerogative of Rome over the fixity of other churches. Möhler was the pupil of Drey, and they made Tübingen the seat of a positive theology, broader and more progressive than that of Munich.

The first eminent thinker whom he saw and heard was Baader, the poorest of writers, but the most instructive and impressive talker in Germany, and the one man who appears to have influenced the direction of his mind. Bishop Martensen has described his amazing powers; and Döllinger, who remembered him with more scant esteem, bore equal testimony to the wealth and worth of his religious philosophy. He probably owed to him his persistent disparagement of Hegel, and more certainly that familiarity with the abstruse literature of mysticism which made him as clear and sure of vision in the twilight of Petrucci and St. Martin as in the congenial company of Duperron. Baader is remembered by those who abstain from sixteen volumes of discordant thought, as the inventor of that system of political insurance which became the Holy Alliance. That authority is as sacred and sovereignty as absolute in the Church as in the State, was an easy and obvious inference, and it has been lately drawn with an energy and literary point to which Baader was a stranger, by the Count de Maistre, who was moreover a student of St. Martin. When the ancient mystic welcomed his new friend, he was full of praises of De Maistre. He impressed upon his earnest listener the importance of the books on the pope and on the Gallican church, and assured him that the spirit which animates them is the genuine Catholicism. These conversations were the origin of Döllinger's specific ultramontanism. It governed one half of his life, and his interest in De Maistre outlasted the assent which he once gave to some of his opinions. Questions arising from the Savoyard's indictment againt Bacon, which he proposed to Liebig, formed the connection between the two laboured attacks on the founder of English philosophy.

Much of that which at any time was unhistoric or presumptive in his mind may be ascribed to this influence; and it divided him from Möhler, who was far before him in the fulness of the enjoyment of his powers and his fame, whom he survived half a century, and never ceased to venerate as the finest theological intellect he had known. The publication of the *Symbolik* made it difficult for the author to remain in Wirtemberg; Tübingen, he said, was a place where he could neither live nor die happy; and having made Döllinger's acquaintance, he conceived an ardent wish to become his colleague at Munich.

"Im Verkehre mit Ihnen, und dem Kreise in dem Sie leben, habe ich mich aufs anmuthigste erheitert, sittlich gestärkt, und religiös getröstet und ermuthigt gefunden; ein Verein von Einwirkungen auf mich wurde mir gewährt, deren aller ich in fast gleichem Grade bedürftig war."

Döllinger negotiated his appointment, overcame the resisting ministerial medium through the intervention of the king, and surrendered his own department of theology, which they both regarded as the most powerful agency in religious instruction. Möhler had visited Göttingen and Berlin, and recognised their superiority. A public address to Planck, praising the Protestant treatment of history, was omitted by Döllinger from the edition of his miscellaneous writings. They differed so widely that one of them hesitated to read Bossuet's *Defensio*, and generally kept the stronger Gallicans out of sight, whilst the other warmly recommended Richer, and Launoy, and Dupin, and cautioned his pupils against Baronius, as a forger and a cheat, who dishonestly attributed to the primitive Church ideas quite foreign to its constitution. He found fault with his friend for undue favour to the Jesuits, and undue severity towards Jansenism. The other advised him to read Fénelon and succeeded in modifying this opinion.

"Sie werden vielleicht um so geneigter sein, mir zu verzeihen, wenn ich Ihnen melde, dass ich inzwischen recht fleissig die Jansenistischen Streitigkeiten, durch Ihre freundliche Zuschrift angeregt, studirt habe, und Ihrer Darstellung ohne Zweifel jetzt weit näher stehe als früher. Selbst die Bulle Unigenitus erscheint mir in einem weit günstigeren Lichte als früher, obschon ich die Censur mancher Quesnel'scher Sätze

immer noch nicht begreifen kann. Sie schrieben mir, dass die Fénelon'sche Correspondenz einen grossen Einfluss auf Ihre Betrachtungs-
weise ausgeübt habe. Auch bei mir ist dieses der Fall."

But in describing the failure of scholastic theology, the exaggeration
of De Maistre, the incompetence of the Roman censorship, the irreligion
of Leo X, and the strength of Luther's case against the Papacy, the
sensitive Suabian made a contrast, then, and long after, with Döllinger's
disciplined coolness and reserve.

"Dann war wirklich die bestehende Form der Kirche im höchsten
Grade tadelhaft, und bedurfte der Reinigung. Die Päpste waren
Despoten, willkührliche Herrscher geworden. Gebräuche hatten sich
angehäuft, die im höchsten Grade dem Glauben und der christlichen
Frömmigkeit entgegen waren. In vielen Punkten hatte Luther immer
Recht, wenn er von Missbräuchen der Römischen Gewalt spricht, dass
dort alles feil sei. Tetzel verfuhr ohnediess auf die empörendste Weise,
und übertrieb, mit einer religiösen Rohheit und einem Stumpfsinn
ohne Gleichen, das Bedenkliche der Sache auf die äusserste Spitze."

The disagreement which made itself felt from time to time between
the famous colleagues was not removed when one of them wished the
other to change his confessor before his last illness.

Möhler claimed the supreme chair of ecclesiastical history as a
matter of course, and by right of seniority. He apologised for venturing
to supersede one who had gained distinction in that lecture-room, but
he hinted that he himself was the least fit of the two for dogmatics.

"Ich habe mich für die historischen Fächer entschieden. Ihr Opfer,
wenn Sie Dogmatik lesen, anerkenne ich, aber ich bitte das meinige
nicht zu überschen. Welcher Entschluss, ich möchte sagen, welche
Unverschämtheit ist es, nach Ihnen und bei Ihren Lebzeiten,
Kirchengeschichte in München zu doziren?"

Döllinger took that branch for the time, but he never afterwards
taught theology proper. As Möhler, who was essentially a theologian,
deserted divinity to compose inferior treatises on the gnostics and the
false decretals, Döllinger, by choice and vocation a divine, having
religion as the purpose of his life, judged that the loftier function, the
more spiritual service, was historical teaching. The problem is to know
how it came to pass that a man who was eminently intelligent and
perspicuous in the exposition of doctrines, but who, in narrative,
description, and knowledge of character, was neither first nor second,
resolved that his mission was history.

In early life he had picked up chance copies of Baronius and Petavius, the pillars of historic theology; but the motives of his choice lay deeper. Church history had long been the weakest point and the cause of weakness among the Catholics, and it was the rising strength of the German Protestants. Therefore it was the post of danger; and it gave to a theologian the command of a public of laymen. The restoration of history coincided with the euthanasia of metaphysic; when the foremost philosophic genius of the time led over to the historic treatment both of philosophy and religion, and Hamilton, Cousin, Comte, severally converted the science into its history. Many men better equipped for speculation than for erudition went the same way; the systematic theology was kept up in the universities by the influence of Rome, where scholasticism went on untouched by the romantic transformation. Writing of England, Wiseman said: "There is still a scholastic hardness in our controversial theology, an unbendingness of outward forms in our explanations of Catholic principles, which renders our theologians dry and unattractive to the most catholicly inclined portion of our Protestants." The choice which these youths made, towards 1830, was, though they did not know it, the beginning of a rift that widened.

Döllinger was more in earnest than others in regarding Christianity as history, and in pressing the affinity between catholic and historical thought. Systems were to him nearly as codes to Savigny, when he exhorted his contemporaries not to consolidate their law, lest, with their wisdom and knowledge, they should incorporate their delusions and their ignorance, and usurp for the state what belonged to the nation. He would send an inquiring student to the *Historia Congregationis de Auxiliis* and the *Historia Pelagiana* rather than to Molina or Lemos, and often gave the advice which, coming from Oriel, disconcerted Morris of Exeter: "I am afraid you will have to read the Jesuit Petavius." He dreaded the predominance of great names which stop the way, and everything that interposes the notions of an epoch, a region, or a school between the Church and the observer.

To an Innsbruck professor, lamenting that there was no philosophy which he could heartily adopt, he replied that philosophies do not subsist in order to be adopted. A Thomist or a Cartesian seemed to him as a captive, or a one-armed combatant. Prizing metaphysicians for the unstrung pearls which they drop beyond the seclusion of system, he loved the *disjecta membra* of Coleridge, and preferred the *Pensieri*, and *Parerga und Paralipomena* to the constructed work of Gioberti and

Schopenhauer. He knew Leibniz chiefly in his letters, and was perceptibly affected by his law of continuous progression, his general optimism, and his eclectic art of extracting from men and books only the good that is in them; but of monadology or pre-established harmony there was not a trace. His colleague, Schelling, no friend to the friends of Baader, stood aloof. The elder Windischmann, whom he particularly esteemed, and who acted in Germany as the interpreter of De Maistre, had hailed Hegel as a pioneer of sound philosophy, with whom he agreed both in thought and word. Döllinger had no such condescension. Hegel remained, in his eyes, the strongest of all the enemies of religion, the guide of Tübingen in its aberrations, the reasoner whose abstract dialectics made a generation of clever men incapable of facing facts. He went on preferring former historians of dogma, who were untainted by the trail of pantheism, Baumgarten-Crusius, and even Muenscher, and by no means admitted that Baur was deeper than the early Jesuits and Oratorians, or gained more than he lost by constriction in the Hegelian coil. He took pleasure in pointing out that the best recent book on the penitential system, Kliefoth's fourth volume, owed its substance to Morinus. The dogmas of pantheistic history offended him too much to give them deep study, and he was ill prepared with counsel for a wanderer lost in the pervading haze. Hegelians said of him that he lacked the constructive unity of idea, and knew the way from effect to cause, but not from cause to law.

His own lectures on the philosophy of religion, which have left no deep furrow, have been praised by Ketteler, who was not an undiscriminating admirer. He sent on one of his pupils to Rosmini, and set another to begin metaphysics with Suarez; and when Lady Ashburton consulted him on the subject, he advised her to read Norris and Malebranche. He encouraged the study of remoter luminaries, such as Cusa and Raymundus, whose *Natural Theology* he preferred to the *Analogy;* and would not have men overlook some who are off the line, like Postel. But although he deemed it the mark of inferiority to neglect a grain of the gold of obsolete and eccentric writers, he always assigned to original speculation a subordinate place, as a good servant but a bad master, without the certainty and authority of history. What one of his English friends writes of a divine they both admired, might fitly be applied to him:

"He was a disciple in the school of Bishop Butler, and had learned as a first principle to recognise the limitations of human knowledge, and the unphilosophical folly of trying to round off into finished and pretentious schemes our fragmentary yet certain notices of our own condition and of God's dealing with it."

He alarmed Archer Gurney by saying that all hope of an understanding is at an end, if logic be applied for the rectification of dogma, and to Dr. Plummer, who acknowledged him as the most capable of modern theologians and historians, he spoke of the hopelessness of trying to discover the meaning of terms used in definitions. To his archbishop he wrote that men may discuss the mysteries of faith to the last day without avail; "we stand here on the solid ground of history, evidence, and fact." Expressing his innermost thought, that religion exists to make men better, and that the ethical quality of dogma constitutes its value, he once said: "Tantum valet quantum ad corrigendum, purgandum, sanctificandum hominem confert." In theology as an intellectual exercise, beyond its action on the soul, he felt less interest, and those disputes most satisfied him which can be decided by appeal to the historian.

From his early reputation and his position at the outpost, confronting Protestant science, he was expected to make up his mind over a large area of unsettled thought and disputed fact, and to be provided with an opinion—a freehold opinion of his own—and a reasoned answer to every difficulty. People had a right to know what he knew about the end of the sixteenth chapter of St. Mark, and the beginning of the eighth chapter of St. John, the lives of St. Patrick and the sources of Erigena, the author of the *Imitation* and of the *Twelve Articles,* the *Nag's Head* and the *Casket Letters*. The suspense and poise of the mind, which is the pride and privilege of the unprofessional scholar, was forbidden him. Students could not wait for the master to complete his studies; they flocked for dry light of knowledge, for something defined and final, to their keen, grave, unemotional professor, who said sometimes more than he could be sure of, but who was not likely to abridge thought by oracular responses, or to give aphorism for argument. He accepted the necessity of the situation. A time came when everybody was invited, once a week, to put any imaginable question from the whole of Church history, and he at once replied. If this was a stimulus to exertion during the years spent in mastering and pondering the immense materials, it served less to promote originality and care than premature certitude and the craving for quick returns. Apart from the constant duty of teaching, his knowledge might not have been so extensive, but his views would have been less decided and therefore less liable to change.

As an historian, Döllinger regarded Christianity as a force more than as a doctrine, and displayed it as it expanded and became the soul of later history. It was the mission and occupation of his life to discover and to disclose how this was accomplished, and to understand the history of civilised Europe, religious and profane, mental and political, by the aid of sources which, being original and authentic, yielded certainty. In his vigorous prime, he thought that it would be within his powers to complete the narrative of the conquest of the world by Christ in a single massive work. The separated churches, the centrifugal forces, were to have been treated apart, until he adopted the ampler title of a history of Christianity. We who look back upon all that the combined and divided labour of a thousand earnest, gifted, and often instructed men has done and left undone in sixty years, can estimate the scientific level of an age where such a dream could be dreamed by such a man, misled neither by imagination nor ambition, but knowing his own limitations and the immeasurable world of books. Experience slowly taught him that he who takes all history for his province is not the man to write a compendium.

The four volumes of *Church History* which gave him a name in literature appeared between 1833 and 1838, and stopped short of the Reformation. In writing mainly for the horizon of seminaries, it was desirable to eschew voyages of discovery and the pathless border-land. The materials were all in print, and were the daily bread of scholars. A celebrated Anglican described Döllinger at that time as more intentional than Fleury; while Catholics objected that he was a candid friend; and Lutherans, probing deeper, observed that he resolutely held his ground wherever he could, and as resolutely abandoned every position that he found untenable. He has since said of himself that he always spoke sincerely, but that he spoke as an advocate—a sincere advocate who pleaded only for a cause which he had convinced himself was just. The cause he pleaded was the divine government of the Church, the fulfilment of the promise that it would be preserved from error, though not from sin, the uninterrupted employment of the powers committed by Christ for the salvation of man. By the absence of false arts he acquired that repute for superior integrity which caused a Tyrolese divine to speak of him as the most chivalrous of the Catholic celebrities; and the nuncio who was at Munich during the first ten years called him the "professeur le plus éclairé, le plus religieux, en un mot le plus distingué de l'université."

Taking his survey from the elevation of general history, he gives less space to all the early heresies together than to the rise of Mohammedanism. His way lies between Neander, who cares for no institutions, and Baur, who cares for no individuals. He was entirely exempt from that impersonal idealism which Sybel laid down at the foundation of his review, which causes Delbrück to complain that Macaulay, who could see facts so well, could not see that they are revelations, which Baur defines without disguise in his *Dreieinigkeitslehre:* "Alle geschichtlichen Personen sind für uns blosse Namen." The two posthumous works of Hegel which turned events into theories had not then appeared. Döllinger, setting life and action above theory, omitted the progress of doctrine. He proposed that Möhler should take that share of their common topic, and the plan, entertained at first, was interrupted, with much besides, by death. He felt too deeply the overwhelming unity of force to yield to that atomic theory which was provoked by the Hegelian excess: "L'histoire n'est pas un simple jeu d'abstractions, et les hommes y sont plus que les doctrines. Ce n'est pas une certaine théorie sur la justification et la rédemption qui a fait la Réforme: c'est Luther, c'est Calvin." But he allows a vast scope to the variable will and character of man. The object of religion upon earth is saintliness, and its success is shown in holy individuals. He leaves law and doctrine, moving in their appointed orbits, to hold up great men and examples of Christian virtue.

Döllinger, who had in youth acted as secretary to Hohenlohe, was always reserved in his use of the supernatural. In the vision of Constantine and the rebuilding of the temple, he gives his reader both the natural explanation and the miraculous. He thought that the witness of the fathers to the continuance of miraculous powers could not be resisted without making history *a priori,* but later on, the more he sifted and compared authorities, the more severe he became. He deplored the uncritical credulity of the author of the *Monks of the West;* and, in examining the Stigmata, he cited the experience of a Spanish convent where they were so common that it became a sign of reprobation to be without them. Historians, he said, have to look for natural causes: enough will remain for the action of Providence, where we cannot penetrate. In his unfinished book on *Ecclesiastical Prophecy* he enumerates the illusions of mediaeval saints when they spoke of the future, and describes them, as he once described Carlyle and Ruskin, as prophets having nothing to foretell. At Frankfort, where he spoilt his watch by depositing it in unexpected holy water, and it was whispered that he had put it there to mend it, everybody knew that there was hardly a Catholic in the Parliament of whom such a fable could be told with more felicitous unfitness.

For twenty years of his life at Munich, Görres was the impressive central figure of a group reputed far and wide, the most intellectual force in the Catholic world. Seeing things by the light of other days, Nippold and Maurenbrecher describe Döllinger himself as its most eminent member. There was present gain and future peril in living amongst a clever but restricted set, sheltered, supported, and restrained by friends who were united in aims and studies, who cherished their sympathies and their enmities in common, and who therefore believed that they were divided by no deep cleft or ultimate principle. Döllinger never outlived the glamour of the eloquence and ascendancy of Görres, and spoke of him long after his death as a man of real knowledge, and of greater religious than political insight. Between the imaginative rhetorician and the measured, scrutinising scholar, the contrast was wide. One of the many pupils and rare disciples of the former complained that his friend supplied interminable matter for the sterile and unavailing *Mystik*, in order to amuse him with ropes of sand: and the severest censure of Döllinger's art as an historian was pronounced by Görres when he said, "I always see analogies, and you always see differences."

At all times, but in his early studies especially, he owed much to the Italians, whose ecclesiastical literature was the first that he mastered, and predominates in his Church history. Several of his countrymen, such as Savigny and Raumer, had composed history on the shoulders of Bolognese and Lombard scholars, and some of their most conspicuous successors to the present day have lived under heavy obligations to Modena and San Marino. During the tranquil century before the Revolution, Italians studied the history of their country with diligence and success. Even such places as Parma, Verona, Brescia, became centres of obscure but faithful work. Osimo possessed annals as bulky as Rome. The story of the province of Treviso was told in twenty volumes. The antiquities of Picenum filled thirty-two folios. The best of all this national and municipal patriotism was given to the service of religion. Popes and cardinals, dioceses and parish churches became the theme of untiring enthusiasts. There too were the stupendous records of the religious orders, their bulls and charters, their biography and their bibliography. In this immense world of patient, accurate, devoted research, Döllinger laid the deep foundations of his historical knowledge. Beginning like everybody with Baronius and Muratori, he gave a large portion of his life to Noris, and to the solid and enlightened scholarship that surrounded Benedict XIV, down to the compilers, Borgia, Fantuzzi, Marini, with whom, in the evil days of regeneration by the French, the grand tradition died away. He has put on record his judgment that Orsi and Saccarelli were the best writers on the general history of the Church. Afterwards, when other layers had been superposed, and the course he took was his own, he relied much on the canonists, Ballerini and Berardi; and he commended Bianchi, De Bennettis, and the author of the anonymous *Confutazione*, as the strongest Roman antidote to Blondel, Buckeridge, and Barrow. Italy possessed the largest extant body of Catholic learning; the whole sphere of Church government was within its range, and it enjoyed something of the official prerogative.

Next to the Italians he gave systematic attention to the French. The conspicuous Gallicans, the Jansenists, from whom at last he derived much support, Richer, Van Espen, Launoy, whom he regarded as the original of Bossuet, Arnauld, whom he thought his superior, are absent from his pages. He never overcame his distrust of Pascal, for his methodical scepticism and his endeavour to dissociate religion from learning; and he rated high Daniel's reply to the *Provinciales*. He esteemed still more the French Protestants of the seventeenth century, who transformed the system of Geneva and Dort. English theology did not come much in his way until he had made himself at home with the Italians and the primary French. Then it abounded. He gathered it in quantities on two journeys in 1851 and 1858, and he possessed the English divines in perfection, at least down to Whitby, and the nonjurors. Early acquaintance with Sir Edward Vavasour and Lord Clifford had planted a lasting prejudice in favour of the English Catholic families, which sometimes tinged his judgments. The neglected literature of the Catholics in England held a place in his scheme of thought, which it never obtained in the eyes of any other scholar, native or foreign. This was the only considerable school of divines who wrote under persecution, and were reduced to an attitude of defence. In conflict with the most learned, intelligent, and conciliatory of controversialists, they developed a remarkable spirit of moderation, discriminating inferior elements from the original and genuine growth of Catholic roots; and their several declarations and manifestoes, from the Restoration onwards, were an inexhaustible supply for irenics. Therefore they powerfully attracted one who took the words of St. Vincent of Lérins not merely for a flash of illumination, but for a scientific formula and guiding principle. Few writers interested him more deeply than Stapleton, Davenport, who anticipated Number XC, Irishmen, such as Caron and Walshe, and the Scots, Barclay, the adversary and friend of Bellarmine, Ramsay, the convert and recorder of Fénelon. It may be that, to an intellect trained in the historic process, stability, continuity, and growth were terms of more vivid and exact significance than to the doctors of Pont-à-Mousson and Lambspring. But when he came forward arrayed in the spoils of Italian libraries and German universities, with the erudition of centuries and the criticism of to-day, he sometimes was content to follow where forgotten Benedictines or Franciscans had preceded, under the later Stuarts.

He seldom quotes contemporary Germans, unless to dispute with them, prefers old books to new, and speaks of the necessary revision and renovation of history. He suspected imported views and foregone conclusions even in Neander; and although he could not say, with Macaulay, that Gieseler was a rascal, of whom he had never heard, he missed no opportunity of showing his dislike for that accomplished artificer in mosaic. Looking at the literature before him, at England, with Gibbon for its one ecclesiastical historian; at Germany, with the most profound of its divines expecting the Church to merge in the State, he inferred that its historic and organic unity would only be recognised by Catholic science, while the soundest Protestant would understand it least. In later years, Kliefoth, Ritschl, Gass, perhaps also Dorner and Uhlhorn, obliged him to modify an opinion which the entire school of Schleiermacher, including the illustrious Rothe, served only to confirm. Germany, as he found it when he began to see the world, little resembled that of his old age, when the work he had pursued for seventy years was carried forward, with knowledge and power like his own, by the best of his countrymen. The proportion of things was changed. There was a religious literature to be proud of, to rely on: other nations, other epochs, had lost their superiority. As his own people advanced, and dominated in the branches of learning to which his life was given, in everything except literary history and epigraphics, and there was no more need to look abroad, Döllinger's cosmopolitan characteristic diminished, he was more absorbed in the national thought and work, and did not object to be called the most German of the Germans.

The idea that religious science is not so much science as religion, that it should be treated differently from other matters, so that he who treats it may rightly display his soul, flourished in his vicinity, inspiring the lives of Saint Elizabeth and Joan of Arc, Möhler's fine lectures on the early fathers, and the book which Gratry chose to entitle a *Commentary on St. Matthew*. Döllinger came early to the belief that history ought to be impersonal, that the historian does well to keep out of the way, to be humble and self-denying, making it a religious duty to prevent the intrusion of all that betrays his own position and quality, his hopes and wishes. Without aspiring to the calm indifference of Ranke, he was conscious that, in early life, he had been too positive, and too eager to persuade. The Belgian scholar who, conversing with him in 1842, was reminded of Fénelon, missed the acuter angles of his character. He, who in private intercourse sometimes allowed himself to persist, to contradict, and even to baffle a bore by frankly falling asleep, would have declined the evocation of Versailles. But in reasonableness, moderation, and charity, in general culture of mind and the sense of the demands of the progress of civilisation, in the ideal church for which he lived, he was more in harmony with Fénelon than with many others who resembled him in the character of their work.

He deemed it Catholic to take ideas from history, and heresy to take them into it. When men gave evidence for the opposite party, and against their own, he willingly took for impartiality what he could not always distinguish from indifference or subdivision. He felt that sincere history was the royal road to religious union, and he specially cultivated those who saw both sides. He would cite with complacency what clever Jesuits, Raynaud and Faure, said for the Reformation, Mariana and Cordara against their society. When a Rhenish Catholic and a Genevese Calvinist drew two portraits of Calvin which were virtually the same, or when, in Ficker's revision of Böhmer, the Catholic defended the Emperor Frederic II against the Protestant, he rejoiced as over a sign of the advent of science. As the Middle Ages, rescued from polemics by the genial and uncritical sympathy of Müller, became an object of popular study, and Royer Collard said of Villemain, *Il a fait, il fait, et il fera toujours son Grégoire VII,* there were Catholics who desired, by a prolonged *sorites,* to derive advantage from the new spirit. Wiseman consulted Döllinger for the purpose. "Will you be kind enough to write me a list of what you consider the best books for the history of the Reformation; Menzel and Buchholz I know; especially any exposing the characters of the leading reformers?" In the same frame of mind he asked him what pope there was whose good name had not been vindicated; and Döllinger's reply, that Boniface VIII wanted a friend, prompted both Wiseman's article and Tosti's book.

In politics, as in religion, he made the past a law for the present, and resisted doctrines which are ready-made, and are not derived from experience. Consequently, he undervalued work which would never have been done from disinterested motives; and there were three of his most eminent contemporaries whom he decidedly underestimated. Having known Thiers, and heard him speak, he felt profoundly the talent of the extraordinary man, before Lanfrey or Taine, Häusser and Bernhardi had so ruined his credit among Germans that Döllinger, disgusted by his advocacy, whether of the Revolution, of Napoleon, or of France, neglected his work. Stahl claims to be accounted an historian by his incomparably able book on the Church government of the Reformation. As a professor at Munich, and afterwards as a parliamentary leader at Berlin, he was always an avowed partisan. Döllinger depreciated him accordingly, and he had the mortification that certain remarks on the sovereign dialectician of European conservatism were on the point of appearing when he died. He so far made it good in his preface that the thing was forgotten when Gerlach came to see the assailant of his friend. But once, when I spoke of Stahl as the greatest man born of a Jewish mother since Titus, he thought me unjust to Disraeli.

Most of all, he misjudged Macaulay, whose German admirers are not always in the higher ranks of literature, and of whom Ranke even said that he could hardly be called an historian at all, tried by the stricter test. He had no doubt seen how his unsuggestive fixity and assurance could cramp and close a mind; and he felt more beholden to the rivals who produced d'Adda, Barillon, and Bonnet, than to the author of so many pictures and so much bootless decoration. He tendered a course of Bacon's Essays, or of Butler's and Newman's Sermons, as a preservative against intemperate dogmatism. He denounced Macaulay's indifference to the merits of the inferior cause, and desired more generous treatment of the Jacobites and the French king. He deemed it hard that a science happily delivered from the toils of religious passion should be involved in political, and made to pass from the sacristy to the lobby, by the most brilliant example in literature. To the objection that one who celebrates the victory of parliaments over monarchs, of democracy over aristocracy, of liberty over authority, declares, not the tenets of a party, but manifest destiny and the irrevocable decree, he would reply that a narrow induction is the bane of philosophy, that the ways of Providence are not inscribed on the surface of things, that religion, socialism, militarism, and revolution possibly reserve a store of cogent surprises for the economist, utilitarian, and whig.

In 1865 he was invited to prepare a new edition of his Church history. Whilst he was mustering the close ranks of folios which had satisfied a century of historians, the world had moved, and there was an increase of raw material to be measured by thousands of volumes. The archives which had been sealed with seven seals had become as necessary to the serious student as his library. Every part of his studies had suffered transformation, except the fathers, who had largely escaped the crucible, and the canon law, which had only just been caught by the historical current. He had begun when Niebuhr was lecturing at Bonn and Hegel at Berlin; before Tischendorf unfolded his first manuscript; before Baur discovered the Tübingen hypothesis in the congregation of Corinth; before Rothe had planned his treatise on the primitive church, or Ranke had begun to pluck the plums for his modern popes. Guizot had not founded the *École des Chartes*, and the school of method was not yet opened at Berlin. The application of instruments of precision was just beginning, and what Prynne calls the heroic study of records had scarcely molested the ancient reign of lives and chronicles. None had worked harder at his science and at himself than Döllinger; and the change around him was not greater than the change within. In his early career as a teacher of religion he had often shrunk from books which bore no stamp of orthodoxy. It was long before he read Sarpi or the *Lettres Provinciales*, or even Ranke's *Popes*, which appeared when he was thirty-five, and which astonished him by the serene ease with which a man who knew so much touched on such delicate ground. The book which he had written in that state of mind, and with that conception of science and religion, had only a prehistoric interest for its author. He refused to reprint it, and declared that there was hardly a sentence fit to stand unchanged. He lamented that he had lost ten years of life in getting his bearings, and in learning, unaided, the most difficult craft in the world. Those years of apprenticeship without a master were the time spent on his *Kirchengeschichte*. The want of training remained. He could impart knowledge better than the art of learning. Thousands of his pupils have acquired connected views of religion passing through the ages, and gathered, if they were intelligent, some notion of the meaning of history; but nobody ever learnt from him the mechanism by which it is written.

Brougham advised the law-student to begin with Dante; and a distinguished physician informs us that Gibbon, Grote, and Mill made him what he is. The men to whom Döllinger owed his historic insight and who mainly helped to develop and strengthen and direct his special faculty, were not all of his own cast, or remarkable in the common description of literary talent. The assistants were countless, but the masters were few, and he looked up with extraordinary gratitude to men like Sigonius, Antonius Augustinus, Blondel, Petavius, Leibniz, Burke, and Niebuhr, who had opened the passes for him as he struggled and groped in the illimitable forest.

He interrupted his work because he found the materials too scanty for the later Middle Ages, and too copious for the Reformation. The defective account of the Albigensian theology, which he had sent to one of his translators, never appeared in German. At Paris he searched the library for the missing information, and he asked Rességuier to make inquiry for the records of the Inquisition in Languedoc, thus laying the foundations of that *Sektengeschichte* which he published fifty years later. Munich offered such inexhaustible supplies for the Reformation that his collections overran all bounds. He completed only that part of his plan which included Lutheranism and the sixteenth century. The third volume, published in 1848, containing the theology of the Reformation, is the most solid of his writings. He had miscalculated, not his resources, of which only a part had come into action, but the possibilities of concentration and compression. The book was left a fragment when he had to abandon his study for the Frankfort barricades.

The peculiarity of his treatment is that he contracts the Reformation into a history of the doctrine of justification. He found that this and this alone was the essential point in Luther's mind, that he made it the basis of his argument, the motive of his separation, the root and principle of his religion. He believed that Luther was right in the cardinal importance he attributed to this doctrine in his system, and he in his turn recognised that it was the cause of all that followed, the source of the reformer's popularity and success, the sole insurmountable obstacle to every scheme of restoration. It was also, for him, the centre and the basis of his antagonism. That was the point that he attacked when he combated Protestantism, and he held all other elements of conflict cheap in comparison, deeming that they are not invariable, or not incurable, or not supremely serious. Apart from this, there was much in Protestantism that he admired, much in its effects for which he was grateful. With the Lutheran view of imputation, Protestant and Catholic were separated by an abyss. Without it, there was no lasting reason why they should be separate at all. Against the communities that hold it he stood in order of battle, and believed that he could scarcely hit too hard. But he distinguished very broadly the religion of the reformers from the religion of Protestants. Theological science had moved away from the symbolical books, the root dogma had been repudiated and contested by the most eminent Protestants, and it was an English bishop who wrote: "Fuit haec doctrina jam a multis annis ipsissimum Reformatae Ecclesiae opprobrium ac dedecus. Est error non levis, error putidissimus." Since so many of the best writers resist or modify that which was the main cause, the sole ultimate cause, of disunion, it cannot be logically impossible to discover a reasonable basis for discussion. Therefore conciliation was always in his thoughts; even his *Reformation* was a treatise on the conditions of reunion. He long purposed to continue it, in narrower limits, as a history of that central doctrine by which Luther meant his church to stand or fall, of the reaction against it, and of its decline. In 1881, when Ritschl, the author of the chief work upon the subject, spent some days with Döllinger, he found him still full of these ideas, and possessing Luther at his fingers' ends.

This is the reason why Protestants have found him so earnest an opponent and so warm a friend. It was this that attracted him towards Anglicans, and made very many of them admire a Roman dignitary who knew the Anglo-Catholic library better than De Lugo or Ripalda. In the same spirit he said to Pusey: "Tales cum sitis jam nostri estis," always spoke of Newman's *Justification* as the greatest masterpiece of theology that England has produced in a hundred years, and described Baxter and Wesley as the most eminent of English Protestants—

meaning Wesley as he was after 1st December 1767, and Baxter as the life-long opponent of that theory which was the source and the soul of the Reformation. Several Englishmen who went to consult him—Hope Scott and Archdeacon Wilberforce—became Catholics. I know not whether he urged them. Others there were, whom he did not urge, though his influence over them might have been decisive. In a later letter to Pusey he wrote: "I am convinced by reading your *Eirenicon* that we are united inwardly in our religious convictions, although externally we belong to two separated churches." He followed attentively the parallel movements that went on in his own country, and welcomed with serious respect the overtures which came to him, after 1856, from eminent historians. When they were old men, he and Ranke, whom, in hot youth, there was much to part, lived on terms of mutual goodwill. Döllinger had pronounced the theology of the *Deutsche Reformation* slack and trivial, and Ranke at one moment was offended by what he took for an attack on the popes, his patrimony. In 1865, after a visit to Munich, he allowed that in religion there was no dispute between them, that he had no fault to find with the Church as Döllinger understood it. He added that one of his colleagues, a divine whose learning filled him with unwonted awe, held the same opinion. Döllinger's growing belief that an approximation of part of Germany to sentiments of conciliation was only a question of time, had much to do with his attitude in Church questions after the year 1860. If history cannot confer faith or virtue, it can clear away the misconceptions and misunderstandings that turn men against one another. With the progress of incessant study and meditation his judgment on many points underwent revision; but with regard to the Reformation the change was less than he supposed. He learnt to think more favourably of the religious influence of Protestantism, and of its efficacy in the defence of Christianity; but he thought as before of the spiritual consequences of Lutheranism proper. When people said of Luther that he does not come well out of his matrimonial advice to certain potentates, to Henry and to Philip, of his exhortations to exterminate the revolted peasantry, of his passage from a confessor of toleration to a teacher of intolerance, he would not have the most powerful conductor of religion that Christianity has produced in eighteen centuries condemned for two pages in a hundred volumes. But when he had refused the test of the weakest link, judging the man by his totals, he was not less severe on his theological ethics.

"Meinerseits habe ich noch eine andre schwere Anklage gegen ihn zu erheben, nämlich die, dass er durch seine falsche Imputationslehre das sittlich-religiöse Bewusstseyn der Menschen auf zwei Jahrhunderte hinaus verwirrt und corrumpirt hat (3rd July 1888)."

The revolution of 1848, during which he did not hold his professorship, brought him forward uncongenially in active public life, and gave him the means of telling the world his view of the constitution and policy of the Church, and the sense and limits of liability in which he gave his advocacy. When lecturing on canon law he was accustomed to dwell on the strict limit of all ecclesiastical authority, admitting none but spiritual powers, and invoking the maxims of pontiffs who professed themselves guardians, not masters, of the established legislation—"Canones ecclesiae solvere non possumus, qui custodes canonum sumus." Acting on these principles, in the Paulskirche, and at Ratisbon, he vindicated Rome against the reproach of oppression, argued that society can only gain by the emancipation of the Church, as it claims no superiority over the State, and that both Gallicans and Jesuits are out of date. Addressing the bishops of Germany in secret session at Würzburg, he exhorted them to avail themselves fully of an order of things which was better than the old, and to make no professions of unconditional allegiance. He told them that freedom is the breath of the Catholic life, that it belongs to the Church of God by right divine, and that whatever they claimed must be claimed for others.

From these discourses, in which the scholar abandoned the details by which science advances for the general principles of the popular orator, the deductions of liberalism proceed as surely as the revolution from the title-page of Sieyès. It should seem that the key to his career lies there. It was natural to associate him with the men whom the early promise of a reforming pope inspired to identify the cause of free societies with the papacy which had Rosmini for an adviser, Ventura for a preacher, Gioberti for a prophet, and to conclude that he thus became a trusted representative, until the revolving years found him the champion of a vanished cause, and the Syllabus exposed the illusion and bore away his ideal. Harless once said of him that no good could be expected from a man surrounded by a ring of liberals. When Döllinger made persecution answer both for the decline of Spain and the fall of Poland, he appeared to deliver the common creed of Whigs; and he did not protest against the American who called him the acknowledged head of the liberal Catholics. His hopefulness in the midst of the movement of 1848, his ready acquiescence in the fall of ancient powers and institutions, his trust in Rome, and in the abstract rights of Germans, suggested a reminiscence of the *Avenir* in 1830.

Lamennais, returning with Montalembert after his appeal to Rome, met Lacordaire at Munich, and during a banquet given in their honour he learnt, privately, that he was condemned. The three friends spent that afternoon in Döllinger's company; and it was after he had left them that Lamennais produced the encyclical and said: *Dieu a parlé*. Montalembert soon returned, attracted as much by Munich art as by religion or literature. The fame of the Bavarian school of Catholic thought spread in France among those who belonged to the wider circles of the *Avenir*; and priests and laymen followed, as to a scientific shrine. In the *Mémoires d'un Royaliste* Falloux has preserved, with local colour, the spirit of that pilgrimage:

"Munich lui fut indiqué comme le foyer d'une grande rénovation religieuse et artistique. Quels nobles et ardents entretiens, quelle passion pour l'Eglise et pour sa cause! Rien n'a plus ressemblé aux discours d'un portique chrétien que les apologies enflammées du vieux Görres, les savantes déductions de Döllinger, la verve originale de Brentano."

Rio, who was the earliest of the travellers, describes Döllinger as he found him in 1830:

"Par un privilège dont il serait difficile de citer un autre exemple, il avait la passion des études théologiques comme s'il n'avait été que prêtre, et la passion des études littéraires appliquées aux auteurs anciens et modernes comme s'il n'avait été que littérateur; à quoi il faut ajouter un autre don qu'il y aurait ingratitude à oublier, celui d'une exposition lucide, patiente et presque affectueuse, comme s'il n'avait accumulé tant de connaissances que pour avoir le plaisir de les communiquer."

For forty years he remained in correspondence with many of these early friends, who, in the educational struggle which ended with the ministry of Falloux in 1850, revived the leading maxims of the rejected master. As Lacordaire said, on his deathbed: "La parole de l'Avenir avait germé de son tombeau comme une cendre féconde." Döllinger used to visit his former visitors in various parts of France, and at Paris he attended the salon of Madame Swetchine. One day, at the seminary, he inquired who were the most promising students; Dupanloup pointed out a youth, who was the hope of the Church, and whose name was Ernest Renan.

Although the men who were drawn to him in this way formed the largest and best-defined cluster with which he came in contact, there was more private friendship than mutual action or consultation between them. The unimpassioned German, who had no taste for ideas released from controlling fact, took little pleasure in the impetuous declamation of the Breton, and afterwards pronounced him inferior to Loyson. Neither of the men who were in the confidence of both has intimated that he made any lasting impression on Lamennais, who took leave of him without discussing the action of Rome. Döllinger never sought to renew acquaintance with Lacordaire, when he had become the most important man in the church of France. He would have a prejudice to overcome against him whom Circourt called the most ignorant man in the Academy, who believed that Erasmus ended his days at Rotterdam, unable to choose between Rome and Wittenberg, and that the Irish obtained through O'Connell the right to worship in their own way. He saw more of Dupanloup, without feeling, as deeply as Renan, the rare charm of the combative prelate. To an exacting and reflective scholar, to whom even the large volume of heavy erudition in which Rosmini defended the *Cinque Piaghe* seemed superficial, there was incongruity in the attention paid to one of whom he heard that he promoted the council, that he took St. Boniface for St. Wilfrid, and that he gave the memorable advice: *Surtout méfiez-vous des sources*. After a visit from the Bishop of Orleans he sat down in dismay to compose the most elementary of his books. Seeing the inferiority of Falloux as a historian, he never appreciated the strong will and cool brain of the statesman who overawed Tocqueville. Eckstein, the obscure but thoughtful originator of much liberal feeling among his own set, encouraged him in the habit of depreciating the attainments of the French clergy, which was confirmed by the writings of the most eminent among them, Darboy, and lasted until the appearance of Duchesne. The politics of Montalembert were so heavily charged with conservatism, that in defiance of such advisers as Lacordaire, Ravignan, and Dupanloup, he pronounced in favour of the author of the *coup d'état*, saying: "Je suis pour l'autorité contre la révolte"; and boasted that, in entering the Academy he had attacked the Revolution, not of '93 but '89, and that Guizot, who received him, had nothing to say in reply. There were many things, human and divine, on which they could not feel alike; but as the most urgent, eloquent, and persevering of his Catholic friends, gifted with knowledge and experience of affairs, and dwelling in the focus, it may be that on one critical occasion, when religion and politics intermingled, he influenced the working of Döllinger's mind. But the plausible reading of his life which explains it by his connection with such public men as Montalembert, De Decker, and Mr. Gladstone is profoundly untrue; and those who deem him a liberal in any scientific use of the term, miss the keynote of his work.

The political party question has to be considered here, because, in fact, it is decisive. A liberal who thinks his thought out to the end without flinching is forced to certain conclusions which colour to the root every phase and scene of universal history. He believes in upward progress, because it is only recent times that have striven deliberately, and with a zeal according to knowledge, for the increase and security of freedom. He is not only tolerant of error in religion, but is specially indulgent to the less dogmatic forms of Christianity, to the sects which have restrained the churches. He is austere in judging the past, imputing not error and ignorance only, but guilt and crime, to those who, in the dark succession of ages, have resisted and retarded the growth of liberty, which he identifies with the cause of morality, and the condition of the reign of conscience. Döllinger never subjected his mighty vision of the stream of time to correction according to the principles of this unsympathising philosophy, never reconstituted the providential economy in agreement with the Whig Théodicée. He could understand the Zoroastrian simplicity of history in black and white, for he wrote: "obgleich man allerdings sagen kann, das tiefste Thema der Weltgeschichte sei der Kampf der Knechtschaft oder Gebundenheit, mit der Freiheit, auf dem intellectuellen, religiösen, politischen und socialen Gebiet." But the scene which lay open before his mind was one of greater complexity, deeper design, and infinite intellect. He imagined a way to truth through error, and outside the Church, not through unbelief and the diminished reign of Christ. Lacordaire in the cathedral pulpit offering his thanks to Voltaire for the good gift of religious toleration, was a figure alien to his spirit. He never substituted politics for religion as the test of progress, and never admitted that they have anything like the dogmatic certainty and sovereignty of religious, or of physical, science. He had all the liberality that consists of common sense, justice, humanity, enlightenment, the wisdom of Canning or Guizot. But revolution, as the breach of continuity, as the renunciation of history, was odious to him, and he not only refused to see method in the madness of Marat, or dignity in the end of Robespierre, but believed that the best measures of Leopold, the most intelligent reformer in the era of repentant monarchy, were vitiated and frustrated by want of adaptation to custom. Common party divisions represented nothing scientific to his mind; and he was willing, like De Quincey, to accept them as corresponding halves of a necessary whole. He wished that he knew half as much as his neighbour, Mrs. Somerville; but he possessed no natural philosophy, and never acquired the emancipating habit which comes from a life spent in securing progress by shutting one's eyes to the past. "Alle Wissenschaft steht und ruht auf ihrer historischen Entwicklung, sie lebt von ihrer traditionellen Vergangenheit, wie der Baum von seiner Wurzel."

He was moved, not by the gleam of reform after the conclave of Pius IX, but by Pius VII. The impression made upon him by the character of that pope, and his resistance to Napoleon, had much to do with his resolution to become a priest. He took orders in the Church in the days of revival, as it issued from oppression and the eclipse of hierarchy; and he entered its service in the spirit of Sailer, Cheverus, and Doyle. The mark of that time never left him. When Newman asked him what he would say of the Pope's journey to Paris, for the coronation of the emperor, he hardly recognised the point of the question. He opposed, in 1853, the renewal of that precedent; but to the end he never felt what people mean when they remark on the proximity of Notre-Dame to Vincennes.

Döllinger was too much absorbed in distant events to be always a close observer of what went on near him; and he was, therefore, not so much influenced by contact with contemporary history as men who were less entirely at home in other centuries. He knew about all that could be known of the ninth: in the nineteenth his superiority deserted him. Though he informed himself assiduously his thoughts were not there. He collected from Hormayr, Radowitz, Capponi, much secret matter of the last generation; and where Brewer had told him about Oxford, and Plantier about Louis Philippe, there were landmarks, as when Knoblecher, the missionary, set down Krophi and Mophi on his map of Africa. He deferred, at once, to the competent authority. He consulted his able colleague Hermann on all points of political economy, and used his advice when he wrote about England. Having satisfied himself, he would not reopen these questions, when, after Hermann's death, he spent some time in the society of Roscher, a not less eminent economist, and of all men the one who most resembled himself in the historian's faculty of rethinking the thoughts and realising the knowledge, the ignorance, the experience, the illusions of a given time.

He had lived in many cities, and had known many important men; he had sat in three parliamentary assemblies, had drawn constitutional amendments, had been consulted upon the policy and the making of ministries, and had declined political office; but as an authority on recent history he was scarcely equal to himself. Once it became his duty to sketch the character of a prince whom he had known. There was a report that this sovereign had only been dissuaded from changing his religion and abolishing the constitution by the advice of an archbishop and of a famous parliamentary jurist; and the point of the story was that the Protestant doctrinaire had prevented the change of religion, and the archbishop had preserved the constitution. It was too early to elucidate these court mysteries; instead of which there is a remarkable conversation about religion, wherein it is not always clear whether the prince is speaking, or the professor, or Schelling.

Although he had been translated into several languages and was widely known in his own country, he had not yet built himself a European name. At Oxford, in 1851, when James Mozley asked whom he would like to see, he said, the men who had written in the *Christian Remembrancer* on Dante and Luther. Mozley was himself one of the two, and he introduced him to the other at Oriel. After thirty-two years, when the writer on Dante occupied a high position in the Church and had narrowly escaped the highest, that visit was returned. But he had no idea that he had once received Döllinger in his college rooms, and hardly believed it when told. In Germany, the serried learning of the *Reformation*, the author's energy and decisiveness in public assemblies, caused him to stand forth as an accepted spokesman, and, for a season, threw back the reticent explorer, steering between the shallows of anger and affection.

In that stage the *Philosophumena* found him, and induced him to write a book of controversy in the shape of history. Here was an anonymous person who, as Newman described it, "calls one pope a weak and venal dunce, and another a sacrilegious swindler, an infamous convict, and an heresiarch *ex cathedra.*" In the Munich Faculty there was a divine who affirmed that the Church would never get over it. Döllinger undertook to vindicate the insulted See of Rome; and he was glad of the opportunity to strike a blow at three conspicuous men of whom he thought ill in point both of science and religion. He spoke of Gieseler as the flattest and most leathern of historians; he accused Baur of frivolity and want of theological conviction; and he wished that he knew as many circumlocutions for untruth as there are Arabian synonyms for a camel, that he might do justice to Bunsen without violation of courtesy. The weight of the new testimony depended on the discovery of the author. Adversaries had assigned it to Hippolytus, the foremost European writer of the time, venerated as a saint and a father of the Church. Döllinger thought them right, and he justified his sincerity by giving further reasons for a conclusion which made his task formidable even for such dexterity as his own. Having thus made a concession which was not absolutely inevitable, he resisted the inference with such richness of illustration that the fears of the doubting colleague were appeased. In France, by Pitra's influence, the book was reviewed without making known that it supported the authorship of Hippolytus, which is still disputed by some impartial critics, and was always rejected by Newman. *Hippolytus und Kallistus,* the high-water mark of Döllinger's official assent and concurrence, came out in 1853. His next book showed the ebb.

He came originally from the romantic school, where history was honeycombed with imagination and conjecture; and the first important book he gave to a pupil in 1850 was Creuzer's *Mythology.* In 1845 he denounced the rationalism of Lobeck in investigating the *Mysteries;* but in 1857 he preferred him as a guide to those who proceed by analogy. With increase of knowledge had come increase of restraining caution and sagacity. The critical acumen was not greater in the *Vorhalle* than when he wrote on the *Philosophumena,* but instead of being employed in a chosen cause, upon fixed lines, for welcome ends, it is applied impartially. Ernst von Lasaulx, a man of rich and noble intellect, was lecturing next door on the philosophy and religion of Greece, and everybody heard about his indistinct mixture of dates and authorities, and the spell which his unchastened idealism cast over students. Lasaulx, who brilliantly carried on the tradition of Creuzer, who had tasted of the mythology of Schelling, who was son-in-law to Baader and nephew to Görres, wrote a volume on the fall of Hellenism which he brought in manuscript and read to Döllinger at a sitting. The effect on the dissenting mind of the hearer was a warning; and there is reason to date from those two hours in 1853 a more severe use of materials, and a stricter notion of the influence which the end of an inquiry may lawfully exert on the pursuit of it.

Heidenthum und Judenthum, which came out in 1857, gave Lasaulx his revenge. It is the most positive and self-denying of histories, and owes nothing to the fancy. The author refused the aid of Scandinavia to illustrate German mythology, and he was rewarded long after, when Caspari of Christiania and Conrad Maurer met at his table and confirmed the discoveries of Bugge. But the account of Paganism ends with a significant parallel. In December 69 a torch flung by a soldier burnt the temple on the Capitol to the ground. In August 70 another Roman soldier set fire to the temple on Mount Sion. The two sanctuaries perished within a year, making way for the faith of men still hidden in the back streets of Rome. When the Hellenist read this passage it struck him deeply. Then he declared that it was hollow. All was over at Jerusalem; but at Rome the ruin was restored, and the smoke of sacrifice went up for centuries to come from the altar of Capitoline Jove.

In this work, designed as an introduction to Christian history, the apologist betrays himself when he says that no Greek ever objected to slavery, and when, out of 730 pages on paganism, half a page is allotted to the moral system of Aristotle. That his Aristotelian chapter was weak, the author knew; but he said that it was not his text to make more of it. He did not mean that a Christian divine may be better employed than in doing honour to a heathen; but, having to narrate events and the action of causes, he regarded Christianity more as an organism employing sacramental powers than as a body of speculative ideas. To cast up the total of moral and religious knowledge attained by Seneca, Epictetus, and Plutarch, to measure the line and rate of progress since Socrates, to compare the point reached by Hermas and Justin, is an inquiry of the highest interest for writers yet to come. But the quantitative difference of acquired precept between the later pagan and the early Christian is not the key to the future. The true problem is to expose the ills and errors which Christ, the Healer, came to remove. The measure must be taken from the depth of evil from which Christianity had to rescue mankind, and its history is more than a continued history of philosophical theories. Newman, who sometimes agreed with Döllinger in the letter, but seldom in the spirit, and who distrusted him as a man in whom the divine lived at the mercy of the scholar, and whose burden of superfluous learning blunted the point and the edge of his mind, so much liked what he heard of this book that, being unable to read it, he had it translated at the Oratory.

The work thus heralded never went beyond the first volume, completed in the autumn of 1860, which was received by the *Kirchen-zeitung* of Berlin as the most acceptable narrative of the founding of Christianity, and as the largest concession ever made by a Catholic divine. The author, following the ancient ways, and taking, with Reuss, the New Testament as it stands, made no attempt to establish the position against modern criticism. Up to this, prescription and tradition held the first place in his writings, and formed his vantage-ground in all controversy. His energy in upholding the past as the rule and measure of the future distinguished him even among writers of his own communion. In *Christenthum und Kirche* he explained his theory of development, under which flag the notion of progress penetrates into theology, and which he held as firmly as the balancing element of perpetuity: "In dem Maass als dogmenhistorische Studien mehr getrieben werden, wird die absolute innere Nothwendigkeit und Wahr-heit der Sache immer allgemeiner einleuchten." He conceived no bounds to the unforeseen resources of Christian thought and faith. A philosopher in whose works he would not have expected to find the scientific expression of his own idea, has a passage bearing close analogy to what he was putting forward in 1861:

"It is then in the change to a higher state of form or composition that development differs from growth. We must carefully distinguish development from mere increase; it is the acquiring, not of greater bulk, but of new forms and structures, which are adapted to higher conditions of existence."

It is the distinction which Uhhorn draws between the terms *Entfaltung* and *Entwickelung*. Just then, after sixteen years spent in the Church of Rome, Newman was inclined to guard and narrow his theory. On the one hand he taught that the enactments and decisions of ecclesiastical law are made on principles and by virtue of prerogatives which *jam antea latitavere* in the Church of the apostles and fathers. But he thought that a divine of the second century on seeing the Roman catechism, would have recognised his own belief in it, without surprise, as soon as he understood its meaning. He once wrote: "If I have said more than this, I think I have not worked out my meaning, and was confused—whether the minute facts of history will bear me out in this view, I leave to others to determine." Döllinger would have feared to adopt a view for its own sake, without knowing how it would be borne out by the minute facts of history. His own theory of development had not the same ingenious simplicity, and he thought Newman's brilliant book unsound in detail. But he took high ground in asserting the undeviating fidelity of Catholicism to its principle. In this, his last book on the Primitive Church, as in his early lectures, he claims the unswerving unity of faith as a divine prerogative. In a memorable passage of the *Symbolik* Möhler had stated that there is no better security than the law which pervades human society, which preserves harmony and consistency in national character, which makes Lutheranism perpetually true to Luther, and Islamism to the Koran.

Speaking in the name of his own university, the rector described him as a receptive genius. Part of his career displays a quality of assimilation, acquiescence, and even adaptation, not always consistent with superior originality or intense force of character. His *Reformation,* the strongest book, with the *Symbolik,* which Catholics had produced in the century, was laid down on known lines, and scarcely effected so much novelty and change as the writings of Kampschulte and Kolde. His book on the first age of the Church takes the critical points as settled, without special discussion. He appeared to receive impulse and direction, limit and colour, from his outer life. His importance was achieved by the force within. Circumstances only conspired to mould a giant of commonplace excellence and average ideas, and their influence on his view of history might long be traced. No man of like spirituality, of equal belief in the supreme dignity of conscience, systematically allowed as much as he did for the empire of chance surroundings and the action of home, and school, and place of worship upon conduct. He must have known that his own mind and character as an historian was not formed by effort and design. From early impressions, and a life spent, to his fiftieth year, in a rather unvaried professional circle, he contracted homely habits in estimating objects of the greater world; and his imagination was not prone to vast proportions and wide horizons. He inclined to apply the rules and observation of domestic life to public affairs, to reduce the level of the heroic and sublime; and history, in his hands, lost something both in terror and in grandeur. He acquired his art in the long study of earlier times, where materials are scanty. All that can be known of Caesar or Charlemagne, or Gregory VII, would hold in a dozen volumes; a library would not be sufficient for Charles V or Lewis XVI. Extremely few of the ancients are really known to us in detail, as we know Socrates, or Cicero, or St. Augustine. But in modern times, since Petrarca, there are at least two thousand actors on the public stage whom we see by the revelations of private correspondence. Besides letters that were meant to be burnt, there are a man's secret diaries, his autobiography and table-talk, the recollections of his friends, self-betraying notes on the margins of books, the report of his trial if he is a culprit, and the evidence for beatification if he is a saint. Here we are on a different footing, and we practise a different art when dealing with Phocion or Dunstan, or with Richelieu or Swift. In one case we remain perforce on the surface of character, which we have not the means of analysing: we have to be content with conjecture, with probable explanations and obvious motives. We must constantly allow the benefit of the doubt, and reserve sentence. The science of character comes in with modern history. Döllinger had lived too long in the ages during which men are seen mostly in outline, and never applied an historical psychology distinct from that of private experience. Great men are something different from an enlarged repetition of average and familiar types, and the working and motive of their minds is in many instances the exact contrary of ordinary men, living to avoid contingencies of danger, and pain, and sacrifice, and the weariness of constant thinking and far-seeing precaution.

"We are apt to judge extraordinary men by our own standard, that is to say, we often suppose them to possess, in an extraordinary degree, those qualities which we are conscious of in ourselves or others. This is the easiest way of conceiving their characters, but not the truest. They differ in kind rather than in degree."

We cannot understand Cromwell or Shaftesbury, Sunderland or Penn, by studies made in the parish. The study of intricate and subtle character was not habitual with Döllinger, and the result was an extreme dread of unnecessary condemnation. He resented being told that Ferdinand I and II, that Henry III and Lewis XIII, were, in the coarse terms of common life, assassins; that Elizabeth tried to have Mary made away with, and that Mary, in matters of that kind, had no greater scruples; that William III ordered the extirpation of a clan, and rewarded the murderers as he had rewarded those of De Witt; that Lewis XIV sent a man to kill him, and James II was privy to the Assassination Plot. When he met men less mercifully given than himself, he said that they were hanging judges with a Malthusian propensity to repress the growth of population. This indefinite generosity did not disappear when he had long outgrown its early cause. It was revived, and his view of history was deeply modified, in the course of the great change in his attitude in the Church which took place between the years 1861 and 1867.

Döllinger used to commemorate his visit to Rome in 1857 as an epoch of emancipation. He had occasionally been denounced; and a keen eye had detected latent pantheism in his *Vorhalle*, but he had not been formally censured. If he had once asserted the value of nationality in the Church, he was vehement against it in religion; and if he had joined in deprecating the dogmatic decree in 1854, he was silent afterwards. By Protestants he was still avoided as the head and front of offending ultramontanism; and when the historical commission was instituted at Munich, by disciples of the Berlin school, he was passed over at first, and afterwards opposed. When public matters took him to Berlin in 1857, he sought no intercourse with the divines of the faculty. The common idea of his *Reformation* was expressed by Kaulbach in a drawing which represented the four chief reformers riding on one horse, pursued by a scavenger with the unmistakable features of their historian. He was received with civility at Rome, if not with cordiality. The pope sent to Cesena for a manuscript which it was reported that he wished to consult; and his days were spent profitably between the Minerva and the Vatican, where he was initiated in the mysteries of Galileo's tower. It was his fortune to have for pilot and instructor a prelate classified in the pigeon-holes of the Wilhelmstrasse as the chief agitator against the State, "dessen umfangreiches Wissen noch durch dessen Feinheit und geistige Gewandtheit übertroffen wird." He was welcomed by Passaglia and Schrader at the Collegio Romano, and enjoyed the privilege of examining San Callisto with De Rossi for his guide. His personal experience was agreeable though he strove unsuccessfully to prevent the condemnation of two of his colleagues by the Index.

There have been men connected with him who knew Rome in his time, and whose knowledge moved them to indignation and despair. One bishop assured him that the Christian religion was extinct there, and only survived in its forms; and an important ecclesiastic on the spot wrote: *Delenda est Carthago.* The archives of the Culturkampf contain a despatch from a Protestant statesman sometime his friend, urging his government to deal with the Papacy as they would deal with Dahomey. Döllinger's impression on his journey was very different. He did not come away charged with visions of scandal in the spiritual order, of suffering in the temporal, or of tyranny in either. He was never in contact with the sinister side of things. Theiner's *Life of Clement the Fourteenth* failed to convince him, and he listened incredulously to his indictment of the Jesuits. Eight years later Theiner wrote to him that he hoped they would now agree better on that subject than when they discussed it in Rome. "Ich freue mich, dass Sie jetzt erkennen, dass mein Urtheil über die Jesuiten und ihr Wirken gerecht war. Im kommenden Jahr, so Gott will, werden wir uns hoffentlich besser verstehen als im Jahr 1857." He thought the governing body unequal to the task of ruling both Church and State; but it was the State that seemed to him to suffer from the combination. He was anxious about the political future, not about the future of religion. The persuasion that government by priests could not maintain itself in the world as it is, grew in force and definiteness as he meditated at home on the things he had seen and heard. He was despondent and apprehensive, but he had no suspicion of what was then so near. In the summer of 1859, as the sequel of Solferino began to unfold itself, he thought of making his observations known. In November a friend wrote: "Je ne me dissimule aucune des misères de tout ordre qui vous ont frappé à Rome." For more than a year he remained silent and uncertain, watching the use France would make of the irresistible authority acquired by the defeat of Austria and the collapse of government in Central Italy.

The war of 1859, portending danger to the temporal power, disclosed divided counsels. The episcopate supported the papal sovereignty, and a voluntary tribute, which in a few years took shape in tens of millions, poured into the treasury of St. Peter. A time followed during which the Papacy endeavoured, by a series of connected measures, to preserve its political authority through the aid of its spiritual. Some of the most enlightened Catholics, Dupanloup and Montalembert, proclaimed a sort of holy war. Some of the most enlightened Protestants, Guizot and Leo, defended the Roman government, as the most legitimate, venerable, and necessary of governments. In Italy there were ecclesiastics like Liverani, Tosti, Capecelatro, who believed with Manzoni that there could be no deliverance without unity, or calculated that political loss might be religious gain. Passaglia, the most celebrated

Jesuit living, and a confidential adviser of the pope, both in dogma and in the preparation of the Syllabus, until Perrone refused to meet him, quitted the Society, and then fled from Rome, leaving the Inquisition in possession of his papers, in order to combat the use of theology in defence of the temporal power. Forty thousand priests, he said, publicly or privately agreed with him; and the diplomatists reported the names of nine cardinals who were ready to make terms with Italian unity, of which the pope himself said: "Ce serait un beau rêve." In this country, Newman did not share the animosity of conservatives against Napoleon III and his action in Italy. When the flood, rising, reached the papal throne, he preserved an embarrassed silence, refusing, in spite of much solicitation, to commit himself even in private. An impatient M.P. took the train down to Edgbaston, and began, trying to draw him: "What times we live in, Father Newman! Look at all that is going on in Italy."—"Yes, indeed! And look at China too, and New Zealand!" Lacordaire favoured the cause of the Italians more openly, in spite of his Paris associates. He hoped, by federation, to save the interests of the Holy See, but he was reconciled to the loss of provinces, and he required religious liberty at Rome. Lamoricière was defeated in September 1860, and in February the fortress of Gaëta, which had become the last Roman outwork, fell. Then Lacordaire, disturbed in his reasoning by the logic of events, and by an earnest appeal to his priestly conscience, as his biographer says: "ébranlé un moment par une lettre éloquente," broke away from his friends:

"Que Montalembert, notre ami commun, ne voie pas dans ce qui se passe en Italie, sauf le mal, un progrès sensible dans ce que nous avons toujours cru le bien de l'église, cela tient à sa nature passionnée. Ce qui le domine aujourd'hui c'est la haine du gouvernement français. Dieu se sert de tout, même du despotisme, même de l'égoïsme; et il y a même des choses qu'il ne peut accomplir par des mains tout à fait pures. Qu'y puis-je? Me déclarer contre l'Italie parce que ses chaînes tombent mal à propos? Non assurément: je laisse à d'autres une passion aussi profonde, et j'aime mieux accepter ce que j'estime un bien de quelque part qu'il vienne. Il est vrai que la situation temporelle du Pape souffre présentement de la libération de l'Italie, et peut-être en souffrira-t-elle encore assez longtemps: mais c'est un malheur qui a aussi ses fins dans la politique mystérieuse de la Providence. Souffrir n'est pas mourir, c'est quelquefois expier et s'éclairer."

This was written on 22nd February 1861. In April Döllinger spoke on the Roman question in the Odeon at Munich, and explained himself more fully in the autumn, in the most popular of all his books.

The argument of *Kirche und Kirchen* was, that the churches which are without the pope drift into many troubles, and maintain themselves at a manifest disadvantage, whereas the church which energetically preserves the principle of unity has a vast superiority which would prevail, but for its disabling and discrediting failure in civil government. That government seemed to him as legitimate as any in the world, and so needful to those for whose sake it was instituted, that if it should be overthrown, it would, by irresistible necessity, be restored. Those for whose sake it was instituted were, not the Roman people, but the catholic world. That interest, while it lasted, was so sacred, that no sacrifice was too great to preserve it, not even the exclusion of the clerical order from secular office.

The book was an appeal to Catholics to save the papal government by the only possible remedy, and to rescue the Roman people from falling under what the author deemed a tyranny like that of the Convention. He had acquired his politics in the atmosphere of 1847, from the potential liberality of men like Radowitz, who declared that he would postpone every political or national interest to that of the Church, Capponi, the last Italian federalist, and Tocqueville, the minister who occupied Rome. His object was not materially different from that of Antonelli and Mérode, but he sought it by exposing the faults of the papal government during several centuries, and the hopelessness of all efforts to save it from the Revolution unless reformed. He wrote to an English minister that it could not be our policy that the head of the Catholic Church should be subject to a foreign potentate:

"Das harte Wort, mit welchem Sie im Parlamente den Stab über Rom gebrochen haben—*hopelessly incurable,* oder *incorrigible*—kann ich mir nicht aneignen; ich hoffe vielmehr, wie ich es in dem Buche dargelegt habe, das Gegentheil. An die Dauerhaftigkeit eines ganz Italien umfassenden Piemontesisch-Italiänischen Reiches glaube ich nicht. Inzwischen tröste ich mich mit dem Gedanken, dass in Rom zuletzt doch *vexatio dabit intellectum,* und dann wird noch alles gut werden."

To these grateful vaticinations his correspondent replied:

"You have exhibited the gradual departure of the government in the states of the church from all those conditions which made it tolerable to the sense and reason of mankind, and have, I think, completely justified, in principle if not in all the facts, the conduct of those who have determined to do away with it."

The policy of exalting the spiritual authority though at the expense of sacrifices in the temporal, the moderation even in the catalogue of faults, the side blow at the Protestants, filling more than half the volume, disarmed for a moment the resentment of outraged Rome. The Pope, on a report from Theiner, spoke of the book as one that might do good. Others said that it was pointless, that its point was not where the author meant it to be, that the handle was sharper than the blade. It was made much more clear that the Pope had governed badly than that Russia or Great Britain would gain by his supremacy. The cold analysis, the diagnosis by the bedside of the sufferer, was not the work of an observer dazzled by admiration or blinded by affection. It was a step, a first unconscious, unpremeditated step, in the process of detachment. The historian here began to prevail over the divine, and to judge Church matters by a law which was not given from the altar. It was the outcome of a spirit which had been in him from the beginning. His English translator had uttered a mild protest against his severe treatment of popes. His censure of the Reformation had been not as that of Bossuet, but as that of Baxter and Bull. In 1845 Mr. Gladstone remarked that he would answer every objection, but never proselytised. In 1848 he rested the claims of the Church on the common law, and bade the hierarchy remember that national character is above free will: "Die Nationalität ist etwas der Freiheit des menschlichen Willens entrücktes, geheimnissvolles und in ihrem letzten Grunde selbst etwas von Gott gewolltes." In his *Hippolytus* he began by surrendering the main point, that a man who so vilified the papacy might yet be an undisputed saint. In the *Vorhalle* he flung away a favourite argument, by avowing that paganism developed by its own lines and laws, untouched by Christianity, until the second century; and as with the Gentiles, so with the sects; he taught, in the suppressed chapter of his history, that their doctrines followed a normal course. And he believed so far in the providential mission of Protestantism, that it was idle to talk of reconciliation until it had borne all its fruit. He exasperated a Munich colleague by refusing to pronounce whether Gregory and Innocent had the right to depose emperors, or Otho and Henry to depose popes; for he thought that historians should not fit theories to facts, but should be content with showing how things worked. Much secret and suppressed antagonism found vent in 1858, when one who had been his assistant in writing the *Reformation* and was still his friend, declared that he would be a heretic whenever he found a backing.

Those with whom he actively coalesced felt at times that he was incalculable, that he pursued a separate line, and was always learning, whilst others busied themselves less with the unknown. This note of distinctness and solitude set him apart from those about him, during his intimacy with the most catholic of Anglican prelates, Forbes, and with the lamented Liddon. And it appeared still more when the denominational barrier of his sympathy was no longer marked, and he, who had stood in the rank almost with De Maistre and Perrone, found himself acting for the same ends with their enemies, when he delivered a studied eulogy on Mignet, exalted the authority of Laurent in religious history and of Ferrari in civil, and urged the Bavarian academy to elect Taine, as a writer who had but one rival in France, leaving it to uncertain conjecture whether the man he meant was Renan. In theory it was his maxim that a man should guard against his friends. When he first addressed the university as Rector, saying that as the opportunity might never come again, he would employ it to utter the thoughts closest to his heart, he exhorted the students to be always true to their convictions and not to yield to surroundings; and he invoked, rightly or wrongly, the example of Burke, his favourite among public men, who, turning from his associates to obey the light within, carried the nation with him. A gap was apparent now between the spirit in which he devoted himself to the service of his Church and that of the men whom he most esteemed. At that time he was nearly the only German who knew Newman well and appreciated the grace and force of his mind. But Newman, even when he was angry, assiduously distinguished the pontiff from his court:

"There will necessarily always be round the Pope second-rate people, who are not subjects of that supernatural wisdom which is his prerogative. For myself, certainly I have found myself in a different atmosphere, when I have left the Curia for the Pope himself."

Montalembert protested that there were things in *Kirche und Kirchen* which he would not have liked to say in public:

"Il est certain que la seconde partie de votre livre déplaira beaucoup, non seulement à Rome, mais encore à la très grande majorité des

Catholiques. Je ne sais donc pas si, dans le cas où vous m'eussiez consulté préalablement, j'aurais eu le courage d'infliger cette blessure à mon père et à mes frères."

Döllinger judged that the prerogative even of natural wisdom was often wanting in the government of the Church; and the sense of personal attachment, if he ever entertained it, had worn away in the friction and familiarity of centuries.

After the disturbing interlude of the Roman question he did not resume the history of Christianity. The second century with its fragments of information, its scope for piercing and conjecture, he left to Lightfoot. With increasing years he lost the disposition to travel on common ground, impregnably occupied by specialists, where he had nothing of his own to tell; and he preferred to work where he could be a pathfinder. Problems of Church government had come to the front, and he proposed to retraverse his subject, narrowing it into a history of the papacy. He began by securing his foundations and eliminating legend. He found so much that was legendary that his critical preliminaries took the shape of a history of fables relating to the papacy. Many of these were harmless: others were devised for a purpose, and he fixed his attention more and more on those which were the work of design. The question, how far the persistent production of spurious matter had permanently affected the genuine constitution and theology of the Church arose before his mind as he composed the *Papstfabeln des Mittelalters*. He indicated the problem without discussing it. The matter of the volume was generally neutral, but its threatening import was perceived, and twenty-one hostile critics sent reviews of it to one theological journal.

Since he first wrote on these matters, thirty years earlier, the advance of competitive learning had made it a necessity to revise statements by all accessible lights, and to subject authorities to a closer scrutiny. The increase in the rigour of the obligation might be measured by Tischendorf, who, after renewing the text of the New Testament in seven editions, had more than three thousand changes to make in the eighth. The old pacific superficial method yielded no longer what would be accepted as certain knowledge. Having made himself master of the reconstructive process that was carried on a little apart from the main chain of durable literature, in academic transactions, in dissertations and periodicals, he submitted the materials he was about to use to the exigencies of the day. Without it, he would have remained a man of the last generation, distanced by every disciple of the new learning. He went to work with nothing but his trained and organised common sense, starting from no theory, and aiming at no conclusion. If he was beyond his contemporaries in the mass of expedient knowledge, he was not before them in the strictness of his tests, or in sharpness or boldness in applying them. He was abreast as a critic, he was not ahead. He did not innovate. The parallel studies of the time kept pace with his; and his judgments are those which are accepted generally. His critical mind was pliant, to assent where he must, to reject where he must, and to doubt where he must. His submission to external testimony appeared in his panegyric of our Indian empire, where he overstated the increase of population. Informed of his error by one of his translators, he replied that the figures had seemed incredible also to him, but having verified, he found the statement so positively made that he did not venture to depart from it. If inclination ever swayed his judgment, it was in his despair of extracting a real available Buddha from the fables of Southern India, which was conquered at last by the ablest of Mommsen's pupils.

He was less apprehensive than most of his English friends in questions relating to the Old Testament; and in the New, he was disposed, at times, to allow some force to Muratori's fragment as to the person of the evangelist who is least favourable to St. Peter; and was puzzled at the zeal of the Speaker's commentator as to the second epistle of the apostle. He held to the epistles of St. Ignatius with the tenacity of a Caroline prelate, and was grateful to De Rossi for a chronological point in their favour. He rejected the attacks of Lucius on the most valued passages in Philo, and stood with Gass against Weingarten's argument on the life of St. Anthony and the origin of Monasticism. He resisted Overbeck on the epistle to Diognetus, and thought Ebrard all astray as to the Culdees. There was no conservative antiquarian whom he prized higher than Le Blant: yet he considered Ruinart credulous in dealing with acts of early martyrs. A pupil on whose friendship he relied, made an effort to rescue the legends of the conversion of Germany; but the master preferred the unsparing demolitions of Rettberg. Capponi and Carl Hegel were his particular friends; but he abandoned them without hesitation for Scheffer Boichorst, the iconoclast of early Italian chronicles, and never consented to read the learned reply of Da Lungo.

The *Pope Fables* carried the critical inquiry a very little way; but he went on with the subject. After the Donation of Constantine came the Forged Decretals, which were just then printed for the first time in an accurate edition. Döllinger began to be absorbed in the long train of hierarchical fictions, which had deceived men like Gregory VII, St. Thomas Aquinas, and Cardinal Bellarmine, which he traced up to the false Areopagite, and down to the Laminae Granatenses. These studies became the chief occupation of his life; they led to his excommunication in 1871, and carried him away from his early system. For this, neither syllabus nor ecumenical council was needed; neither crimes nor scandals were its distant cause. The history of Church government was the influence which so profoundly altered his position. Some trace of his researches, at an early period of their progress, appears in what he wrote on the occasion of the Vatican Council, especially in the fragment of an ecclesiastical pathology which was published under the name of Janus. But the history itself, which was the main and characteristic work of his life, and was pursued until the end, was never published or completed. He died without making it known to what extent, within what limit, the ideas with which he had been so long identified were changed by his later studies, and how wide a trench had opened between his earlier and his later life. Twenty years of his historical work are lost for history.

The revolution in method since he began to write was partly the better use of old authorities, partly the accession of new. Döllinger had devoted himself to the one in 1863; he passed to the other in 1864. For definite objects he had often consulted manuscripts, but the harvest was stacked away, and had scarcely influenced his works. In the use and knowledge of unpublished matter he still belonged to the old school, and was on a level with Neander. Although, in later years, he printed six or seven volumes of Inedita, like Mai and Theiner he did not excel as an editor: and this part of his labours is notable chiefly for its effect on himself. He never went over altogether to men like Schottmüller, who said of him that he made no research—*er hat nicht geforscht*—meaning that he had made his mind up about the Templars by the easy study of Wilkins, Michelet, Schottmüller himself, and perhaps a hundred others, but had not gone underground to the mines they delved in. Fustel de Coulanges, at the time of his death, was promoting the election of the Bishop of Oxford to the Institute, on the ground that he surpassed all other Englishmen in his acquaintance with manuscripts. Döllinger agreed with their French rival in his estimate of our English historian, but he ascribed less value to that part of his acquirements. He assured the Bavarian Academy that Mr. Freeman, who reads print, but nevertheless mixes his colours with brains, is the author of the most profound work on the Middle Ages ever written in this country, and is not only a brilliant writer and a sagacious critic, but the most learned of all our countrymen. Ranke once drew a line at 1514, after which, he said, we still want help from unprinted sources. The world had moved a good deal since that cautious innovation, and after 1860, enormous and excessive masses of archive were brought into play. The Italian Revolution opened tempting horizons. In 1864 Döllinger spent his vacation in the libraries of Vienna and Venice. At Vienna, by an auspicious omen, Sickel, who was not yet known to Greater Germany as the first of its mediaeval palaeographers, showed him the sheets of a work containing 247 Carolingian acts unknown to Böhmer, who had just died with the repute of being the best authority on Imperial charters. During several years Döllinger followed up the discoveries he now began. Theiner sent him documents from the *Archivio Segreto*; one of his friends shut himself up at Trent, and another at Bergamo. Strangers ministered to his requirements, and huge quantities of transcripts came to him from many countries. Conventional history faded away; the studies of a lifetime suddenly underwent transformation; and his view of the last six centuries was made up from secret information gathered in thirty European libraries and archives. As many things remote from current knowledge grew to be certainties, he became more confident, more independent, and more isolated. The ecclesiastical history of his youth went to pieces against the new criticism of 1863, and the revelation of the unknown which began on a very large scale in 1864.

During four years of transition occupied by this new stage of study, he abstained from writing books. Whenever some local occasion called upon him to speak, he spoke of the independence and authority of history. In cases of collision with the Church, he said that a man should seek the error in himself; but he spoke of the doctrine of the universal Church, and it did not appear that he thought of any living voice or present instructor. He claimed no immunity for philosophy; but history, he affirmed, left to itself and pursued disinterestedly, will heal the ills it causes; and it was said of him that he set the university in the place of the hierarchy. Some of his countrymen were deeply moved by the measures which were being taken to restore and to confirm the authority of Rome; and he had impatient colleagues at the university who pressed him with sharp issues of uncompromising logic. He himself was reluctant to bring down serene research into troublesome disputation, and wished to keep history and controversy apart. His hand was forced at last by his friends abroad. Whilst he pursued his isolating investigations he remained aloof from a question which in other countries and other days was a summary and effective test of impassioned controversy. Persecution was a problem that had never troubled him. It was not a topic with theoretical Germans; the necessary books were hardly available, and a man might read all the popular histories and theologies without getting much further than the Spanish Inquisition. Ranke, averse from what is unpleasant, gave no details. The gravity of the question had never been brought home to Döllinger in forty years of public teaching. When he approached it, as late as 1861, he touched lightly, representing the intolerance of Protestants to their disadvantage, while that of Catholics was a bequest of Imperial Rome, taken up in an emergency by secular powers, in no way involving the true spirit and practice of the Church. With this light footfall the topic which has so powerful a leverage slipped into the current of his thought. The view found favour with Ambrose de Lisle, who, having read the *Letters to a Prebendary*, was indignant with those who commit the Church to a principle often resisted or ignored. Newman would admit to no such compromise:

"Is not the miraculous infliction of judgments upon blasphemy, lying, profaneness, etc., in the apostles' day a sanction of infliction upon the same by a human hand in the times of the Inquisition? Ecclesiastical rulers may punish with the sword, if they can, and if it is expedient or necessary to do so. The church has a right to make laws and to enforce them with temporal punishments."

The question came forward in France in the wake of the temporal power. Liberal defenders of a government which made a principle of persecution had to decide whether they approved or condemned it. Where was their liberality in one case, or their catholicity in the other? It was the simple art of their adversaries to press this point, and to make the most of it; and a French priest took upon him to declare that intolerance, far from being a hidden shame, was a pride and a glory: "L'Eglise regarde l'Inquisition comme l'apogée de la civilisation chrétienne, comme le fruit naturel des époques de foi et de catholicisme national." Gratry took the other side so strongly that there would have been a tumult at the Sorbonne, if he had said from his chair what he wrote in his book; and certain passages were struck out of the printed text by the cautious archbishop's reviser. He was one of those French divines who had taken in fuel at Munich, and he welcomed *Kirche und Kirchen:* "Quant au livre du docteur Döllinger sur la Papauté, c'est, selon moi, le livre décisif. C'est un chef-d'oeuvre admirable à plusieurs égards, et qui est destiné à produire un bien incalculable et à fixer l'opinion sur ce sujet; c'est ainsi que le juge aussi M. de Montalembert. Le docteur Döllinger nous a rendu à tous un grand service." This was not the first impression of Montalembert. He deplored the Odeon lectures as usurping functions divinely assigned not to professors, but to the episcopate, as a grief for friends and a joy for enemies. When the volume came he still objected to the policy, to the chapter on England, and to the cold treatment of Sixtus V. At last he admired without reserve. Nothing better had been written since Bossuet; the judgment on the Roman government, though severe, was just, and contained no more than the truth. There was not a word which he would not be able to sign. A change was going on in his position and his affections, as he came to regard toleration as the supreme affair. At Malines he solemnly declared that the Inquisitor was as horrible as the Terrorist, and made no distinction in favour of death inflicted for religion against death for political motives: "Les bûchers allumés par une main catholique me font autant d'horreur que les échafauds où les Protestants ont immolé tant de martyrs." Wiseman, having heard him once, was not present on the second day; but the Belgian cardinal assured him that he had spoken like a sound divine. He described Dupanloup's defence of the Syllabus as a masterpiece of eloquent subterfuge, and repudiated his *interprétations équivoques*. A journey to Spain in 1865 made him more vehement than ever; although, from that time, the political opposition inflamed him less. He did not find imperialism intolerable. His wrath was fixed on the things of which Spain had reminded him: "C'est là qu'il faut aller pour voir ce que le catholicisme exclusif a su faire d'une des plus grandes et des plus héroïques nations de la terre. Je rapporte un surcroît d'horreur pour les doctrines fanatiques et absolutistes qui ont cours aujourd'hui chez les catholiques du monde entier." In 1866 it became difficult, by the aid of others, to overcome Falloux's resistance to the admission of an article in the *Correspondant,* and by the end of the year his friends were unanimous to exclude him. An essay on Spain, his last work—

"dernier soupir de mon âme indignée et attristée"—was, by Dupanloup's advice, not allowed to appear. Repelled by those whom he now designated as spurious, servile, and prevaricating liberals, he turned to the powerful German with whom he thought himself in sympathy. He had applauded him for dealing with one thing at a time, in his book on Rome: "Vous avez bien fait de ne rien dire de l'absolutisme spirituel, quant à présent. *Sat prata biberunt.* Le reste viendra en son temps." He avowed that spiritual autocracy is worse than political; that evil passions which had triumphed in the State were triumphant in the Church; that to send human beings to the stake, with a crucifix before them, was the act of a monster or a maniac. He was dying; but whilst he turned his face to the wall, lamenting that he had lived too long, he wished for one more conference with the old friend with whom, thirty-five years before, in a less anxious time, he had discussed the theme of religion and liberty. This was in February 1867, and for several years he had endeavoured to teach Döllinger his clear-cut antagonism, and to kindle in him something of his gloomy and passionate fervour, on the one point on which all depended.

Döllinger arrived slowly at the contemplation of deeper issues than that of churchmen or laymen in political offices, of Roman or German pupils in theological chairs. After seeing Baron Arnim, in 1865, he lost the hope of saving the papal government, and ceased to care about the things he had contended for in 1861; and a time came when he thought it difficult to give up the temporal power, and yet revere the Holy See. He wrote to Montalembert that his illusions were failing: "Ich bin sehr ernüchtert. Es ist so vieles in der Kirche anders gekommen, als ich es mir vor 20–30 Jahren gedacht, und rosenfarbig ausgemalt hatte." He learnt to speak of spiritual despotism almost in the words of his friend. The point of junction between the two orders of ideas is the use of fire for the enforcement of religion on which the French were laying all their stress: "In Frankreich bewegt sich der Gegensatz blos auf dem socialpolitischen Gebiete, nicht auf dem theologisch-wissenschaftlichen, weil es dort genau genommen eine theologische Wissenschaft nicht gibt" (16th October 1865). The Syllabus had not permanently fixed his attention upon it. Two years later, the matter was put more definitely, and he found himself, with little real preparation, turning from antiquarian curiosities, and brought face to face with the radical question of life and death. If ever his literary career was influenced by his French alliances, by association with men in the throng, for whom politics decided, and all the learning of the schools did not avail, the moment was when he resolved to write on the Inquisition.

The popular account which he drew up appeared in the newspapers in the summer of 1867; and although he did not mean to burn his ships, his position as an official defender of the Holy See was practically at an end. He wrote rapidly, at short notice, and not in the steady course of progressive acquisition. Ficker and Winkelmann have since given a different narrative of the step by which the Inquisition came into existence; and the praise of Gregory X, as a man sincerely religious who kept aloof, was a mark of haste. In the work which he was using, there was no act by that pontiff; but if he had had time to look deeper he would not have found him, in this respect, different from his contemporaries. There is no uncertainty as to the author's feeling towards the infliction of torture and death for religion, and the purpose of his treatise is to prevent the nailing of the Catholic colours to the stake. The spirit is that of the early lectures, in which he said: "Diese Schutzgewalt der Kirche ist rein geistlich. Sie kann also auch einen solchen öffentlichen hartnäckigen und sonst unheilbaren Gegner der Kirche nur seiner rein geistlichen kirchlichen Rechte berauben." Compared with the sweeping vehemence of the Frenchmen who preceded, the restrained moderation of language, the abstinence from the use of general terms, leaves us in doubt how far the condemnation extended, and whether he did more, in fact, than deplore a deviation from the doctrine of the first centuries. "Kurz darauf trat ein Umschwung ein, den man wohl einen Abfall von der alten Lehre nennen darf, und der sich ausnimmt, als ob die Kaiser die Lehrmeister der Bischöfe geworden seien." He never entirely separated himself in principle from the promoters, the agents, the apologists. He did not believe, with Hefele, that the spirit survives, that there are men, not content with eternal flames, who are ready to light up new Smithfields. Many of the defenders were his intimate friends. The most conspicuous was the only colleague who addressed him with the familiar German *Du*. Speaking of two or three men, of whom one, Martens, had specially attacked the false liberalism which sees no good in the Inquisition, he wrote: "Sie werden sich noch erinnern . . . wie hoch ich solche Männer stelle." He differed from them widely, but he differed academically; and this was not the polish or precaution of a man who knows that to assail character is to degrade and to betray one's cause. The change in his own opinions was always before him. Although convinced that he had been wrong in many of the ideas and facts with which he started, he was also satisfied that he had been as sincere and true to his lights in 1835 as in 1865. There was no secret about the Inquisition, and its observances were published and republished in fifty books; but in his early days he had not read them, and there was not a German, from Basel to Königsberg, who could have faced a *viva voce* in the *Directorium* or the *Arsenale*, or who had ever read Percin or Paramo. If Lacordaire disconnected St. Dominic from the practice of persecution, Döllinger had done the same thing before him.

"Weit entfernt, wie man ihm wohl vorgeworfen hat, sich dabei Gewalt und Verfolgung zu erlauben, oder gar der Stifter der Inquisition zu werden, wirkte er, nicht den Irrenden, sondern den Irrthum befehdend, nur durch ruhige Belehrung und Erörterung."

If Newman, a much more cautious disputant, thought it substantial truth to say that Rome never burnt heretics, there were things as false in his own early writings. If Möhler, in the religious wars, diverted attention from Catholic to Protestant atrocities, he took the example from his friend's book, which he was reviewing. There may be startling matter in Locatus and Pegna, but they were officials writing under the strictest censorship, and nobody can tell when they express their own private thoughts. There is a copy of Suarez on which a priest has written the marginal ejaculation: "Mon Dieu, ayez pitié de nous!" But Suarez had to send the manuscript of his most aggressive book to Rome for revision, and Döllinger used to insist, on the testimony of his secretary, in Walton's *Lives*, that he disavowed and detested the interpolations that came back.

The French group, unlike him in spirit and motive, but dealing with the same opponents, judged them freely, and gave imperative utterance to their judgments. While Döllinger said of Veuillot that he meant well, but did much good and much evil, Montalembert called him a hypocrite: "L'Univers, en déclarant tous les jours qu'il ne veut pas d'autre liberté que la sienne, justifie tout ce que nos pires ennemis ont jamais dit sur la mauvaise foi et l'hypocrisie des polémistes chrétiens." Lacordaire wrote to a hostile bishop: "L'Univers est à mes yeux la négation de tout esprit chrétien et de tout bon sens humain. Ma consolation au milieu de si grandes misères morales est de vivre solitaire, occupé d'une oeuvre que Dieu bénit, et de protester par mon silence, et de temps en temps par mes paroles, contre la plus grande insolence qui se soit encore authorisée au nom de Jésus-Christ." Gratry was a man of more gentle nature, but his tone is the same: "Esprits faux ou nuls, consciences intellectuelles faussées par l'habitude de l'apologie sans franchise: *partemque ejus cum hypocritis ponet.* Cette école est bien en vérité une école de mensonge. C'est cette école qui est depuis des siècles, et surtout en ce siècle, l'opprobre de notre cause et le fléau de la religion. Voilà notre ennemi commun; voilà l'ennemi de l'Eglise."

Döllinger never understood party divisions in this tragic way. He was provided with religious explanations for the living and the dead; and his maxims in regard to contemporaries governed and attenuated his view of every historical problem. For the writers of his acquaintance who were unfaltering advocates of the Holy Office, for Philips and Gams, and for Theiner, who expiated devious passages of early youth, amongst other penitential works, with large volumes in honour of Gregory XIII, he had always the same mode of defence: "Mir begegnet es noch jede Woche, dass ich irgend einem Irrthum, mitunter einem lange gepflegten, entsage, ihn mir gleichsam aus der Brust herausreissen muss. Da sollte man freilich höchst duldsam und nachsichtig gegen fremde Irrthümer werden" (5th October 1866). He writes in the same terms to another correspondent sixteen years later: "Mein ganzes Leben ist ein successives Abstreifen von Irrthümern gewesen, von Irrthümern, die ich mit Zähigkeit festhielt, gewaltsam gegen die mir aufdämmernde bessere Erkenntniss mich stemmend; und doch meine ich sagen zu dürfen, dass ich dabei nicht *dishonest* war. Darf ich andre verurtheilen *in eodem luto mecum haerentes?*" He regretted as he grew old the hardness and severity of early days, and applied the same inconclusive deduction from his own experience to the past. After comparing Baronius and Bellarmine with Bossuet and Arnauld he goes on: "Wenn ich solche Männer auf einem Irrthum treffe, so sage ich mir: 'Wenn Du damals gelebt, und an seiner Stelle gestanden wärest, hättest Du nicht den allgemeinen Wahn getheilt; und er, wenn er die Dir zu Theil gewordenen Erkenntnissmittel besessen, würde er nicht besseren Gebrauch davon gemacht haben, die Wahrheit nicht früher erkannt und bekannt haben, als Du?' "

He sometimes distrusted his favourite argument of ignorance and early prepossessions, and felt that there was presumption and unreality in tendering such explanations to men like the Bollandist De Buck, De Rossi, whom the Institute elected in preference to Mommsen, or

Windischmann, whom he himself had been accused of bringing forward as a rival to Möhler. He would say that knowledge may be a burden and not a light, that the faculty of doing justice to the past is among the rarest of moral and intellectual gifts: "Man kann viel wissen, viele Notizen im Kopf haben, ohne das rechte wissenschaftliche Verständniss, ohne den historischen Sinn. Dieser ist, wie Sie wohl wissen, gar nicht so häufig; und wo er fehlt, da fehlt auch, scheint mir, die volle Verantwortlichkeit für das gewusste."

In 1879 he prepared materials for a paper on the Massacre of St. Bartholomew. Here he was breaking new ground, and verging on that which it was the policy and the aspiration of his life to avoid. Many a man who gives no tears to Cranmer, Servetus, or Bruno, who thinks it just that the laws should be obeyed, who deems that actions done by order are excused, and that legality implies morality, will draw the line at midnight murder and wholesale extermination. The deed wrought at Paris and in forty towns of France in 1572, the arguments which produced it, the arguments which justified it, left no room for the mists of mitigation and compromise. The passage from the age of Gregory IX to that of Gregory XIII, from the Crusades to the wars of Religion, brought his whole system into jeopardy. The historian who was at the heels of the divine in 1861, and level with him in 1867, would have come to the front. The discourse was never delivered, never composed. But the subject of toleration was absent no more from his thoughts, filling space once occupied by Julian of Eclanum and Duns Scotus, the Variata and the Five Propositions. To the last days of 1889 he was engaged in following the doctrines of intolerance back to their root, from Innocent III to the Council of Rheims, from Nicholas I to St. Augustine, narrowing the sphere of individual responsibility, defending agents, and multiplying degrees so as to make them imperceptible. Before the writings of Priscillian were published by the Vienna Academy the nature of their strange contents was disclosed. It then appeared that a copy of the *Codex unicus* had been sent to Döllinger from Würzburg years before; and that he had never adverted to the fact that the burning of heretics came, fully armed, from the brain of one man, and was the invention of a heretic who became its first victim.

At Rome he discussed the council of Trent with Theiner, and tried to obtain permission for him to publish the original acts. Pius IX objected that none of his predecessors had allowed it, and Theiner answered that none of them had defined the Immaculate Conception. In a paper which Döllinger drew up, he observed that Pallavicini cannot convince; that far from proving the case against the artful Servite, the pettiness of his charges indicates that he has no graver fault to find; so that nothing but the production of the official texts can enforce or disprove the imputation that Trent was a scene of tyranny and intrigue. His private belief then was that the papers would disprove the imputation and vindicate the council. When Theiner found it possible to publish his *Acta Authentica*, Döllinger also printed several private diaries, chiefly from Mendham's collection at the Bodleian. But the correspondence between Rome and the legates is still, in its integrity, kept back. The two friends had examined it; both were persuaded that it was decisive; but they judged that it decided in opposite ways. Theiner, the official guardian of the records, had been forbidden to communicate them during the Vatican Council; and he deemed the concealment prudent. What passed in Rome under Pius IX would, he averred, suffer by comparison. According to Döllinger, the suppressed papers told against Trent.

"Wenn wir nicht allen unseren henotischen Hoffnungen entsagen und uns nicht in schweren Konflikt mit der alten (vormittelalterigen) Kirche bringen wollen, werden wir doch auch da das Korrektiv des Vincentianischen Prinzips (*semper, ubique, ab omnibus*) zur Anwendung bringen müssen."

After his last visit to the Marciana he thought more favourably of Father Paul, sharing the admiration which Venetians feel for the greatest writer of the Republic, and falling little short of the judgments which Macaulay inscribed, after each perusal, in the copy at Inveraray. Apart from his chief work he thought him a great historian, and he rejected the suspicion that he professed a religion which he did not believe. He even fancied that the manuscript, which in fact was forwarded with much secrecy to Archbishop Abbot, was published against his will. The intermediate seekers, who seem to skirt the border, such as Grotius, Ussher, Praetorius, and the other celebrated Venetian, De Dominis, interested him deeply, in connection with the subject of Irenics, and the religious problem was part motive of his incessant study of Shakespeare, both in early life, and when he meditated joining in the debate between Simpson, Rio, Bernays, and the *Edinburgh Review*.

His estimate of his own work was low. He wished to be remembered as a man who had written certain books, but who had not written many more. His collections constantly prompted new and attractive schemes, but his way was strewn with promise unperformed, and abandoned from want of concentration. He would not write with imperfect materials, and to him the materials were always imperfect. Perpetually engaged in going over his own life and reconsidering his conclusions, he was not depressed by unfinished work. When a sanguine friend hoped that all the contents of his hundred note-books would come into use, he answered that perhaps they might, if he lived for a hundred and fifty years. He seldom wrote a book without compulsion, or the aid of energetic assistants. The account of mediaeval sects, dated 1890, was on the stocks for half a century. The discourse on the Templars, delivered at his last appearance in public, had been always before him since a conversation with Michelet about the year 1841. Fifty-six years lay between his text to the *Paradiso* of Cornelius and his last return to Dante.

When he began to fix his mind on the constitutional history of the Church, he proposed to write, first, on the times of Innocent XI. It was the age he knew best, in which there was most interest, most material, most ability, when divines were national classics, and presented many distinct types of religious thought, when biblical and historical science was founded, and Catholicism was presented in its most winning guise. The character of Odescalchi impressed him, by his earnestness in sustaining a strict morality. Fragments of this projected work reappeared in his lectures on Louis XIV, and in his last publication on the Casuists. The lectures betray the decline of the tranquil idealism which had been the admiration and despair of friends. Opposition to Rome had made him, like his ultramontane allies in France, more indulgent to the ancient Gallican enemy. He now had to expose the vice of that system, which never roused the king's conscience, and served for sixty years, from the remonstrance of Caussin to the anonymous warning of Fénelon, as the convenient sanction of absolutism. In the work on seventeenth-century ethics, which is his farthest, the moral point of view prevails over every other, and conscience usurps the place of theology, canon law, and scholarship. This was his tribute to a new phase of literature, the last he was to see, which was beginning to put ethical knowledge above metaphysics and politics, as the central range of human progress. Morality, veracity, the proper atmosphere of ideal history, became the paramount interest.

When he was proposed for a degree, the most eloquent lips at

Oxford, silenced for ever whilst I write this page, pointed to his excellence in those things which are the merit of Germans. "Quaecunque in Germanorum indole admiranda atque imitanda fere censemus, ea in Doellingero maxime splendent." The patriotic quality was recognised in the address of the Berlin professors, who say that by upholding the independence of the national thought, whilst he enriched it with the best treasure of other lands, he realised the ideal of the historian. He became more German in extreme old age, and less impressive in his idiomatic French and English than in his own language. The lamentations of men he thought good judges, Mazade and Taine, and the first of literary critics, Montégut, diluted somewhat his admiration for the country of St. Bernard and Bossuet. In spite of politics, his feeling for English character, for the moral quality of English literature, never changed; and he told his own people that their faults are not only very near indeed to their virtues, but are sometimes more apparent to the observer. The belief in the fixity and influence of national type, confirmed by his authorities, Ganganelli and Möhler, continued to determine his judgments. In his last letter to Mr. Gladstone, he illustrated the Irish question by means of a chronicle describing Ireland a thousand years ago.

Everybody has felt that his power was out of proportion to his work, and that he knew too much to write. It was so much better to hear him than to read all his books, that the memory of what he was will pass away with the children whom he loved. Hefele called him the first theologian in Germany, and Höfler said that he surpassed all men in the knowledge of historical literature; but Hefele was the bishop of his predilection, and Höfler had been fifty years his friend, and is the last survivor of the group which once made Munich the capital of citramontane Catholicity. Martensen, the most brilliant of Episcopalian divines, describes him as he talked with equal knowledge and certainty of every age, and understood all characters and all situations as if he had lived in the midst of them. The best ecclesiastical historian now living is the fittest judge of the great ecclesiastical historian who is dead. Harnack has assigned causes which limited his greatness as a writer, perhaps even as a thinker; but he has declared that no man had the same knowledge and intelligence of history in general, and of religious history which is its most essential element, and he affirms, what some have doubted, that he possessed the rare faculty of entering into alien thought. None of those who knew Professor Döllinger best, who knew him in the third quarter of the century, to which he belonged by the full fruition of his powers and the completeness of his knowledge, will ever qualify these judgments. It is right to add that, in spite of boundless reading, there was no lumber in his mind, and in spite of his classical learning, little ornament. Among the men to be commemorated here, he stands alone. Throughout the measureless distance which he traversed, his movement was against his wishes, in pursuit of no purpose, in obedience to no theory, under no attraction but historical research alone. It was given to him to form his philosophy of history on the largest induction ever available to man; and whilst he owed more to divinity than any other historian, he owed more to history than any other divine.

[22]
Talleyrand's *Memoirs*

The reality of History is so unlike the report that we continue, in spite of much disappointment, to look for revelations as often as an important personage leaves us his reminiscences. The famous book which has been so eagerly expected and so long withheld will not satisfy those who, like the first Queen of Prussia, demand to know *le pourquoy du pourquoy*. The most experienced and sagacious of men discourses about certain selected events that concerned him, and passes sentence on two generations of contemporaries; but he betrays few secrets and prepares no surprises. Nothing could increase the lustre of the talents which he is known—by the malevolent testimony of Vitrolles—to have displayed at the first restoration, or which are proved by his own correspondence from Vienna. But we are made to know him better; and all that he says and much that he conceals brings into vivid light one of the wonders of modern politics.

Three months after the fall of Napoleon, Talleyrand went out of office, opposed by Russia, disliked by the King, hated by the triumphant Royalists. Under that constellation, mainly in the year 1816, he wrote these Memoirs. The undercurrent of motive is to explain, or to explain away, the earlier part of his career; to expose his incomparable services to the crown, the country, and the dominant party; to show that nothing in the various past disqualifies him for the first place in the councils of the monarchy he had restored. It is not the plea of a vulgar competitor; for, with all his sleepless ambition, he writes with studied moderation and reserve. He has not the tone of a man contemplating from aloft his own achievements, his immense renown, his assured place in the central history of the world. Talleyrand is dissatisfied, satirical, and almost always bitter in his judgment of men. The better

Published in the *Nineteenth Century* 29 (1891):670–684. Reprinted in Acton, *Historical Essays*, pp. 393–413.

to dissociate himself from evil communications, he interpolates a laboured attack on the Duke of Orleans, which would be a blot on the composition but for the redeeming paragraph on Sieyès, the best of all the characters he has drawn. He slurs over his own share in the work of the National Assembly, justifies his attitude under Napoleon by the pressing need for monarchy, and by his breach with him on the affairs of Spain, and puts himself straight with the Church by a detailed narrative of the disputes with Rome.

He was reputed too idle a man to be a good writer, and it was supposed that Des Renaudes held the pen for him at one time and La Besnardière at another. Chateaubriand, who devoted his most tremendous sentences to the business of denouncing him as a traitor in politics and religion, and who insisted that the last action of his life was a deceitful comedy, quotes a letter to himself as evidence that Talleyrand was deficient in ideas, and wrote an unsubstantial style. These volumes are composed with much art, and, in the passage which is an express vindication, with uncommon power. Sometimes the author shows that he is accustomed to careless converse with inferior minds. He has more good sense than orginality, and few gleams of unexpected light, like his friend Hamilton, or his master Machiavelli.

Although Talleyrand was in the habit of showing portions of the Memoirs to many persons in his time, his literary executor, Bacourt, determined that they should not be published until the year 1888. At that time they were the property of M. Andral, who would have liked to protract the suppression. This excessive caution has not been explained. Andral, the grandson of Royer-Collard, who presided over the Council of State under MacMahon, and, in the struggle for class government, was once thought of as the head of an extra-parliamentary Ministry on the American model, was much consulted as a shrewd adviser, steeped in the knowledge of public and private affairs. The business of the day left him without time or care for remoter things, and he lightly eluded inquiry into his precious deposit. He communicated the manuscript to the Count of Paris, though he refused it to his friend Thiers; and he died, bequeathing it to the distinguished writer, who is at the same time a party leader and the bearer of an historic name.

Talleyrand is not favourable to men in authority, or to precepts of attachment and respect. His Memoirs forcibly proclaim that there is no such thing in reason as personal loyalty to a party or a man; that whoever serves one order of things, does well to be preparing for the next; that it is the note of a strong man to employ principles, and of a weak man to obey them. They are especially injurious to the house of Orleans; and a passage relating to Philippe Egalité is the one portion of the manuscript which has been allowed to disappear. This hiatus of several sheets raises the question of the second copy. The Duke de Broglie publishes the final and authentic text; but an earlier transcript exists, and bears marks of having been retouched by the author himself. For appreciable reasons, its possessor has never chosen, hitherto, to make any use of it; but it will now be known whether it completes the published text and throws light on the successive growth of the Memoirs. Two or three passages are evidently later insertions; some were written earlier; and it will be interesting to inquire whether the Spanish and the Roman chapters are entirely the work of Talleyrand himself. One of them is hardly in keeping with the usually secular turn of his mind, and both are out of perspective.

French critics will easily detect inaccuracies, besides those which the editor has pointed out and corrected. It is not true that the Austrians were defeated in Germany in 1796; Carnot never was at Cayenne; Oudinot was not a marshal in 1808. In one of his letters, Talleyrand showed how little he knew about English politics, when he says that the Whigs were seldom in power for more than a short time since 1688. Slips of memory and involuntary mistakes will not discredit the Memoirs. The omissions are more suspicious and indicate design. The remark that Marengo also made Hohenlinden superfluous, curiously ignores the treaty with St. Julien, one of the less creditable transactions in the life of the French negotiator. But it would be unjust to insist on things untold; for if the author, sweeping a vast horizon, passes discreetly over treacherous places, he has not sought opportunities for vainglory, and is too well bred to record the scenes which exhibit his promptness in emergencies and the ease with which he disconcerted opponents. He describes neither the deliberations of the provisional government nor the arts of management by which a senate peopled with regicides was brought to declare for the Bourbons. He does even less than justice to himself when he relates that Napoleon, refusing to preserve his crown by reducing the territory, said, "Find other masters—je suis trop grand pour vous." This saying, made known last year, and bearing the mark of the lion's claw, proved that the mysterious duplicate is authentic. What Talleyrand does not say is that Napoleon, after these heroic words, assented at last to the conditions offered at Châtillon; and that he himself, in May, signed peace on more favourable terms. Instances of this kind are so many, that the Duke de Broglie esteems that the work he has published was not designed for an apology.

He complains that Madame de Staël is not mentioned among those who procured the author's recall from proscription. But Talleyrand acknowledges that he owed to her his introduction to Barras, and his first appointment to the Ministry of Foreign Affairs. He affirms that he, for his own part, would have preferred to stand aloof, and that he yielded reluctantly to her influence. He allows full credit to her initiative in a step which was to lead so far. The story has been told in another shape. Talleyrand, it is said, declared to Madame de Staël that his money was exhausted, and that he would have to blow out his brains if, in a month, she could not find him a way to supplies. This is the version of Barante, the least inventive of men, who knew them both well, who had seen the Memoirs, and who goes on to describe the meeting with the director and the scene at Suresnes, as they do. If the well-informed and disinterested historian deserves credit, the Memoirs must be discarded as a concatenation of insincerity. But he is not a sufficient witness to carry such a verdict. For he says that the friends soon afterwards quarrelled, that Talleyrand never ceased to detest the woman to whom he owed so much, and that she, in her anger, never again dreamed of a reconciliation. Nevertheless, in February 1809, she entreated his intervention with the Emperor, in terms which would have been barely dignified in any circumstances, and are incompatible with unforgiveness. The breach on her side cannot have been as incurable as Barante has described it. Yet the occasion was one which might have justified strong feelings.

The American envoys made it known that they had been invited to bestow a present of money on the French minister, and Talleyrand had laughed at the idea of being challenged to repel the accusation. The reproach of official corruption is, perhaps, the most difficult to meet of all those that he incurred. Count Senfft, who, when I knew him, was an inmate of the Jesuits' College at Innsbruck, but who had been Talleyrand's warm admirer and friend as early as 1806, relates that he caused a sum of four millions of florins to be returned to the Poles, when he found that he was unable to serve their cause; but that he accepted gifts of money from the German princes, whose interest he promoted, including one payment of forty thousand pounds from the King of Saxony. Senfft himself was Saxon Minister, and as such in the secrets both of Dresden and Warsaw. Bacourt, who has been careful to ascertain that Metternich and Nesselrode received no millions from France, says nothing in exoneration of his chief and patron. The next volume, which will contain Talleyrand's account of the execution of Enghien, may possibly give some reply to this more formidable imputation. In one of his earliest despatches he censures the venality of Thugut; but his papers, so far as we have them, say nothing of his own. It might be urged that what he did was not really done in secret, that the reconstruction of the European ruin after the revolutionary war, during the confederation of the Rhine and at the Congress of Vienna, afforded opportunities so exceptional that they amount to excuses; that Napoleon, who allowed his brother to bring back bags of diamonds from Madrid, admitted the practice of diplomatic *douceurs*, and distributed enormous sums in that way. Enemies of the United States used to affirm that the Ashburton treaty was carried by a method which may be traced in the books of Barings.

Talleyrand gives himself all the advantage to be got by depreciating others. He speaks warmly of Hamilton, and respectfully of Lansdowne and Fox in England, of Mollien and Caulaincourt in France; and he is above the vulgar and inefficacious error of reviling enemies. Friends enjoy no immunity from his satiric temper; and he is severe towards his tutor, Langfois, his secretary, Des Renaudes, and his intimate associate, Narbonne. He says that the choice of Necker was the worst the King could have made; Lafayette is beneath the level of mediocrity; Breteuil is fit for the second place anywhere; Sieyès would not be a rogue if he was not a coward; the hands of Carnot are dripping with blood; Fesch is a corsair disguised as a cardinal; Joseph and Jerome are inglorious libertines; the most prosperous of the marshals, Suchet, is *quelque peu bel esprit*; his own successor, Champagny, begins every day trying to repair his blunders of the day before; Humboldt is a bore; Metternich is tortuous and second-rate; Wellington has no head for principles; Castlereagh strains the Englishman's prerogative of ignorance.

Most historical characters will probably suffer if we try them fairly by a fixed standard; but Talleyrand displays no such thing as a standard of public or private morality. He tells how, greatly to his honour, he remonstrated with the Emperor upon his Spanish policy, saying that much evil-doing may be condoned, but that a mere cheat becomes contemptible. He was ready to make sacrifices to his sense, not of duty, but of propriety. The thing that shocks him is the indignity offered to the royal family, not the wrong done to the Spanish nation, for he himself had proposed that France should annex Catalonia. This passage, jointly with one or two others, gives the measure of his notion of right and wrong. He relates that, as a student at the seminary, he was silent, resentful, and morose, and was rescued from this unhealthy condition by an actress, whom he met under an umbrella, and with whom he lived for two years. He confesses that she was stupid; but he adds, with unmixed complacency, that the improvement of his manners and disposition was very much her work, and that the authorities had learned not to interfere with a youth of good family, predestined to become a Minister of State, a cardinal, perhaps even the dispenser of Crown patronage. To write like this in Memoirs addressed to the society of the Restoration shows more than a flaw in his knowledge of good and evil. Elsewhere he tells how a lady, whose intimacy with himself had not been free from scandal, requested him to stay away from the place where she was residing, as his presence might hinder her intended marriage. He publishes her name, and adds that the marriage came off without impediment, although there were others about who might have been as much in the way as himself. Here it must be admitted that the great master of ceremonials and the social art touches low-water mark, and we learn to suspect that a low moral vitality had as much to do with the stains on his life as violent passions or extreme temptation.

Talleyrand means it to be understood that, in all his versatile career, he was not the mere servant of opportunity, but that he was a man steering by fixed stars, applying principles to policy, occupied and possessed by certain general ideas superior to time and place. Many volumes of his letters produced in the least ten years show what truth there is in this thesis of the Memoirs. They show that Talleyrand accepted the essential philosophy of Liberalism, construed from Montesquieu and Turgot, Smith and Bentham. In 1786 he defends the Commercial Treaty as a policy based on the true natural laws that will put an end to the rivalry of nations. He believes, even then, that France and England ought to be inseparable in the cause of reason and justice against the world of divine right. A little later he declares that the traditional alliances terminate with the traditional monarchy;

and anticipating in 1792 the language of James Mill, argues that arbitrary governments labour for their own good, and free governments for the good of mankind. At a time when it was said that there were only two tolerant prelates in the Church of France, he was one of them. If it cost a sceptic no meritorious effort to emancipate the Jews, the ex-Bishop of Autun attested his sincerity in an hour of passion and peril, by insisting that the State has no authority over the conscience of citizen or monarch, and that the priest who refused the oath must be protected against the popular rage. He deems it the interest and the duty of France to rest content within her own wide borders, and to respect the integrity and independence of other countries by the same law as her own. He pleads for non-intervention in 1792, and still more in 1798, as plainly as in 1830. He acknowledged more and more that every people has the right to shape its own government, and maintained that France would have done well to create a united Italy, an independent Poland. As an avowed convert to the doctrine of Nationality and Revolution, he doubted the supreme masterpiece of political compromise and half measures, the Orleanist monarchy, and exhorted Lamartine to reserve his genius for a worthier cause than the support of a baseless throne. At the height of authority and fame he defies the wrath of his Government, and compels Louis Philippe to refuse for his son the proffered crown of Belgium.

When we touch the hard formation and come to the convictions he expressed when circumstances did not sway him, and his language was apart from his interest, this is what we find. His Memoirs, letters, and State papers contain a buried picture not unlike the familiar one on the surface of history. The old lines are not effaced. We have not got to expunge from memory the unscrupulous priest, the money-getting Sybarite, the patient auxiliary of the conqueror and the tyrant, the Royalist who defended the tenth of August, the Republican minister who brought on the Empire, the imperial dignitary who restored the Bourbons, the apostle of legitimacy who hailed its fall. The Talleyrand of manifold tradition remains, and he remains a more valuable study than the most consistent doctrinaire.

But the doctrine is there as well as the policy, and the contrast gives an import to his life beyond any measure of practical success. It was characteristic of his public conduct repeatedly to undo his own work, and the problem is to find any constant motive under the glaring outer inconsistencies. Principles, in his easy philosophy, depended a good deal upon circumstances for their available use; and his saying that non-intervention is a term that means about the same thing as intervention, was more than a jest. Accustomed to hold dogmas loosely and conditionally, even in the science of which he was master, he described his own principle of legitimacy as nothing more than a supreme expedient. He gives the keynote at once by declaring that he will not call his Memoirs "My view of the events of my time," because that would be too positive a title for the work of a man *qui a autant que moi douté dans sa vie.* He understands the economists and believes in their doctrines, but he confesses that, having found human nature a poor material to carry them out with, he cheerfully ceased to care about them. Wessenberg records that he heard him say, *"Le seul bon principe est de n'en avoir aucun."* The interior Talleyrand is a man with a nucleus of distinct opinions, which have not enough sanctity, or even certainty, to be worth the waste of an existence. He knows his shortcomings, his failures, his mistakes, but he assigns most of the blame to others. He brings an indictment against the many resisting and disturbing influences under which he strayed; and the times he lived in, like nothing else in history, have to answer for much deviation. The first enemy was his father.

The accident that lamed him robbed him both of his birthright and of his home. During boyhood he never spent a week in the house of his parents. They not only showed him no affection, but gave him no encouragement, lest success should awaken importunate hopes and claims. They did not even inform him that the meaning of all this coldness, humiliation, and neglect was that he had been dedicated to the service of God. At last he was sent to Rheims, to his uncle the coadjutor, that he might be made aware of the sweets of episcopal life; and he went through his course at St. Sulpice and the Sorbonne. He never had the choice of an alternative or the opportunity of escape. His father would give him no other provision, and the cost of his education was paid out of his first benefice. The family insisted absolutely on putting him into the Church; and the Church received him as he was, without moral fitness, and apparently without religious faith. He was not more unworthy than others of the French clergy in his time, and he was far the ablest. His narrative, with measured but repeated touches, produces an impression stronger than his words. It is not he that sinned, but his parents. If, by taking orders without vocation he became a sacrilegious priest, destined in his long life never to know the security of a tranquil conscience, the crime was theirs. In this man, yet more than in Mirabeau, the ancient order of society operating in conformity with accepted usage, prepared its doom.

When he last appeared before the world, mindful of his early training, he said that theology imparts certain qualities to the mind—*une force et en même temps une souplesse de raisonnement*—conducive to political excellence. He names the example of Lionne, who, having been educated for the Church, became the chief organiser in France of that diplomatic subtlety and finesse which Richelieu and the Père Joseph developed between them. He had in mind that which divines learn on the benches of the schools, the extreme subdivision of thought, the habit of threshing out all the contents of a proposition, the dialectics verging on hair-splitting and sophistry, inherited from long ages that were undeterred by observation; not the advantages of a system with imposing traditions, fixed maxims, and a constant policy, whose agents are never taken by surprise and know the uses of time. He was thinking of the priesthood negotiating more than governing. He had seen in his own vicinity, in his own person, things more memorable than the diplomatic art of Cardinal du Bellay and Cardinal de Bernis. The Revolution had been started by one priest; the Republic had been proposed by another. Three out of eight in the Constitutional Committee were ecclesiastics. The Constitution of the year III, as well as that of the year VIII, were chiefly devised by divines. The four ministers who, at the Restoration, inaugurated parliamentary government belonged to the clergy.

His own studies were principally profane. The first book he mentions is the *Memoirs of Cardinal de Retz*, a man often compared to him in point of character and ability. He tells us that he read political writers and historians; but when he puts Polignac next to d'Ossat among negotiators, he betrays the limits of his knowledge in that sort of literature. He had read Montesquieu, and, like all the best minds of that age, he was influenced by the *Esprit des Lois*. He pays Machiavelli the tribute of intelligent imitation, and fortifies his legitimacy by the authority of a grim passage from *The Prince*. He collected a choice library; but he was too much a man of the world to resign himself to study and the dominion of silent masters. Books, he says, have enlightened him; he has never allowed them to govern him. He describes how much he owed to conversation in chosen society and how he picked the brains of specialists.

In old age Talleyrand used to say that life had never had so much to recommend it as at Paris in his youth. In the Memoirs he speaks of a diminution of refinement and a falling-off from what had been before the approach of revolution. He regards himself as belonging to a higher and earlier epoch of good manners, and describes as bearing an inferior stamp men who were the guide of contemporaries and their mould of form. Choiseul, the man he liked best, gesticulates too much, and has a cold heart. Narbonne's cleverness is all for show, and is exhausted by a joke; his spirits are higher than good taste allows, his familiar grace makes him friends, especially among rather vulgar men. *Il a une politesse sans nuances.* Nevertheless, they were all such good friends that their intimacy, in the course of five years, was never disturbed by tittle-tattle or misunderstanding. He attributes his own reputation for wit a good deal to the power of holding his tongue. He explains what he considers that the best conversation should be, by the example of his mother, whose charm consisted in pleasing and passing on, without saying a word that could strike or remain. *Elle ne parlait que par nuances; jamais elle n'a dit un bon mot: c'était quelque chose de trop exprimé.* Much of the thought, the talent, the discipline, the exertion which goes, with other men, to the conduct of affairs, the making of speeches, the writing of books, was concentrated, by him, on the business of pleasant intercourse. His perfect mastery of so much that makes mere society enjoyable, acquired among men who had beheld the evening rays of Louis the Fourteenth, became one of the elements of his superiority; and he spoke with meaning when, after an outbreak of Napoleon's fury, he said that it was a pity so great a man had been so ill brought up. An ambassador described him in 1814 as one *"qui posséda si éminemment l'art de la société, et qui en a si souvent usé avec succès, tantôt pour en imposer à ceux qu'on voulait détruire, en leur faisant perdre contenance, tantôt pour attirer à lui ceux dont on voulait se servir."* The prestige of his grand manner, of his lofty distinction was a weapon both for attack and defence. The Emperor himself recognised the political force residing in the region where his aristocratic minister was supreme, when a report from Madame de Genlis on the conversations of the Faubourg St. Germain, which Talleyrand read to him, put him beside himself with anger, on the evening of Austerlitz.

The young Abbé de Perigord was so obviously marked out for promotion that he was made agent-general of the clergy before he was ordained. In that capacity he relates that he endeavoured to be more than a man of his cloth, and attempted measures of general use. He generally failed; and he professes to have failed because of that common vice of inexperienced men, too much idealism, and an artless belief in human nature. He was so conspicuous that he was spoken of for the Archbishopric of Bourges, and looked forward to a position which would have given scope to his talents as an administrator. The Pope, urged by Gustavus the Third, who came to Rome in 1784, consented to make him a cardinal. But Perigord, being connected with the Rohans, shared the disgrace which the Diamond Necklace brought upon them; and the Queen, through Count Mercy, who calls him a scoundrel, prevented the appointment. Louis the Sixteenth hesitated for months before nominating him to the See of Autun, which happened just before the meeting of the States-General.

Talleyrand appeared at Versailles with the reputation of a man of business, expert in money-matters. By his management of the affairs of the clergy and his association with Calonne, he was better known by his head for figures than as a master of ecclesiastical policy. Mirabeau, with whom he had had a serious quarrel, meant to offer him the department of Finance. At that time he is described as a man without enthusiasm or illusions, pliant, patient, and calm, sure of rising to the greatest elevation. He was no orator, and obtained no popular ascendency. In his address to his clergy, he demanded the Habeas Corpus, trial by jury, free trade, a free press, and the codification of the law. But he thought it madness to double the Third Estate, and wished that the King would dissolve the Assembly and summon another on different lines, with a definite plan of action, which Talleyrand had prepared. He took the lead in discarding instructions and the division of the orders; but, after the fall of the Bastille, he, with his friends, called on Louis the Sixteenth to adopt their policy. At midnight, on the 16th of July, he roused the Count of Artois, explained to him during two hours what would happen if the unresisted Assembly was allowed to send France down the entire cataract of deductive logic, and made him get out of bed and carry the ultimatum to the King. Louis, judging that this was a bid for office by a man who had given no extraordinary proof of capacity, and who in public had taken the opposite line of submission to the majority, rejected the warning, and the Count came back, protesting that the game was lost and that he would be off for the frontier in the morning. Talleyrand vainly dissuaded him from emigrating. At last he said, "Then, sir, as the King and the princes abandon the monarchy, nothing remains for

us but to shift for ourselves." Twenty-five years later when, as head
of the Government, he invited the Count to return, he was able to
remind him that the advice he had given at their last meeting was
good.

The famous decree with which Talleyrand is identified, though it
altered fundamentally the conditions of religion in France, was a
financial measure, not the outcome of a scheme of Church government.
At a Conference held in May, the Archbishop of Arles made, with
applause, the insane proposal that they should take the opportunity
to have the debt of the clergy paid by the State. It was soon apparent
that the clergy would be called on to supply the deficit of the State,
and after the 4th of August, and the abolition of tithes, the property
of the Church could not be saved. As soon as the assembly had
removed to Paris, the Bishop of Autun, quick to recognise the inevitable,
moved that the nation should take over the Church property, allowing
a pension exceeding by a million sterling that which is now paid,
which, while reducing the income of prelates, improved the situation
of the parish clergy. The effect was not what he intended, for he did
not save the public credit, and he ruined the Gallican Church. The
Assembly would neither leave the patronage to the executive, nor
salary a body of men to be nominated by the Pope. It therefore adopted
the principle of election, which was the substance of the *Constitution
Civile*. In questions of Canon Law, ancient or modern, Talleyrand was
neither competent nor interested. The scheme was not of his devising,
but it was executed by his instrumentality; he consecrated the first of
the new bishops. Writing amid the environments of 1816, he states his
reason. Nearly all the bishops had refused the Constitutional oath. If
none had accepted, and if there had, consequently, been nobody to
transmit the succession, the State might have lapsed into Presbyteri-
anism, which was a form that harmonised with the spirit of the new
institutions, and Calvinism would have been established. This farfetched argument may have been a genuine reminiscence of Bossuet,
and of the doctrine familiar to Gallican divines, that a Huguenot is a
Republican, that a Presbyterian is the same as a Whig, and that
hierarchy in the Church responds to monarchy in the State.

It may be that the bishop employed schism as a supreme preservative
against Democratic heresy. The establishment of the new episcopate
gave him a welcome opportunity of abandoning his position in the
Church and seeking a new career. There was no French abbé on whom

his orders sat more lightly, or who was so secular in his conduct. But though he wore no mask of hypocrisy, and submitted to little restraint, when he could not win twelve hundreds at play without being made the talk of the town, the falseness of his position became intolerable. He resigned his bishopric, and refused to have himself put forward for the See of Paris. Three years later, when, riding at night in an American forest, he called out to his servant, and a voice answered, "Here I am, Monseigneur," he could not help laughing at this reminder of distant Autun. In 1802 Pius the Seventh, although he loved his excommunicated brother less than he will have it, secularised him for his services to the Concordat. The Memoirs specially observe the tone of ecclesiastical decorum; and once, addressing Louis the Eighteenth, Talleyrand is aghast at the incredulity of the age.

For a short time, when his Parisian rival, Narbonne, became Minister, he obtained considerable influence, and came to England early in 1792 on an acknowledged, but necessarily unofficial, mission, to ensure the neutrality of Pitt. In August he was again in Paris, and witnessed the overthrow of the monarchy. He induced Danton to send him back to London, under cover of some scientific negotiation, and was thus able to declare that he had not incurred the pains of emigration, and yet to assure Grenville that he was not in the service of the Republic. But with all his dexterity and coolness he could not hold a position between the upper and the nether millstone. He was outlawed in France, he was expelled from England; and having sold his books in London, he sailed for Philadelphia. He would have been glad to get a passage to India, to be shrouded in sufficient obscurity until his time came.

It came at the end of two years. In 1796 he found himself restored to France, in the embarrassing company of a lady who had got Francis into trouble before him, and having no position but that of a member of the Institute. In the scheme for a national system of education, which he presented to the Assembly, the whole was to have been directed by a central board composed of the ablest men in France; so that the idea of the Institute may be said to belong to him. The Duke de Broglie, following his father's *Souvenirs*, believes that Talleyrand's Report was not his own work; while Jules Simon affirms the contrary, and the Memoirs claim that he drew it up after consulting Lavoisier, Laplace, and the scientific men of the day. In his new character he read two papers exposing the wisdom he had gathered in exile. During his two years' stay in England he had made a friend of Lord Lansdowne, and in the Bowood circle had met men who were working the problems of the hour on different lines from those he had learned at home. In the United States he came under the influence of Alexander Hamilton. He had gone away a disciple in economics of Dupont de Nemours, without his dogmatism and without his fervour. He came back a believer in the doctrine of Utility, in the colonial system of Adam Smith; and he informs his countrymen that nations act by self-interest, not by gratitude or resentment, and that nothing can divert the trade of America from England to France. He said afterwards that a sound political economy was the talisman which made England, for thirty years, the first of European Powers.

Academic exercises were not the road to greatness; and Madame de Staël rescued him from penury by telling Barras what manner of man he was. Talleyrand's fortune was made that day. He grasped his opportunity; fascinated the director by that pleasant talk which aged men still remember with admiration; and was appointed Minister of Foreign Affairs by a bare majority over the most obscure of competitors. With an interval of four months in 1799, he held the office during the ten extraordinary years from Campo Formio to Tilsit. His despatches, written for the Directory, have been published by M. Pallain, who, but for names and dates, would be an excellent editor, and they are not worthy of his later fame. As the executive agent of a deliberative and fluctuating body, he is not seen to advantage. His employers distrusted him, and he despised his employers. The Swiss and Italian questions were decided without him; the question of the negotiations at Lille was settled against him. He made way slowly, and carried to extremes the compliance which is expected in a subordinate and in a colleague. He tried in vain to be elected one of the directors, and the Prussian envoy writes that his elevation would put an end to the convulsions of Europe. He craved for a master more intelligent than the directors, or at least firmer and more constant. Together with Sieyès he thought of Moreau, of Joubert, of the Duke of Brunswick, the grand illusion of the time. Together they contrived the Eighteenth of Brumaire. He had seen from the beginning that Bonaparte had more than a military genius. He felt for monarchy like the Vendéan chief who, when he was asked in whose name he fought, replied, "In the name of the King, that is, of any man who may occupy the throne."

He had found what he wanted, a master worthy of such a minister. By the account which he gives of his own system, his endurance in office during all the ascending years is a prodigy of suppleness. Talleyrand at all times wished to restrict the limits of France to the Rhine. He would have made terms with England by the sacrifice of Malta, and thought us justified in the breach of the peace of Amiens. He regarded Austria as the natural and necessary ally, and would have granted overwhelming compensation, by the partition of Turkey, for her losses in the sphere of French influence. He advised the restoration of Venice, and exposed the folly of surrounding the Empire with a girdle of helpless Bonapartes. On the topics of agreement with Napoleon he does not enlarge, and asserts some merit for sympathy and generosity shown to the vanquished Hohenzollerns. But in his political construction Prussia was the inevitable adversary. He constantly described it as a neighbour on whom there was no reliance, with a barren territory and an open frontier, compelled by nature to be ambitious and aggressive, and to scheme for the subjugation of Germany. *Tout prétexte lui est bon. Nul scrupule ne l'arrête. La convenance est son droit.* His encounter at Vienna with the Prussian statesmen, when he got the better of William Humboldt, must have been a prouder moment than when he set up his chancery at Berlin.

From his entrance into office he pursued the policy of secularisation. From Salzburg all round to Liége Europe was covered with ecclesiastical proprietors and potentates, and it was an opportune and congenial resource to suppress them in order to satisfy the princes who had to be consoled for the conquests of Bonaparte. This process of ecclesiastical liquidation was Talleyrand's element. He had destroyed the Church of France as a privileged and proprietary corporation; and by the like impulse he helped to deprive the clergy of the Empire of their political prerogative. And he was still on the same ground at the Congress, when he reduced political right to the hereditary rights of families, and the Prince of Reuss was a weightier personage than a doge of Venice or an Archbishop of Cologne. There was little to boast of in following with a despatch-box where the sword of Napoleon cleared the way; but Talleyrand claims to have done his best for the victims, and he angered his master by drawing clauses from which he could not escape. He had to submit to be the instrument of violence, to see his State papers transformed; and, as in the Lauderdale correspondence, to publish as authentic letters he had been too wise to send.

Not much in the description of Napoleon is new. There is a good deal between the lines of the grotesque account of the Spanish princes at Valençay; and in the complacent details of the interview at Erfurt, the point of the dialogue with Wieland has been lost. But the portrait of the Emperor by the most intelligent man in the Empire will always retain its value. The idea it suggests is that Napoleon failed by excess of talent. The flaw in the reckoning was that he calculated too much, and carried his thinking too far. He set himself to provide against contingencies which he could detect, but which were so remote that they practically did not exist, and weakened himself by defences against dangers not likely to take shape amongst obvious-minded men. He brought on perpetual war because the increase of France having been the work of other generals, he was afraid of their renown. Therefore he annexed Piedmont as a trophy of his own campaigns. In the same way he thought that Spain could never be reduced to a trusty satellite, as the King would some day remember who the Bourbons were, and how they came to reign beyond the Pyrenees.

In 1807, when the Empire was at its best, Talleyrand resigned his office; but as a great dignitary of State he continued to be consulted and employed. His proper place at that time was in opposition. He implored Alexander not to ruin his master by too much yielding. His advice to Metternich was an encouragement to Austria to prepare for the war of 1809. Napoleon proposed to send him to Warsaw in 1812, and made the mistake of changing his mind. In the following year he again offered him the Foreign Office. Talleyrand refused; he was not good on a sinking ship. It does not suit everybody, as he said to Savary, to be buried in the impending crash. Before Napoleon started for the campaign in France, that scene of violence occurred which Molé described to Dalling. Talleyrand offered to resign his dignities. Insult had released him from personal obligation; and when the fortune of war turned, after the victories of February, he allowed his friends to open communication with the invaders. Their emisssary made his way through the French lines to headquarters, carrying two names as a password, names which had a meaning for Stadion; and, for Nesselrode, these dangerous and significant words traced in invisible ink: "You march on crutches." The bearer of these credentials was the most acute, the most alert, and the boldest of Royalists. He found, in the middle of March, less than a fortnight before the capitulation of Paris, that the allies were agreed in rejecting the Bourbons. This mission of the Baron de Vitrolles, of which there are three narratives in the second volume, is an epoch in the life of Talleyrand. When he knew that Louis the Eighteenth, who was forgotten in France, was repudiated by Europe, he resolved that he should be king. It was the one solution entirely his own. And he made him king, imposing his choice with invincible ease on an Assembly of Republicans and Bonapartists, and on the wavering and bewildered master of twenty legions. It is the stroke of genius in his career. The conquerors of Napoleon found themselves at Paris in the hands of a gracious cripple in powder, who, without emphasis or exertion, crumpled up their schemes, and quietly informed them that the Bourbons alone were a principle.

With those words he legislated for Europe. By that law, so convincing to his generation, he was providing an organic force that enabled him at Vienna to subdue the Congress, to scatter the victorious allies, and to achieve his own chosen scheme of an alliance between England, Austria, and France. The implacable analysis of history has since made known that the doctrine which makes hereditary right paramount in politics is unscientific, and cannot combine with the rights of nations. Talleyrand was no advocate of arbitrary power, either at Paris or at Vienna. He was disgusted with those who sent Ferdinand the Seventh to reign without conditions. Although it was not his hand that drew up the Charte, it was his mind chiefly that inspired it. In 1815 he denounced the reactionary counsels of the Count of Artois before the King and the Count himself, and insisted on the principle of a homogeneous and responsible ministry; and he retired before the Holy Alliance. The Bourbons, if they had reigned by his advice, would not have fallen. When he wrote his narrative of the events in which he performed the part of king-maker, he did not see that he had made a blunder. The dynasty he had enthroned persisted for fifteen years in excluding him from power. After 1830 he regrets that he had forgotten Fox's saying that the worst sort of Revolution is a Restoration. When Madame de Lieven affected surprise that the man who had crowned Louis the Eighteenth should appear in London as the plenipotentiary of Louis Philippe, he replied that the King he served would have been the choice of Alexander in 1814. They do not seem to have remembered who it was that prevented it.

[23]

Introduction to Burd's Edition
of *Il Principe* by Machiavelli

Mr. Burd has undertaken to redeem our long inferiority in Machiavellian studies, and it will, I think, be found that he has given a more completely satisfactory explanation of *The Prince* than any country possessed before. His annotated edition supplies all the solvents of a famous problem in the history of Italy and the literature of politics. In truth, the ancient problem is extinct, and no reader of this volume will continue to wonder how so intelligent and reasonable a man came to propose such flagitious counsels. When Machiavelli declared that extraordinary objects cannot be accomplished under ordinary rules, he recorded the experience of his own epoch, but also foretold the secret of men since born. He illustrates not only the generation which taught him, but the generations which he taught, and has no less in common with the men who had his precepts before them than with the Viscontis, Borgias, and Baglionis who were the masters he observed. He represents more than the spirit of his country and his age. Knowledge, civilisation, and morality have increased; but three centuries have borne enduring witness to his political veracity. He has been as much the exponent of men whom posterity esteems as of him whose historian writes: "Cet homme que Dieu, après l'avoir fait si grand, avait fait bon aussi, n'avait rien de la vertu." The authentic interpreter of Machiavelli, the *Commentarius Perpetuus* of the *Discorsi* and *The Prince*, is the whole of later history.

Michelet has said: "Rapportons-nous-en sur ceci à quelqu'un qui fut bien plus Machiavéliste que Machiavel, à la république de Venise." Before his day, and long after, down almost to the time when a price

Published as pp. xix–xl of *Il Principe*, ed. L. A. Burd (Oxford, 1891). Reprinted in Acton, *History of Freedom*, pp. 212–231.

was set on the heads of the Pretender and of Pontiac, Venice employed assassins. And this was not the desperate resource of politicians at bay, but the avowed practice of decorous and religious magistrates. In 1569 Soto hazards an impersonal doubt whether the morality of the thing was sound: "Non omnibus satis probatur Venetorum mos, qui cum complures a patria exules habeant condemnatos, singulis facultatem faciunt, ut qui alium eorum interfecerit, vita ac libertate donetur." But his sovereign shortly after obtained assurance that murder by royal command was unanimously approved by divines: "A los tales puede el Principe mandarlos matar, aunque esten fuera de su distrito y reinos. Sin ser citado, secretamente se le puede quitar la vita. Esta es doctrina comun y cierta y recevida de todos los theologos." When the King of France, by despatching the Guises, had restored his good name in Europe, a Venetian, Francesco da Molino, hoped that the example would not be thrown away on the Council of Ten: "Permeti sua divina bontà che questo esempio habbi giovato a farlo proceder come spero con meno fretta e più sodamente a cose tali e d' importanza." Sarpi, their ablest writer, their official theologian, has a string of maxims which seem to have been borrowed straight from the Florentine predecessor: "Proponendo cosa in apparenza non honesta, scusarla come necessaria, come practicata da altri, come propria al tempo, che tende a buon fine, et conforme all' opinione de' molti. La vendetta non giova se non per fugir lo sprezzo. Ogn' huomo ha opinione che il mendacio sia buono in ragion di medicina, et di far bene a far creder il vero et utile con premesse false." One of his countrymen, having examined his writings, reports: "I ricordi di questo grand' uomo furono più da politico che da christiano." To him was attributed the doctrine of secret punishment, and the use of poison against public enemies: "In casi d' eccessi incorrigibili si punissero secretamente, a fine che il sangue patrizio non resti profanato. Il veleno deve esser l' unico mezzo per levarli dal mondo, quando alla giustizia non complisse farli passare sotto la manaia del carnefice." Venice, otherwise unlike the rest of Europe, was, in this particular, not an exception.

Machiavelli enjoyed a season of popularity even at Rome. The Medicean popes refused all official employment to one who had been the brain of a hostile government; but they encouraged him to write, and were not offended by the things he wrote for them. Leo's own dealings with the tyrant of Perugia were cited by jurists as a suggestive model for men who have an enemy to get rid of. Clement confessed to

Contarini that honesty would be preferable, but that honest men get the worst of it: "Io cognosco certo che voi dicete il vero, et che ad farla da homo da bene, et a far il debito, seria proceder come mi aricordate; ma bisognerebbe trovar la corrispondentia. Non vedete che il mondo è ridutto a un termine che colui il qual è più astuto et cum più trame fa il fatto suo, è più laudato, et estimato più valente homo, et più celebrato, et chi fa il contrario vien detto di esso: quel tale è una bona persona, ma non val niente? Et se ne sta cum quel titulo solo di bona persona. Chi va bonamente vien trata da bestia." Two years after this speech the astute Florentine authorised *The Prince* to be published at Rome.

It was still unprinted when Pole had it pressed on his attention by Cromwell, and Brosch consequently suspects the story. Upon the death of Clement, Pole opened the attack; but it was not pursued during the reaction against things Medicean which occupied the reign of Farnese. Machiavelli was denounced to the Inquisition on the 11th of November 1550, by Muzio, a man much employed in controversy and literary repression, who, knowing Greek, was chosen by Pius V for the work afterwards committed to Baronius: "Senza rispetto alcuno insegna a non servar ne fede, ne charità, ne religione; et dice che di queste cose, gli huomini se ne debbono servire per parer buoni, et per le grandezze temporali, alle quali quando non servono non se ne dee fare stima. Et non è questo peggio che heretica dottrina? Vedendosi che ciò si comporta, sono accettate come opere approvate dalla Santa Madre chiesa." Muzio, who at the same time recommended the *Decamerone,* was not acting from ethical motives. His accusation succeeded. When the Index was instituted, in 1557, Machiavelli was one of the first writers condemned, and he was more rigorously and implacably condemned than anybody else. The Trent Commissioners themselves prepared editions of certain prohibited authors, such as Clarius and Flaminius; Guicciardini was suffered to appear with retrenchments; and the famous revision of Boccaccio was carried out in 1573. This was due to the influence of Victorius, who pleaded in vain for a castigated text of Machiavelli. He continued to be specially excepted when permission was given to read forbidden books. Sometimes there were other exceptions, such as Dumoulin, Marini, or Maimbourg; but the exclusion of Machiavelli was permanent, and when Lucchesini preached against him at the Gesù, he had to apply to the Pope himself for license to read him. Lipsius was advised by his Roman censors to mix a little Catholic salt in his Machiavellism, and to suppress a seeming protest against the universal hatred for a writer *qui misera qua non manu hodie vapulat.* One of the ablest but most contentious of the Jesuits, Raynaud, pursued his memory with a story like that with which Tronchin improved the death of Voltaire: "Exitus impiissimi nebulonis metuendus est eius aemulatoribus, nam blasphemans evomuit reprobum spiritum."

In spite of this notorious disfavour, he has been associated with the excesses of the religious wars. The daughter of the man to whom he addressed *The Prince* was Catharine of Medici, and she was reported to have taught her children "surtout des traictz de cet athée Machiavel." Boucher asserted that Henry III carried him in his pocket: "qui perpetuus ei in sacculo atque manibus est"; and Montaigne confirms the story when he says: "Et dict on, de ce temps, que Machiavel est encores ailleurs en crédit." The pertinently appropriate quotation by which the Queen sanctified her murderous resolve was supplied, not by her father's rejected and discredited monitor, but by a bishop at the Council of Trent, whose sermons had just been published: "Bisogna esser severo et acuto, non bisogna esser clemente; è crudeltà l' esser pietoso, è pietà l' esser crudele." And the argument was afterwards embodied in the *Controversies* of Bellarmin: "Haereticis obstinatis beneficium est, quod de hac vita tollantur, nam quo diutius vivunt, eo plures errores excogitant; plures pervertunt, et majorem sibi damnationem acquirunt."

The divines who held these doctrines received them through their own channels straight from the Middle Ages. The germ theory, that the wages of heresy is death, was so expanded as to include the rebel, the usurper, the heterodox or rebellious town, and it continued to develop long after the time of Machiavelli. At first it had been doubtful whether a small number of culprits justified the demolition of a city: "Videtur quod si aliqui haeretici sunt in civitate potest exuri tota civitas." Under Gregory XIII the right is asserted unequivocally: "Civitas ista potest igne destrui, quando in ea plures sunt haeretici." In case of sedition, fire is a less suitable agent: "Propter rebellionem civitas quandoque supponitur aratro et possunt singuli decapitari." As to heretics the view was: "Ut hostes latronesque occidi possunt etiamsi sunt clerici." A king, if he was judged a usurper, was handed over to extinction: "Licite potest a quolibet de populo occidi, pro libertate populi, quando non est recursus ad superiorem, a quo possit iustitia fieri." Or, in the words of the scrupulous Soto: "Tunc quisque ius habet ipsum extinguendi." To the end of the seventeenth century theologicans taught: "Occidatur, seu occidendus proscribatur, quando non alitur potest haberi tranquillitas Reipublicae."

This was not mere theory, or the enforced logic of men in thrall to mediaeval antecedents. Under the most carnal and unchristian king, the Vaudois of Provence were exterminated in the year 1545, and Paul Sadolet wrote as follows to Cardinal Farnese just before and just after the event: "Aggionta hora questa instantia del predetto paese di Provenza a quella che da Mons. Nuntio s' era fatta a Sua Maestà Christianissima a nome di Sua Beatitudine et di Vostra Reverendissima Signoria, siamo in ferma speranza, che vi si debbia pigliare qualche bono expediente et farci qualche gagliarda provisione. È seguito, in questo paese, quel tanto desiderato et tanto necessario effetto circa le cose di Cabrieres, che da vostra Signoria Reverendissima è stato si lungamente ricordato et sollicitato et procurato." Even Melanchthon was provoked by the death of Cromwell to exclaim that there is no better deed than the slaughter of a tyrant; "Utinam Deus alicui forti viro hanc mentem inserat!" And in 1575 the Swedish bishops decided that it would be a good work to poison their king in a basin of soup—an idea particularly repugnant to the author of *De Rege et Regis Institutione*. Among Mariana's papers I have seen the letter from Paris describing the murder of Henry III, which he turned to such account in the memorable sixth chapter: "Communicò con sus superiores, si peccaria mortalmente un sacerdote que matase a un tirano. Ellos le diceron que non era pecado, mas que quedaria irregular. Y no contentandose con esto, ni con las disputas que avia de ordinario en la Sorbona sobre la materia, continuando siempre sus oraciones, lo preguntò a otros theologos, que le afirmavan lo mismo; y con esto se resolviò enteramente de executarlo. Por el successo es de collegir que tuvo el fraile alguna revelacion de Nuestro Señor en particular, y inspiracion para executar el caso." According to Maffei, the Pope's biographer, the priests were not content with saying that killing was no sin: "Cum illi posse, nec sine magno quidem merito censuissent." Regicide was so acceptable a work that it seemed fitly assigned to a divine interposition.

When, on the 21st of January 1591, a youth offered his services to make away with Henry IV, the Nuncio remitted the matter to Rome: "Quantunque mi sia parso di trovarlo pieno di tale humilità, prudenza, spirito et cose che arguiscono che questa sia inspiratione veramente piuttosto che temerità e leggerezza." In a volume which, though recent, is already rare, the Foreign Office published D'Avaux's advise to treat the Protestants of Ireland much as William treated the Catholics of Glencoe; and the argument of the Assassination Plot came originally from a Belgian seminary. There were at least three men living far into the eighteenth century who defended the massacre of St. Bartholomew in their books; and it was held as late as 1741 that culprits may be killed before they are condemned: "Etiam ante sententiam impune occidi possunt, quando de proximo erant banniendi, vel quando eorum delictum est notorium, grave, et pro quo poena capitis infligenda esset."

Whilst these principles were current in religion as well as in society, the official censures of the Church and the protests of every divine since Catharinus were ineffectual. Much of the profaner criticism uttered by such authorities as the Cardinal de Retz, Voltaire, Frederic the Great, Daunou, and Mazzini is not more convincing or more real. Linguet was not altogether wrong in suggesting that the assailants knew Machiavelli at second hand: "Chaque fois que je jette les yeux sur les ouvrages de ce grand génie, je ne saurais concevoir, je l'avoue, la cause du décri où il est tombé. Je soupçonne fortement que ses plus grands ennemis sont ceux qui ne l'ont pas lu." Retz attributed to him a proposition which is not in his writings. Frederic and Algernon Sidney had read only one of his books, and Bolingbroke, a congenial spirit, who quotes him so often, knew him very little. Hume spoils a serious remark by a glaring eighteenth-century comment: "There is scarcely any maxim in *The Prince* which subsequent experience has not entirely refuted. The errors of this politician proceeded, in a great measure, from his having lived in too early an age of the world to be a good judge of political truth." Bodin had previously written: "Il n'a jamais sondé le gué de la science politique." Mazzini complains of his *analisi cadaverica ed ignoranza della vita*; and Barthélemy St. Hilaire, verging on paradox, says: "On dirait vraiment que l'histoire ne lui a rien appris, non plus que la conscience." That would be more scientific treatment than the common censure of moralists and the common applause of politicians. It is easier to expose errors in practical politics than to remove the ethical basis of judgments which the modern world employs in common with Machiavelli.

By plausible and dangerous paths men are drawn to the doctrine of the justice of History, of judgment by results, the nursling of the nineteenth century, from which a sharp incline leads to *The Prince*. When we say that public life is not an affair of morality, that there is no available rule of right and wrong, that men must be judged by their age, that the code shifts with the longitude, that the wisdom which governs the event is superior to our own, we carry obscurely tribute to the system which bears so odious a name. Few would scruple to maintain with Mr. Morley that the equity of history requires that we shall judge men of action by the standards of men of action; or with Retz: "Les vices d'un archevêque peuvent être, dans une infinité de rencontres, les vertus d'un chef de parti." The expounder of Adam Smith to France, J. B. Say, confirms the ambitious coadjutor: "Louis XIV et son despotisme et ses guerres n'ont jamais fait le mal qui serait résulté des conseils de ce bon Fénelon, l'apôtre et le martyr de la vertu et du bien des hommes." Most successful public men deprecate what Sir Henry Taylor calls much weak sensibility of conscience, and approve Lord Grey's language to Princess Lieven: "I am a great lover of morality, public and private; but the intercourse of nations cannot be strictly regulated by that rule." While Burke was denouncing the Revolution, Walpole wrote: "No great country was ever saved by good men, because good men will not go the lengths that may be necessary." All which had been formerly anticipated by Pole: "Quanto quis privatam vitam agens Christi similior erit tanto minus aptus ad regendum id munus iudicio hominum existimabitur." The main principle of Machiavelli is asserted by his most eminent English disciple: "It is the solecism of power to think, to command the end, and yet not to endure the means." And Bacon leads up to the familiar Jesuit: "Cui licet finis, illi et media permissa sunt."

The austere Pascal has said: "On ne voit rien de juste ou d'injuste qui ne change de qualité en changeant de climat" (the reading *presque* rien was the precaution of an editor). The same underlying scepticism is found not only in philosophers of the Titanic sort, to whom remorse is a prejudice of education, and the moral virtues are "the political offspring which flattery begat upon pride," but among the masters of living thought. Locke, according to Mr. Bain, holds that we shall scarcely find any rule of morality, excepting such as are necessary to hold society together, and these too with great limitations, but what is somewhere or other set aside, and an opposite established by whole societies of men. Maine de Biran extracts this conclusion from the

Esprit des Lois: "Il n'y a rien d'absolu ni dans la religion, ni dans la morale, ni, à plus forte raison, dans la politique." In the mercantile economists Turgot detects the very doctrine of Helvetius: "Il établit qu'il n'y a pas lieu à la probité entre les nations, d'où suivroit que le monde doit être éternellement un coupegorge. En quoi il est bien d'accord avec les panégyristes de Colbert."

These things survive, transmuted, in the edifying and popular epigram: "Die Weltgeschichte ist das Weltgericht." Lacordaire, though he spoke so well of "L'empire et les ruses de la durée," recorded his experience in these words: "J'ai toujours vu Dieu se justifier à la longue." Reuss, a teacher of opposite tendency and greater name, is equally consoling: "Les destinées de l'homme s'accomplissent ici-bas; la justice de Dieu s'exerce et se manifeste sur cette terre." In the infancy of exact observation Massillon could safely preach that wickedness ends in ignominy: "Dieu aura son tour." The indecisive Providentialism of Bossuet's countrymen is shared by English divines. "Contemporaries," says Hare, "look at the agents, at their motives and characters; history looks rather at the acts and their consequences." Thirlwall hesitates to say that whatever is, is best; "but I have a strong faith that it is for the best, and that the general stream of tendency is toward good." And Sedgwick, combining induction with theology, writes: "If there be a superintending Providence, and if His will be manifested by general laws, operating both on the physical and moral world, then must a violation of those laws be a violation of His will, and be pregnant with inevitable misery."

Apart from the language of Religion, an optimism ranging to the bounds of fatalism is the philosophy of many, especially of historians: "Le vrai, c'est, en toutes choses, le fait." Sainte-Beuve says: "Il y a dans tout fait général et prolongé une puissance de démonstration insensible"; and Scherer describes progress as "une espèce de logique objective et impersonelle qui résout les questions sans appel." Ranke has written: "Der beste Prüfstein ist die Zeit"; and Sybel explains that this was not a short way out of confusion and incertitude, but a profound generalisation: "Ein Geschlecht, ein Volk löst das andere ab, und der Lebende hat Recht." A scholar of a different school and fibre, Stahr the Aristotelian, expresses the same idea: "Die Geschichte soll die Richtigkeit des Denkens bewähren." Richelieu's maxim: "Les grands desseins et notables entreprises ne se vérifient jamais autrement que par le succès"; and Napoleon's: "Je ne juge les hommes que par les résultats," are seriously appropriated by Fustel de Coulanges: "Ce qui caractérise le véritable homme d'état, c'est le succès, on le reconnaît surtout à ce signe, qu'il réussit." One of Machiavelli's gravest critics applied it to him: "Die ewige Aufgabe der Politik bleibt unter den gegebenen Verhältnissen und mit den vorhandenen Mitteln etwas zu erreichen. Eine Politik, die das verkennt, die auf den Erfolg verzichtet, sich auf eine theoretische Propaganda, auf ideale Gesichtspunkte beschränkt, von einer verlorenen Gegenwart an eine künftige Gerechtigkeit appellirt, ist keine Politik mehr." One of the mediaeval pioneers, Stenzel, delivered a formula of purest Tuscan cinquecento: "Was bei anderen Menschen gemeine Schlechtigkeit ist, erhält, bei den ungewöhnlichen Geistern, den Stempel der Grösse, der selbst dem Verbrechen sich aufdrückt. Der Maassstab ist anders; denn das Ausserordentliche lässt sich nur durch Ausserordentliches bewirken." Treitschke habitually denounces the impotent Doctrinaires who do not understand "dass der Staat Macht ist und der Welt des Willens angehört," and who know not how to rise "von der Politik des Bekenntnisses zu der Politik der That." Schäfer, though a less pronounced partisan, derides Macaulay for thinking that human happiness concerns political science: "Das Wesen des Staates ist die Macht, und die Politik die Kunst ihn zu erhalten." Rochau's *Realpolitik* was a treatise in two volumes written to prove "dass der Staat durch seine Selbsterhaltung das oberste Gebot der Sittlichkeit erfüllt." Wherefore, nobody finds fault when a State in its decline is subjugated by a robust neighbour. In one of those telling passages which moved Mr. Freeman to complain that he seems unable to understand that a small State can have any rights, or that a generous or patriotic sentiment can find a place anywhere except in the breast of a fool, Mommsen justifies the Roman conquests: "Kraft des Gesetzes, dass das zum Staat entwickelte Volk die politisch unmündigen, das civilisirte die geistig unmündigen in sich auflöst." The same idea was imparted into the theory of ethics by Kirchmann, and appears, with a sobering touch, in the *Geschichte Jesu* of Hase, the most popular German divine: "Der Einzelne wird nach der Grösse seiner Ziele, nach den Wirkungen seiner Thaten für das Wohl der Völker gemessen, aber nicht nach dem Maasse der Moral und des Rechts. Vom Leben im Geiste seiner Zeit hängt nicht der sittliche Werth eines Menschen, aber seine geschichtliche Wirksamkeit ab." Rümelin, both in politics and literature the most brilliant Suabian of his time, and a strenuous adversary of Machiavelli, wrote thus in 1874: "Für den Einzelnen im

Staat gilt das Princip der Selbsthingabe, für den Staat das der
Selbstbehauptung. Der Einzelne dient dem Recht; der Staat handhabt,
leitet und schafft dasselbe. Der Einzelne ist nur ein flüchtiges Glied in
dem sittlichen Ganzen; der Staat ist, wenn nicht dieses Ganze selbst,
doch dessen reale, ordnende Macht; er ist unsterblich und sich selbst
genug. Die Erhaltung des Staats rechtfertigt jedes Opfer und steht
über jedem Gebot." Nefftzer, an Alsatian borderer, says: "Le devoir
suprême des individus est de se dévouer, celui des nations est de se
conserver, et se confond par conséquent avec leur intérêt." Once, in a
mood of pantheism, Renan wrote: "L'humanité a tout fait, et, nous
voulons le croire, tout bien fait." Or, as Michelet abridges the *Scienza
Nuova*: "L'humanité est son oeuvre à elle-même. Dieu agit sur elle,
mais par elle." Mr. Leslie Stephen thus lays down the philosophy of
history according to Carlyle, "that only succeeds which is based on
divine truth, and permanent success therefore proves the right, as the
effect proves the cause." Darwin, having met Carlyle, notes that "in
his eyes might was right," and adds that he had a narrow and
unscientific mind; but Mr. Goldwin Smith discovers the same lesson:
"History, of itself, if observed as science observes the facts of the
physical world, can scarcely give man any principle or any object of
allegiance, unless it be success." Dr. Martineau attributes this doctrine
to Mill: "Do we ask what determines the moral quality of actions? We
are referred, not to their spring, but to their consequences." Jeremy
Bentham used to relate how he found the greatest happiness principle
in 1768, and gave a shilling for it, at the corner of Queen's College.
He found it in Priestley, and he might have gone on finding it in
Beccaria and Hutcheson, all of whom trace their pedigree to the
Mandragola: "Io credo che quello sia bene che facci bene a' più, e che
i più se ne contentino." This is the centre of unity in all Machiavelli,
and gives him touch, not with unconscious imitators only, but with
the most conspicuous race of reasoners in the century.

English experience has not been familiar with a line of thought
plainly involving indulgence to Machiavelli. Dugald Stewart raises
him high, but raises him for a heavy fall: "No writer, certainly, either
in ancient or in modern times, has ever united, in a more remarkable
degree, a greater variety of the most dissimilar and seemingly the most
discordant gifts and attainments. To his maxims the royal defenders
of the Catholic faith have been indebted for the spirit of that policy
which they have uniformly opposed to the innovations of the reformers."

Hallam indeed has said: "We continually find a more flagitious and undisguised abandonment of moral rules for the sake of some idol of a general principle than can be imputed to *The Prince* of Machiavel." But the unaccustomed hyperbole had been hazarded a century before in the obscurity of a Latin dissertation by Feuerlein: "Longe detestabiliores errores apud alios doctores politicos facile invenias, si eidem rigorosae censurae eorum scripta subiicienda essent." What has been, with us, the occasional aphorism of a masterful mind, encountered support abroad in accredited systems, and in a vast and successful political movement. The recovery of Machiavelli has been essentially the product of causes operating on the Continent.

When Hegel was dominant to the Rhine, and Cousin beyond it, the circumstances favoured his reputation. For Hegel taught: "Der Gang der Weltgeschichte steht ausserhalb der Tugend, des Lasters, und der Gerechtigkeit." And the great eclectic renewed, in explicit language, the worst maxim of the *Istorie Fiorentine*: "L'apologie d'un siècle est dans son existence, car son existence est un arrêt et un jugement de Dieu même, ou l'histoire n'est qu'une fantasmagorie insignifiante. Le caractère propre, le signe d'un grand homme, c'est qu'il réussit. Ou nul guerrier ne doit être appelé grand homme, ou, s'il est grand, il faut l'absoudre, et absoudre en masse tout ce qu'il a fait. Il faut prouver que le vainqueur non seulement sert la civilisation, mais qu'il est meilleur, plus moral, et que c'est pour cela qu'il est vainqueur. Maudire la puissance (j'entends une puissance longue et durable) c'est blasphémer l'humanité."

This primitive and everlasting problem assumed a peculiar shape in theological controversy. The Catholic divines urged that prosperity is a sign by which, even in the militant period, the true Church may be known; coupling *Felicitas Temporalis illis collata qui ecclesiam defenderunt* with *Infelix exitus eorum qui ecclesiam oppugnant*. Le Blanc de Beaulieu, a name famous in the history of pacific disputation, holds the opposite opinion: "Crucem et perpessiones esse potius ecclesiae notam, nam denunciatum piis in verbo Dei fore ut in hoc mundo persecutionem patiantur, non vero ut armis sint adversariis suis superiores." Renan, outbidding all, finds that honesty is the worst policy: "En général, dans l'histoire, l'homme est puni de ce qu'il fait de bien, et récompensé de ce qu'il fait de mal. L'histoire est tout le contraire de la vertu récompensée."

The national movement which united, first Italy and then Germany, opened a new era for Machiavelli. He had come down, laden with the distinctive reproach of abetting despotism; and the men who, in the seventeenth century, levelled the course of absolute monarchy, were commonly known as *novi politici et Machiavellistae*. In the days of Grotius they are denounced by Besold: "Novi politici, ex Italia redeuntes qui quavis fraude principibus a subditis pecuniam extorquere fas licitumque esse putant, Machiavelli plerumque praeceptis et exemplis principum, quorum rationes non capiunt, ad id abutentes." But the immediate purpose with which Italians and Germans effected the great change in the European constitution was unity, not liberty. They constructed, not securities, but forces. Machiavelli's time had come. The problems once more were his own: and in many forward and resolute minds the spirit also was his, and displayed itself in an ascending scale of praise. He was simply a faithful observer of facts, who described the fell necessity that governs narrow territories and unstable fortunes; he discovered the true line of progress and the law of future society; he was a patriot, a republican, a Liberal, but above all this, a man sagacious enough to know that politics is an inductive science. A sublime purpose justifies him, and he has been wronged by dupes and fanatics, by irresponsible dreamers and interested hypocrites.

The Italian Revolution, passing from the Liberal to the national stage, at once adopted his name and placed itself under his invocation. Count Sclopis, though he declared him *Penseur profond, écrivain admirable*, deplored this untimely preference: "Il m'a été pénible de voir le gouvernement provisoire de la Tuscane, en 1859, le lendemain du jour où ce pays recouvrait sa liberté, publier un décret, portant qu'une édition complète des oeuvres de Machiavel serait faite aux frais de l'état." The research even of our best masters, Villari and Tommasini, is prompted by admiration. Ferrari, who comes so near him in many qualities of the intellect, proclaims him the recorder of fate: "Il décrit les rôles que la fatalité distribue aux individus et aux masses dans ces moments funestes et glorieux où ils sont appelés à changer la loi et la foi des nations." His advice, says La Farina, would have saved Italy. Canello believes that he is disliked because he is mistaken for a courtier: "L' orrore e l' antipatia che molti critici hanno provato per il Machiavelli son derivati dal pensare che tutti i suoi crudi insegnamenti fossero solo a vantaggio del Principe." One biographer, Mordenti, exalts him as the very champion of conscience: "Risuscitando la dignità dell' umana coscienza, ne affermò l' esistenza in faccia alla ragione." He adds, more truly, "È uno dei personaggi del dramma che si va svolgendo nell' età nostra."

That is the meaning of Laurent when he says that he has imitators but no defenders: "Machiavel ne trouve plus un seul partisan au XIXᵉ siècle. La postérité a voué son nom à l'infamie, tout en pratiquant sa doctrine." His characteristic universality has been recognised by Baudrillart: "En exprimant ce mauvais côté, mais ce mauvais côté, hélas, éternel! Machiavel n'est plus seulement le publiciste de son pays et de son temps; il est le politique de tous les siècles. S'il fait tout dépendre de la puissance individuelle, et de ses facultés de force, d'habileté, de ruse, c'est que, plus le théâtre se rétrécit, plus l'homme influe sur la marche des événements." Matter finds the same merits which are applauded by the Italians: "Il a plus innové pour la liberté que pour le despotisme, car autour de lui la liberté était inconnue, tandis que le despotisme lui posait partout." And his reviewer, Longpérier, pronounces the doctrine "parfaitement appropriée aux états d'Italie." Nourrisson, with Fehr, one of the few religious men who still have a good word for the Secretary, admires his sincerity: "*Le Prince* est un livre de bonne foi, où l'auteur, sans songer à mal, n'a fait que traduire en maximes les pratiques habituelles à ses contemporains." Thiers, though he surrendered *The Prince*, clung to the *Discorsi*—the *Discorsi*, with the pointed and culminating text produced by Mr. Burd. In the archives of the ministry he might have found how the idea struck his successful predecessor, Vergennes: "Il est des choses plus fortes que les hommes, et les grands intérêts des nations sont de ce genre, et doivent par conséquent l'emporter sur la façon de penser de quelques particuliers."

Loyalty to Frederic the Great has not restrained German opinion, and philosophers unite with historians in rejecting his youthful moralities. Zimmerman wonders what would have become of Prussia if the king had practised the maxims of the crown prince; and Zeller testifies that the *Anti-Machiavel* was not permitted to influence his reign: "Wird man doch weder in seiner Staatsleitung noch in seinen politischen Grundsätzen etwas von dem vermissen, worauf die Ueberlegenheit einer gesunden Realpolitik allem liberalen oder conservativen, radikalen oder legitimistischen, Doktrinarismus gegenüber beruht." Ahrens and Windelband insist on the virtue of a national government: "Der Staat ist sich selbst genug, wenn er in einer Nation wurzelt, das ist der Grundgedanke Machiavelli's." Kirchmann celebrates the emancipation of the State from the moral yoke: "Man hat Machiavelli zwar in der Theorie bekämpft, allein die Praxis der Staaten hat seine Lehren immer eingehalten. Wenn seine Lehre verletzt, so kommt diess nur von der Kleinheit der Staaten und Fürsten, auf die er sie verwendet. Es spricht nur für seine tiefe Erkenntniss des Staatswesens, dass er die Staatsgewalt nicht den Regeln der Privatmoral unterwirft, sondern selbst vor groben Verletzungen dieser Moral durch den Fürsten nicht zurückschreckt, wenn das Wohl des Ganzen und die Freiheit des Vaterlandes nicht anders vorbereitet und vermittelt werden kann." In Kuno Fischer's progress through the systems of metaphysics Machiavelli appears at almost every step; his influence is manifest to Dr. Abbott throughout the whole of Bacon's political writings: Hobbes followed up his theory to the conclusions which he abstained from; Spinoza gave him the benefit of a liberal interpretation; Leibniz, the inventor of the acquiescent doctrine which Bolingbroke transmitted to the *Essay on Man*, said that he drew a good likeness of a bad prince; Herder reports him to mean that a rogue need not be a fool; Fichte frankly set himself to rehabilitate him. In the end, the great master of modern philosophy pronounces in his favour, and declares it absurd to robe a prince in the cowl of a monk: "Ein politischer Denker und Künstler, dessen erfahrener und tiefer Verstand aus den geschichtlich gegebenen Verhältnissen besser als aus den Grundsätzen der Metaphysik, die politischen Nothwendigkeiten, den Charakter, die Bildung und Aufgabe weltlicher Herrschaft zu begreifen wusste. Da man weiss, dass politische Machtfragen nie, am Wenigsten in einem verderbten Volke, mit den Mitteln der Moral zu lösen sind, so ist es unverständig, das Buch vom Fürsten zu verschreien. Machiavelli hatte einen Herrscher zu schildern, keinen Klosterbruder."

Ranke was a grateful student of Fichte when he spoke of Machiavelli as a meritorious writer, maligned by people who could not understand him: "Einem Autor von höchstem Verdienst, und der keineswegs ein böser Mensch war. Die falsche Auffassung des *Principe* beruht eben darauf, dass man die Lehren Machiavells als allgemeine betrachtet, während sie bloss Anweisungen für einen bestimmten Zweck sind." To Gervinus, in 1853, he is "der grosse Seher," the prophet of the modern world. "Er errieth den Geist der neuern Geschichte." Gervinus was a democratic Liberal, and, taken with Gentz from another quarter, he shows how widely the elements of the Machiavellian restoration were spread over Europe. Gentz had not forgotten his classics in the service of Austria when he wrote to a friend: "Wenn selbst das Recht je verletzt werden darf, so geschehe es, um die rechtmässige Macht zu erhalten; in allem Uebrigen herrsche es unbedingt." Twesten is as well persuaded as Machiavelli that the world cannot be governed "con Pater nostri in mano," and he deemed that patriotism atoned for his errors: "Dass der weltgeschichtliche Fortschritt nicht mit Schonung und Gelindigkeit, nicht in den Formen des Rechts vollzogen werden konnte, hat die Geschichte aller Länder bestätigt. Auch Machiavellis Sünden mögen wir als gesühnt betrachten, durch das hochsinnige Streben für das Grosse und das Ansehen seines Volkes." One censor of Frederic, Boretius, makes him answerable for a great deal of presuming criticism: "Die Gelehrten sind bis heute in ihrem Urtheil über Machiavelli nicht einig, die öffentliche Meinung ist hierin glücklicher. Die öffentliche Meinung kann sich für alle diese Weisheit beim alten Fritz bedanken." On the eve of the campaign in Bohemia, Herbst pointed out that Machiavelli, though previously a republican, sacrificed liberty to unity: "Der Einheit soll die innere Freiheit—Machiavelli war kurz zuvor noch begeisterter Anhänger der Republik—geopfert werden." According to Feuerlein the heart of the writer was loyal, but the conditions of the problem were inexorable; and Klein detects in *The Prince*, and even in the *Mandragola*, "die reformatorische Absicht eines Sittenspiegels." Chowanetz wrote a book to hold up Machiavelli as a teacher of all ages, but especially of our own: "Die Absicht aber, welche Machiavel mit seinem Buche verband, ist trefflich für alle Zeiten." And Weitzel hardly knows a better writer, or one less worthy of an evil name: "Im Interesse der Menschheit und gesetzmässiger Verfassungen kann kaum ein besseres Werk geschrieben werden. Wohl ist mancher in der Geschichte, wie in der Tradition der Völker, auf eine unschuldige Weise um seinen verdienten, oder zu einem unverdienten Rufe gekommen, aber keiner vielleicht unschuldiger als Machiavelli."

These are remote and forgotten names. Stronger men of the imperial epoch have resumed the theme with better means of judging, and yet with no harsher judgment. Hartwig sums up his penetrating and severe analysis by confessing that the world as Machiavelli saw it, without a conscience, is the real world of history as it is: "Die Thatsachen selbst scheinen uns das Geheimniss ihrer Existenz zu verrathen; wir glauben vor uns die Fäden sich verknüpfen und verschlingen zu sehen, deren Gewebe die Weltgeschichte ist." Gaspary thinks that he hated iniquity, but that he knew of no righteousness apart from the State: "Er lobte mit Wärme das Gute und tadelte mit Abscheu das Böse; aber er studirte auch dieses mit Interesse. Er erkennt eben keine Moral, wie keine Religion, über dem Staate, sondern nur in demselben; die Menschen sind von Natur schlecht, die Gesetze machen sie gut. Wo es kein Gericht giebt, bei dem man klagen könnte, wie in den Handlungen der Fürsten, betrachtet man immer das Ende." The common opinion is expressed by Baumgarten in his *Charles the Fifth*, that the grandeur of the purpose assures indulgence to the means proposed: "Wenn die Umstände zum Wortbruch, zur Grausamkeit, Habgier, Lüge treiben, so hat man sich nicht etwa mit Bedauern, dass die Not dazu zwinge, sondern schlechtweg, weil es eben politisch zweckmässig ist und ohne alles Bedenken so zu verhalten. Ihre Deduktionen sind uns unerträglich, wenn wir nicht sagen können: alle diese schrecklichen Dinge empfahl Machiavelli, weil er nur durch sie die Befreiung seines Vaterlandes zu erreichen hoffte. Dieses erhabene Ziel macht uns die fürchterlichen Mittel annehmbar, welche Machiavelli seinem Fürsten empfiehlt." Hillebrand was a more international German; he had swum in many European waters, and wrote in three languages. He is scarcely less favourable in his interpretation: "Cette dictature, il ne faut jamais le perdre de vue, ne serait jamais que transitoire, et devrait faire place à un gouvernement libre dès que la grande réforme nationale et sociale serait accomplie. Il a parfaitement conscience du mal. L'atmosphère ambiante de son siècle et de son pays n'a nullement oblitéré son sens moral. Il a si bien conscience de l'énormité de ces crimes, qu'il la condamne hautement lorsque la dernière nécessité ne les impose pas."

Among these utterances of capable and distinguished men, it will be seen that some are partially true, and others, without a particle of truth, are at least representative and significant, and serve to bring Machiavelli within fathomable depth. He is the earliest conscious and articulate exponent of certain living forces in the present world. Religion, progressive enlightenment, the perpetual vigilance of public opinion, have not reduced his empire, or disproved the justice of his conception of mankind. He obtains a new lease of life from causes that are still prevailing, and from doctrines that are apparent in politics, philosophy, and science. Without sparing censure, or employing for comparison the grosser symptoms of the age, we find him near our common level, and perceive that he is not a vanishing type, but a constant and contemporary influence. Where it is impossible to praise, to defend, or to excuse, the burden of blame may yet be lightened by adjustment and distribution, and he is more rationally intelligible when illustrated by lights falling not only from the century he wrote in, but from our own, which has seen the course of its history twenty-five times diverted by actual or attempted crime.

[24]
Review of Flint's
Historical Philosophy

When Dr. Flint's former work appeared, a critic, who, it is true, was also a rival, objected that it was diffusely written. What then occupied three hundred and thirty pages has now expanded to seven hundred, and suggests a doubt as to the use of criticism. It must at once be said that the increase is nearly all material gain. The author does not cling to his main topic, and, as he insists that the science he is adumbrating flourishes on the study of facts only, and not on speculative ideas, he bestows some needless attention on historians who professed no philosophy, or who, like Daniel and Velly, were not the best of their kind. Here and there, as in the account of Condorcet, there may be an unprofitable or superfluous sentence. But on the whole the enlarged treatment of the philosophy of history in France is accomplished not by expansion, but by solid and essential addition. Many writers are included whom the earlier volume passed over, and Cousin occupies fewer pages now than in 1874, by the aid of smaller type and the omission of a passage injurious to Schelling. Many necessary corrections and improvements have been made, such as the transfer of Ballanche from theocracy to the liberal Catholicism of which he is supposed to be the founder.

Dr. Flint's unchallenged superiority consists alike in his familiarity with obscure, but not irrelevant authors, whom he has brought into line, and in his scrupulous fairness towards all whose attempted systems he has analysed. He is hearty in appreciating talent of every kind, but he is discriminating in his judgment of ideas, and rarely sympathetic. Where the best thoughts of the ablest men are to be displayed, it

Robert Flint, *Historical Philosophy in France and French Belgium and Switzerland* (London: W. Blackwood, 1893). This review was published in the *English Historical Review* 10 (1895):108–113. Reprinted in Acton, *History of Freedom*, pp. 588–596.

would be tempting to present an array of luminous points or a chaplet of polished gems. In the hands of such artists as Stahl or Cousin they would start into high relief with a convincing lucidity that would rouse the exhibited writers to confess that they had never known they were so clever. Without transfiguration the effect might be attained by sometimes stringing the most significant words of the original. Excepting one unduly favoured competitor, who fills two pages with untranslated French, there is little direct quotation. Cournot is one of those who, having been overlooked at first, are here raised to prominence. He is urgently, and justly, recommended to the attention of students. "They will find that every page bears the impress of patient, independent, and sagacious thought. I believe I have not met with a more genuine thinker in the course of my investigations. He was a man of the finest intellectual qualities, of a powerful and absolutely truthful mind." But then we are warned that Cournot never wrote a line for the general reader, and accordingly he is not permitted to speak for himself. Yet it was this thoughtful Frenchman who said: "Aucune idée parmi celles qui se réfèrent à l'ordre des faits naturels ne tient de plus près à la famille des idées religieuses que l'idée du progrès, et n'est plus propre à devenir le principe d'une sorte de foi religieuse pour ceux qui n'en ont pas d'autres. Elle a, comme la foi religieuse, la vertu de relever les âmes et les caractères."

The successive theories gain neither in clearness nor in contrast by the order in which they stand. As other countries are reserved for other volumes, Cousin precedes Hegel, who was his master, whilst Quetelet is barely mentioned in his own place, and has to wait for Buckle, if not for Oettingen and Rümelin, before he comes on for discussion. The finer threads, the underground currents, are not carefully traced. The connection between the *juste milieu* in politics and eclecticism in philosophy was already stated by the chief eclectic; but the subtler link between the Catholic legitimists and democracy seems to have escaped the author's notice. He says that the republic proclaimed universal suffrage in 1848, and he considers it a triumph for the party of Lafayette. In fact, it was the triumph of an opposite school—of those legitimists who appealed from the narrow franchise which sustained the Orleans dynasty to the nation behind it. The chairman of the constitutional committee was a legitimist, and he, inspired by the abbé de Genoude, of the *Gazette de France,* and opposed by Odilon Barrot, insisted on the pure logic of absolute democracy.

It is an old story now that the true history of philosophy is the true evolution of philosophy, and that when we have eliminated whatever has been damaged by contemporary criticism or by subsequent advance, and have assimilated all that has survived through the ages, we shall find in our possession not only a record of growth, but the full-grown fruit itself. This is not the way in which Dr. Flint understands the building up of his department of knowledge. Instead of showing how far France has made a way towards the untrodden crest, he describes the many flowery paths, discovered by the French, which lead elsewhere, and I expect that in coming volumes it will appear that Hegel and Buckle, Vico and Ferrari, are scarcely better guides than Laurent or Littré. Fatalism and retribution, race and nationality, the test of success and of duration, heredity and the reign of the invincible dead, the widening circle, the emancipation of the individual, the gradual triumph of the soul over the body, of mind over matter, reason over will, knowledge over ignorance, truth over error, right over might, liberty over authority, the law of progress and perfectibility, the constant intervention of providence, the sovereignty of the developed con-science—neither these nor other alluring theories are accepted as more than illusions or half-truths. Dr. Flint scarcely avails himself of them even for his foundations or his skeleton framework. His critical faculty, stronger than his gift of adaptation, levels obstructions and marks the earth with ruin. He is more anxious to expose the strange unreason of former writers, the inadequacy of their knowledge, their want of aptitude in induction, than their services in storing material for the use of successors. The result is not to be the sifted and verified wisdom of two centuries, but a future system, to be produced when the rest have failed by an exhaustive series of vain experiments. We may regret to abandon many brilliant laws and attractive generalisations that have given light and clearness and simplicity and symmetry to our thought; but it is certain that Dr. Flint is a close and powerful reasoner, equipped with satisfying information, and he establishes his contention that France has not produced a classic philosophy of history, and is still waiting for its Adam Smith or Jacob Grimm.

The kindred topic of development recurs repeatedly, as an important factor in modern science. It is still a confused and unsettled chapter, and in one place Dr. Flint seems to attribute the idea to Bossuet; in another he says that it was scarcely entertained in those days by Protestants, and not at all by Catholics; in a third he implies that its celebrity in the nineteenth century is owing in the first place to Lamennais. The passage, taken from Vinet, in which Bossuet speaks of the development of religion is inaccurately rendered. His words are the same which, on another page, are rightly translated "the course of religion"—*la suite de la religion*. Indeed, Bossuet was the most powerful adversary the theory ever encountered. It was not so alien to Catholic theology as is here stated, and before the time of Jurieu is more often found among Catholic than Protestant writers. When it was put forward, in guarded, dubious, and evasive terms, by Petavius, the indignation in England was as great as in 1846. The work which contained it, the most learned that Christian theology had then produced, could not be reprinted over here, lest it should supply the Socinians with inconvenient texts. Nelson hints that the great Jesuit may have been a secret Arian, and Bull stamped upon his theory amid the grateful applause of Bossuet and his friends. Petavius was not an innovator, for the idea had long found a home among the Franciscan masters: "Proficit fides secundum statum communem, quia secundum profectum temporum efficiebantur homines magis idonei ad percipienda et intelligenda sacramenta fidei. Sunt multae conclusiones necessario inclusae in articulis creditis, sed antequam sunt per Ecclesiam declaratae et explicatae non oportet quemcumque eas credere. Oportet tamen circa eas sobrie opinari, ut scilicet homo sit paratus eas tenere pro tempore, pro quo veritas fuerit declarata." Cardinal Duperron said nearly the same thing as Petavius a generation before him: "L'Arien trouvera dans sainct Irénée, Tertullien et autres qui nous sont restez en petit nombre de ces siècles-là, que le Fils est l'instrument du Père, que le Père a commandé au Fils lors qu'il a esté question de la création des choses, que le Père et le Fils sont *aliud et aliud;* choses que qui tiendroit aujourd'huy, que le langage de l'Eglise est plus examiné, seroit estimé pour Arien luymesme." All this does not serve to supply the pedigree which Newman found it so difficult to trace. Development, in those days, was an expedient, an hypothesis, and not even the thing so dear to the Oxford probabilitarians, a working hypothesis. It was not more substantial than the gleam in Robinson's farewell to the pilgrims: "I am very confident that the Lord has more truth yet to break forth out of His holy word." The reason why it possessed no scientific basis is explained by Duchesne: "Ce n'est guère avant la seconde moitié du xviie siècle qu'il devint impossible de soutenir l'authenticité des fausses décrétales, des constitutions apostoliques, des

'Récognitions Clémentines,' du faux Ignace, du pseudo-Dionys et de l'immense fatras d'œuvres anonymes ou pseudonymes qui grossissait souvent du tiers ou de la moitié l'héritage littéraire des auteurs les plus considérables. Qui aurait pu même songer à un développement dogmatique?" That it was little understood, and lightly and loosely employed, is proved by Bossuet himself, who alludes to it in one passage as if he did not know that it was the subversion of his theology: "Quamvis ecclesia omnem veritatem funditus norit, ex haeresibus tamen discit, ut aiebat magni nominis Vincentius Lirinensis, aptius, distinctius, clariusque eandem exponere."

The account of Lamennais suffers from the defect of mixing him up too much with his early friends. No doubt he owed to them the theory that carried him through his career, for it may be found in Bonald, and also in De Maistre, though not, perhaps, in the volumes he had already published. It was less original than he at first imagined, for the English divines commonly held it from the seventeenth century, and its dirge was sung only the other day by the Bishop of Gloucester and Bristol.[1] A Scottish professor would even be justified in claiming it for Reid. But of course it was Lamennais who gave it most importance, in his programme and in his life. And his theory of the common sense, the theory that we can be certain of truth only by the agreement of mankind, though vigorously applied to sustain authority in State and Church, gravitated towards multitudinism, and marked him off from his associates. When he said *quod semper, quod ubique, quod ab omnibus,* he was not thinking of the Christian Church, but of Christianity as old as the creation; and the development he meant led up to the Bible, and ended at the New Testament instead of beginning there. That is the theory which he made so famous, which founded his fame and governed his fate, and to which Dr. Flint's words apply when he speaks of celebrity. In that sense it is a mistake to connect Lamennais with Möhler and Newman; and I do not believe that he anticipated their teaching, in spite of one or two passages which do not, on the face of them, bear date B.C., and may, no doubt, be quoted for the opposite opinion.

In the same group Dr. Flint represents De Maistre as the teacher of Savigny, and asserts that there could never be a doubt as to the liberalism of Chateaubriand. There was none after his expulsion from

---

[1] [Dr. Ellicott.]

office; but there was much reason for doubting in 1815, when he entreated the king to set bounds to his mercy; in 1819, when he was contributing to the *Conservateur;* and in 1823, when he executed the mandate of the absolute monarchs against the Spanish constitution. His zeal for legitimacy was at all times qualified with liberal elements, but they never became consistent or acquired the mastery until 1824. De Maistre and Savigny covered the same ground at one point; they both subjected the future to the past. This could serve as an argument for absolutism and theocracy, and on that account was lovely in the eyes of De Maistre. If it had been an argument the other way he would have cast it off. Savigny had no such ulterior purpose. His doctrine, that the living are not their own masters, could serve either cause. He rejected a mechanical fixity, and held that whatever has been made by process of growth shall continue to grow and suffer modification. His theory of continuity has this significance in political science, that it supplied a basis for conservatism apart from absolutism and compatible with freedom. And, as he believed that law depends on national tradition and character, he became indirectly and through friends a founder of the theory of nationality.

The one writer whom Dr. Flint refuses to criticise, because he too nearly agrees with him, is Renouvier. Taking this avowal in conjunction with two or three indiscretions on other pages, we can make a guess, not at the system itself, which is to console us for so much deviation, but at its tendency and spirit. The fundamental article is belief in divine government. As Kant beheld God in the firmament of heaven, so too we can see him in history on earth. Unless a man is determined to be an atheist, he must acknowledge that the experience of mankind is a decisive proof in favour of religion. As providence is not absolute, but reigns over men destined to freedom, its method is manifested in the law of progress. Here, however, Dr. Flint, in his agreement with Renouvier, is not eager to fight for his cause, and speaks with a less jubilant certitude. He is able to conceive that providence may attain its end without the condition of progress, that the divine scheme would not be frustrated if the world, governed by omnipotent wisdom, became steadily worse. Assuming progress as a fact, if not a law, there comes the question wherein it consists, how it is measured, where is its goal. Not religion, for the Middle Ages are an epoch of decline. Catholicism has since lost so much ground as to nullify the theories of Bossuet; whilst Protestantism never succeeded in France, either after the

Reformation, when it ought to have prevailed, nor after the Revolution, when it ought not. The failure to establish the Protestant Church on the ruins of the old *régime*, to which Quinet attributes the breakdown of the Revolution, and which Napoleon regretted almost in the era of his concordat, is explained by Mr. Flint on the ground that Protestants were in a minority. But so they were in and after the wars of religion; and it is not apparent why a philosopher who does not prefer orthodoxy to liberty should complain that they achieved nothing better than toleration. He disproves Bossuet's view by that process of deliverance from the Church which is the note of recent centuries, and from which there is no going back. On the future I will not enlarge, because I am writing at present in the *Historical*, not the *Prophetical, Review*. But some things were not so clear in France in 1679 as they are now at Edinburgh. The predominance of Protestant power was not foreseen, except by those who disputed whether Rome would perish in 1710 or about 1720. The destined power of science to act upon religion had not been proved by Newton or Simon. No man was able to forecast the future experience of America, or to be sure that observations made under the reign of authority would be confirmed by the reign of freedom.

If the end be not religion, is it morality, humanity, civilisation, knowledge? In the German chapters of 1874 Dr. Flint was severe upon Hegel, and refused his notion that the development of liberty is the soul of history, as crude, one-sided, and misunderstood. He is more lenient now, and affirms that liberty occupies the final summit, that it profits by all the good that is in the world, and suffers by all the evil, that it pervades strife and inspires endeavour, that it is almost, if not altogether, the sign, and the prize, and the motive in the onward and upward advance of the race for which Christ was crucified. As that refined essence which draws sustenance from all good things it is clearly understood as the product of civilisation, with its complex problems and scientific appliances, not as the elementary possession of the noble savage, which has been traced so often to the primeval forest. On the other hand, if sin not only tends to impair, but does inevitably impair and hinder it, providence is excluded from its own mysterious sphere, which, as it is not the suppression of all evil and present punishment of wrong, should be the conversion of evil into an instrument to serve the higher purpose. But although Dr. Flint has come very near to Hegel and Michelet, and seemed about to elevate their teaching to a higher level and a wider view, he ends by treating it coldly, as a partial truth requiring supplement, and bids us wait until many more explorers have recorded their soundings. That, with the trained capacity for misunderstanding and the smouldering dissent proper to critics, I might not mislead any reader, or do less than justice to a profound though indecisive work, I should have wished to piece together the passages in which the author indicates, somewhat faintly, the promised but withheld philosophy which will crown his third or fourth volume. Any one who compares pages 125, 135, 225, 226, 671, will understand better than I can explain it the view which is the master-key to the book.

[25]
The Study of History

Fellow Students—I look back to-day to a time before the middle of the century, when I was reading at Edinburgh and fervently wishing to come to this University. At three colleges I applied for admission, and, as things then were, I was refused by all. Here, from the first, I vainly fixed my hopes, and here, in a happier hour, after five-and-forty years, they are at last fulfilled.

I desire, first, to speak to you of that which I may reasonably call the Unity of Modern History, as an easy approach to questions necessary to be met on the threshold by anyone occupying this place, which my predecessor has made so formidable to me by the reflected lustre of his name.

You have often heard it said that modern history is a subject to which neither beginning nor end can be assigned. No beginning, because the dense web of the fortunes of man is woven without a void; because, in society as in nature, the structure is continuous, and we can trace things back uninterruptedly, until we dimly descry the Declaration of Independence in the forests of Germany. No end, because, on the same principle, history made and history making are scientifically inseparable and separately unmeaning.

"Politics," said Sir John Seeley, "are vulgar when they are not liberalised by history, and history fades into mere literature when it loses sight of its relation to practical politics." Everybody perceives the sense in which this is true. For the science of politics is the one science that is deposited by the stream of history, like grains of gold in the sand of a river; and the knowledge of the past, the record of truths revealed by experience, is eminently practical, as an instrument

Acton's Inaugural Lecture as Regius Professor of Modern History at Cambridge. Delivered June 11, 1895. Published as *A Lecture on the Study of History* (London, 1895). Reprinted in Acton, *Lectures on Modern History*, pp. 1–28, 319–342; Acton, *Freedom and Power*, pp. 3–29, 399–428; *Liberal Interpretation of History*, pp. 300–359.

of action and a power that goes to the making of the future.[1] In France, such is the weight attached to the study of our own time, that there is an appointed course of contemporary history, with appropriate text-books.[2] That is a chair which, in the progressive division of labour by which both science and government prosper,[3] may some day be founded in this country. Meantime, we do well to acknowledge the points at which the two epochs diverge. For the contemporary differs from the modern in this, that many of its facts cannot by us be definitely ascertained. The living do not give up their secrets with the candour of the dead; one key is always excepted, and a generation passes before we can ensure accuracy. Common report and outward seeming are bad copies of the reality, as the initiated know it. Even of a thing so memorable as the war of 1870, the true cause is still obscure; much that we believed has been scattered to the winds in the last six months, and further revelations by important witnesses are about to appear. The use of history turns far more on certainty than on abundance of acquired information.

Beyond the question of certainty is the question of detachment. The process by which principles are discovered and appropriated is other than that by which, in practice, they are applied; and our most sacred and disinterested convictions ought to take shape in the tranquil regions of the air, above the tumult and the tempest of active life.[4] For a man is justly despised who has one opinion in history and another in politics, one for abroad and another at home, one for opposition and another for office. History compels us to fasten on abiding issues, and

---

[1] No political conclusions of any value for practice can be arrived at by direct experience. All true political science is, in one sense of the phrase, *a priori,* being deduced from the tendencies of things, tendencies known either through our general experience of human nature, or as the result of an analysis of the course of history, considered as a progressive evolution.—Mill, *Inaugural Address,* 51.

[2] Contemporary history is, in Dr. Arnold's opinion, more important than either ancient or modern; and in fact superior to it by all the superiority of the end to the means.—Seeley, *Lectures and Essays,* 306.

[3] The law of all progress is one and the same, the evolution of the simple into the complex by successive differentiation.—*Edinburgh Review,* CLVII, 248. Die Entwickelung der Völker vollzieht sich nach zwei Gesetzen. Das erste Gesetz ist das der Differenzierung. Die primitiven Einrichtungen sind einfach und einheitlich, die der Civilisation zusammengesetzt und geteilt, und die Arbeitsteilung nimmt beständig zu.—Sickel, *Goettingen Gelehrte Anzeigen,* 1890, 563.

[4] Nous risquons toujours d'être influencés par les préjugés de notre époque; mais nous sommes libres des préjugés particuliers aux époques antérieures.—E. Naville, *Christianisme de Fénelon,* 9.

rescues us from the temporary and transient. Politics and history are interwoven, but are not commensurate. Ours is a domain that reaches farther than affairs of state, and is not subject to the jurisdiction of governments. It is our function to keep in view and to command the movement of ideas, which are not the effect but the cause of public events;[5] and even to allow some priority to ecclesiastical history over civil, since, by reason of the graver issues concerned, and the vital consequences of error, it opened the way in research, and was the first to be treated by close reasoners and scholars of the higher rank.[6]

In the same manner, there is wisdom and depth in the philosophy which always considers the origin and the germ, and glories in history as one consistent epic.[7] Yet every student ought to know that mastery is acquired by resolved limitation. And confusion ensues from the theory of Montesquieu and of his school, who, adapting the same term to things unlike, insist that freedom is the primitive condition of the race from which we are sprung.[8] If we are to account mind not matter, ideas not force, the spiritual property that gives dignity and grace and intellectual value to history, and its action on the ascending life of man, then we shall not be prone to explain the universal by the

---

[5] La nature n'est qu'un écho de l'esprit. L'idée est la mère du fait, elle façonne graduellement le monde à son image.—Feuchtersleben, in Caro, *Nouvelles Études Morales*, 132. Il n'est pas d'étude morale qui vaille l'histoire d'une idée.—Laboulaye, *Liberté Religieuse*, 25.

[6] Il y a des savants qui raillent le sentiment religieux. Ils ne savent pas que c'est à ce sentiment, et par son moyen, que la science historique doit d'avoir pu sortir de l'enfance. . . . Depuis des siècles les âmes indépendantes discutaient les textes et les traditions de l'église, quand les lettrés n'avaient pas encore eu l'idée de porter un regard critique sur les textes de l'antiquité mondaine.—*La France Protestante*, II, 17.

[7] In our own history, above all, every step in advance has been at the same time a step backwards. It has often been shown how our latest constitution is, amidst all external differences, essentially the same as our earliest, how every struggle for right and freedom, from the thirteenth century onwards, has simply been a struggle for recovering something old.—Freeman, *Historical Essays*, IV, 253. Nothing but a thorough knowledge of the social system, based upon a regular study of its growth, can give us the power we require to affect it.—Harrison, *Meaning of History*, 19. Eine Sache wird nur völlig auf dem Wege verstanden, wie sie selbst entsteht.—In dem genetischen Verfahren sind die Gründe der Sache, auch die Gründe des Erkennens.—Trendelenburg, *Logische Untersuchungen*, II, 395, 388.

[8] Une telle liberté . . . n'a rien de commun avec le savant système de garanties qui fait libres les peuples modernes.—Boutmy, *Annales des Sciences Politiques*, I, 157. Les trois grandes réformes qui ont renouvelé l'Angleterre, la liberté religieuse, la réforme parlementaire, et la liberté économique, ont été obtenues sous la pression des organisations extra-constitutionnelles.—Ostrogorski, *Revue Historique*, LII, 272.

national, and civilization by custom.[9] A speech of Antigone, a single sentence of Socrates, a few lines that were inscribed on an Indian rock before the Second Punic War, the footsteps of a silent yet prophetic people who dwelt by the Dead Sea, and perished in the fall of Jerusalem, come nearer to our lives than the ancestral wisdom of barbarians who fed their swine on the Hercynian acorns.

For our present purpose, then, I describe as modern history that which begins four hundred years ago, which is marked off by an evident and intelligible line from the time immediately preceding, and displays in its course specific and distinctive characteristics of its own.[10] The modern age did not proceed from mediaeval by normal succession, with outward tokens of legitimate descent. Unheralded, it founded a new order of things, under a law of innovation, sapping the ancient reign of continuity. In those days Columbus subverted the notions of the world, and reversed the conditions of production, wealth, and power; in those days Machiavelli released government from the restraint of law; Erasmus diverted the current of ancient learning from profane into Christian channels; Luther broke the chain of authority and tradition at the strongest link; and Copernicus erected an invincible power that set forever the mark of progress upon the time that was to come. There is the same unbound originality and disregard for inherited sanctions in the rare philosophers as in the discovery of Divine Right, and the intruding Imperialism of Rome. The like effects are visible everywhere, and one generation beheld them all. It was an awakening of new life; the world revolved in a different orbit, determined by influences unknown before. After many ages persuaded of the headlong

---

[9] The question which is at the bottom of all constitutional struggles, the question between the national will and the national law.—Gardiner, *Documents*, XVIII. Religion, considered simply as the principle which balances the power of human opinion, which takes man out of the grasp of custom and fashion, and teaches him to refer himself to a higher tribunal, is an infinite aid to moral strength and elevation.—Channing, *Works*, IV, 83. Je tiens que le passé ne suffit jamais au présent. Personne n'est plus disposé que moi à profiter de ses leçons; mais en même temps, je le demande, le présent ne fournit-il pas toujours les indications qui lui sont propres?—Molé, in Falloux, *Etudes et Souvenirs*, 130. Admirons la sagesse de nos pères, et tâchons de l'imiter, en faisant ce qui convient à notre siècle.—Galiani, *Dialogues*, 40.

[10] Ceterum in legendis Historiis malim te ductum animi, quam anxias leges sequi. Nullae sunt, quae non magnas habeant utilitates; et melius haerent, quae libenter legimus. In universum tamen, non incipere ab antiquissimis, sed ab his, quae nostris temporibus nostraeque notitiae propius cohaerent, ac paulatim deinde in remotiora eniti, magis e re arbitror.—Grotius, *Epistolae*, 18.

decline and impending dissolution of society,[11] and governed by usage
and the will of masters who were in their graves, the sixteenth century
went forth armed for untried experience, and ready to watch with
hopefulness a prospect of incalculable change.

That forward movement divides it broadly from the older world;
and the unity of the new is manifest in the universal spirit of investigation
and discovery which did not cease to operate, and withstood the
recurring efforts of reaction, until, by the advent of the reign of general
ideas which we call the Revolution, it at length prevailed.[12] This
successive deliverance and gradual passage, for good and evil, from
subordination to independence is a phenomenon of primary import to
us, because historical science has been one of its instruments.[13] If the

---

[11] The older idea of a law of degeneracy, of a "fatal drift towards the worse," is as
obsolete as astrology or the belief in witchcraft. The human race has become hopeful,
sanguine.—Seeley, *Rede Lecture*, 1887. *Fortnightly Review*, July, 1887, 124.

[12] Formuler des idées générales, c'est changer le salpêtre en poudre.—A. DeMusset,
Confessions d'un Enfant du Siècle, 15. Les révolutions c'est l'avènement des idées libérales.
C'est presque toujours par les révolutions qu'elles prévalent et se fondent, et quand les
idées libérales en sont véritablement le principe et le but, quand elles leur ont donné
naissance, et quand elles les couronnent à leur dernier jour, alors ces révolutions sont
légitimes.—Rémusat, 1839, in *Revue des Deux Mondes*, 1875, VI, 335. Il y a même des
personnes de piété qui prouvent par raison qu'il faut renoncer à la raison; que ce n'est
point la lumière, mais la foi seule qui doit nous conduire, et que l'obéissance aveugle
est la principale vertu des chrétiens. La paresse des inférieurs et leur esprit flatteur
s'accommode souvent de cette vertu prétendue, et l'orgueil de ceux qui commandent en
est toujours très content. De sorte qu'il se trouvera peut-être des gens qui seront
scandalisés que je fasse cet honneur à la raison, de l'élever au-dessus de toutes les
puissances, et qui s'imagineront que je me révolte contre les autorités légitimes à cause
que je prends son parti et que je soutiens que c'est à elle à décider et à régner.—
Malebranche, *Morale*, I, 2, 13. That great statesman (Mr. Pitt) distinctly avowed that
the application of philosophy to politics was at that time an innovation, and that it was
an innovation worthy to be adopted. He was ready to make the same avowal in the
present day which Mr. Pitt had made in 1792.—Canning, 1st June, 1827. *Parliamentary
Review*, 1828, 71. American history knows but one avenue of success in American
legislation, freedom from ancient prejudice. The best law givers in our colonies first
became as little children.—Bancroft, *History of the United States*, I, 494. Every American,
from Jefferson and Gallatin down to the poorest squatter, seemed to nourish an idea
that he was doing what he could to overthrow the tyranny which the past had fastened
on the human mind.—Adams, *History of the United States*, I, 175.

[13] The greatest changes of which we have had experience as yet are due to our
increasing knowledge of history and nature. They have been produced by a few minds
appearing in three or four favoured nations, in comparatively a short period of time.
May we be allowed to imagine the minds of men everywhere working together during
many ages for the completion of our knowledge? May not the increase of knowledge
transfigure the world?—Jowett, *Plato*, I, 414. Nothing, I believe, is so likely to beget in

Past has been an obstacle and a burden, knowledge of the Past is the safest and the surest emancipation. And the earnest search for it is one of the signs that distinguish the four centuries of which I speak from those that went before. The Middle Ages, which possessed good writers of contemporary narrative, were careless and impatient of older fact. They became content to be deceived, to live in a twilight of fiction, under clouds of false witness, inventing according to convenience, and glad to welcome the forger and the cheat.[14] As time went on, the atmosphere of accredited mendacity thickened, until in the Renaissance, the art of exposing falsehood dawned upon keen Italian minds. It was then that history as we understand it began to be understood, and the illustrious dynasty of scholars arose to whom we still look both for method and material. Unlike the dreaming prehistoric world, ours knows the need and the duty to make itself master of the earlier times, and to forfeit nothing of their wisdom or their warnings,[15] and has devoted its best energy and treasure to the sovereign purpose of detecting error and vindicating entrusted truth.[16]

In this epoch of full-grown history men have not acquiesced in the given conditions of their lives. Taking little for granted they have sought to know the ground they stand on, and the road they travel, and the reason why. Over them, therefore, the historian has obtained an increasing ascendancy.[17] The law of stability was overcome by the power of ideas, constantly varied and rapidly renewed;[18] ideas that

---

us a spirit of enlightened liberality, of christian forbearance, of large-hearted moderation, as the careful study of the history of doctrine and the history of interpretation.—Perowne, *Psalms*, I, p. xxxi.

[14] Ce n'est guère avant la seconde moitié du XVIIe siècle qu'il devient impossible de soutenir l'authenticité des fausses décrétales, des Constitutions apostoliques, des Récognitions Clémentines, du faux Ignace, du pseudo-Dionys et de l'immense fatras d'oeuvres anonymes ou pseudonymes qui grossissait souvent du tiers ou de la moitié l'héritage littéraire des auteurs les plus considérables.—Duchesne, *Témoins anténicéens de la Trinité*, 1883, 36.

[15] A man who does not know what has been thought by those who have gone before him is sure to set an undue value upon his own ideas.—M. Pattison, *Memoirs*, 78.

[16] Travailler à discerner, dans cette discipline, le solide d'avec l'opinion, ce qui forme le jugement d'avec ce qui ne fait que charger la mémoire.—Lamy, *Connoissance de soi-même*, V, 459.

[17] All our hopes of the future depend on a sound understanding of the past.—Harrison, *The Meaning of History*, 6.

[18] The real history of mankind is that of the slow advance of resolved deed following laboriously just thought; and all the greatest men live in their purpose and effort more than it is possible for them to live in reality. The things that actually happened were of

give life and motion, that take wing and traverse seas and frontiers, making it futile to pursue the consecutive order of events in the seclusion of a separate nationality.[19] They compel us to share the existence of societies wider than our own, to be familiar with distant and exotic types, to hold our march upon the loftier summits, along the central range, to live in the company of heroes, and saints, and men of genius, that no single country could produce. We cannot afford wantonly to lose sight of great men and memorable lives, and are bound to store up objects for admiration as far as may be;[20] for the effect of implacable research is constantly to reduce their number. No intellectual exercise, for instance, can be more invigorating than to watch the working of the mind of Napoleon, the most entirely known as well as the ablest of historic men. In another sphere, it is the vision of a higher world to be intimate with the character of Fénelon, the cherished model of politicians, ecclesiastics, and men of letters, the witness against one century and precursor of another, the advocate of the poor against oppression, of liberty in an age of arbitrary power, of tolerance in an age of persecution, of the humane virtues among men

small consequence—the thoughts that were developed are of infinite consequence.— Ruskin. Facts are the mere dross of history. It is from the abstract truth which interpenetrates them, and lies latent among them like gold in the ore, that the mass derives its value.—Macaulay, *Works*, V, 131.

[19] Die Gesetze der Geschichte sind eben die Gesetze der ganzen Menschheit, gehen nicht in die Geschicke eines Volkes, einer Generation oder gar eines Einzelnen auf. Individuen und Geschlechter, Staaten und Nationen, können zerstäuben, die Menschheit bleibt.—A. Schmidt, *Züricher Monatsschrift*, i, 45.

[20] Le grand péril des âges démocratiques, soyez-en sûr, c'est la destruction ou l'affaiblissement excessif des parties du corps social en présence du tout. Tout ce qui relève de nos jours l'idée de l'individu est sain.—Tocqueville, 3rd January, 1840, *Œuvres*, VII, 97. En France, il n'y a plus d'hommes. On a systématiquement tué l'homme au profit du peuple, des masses, comme disent nos législateurs écervelés. Puis un beau jour, on s'est aperçu que ce peuple n'avait jamais existé qu'en projet, que ces masses étaient un troupeau mi-parti de moutons et de tigres. C'est une triste histoire. Nous avons à relever l'âme humaine contre l'aveugle, et brutale tyrannie des multitudes.— Lanfrey, 23rd March, 1855. M. duCamp, *Souvenirs Littéraires*, II, 273. C'est le propre de la vertu d'être invisible, même dans l'histoire, à tout autre œil que celui de la conscience.— Vachesat, *Comptes Rendus de l'Institut*, LXIX, 319. Dans l'histoire où la bonté est la perle rare, qui a été bon passe presque avant qui a été grand.—V. Hugo, *Les Misérables*, VII, 46. Grosser Maenner Leben und Tod der Wahrheit gemaess mit Liebe zu schildern, ist zu allen Zeiten herzerhebend; am meisten aber dann, wenn im Kreislauf der irdischen Dinge die Sterne wieder aehnlich stehen wie damals als sie unter uns lebten.—Lasaulx, *Sokrates*, 3. Instead of saying that the history of mankind is the history of the masses, it would be much more true to say that the history of mankind is the history of its great men.—Kingsley, *Lectures*, 329.

accustomed to sacrifice them to authority, the man of whom one enemy says that his cleverness was enough to strike terror, and another, that genius poured in torrents from his eyes. For the minds that are greatest and best alone furnish the instructive examples. A man of ordinary proportion or inferior metal knows not how to think out the rounded circle of his thought, how to divest his will of its surroundings and to rise above the pressure of time and race and circumstances,[21] to choose the star that guides his course, to correct and test, and assay his convictions by the light within,[22] and, with a resolute conscience and ideal courage, to remodel and reconstitute the character which birth and education gave him.[23]

For ourselves, if it were not the quest of the higher level and the extended horizon, international history would be imposed by the exclusive and insular reason that parliamentary reporting is younger than parliaments. The foreigner has no mystic fabric in his government, and no *arcanum imperii*. For him the foundations have been laid bare; every motive and function of the mechanism is accounted for as distinctly as the works of a watch. But with our indigenous constitution, not made with hands or written upon paper, but claiming to develop by a law of organic growth; with our disbelief in the virtue of definitions and general principles and our reliance on relative truths, we can have nothing equivalent to the vivid and prolonged debates in which other communities have displayed the inmost secrets of political science to every man who can read. And the discussions of constituent assemblies, at Philadelphia, Versailles and Paris, at Cadiz and Brussels, at Geneva,

---

[21] Le génie n'est que la plus complète émancipation de toutes les influences de temps, de mœurs et de pays.—Nisand, *Souvenirs*, II, 43.

[22] Meine kritische Richtung zieht mich in der Wissenschaft durchaus zur Kritik meiner eigenen Gedanken hin, nicht zu der des Gedanken Anderer.—Rothe, *Ethik*, I, p. xi.

[23] When you are in young years the whole mind is, as it were, fluid, and is capable of forming itself into any shape that the owner of the mind pleases to order it to form itself into.—Carlyle, *On the Choice of Books*, 131. Nach allem erscheint es somit unzweifelhaft als eine der psychologischen Voraussetzungen des Strafrechts, ohne welche der Zurechnungsbegriff nicht haltbar wäre, dass der Mensch für seinen Karakter verantworthlich ist und ihn muss abändern können.—Rumelin, *Reden und Aufsätze*, II, 60. An der tiefen und verborgenen Quelle, woraus der Wille entspringt, an diesem Punkt, nur hier steht die Freiheit, und führt das Steuer und lenkt den Willen. Wer nicht bis zu dieser Tiefe in sich einkehren und seinen natürlichen Karakter von hier aus bemeistern kann, der hat nicht den Gebrauch seiner Freiheit, der ist nicht frei, sondern, unterworfen dem Triebwerk seiner Interessen, und dadurch in der Gewalt des Weltlaufs, worin jede Begebenheit und jede Handlung eine notwendige Folge ist aller vorhergehenden.—Fischer, *Problem der Freiheit*, 27.

Frankfort and Berlin, above nearly all, those of the most enlightened States in the American Union, when they have recast their institutions, are paramount in the literature of politics, and proffer treasures which at home we have never enjoyed.

To historians the later part of their enormous subject is precious because it is inexhaustible. It is the best to know because it is the best known and the most explicit. Earlier scenes stand out from a background of obscurity. We soon reach the sphere of hopeless ignorance and unprofitable doubt. But hundreds and even thousands of the moderns have borne testimony against themselves, and may be studied in their private correspondence and sentenced on their own confession. Their deeds are done in the daylight. Every country opens its archives and invites us to penetrate the mysteries of State. When Hallam wrote his chapter on James II, France was the only Power whose reports were available. Rome followed, and the Hague; and then came the stores of the Italian States, and at last the Prussian and the Austrian papers, and partly those of Spain. Where Hallam and Lingard were dependent on Barillon, their successors consult the diplomacy of ten governments. The topics, indeed, are few on which the resources have been so employed that we can be content with the work done for us and never wish it to be done over again. Part of the lives of Luther and Frederic, a little of the Thirty Years' War, much of the American Revolution and the French Restoration, the early years of Richelieu and Mazarin, and a few volumes of Mr. Gardiner, show here and there like Pacific islands in the ocean. I should not even venture to claim for Ranke, the real originator of the heroic study of records, and the most prompt and fortunate of European pathfinders, that there is one of his seventy volumes that has not been overtaken and in part surpassed. It is through his accelerating influence mainly that our branch of study has become progressive, so that the best master is quickly distanced by the better pupil.[24] The Vatican archives alone, now made accessible to the world, filled 3,239 cases when they were sent to France; and they are not the richest. We are still at the beginning of the documentary

---

[24] I must regard the main duty of a Professor to consist, not simply in communicating information, but in doing this in such a manner, and with such an accompaniment of subsidiary means, that the information he conveys may be the occasion of awakening his pupils to a vigorous and varied exertion of their faculties.—Sir W. Hamilton, *Lectures*, I, 14. No great man really does his work by imposing his maxims on his disciples, he evokes their life. The pupil may become much wiser than his instructor, he may not accept his conclusions, but he will own, "You awakened me to be myself; for that I thank you."—Maurice, *The Conscience*, 7, 8.

age, which will tend to make history independent of historians, to develop learning at the expense of writing, and to accomplish a revolution in other sciences as well.[25]

To men in general I would justify the stress I am laying on modern history, neither by urging its varied wealth, nor the rupture with precedent, nor the perpetuity of change and increase of pace, nor the growing predominance of opinion over belief, and of knowledge over opinion, but by the argument that it is a narrative told of ourselves, the record of a life which is our own, of efforts not yet abandoned to repose, of problems that still entangle the feet and vex the hearts of men. Every part of it is weighty with inestimable lessons that we must learn by experience and at a great price, if we know not how to profit by the example and teaching of those who have gone before us, in a society largely resembling the one we live in.[26] Its study fulfills its purpose even if it only makes us wiser, without producing books, and gives us the gift of historical thinking, which is better than historical learning.[27] It is a most powerful ingredient in the formation of character and the training of talent, and our historical judgments have as much

[25] Ich sehe die Zeit kommen, wo wir die neuere Geschichte nicht mehr auf die Berichte selbst nicht der gleichzeitigen Historiker, ausser in so weit ihnen neue originale Kenntniss beiwohnte, geschweige denn auf die weiter abgeleiteten Bearbeitungen zu gründen haben, sondern aus den Relationen der Augenzeugen und der ächten und unmittelbarsten Urkunden aufbauen werden.—Ranke, *Reformation*, Preface, 1838. Ce qu'on a trouvé et mis en œuvre est considérable en soi: c'est peu de chose au prix de ce qui reste à trouver et à mettre en œuvre.—Aulard, *Études sur la Révolution*, 21.

[26] N'attendez donc pas les leçons de l'expérience; elles coûtent trop cher aux nations.—O. Barrot, *Mémoire*, II, 435. Il y a des leçons dans tous les temps, pour tous le temps; et celles qu'on emprunte à des ennemis ne sont pas les moins précieuses.—Lanfrey, *Napoléon*, v. p. II. Old facts may always be fresh, and may give out a fresh meaning for each generation.—Maurice, *Lectures*, 62. The object is to lead the student to attend to them; to make him take interest in history not as a mere narrative, but as a chain of causes and effects still unwinding itself before our eyes, and full of momentous consequences to himself and his descendants—an unremitting conflict between good and evil powers, of which every act done by anyone of us, insignificant as we are, forms one of the incidents; a conflict in which even the smallest of us cannot escape from taking part, in which whoever does not help the right side is helping the wrong.—Mill, *Inaugural Address*, 59.

[27] I hold that the degree in which Poets dwell in sympathy with the Past, marks exactly the degree of their poetical faculty.—Wadsworth, in C. Fox, *Memoirs*, June 1842. In all political, all social, all human questions whatever, history is the main resource of the inquirer.—Harrison, *Meaning of History*, 15. There are no truths which more readily gain the assent of mankind, or are more firmly retained by them, than those of an historical nature, depending upon the testimony of others.—Priestley, *Letters to French Philosophers*, 9. Improvement consists in bringing our opinions into nearer agreement with facts; and we shall not be likely to do this while we look at facts only through glasses coloured by those very opinions.—Mill, *Inaugural Address*, 25.

to do with hopes of heaven as public or private conduct. Convictions that have been strained through the instances and the comparisons of modern times differ immeasurably in solidity and force from those which every new fact perturbs, and which are often little better than illusions or unsifted prejudice.[28]

The first of human concerns is religion, and it is the salient feature of modern centuries. They are signalised as the scene of Protestant developments. Starting from a time of extreme indifference, ignorance, and decline, they were at once occupied with that conflict which was to rage so long, and of which no man could imagine the infinite consequences. Dogmatic conviction—for I shun to speak of faith in connection with many characters of those days—dogmatic conviction rose to be the centre of universal interest, and remained down to Cromwell the supreme influence and motive of public policy. A time came when the intensity of prolonged conflict, when even the energy of antagonistic assurance abated somewhat, and the controversial spirit began to make room for the scientific; and as the storm subsided, and the area of settled questions emerged, much of the dispute was abandoned to the serene and soothing touch of historians, invested as they are with the prerogative of redeeming the cause of religion from many unjust reproaches, and from the graver evil of reproaches that are just. Ranke used to say that Church interests prevailed in politics

---

[28] He who has learnt to understand the true character and tendency of many succeeding ages is not likely to go very far wrong in estimating his own.—Lecky, *Value of History*, 21. C'est à l'histoire qu'il faut se prendre, c'est le fait que nous devons interroger, quand l'idée vacille et fuit à nos yeux.—Michelet, *Disc. d'Ouverture*, 263. C'est la loi des faits telle qu'elle se manifeste dans leur succession. C'est la règle de conduite donnée par la nature humaine et indiquée par l'histoire. C'est la logique, mais cette logique qui ne fait qu'un avec l'enchaînement des choses. C'est l'enseignement de l'expérience.— Scherer, *Mélanges*, 558. Wer seine Vergangenheit nicht als seine Geschichte hat und weiss, wird und ist karacterlos. Wem ein Ereigniss sein Sonst plötzlich abreisst von seinem Jetzt, wird leicht wurzellos.—Kliefoth, *Rheinwalds Repertorium*, XLIV, 20. La politique est une des meilleures écoles pour l'esprit. Elle force à chercher la raison de toutes choses, et ne permet pas cependant de la chercher hors des faits.—Rémusat, *Le Temps Passé*, I, 31. It is an unsafe partition that divides opinions without principle from unprincipled opinions.—Coleridge, *Lay Sermons*, 373.

> Wer nicht von drei tausend Jahren sich weiss Rechenschaft zu geben,
> Bleib' im Dunkeln unerfahren, mag von Tag zu Tage leben!
>
> Goethe.

What can be rationally required of the student of philosophy is not a preliminary and absolute, but a gradual and progressive, abrogation of prejudices.—Sir W. Hamilton, *Lectures*, IV, 92.

until the Seven Years' War, and marked a phase of society that ended when the hosts of Brandenburg went into action at Leuthen, chaunting their Lutheran hymns.[29] That bold proposition would be disputed even if applied to the present age. After Sir Robert Peel had broken up his party, the leaders who followed him declared that no popery was the only basis on which it could be reconstructed.[30] On the other side may be urged that, in July 1870, at the outbreak of the French war, the only government that insisted on the abolition of the temporal power was Austria; and since then we have witnessed the fall of Castelar, because he attempted to reconcile Spain with Rome.

Soon after 1850 several of the most intelligent men in France, struck by the arrested increase of their own population and by the telling statistics from Further Britain, foretold the coming preponderance of the English race. They did not foretell, what none could then foresee, the still more sudden growth of Prussia, or that the three most important countries of the globe would, by the end of the century, be those that chiefly belonged to the conquests of the Reformation. So that in Religion, as in so many things, the product of these centuries has favoured the new elements; and the centre of gravity, moving from the Mediterranean nations to the Oceanic, from the Latin to the Teuton, has also passed from the Catholic to the Protestant.[31]

Out of these controversies proceeded political as well as historical science. It was in the Puritan phase, before the restoration of the Stuarts, that theology, blending with politics, effected a fundamental change. The essentially English reformation of the seventeenth century was less a struggle between churches than between sects, often subdivided by questions of discipline and self-regulation rather than

[29] Die Schlacht bei Leuthen ist wohl die letzte, in welcher diese religiösen Gegensätze entscheidend eingewirkt haben.—Ranke, *Allgemeine Deutsche Biographie*, VII, 70.

[30] The only real cry in the country is the proper and just old No Popery cry.—*Major Beresford*, July 1847. Unfortunately the strongest bond of union amongst them is an apprehension of Popery.—*Stanley*, 12th September 1847. The great Protestionist party having degenerated into a No Popery, No Jew Party, I am still more unfit now than I was in 1846 to lead it.—*G. Bentinck*, 26th December 1847; *Croker's Memoirs*, III, 116, 132, 157.

[31] In the case of Protestantism, this constitutional instability is now a simple matter of fact, which has become too plain to be denied. The system is not fixed, but in motion; and the motion is for the time in the direction of complete self-dissolution. We take it for a transitory scheme, whose breaking up is to make room in due time for another and far more perfect state of the Church. The new order in which Protestantism is to become thus complete cannot be reached without the co-operation and help of Romanism.—Nevin, *Mercersburg Review*, IV, 48.

by dogma. The sectaries cherished no purpose or prospect of prevailing over the nations; and they were concerned with the individual more than with the congregation, with conventicles, not with State churches. Their view was narrowed, but their sight was sharpened. It appeared to them that governments and institutions are made to pass away, like things of earth, whilst souls are immortal; that there is no more proportion between liberty and power than between eternity and time; that, therefore, the sphere of enforced command ought to be restricted within fixed limits, and that which had been done by authority, and outward discipline, and organised violence, should be attempted by division of power, and committed to the intellect and the conscience of free men.[32] Thus was exchanged the dominion of will over will for the dominion of reason over reason. The true apostles of toleration are not those who sought protection for their own beliefs, or who had none to protect; but men to whom, irrespective of their cause, it was a political, a moral, and a theological dogma, a question of conscience involving both religion and policy.[33] Such a man was Socinus; and others arose in the smaller sects—the Independent founder of the colony of Rhode Island, and the Quaker patriarch of Pennsylvania. Much of the energy and zeal which had laboured for authority of doctrine was employed for liberty of prophesying. The air was filled with the enthusiasm of a new cry; but the cause was still the same. It

[32] Diese Heiligen waren es, die aus dem unmittelbaren Glaubensleben und den Grundgedanken der christlichen Freiheit zuerst die Idee allgemeiner Menschenrechte abgeleitet und rein von Selbstsucht vertheidigt haben.—Weingarten, *Revolutionskirchen*, 447. Wie selbst die Idee allgemeiner Menschenrechte, die in dem gemeinsamen Character der Ebenbildlichkeit Gottes gegründet sind, erst durch das Christenthum zum Bewusstsein gebracht werden, während jeder andere Eifer für politische Freiheit als ein mehr oder weniger selbstsüchtiger und beschränkter sich erwiesen hat.—Neander, *Pref. to Uhden's Wilberforce*, p. v. The rights of individuals and the justice due to them are as dear and precious as those of states; indeed the latter are founded on the former, and the great end and object of them must be to secure and support the rights of individuals, or else vain is government.—Cushing, in Conway, *Life of Paine*, I, 217. As it is owned the whole scheme of Scripture is not yet understood; so, if it ever comes to be understood, before the restitution of all things, and without miraculous interpositions, it must be in the same way as natural knowledge is come at—by the continuance and progress of learning and liberty.—Butler, *Analogy*, II, 3.

[33] Comme les lois elles-mêmes sont faillibles, et qu'il peut y avoir une autre justice que la justice écrite, les sociétés modernes ont voulu garantir les droits de la conscience à la poursuite d'une justice meilleure que celle qui existe; et là est le fondement de ce qu'on appelle liberté de conscience, liberté d'écrire, liberté de pensée.—Janet, *Philosophie Contemporaine*, 308. Si la force matérielle a toujours fini par céder à l'opinion, combien plus ne serait-elle pas contrainte de céder à la conscience? Car la conscience, c'est l'opinion renforcée par le sentiment de l'obligation.—Vinet, *Liberté Religieuse*, 3.

became a boast that religion was the mother of freedom, that freedom was the lawful offspring of religion; and this transmutation, this subversion of established forms of political life by the development of religious thought, brings us to the heart of my subject, to the significant and central feature of the historical cycles before us. Beginning with the strongest religious movement and the most refined despotism ever known, it has led to the superiority of politics over divinity in the life of nations, and terminates in the equal claim of every man to be unhindered by man in the fulfillment of duty to God[34]—a doctrine laden with storm and havoc, which is the secret essence of the Rights of Man, and indestructible soul of Revolution.

When we consider what the adverse forces were, their sustained resistance, their frequent recovery, the critical moments when the struggle seemed for ever desperate, in 1685, in 1772, in 1808, it is no hyperbole to say that the progress of the world towards self-government would have been arrested but for the strength afforded by the religious motive in the seventeenth century. And this constancy of progress, of progress in the direction of organised and assured freedom, is the characteristic fact of modern history, and its tribute to the theory of Providence.[35] Many persons, I am well assured, would detect that this

---

[34] Après la volonté d'un homme, la raison d'état; après la raison d'état, la religion; après la religion, la liberté. Voilà toute la philosophie de l'histoire.—Flottes, *La Souveraineté du Peuple*, 1851, 192. La répartition plus égale des biens et des droits dans ce monde est le plus grand objet que doivent se proposer ceux qui mènent les affaires humaines. Je veux seulement que l'égalité en politique consiste à être également libre.—Tocqueville, 10th September 1856. *Mme. Swetchine*, I, 455. On peut concevoir une législation très simple, lorsqu'on voudra en écarter tout ce qui est arbitraire, ne consulter que les deux premières lois de la liberté et de la propriété, et ne point admettre de lois positives qui ne tirent leur raison de ces deux lois souveraines de la justice essentielle et absolue.—Letrosne, *Vues sur la Justice Criminelle*, 16. Summa enim libertas est, ad optimum recta ratione cogi.—Nemo optat sibi hanc libertatem, volendi quae velit, sed potius volendi optima.—Leibniz, *De Facto*. Trendelenburg, *Beiträge zur Philosophie*, II, 190.

[35] All the world is, by the very law of its creation, in eternal progress; and the cause of all the evils of the world may be traced to that natural, but most deadly error of human indolence and corruption, that our business is to preserve and not to improve.—Arnold, *Life*, I, 259. In whatever state of knowledge we may conceive man to be placed, his progress towards a yet higher state need never fear a check, but must continue till the last existence of society.—Herschel, *Prel. Dis.*, 360. It is in the development of thought as in every other development; the present suffers from the past, and the future struggles hard in escaping from the present.—Max Müller, *Science of Thought*, 617. Most of the great positive evils of the world are in themselves removable, and will, if human affairs continue to improve, be in the end reduced within narrow limits. Poverty in any of society combined with the good sense and providence of individuals. All the grand sources, in short, of human suffering are in a great degree, many of them almost entirely,

conquerable by human care and effort.—J. S. Mill, *Utilitarianism*, 21, 22. The ultimate standard of worth is personal worth, and the only progress that is worth striving after, the only acquisition that is truly good and enduring, is the growth of the soul.—Bixby, *Crisis of Morals*, 210. La science, et l'industrie qu'elle produit, ont, parmi tous les autres enfants du génie de l'homme, ce privilège particulier, que leur vol non-seulement ne peut pas s'interrompre, mais qu'il s'accélère sans cesse.—Cuvier, *Discours sur la Marche des Sciences*, 24 Avril, 1816. Aucune idée parmi celles qui se réfèrent à l'ordre des faits naturels ne tient de plus près à la famille des idées religieuses que l'idée du progrès, et n'est plus propre à devenir le principe d'une sorte de foi religieuse pour ceux qui n'en ont pas d'autres. Elle a, comme la foi religieuse, la vertu de relever les âmes et les caractères.—Cournot, *Marche des Idées*, II, 425. Dans le spectacle de l'humanité errante, souffrante et travaillant toujours à mieux voir, à mieux penser, à mieux agir, à diminuer l'infirmité de l'être humain, à apaiser l'inquiétude de son cœur, la science découvre une direction et un progrès.—A. Sorel, *Discours de Réception*, 14. Le jeune homme qui commence son éducation quinze ans après son père, à une époque où celui-ci, engagé dans une profession spéciale et active, ne peut que suivre les anciens principes, acquiert une supériorité théorique dont on doit tenir compte dans la hiérarchie sociale. Le plus souvent le père n'est-il pas pénétré de l'esprit de routine, tandis que le fils représente et défend la science progressive? En diminuant l'écart qui existait entre l'influence des jeunes générations et celle de la vieillesse ou de l'âge mûr, les peuples modernes n'auraient donc fait que reproduire dans leur ordre social un changement de rapports qui s'était déjà accompli dans la nature intime des choses.—Boutmy, *Revue Nationale*, XXI, 393. Il y a dans l'homme individuel des principes de progrès viager; il y a, en toute société, des causes constantes qui transforment ce progrès viager en progrès héréditaire. Une société quelconque tend à progresser tant que les circonstances ne touchent pas aux causes de progrès que nous avons reconnues, l'imitation des devanciers par les successeurs, des étrangers par les indigènes.—Lacombe, *L'Histoire comme Science*, 292. Veram creatae mentis beatitudinem consistere in non impedito progressu ad bona majora.—Leibniz to Wolf, 21st February 1705. In cumulum etiam pulchritudinis perfectionisque universalis operum divinorum progressus quidam perpetuus liberrimusque totius universi est agnoscendus, ita ut ad majorem semper cultum procedat.— Leibniz ed. Erdmann, 150*a*. Der Creaturen und auch unsere Vollkommenheit bestehen in einem ungehinderten starken Forttrieb zu neuen und neuen Vollkommenheiten.— Leibniz, *Deutsche Schriften*, II, 36. Hegel, welcher annahm, der Fortschritt der Neuzeit gegen das Mittelalter sei dieser, dass die Principien der Tugend und des Christenthums, welche im Mittelalter sich allein im Privatleben und der Kirche zur Geltung gebracht hätten, nun auch anfingen, das politische Leben zu durchdringen.—Fortlage, *Allg. Monatsschrift*, 1853, 777. Wir Slawen wissen, dass die Geister einzelner Menschen und ganzer Völker sich nur durch die Stufe ihrer Entwicklung unterscheiden.—Mickiewicz, *Slawische Literatur*, II, 436. Le progrès ne disparait jamais, mais il se déplace souvent. Il va des gouvernants aux gouvernés. La tendance des révolutions est de le ramener toujours parmi les gouvernants. Lorsqu'il est à la tête des sociétés, il marche hardiment, car il conduit. Lorsqu'il est dans la masse, il marche à pas lents, car il lutte.—Napoléon III, *Des Idées Napoléoniennes*. La loi du progrès avait jadis l'inexorable rigueur du destin; elle prend maintenant de jour en jour la douce puissance de la Providence. C'est l'erreur, c'est l'iniquité, c'est le vice, que la civilisation tend à emporter dans sa marche irrésistible; mais la vie des individus et des peuples est devenue pour elle une chose sacrée. Elle transforme plutôt qu'elle ne détruit les choses qui s'opposent a son développement; elle procède par absorption graduelle plutôt que par brusque exécution; elle aime à conquérir par l'influence des idées plutôt que par la force des armes, un peuple, une classe, une institution qui résiste au progrès.—Vacherot, *Essais de Philosophie Critique*, 443. Peu à peu l'homme intellectuel finit par effacer l'homme physique.—Quetelet, *De l'Homme*, II,

is a very old story, and a trivial commonplace, and would challenge proof that the world is making progress in aught but intellect, that it is gaining in freedom, or that increase in freedom is either a progress or a gain. Ranke, who was my own master, rejected the view that I have stated;[36] Comte, the master of better men, believed that we drag a lengthening chain under the gathered weight of the dead hand;[37] and many of our recent classics—Carlyle, Newman, Froude—were

---

285. In dem Fortschritt der ethischen Anschauungen liegt daher der Kern des geschichtlichen Fortschritts überhaupt.—Schäfer, *Arbeitsgebiet der Geschichte*, 24. Si l'homme a plus de devoirs à mesure qu'il avance en âge, ce qui est mélancolique, mais ce qui est vrai, de même aussi l'humanité est tenue d'avoir une morale plus sévère à mesure qu'elle prend plus de siècles.—Faguet, *Revue des Deux Mondes*, 1894, III, 871. Si donc il y a une loi du progrès, elle se confond avec la loi morale, et la condition fondamentale du progrès, c'est la pratique de cette loi.—Carrau, *Ib.* 1875, V, 585. L'idée du progrès, du développement, me parait être l'idée fondamentale contenue sous le mot de civilisation.—Guizot, *Cours d'Histoire*, 1828, 15. Le progrès social est continu. Il a ses périodes de fièvre ou d'atonie, de surexcitation ou de léthargie; il a ses soubresauts et ses haltes, mais il avance toujours.—De Decker, *La Providence*, 174. Ce n'est pas au bonheur seul, c'est au perfectionnement que notre destin nous appelle; et la liberté politique est le plus puissant, le plus énergique moyen de perfectionnement que le ciel nous ait donné.—B. Constant, *Cours de Politique*, II, 559. To explode error, on whichever side it lies, is certainly to secure progress.—Martineau, *Essays*, I, 114. Die sämmtlichen Freiheitsrechte, welche der heutigen Menschheit so theuer sind, sind im Grunde nur Anwendungen des Rechts der Entwickelung.—Bluntschli, *Kleine Schriften*, I, 51. Geistiges Leben ist auf Freiheit beruhende Entwicklung, mit Freiheit vollzogene That und geschichtlicher Fortschritt.—*Münchner Gel. Anzeigen*, 1849, II, 83. Wie das Denken erst nach und nach reift, so wird auch der freie Wille nicht fertig geboren, sondern in der Entwickelung erworben.—Trendelenburg, *Logische Untersuchungen*, II, 94. Das Liberum Arbitrium im vollen Sinne (die vollständig aktuelle Macht der Selbstbestimmung) lässt sich seinem Begriff zufolge schlechterdings nicht unmittelbar geben; es kann nur erworben werden durch das Subjekt selbst, in sich moralisch hervorgebracht werden kraft seiner eigenen Entwickelung.—Rothe, *Ethik*, I, 360. So gewaltig sei der Andrang der Erfindungen und Entdeckungen, dass "Entwicklungsperioden, die in früheren Zeiten erst in Jahrhunderten durchlaufen wurden die im Beginn unserer Zeitperiode noch der Jahrzehnte bedurften, sich heute in Jahren vollenden, häufig schon in voller Ausbildung ins Dasein treten."—Philippovich, *Fortschritt und Kulturentwicklung*, 1892, I, quoting Siemens, 1886. Wir erkennen, dass dem Menschen die schwere körperliche Arbeit, von der er in seinem Kampfe um's Dasein stets schwer niedergedrückt war und grossenteils noch ist, mehr und mehr durch die wachsende Benutzung der Naturkräfte zur mechanischen Arbeitsleistung abgenommen wird, dass die ihm zufallende Arbeit immer mehr eine intellektuelle wird.—Siemens, 1886, *Ib.* 6.

[36] Once, however, he wrote:—Darin könnte man den idealen Kern der Geschichte des menschlichen Geschlechtes überhaupt sehen, dass in den Kämpfen, die sich in den gegenseitigen Interessen der Staaten und Völker vollziehen, doch immer höhere Potenzen emporkommen, die das Allgemeine demgemäss umgestalten und ihm wieder einen anderen Charakter verleihen.—Ranke, *Weltgeschichte*, III, I, 6.

[37] Toujours et partout, les hommes furent de plus en plus dominés par l'ensemble de leurs prédécesseurs, dont ils purent seulement modifier l'empire nécessaire.—Comte, *Politique Positive*, III, 621.

persuaded that there is no progress justifying the ways of God to man, and that the mere consolidation of liberty is like the motion of creatures whose advance is in the direction of their tails. They deem that anxious precaution against bad government is an obstruction to good, and degrades morality and mind by placing the capable at the mercy of the incapable, dethroning enlightened virtue for the benefit of the average man. They hold that great and salutary things are done for mankind by power concentrated, not by power balanced and cancelled and dispersed, and that the whig theory, sprung from decomposing sects, the theory that authority is legitimate only by virtue of its checks, and that the sovereign is dependent on the subject, is rebellion against the divine will manifested all down the stream of time.

I state the objection not that we may plunge into the crucial controversy of a science that is not identical with ours, but in order to make my drift clear by the defining aid of express contradiction. No political dogma is as serviceable to my purpose here as the historian's maxim to do the best he can for the other side, and to avoid pertinacity or emphasis on his own. Like the economic precept *laissez faire*,[38] which the eighteenth century derived from Colbert, it has been an important, if not a final step in the making of method. The strongest and most impressive personalities, it is true, like Macaulay, Thiers, and the two greatest of living writers, Mommsen and Treitschke, project their own broad shadow upon their pages. This is a practice proper to great men, and a great man may be worth several immaculate historians. Otherwise there is virtue in the saying that a historian is seen at his best when he does not appear.[39] Better for us is the example of the Bishop of Oxford, who never lets us know what he thinks of anything but the matter before him; and of his illustrious French rival, Fustel de Coulanges, who said to an excited audience: "Do not imagine you are listening to me; it is history itself that speaks."[40] We can found no

---

[38] La liberté est l'âme du commerce.—Il faut laisser faire les hommes qui s'appliquent sans peine à ce qui convient le mieux; c'est ce qui apporte le plus d'avantage.—Colbert, in *Comptes Rendus de l'Institut*, XXXIX, 93.

[39] Il n'y a que les choses humaines exposées dans leur vérité, c'est-à-dire avec leur grandeur, leur variété, leur inépuisable fécondité, qui aient le droit de retenir le lecteur et qui le retiennent en effet. Si l'écrivain paraît une fois, il ennuie ou fait sourire de pitié les lecteurs sérieux.—Thiers to Ste. Beuve, *Lundis*, III, 195. Comme l'a dit Taine, la disparition du style, c'est la perfection du style.—Faguet, *Revue Politique*, LIII, 67.

[40] Ne m'applaudissez pas; ce n'est pas moi qui vous parle; c'est l'histoire qui parle par ma bouche.—*Revue Historique*, XLI, 278.

philosophy on the observation of four hundred years, excluding three thousand. It would be an imperfect and a fallacious induction. But I hope that even this narrow and disedifying section of history will aid you to see that the action of Christ who is risen on mankind whom he redeemed fails not, but increases;[41] that the wisdom of divine rule appears not in the perfection but in the improvement of the world[42] and that achieved liberty is the one ethical result that rests on the converging and combined conditions of advancing civilisation.[43] Then

[41] Das Evangelium trat als Geschichte in die Welt, nicht als Dogma—wurde als Geschichte in der christlichen Kirche deponirt.—Rothe, *Kirchengeschichte*, II, p. x. Das Christenthum ist nicht der Herr Christus, sondern dieser macht es. Es ist sein Werk, und zwar ein Werk, das er stets unter der Arbeit hat. Er selbst, Christus der Herr, bleibt, der er ist in alle Zukunft, dagegen liegt es ausdrücklich im Begriffe seines Werks, des Christenthums, dass es nicht so bleibt, wie es anhebt.—Rothe, *Allgemeine kirchliche Zeitschrift*, 1864, 299. Diess Werk, weil es dem Wesen der Geschichte zufolge eine Entwickelung ist, muss über Stufen hinweggehen, die einander ablösen, und von denen jede folgende neue immer nur unter der Zertrümmerung der ihr vorangehenden Platz greifen kann.—Rothe, *Ib.* 19th April, 1865. Je grösser ein geschichtliches Princip ist, desto langsamer und über mehr Stufen hinweg entfaltet es seinen Gehalt; desto langlebiger ist es aber ebendeshalb auch in diesen seinen unaufhörlichen Abwandelungen.—Rothe, *Stille Stunden*, 301. Der christliche Glaube geht nicht von der Anerkennung abstracter Lehrwahrheiten aus, sondern von der Anerkennung einer Reihe von Thatsachen, die in der Erscheinung Jesu ihren Mittelpunkt haben.—Nitzsch, *Dogmengeschichte*, I, 17. Der Gedankengang der evangelischen Erzählung gibt darum auch eine vollständige Darstellung der christlichen Lehre in ihren wesentlichen Grundzügen; aber er gibt sie im allseitigen lebendigen Zusammenhange mit der Geschichte der christlichen Offenbarung, und nicht in einer theoretisch zusammenhängenden Folgenreihe von ethischen und dogmatischen Lehrsätzen.—Deutinger, *Reich Gottes*, I, p. v.

[42] L'Univers ne doit pas être considéré seulement dans ce qu'il est; pour le bien connoître, il faut le voir aussi dans ce qu'il doit estre. C'est cet avenir surtout qui a été le grand objet de Dieu dans la création, et c'est pour cet avenir seul que le présent existe.—D'Houteville, *Essai sur la Providence*, 273. La Providence emploie les siècles à élever toujours un plus grand nombre de familles et d'individus à ces biens de la liberté et de l'égalité légitimes que, dans l'enfance des sociétés, la force avait rendus le privilège de quelques-uns.—Guizot, *Gouvernement de la France*, 1820, 9. La marche de la Providence n'est pas assujettie à d'étroites limites; elle ne s'inquiète pas de tirer aujourd'hui la conséquence du principe qu'elle a posé hier; elle la tirera dans des siècles, quand l'heure sera venue; et pour raisonner lentement selon nous, sa logique n'est pas moins sûre.—Guizot, *Histoire de la Civilisation*, 20. Der Keim fortschreitender Entwicklung ist, auch auf göttliches Geheisse, der Menschheit eingepflanzt. Die Weltgeschichte ist der blosse Ausdruck einer vorbestimmten Entwicklung.—A. Humboldt, 2nd January, 1842, *Im Neuen Reich*, 1872, I, 197. Das historisch grosse ist religiös gross; es ist die Gottheit selbst, die sich offenbart.—Raumer, April, 1807, *Erinnerungen*, I, 85.

[43] Je suis arrivé à l'âge où je suis, à travers bien des événements différents, mais avec une seule cause, celle de la liberté régulière.—Tocqueville, 1st May 1852, *Œuvres Inédites*, II, 185. Me trouvant dans un pays où la religion et le libéralisme sont d'accord, j'avais respiré. J'exprimais ce sentiment, il y a plus de vingt ans, dans l'avant-propos de la

Démocratie. Je l'éprouve aujourd'hui aussi vivement que si j'étais encore jeune, et je ne sais s'il y a une seule pensée qui ait été plus constamment présente à mon esprit.—5th August 1857, *Œuvres*, VI, 395. Il n'y a que la liberté (j'entends la modérée et la régulière) et la religion, qui, par un effort combiné, puissent soulever les hommes au-dessus du bourbier où l'égalité démocratique les plonge naturellement.—1st December 1852, *Œuvres*, VII, 295. L'un de mes rêves, le principal en entrant dans la vie politique, était de travailler à concilier l'esprit libéral et l'esprit de religion, la société nouvelle et l'église.—15th November 1843, *Œuvres Inédites*, II, 121. La véritable grandeur de l'homme n'est que dans l'accord du sentiment libéral et du sentiment religieux.—17 September 1853, *Œuvres Inédites*, II, 228. Qui cherche dans la liberté autre chose qu'elle-même est fait pour servir.—*Ancien Régime*, 248. Je regarde, ainsi que je l'ai toujours fait, la liberté comme le premier des biens; je vois toujours en elle l'une des sources les plus fécondes des vertus mâles et des actions grandes. Il n'y a pas de tranquillité ni de bien-être qui puisse me tenir lieu d'elle.—7th January 1856, *Mme. Swetchine*, I, 452. La liberté a un faux air d'aristocratie; en donnant pleine carrière aux facultés humaines, en encourageant le travail et l'économie, elle fait ressortir les supériorités naturelles ou acquises.— Laboulaye, *L'Etat et ses Limites*, 154. Dire que la liberté n'est point par elle-même, qu'elle dépend d'une situation, d'une opportunité, c'est lui assigner une valeur négative. La liberté n'est pas dès qu'on la subordonne. Elle n'est pas un principe purement négatif, un simple élément de contrôle et de critique. Elle est le principe actif, créateur, organisateur par excellence. Elle est le moteur et la règle, la source de toute vie, et le principe de l'ordre. Elle est, en un mot, le nom que prend la conscience souveraine, lorsque, se posant en face du monde social et politique, elle émerge du moi pour modeler les sociétés sur les données de la raison.—Brisson, *Revue Nationale*, XXIII, 214. Le droit, dans l'histoire, est le développement progressif de la liberté, sous la loi de la raison.— Lerminier, *Philosophie du Droit*, I, 211. En prouvant par les leçons de l'histoire que la liberté fait vivre les peuples et que le despotisme les tue, en montrant que l'expiation suit la faute et que la fortune finit d'ordinaire par se ranger du côté de la vertu, Montesquieu n'est ni moins moral ni moins religieux que Bossuet.—Laboulaye, *Œuvres de Montesquieu*, II, 109. Je ne comprendrais pas qu'une nation ne plaçât pas les libertés politiques au premier rang, parce que c'est des libertés politiques que doivent découler toutes les autres.—Thiers, *Discours*, X, 8, 28th March 1865. Nous sommes arrivés à une époque où la liberté est le but sérieux de tous, où le reste n'est plus qu'une question de moyens.—J. Lebeau, *Observations sur le Pouvoir Royal:* Liège, 1830, p. 10. Le libéralisme, ayant la prétention de se fonder uniquement sur les principes de la raison, croit d'ordinaire n'avoir pas besoin de tradition. Là est son erreur. L'erreur de l'école libérale est d'avoir trop cru qu'il est facile de créer la liberté par la réflexion, et de n'avoir pas vu qu'un établissement n'est solide que quand il a des racines historiques.—Renan, 1858, *Nouvelle Revue*, LXXIX, 596. Le respect des individus et des droits existants est autant au-dessus du bonheur de tous, qu'un intérêt moral surpasse un intérêt purement temporel.—Renan, 1858, *Ib.* LXXIX, 597. Die Rechte gelten nichts, wo es sich handelt um das Recht, und das Recht der Freiheit kann nie verjähren, weil es die Quelle alles Rechtes selbst ist.—C. Frantz, *Ueber die Freiheit*, 110. Wir erfahren hienieden nie die ganze Wahrheit: wir geniessen nie die ganze Freiheit.—Reuss, *Reden*, 56. Le gouvernement constitutionnel, comme tout gouvernement libre, présente et doit présenter un état de lutte permanent. La liberté est la perpétuité de la lutte.—De Serre. Broglie, *Nouvelles Etudes*, 243. The experiment of free government is not one which can be tried once for all. Every generation must try it for itself. As each new generation starts up to the responsibilities of manhood, there is, as it were, a new launch of Liberty, and its voyage of experiment begins afresh.—Winthrop, *Addresses*, 163. L'histoire perd son véritable caractère du moment que la liberté en a disparu; elle devient une sorte de physique sociale. C'est l'élément personnel de l'histoire qui en fait la réalité.—Vacherot, *Revue des*

you will understand what a famous philosopher said, that history is the true demonstration of religion.[44]

But what do people mean who proclaim that liberty is the palm, and the prize, and the crown, seeing that it is an idea of which there are two hundred definitions, and that this wealth of interpretation has caused more bloodshed than anything, except theology? Is it Democracy

---

Deux Mondes, 1869, IV, 215. Demander la liberté pour soi et la refuser aux autres, c'est la définition du despotisme.—Laboulaye, 4th December 1874. Les causes justes profitent de tout, des bonnes intentions comme des mauvaises, des calculs personnels comme des dévouements courageux, de la démence, enfin, comme de la raison.—B. Constant, *Les Cent Jours,* II, 29. Sie ist die Kunst, das Gute der schon weit gediehenen Civilisation zu sichern.—Baltisch, *Politische Freiheit,* 9. In einem Volke, welches sich zur bürgerlichen Gesellschaft, überhaupt zum Bewusstseyn der Unendlichkeit des Freien—entwickelt hat, ist nur die constitutionelle Monarchie möglich.—Hegel's *Philosophie des Rechts,* § 137, *Hegel und Preussen,* 1841, 31. Freiheit ist das höchste Gut. Alles andere ist nur das Mittel dazu: gut falls es ein Mittel dazu ist, übel falls es dieselbe hemmt.—Fichte, *Werke,* IV, 403. You are not to inquire how your trade may be increased, nor how you are to become a great and powerful people, but how your liberties can be secured. For liberty ought to be the direct end of your government.—Patrick Henry, 1788; Wirt, *Life of Henry,* 272.

[44] Historiae ipsius praeter delectationem utilitas nulla est, quam ut religionis Christianae veritas demonstretur, quod aliter quam per historiam fieri non potest.—Leibniz, *Opera,* ed. Dutens, VI, 297. The study of Modern History is, next to Theology itself, and only next in so far as Theology rests on a divine revelation, the most thoroughly religious training that the mind can receive. It is no paradox to say that Modern History, including Medieval History in the term, is co-extensive in its field of view, in its habits of criticism, in the persons of its most famous students, with Ecclesiastical History.—Stubbs, *Lectures,* 9. Je regarde donc l'étude de l'histoire comme l'étude de la providence.—L'histoire est vraiment une seconde philosophie.—Si Dieu ne parle pas toujours, il agit toujours en Dieu.—D'Aguesseau, *Œuvres,* XV, 34, 31, 35. Für diejenigen, welche das Wesen der menschlichen Freiheit erkannt haben, bildet die denkende Betrachtung der Weltgeschichte, besonders des christlichen Weltalters, die höchste, und umfassendste Theodicee.—Vatke, *Die Menschliche Freiheit,* 1841, 516. La théologie, que l'on regarde volontiers comme la plus étroite et la plus stérile des sciences, en est, au contraire, la plus étendue et la plus féconde. Elle confine à toutes les études et touche à toutes les questions. Elle renferme tous les éléments d'une instruction libérale.—Scherer, *Mélanges,* 522. The belief that the course of events and the agency of man are subject to the laws of a divine order, which it is alike impossible for any one either fully to comprehend or effectually to resist—this belief is the ground of all our hope for the future destinies of mankind.—Thirlwall, *Remains,* III, 282. A true religion must consist of ideas and facts both; not of ideas alone without facts, for then it would be mere philosophy; nor of facts alone without ideas, of which those facts are the symbols, or out of which they are grounded; for then it would be mere history.—Coleridge, *Table Talk,* 144. It certainly appears strange that the men most conversant with the order of the visible universe should soonest suspect it empty of directing mind; and, on the other hand, that humanistic, moral and historical studies—which first open the terrible problems of suffering and grief, and contain all the reputed provocatives of denial and despair—should confirm, and enlarge rather than disturb, the prepossessions of natural piety.—Martineau, *Essays,* I, 122. Die Religion hat nur dann eine Bedeutung für den Menschen,

as in France, or Federalism as in America, or the national independence
which bounds the Italian view, or the reign of the fittest, which is the
ideal of Germans?[45] I know not whether it will ever fall within my
sphere of duty to trace the slow progress of that idea through the
chequered scenes of our history, and to describe how subtle speculations
touching the nature of conscience promoted a nobler and more spiritual
conception of the liberty that protects it,[46] until the guardian of rights
developed into the guardian of duties which are the cause of rights,[47]
and that which had been prized as the material safeguard for treasures
of earth became sacred as security for things that are divine. All that
we require is a work-day key to history, and our present need can be
supplied without pausing to satisfy philosophers. Without inquiring
how far Sarasa or Butler, Kant or Vinet, is right as to the infallible
voice of God in man, we may easily agree in this, that where absolutism
reigned, by irresistible arms, concentrated possessions, auxiliary churches,
and inhuman laws, it reigns no more; that commerce having risen
against land, labour against wealth, the State against the forces
dominant in society,[48] the division of power against the State, the

wenn er in der Geschichte einen Punkt findet, dem er sich völlig unbedingt hingeben
kann.—Steffens, *Christliche Religionsphilosophie,* 440, 1839. Wir erkennen darin nur eine
Thätigkeit des zu seinem ächten and wahren Leben, zu seinem verlornen, objectiven
Selbstverständnisse sich zurücksehnenden christlichen Geistes unserer Zeit, einen Ausdruck für das Bedürfniss desselben, sich aus den unwahren und unächten Verkleidungen,
womit ihn der moderne, subjective Geschmack der letzten Entwickelungsphase des
theologischen Bewusstseyns umhüllt hat, zu seiner historischen allein wahren und
ursprünglichen Gestalt wiederzugebären, zu derjenigen Bedeutung zurückzukehren, die
ihm in dem Bewusstseyn der Geschichte allein zukommt und deren Verständniss in
dem wogenden luxuriösen Leben der modernen Theologie längst untergegangen ist.—
Georgii, *Zeitschrift für Hist. Theologie,* IX, 5, 1839.

[45] Liberty, in fact, means just so far as it is realised, the right man in the right place.—
Seeley, *Lectures and Essays,* 109.

[46] In diesem Sinne ist Freiheit und sich entwickelnde moralische Vernunft und
Gewissen gleichbedeutend. In diesem Sinne ist der Mensch frei, sobald sich das Gewissen
in ihm entwickelt.—Scheidler, *Ersch und Gruber,* XLIX, 20. Aus der unendlichen und
ewigen Geltung der menschlichen Persönlichkeit vor Gott, aus der Vorstellung von der
in Gott freien Persönlichkeit, folgt auch der Anspruch auf das Recht derselben in der
weltlichen Sphäre, auf bürgerliche und politische Freiheit, auf Gewissen und Religions-
freiheit, auf freie wissenschaftliche Forschung u.s.w., und namentlich die Forderung,
dass niemand lediglich zum Mittel für andere diene.—Martensen, *Christliche Ethik,* I,
50.

[47] Es giebt angeborne Menschenrechte, weil es angeborne Menschenpflichten giebt.—
Wolff, *Naturrecht;* Loeper, *Einleitung zu Faust,* LVII.

[48] La constitution de l'état reste jusqu'à un certain point à notre discrétion. La
constitution de la société ne dépend pas de nous; elle est donnée par la force des choses,

thought of individuals against the practice of ages, neither authorities, nor minorities, nor majorities can command implicit obedience; and, where there has been long and arduous experience, a rampart of tried conviction and accumulated knowledge,[49] where there is a fair level of general morality, education, courage, and self-restraint, there, if there only, a society may be found that exhibits the condition of life towards which, by elimination of failures, the world has been moving through the allotted space.[50] You will know it by outward signs: Representation, the extinction of slavery, the reign of opinion, and the like; better still by less apparent evidences: the security of the weaker groups[51] and the liberty of conscience, which, effectually secured, secures the rest.

Here we reach a point at which my argument threatens to abut on a contradiction. If the supreme conquests of society are won more often by violence than by lenient arts, if the trend and drift of things is towards convulsions and catastrophes,[52] if the world owes religious liberty to the Dutch Revolution, constitutional government to the English, federal republicanism to the American, political equality to

et si l'on veut élever le langage, elle est l'œuvre de la Providence.—Rémusat, *Revue des Deux Mondes*, 1861, V, 795.

[49] Die Freiheit ist bekanntlich kein Geschenk der Götter, sondern ein Gut, das jedes Volk sich selbst verdankt und das nur bei dem erforderlichen Mass moralischer Kraft und Würdigkeit gedeiht.—Ihering, *Geist des Römischen Rechts*, II, 290. Liberty, in the very nature of it, absolutely requires, and even supposes, that people be able to govern themselves in those respects in which they are free; otherwise their wickedness will be in proportion to their liberty, and this greatest of blessings will become a curse.—Butler, *Sermons*, 331. In each degree and each variety of public development there are corresponding institutions, best answering the public needs; and what is meat to one is poison to another. Freedom is for those who are fit for it.—Parkman, *Canada*, 396. Die Freiheit ist die Wurzel einer neuen Schöpfung.—Sederholm, *Die ewigen Thatsachen*, 86.

[50] La liberté politique, qui n'est qu'une complexité plus grande, de plus en plus grande, dans le gouvernement d'un peuple, à mesure que le peuple lui-même contient un plus grand nombre de forces diverses ayant droit et de vivre et de participer à la chose publique, est un fait de civilisation qui s'impose lentement à une société organisée, mais qui n'apparaît point comme un principe à une société qui s'organise.—Faguet, *Revue des Deux Mondes*, 1889, II, 942.

[51] Il y a bien un droit du plus sage, mais non pas un droit du plus fort.—La justice est le droit du plus faible.—Joubert, *Pensées*, I, 355, 358.

[52] Nicht durch ein pflanzenähnliches Wachsthum, nicht aus den dunklen Gründen der Volksempfindung, sondern durch den männlichen Willen, durch die Ueberzeugung, durch die That, durch den Kampf entsteht, behauptet, entwickelt sich das Recht. Sein historisches Werden ist ein bewusstes, im hellen Mittagslicht der Erkenntniss und der Gesetzgebung.—*Rundschau*, November, 1893, 13. Nicht das Normale, Zahme, sondern das Abnorme, Wilde, bildet überall die Grundlage und den Anfang einer neuen Ordnung.—Lasaulx, *Philosophie der Geschichte*, 143.

the French and its successors,[53] what is to become of us, docile and attentive students of the absorbing past? The triumph of the Revolutionist annuls the historian.[54] By its authentic exponents, Jefferson and Sieyès, the Revolution of the last century repudiates history. Their followers renounced acquaintance with it, and were ready to destroy its records and to abolish its inoffensive professors. But the unexpected truth, stranger than fiction, is that this was not the ruin but the renovation of history. Directly and indirectly, by process of development and by process of reaction, an impulse was given which made it infinitely more effectual as a factor of civilisation than ever before, and a movement began in the world of minds which was deeper and more serious than the revival of ancient learning.[55] The dispensation under which we live and labour consists first in the recoil from the negative spirit that rejected the law of growth, and partly in the endeavour to classify and adjust the Revolution, and to account for it by the natural working of historic causes. The Conservative line of writers, under the name of the Romantic or Historical School, had its seat in Germany, looked upon the Revolution as an alien episode, the error of an age, a disease to be treated by the investigation of its origin, and strove to unite the broken threads and to restore the normal conditions of

---

[53] Um den Sieg zu vervollständigen, erübrigte das zweite Stadium oder die Aufgabe: die Berechtigung der Mehrheit nach allen Seiten hin zur gleichen Berechtigung aller zu erweitern, d.h. bis zur Gleichstellung aller Bekenntnisse im Kirchenrecht, aller Völker im Völkerrecht, aller Staatsbürger im Staatsrecht und aller socialen Interessen im Gesellschaftsrecht fortzuführen.—A. Schmidt, *Züricher Monatschrift*, I, 68.

[54] Notre histoire ne nous enseignait nullement la liberté. Le jour où la France voulut être libre, elle eut tout à créer, tout à inventer dans cet ordre de faits.—Cependant il faut marcher, l'avenir appelle les peuples. Quand on n'a point pour cela l'impulsion du passé, il faut bien se confier à la raison.—Dupont White, *Revue des Deux Mondes*, 1861, VI, 191. Le peuple français a peu de goût pour le développement graduel des institutions. Il ignore son histoire, il ne s'y reconnaît pas, elle n'a pas laissé de trace dans sa conscience.—Scherer, *Etudes Critiques*, I, 100. Durch die Revolution befreiten sich die Franzosen von ihrer Geschichte.—Rosenkranz, *Aus einem Tagebuch*, 199.

[55] The discovery of the comparative method in philology, in mythology—let me add in politics and history and the whole range of human thought—marks a stage in the progress of the human mind at least as great and memorable as the revival of Greek and Latin learning.—Freeman, *Historical Essays*, IV, 301. The diffusion of a critical spirit in history and literature is affecting the criticism of the Bible in our own day in a manner not unlike the burst of intellectual life in the fifteenth and sixteenth centuries.—Jowett, *Essays and Reviews*, 346. As the revival of literature in the sixteenth century produced the Reformation, so the growth of the critical spirit, and the change that has come over mental science, and the mere increase of knowledge of all kinds, threaten now a revolution less external but not less profound.—Haddan, *Replies*, 348.

organic evolution. The Liberal School, whose home was France, explained and justified the Revolution as a true development, and the ripened fruit of all history.[56] These are the two main arguments of the generation to which we owe the notion and the scientific methods that make history so unlike what it was to the survivors of the last century. Severally, the innovators were not superior to the men of old. Muratori was as widely read, Tillemont as accurate, Leibniz as able, Freret as acute, Gibbon as masterly in the craft of composite construction. Nevertheless, in the second quarter of this century, a new era began for historians.

I would point to three things in particular, out of many, which constitute the amended order. Of the incessant deluge of new and unsuspected matter I need say little. For some years, the secret archives of the papacy were accessible at Paris; but the time was not ripe, and almost the only man whom they availed was the archivist himself.[57]

[56] In his just contempt and detestation of the crimes and follies of the Revolutionists, he suffers himself to forget that the revolution itself is a process of the Divine Providence, and that as the folly of men is the wisdom of God, so are their iniquities instruments of His goodness.—Coleridge, *Biographia Literaria,* II, 240. In other parts of the world, the idea of revolutions in government is, by a mournful and indissoluble association, connected with the idea of wars, and all the calamities attendant on wars. But happy experience teaches us to view such revolutions in a very different light—to consider them only as progressive steps in improving the knowledge of government, and increasing the happiness of society and mankind.—J. Wilson, 26th November, 1787, *Works,* III, 293. La Révolution, c'est-à-dire l'œuvre des siècles, ou, si vous voulez, le renouvellement progressif de la société, ou encore, sa nouvelle constitution.—Rémusat, *Correspondance,* 11th October, 1818. A ses yeux, loin d'avoir rompu le cours naturel des événements, ni la Révolution d'Angleterre, ni la nôtre, n'ont rien dit, rien fait, qui n'eût été dit, souhaité, fait, ou tenté cent fois avant leur explosion. "Il faut en ceci," dit-il, "tout accorder à leurs adversaires, les surpasser même en sévérité, ne regarder à leurs accusations que pour y ajouter, s'ils en oublient; et puis les sommer de dresser, à leur tour, le compte des erreurs, des crimes, et des maux de ces temps et de ces pouvoirs qu'ils ont pris sous leur garde."—*Revue de Paris,* XVI, 303, on Guizot. Quant aux nouveautés mises en œuvre par la Révolution Française on les retrouve une à une, en remontant d'âge en âge, chez les philosophes du XVIIIᵉ siècle, chez les grands penseurs du XVIᵉ, chez certains Pères d'Église et jusque dans la République de Platon.—En présence de cette belle continuité de l'histoire, qui ne fait pas plus de sauts que la nature, devant cette solidarité nécessaire des révolutions avec le passé qu'elles brisent.—Krantz, *Revue Politique,* XXXIII, 264. L'esprit du XIXᵉ siècle est de comprendre et de juger les choses du passé. Notre oeuvre est d'expliquer ce que le XVIIIᵉ siècle avait mission de nier.— Vacherot, *De la Démocratie,* pref., 28.

[57] La commission recherchera, dans toutes les parties des archives pontificales, les pièces relatives à l'abus que les papes ont fait de leur ministère spirituel contre l'autorité des souverains et la tranquillité des peuples.—Daunou, *Instructions,* 3rd January, 1811. Laborde, *Inventaires,* p. cxii.

Towards 1830 the documentary studies began on a large scale, Austria leading the way. Michelet, who claims, towards 1836, to have been the pioneer,[58] was preceded by such rivals as Mackintosh, Bucholtz, and Mignet. A new and more productive period began thirty years later, when the war of 1859 laid open the spoils of Italy. Every country in succession has now allowed the exploration of its records, and there is more fear of drowning than of drought. The result has been that a lifetime spent in the largest collection of printed books would not suffice to train a real master of modern history. After he had turned from literature to sources, from Burnet to Pocock, from Macaulay to Madame Campana, from Thiers to the interminable correspondence of the Bonapartes, he would still feel instant need of inquiry at Venice or Naples, in the Ossuna library or at the Hermitage.[59]

These matters do not now concern us. For our purpose, the main thing to learn is not the art of accumulating material, but the sublimer art of investigating it, of discerning truth from falsehood and certainty from doubt. It is by solidity of criticism more than by the plenitude of erudition, that the study of history strengthens, and straightens, and extends the mind.[60] And the accession of the critic in the place of the

[58] Aucun des historiens remarquables de cette époque n'avait senti encore le besoin de chercher les faits hors des livres imprimés, aux sources primitives, la plupart inédites alors, aux manuscrits de nos bibliothèques, aux documents de nos archives.—Michelet, *Histoire de France*, 1869, I, 2.

[59] Doch besteht eine Grenze, wo die Geschichte aufhört und das Archiv anfängt, und die von der Geschichtschreibung nicht überschritten werden sollte. *Unsere Zeit*, 1866, II, 635. Il faut avertir nos jeunes historiens à la fois de la nécessité inéluctable du document et, d'autre part, du danger qu'il présente.—M. Hanotaux.

[60] This process consists in determining with documentary proofs, and by minute investigations duly set forth, the literal, precise, and positive inferences to be drawn at the present day from every authentic statement, without regard to commonly received notions, to sweeping generalities, or to possible consequences.—Harrisse, *Discovery of America*, 1892, p. VI. Perhaps the time has not yet come for synthetic labours in the sphere of History. It may be that the student of the Past must still content himself with critical inquiries.—*Ib.* p. v. Few scholars are critics, few critics are philosophers, and few philosophers look with equal care on both sides of a question.—W. S. Landor in Holyoake's *Agitator's Life*, II, 15. Introduire dans l'histoire, et sans tenir compte des passions politiques et religieuses, le doute méthodique que Descartes, le premier, appliqua à l'étude de la philosophie, n'est-ce pas là une excellente méthode? N'est-ce pas même la meilleure?—Chantelauze, *Correspondant*, 1883, I, 129. La critique historique ne sera jamais populaire. Comme elle est de toutes les sciences la plus délicate, la plus déliée, elle n'a de crédit qu'auprès des esprits cultivés.—Cherbuliez, *Revue des Deux Mondes*, XCVII, 517. Nun liefert aber die Kritik, wenn sie rechter Art ist, immer nur einzelne Data, gleichsam die Atome des Thatbestandes, und jede Kombination, jede

indefatigable compiler, of the artist in coloured narrative, the skilled limner of character, the persuasive advocate of good, or other, causes, amounts to a transfer of government, to a change of dynasty, in the historic realm. For the critic is one who, when he lights on an interesting statement, begins by suspecting it. He remains in suspense until he has subjected his authority to three operations. First, he asks whether he has read the passage as the author wrote it. For the transcriber, and the editor, and the official or officious censor on the top of the editor, have played strange tricks, and have much to answer for. And if they are not to blame, it may turn out that the author wrote his book twice over, that you can discover the first jet, the progressive variations, things added, and things struck out. Next is the question where the writer got his information. If from a previous writer, it can be ascertained, and the inquiry has to be repeated. If from unpublished papers, they must be traced, and when the fountainhead is reached, or the track disappears, the question of veracity arises. The responsible writer's character, his position, antecedents, and probable motives have to be examined into; and this is what, in a different and adapted sense of the word, may be called the higher criticism, in comparison with the servile and often mechanical work of pursuing statements to their root. For a historian has to be treated as a witness, and not believed unless his sincerity is established.[61] The maxim that a man must be presumed to be innocent until his guilt is proved, was not made for him.

For us, then, the estimate of authorities, the weighing of testimony, is more meritorious than the potential discovery of new matter.[62] And modern history, which is the widest field of application, is not the best

Zusammenfassung und Schlussfolgerung, ohne die es doch einmal nicht abgeht, ist ein subjektiver Akt des Forschers. Demnach blieb Waitz, bei der eigenen Arbeit wie bei jener des anderen, immer höchst mistrauisch gegen jedes Résumé, jede Definition, jedes abschliessende Wort.—Sybel, *Historische Zeitschrift*, LVI, 484. Mit blosser Kritik wird darin nichts ausgerichtet, denn die ist nur eine Vorarbeit, welche da aufhört, wo die echte historische Kunst anfängt.—Lasaulx, *Philosophie der Künste*, 212.

[61] The only case in which such extraneous matters can be fairly called in is when facts are stated resting on testimony; then it is not only just, but it is necessary for the sake of truth, to inquire into the habits of mind of him by whom they are adduced.—Babbage, *Bridgewater Treatise*, p. xiv.

[62] There is no part of our knowledge which it is more useful to obtain at first hand—to go to the fountain-head for—than our knowledge of History.—J. S. Mill, *Inaugural Address*, 34. The only sound intellects are those which, in the first instance, set their standard of proof high.—J. S. Mill, *Examination of Hamilton's Philosophy*, 525.

to learn our business in; for it is too wide, and the harvest has not been winnowed as in antiquity, and further on to the Crusades. It is better to examine what has been done for questions that are compact and circumscribed, such as the sources of Plutarch's *Pericles,* the two tracts on Athenian government, the origin of the epistle to Diognetus, the date of the life of St. Antony; and to learn from Schwegler how this analytical work began. More satisfying because more decisive has been the critical treatment of the mediaeval writers, parallel with the new editions, on which incredible labour has been lavished, and of which we have no better examples than the prefaces of Bishop Stubbs. An important event in this series was the attack on Dino Compagni, which, for the sake of Dante, roused the best Italian scholars to a not unequal contest. When we are told that England is behind the continent in critical faculty, we must admit that this is true as to quantity, not as to quality of work. As they are no longer living, I will say of two Cambridge professors, Lightfoot and Hort, that they were critical scholars whom neither Frenchman nor German has surpassed.

The third distinctive note of the generation of writers who dug so deep a trench between history as known to our grandfathers and as it appears to us is their dogma of impartiality. To an ordinary man the word means no more than justice. He considers that he may proclaim the merits of his own religion, of his prosperous and enlightened country, of his political persuasion, whether democracy, or liberal monarchy, or historical conservatism, without transgression or offense, so long as he is fair to the relative, though inferior, merits of others, and never treats men as saints or as rogues for the side they take. There is no impartiality, he would say, like that of a hanging judge. The men who, with the compass of criticism in their hands, sailed the uncharted sea of original research proposed a different view. History, to be above evasion or dispute, must stand on documents, not on opinions. They had their own notion of truthfulness, based on the exceeding difficulty of finding truth, and the still greater difficulty of impressing it when found. They thought it possible to write, with so much scruple, and simplicity, and insight, as to carry along with them every man of good will, and, whatever his feelings, to compel his assent. Ideas which, in religion and in politics, are truths, in history are forces. They must be respected; they must not be affirmed. By dint of a supreme reserve, by much self-control, by a timely and discreet indifference, by secrecy in the matter of the black cap, history might be lifted above contention, and made an accepted tribunal, and the same for all.[63] If men were truly sincere, and delivered judgment by no canons but those of evident morality, then Julian would be described in the same terms by Christian and pagan, Luther by Catholic and Protestant, Washington by Whig and Tory, Napoleon by patriotic Frenchman and patriotic German.[64]

---

[63] There are so few men mentally capable of seeing both sides of a question; so few with consciences sensitively alive to the obligation of seeing both sides; so few placed under conditions either of circumstance or temper, which admit of their seeing both sides.—Greg, *Political Problems*, 1870, 173. Il n'y a que les Allemands qui sachent être aussi complètement objectifs. Ils se dédoublent, pour ainsi dire, en deux hommes, l'un qui a des principes très arrêtés et des passions très vives, l'autre qui sait voir et observer comme s'il n'en avait point.—Laveleye, *Revue des Deux Mondes*, 1868, I, 431. L'écrivain qui penche trop dans le sens où il incline, et qui ne se défie pas de ses qualités presque autant que de ses défauts, cet écrivain tourne à la manière.—Scherer, *Mélanges*, 484. Il faut faire volte-face, et vivement, franchement, tourner le dos au moyen âge, à ce passé morbide, qui, même quand il n'agit pas, influe terriblement par la contagion de la mort. Il ne faut ni combattre, ni critiquer, mais oublier. Oublions et marchons!—Michelet, *La Bible de l'Humanité*, 483. It has excited surprise that Thucydides should speak of Antiphon, the traitor to the democracy, and the employer of assassins, as "a man inferior in virtue to none of his contemporaries." But neither here nor elsewhere does Thucydides pass moral judgments.—Jowett, *Thucydides*, II, 501.

[64] Non theologi provinciam suscepimus; scimus enim quantum hoc ingenii nostri tenuitatem superet: ideo sufficit nobis τὸ ὅτι fideliter ex antiquis auctoribus retulisse.—Morinus, *De Poenitentia*, IX, 10.—Il faut avouer que la religion chrétienne a quelque chose d'étonnant! C'est parce que vous y êtes né, dira-t-on. Tant s'en faut, je me roidis contre par cette raison-là même, de peur que cette prévention ne me suborne.—Pascal, *Pensées*, XVI, 7.—I was fond of Fleury for a reason which I express in the advertisement; because it presented a sort of photograph of ecclesiastical history without any comment upon it. In the event, that simple representation of the early centuries had a good deal to do with unsettling me.—Newman, *Apologia*, 152. Nur was sich vor dem Richterstuhl einer ächten, unbefangenen, nicht durch die Brille einer philosophischen oder dogmatischen Schule stehenden Wissenschaft als wahr bewährt, kann zur Erbauung, Belehrung und Warnung tüchtig seyn.—Neander, *Kirchengeschichte*, I, p. vii. Wie weit bei katholischen Publicisten bei der Annahme der Ansicht von der Staatsanstalt apologetische Gesichtspunkte massgebend gewesen sind, mag dahingestellt bleiben. Der Historiker darf sich jedoch nie durch apologetische Zwecke leiten lassen; sein einziges Ziel soll die Ergründung der Wahrheit sein.—Pastor, *Geschichte der Päbste*, II, 545. Church history falsely written is a school of vainglory, hatred, and uncharitableness; truly written, it is a discipline of humility, of charity, of mutual love.—Sir W. Hamilton, *Discussions*, 506. The more trophies and crowns of honour the Church of former ages can be shown to have won in the service of her adorable head, the more tokens her history can be brought to furnish of his powerful presence in her midst, the more will we be pleased and rejoice, Protestant though we be.—Nevin, *Mercersburg Review*, 1851, 168. S'il est une chose à laquelle j'ai donné tous mes soins, c'est à ne pas laisser influencer mes jugements par les opinions politiques ou religieuses; que si j'ai quelquefois péché par quelque excès, c'est par la bienveillance pour les œuvres de ceux qui pensent autrement que moi.—Monod, *R.*

I speak of this school with reverence, for the good it has done, by the assertion of historic truth and of its legitimate authority over the minds of men. It provides a discipline which every one of us does well to undergo, and perhaps also well to relinquish. For it is not the whole truth. Lanfrey's essay on Carnot, Chuquet's wars of the Revolution, Ropes' military histories, Roget's Geneva in the time of Calvin, will supply you with examples of a more robust impartiality than I have described. Renan calls it the luxury of an opulent and aristocratic society, doomed to vanish in an age of fierce and sordid striving. In our universities it has a magnificent and appointed refuge; and to serve its cause, which is sacred, because it is the cause of truth and honour, we may import a profitable lesson from the highly unscientific region of public life. There a man does not take long to find out that he is opposed by some who are abler and better than himself. And, in order to understand the cosmic force and the true connection of ideas, it is a source of power, and an excellent school of principle, not to rest until, by excluding the fallacies, the prejudices, the exaggerations which perpetual contention and the consequent precautions breed, we have made out for our opponents a stronger and more impressive case than they present themselves.[65] Excepting one to which we are coming

---

Hist., XVI, 184. Nous n'avons nul intérêt à faire parler l'histoire en faveur de nos propres opinions. C'est son droit imprescriptible que le narrateur reproduise tous les faits sans aucune réticence et range toutes les évolutions dans leur ordre naturel. Notre récit restera complètement en dehors des préoccupations de la dogmatique et des déclamations de la polémique. Plus les questions auxquelles nous aurons à toucher agitent et passionnent de nos jours les esprits, plus il est du devoir de l'historien de s'effacer devant les faits qu'il veut faire connaître.—Reuss, *Nouvelle Revue de Théologie*, VI, 193, 1860. To love truth for truth's sake is the principal part of human perfection in this world, and the seed-plot of all other virtues.—Locke, *Letter to Collins*. Il n'est plus possible aujourd'hui à l'historien d'être national dans le sens étroit du mot. Son patriotisme à lui c'est l'amour de la vérité. Il n'est pas l'homme d'une race ou d'un pays, il est l'homme de tous les pays, il parle au nom de la civilisation générale.—Lanfrey, *Hist. de Nap.* III, 2, 1870. Juger avec les parties de soi-même qui sont le moins des formes du tempérament, et le plus des facultés pénétrées et modelées par l'expérience, par l'étude, par l'investigation, par le non-moi.—Faguet, *R. de Paris*, I, 151. Aucun critique n'est aussi impersonnel que lui, aussi libre de partis pris et d'opinions préconçues, aussi objectif. Il ne mêle ou paraît mêler à ses appréciations ni inclinations personnelles de goût ou d'humeur, ou théories d'aucune sorte.—G. Monod, of Faguet, *Revue Historique*, XLII, 417. On dirait qu'il a peur, en généralisant ses observations, en systématisant ses connaissances, de mêler de lui-même aux choses. Je lis tout un volume de M. Faguet, sans penser une fois à M. Faguet; je ne vois que les originaux qu'il montre. J'envisage toujours une réalité objective, jamais l'idée de M. Faguet, jamais la doctrine de M. Faguet.—Lanson, *Revue Politique*, 1894, I, 98.

[65] It should teach us to disentangle principles first from parties, and again from one

before I release you, there is no precept less faithfully observed by historians.

Ranke is the representative of the age which instituted the modern study of history. He taught it to be critical, to be colourless, and to be new. We meet him at every step, and he has done more for us than any other man. There are stronger books than any one of his, and some may have surpassed him in political, religious, philosophic insight, in vividness of the creative imagination, in originality, elevation, and depth of thought; but by the extent of important work well executed, by his influence on able men, and by the amount of knowledge which mankind receives and employs with the stamp of his mind upon it, he stands without a rival. I saw him last in 1877, when he was feeble, sunken, and almost blind, and scarcely able to read or write. He uttered his farewell with a kindly emotion, and I feared that the next I should hear of him would be the news of his death. Two years later he began a Universal History, which is not without traces of weakness, but which, composed after the age of eighty-three, and carried, in seventeen volumes, far into the Middle Ages, brings to a close the most astonishing career in literature.

His course had been determined, in early life, by *Quentin Durward*. The shock of the discovery that Scott's Lewis the Eleventh was inconsistent with the original in Commynes made him resolve that his object thenceforth should be above all things to follow, without swerving, and in stern subordination and surrender, the lead of his authorities. He decided effectually to repress the poet, the patriot, the religious or political partisan, to sustain no cause, to vanish himself from his books, and to write nothing that would gratify his own feelings

---

another; first of all as showing how imperfectly all parties represent their own principles, and then how the principles themselves are a mingled tissue.—Arnold, *Modern History*, 184. I find it a good rule, when I am contemplating a person from whom I want to learn, always to look out for his strength, being confident that the weakness will discover itself.—Maurice, *Essays*, 305. We may seek for agreement somewhere with our neighbours, using that as a point of departure for the sake of argument. It is this latter course that I wish here to explain and defend. The method is simple enough, though not yet very familiar. It aims at conciliation; it proceeds by making the best of our opponent's case, instead of taking him at his worst. The most interesting part of every disputed question only begins to appear when the rival ideals admit each other's right to exist.—A. Sidgwick, *Distinction and the Criticism of Beliefs*, 1892, 211. That cruel reticence in the breasts of wise men which makes them always hide their deeper thought.—Ruskin, *Sesame and Lilies*, I, 16. Je offener wir die einzelnen Wahrheiten des Sozialismus anerkennen, desto erfolgreicher können wir seine fundamentalen Unwahrheiten widerlegen.—Roscher, *Deutsche Vierteljahrschrift*, 1849, I, 177.

or disclose his private convictions.[66] When a strenuous divine, who, like him, had written on the Reformation, hailed him as a comrade, Ranke repelled his advances. "You," he said, "are in the first place a Christian: I am in the first place a historian. There is a gulf between us."[67] He was the first eminent writer who exhibited what Michelet calls *le désintéressement des morts*. It was a moral triumph for him when he could refrain from judging, show that much might be said on both sides, and leave the rest to Providence.[68] He would have felt sympathy with the two famous London physicians of our day, of whom it is told that they could not make up their minds on a case and reported dubiously. The head of the family insisted on a positive opinion. They answered that they were unable to give one, but he might easily find fifty doctors who could.

Niebuhr had pointed out that chroniclers who wrote before the invention of printing generally copied one predecessor at a time, and knew little about sifting or combining authorities. The suggestion became luminous in Ranke's hands, and with his light and dexterous

---

[66] Dann habe ihn die Wahrnehmung, dass manche Angaben in den historischen Romanen Walter Scott's, mit den gleichzeitigen Quellen im Widerspruch standen, "mit Erstaunen" erfüllt, und ihn zu dem Entschlusse gebracht, auf das Gewissenhafteste an der Ueberlieferung der Quellen festzuhalten.—Sybel, *Gedächtnissrede auf Ranke. Akad. der Wissenschaften,* 1887, p. 6. Sich frei zu halten von allem Widerschein der Gegenwart, sogar, soweit das menschenmöglich, von dem der eignen subjektiven Meinung in den Dingen des Staates, der Kirche und der Gesellschaft.—A. Dove, *Im Neuen Reich,* 1875, II, 967. Wir sind durchaus nicht für die leblose und schemenartige Darstellungsweise der Ranke'schen Schule eingenommen; es wird uns immer kühl bis ans Herz heran, wenn wir derartige Schilderungen der Reformation und der Revolution lesen, welche so ganz im kühlen Element des Pragmatismus sich bewegen und dabei so ganz Undinenhaft sind und keine Seele haben.—Wir lassen es uns lieber gefallen, dass die Männer der Geschichte hier und dort gehofmeistert werden, als dass sie uns mit Glasaugen ansehen, so meisterhaft immer die Kunst sein mag, die sie ihnen eingesetzt hat.—Gottschall, *Unsere Zeit,* 1866, II, 636, 637. A vivre avec des diplomates, il leur a pris des qualités qui sont un défaut chez un historien. L'historien n'est pas un témoin, c'est un juge; c'est à lui d'accuser et de condamner au nom du passé opprimé et dans l'intérêt de l'avenir.—Laboulaye on Ranke; *Débats,* 12th January, 1852.

[67] Un théologien qui a composé une éloquente histoire de la Réformation, recontrant à Berlin un illustre historien qui, lui aussi, a raconté Luther et le XVIᵉ siècle, l'embrassa avec effusion en le traitant de confrère. "Ah! permettez," lui répondit l'autre en se dégageant, "il y a une grande différence entre nous: vous êtes avant tout chrétien, et je suis avant tout historien."—Cherbuliez, *Revue des Deux Mondes,* 1872, I, 537.

[68] Nackte Wahrheit ohne allen Schmuck; gründliche Erforschung des Einzelnen; das Uebrige, Gott befohlen.—*Werke,* XXXIV, 24. Ce ne sont pas les théories qui doivent nous servir de base dans la recherche des faits, mais ce sont les faits qui doivent nous servir de base pour la composition des théories.—Vincent, *Nouvelle Revue de Théologie,* 1859, II, 252.

touch he scrutinised and dissected the principal historians, from Machiavelli to the *Mémoires d'un Homme d'État,* with a rigour never before applied to moderns. But whilst Niebuhr dismissed the traditional story, replacing it with a construction of his own, it was Ranke's mission to preserve, not to undermine, and to set up masters whom, in their proper sphere, he could obey. The many excellent dissertations in which he displayed this art, though his successors in the next generation matched his skill and did still more thorough work, are the best introduction from which we can learn the technical process by which within living memory the study of modern history has been renewed. Ranke's contemporaries, weary of his neutrality and suspense, and of the useful but subordinate work that was done by beginners who borrowed his wand, thought that too much was made of these obscure preliminaries which a man may accomplish for himself, in the silence of his chamber, with less demand on the attention of the public.[69] That may be reasonable in men who are practised in these fundamental technicalities. We who have to learn them must immerse ourselves in the study of the great examples.

Apart from what is technical, method is only the reduplication of common sense, and is best acquired by observing its use by the ablest men in every variety of intellectual employment.[70] Bentham acknowl-

---

[69] Die zwanglose Anordnungs—die leichte und leise Andeutungskunst des grossen Historikers voll zu würdigen, hinderte ihn in früherer Zeit sein Bedürfniss nach scharfer begrifflicher Ordnung und Ausführung, später, und in immer zunehmendem Grade, sein Sinn für Strenge, Sachlichkeit, und genaue Erforschung der ursächlichen Zusammenhänge, noch mehr aber regte sich seine geradherzige Offenheit, seine männliche Ehrlichkeit, wenn er hinter den fein verstrichenen Farben der Rankeschen Erzählungsbilder die gedeckte Haltung des klugen Diplomaten zu entdecken glaubte.—Haym, *Duncker's Leben,* 437. The ground of criticism is indeed, in my opinion, nothing else but distinct attention, which every reader should endeavour to be master of.—Hare, December, 1736; *Warburton's Works,* XIV, 98. Wenn die Quellenkritik so verstanden wird, als sei sie der Nachweis, wie ein Autor den andern benutzt hat, so ist das nur ein gelegentliches Mittel—eins unter anderen—ihre Aufgabe, den Nachweis der Richtigkeit zu lösen oder vorzubereiten.—Droysen, *Historik,* 18.

[70] L'esprit scientifique n'est autre en soi que l'instinct du travail et de la patience, le sentiment de l'ordre, de la réalité et de la mesure.—Papillon, *R. des Deux Mondes,* 1873, V, 704. Non seulement les sciences, mais toutes les institutions humaines s'organisent de même, et sous l'empire des mêmes idées régulatrices.—Cournot, *Idées Fondamentales,* I, 4. There is no branch of human work whose constant laws have not close analogy with those which govern every other mode of man's exertion. But more than this, exactly as we reduce to greater simplicity and surety any one group of these practical laws, we shall find them passing the mere condition of connection or analogy, and becoming the actual expression of some ultimate nerve or fibre of the mighty laws which govern the

edged that he learned less from his own profession than from writers like Linnaeus and Cullen; and Brougham advised the student of Law to begin with Dante. Liebig described his *Organic Chemistry* as an application of ideas found in Mill's *Logic*, and a distinguished physician, not to be named lest he should overhear me, read three books to enlarge his medical mind; and they were Gibbon, Grote, and Mill. He goes on to say, "An educated man cannot become so on one study alone, but must be brought under the influence of natural, civil, and moral modes of thought."[71] I quote my colleague's golden words in order to reciprocate them. If men of science owe anything to us, we may learn much from them that is essential.[72] For they can show how to test proof, how to secure fulness and soundness in induction, how to restrain and to employ with safety hypothesis and analogy. It is

---

moral world.—Ruskin, *Seven Lamps*, 4. The sum total of all intellectual excellence is good sense and method. When these have passed into the instinctive readiness of habit, when the wheel revolves so rapidly that we cannot see it revolve at all, then we call the combination genius. But in all modes alike, and in all professions, the two sole component parts, even of genius, are good sense and method.—Coleridge, June, 1814, *Mem. of Coleorton*, II, 172. Si l'exercice d'un art nous empêche d'en apprendre un autre, il n'en est pas ainsi dans les sciences: la connoissance d'une vérité nous aide à en découvrir une autre. Toutes les sciences sont tellement liées ensemble qu'il est bien plus facile de les apprendre toutes à la fois que d'en apprendre une seule en la détachant des autres.— Il ne doit songer qu'à augmenter les lumières naturelles de sa raison, non pour résoudre telle ou telle difficulté de l'école, mais pour que dans chaque circonstance de la vie son intelligence montre d'avance à sa volonté le parti qu'elle doit prendre.—Descartes, *Œuvres Choisies*, 300, 301. *Règles pour la Direction de l'Esprit*. La connaissance de la méthode qui a guidé l'homme de génie n'est pas moins utile au progrès de la science et même à sa propre gloire, que ses découvertes.—Laplace, *Système du Monde*, II, 371. On ne fait rien sans idées préconçues, il faut avoir seulement la sagesse de ne croire à leurs déductions qu'autant que l'expérience les confirme. Les idées préconçues, soumises au contrôle sévère de l'expérimentation, sont la flamme vivante des sciences d'observation; les idées fixes en sont le danger.—Pasteur, in *Histoire d'un Savant*, 284. Douter des vérités humaines, c'est ouvrir la porte aux découvertes; en faire des articles de foi, c'est la fermer.—Dumas, *Discours*, I, 123.

[71] We should not only become familiar with the laws of phenomena within our own pursuit, but also with the modes of thought of men engaged in other discussions and researches, and even with the laws of knowledge itself, that highest philosophy. Above all things, know that we call you not here to run your minds into our moulds. We call you here on an excursion, on an adventure, on a voyage of discovery into space as yet uncharted.—Allbutt, *Introductory Address at St. George's*, October, 1889. Consistency in regard to opinions is the slow poison of intellectual life.—Davy, *Memoirs*, 68.

[72] Ce sont vous autres physiologistes des corps vivants, qui avez appris à nous autres physiologistes de la société (qui est aussi un corps vivant) la manière de l'observer et de tirer des conséquences de nos observations.—J. B. Say to De Candolle, 1st June, 1827; De Candolle, *Mémoires*, 567.

they who hold the secret of the mysterious property of the mind by which error ministers to truth, and truth slowly but irrevocably prevails.[73] Theirs is the logic of discovery,[74] the demonstration of the advance of knowledge and the development of ideas, which as the earthly wants and passions of men remain almost unchanged, are the charter of progress and the vital spark in history. And they often give

---

[73] Success is certain to the pure and true: success to falsehood and corruption, tyranny and aggression, is only the prelude to a greater and an irremediable fall.—Stubbs, *Seventeen Lectures*, 20. The Carlylean faith, that the cause we fight for, so far as it is true, is sure of victory, is the necessary basis of all effective activity for good.—Caird, *Evolution of Religion*, II, 43. It is the property of truth to be fearless, and to prove victorious over every adversary. Sound reasoning and truth, when adequately communicated, must always be victorious over error.—Godwin, *Political Justice* (Conclusion). Vice was obliged to retire and give place to virtue. This will always be the consequence when truth has fair play. Falsehood only dreads the attack, and cries out for auxiliaries. Truth never fears the encounter; she scorns the aid of the secular arm, and triumphs by her natural strength.—Franklin, *Works,* II, 292. It is a condition of our race that we must ever wade through error in our advance towards truth; and it may even be said that in many cases we exhaust almost every variety of error before we attain the desired goal.—Babbage, *Bridgewater Treatise*, 27. Les hommes ne peuvent, en quelque genre que ce soit, arriver à quelque chose de raisonnable qu'après avoir, en ce même genre, épuisé toutes les sottises imaginables. Que de sottises ne dirions-nous pas maintenant, si les anciens ne les avaient pas déjà dites avant nous, et ne nous les avaient, pour ainsi dire, enlevées!—Fontenelle. Without premature generalisations the true generalisation would never be arrived at.—H. Spencer, *Essays,* II, 57. The more important the subject of difference, the greater, not the less, will be the indulgence of him who has learned to trace the sources of human error—of error, that has its origin not in our weakness and imperfection merely, but often in the most virtuous affections of the heart.—Brown, *Philosophy of the Human Mind,* I, 48, 1824. Parmi les châtiments du crime qui ne lui manquent jamais, à côté de celui que lui inflige la conscience, l'histoire lui en inflige un autre encore, éclatant et manifeste, l'impuissance.—Cousin, *Phil. Mod.,* II, 24. L'avenir de la science est garanti; car dans le grand livre scientifique tout s'ajoute et rien ne se perd. L'erreur ne fonde pas; aucune erreur ne dure très longtemps.—Renan, *Feuilles Détachées,* XIII. Toutes les fois que deux hommes sont d'un avis contraire sur la même chose, à coup sûr, l'un ou l'autre se trompe; bien plus, aucun ne semble posséder la vérité; car si les raisons de l'un étoient certaines et évidentes, il pourroit les exposer à l'autre de telle manière qu'il finiroit par le convaincre également.—Descartes, *Règles; Œuvres Choisies,* 302. Le premier principe de la critique est qu'une doctrine ne captive ses adhérents que par ce qu'elle a de légitime.—Renan, *Essais de Morale,* 184. Was dem Wahn solche Macht giebt ist wirklich nicht er selbst, sondern die ihm zu Grunde liegende und darin nur verzerrte Wahrheit.—Frantz, *Schelling's Philosophie,* I, 62. Quand les hommes ont vu une fois la vérité dans son éclat, ils ne peuvent plus l'oublier. Elle reste debout, et tôt ou tard elle triomphe, parce qu'elle est la pensée de Dieu et le besoin du monde.—Mignet, *Portraits,* II, 295. C'est toujours le sens commun inaperçu qui fait la fortune des hypothèses auxquelles il se mêle.—Cousin, *Fragments Phil.* I, 51, Preface of 1826. Wer da sieht, wie der Irrthum selbst ein Träger mannigfaltigen und bleibenden Fortschritts wird, der wird auch nicht so leicht aus dem thatsächlichen Fortschritt der

us invaluable counsel when they attend to their own subjects and address their own people. Remember Darwin taking note only of those passages that raised difficulties in his way; the French philosopher complaining that his work stood still, because he found no more contradicting facts; Baer, who thinks error treated thoroughly nearly as remunerative as truth, by the discovery of new objections; for, as Sir Robert Ball warns us, it is by considering objections that we often learn.[75] Faraday declared that "in knowledge, that man only is to be

---

Gegenwart auf Unumstösslichkeit unserer Hypothesen schliessen. Das richtigste Resultat der geschichtlichen Betrachtung ist die akademische Ruhe, mit welcher unsere Hypothesen und Theorien ohne Feindschaft und ohne Glauben als das betrachtet werden, was sie sind; als Stufen in jener unendlichen Annäherung an die Wahrheit, welche die Bestimmung unserer intectuellen Entwickelung zu sein scheint.—Lange, *Geschichte des Materialismus*, 502, 503. Hominum errores divina providentia reguntur, ita ut saepe male jacta bene cadant.—Leibniz, ed. Klopp, I, p. lii. Sainte-Beuve n'était même pas de la race des libéraux, c'est-à-dire de ceux qui croient que, tout compte fait, et dans un état de civilisation donné, le bien triomphe du mal à armes égales, et la vérité de l'erreur.—D'Haussonville, *Revue des Deux Mondes*, 1875, I, 567. In the progress of the human mind, a period of controversy amongst the cultivators of any branch of science must necessarily precede the period of unanimity.—Torrens, *Essay on the Production of Wealth*, 1821, p. xiii. Even the spread of an error is part of the wide-world process by which we stumble into mere approximations to truth.—L. Stephen, *Apology of an Agnostic*, 81. Errors, to be dangerous, must have a great deal of truth mingled with them; it is only from this alliance that they can ever obtain an extensive circulation.—S. Smith, *Moral Philosophy*, 7. The admission of the few errors of Newton himself is at least of as much importance to his followers in science as the history of the progress of his real discoveries.—Young, *Works*, III, 621. Error is almost always partial truth, and so consists in the exaggeration or distortion of one verity by the suppression of another, which qualifies and modifies the former.—Mivart, *Genesis of Species*, 3. The attainment of scientific truth has been effected, to a great extent, by the help of scientific errors.—Huxley: Ward, *Reign of Victoria*, II, 337. Jede neue tief eingreifende Wahrheit hat meiner Ansicht nach erst das Stadium der Einseitigkeit durchzumachen.—Ihering, *Geist des R. Rechts*, II, 22. The more readily we admit the possibility of our own cherished convictions being mixed with error, the more vital and helpful whatever is right in them will become.—Ruskin, *Ethics of the Dust*, 225. They hardly grasp the plain truth unless they examine the error which it cancels.—Cory, *Modern English History*, 1880, I, 109. Nur durch Irrthum kommen wir, der eine kürzeren und glücklicheren Schrittes, als der andere, zur Wahrheit; und die Geschichte darf nirgends diese Verirrungen übergehen, wenn sie Lehrerin und Warnerin für die nachfolgenden Geschlechter werden will.—*München Gel. Anzeigen*, 1840, I, 737.

[74] Wie die Weltgeschichte das Weltgericht ist, so kann in noch allgemeinerem Sinne gesagt werden, dass das gerechte Gericht, d.h. die wahre Kritik einer Sache, nur in ihrer Geschichte liegen kann. Insbesondere in der Hinsicht lehrt die Geschichte denjenigen, der ihr folgt, ihre eigene Methode, das ihr Fortschritt niemals ein reines Vernichten, sondern nur ein Aufheben im philosophischen Sinne ist.—Strauss, *Hallische Jahrbücher*, 1839, 120.

[75] Dans tous les livres qu'il lit, et il en dévore des quantités, Darwin ne note que les passages qui contrarient ses idées systématiques.—Il collectionne les difficultés, les cas

condemned and despised who is not in a state of transition." And John Hunter spoke for all of us when he said: "Never ask me what I have said or what I have written; but if you will ask me what my present opinions are, I will tell you."

From the first years of the century we have been quickened and enriched by contributors from every quarter. The jurists brought us that law of continuous growth which has transformed history from a chronicle of casual occurrences into the likeness of something organic.[76] Towards 1820 divines began to recast their doctrines on the lines of development, of which Newman said, long after, that evolution had come to confirm it.[77] Even the economists, who were practical men,

---

épineux, les critiques possibles.—Vernier, *Le Temps*, 6th Décembre, 1887. Je demandais à un savant célèbre où il en était de ses recherches. "Cela ne marche plus," me dit-il, "je ne trouve plus de faits contradictoires." Ainsi le savant cherche à se contredire lui-même pour faire avancer sa pensée.—Janet, *Journal des Savants*, 1892, 20. Ein Umstand, der uns die Selbständigkeit des Ganges der Wissenschaft anschaulich machen kann, ist auch der: dass der Irrthum, wenn er nur gründlich behandelt wird, fast ebenso fördernd ist als das Finden der Wahrheit, denn er erzeugt fortgesetzten Widerspruch.—Baer, *Blicke auf die Entwicklung der Wissenschaft*, 120. It is only by virtue of the opposition which it has surmounted that any truth can stand in the human mind.—Archbishop Temple; Kinglake, *Crimea, Winter Troubles*, app. 104. I have for many years found it expedient to lay down a rule for my own practice, to confine my reading mainly to those journals the general line of opinions in which is adverse to my own.—Hare, *Means of Unity*, I, 19. Kant had a harder struggle with himself than he could possibly have had with any critic or opponent of his philosophy.—Caird, *Philosophy of Kant*, 1889, I, p. ix.

[76] The social body is no more liable to arbitrary changes than the individual body. A full perception of the truth that society is not a mere aggregate, but an organic growth, that it forms a whole, the laws of whose growth can be studied apart from those of the individual atom, supplies the most characteristic postulate of modern speculation.—L. Stephen, *Science of Ethics*, 31. Wie in dem Leben des einzelnen Menschen kein Augenblick eines vollkommenen Stillstandes wahrgenommen wird, sondern stete organische Entwicklung, so verhält es sich auch in dem Leben der Völker, und in jedem einzelnen Element, woraus dieses Gesammtleben besteht. So finden wir in der Sprache stete Fortbildung und Entwicklung, und auf gleiche Weise in dem Recht. Und auch diese Fortbildung steht unter demselben Gesetz der Erzeugung aus innerer Kraft und Nothwendigkeit, unabhängig von Zufall und individueller Willkür, wie die ursprüngliche Entstehung.—Savigny, *System*, I, 16, 17. Seine eigene Entdeckung, dass auch die geistige Produktion, bis in einem gewissen Punkte wenigstens, unter dem Gesetze der Kausalität steht, dass jedeiner nur geben kann, was er hat, nur hat, was er irgendwoher bekommen, muss auch für ihn selber gelten.—Bekker, *Das Recht des Besitzes bei den Römern*, 3, 1880. Die geschichtliche Wandlung des Rechts, in welcher vergangene Jahrhunderte halb ein Spiel des Zufalls und halb ein Werk vernünftelnder Willkür sahen, als gesetzmässige Entwickelung zu begreifen, war das unsterbliche Verdienst der von Männern wie Savigny, Eichhorn und Jacob Grimm geführten historischen Rechtsschule.—Gierke, *Rundschau*, XVIII, 205.

[77] The only effective way of studying what is called the philosophy of religion, or the philosophical criticism of religion, is to study the history of religion. The true science of

dissolved their science into liquid history, affirming that it is not an auxiliary, but the actual subject-matter of their inquiry.[78] Philosophers claim that, as early as 1804, they began to bow the metaphysical neck beneath the historical yoke. They taught that philosophy is only the amended sum of all philosophies, that systems pass with the age whose

war is the history of war, the true science of religion is, I believe, the history of religion.—M. Müller, *Theosophy*, 3, 4. La théologie ne doit plus être que l'histoire des efforts spontanés tentés pour résoudre le problème divin. L'histoire, en effet, est la forme nécessaire de la science de tout ce qui est soumis aux lois de la vie changeante et successive. La science de l'esprit humain, c'est de même, l'histoire de l'esprit humain.—Renan, *Averroës*, Pref. vi.

[78] Political economy is not a science, in any strict sense, but a body of systematic knowledge gathered from the study of common processes, which have been practised all down the history of the human race in the production and distribution of wealth.—Bonamy Price, *Social Science Congress*, 1878. Such a study is in harmony with the best intellectual tendencies of our age, which is, more than anything else, characterised by the universal supremacy of the historical spirit. To such a degree has this spirit permeated all our modes of thinking, that with respect to every branch of knowledge, no less than with respect to every institution and every form of human activity, we almost instinctively ask, not merely what is its existing condition, but what were its earliest discoverable germs, and what has been the course of its development.—Ingram, *History of Political Economy*, 2. Wir dagegen stehen keinen Augenblick an, die Nationalökonomie für eine reine Erfahrungswissenschaft zu erklären, und die Geschichte ist uns daher nicht Hülfsmittel, sondern Gegenstand selber.—Roscher, *Deutsche Vierteljahrschrift*, 1849, I, 182. Der bei weitem grösste Theil menschlicher Irrthümer beruhet darauf, dass man zeitlich und örtlich Wahres oder Heilsames für absolut wahr oder heilsam ausgiebt. Für jede Stufe der Volksentwickelung passt eine besondere Staatsverfassung, die mit allen übrigen Verhältnissen des Volks als Ursache und Wirkung auf's Innigste verbunden ist; so passt auch für jede Entwickelungsstufe eine besondere Landwirthschaftsverfassung.—Roscher, *Archiv f. p. Oek.*, VIII, 2, Heft, 1845. Seitdem vor allen Roscher; Hildebrand und Knies den Werth, die Berechtigung und die Nothwendigkeit derselben unwiderleglich dargethan, hat sich immer allgemeiner der Gedanke Bahn gebrochen, dass diese Wissenschaft, die bis dahin nur auf die Gegenwart, auf die Erkenntniss der bestehenden Verhältnisse und die in ihnen sichtbaren Gesetze den Blick gerichtet hatte, auch in die Vergangenheit, in die Erforschung der bereits hinter uns liegenden wirthschaftlichen Entwicklung der Völker sich vertiefen müsse.—Schonberg, *Jahrbücher f. Nationalökonomie und Statistik*, Neue Folge, 1867, I, 1. Schmoller, moins dogmatique et mettant comme une sorte de coquetterie à être incertain, démontre, par les faits, la fausseté ou l'arbitraire de tous ces postulats, et laisse l'économie politique se dissoudre dans l'histoire.—Breton, *R. de Paris*, IX, 67. Wer die politische Oekonomie Feuerlands unter dieselben Gesetze bringen wollte mit der des heutigen Englands, würde damit augenscheinlich nichts zu Tage fördern als den allerbanalsten Gemeinplatz. Die politische Oekonomie ist somit wesentlich eine historische Wissenschaft. Sie behandelt einen geschichtlichen, das heisst einen stets wechselnden Stoff. Sie untersucht zunächst die besondern Gesetze jeder einzelnen Entwicklungsstufe der Produktion und des Austausches, und wird erst am Schluss dieser Untersuchung die wenigen, für Produktion und Austausch überhaupt geltenden, ganz allgemeinen Gesetze aufstellen können.—Engels, *Dührings Umwälzung der Wissenschaft*, 1878, 121.

impress they bear,[79] that the problem is to focus the rays of wandering but extant truth, and that history is the source of philosophy, if not quite a substitute for it.[80] Comte begins a volume with the words that the preponderance of history over philosophy was the characteristic of the time he lived in.[81] Since Cuvier first recognized the conjunction between the course of inductive discovery and the course of civilisation,[82] science had its share in saturating the age with historic ways of thought,

[79] History preserves the student from being led astray by a too servile adherence to any system.—Wolowski. No system can be anything more than a history, not in the order of impression, but in the order of arrangement by analogy.—Davy, *Memoirs*, 68. Avec des matériaux si nombreux et si importants, il fallait bien du courage pour résister à la tentation de faire un système. De Saussure eut ce courage, et nous en ferons le dernier trait et le trait principal de son éloge.—Cuvier, *Éloge de Saussure*, 1810.

[80] C'était, en 1804, une idée heureuse et nouvelle, d'appeler l'histoire au secours de la science, d'interroger les deux grandes écoles rivales au profit de la vérité.—Cousin, *Fragments Littéraires*, 1843, 95, on Dégerando. No branch of philosophical doctrine, indeed, can be fairly investigated or apprehended apart from its history. All our systems of politics, morals, and metaphysics would be different if we knew exactly how they grew up, and what transformations they have undergone; if we knew, in short, the true history of human ideas.—Cliffe Leslie, *Essays in Political and Moral Philosophy*, 1879, 149. The history of philosophy must be rational and philosophic. It must be philosophy itself, with all its elements, in all their relations, and under all their laws represented in striking characters by the hands of time and of history, in the manifested progress of the human mind.—Sir William Hamilton, *Edin. Rev.* I, 200, 1829. Il n'est point d'étude plus instructive, plus utile que l'étude de l'histoire de la philosophie; car on y apprend à se désabuser des philosophes, et l'on y désapprend la fausse science de leurs systèmes.— Royer Collard, *Œuvres de Reid*, IV, 426. On ne peut guère échapper à la conviction que toutes les solutions des questions philosophiques n'aient été développées ou indiquées avant le commencement du dix-neuvième siècle, et que par conséquent il ne soit très difficile, pour ne pas dire impossible, de tomber, en pareille matière, sur une idée neuve de quelque importance. Or si cette conviction est fondée, il s'ensuit que la science est faite.—Jouffroy, in Damiron, *Philosophie du XIXᵉ Siècle*, 363. Le but dernier de tous mes efforts, l'âme de mes écrits et de tout mon enseignement, c'est l'identité de la philosophie et de son histoire.—Cousin, *Cours de* 1829. Ma route est historique, il est vrai, mais mon but est dogmatique; je tends à une théorie, et cette théorie je la demande à l'histoire.— Cousin, *Ph. du XVIIIᵉ Siècle*, 15. L'histoire de la philosophie est contrainte d'emprunter d'abord à la philosophie la lumière qu'elle doit lui rendre un jour avec usure.—Cousin, *Du Vrai*, 1855, 14. M. Cousin, durant tout son professorat de 1816 à 1829, a pensé que l'histoire de la philosophie était la source de la philosophie même. Nous ne croyons pas exagérer en lui prêtant cette opinion.—B. St. Hilaire, *Victor Cousin*, I, 302. Il se hâta de convertir le fait en loi, et proclama que la philosophie, étant identique à son histoire, ne pouvait avoir une loi différente, et était vouée à jamais à l'évolution fatale des quatre systèmes, se contredisant toujours, mais se limitant, et se modérant, par cela même de manière à maintenir l'équilibre, sinon l'harmonie de la pensée humaine.—Vacherot, *Revue des Deux Mondes*, 1868, III, 957. Er hat überhaupt das unvergängliche Verdienst, zuerst in Frankreich zu der Erkenntniss gelangt zu sein, dass die menschliche Vernunft nur durch das Studium des Gesetzes ihrer Entwickelungen begriffen werden kann.— Lauser, *Unsere Zeit*, 1868, I, 459. Le philosophe en quête du vrai en soi, n'est plus réduit

à ses conceptions individuelles; il est riche du trésor amassé par l'humanité.—Boutroux, *Revue Politique*, XXXVII, 802. L'histoire, je veux dire l'histoire de l'esprit humain, est en ce sens la vraie philosophie de notre temps.—Renan, *Études de Morale*, 83. Die Philosophie wurde eine höchst bedeutende Hülfswissenschaft der Geschichte, sie hat ihre Richtung auf das Allgemeine gefördert, ihren Blick für dasselbe geschärft, und sie, wenigstens durch ihre Vermittlung, mit Gesichtspuncten, Ideen, bereichert, die sie aus ihrem eigenen Schoosse sobald noch nicht erzeugt haben würde. Weit die fruchtbarste darunter war die aus der Naturwissenschaft geschöpfte Idee des organischen Lebens, dieselbe auf der die neueste Philosophie selbst beruht. Die seit zwei bis drei Jahrzehnten in der Behandlung der Geschichte eingetretene durchgreifende Veränderung, wie die nach völlige Umgestaltung so mancher anderen Wissenschaft . . . ist der Hauptsache nach ihr Werk.—Haug, *Allgemeine Geschichte*, 1841, I, 22. Eine Geschichte der Philosophie im eigentlichen Sinne wurde erst möglich, als man an die Stelle der Philosophen deren Systeme setzte, den inneren Zusammenhang zwischen diesen feststellte und—wie Dilthey sagt—mitten im Wechsel der Philosophien ein siegreiches Fortschreiten zur Wahrheit nachwies. Die Gesammtheit der Philosophie stellt sich also dar als eine geschichtliche Einheit.—Saul, *Rundschau*, February, 1894, 307. Warum die Philosophie eine Geschichte habe und haben müsse, blieb unerörtert, ja ungeahnt, dass die Philosophie am meisten von allen Wissenschaften historisch sei, denn man hatte in der Geschichte den Begriff der Entwicklung nicht entdeckt.—Marbach, *Griechische Philosophie*, 15. Was bei oberfläch-licher Betrachtung nur ein Gewirre einzelner Personen und Meinungen zu sein schien, zeigt sich bei genauerer und gründlicherer Untersuchung als eine geschichtliche Entwicklung, in der alles, bald näher, bald entfernter, mit allem anderen zusammen-hängt.—Zeller, *Rundschau*, February, 1894, 307. Nur die Philosophie, die an die geschichtliche Entwickelung anknüpft kann auf bleibenden Erfolg auch für die Zukunft rechnen und fortschreiten zu dem, was in der bisherigen philosophischen Entwickelung nur erst unvollkommen erreicht oder angestrebt worden ist. Kann sich doch die Philosophie überhaupt und insbesondere die Metaphysik ihrer eigenen geschichtlichen Entwickelung nicht entschlagen, sondern hat eine Geschichte der Philosophie als eigene und zwar zugleich historische und spekulative Disziplin, in deren geschichtlichen Entwickelungsphasen und geschichtlich aufeinanderfolgenden Systemen der Philosophen die neuere Spekulation seit Schelling und Hegel zugleich die Philosophie selbst als ein die verschiedenen geschichtlichen Systeme umfassendes ganzes in seiner dialektischen Gliederung erkannt hat.—Gloatz, *Spekulative Theologie*, I, 23. Die heutige Philosophie führt uns auf einen Standpunkt von dem aus die philosophische Idee als das innere Wesen der Geschichte selbst erscheint. So trat an die Stelle einer abstrakt philosophischen Richtung, welche das Geschichtliche verneinte, eine abstrakt geschichtliche Richtung, welche das Philosophische verläugnete. Beide Richtungen sind als überschrittene und besiegte zu betrachten.—Berner, *Strafrecht*, 75. Die Geschichte der Philosophie hat uns fast schon die Wissenschaft der Philosophie selbst ersetzt.—Hermann, *Phil. Monatshefte*, II, 198, 1889.

[81] Le siècle actuel sera principalement caractérisé par l'irrévocable prépondérance de l'histoire, en philosophie, en politique, et même en poésie.—Comte, *Politique Positive*, III, 1.

[82] The historical or comparative method has revolutionised not only the sciences of law, mythology, and language, of anthropology and sociology, but it has forced its way even into the domain of philosophy and natural science. For what is the theory of evolution itself, with all its far-reaching consequences, but the achievement of the historical method?—Prothero, *Inaugural; National Review*, December, 1894, 461. To facilitate the advancement of all the branches of useful science, two things seem to be principally requisite. The first is, an historical account of their rise, progress, and present state. Without the former of these helps, a person every way qualified for extending the

and subjecting all things to that influence for which the depressing names historicism and historical-mindedness have been devised.

There are certain faults which are corrigible mental defects on which I ought to say a few denouncing words, because they are common to us all. First: the want of an energetic understanding of the sequence and real significance of events, which would be fatal to a practical politician, is ruin to a student of history, who is the politician with his face turned backwards.[83] It is playing at study, to see nothing but the unmeaning and unsuggestive surface, as we generally do. Then we have a curious proclivity to neglect, and by degrees to forget, what has been certainly known. An instance or two will explain my idea. The most popular English writer relates how it happened in his presence that the title of Tory was conferred upon the Conservative party. For it was an opprobrious name at the time, applied to men for whom the Irish Government offered head-money; so that if I have made too sure of progress, I may at least complacently point to this instance of our mended manners. One day, Titus Oates lost his temper with the men who refused to believe him, and, after looking about for a scorching imprecation, he began to call them Tories.[84] The name

bounds of science labours under great disadvantages; wanting the lights which have been struck out by others, and perpetually running the risk of losing his labour, and finding himself anticipated.—Priestley, *History of Vision*, 1772, I, Pref. i. Cuvier se proposait de montrer l'enchaînement scientifique des découvertes, leurs relations avec les grands événements historiques, et leur influence sur le progrès et le développement de la civilisation.—Dareste, *Biographie Générale*, XII, 685. Dans ses éloquentes leçons, l'histoire des sciences est devenue l'histoire même de l'esprit humain; car, remontant aux causes de leurs progrès et de leurs erreurs, c'est toujours dans les bonnes ou mauvaises routes suivies par l'esprit humain, qu'il trouve ces causes.—Flourens, *Eloge de Cuvier*, XXXI. Wie keine fortlaufende Entwickelungsreihe von nur Einem Punkte aus vollkommen aufzufassen ist, so wird auch keine lebendige Wissenschaft nur aus der Gegenwart begriffen werden können. Deswegen ist aber eine solche Darstellung doch noch nicht der gesammten Wissenschaft adäquat, und sie birgt, wenn sie damit verwechselt wird, starke Gefahren der Einseitgkeit, des Dogmatismus und damit der Stagnation in sich. Diesen Gefahren kann wirksam nur begegnet werden durch die verständige Betrachtung der Geschichte der Wissenschaften, welche diese selbst in stetem Flusse zeigt und die Tendenz ihres Fortschreitens in offenbarer und sicherer Weise klarlegt.—Rosenberg, *Geschichte der Physik*, III, p. vi. Die Continuität in der Ausbildung aller Auffassungen tritt um so deutlicher hervor, je vollständiger man sich damit wie sie zu verschiedenen Zeiten waren, vertraut macht.—Kopp, *Entwickelung der Chemie*, 814.

[83] Die Geschichte und die Politik sind ein und derselbe Janus mit dem Doppelgesicht, das in der Geschichte in die Vergangenheit, in der Politik in die Zukunft hinschaut.—Gügler's *Leben*, II, 59.

[84] The papers inclosed, which give an account of the killing of two men in the county of Londonderry; if they prove to be Tories, 'tis very well they are gone.—I think it will

remained; but its origin, attested by Defoe, dropped out of common memory, as if one party were ashamed of their godfather, and the other did not care to be identified with his cause and character. You all know, I am sure, the story of the news of Trafalgar, and how, two days after it had arrived, Mr. Pitt, drawn by an enthusiastic crowd, went to dine in the city. When they drank the health of the minister who had saved his country, he declined the praise. "England," he said, "has saved herself by her own energy; and I hope that after having saved herself by her energy, she will save Europe by her example." In 1814, when this hope had been realised, the last speech of the great orator was remembered, and a medal was struck upon which the whole sentence was engraved, in four words of compressed Latin: *Seipsam virtute, Europam exemplo.* Now it was just at the time of his last appearance in public that Mr. Pitt heard of the overwhelming success of the French in Germany, and of the Austrian surrender at Ulm. His friends concluded that the contest on land was hopeless, and that it was time to abandon the Continent to the conqueror, and to fall back upon our new empire of the sea. Pitt did not agree with them. He said that Napoleon would meet with a check whenever he encountered a national resistance; and he declared that Spain was the place for it, and that then England would intervene.[85] General Wellesley, fresh from India, was present. Ten years later, when he had accomplished that which Pitt had seen in the lucid prescience of his last days, he related at Paris what I scarcely hesitate to call the most astounding and profound prediction in all political history, where such things have not been rare.

---

not only be necessary to grant those a pardon who killed them, but also that they have some reward for their own and others' encouragement.—Essex, *Letters*, 10, 10th January, 1675. The author of this happened to be present. There was a meeting of some honest people in the city, upon the occasion of the discovery of some attempt to stifle the evidence of the witnesses.—Bedloe said he had letters from Ireland, that there were some Tories to be brought over hither, who were privately to murder Dr. Oates and the said Bedloe. The doctor, whose zeal was very hot, could never after this hear any man talk against the plot, or against the witnesses, but he thought he was one of these Tories, and called almost every man a Tory that opposed him in discourse; till at last the word Tory became popular.—Defoe, *Edinburgh Review*, I, 403.

[85] La España serà el primer pueblo en donde se encenderá esta guerra patriotica que solo puede libertar á Europa.—Hemos oido esto en Inglaterra á varios de los que estaban alli presentes. Muchas veces ha oido lo mismo al duque de Wellington el general Don Miguel de Alava, y dicho duque refirió el suceso en una comida diplomatica que dió en Paris el duque de Richelieu en 1816.—Toreno, *Historia del Levantamiento de España*, 1838, I, 508.

I shall never again enjoy the opportunity of speaking my thoughts to such an audience as this, and on so privileged an occasion a lecturer may well be tempted to bethink himself whether he knows of any neglected truth, any cardinal proposition, that might serve as his selected epigraph, as a last signal, perhaps even as a target. I am not thinking of those shining precepts which are the registered property of every school; that is to say—Learn as much by writing as by reading; be not content with the best book; seek sidelights from the others; have no favourites; keep men and things apart; guard against the prestige of great names;[86] see that your judgments are your own, and do not shrink from disagreement; no trusting without testing; be more severe to ideas than to actions;[87] do not overlook the strength of the bad cause or the weakness of the good;[88] never be surprised by the crumbling of an idol or the disclosure of a skeleton; judge talent at its best and character at its worst; suspect power more than vice,[89] and study problems in preference to periods; for instance: the derivation of Luther, the scientific influence of Bacon, the predecessors of Adam Smith, the mediaeval masters of Rousseau, the consistency of Burke, the identity

[86] Nunquam propter auctoritatem illorum, quamvis magni sint nominis (supponimus scilicet semper nos cum eo agere qui scientiam historicam vult consequi), sententias quas secuti sunt ipse tamquam certas admittet, sed solummodo ob vim testimoniorum et argumentorum quibus eas confirmarunt.—De Smedt, *Introductio ad historiam critice tractandam*, 1866, I, 5.

[87] Hundert schwere Verbrechen wiegen nicht so schwer in der Schale der Unsittlichkeit, als ein unsittliches Princip.—*Hallische Jahrbücher*, 1839, 308. Il faut flétrir les crimes; mais il faut aussi, et surtout, flétrir les doctrines et les systèmes qui tendent à les justifier.—Mortimer Ternaux, *Histoire de la Terreur*.

[88] We see how good and evil mingle in the best of men and in the best of causes; we learn to see with patience the men whom we like best often in the wrong, and the repulsive men often in the right; we learn to bear with patience the knowledge that the cause which we love best has suffered, from the awkwardness of its defenders, so great disparagement, as in strict equity to justify the men who were assaulting it.—Stubbs, *Seventeen Lectures*, 97.

[89] *Caeteris paribus*, on trouvera toujours que ceux qui ont plus puissance sont sujets à pécher davantage; et il n'y a point de théorème de géométrie qui soit plus asseuré que cette proposition.—Leibniz, 1688, ed. Rommel, II, 197. Il y a toujours eu de la malignité dans la grandeur, et de l'opposition à l'esprit de l'Évangile; mais maintenant il y en a plus que jamais, et il semble que comme le monde va à sa fin, celui qui est dans l'élévation fait tous ses efforts pour dominer avec plus de tyrannie, et pour étouffer les maximes du Christianisme et le règne de Jésus-Christ, voiant qu'il s'approche.—Godeau, *Lettres*, 423, 27th March, 1667. There is, in fact, an unconquerable tendency in all power, save that of knowledge, acting by and through knowledge, to injure the mind of him by whom that power is exercised.—Wordsworth, 22nd June, 1817; *Letters of Lake Poets*, 369.

of the first Whig. Most of this, I suppose, is undisputed, and calls for no enlargement. But the weight of opinion is against me when I exhort you never to debase the moral currency or to lower the standard of rectitude, but to try others by the final maxim that governs your own lives, and to suffer no man and no cause to escape the undying penalty which history has the power to inflict on wrong.[90] The plea in extenuation of guilt and mitigation of punishment is perpetual. At every step we are met by arguments which go to excuse, to palliate, to confound right and wrong, and reduce the just man to the level of the reprobate. The men who plot to baffle and resist us are, first of all, those who made history what it has become. They set up the principle that only a foolish Conservative judges the present time with the ideas of the past; that only a foolish Liberal judges the past with the ideas of the present.[91]

The mission of that school was to make distant times, and especially the Middle Ages, then most distant of all, intelligible and acceptable to a society issuing from the eighteenth century. There were difficulties in the way; and among others this, that, in the first fervour of the Crusades, the men who took the Cross, after receiving communion, heartily devoted the day to the extermination of Jews. To judge them by a fixed standard, to call them sacrilegious fanatics or furious hypocrites, was to yield a gratuitous victory to Voltaire. It became a rule of policy to praise the spirit when you could not defend the deed. So that we have no common code; our moral notions are always fluid; and you must consider the times, the class from which men sprang, the surrounding influences, the masters in their schools, the preachers in their pulpits, the movement they obscurely obeyed, and so on, until responsibility is merged in numbers, and not a culprit is left for execution.[92] A murderer was no criminal if he followed local custom,

---

[90] I cieli han messo sulla terra due giudici delle umane azioni, la coscienza e la storia.—Colletta. Wenn gerade die edelsten Männer um des Nachruhmes willen gearbeitet haben, so soll die Geschichte ihre Belohnung sein, sie auch die Strafe für die Schlechten.—Lasaulx, *Philosophie der Künste*, 211. Pour juger ce qui est bon et juste dans la vie actuelle ou passée, il faut posséder un criterium, qui ne soit pas tiré du passé ou du présent, mais de la nature humaine.—Ahrens, *Cours de Droit Naturel*, I, 67.

[91] L'homme de notre temps! La conscience moderne! Voilà encore de ces termes qui nous ramènent la prétendue philosophie de l'histoire et la doctrine du progrès, quand il s'agit de la justice, c'est-à-dire de la conscience pure et de l'homme rationnel, que d'autres siècles encore que le nôtre ont connu.—Renouvier, *Crit. Phil.*, 1873, II, 55.

[92] Il faut pardonner aux grands hommes le marchepied de leur grandeur.—Cousin,

if neighbours approved, if he was encouraged by official advisers or prompted by just authority, if he acted for the reason of state or the pure love of religion, or if he sheltered himself behind the complicity of the Law. The depression of morality was flagrant; but the motives were those which have enabled us to contemplate with distressing complacency the secret of unhallowed lives. The code that is greatly modified by time and place will vary according to the cause. The amnesty is an artifice that enables us to make exceptions, to tamper with weights and measures, to deal unequal justice to friends and enemies.

It is associated with that philosophy which Cato attributes to the gods. For we have a theory which justifies Providence by the event, and holds nothing so deserving as success, to which there can be no victory in a bad cause; prescription and duration legitimate;[93] and

in J. Simon, *Nos Hommes d'État*, 1887, 55. L'esprit du XVIIIᵉ siècle n'a pas besoin d'apologie: l'apologie d'un siècle est dans son existence.—Cousin, *Fragments*, III, 1826. Suspendus aux lèvres éloquentes de M. Cousin, nous l'entendîmes s'écrier que la meilleure cause l'emportait toujours, que c'était la loi de l'histoire, le rhythme immuable du progrès.—Gasparin, *La Liberté Morale*, II, 63. Cousin verurtheilen heisst darum nichts Anderes als jenen Geist historischer Betrachtung verdammen, durch welchen das 19. Jahrhundert die revolutionäre Kritik des 18. Jahrhunderts ergänzt, durch welchen insbesondere Deutschland die geistigen Wohlthaten vergolten hat, welche es im Zeitalter der Aufklärung von seinen westlichen Nachbarn empfangen.—Iodl, *Gesch. der Ethik*, II, 295. Der Gang der Weltgeschichte steht ausserhalb der Tugend, des Lasters, und der Gerechtigkeit.—Hegel, *Werke*, VIII, 425. Die Vermischung des Zufälligen im Individuum mit dem an ihm Historischen führt zu unzähligen falschen Ansichten und Urtheilen. Hierzu gehört namentlich alles Absprechen über die moralische Tüchtigkeit der Individuen, und die Verwunderung, welche bis zur Verzweiflung an göttlicher Gerechtigkeit sich steigert, dass historisch grosse Individuen moralisch nichtswürdig erscheinen können. Die moralische Tüchtigkeit besteht in der Unterordnung alles dessen, was zufällig am Einzelnen unter das an ihm den Allgemeinen Angehörige.—Marbach, *Geschichte der Griechischen Philosophie*, 7. Das Sittliche der Neuseeländer, der Mexikaner ist vielmehr ebenso sittlich, wie das der Griechen, der Römer; und das Sittliche der Christen des Mittelalters ist ebenso sittlich, wie das der Gegenwart.—Kirchmann, *Grundbegriffe des Rechts*, 194. Die Geschichtswissenschaft als solche kennt nur ein zeitliches und mithin auch nur ein relatives Maass der Dinge. Alle Werthbeurtheilung der Geschichte kann daher nur relativ und aus zeitlichen Momenten fliessen, und wer sich nicht selbst täuschen und den Dingen nicht Gewalt anthun will, muss ein für allemal in dieser Wissenschaft auf absolute Werthe verzichten.—Lorenz, *Schlosser*, 80. Only according to his faith is each man judged. Committed as this deed has been by a pure-minded, pious youth, it is a beautiful sign of the time.—De Wette to Sand's Mother; Cheyne, *Founders of Criticism*, 44. The men of each age must be judged by the ideal of their own age and country, and not by the ideal of ours.—Lecky, *Value of History*, 50.

[93] La durée ici-bas, c'est le droit, c'est la sanction, de Dieu.—Guiraud, *Philosophie Catholique de l'Histoire*.

whatever exists is right and reasonable; and as God manifests His will by that which He tolerates, we must conform to the divine decree by living to shape the future after the ratified image of the past.[94] Another theory, less confidently urged, regards history as our guide, as much by showing errors to evade as examples to pursue. It is suspicious of illusions in success, and, though there may be hope of ultimate triumph for what is true, if not by its own attraction, by the gradual exhaustion of error, it admits no corresponding promise for what is ethically right. It deems the canonisation of the historic past more perilous than ignorance or denial, because it would perpetuate the reign of sin and acknowledge the sovereignty of wrong, and conceives it the part of real greatness to know how to stand and fall alone, stemming, for a lifetime, the contemporary flood.[95]

Ranke relates, without adornment, that William III ordered the extirpation of a Catholic clan, and scouts the faltering excuse of his defenders. But when he comes to the death and character of the international deliverer, Glencoe is forgotten, the imputation of murder drops, like a thing unworthy of notice.[96] Johannes Mueller, a great

---

[94] Ceux qui ne sont pas contens de l'ordre des choses ne sçauroient se vanter d'aimer Dieu comme il faut. Il faut toujours estre content de l'ordre du passé, parce qu'il est conforme à la volonté de Dieu absolue, qu'on connoît par l'événement. Il faut tâcher de rendre l'avenir, autant qu'il dépend de nous, conforme à la volonté de Dieu présomptive.—Leibniz, *Werke*, ed. Gerhardt, II, 136. Ich habe damals bekannt und bekenne jetzt, dass die politische Wahrheit aus denselben Quellen zu schöpfen ist, wie alle anderen, aus dem göttlichen Willen und dessen Kundgebung in der Geschichte des Menschengeschlechts.—Radowitz, *Neue Gespräche,* 65.

[95] A man is great as he contends best with the circumstances of his age.—Froude, *Short Studies,* I, 388. La persuasion que l'homme est avant tout une personne morale et libre, et qu'ayant conçu, seul, dans sa conscience et devant Dieu, la règle de sa conduite, il doit s'employer tout entier à l'appliquer en lui, hors de lui, absolument, obstinément, inflexiblement, par une résistance perpétuelle opposée aux autres; et par une contrainte perpétuelle exercée sur soi, voilà la grande idée anglaise.—Taine; Sorel, *Discours de Réception,* 24. In jeder Zeit des Christenthums hat es einzelne Männer gegeben, die über ihrer Zeit standen und von ihren Gegensätzen nicht berührt wurden.—Bachmann, *Hengstenberg,* I, 160. Eorum enim qui de iisdem rebus mecum aliquid ediderunt, aut solus insanio ego, aut solus non insanio; tertium enim non est, nisi (quod dicet forte aliquis) insaniamus omnes.—Hobbes, quoted by De Morgan, 3rd June, 1858: *Life of Sir W. R. Hamilton,* III, 552.

[96] I have now to exhibit a rare combination of good qualities, and a steady perseverance in good conduct, which raised an individual to be an object of admiration and love to all his contemporaries, and have made him to be regarded by succeeding generations as a model of public and private virtue. The evidence shows that upon this occasion he was not only under the influence of the most vulgar credulity, but that he violated the plainest rules of justice, and that he really was the murderer of two innocent women.

Swiss celebrity, writes that the British Constitution occurred to somebody, perhaps to Halifax. This artless statement might not be approved by rigid lawyers as a faithful and felicitous indication of the manner of that mysterious growth of ages, from occult beginnings, that was never profaned by the invading wit of man;[97] but it is less grotesque than it appears. Lord Halifax was the most original writer of political tracts in the pamphleteering crowd between Harrington and Bolingbroke; and in the Exclusion struggle he produced a scheme of limitations which, in substance, if not in form, foreshadowed the position of the monarchy in the later Hanoverian reigns. Although Halifax did not believe in the plot,[98] he insisted that innocent victims should be sacrificed to content the multitude. Sir William Temple writes: "We only disagreed in one point, which was the leaving some priests to the law upon the accusation of being priests only, as the House of Commons had desired; which I thought wholly unjust. Upon this point Lord Halifax and I had so sharp a debate at Lord Sunderland's lodgings, that he told me, if I would not concur in points which were so necessary for the people's satisfaction, he would tell everybody I was a Papist. And upon his affirming that the plot must be handled as if it were true, whether it were so or no, in those points that were so generally believed." In spite of this accusing passage,

---

Hale's motives were most laudable.—Campbell's *Lives of the Chief Justices*, I, 512, 561, 566. It was not to be expected of the colonists of New England that they should be the first to see through a delusion which befooled the whole civilised world, and the gravest and most knowing persons in it. The people of New England believed what the wisest men of the world believed at the end of the seventeenth century.—Palfrey, *New England*, IV, 127, 129 (also speaking of witchcraft). Il est donc bien étrange que sa sévérité tardive s'exerce aujourd'hui sur un homme auquel elle n'a d'autre reproche à faire que d'avoir trop bien servi l'état par des mesures politiques, injustes peut-être, violentes, mais qui, en aucune manière, n'avaient l'intérêt personnel du coupable pour objet. M. Hastings peut sans doute paraître répréhensible aux yeux des étrangers, des particuliers même, mais il est assez extraordinaire qu'une nation usurpatrice d'une partie de l'Indostan veuille mêler les règles de la morale à celles d'une administration forcée, injuste et violente par essence, et à laquelle il faudrait renoncer à jamais pour être conséquent.—Mallet Du Pan, *Mémoires*, ed. Sayous, I, 102.

[97] On parle volontiers de la stabilité de la constitution anglaise. La vérité est que cette constitution est toujours en mouvement et en oscillation et qu'elle se prête merveilleuse-ment au jeu de ses différentes parties. Sa solidité vient de sa souplesse; elle plie et ne rompt pas.—Boutmy, *Nouvelle Revue*, 1878, 49.

[98] This is not an age for a man to follow the strict morality of better times, yet sure mankind is not yet so debased but that there will ever be found some few men who will scorn to join concert with the public voice when it is not well grounded.—*Savile Correspondence*, 173.

Macaulay, who prefers Halifax to all the statesmen of his age, praises him for his mercy: "His dislike of extremes, and a forgiving and compassionate temper which seems to have been natural to him, preserved him from all participation in the worst crimes of his time."

If, in our uncertainty, we must often err, it may be sometimes better to risk excess in rigour than in indulgence, for then at least we do no injury by loss of principle. As Bayle has said, it is more probable that the secret motives of an indifferent action are bad than good;[99] and this discouraging conclusion does not depend upon theology, for James Mozley supports the sceptic from the other flank, with all the artillery of Tractarian Oxford. "A Christian," he says, "is bound by his very creed to suspect evil, and cannot release himself. . . . He sees it where others do not; his instinct is divinely strengthened; his eye is super-naturally keen; he has a spiritual insight, and senses exercised to discern. . . . He owns the doctrine of original sin; that doctrine puts him necessarily on his guard against appearances, sustains his appre-hension under perplexity, and prepares him for recognising anywhere what he knows to be everywhere."[100] There is a popular saying of Madame de Staël, that we forgive whatever we really understand. The paradox has been judiciously pruned by her descendant, the Duke de Broglie, in the words: "Beware of too much explaining, lest we end by too much excusing."[101] History, says Froude, does teach that right and

---

[99] Cette proposition: L'homme est incomparablement plus porté au mal qu'au bien, et il se fait dans le monde incomparablement plus de mauvaises actions que de bonnes—est aussi certaine qu'aucun principe de métaphysique. Il est donc incomparablement plus probable qu'une action faite par un homme est mauvaise, qu'il n'est probable qu'elle soit bonne. Il est incomparablement plus probable que ces secrets ressorts qui l'ont produite sont corrompus, qu'il n'est probable qu'ils soient honnêtes. Je vous avertis que je parle d'une action qui n'est point mauvaise extérieurement.—Bayle, Œuvres, II, 248.

[100] A Christian is bound by his very creed to suspect evil, and cannot release himself.—His religion has brought evil to light in a way in which it never was before; it has shown its depth, subtlety, ubiquity; and a revelation, full of mercy on the one hand, is terrible in its exposure of the world's real state on the other. The Gospel fastens the sense of evil upon the mind; a Christian is enlightened, hardened, sharpened, as to evil; he sees it where others do not.—Mozley, Essays, I, 308. All satirists, of course, work in the direction of Christian doctrine, by the support they give to the doctrine of original sin, making a sort of meanness and badness a law of society.—Mozley, Letters, 333. Les critiques, même malveillants, sont plus près de la vérité dernière que les admirateurs.—Nisard, Lit. fr., Conclusion. Les hommes supérieurs doivent nécessairement passer pour méchants. Où les autres ne voient ni un défaut, ni un ridicule, ni un vice, leur implacable œil l'aperçoit.—Barbey d'Aurevilly, Figaro, 31st March, 1888.

[101] Prenons garde de ne pas trop expliquer, pour ne pas fournir des arguments à ceux qui veulent tout excuser.—Broglie, Réception de Sorel, 46.

wrong are real distinctions. Opinions alter, manners change, creeds rise and fall, but the moral law is written on the tablets of eternity.[102] And if there are moments when we may resist the teaching of Froude, we have seldom the chance of resisting when he is supported by Mr. Goldwin Smith: "A sound historical morality will sanction strong measures in evil times; selfish ambition, treachery, murder, perjury, it will never sanction in the worst of times, for these are the things that make times evil—Justice has been justice, mercy has been mercy, honour has been honour, good faith has been good faith, truthfulness has been truthfulness from the beginning." The doctrine that, as Sir Thomas Browne says, morality is not ambulatory,[103] is expressed as follows by Burke, who, when true to himself, is the most intelligent of our instructors: "My principles enable me to form my judgment upon men and actions in history, just as they do in common life; and are not formed out of events and characters, either present or past. History is a preceptor of prudence, not of principles. The principles of true politics are those of morality enlarged; and I neither now do, nor ever will admit of any other."[104]

[102] The eternal truths and rights of things exist, fortunately, independent of our thoughts or wishes, fixed as mathematics, inherent in the nature of man and the world. They are no more to be trifled with than gravitation.—Froude, *Inaugural Lecture at St. Andrews,* 1869, 41. What have men to do with interests? There is a right way and a wrong way. That is all we need think about.—Carlyle to Froude, *Longman's Magazine,* December, 1892, 151. As to History, it is full of indirect but very effective moral teaching. It is not only, as Bolingbroke called it, "Philosophy teaching by examples," but it is morality teaching by examples.—It is essentially the study which best helps the student to conceive large thoughts.—It is impossible to overvalue the moral teaching of History.— Fitch, *Lectures on Teaching,* 432. Judging from the past history of our race, in ninety-nine cases out of a hundred, war is a folly and a crime.—Where it is so, it is the saddest and the wildest of all follies, and the most heinous of all crimes.—Greg, *Essays on Political and Social Science,* 1853, I, 562. La volonté de tout un peuple ne peut rendre juste ce qui est injuste: les représentants d'une nation n'ont pas le droit de faire ce que la nation n'a pas le droit de faire elle-même.—B. Constant, *Principes de Politique,* I, 15.

[103] Think not that morality is ambulatory; that vices in one age are not vices in another, or that virtues, which are under the everlasting seal of right reason, may be stamped by opinion.—Sir Thomas Browne, *Works,* IV, 64.

[104] Osons croire qu'il seroit plus à propos de mettre de côté ces traditions, ces usages, et ces coutumes souvent si imparfaites, si contradictoires, si incohérentes, ou de ne les consulter que pour saisir les inconvénients et les éviter; et qu'il faudroit chercher non-seulement les éléments d'une nouvelle législation, mais même ses derniers détails dans une étude approfondie de la morale.—Letrosne, *Réflexions sur la Législation Criminelle,* 137. M. Renan appartient à cette famille d'esprits qui ne croient pas en réalité la raison, la conscience, le droit applicables à la direction des sociétés humaines, et qui demandent à l'histoire, à la tradition, non à la morale, les règles de la politique. Ces esprits sont atteints de la maladie du siècle, le scepticisme moral.—Pillon, *Critique Philosophique,* I, 49.

Whatever a man's notions of these later centuries are, such, in the main, the man himself will be. Under the name of History, they cover the articles of his philosophic, his religious, and his political creed.[105] They give his measure; they denote his character: and, as praise is the shipwreck of historians, his preferences betray him more than his aversions. Modern history touches us so nearly, it is so deep a question of life and death, that we are bound to find our own way through it, and to owe our insight to ourselves. The historians of former ages, unapproachable for us in knowledge and in talent, cannot be our limit. We have the power to be more rigidly impersonal, disinterested and just than they; and to learn from undisguised and genuine records to look with remorse upon the past, and to the future with assured hope of better things; bearing this in mind, that if we lower our standard in history, we cannot uphold it in Church or State.

[105] The subject of modern History is of all others, to my mind, the most interesting, inasmuch as it includes all questions of the deepest interest relating not to human things only, but to divine.—Arnold, *Modern History,* 311.

Index

The typeface for the text of this book is *Baskerville*. Its creator, John Baskerville (1706–1775), broke with tradition to reflect in his type the rounder, yet more sharply cut lettering of eighteenth-century stone inscriptions and copy books. The type foreshadows modern design in such novel characteristics as the increase in contrast between thick and thin strokes and the shifting of stress from the diagonal to the vertical strokes. Realizing that this new style of letter would be most effective if cleanly printed on smooth paper with genuinely black ink, he built his own presses, developed a method of hot-pressing the printed sheet to a smooth, glossy finish, and experimented with special inks. However, Baskerville did not enter into general commercial use in England until 1923.

Book design by Hermann Strohbach, New York, New York
Editorial service and index by Harkavy Publishing Service,
New York, New York
Typography by Monotype Composition Co., Inc., Baltimore, Maryland
Printed and bound by Worzalla Publishing Company,
Stevens Point, Wisconsin